SOCIAL WORK
ALMANAC
2nd
Edition

SOCIAL WORK ALMANAC

2nd Edition

by Leon Ginsberg

NASW PRESS

National Association of Social Workers
Washington, DC

Ann A. Abbott, PhD, ACSW, *President*
Sheldon R. Goldstein, ACSW, LISW, *Executive Director*

Linda Beebe, Executive Editor
Nancy Winchester, Editorial Services Director
Hyde Loomis, Senior Editor and Project Manager
Ida Audeh, Copyeditor
Donna Brodsky, Proofreader
Sue Nedrow, Proofreader
Marina Rota, Proofreader
Vivian Mason, Proofreader
Louise Goines, Proofreader
Editorial Experts, Inc., Proofreader
Robert Elwood, Indexer

Library of Congress Cataloging-in-Publication Data

Ginsberg, Leon H.
    Social work almanac / Leon Ginsberg.—2nd ed.
        p.   cm.
    "National Association of Social Workers."
    Includes bibliographical references (p.   ) and index.
    ISBN 0-87101-248-0 (acid-free paper)
    1. Social service—United States—Statistics.   2. United States—
Population—Statistics.   3. United States—Social conditions—1980-
—Statistics.   I. National Association of Social Workers.
II. Title.
HV90.G53   1995
361.973—dc 20   94-48860
                                                        CIP

Printed in the United States of America
Cover and interior design by G. Quinn Information Design

CONTENTS

ILLUSTRATIONS

CHAPTER 3

CHAPTER 4

CHAPTER 5

Chapter 6   TABLE

CHAPTER 7   TABLE

FIGURE

ACKNOWLEDGMENTS

My thanks go to several people at the University of South Carolina who assisted me in the research for and preparation of this manuscript. Especially, I extend my gratitude to Janet Bradshaw, MSW, for her government document research and Kevin Colligan for his assistance with manuscript preparation while they were graduate assistants at the University of South Carolina College of Social Work. I also am indebted to Joyce Shaw, a member of the College of Social Work support staff, for her help in preparing the manuscript for this book.

The University of South Carolina provided me a sabbatical during the spring semester of 1993, which made it possible for me to begin work on this edition of *Social Work Almanac*.

The National Association of Social Workers has also been central, of course, to the development of this project. Hyde Loomis, senior editor for NASW, has been a rigorous and helpful critic and designer of the work. In many ways, it is her book, too, as was the first edition. Linda Beebe, associate executive director, provided the kind of support and attention to this project,

including helping design it, that has made the difference between its being published and its having been only a good idea. Richard Edwards and the editorial committee for the 19th edition of *The Encyclopedia of Social Work* showed their support for this book by making it part of that overall effort.

Special gratitude, too, goes to the hundreds of government scientists and statisticians, as well as many in voluntary organizations, who collected and organized the data that is the basis for this work.

My family has always supported me and encouraged this latest publications effort, and I am grateful to them, as well.

This project owes special thanks to the Social Work Librarians Group, who understood the value of a social welfare statistics compendium and who encouraged its publication and use.

And, of course, my gratitude to the thousands of educators, students, and human service practitioners who purchased and used the first edition and made it clear that a second edition was needed and of value.

Introduction

Understanding social problems, policies, and programs requires mastery of and knowledge about facts. This is a book about the major social issues and social programs of the 1990s. It is the second edition of a book that combines national and some international information on population, children, crime and corrections, education, health and mortality, mental health, older adults, and the social work profession itself. It also describes major social welfare and assistance programs, entitlements as well as means-tested benefits, that serve all age groups and address social needs.

Organization

This volume is organized into nine chapters, arranged alphabetically by subject. Not all the information in a chapter is related only to that chapter's subject, because some groups are so important that no one chapter could cover all that needs to be included. For example, although there is no specific chapter on families, which are the central focus of much social work study and practice, every chapter has something to say about families. Likewise, there are no separate chapters on ethnic minorities or women, although both are covered extensively in each chapter. Information on children and older adults, although covered in individual chapters, is also discussed in some way in most chapters, partly because these groups, too, are of great interest to social workers. The index will help the reader find information on various subjects throughout the book.

The most difficult task was deciding what to include and exclude. The same information is frequently provided in a variety of different ways in several reports. Therefore, I tried to select the most relevant data for social workers and to avoid, when possible, long and complicated reports on complex issues. I did not want to duplicate existing volumes.

Sources of Information

As the reference list demonstrates, diverse sources were used in preparing this book. Most of the material presented comes from data collected, analyzed, and disseminated by researchers and statisticians in the various departments and branches of the U.S. government. One of the primary functions of the executive branch of a federal government such as that of the United States, in which the states exercise most of the power and operate most of the programs, is to collect information that supports the states in their efforts to serve their people.

The *Statistical Abstract of the United States,* which is published every year by the U.S. Bureau of the Census, is a must for those who want to understand basic facts about the United States. Although social statistics and population data are only a part of the annual volumes, they are an important part. The *Statistical Abstract* publishes much of the most current and pertinent data on matters that are of concern to social workers. It also has a wealth of other kinds of information, from data on agricultural production to almost every kind of economic issue.

Another especially important source for the student of social welfare is the *Green Book,* which is published annually by the Committee on Ways and Means of the U.S. House of Representatives. The *Green Book* is a study of all the statistical information available on entitlement programs for children and older adults, including health services and antipoverty programs such as Aid to Families with Dependent Children (AFDC) and the Food

Stamp program. It is probably the single best and most complete source on those issues.

Certain commercial publishing ventures also publish useful data. The *Universal Almanac,* which is published annually, has been useful in identifying the available data for this book. It is substantially different from two other widely circulated almanacs, the *Information Please Almanac* and the *World Almanac and Book of Facts,* in that it contains more information on U.S. and world populations, government social programs, and health and social statistics. The almanacs, however, are published in the fall for the forthcoming year. Therefore, the 1994 editions have no facts on 1994 and only incomplete information on 1993.

Most of the social welfare information in all these publications is available from several sources. It is constructed from periodic reports by voluntary organizations such as the American Humane Association, the American Public Welfare Association, the American Heart Association, and the American Cancer Society, as well as by government agencies. One will find a variety of data from those voluntary organizations sprinkled throughout the basic federal government sources and the commercially published almanacs.

Most of the statistics come from federal government agencies such as the U.S. Bureau of the Census, the U.S. Department of Health and Human Services, the U.S. Public Health Service, the U.S. Department of Education, the U.S. Department of Agriculture, the U.S. Department of Justice, and the U.S. Department of Commerce. All these agencies publish periodic updates on various population, social, and economic issues and periodic special reports on selected issues. These pamphlets and bulletins are available in many public college and university libraries, as well as in state government libraries. When looking for such reports, one should find a federal repository—a library that receives copies of federal government publications. However, the accessibility of these documents depends, in part, on the ability of those seeking information to find and use them and on the ability of the repository to file them properly and make them readily available to researchers.

The reference list also includes non-government literature and information published by the National Association of Social Workers and by other organizations, some of them with federal financial support. In addition, many voluntary health and disease-related organizations collect and provide statistics as part of their public information efforts. Some of the sources that were used for this edition came from suggestions by readers—social work students, a journal book reviewer, and practitioners—of the first edition. Other sources emerged serendipitously—from reading reports in newspapers and magazines on such issues as home schooling, labor patterns around the world, and other specific issues that lent themselves to statistical description. When the periodicals did not include sufficient detail for inclusion in the *Social Work Almanac,* I called or wrote the sources for the full reports. I used statistics that were based on surveys taken by the organizations or adapted from other studies after assuring myself that the bases for their data were explained in their reports and that the data were reasonably reliable and valid.

The Material

The tables and figures in this book cover a large spectrum of the human services and social welfare fields. In this edition, there are more tables and figures on more subjects—for example, health and crime and corrections—than there were in the first edition. Because the tables communicate a great deal of information in effective ways, most of them are presented exactly the way the government statisticians developed them.

Readers will note that some of the information presented in this book is based on studies of whole populations. Much of it comes from the 1990 census and later projections from that census. The decennial census is a study of the total U.S. population, and the projections are the result of analyses by statisticians who work in the U.S. Bureau of the Census.

Whereas some of the data represent all of the clients who receive specific services or all of the dollars spent for specific programs, other data (including several reports from *Current*

Population Surveys, which are part of the effort of the U.S. Bureau of the Census) are based on population samples. Estimates and projections that are based on samples, studies, and surveys are probably as accurate as the studies of the whole population. Modern statistical analyses are based on carefully selected and reliable samples that reflect the entire populations from which they are drawn. A study based on a well-constructed sample has as little chance for error as does the collection of information from a large body of people or a whole population. Equal or greater numbers of errors are possible when studying populations as when working with a carefully constructed research project.

However, readers may want to take note of the sources of the information provided and may want to evaluate the data presented in terms of the ways in which they were collected and processed. In its original version, each report contains details on how the data were collected and processed and what assumptions may be made about their margins of error.

It is important to understand exactly what the tables and figures in this book say. Many of them contain great quantities of information in very small amounts of space. Some of the tables and figures provide raw or total numbers of cases, dollars, facilities, or incidents. In such cases it is important to read the numbers accurately. Many are in thousands, and some are in hundreds of thousands. The tables and figures indicate their numerical bases. If a table is in thousands, the reader simply must add three zeroes so that, for example, the figure 1,216 is understood to be 1,216,000. If the figure is in 100,000 increments, then the reader should add five zeroes so that 1,216 would be understood to be 121,600,000.

Some information is provided in percentages, and when that is the case, the tables say so. In other cases "rates" are quoted. The rates may be based on every hundred, thousand, ten thousand, or hundred thousand people. A rate per hundred, for example, is comparable to a percentage, which tells the reader how many cases of the phenomenon being described one finds among every 100 people. Rates based on larger segments of the population allow for useful analyses of relatively rare phenomena.

It is also important and worthwhile to note the publication dates of the data presented in the book. Some information is quite recent and represents data collected only a few months before the manuscript was completed, whereas other information may be several years old. However, all of the data represent the most current information available to me at the time the book was written. Some of the information was costly and time consuming to collect, and therefore the studies that yielded the information are not frequently—or ever—repeated.

Although there is a general preference for current information, older data can be very useful, because the statistical realities of large populations do not change very rapidly. For example, the center of population of the United States has very gradually moved from the East Coast to a point in Missouri. According to the *Statistical Abstract of the United States: 1993* (U.S. Bureau of the Census, 1993), it was 9.7 miles southeast of Steelville, Missouri, in 1993. However, population movements are so slow that the center of population is only inching its way westward. In 1950, for example, it was on the eastern side of Illinois. For another example, states such as mine—South Carolina—have become much more prosperous in recent years than they have ever been before. However, the state is still near the bottom on most of the indicators of quality of life such as per capita income, educational levels, and health status. That is because the relative positions of states change very slowly: While some states improve, all the other states are probably improving to some degree, as well. Therefore, all or most of the states may be better off, but the relative positions of the states change only slightly over long periods of time. Thus, older information may be just as valid for understanding and analysis as newly collected data.

This book provides descriptive statistics—information about the way things are. However, much of the data in the book also provides information on the way things have been and projects, on the basis of statistical formulas, the way things might become. Descriptive statistics provide information on the current status of whatever they are describing as well as information on the way phenomena change over time. (The other broad category of statistics is inferential, which is used to predict how variables may interact with or affect one another; although such data are useful in social work, this book primarily emphasizes the descriptive.)

Use

Some readers will read this book and study its tables for general background knowledge or for pleasure. Readers of the first edition reported that they read specific parts of the book to satisfy their curiosity about a given subject or that they used it to prepare speeches, reports, fundraising proposals, term papers, and the like.

Just as the *Encyclopedia of Social Work* and its supplements provide basic information on major issues in the field and just as *The Social Work Dictionary* defines specific social work terms, the *Social Work Almanac* provides basic data on fundamental information about social issues. Students who use statistics in preparing term papers, theses, dissertations, and other reports and instructors who cite statistics about issues they are teaching are bound to be more persuasive than those who simply offer conjecture or generalities about issues.

Similarly, social services planners can use statistical information to design effective programs and services. In addition, those who seek financial assistance from private and public funding agencies can also help build their cases by drawing on data from this book.

Administrators who are trying to convince their boards, local United Ways, or legislatures of the need for special help; attempting to demonstrate where their state or locality stands in relation to national norms; or seeking to show where improvements are needed—or

where the state or locality is doing the best job it can—can bolster their positions with data from this book. Administrators and others who are interviewed by the media should also be able to make effective use of this book in providing information to reporters, who often ask statistical questions and want to use statistical data in their stories.

For those who are statistics lovers—and there are many—it is hoped that this book will be a solid addition to statistical libraries. For those who have only a passing interest in statistics, it is hoped that they will become enthusiastic consumers of statistical information to inform their practice and enhance their advocacy. For example, it is possible to understand some of the discontents that contributed to the Los Angeles riots of April and May 1992 from the data in this book, especially the chapters that show the failure of social welfare programs to keep pace with social needs, the increasing disparities among income groups, and the disadvantages encountered by many minority group members. The statistics provided in this book thus can be used to shed light on the conditions social workers and their clients face.

People who want to delve further into subjects than the *Social Work Almanac* can take them may want to consult the sources from which the tables and figures were taken. In most cases, those sources have additional information on the same subject. For serious students of specific issues, the *Social Work Almanac* should be used as a guide or introduction rather than the final word on any subject.

This reference book is revised and updated periodically, and those who have been involved in producing it welcome suggestions and ideas about other items that could be included or materials that should be clarified. Comments may be addressed to the author and sent to NASW Press, the publisher.

1

BASIC DEMOGRAPHIC DATA ON THE POPULATION OF THE UNITED STATES

U.S. Population and Age Distribution

The population of the United States has grown dramatically during the 20th century. Table 1-1 presents figures for the total population and percentage increases from 1900 to 1992. Although the percentage increases are always small, the United States is 100 million people larger than it was in 1950, a year that many living Americans remember well. There are 50 million more Americans than there were in 1968, a year with historical significance for a variety of social and political reasons. Fifty million people is more than the populations of most nations, and only a few of the very largest nations have more than 100 million people.

It is important to examine rates of various social and health phenomena because they help account for the real significance of absolute increases. For example, although there have been increases in the total numbers of violent crimes, as chapter 3 shows, the rates of violent crimes have actually declined in recent years. When there are more people, there is more of everything—more cases of cancer, more serial murderers, more people with mental illness. However, when rates are calculated, the incidence of such phenomena per 100,000 population—the basis of most of the rates shown in this book—has often decreased. Much is different about the United States as it enters the 21st century, certainly different than it was in the memories of most readers of this book. However, many of those differences result from the large increases in the population, which have an impact on everything else.

The population of the United States now exceeds 250,000,000 people. In 1992 it was estimated to be about 255,082,000. Table 1-2 provides 1992 population figures by state and region, as well as the percentage of population increase since 1990, population age 65 and over, U.S. residents who were foreign born, and residents who spoke a language other than English. Ranks for each of the states in each of these categories are also shown for each of the measures.

The state with the largest population is California (30,867,000) followed by New York (18,119,000), Texas (17,656,000), and Florida (13,488,000). Regionally, the South had the largest population, whereas the Northeast had the lowest. The states with the largest percentage population increase since the 1990 census were Nevada (10.4), Alaska (6.7), and Idaho (6.0). California and New York are the states with the largest foreign-born populations. Florida, which remained popular with retirees, has the largest population over age 65 (18.4 percent of the total).

Table 1-3 shows the projected population through 2050, calculated according to three levels of projections. The actual population changes may reflect any one of these three models—or something in between them—depending on trends in birth rates, immigration, and life expectancy. By 2050 the population will probably be between 275 million and 500 million people, both of which are substantial increases over today's figures.

Table 1-4 shows the age distribution of the population of each state in 1992. The U.S. population is aging; in 1992, 12.7 percent of the population was 65 years or older. The largest number of young people and the largest number of people age 65 and older live in the South.

Population changes have significant consequences for business and government. Increased populations build the viability of a city

TABLE 1-1 U.S. Population: 1900 to 1992 (Numbers in thousands)

Year	Total Population	Total Percent Change	Resident Population	Civilian Population
1900			76,094	
1905			83,822	
1910			92,407	
1915			100,546	
1920			106,461	
1925			115,829	
1930			123,077	
1935			127,250	
1940			132,457	
1941			133,669	
1942			134,617	
1943			135,107	
1944			133,915	
1945			133,434	
1946			140,686	
1947			144,083	
1948			146,730	
1949			149,304	
1950			152,271	
1951			153,982	
1952			156,393	
1953	160,184	1.67	158,956	156,595
1954	163,026	1.77	161,884	159,695
1955	165,931	1.78	165,069	162,967
1956	168,903	1.79	168,088	166,055
1957	171,984	1.82	171,187	169,110
1958	174,882	1.68	174,149	172,226
1959	177,830	1.69	177,135	175,277
1960	180,671	1.60	179,979	178,140
1961	183,691	1.67	182,992	181,143
1962	186,538	1.55	185,771	183,677
1963	189,242	1.45	188,483	186,493
1964	191,889	1.40	191,141	189,141
1965	194,303	1.26	193,526	191,605
1966	196,560	1.16	195,576	193,420
1967	198,712	1.09	197,457	195,264
1968	200,706	1.00	199,399	197,113
1969	202,677	0.98	201,385	199,145
1970	205,052	1.17	203,984	201,895
1971	207,661	1.27	206,827	204,866
1972	209,896	1.08	209,284	207,511
1973	211,909	0.96	211,357	209,600
1974	213,854	0.92	213,342	211,636
1975	215,973	0.99	215,465	213,789
1976	218,035	0.95	217,563	215,894
1977	220,239	1.01	219,760	218,106
1978	222,585	1.06	222,095	220,467
1979	225,055	1.11	224,567	222,969
1980	227,726	1.19	227,225	225,621
1981	229,966	0.98	229,466	227,818
1982	232,188	0.97	231,664	229,995
1983	234,307	0.91	233,792	232,097
1984	236,348	0.87	235,825	234,110
1985	238,466	0.90	237,924	236,219
1986	240,651	0.92	240,133	238,412
1987	242,804	0.89	242,289	240,550
1988	245,021	0.91	244,499	242,817
1989	247,342	0.95	246,819	245,131
1990	249,900	1.03	249,391	247,751
1991	252,671	1.11	252,160	250,549
1992	255,462	1.10	255,082	253,497

Notes: Prior to 1940, excludes Alaska and Hawaii. Total population includes Armed Forces abroad; civilian population excludes Armed Forces.

Source: Reprinted from U.S. Bureau of the Census. (1993). *Statistical abstract of the United States: 1993* (113th ed., p. 8). Austin, TX: Reference Press.

TABLE 1-2 State Rankings, by Resident Population Size and Selected Characteristics: 1992

Region and State	Total, 1992 Number (1,000)	Rank	Percent Increase, 1990–92 Percent	Rank	65 Years Old and Over, 1992 Percent	Rank	Foreign-Born, 1990 Percent	Rank	Speak a Language Other Than English,[a] 1990 Percent	Rank
United States	255,082	NA	2.6	NA	12.7	NA	7.9	NA	13.8	NA
Northeast	51,118	NA	0.6	NA	13.9	NA	10.3	NA	16.5	NA
Connecticut	3,281	27	−0.2	48	13.9	11	8.5	10	15.2	10
Maine	1,235	39	0.6	45	13.6	15	3.0	26	9.2	17
Massachusetts	5,998	13	−0.3	49	13.9	12	9.5	6	15.2	11
New Hampshire	1,111	41	0.1	47	11.8	35	3.7	21	8.7	20
New Jersey	7,789	9	0.8	43	13.6	16	12.5	5	19.5	7
New York	18,119	2	0.7	44	13.1	22	15.9	2	23.3	5
Pennsylvania	12,009	5	1.1	41	15.7	2	3.1	25	7.3	24
Rhode Island	1,005	43	0.2	46	15.2	4	9.5	7	17.0	9
Vermont	570	49	1.2	40	12.0	33	3.1	24	5.8	30
Midwest	60,713	NA	1.8	NA	13.1	NA	3.6	NA	7.1	NA
Illinois	11,631	6	1.8	32	12.6	27	8.3	11	14.2	12
Indiana	5,662	14	2.1	27	12.7	26	1.7	38	4.8	39
Iowa	2,812	30	1.3	39	15.4	3	1.6	41	3.9	42
Kansas	2,523	32	1.8	31	13.9	13	2.5	30	5.7	32
Michigan	9,437	8	1.5	37	12.2	32	3.8	20	6.6	27
Minnesota	4,480	20	2.4	23	12.5	28	2.6	29	5.6	34
Missouri	5,193	15	1.5	38	14.1	10	1.6	40	3.8	43
Nebraska	1,606	36	1.7	33	14.1	9	1.8	35	4.8	38
North Dakota	636	47	−0.5	50	14.6	8	1.5	42	7.9	21
Ohio	11,016	7	1.6	36	13.2	21	2.4	32	5.4	35
South Dakota	711	45	2.2	26	14.7	7	1.1	45	6.5	28
Wisconsin	5,007	18	2.3	25	13.3	20	2.5	31	5.8	31
South	88,143	NA	3.2	NA	12.7	NA	5.4	NA	10.9	NA
Alabama	4,136	22	2.4	24	13.0	23	1.1	46	2.9	46
Arkansas	2,399	33	2.0	29	14.9	6	1.1	47	2.8	48
Delaware	689	46	3.5	15	12.3	31	3.3	23	6.9	26
District of Columbia	589	NA	−3.0	NA	13.1	NA	9.7	NA	12.5	NA
Florida	13,488	4	4.2	11	18.4	1	12.9	4	17.3	8
Georgia	6,751	11	4.2	12	10.1	47	2.7	28	4.8	40
Kentucky	3,755	24	1.9	30	12.7	25	0.9	48	2.5	50
Louisiana	4,287	21	1.6	35	11.2	39	2.1	34	10.1	16
Maryland	4,908	19	2.7	22	11.0	41	6.6	14	8.9	19
Mississippi	2,614	31	1.6	34	12.5	29	0.8	50	2.8	47
North Carolina	6,843	10	3.2	17	12.4	30	1.7	36	3.9	41
Oklahoma	3,212	28	2.1	28	13.5	17	2.1	33	5.0	37
South Carolina	3,603	25	3.3	16	11.6	37	1.4	43	3.5	44
Tennessee	5,024	17	3.0	20	12.7	24	1.2	44	2.9	45
Texas	17,656	3	3.9	13	10.2	46	9.0	8	25.4	3
Virginia	6,377	12	3.1	19	10.9	43	5.0	16	7.3	23
West Virginia	1,812	35	1.0	42	15.2	5	0.9	49	2.6	49
West	55,108	NA	4.4	NA	11.0	NA	14.8	NA	23.5	NA
Alaska	587	48	6.7	2	4.3	50	4.5	18	12.1	14
Arizona	3,832	23	4.6	9	13.4	19	7.6	12	20.8	6
California	30,867	1	3.7	14	10.5	45	21.7	1	31.5	2
Colorado	3,470	26	5.3	5	10.0	48	4.3	19	10.5	15
Hawaii	1,160	40	4.6	8	11.4	38	14.7	3	24.8	4
Idaho	1,067	42	6.0	3	11.9	34	2.9	27	6.4	29
Montana	824	44	3.1	18	13.4	18	1.7	37	5.0	36
Nevada	1,327	38	10.4	1	11.0	40	8.7	9	13.2	13
New Mexico	1,581	37	4.4	10	10.9	42	5.3	15	35.5	1
Oregon	2,977	29	4.8	7	13.8	14	4.9	17	7.3	25
Utah	1,813	34	5.2	6	8.8	49	3.4	22	7.8	22
Washington	5,136	16	5.5	4	11.7	36	6.6	13	9.0	18
Wyoming	466	50	2.8	21	10.7	44	1.7	39	5.7	33

Notes: When states share the same rank, the next lower rank is omitted. Because of rounded data, states may have identical values shown but different ranks. NA = not applicable.

Source: Reprinted from U.S. Bureau of the Census. (1993). *Statistical abstract of the United States: 1993* (113th ed., p. xii). Austin, TX: Reference Press.

[a]People 5 years old or older.

or a state's economy. Additional schools are required for the larger child population, and the health and social services needs of the adult population increase. When the official population statistics are determined during the Census, which is conducted every 10 years (the last was in 1990), population changes become the bases for allocating the 435 members of Congress among the states and determining the provision of federal funds under some programs. States with large increases in residents gain greater representation and funding, and those with large decreases lose members of Congress and federal money. State per capita income, which is calculated annually, is the basis for determining the percentage of federal funds provided for such programs as Medicaid and Aid to Families with Dependent Children. The matching percentage is redetermined every other year.

Race and Ethnicity

Table 1-5 shows the distribution of the American population by age, race (white; African American; Native American; and Asian and Pacific Islander), and gender from 1980 to 1991. Projections from 1995 through the year 2025 are presented in Table 1-6.

TABLE 1-3 **Resident Population Projections: Selected Years, 1992 to 2050 (Numbers in thousands)**

Year	Middle Series[a]	Lowest Series[b]	Highest Series[c]	Fertility		Life Expectancy		Net Immigration	
				Low	High	Low	High	Low	High
1992	254,922	254,678	255,147	254,922	254,922	254,890	254,951	254,710	255,118
1993	257,592	256,930	258,211	257,549	257,638	257,508	257,670	257,057	258,087
1994	260,202	258,932	261,399	260,059	260,355	260,046	260,347	259,230	261,101
1995	262,754	260,715	264,685	262,483	263,042	262,507	262,984	261,229	264,165
1996	265,251	262,386	267,976	264,825	265,704	264,897	265,584	263,161	267,187
1997	267,700	263,954	271,278	267,092	268,346	267,220	268,154	265,032	270,172
1998	270,106	265,426	274,597	269,288	270,975	269,485	270,698	266,848	273,126
1999	272,476	266,808	277,938	271,421	273,597	271,698	273,222	268,617	276,055
2000	274,815	268,108	281,306	273,496	276,218	273,864	275,732	270,345	278,965
2005	286,324	273,605	298,773	283,271	289,624	284,206	288,238	278,644	293,467
2010	298,109	278,078	317,895	292,579	304,258	294,382	301,184	287,022	308,443
2015	310,370	282,045	338,580	301,815	320,102	304,674	314,733	295,720	324,049
2020	322,602	285,200	360,123	310,681	336,421	314,582	328,401	304,227	339,786
2025	334,216	286,854	382,281	318,465	352,849	323,542	341,678	311,930	355,089
2030	344,951	286,710	405,130	324,798	369,357	331,339	354,367	318,564	369,700
2040	364,349	282,286	453,687	333,694	403,559	344,512	378,378	329,321	397,285
2050	382,674	275,647	506,740	339,701	440,955	357,028	401,359	338,650	424,161

Source: Reprinted from U.S. Bureau of the Census. (1993). *Statistical abstract of the United States: 1993* (113th ed., p. 9). Austin, TX: Reference Press.

[a]Ultimate total fertility rate = 2,119; life expectancy in 2050 = 82.1 years; annual net immigration = 880,000.
[b]Ultimate total fertility rate = 1,846; life expectancy in 2050 = 75.3 years; annual net immigration = 350,000.
[c]Ultimate total fertility rate = 2,507; life expectancy in 2050 = 87.6 years; annual net immigration = 1,370,000.

TABLE 1-4 Resident Population, by Age Group and State: 1992 (Numbers in thousands)

Region and State	Total	Under 5 Years	5 to 17 Years	18 to 24 Years	25 to 34 Years	35 to 44 Years	45 to 54 Years	55 to 64 Years	65 to 74 Years	75 to 84 Years	85 Years and Over	16 Years and Over	Percent 65 Years and Over
United States	255,082	19,512	46,655	25,919	42,463	39,904	27,418	20,927	18,461	10,565	3,259	195,672	12.7
Northeast	51,118	3,702	8,547	5,052	8,480	8,012	5,706	4,494	4,047	2,344	734	40,124	13.9
Connecticut	3,281	239	532	306	554	526	383	283	255	152	49	2,586	13.9
Maine	1,235	83	223	122	195	203	136	106	94	56	19	962	13.6
Massachusetts	5,998	434	950	632	1,067	943	646	491	461	279	95	4,750	13.9
New Hampshire	1,111	82	198	110	193	190	122	85	74	43	14	858	11.8
New Jersey	7,789	573	1,290	713	1,310	1,244	905	696	615	343	99	6,117	13.6
New York	18,119	1,366	3,056	1,810	3,067	2,813	2,037	1,596	1,345	777	252	14,151	13.1
Pennsylvania	12,009	813	2,031	1,185	1,837	1,843	1,308	1,109	1,080	621	181	9,465	15.7
Rhode Island	1,005	71	162	111	166	154	104	83	86	51	16	795	15.2
Vermont	570	40	104	63	90	97	63	44	38	22	8	441	12.0
Midwest	60,713	4,493	11,441	6,126	9,736	9,392	6,487	5,077	4,434	2,647	881	46,442	13.1
Illinois	11,631	899	2,130	1,167	1,953	1,802	1,255	962	822	489	153	8,912	12.6
Indiana	5,662	405	1,056	610	896	875	621	480	408	235	75	4,361	12.7
Iowa	2,812	194	541	281	411	418	291	244	227	150	57	2,156	15.4
Kansas	2,523	187	491	251	396	388	255	204	186	119	44	1,913	13.9
Michigan	9,437	724	1,785	978	1,516	1,483	1,024	776	669	369	113	7,190	12.2
Minnesota	4,480	335	871	425	755	717	470	345	297	193	71	3,393	12.5
Missouri	5,193	377	973	506	820	777	559	448	399	249	86	3,983	14.1
Nebraska	1,606	119	320	157	246	243	160	133	118	78	30	1,212	14.1
North Dakota	636	45	127	67	98	96	60	51	47	34	12	482	14.6
Ohio	11,016	793	2,027	1,119	1,739	1,714	1,204	964	845	466	146	8,497	13.2
South Dakota	711	54	150	69	104	104	67	59	55	36	14	528	14.7
Wisconsin	5,007	360	970	497	801	777	522	411	361	230	78	3,815	13.3
South	88,143	6,633	16,226	9,164	14,553	13,602	9,494	7,315	6,451	3,634	1,070	67,678	12.7
Alabama	4,136	298	778	449	639	621	449	363	307	178	52	3,181	13.0
Arkansas	2,399	171	458	244	349	344	262	213	198	123	37	1,841	14.9
Delaware	689	52	120	72	120	106	75	60	52	25	8	534	12.3
District of Columbia	589	41	76	70	119	94	63	48	44	25	8	483	13.1
Florida	13,488	943	2,163	1,173	2,081	1,946	1,415	1,282	1,414	838	232	10,690	18.4
Georgia	6,751	530	1,270	732	1,184	1,089	749	514	399	220	62	5,138	10.1
Kentucky	3,755	258	706	402	596	580	415	322	270	157	50	2,901	12.7
Louisiana	4,287	340	898	462	691	646	435	335	281	154	45	3,180	11.2
Maryland	4,908	383	843	465	888	819	574	397	324	166	50	3,798	11.0
Mississippi	2,614	203	545	302	388	372	265	214	182	110	34	1,951	12.5

Continued on next page

TABLE 1-4 Continued

Region and State	Total	Under 5 Years	5 to 17 Years	18 to 24 Years	25 to 34 Years	35 to 44 Years	45 to 54 Years	55 to 64 Years	65 to 74 Years	75 to 84 Years	85 Years and Over	16 Years and Over	Percent 65 Years and Over
North Carolina	6,843	491	1,171	767	1,140	1,070	764	594	501	268	76	5,359	12.4
Oklahoma	3,212	232	626	330	493	481	344	272	241	145	48	2,447	13.5
South Carolina	3,603	273	672	409	589	557	390	296	255	128	34	2,760	11.6
Tennessee	5,024	353	893	529	807	787	574	440	367	211	63	3,915	12.7
Texas	17,656	1,489	3,583	1,881	3,084	2,755	1,781	1,285	1,042	576	179	13,098	10.2
Virginia	6,377	468	1,094	688	1,136	1,050	735	509	415	217	64	4,974	10.9
West Virginia	1,812	108	330	191	250	284	204	171	158	91	27	1,429	15.2
West	55,108	4,684	10,442	5,577	9,693	8,897	5,730	4,041	3,529	1,940	574	41,427	11.0
Alaska	587	57	128	57	111	114	63	32	17	6	1	417	4.3
Arizona	3,832	320	727	384	634	568	381	305	303	167	43	2,887	13.4
California	30,867	2,763	5,660	3,195	5,714	4,925	3,158	2,207	1,897	1,036	313	23,217	10.5
Colorado	3,470	262	647	341	607	622	384	259	204	109	35	2,651	10.0
Hawaii	1,160	91	202	119	202	193	125	95	82	40	11	895	11.4
Idaho	1,067	83	241	108	151	166	110	80	71	44	13	779	11.9
Montana	824	58	168	75	117	136	91	69	61	38	11	623	13.4
Nevada	1,327	106	232	118	246	213	153	113	96	41	9	1,021	11.0
New Mexico	1,581	133	336	156	251	247	162	124	102	56	16	1,160	10.9
Oregon	2,977	211	555	274	451	507	335	233	230	138	42	2,291	13.8
Utah	1,813	176	478	215	281	244	151	108	93	52	15	1,227	8.8
Washington	5,136	390	965	488	860	880	570	383	343	197	60	3,915	11.7
Wyoming	466	34	104	46	70	80	48	34	29	16	5	343	10.7

Source: Reprinted from U.S. Bureau of the Census. (1993). *Statistical abstract of the United States: 1993* (113th ed., p. 33). Austin, TX: Reference Press.

TABLE 1-5 Resident Population, by Age Group, Gender, and Race: 1980, 1990, and 1991 (Numbers in thousands)

Year, Gender, and Race	Total, All Years	Under 5 Years	5-9 Years	10-14 Years	15-19 Years	20-24 Years	25-29 Years	30-34 Years	35-39 Years	40-44 Years	45-49 Years	50-54 Years	55-59 Years	60-64 Years	65-74 Years	75-84 Years	85 Years and Over
All Races																	
1980	226,546	16,348	16,700	18,242	21,168	21,319	19,521	17,561	13,965	11,669	11,090	11,710	11,615	10,088	15,581	7,729	2,240
1990	248,710	18,758	18,035	17,060	17,882	19,132	21,328	21,833	19,846	17,589	13,744	11,313	10,487	10,625	18,045	10,012	3,021
1991	252,177	19,222	18,237	17,671	17,205	19,194	20,518	22,159	20,518	18,754	14,094	11,645	10,423	10,582	18,280	10,314	3,160
Male	122,979	9,836	9,337	9,051	8,834	9,775	10,393	11,034	10,174	9,258	6,907	5,656	4,987	4,945	8,022	3,888	881
Female	129,198	9,386	8,900	8,620	8,371	9,419	10,325	11,125	10,344	9,496	7,188	5,989	5,436	5,637	10,258	6,426	2,279
White																	
1980	194,713	13,414	13,717	15,095	17,681	18,072	16,658	15,157	12,122	10,110	9,693	10,360	10,394	9,078	14,045	7,057	2,060
1990	208,704	14,960	14,502	13,670	14,351	15,637	17,638	18,190	16,652	15,001	11,826	9,744	9,131	9,381	16,175	9,084	2,761
1991	210,899	15,168	14,634	14,122	13,749	15,630	17,036	18,424	17,170	15,927	12,097	10,013	9,037	9,312	16,338	9,356	2,886
Male	103,268	7,780	7,512	7,254	7,078	8,006	8,620	9,272	8,608	7,948	5,984	4,908	4,367	4,396	7,212	3,529	795
Female	107,631	7,388	7,123	6,868	6,671	7,625	8,416	9,152	8,562	7,980	6,113	5,105	4,669	4,916	9,125	5,827	2,090
Black																	
1980	26,683	2,459	2,509	2,691	3,007	2,749	2,342	1,904	1,469	1,260	1,150	1,135	1,041	874	1,344	588	159
1990	30,483	2,939	2,711	2,629	2,714	2,655	2,780	2,718	2,359	1,882	1,413	1,178	1,041	972	1,498	772	223
1991	31,164	3,099	2,747	2,722	2,647	2,671	2,753	2,763	2,463	2,055	1,451	1,211	1,050	979	1,536	786	232
Male	14,753	1,568	1,391	1,376	1,339	1,309	1,311	1,291	1,144	949	661	544	464	422	631	282	69
Female	16,412	1,531	1,356	1,346	1,307	1,361	1,442	1,472	1,318	1,106	790	666	586	557	905	504	163
Native American																	
1980	1,420	149	147	156	170	149	125	107	84	69	58	52	45	34	48	21	6
1990	2,065	220	209	197	191	179	188	181	157	132	99	79	64	53	73	34	9
1991	2,117	234	212	207	186	183	184	183	162	138	103	81	65	54	76	36	11
Male	1,050	119	108	105	95	95	93	90	79	67	50	39	31	26	34	14	4
Female	1,068	115	105	102	91	88	91	93	83	71	53	42	34	29	42	21	7
Asian, Pacific Islander																	
1980	3,729	326	328	300	310	349	396	393	291	230	188	163	135	101	143	63	15
1990	7,458	638	612	564	626	661	722	745	678	574	405	312	252	220	300	122	29
1991	7,996	720	644	621	623	710	744	788	723	633	444	340	271	237	329	135	32
Male	3,909	369	327	316	321	365	369	381	343	294	212	165	124	102	145	63	13
Female	4,087	352	317	305	302	345	375	407	380	339	232	175	147	135	184	74	19
Percent: Total, 1991	100.0	7.6	7.2	7.0	6.8	7.6	8.2	8.8	8.1	7.4	5.6	4.6	4.1	4.2	7.7	4.1	1.3
White	100.0	7.2	6.9	6.7	6.5	7.4	8.1	8.7	8.1	7.6	5.7	4.7	4.3	4.4	7.7	4.4	1.4
Black	100.0	9.9	8.8	8.7	8.5	8.6	8.8	8.9	7.9	6.6	4.7	3.9	3.4	3.1	4.9	2.5	0.7
Native American	100.0	11.1	10.0	9.8	8.8	8.6	8.7	8.6	7.7	6.5	4.9	3.8	3.1	2.6	3.6	1.7	0.5
Asian, Pacific Islander	100.0	9.0	8.1	7.8	7.8	8.9	9.3	9.9	9.0	7.9	5.6	4.3	3.4	3.0	4.1	1.7	0.4

Source: Reprinted from U.S. Bureau of the Census. (1993). Statistical abstract of the United States: 1993 (113th ed., p. 21). Austin, TX: Reference Press.

TABLE 1-6 Projections of Resident Population, by Age Group, Race, and Gender: Selected Years, 1995 to 2025 (Numbers in thousands)

Age, Race, and Gender	Population 1995	Population 2000	Population 2005	Population 2010	Population 2025	Percent Distribution 2000	Percent Distribution 2010	Percent Distribution 2025
Total	262,754	274,815	286,324	298,109	334,216	100.0	100.0	100.0
Under 5 years old	19,553	18,908	18,959	19,730	21,682	6.9	6.6	6.5
5 to 13 years old	34,372	36,051	35,782	35,425	39,547	13.1	11.9	11.8
14 to 17 years old	14,754	15,734	17,020	16,908	17,652	5.7	5.7	5.3
18 to 24 years old	24,903	26,117	28,111	30,007	30,005	9.5	10.1	9.0
25 to 34 years old	40,844	37,416	36,495	38,367	43,129	13.6	12.9	12.9
35 to 44 years old	42,500	44,662	42,284	38,853	42,541	16.3	13.0	12.7
45 to 54 years old	31,082	37,054	41,610	43,737	37,346	13.5	14.7	11.2
55 to 64 years old	21,153	23,988	29,647	35,378	39,892	8.7	11.9	11.9
65 to 74 years old	18,800	18,258	18,523	21,235	35,820	6.6	7.1	10.7
75 to 84 years old	11,154	12,339	12,955	12,767	19,565	4.5	4.3	5.9
85 years old and over	3,638	4,289	4,937	5,702	7,038	1.6	1.9	2.1
Male	128,292	134,338	140,097	146,012	164,054	48.9	49.0	49.1
Female	134,461	140,477	146,227	152,097	170,162	51.1	51.0	50.9
White, total	217,511	224,594	230,993	237,412	256,425	100.0	100.0	100.0
Under 5 years old	15,321	14,496	14,254	14,617	15,461	6.5	6.2	6.0
5 to 13 years old	27,201	28,043	27,303	26,455	28,361	12.5	11.1	11.1
14 to 17 years old	11,662	12,322	13,068	12,764	12,601	5.5	5.4	4.9
18 to 24 years old	19,862	20,615	21,997	23,107	21,828	9.2	9.7	8.5
25 to 34 years old	33,296	29,825	28,603	29,813	32,125	13.3	12.6	12.5
35 to 44 years old	35,336	36,660	34,110	30,634	32,436	16.3	12.9	12.6
45 to 54 years old	26,548	31,203	34,536	35,860	28,928	13.9	15.1	11.3
55 to 64 years old	18,242	20,554	25,265	29,772	32,180	9.2	12.5	12.5
65 to 74 years old	16,652	15,906	15,899	18,136	29,764	7.1	7.6	11.6
75 to 84 years old	10,093	11,111	11,538	11,191	16,798	4.9	4.7	6.6
85 years old and over	3,299	3,862	4,419	5,064	5,944	1.7	2.1	2.3
Male	106,684	110,359	113,689	117,043	126,877	49.1	49.3	49.5
Female	110,827	114,235	117,304	120,369	129,548	50.9	50.7	50.5
Black, total	33,147	35,525	37,907	40,429	48,388	100.0	100.0	100.0
Under 5 years old	3,177	3,183	3,299	3,529	4,088	9.0	8.7	8.4
5 to 13 years old	5,337	5,829	5,939	6,081	7,221	16.4	15.0	14.9
14 to 17 years old	2,296	2,418	2,786	2,803	3,189	6.8	6.9	6.6
18 to 24 years old	3,703	3,923	4,197	4,701	5,095	11.0	11.6	10.5
25 to 34 years old	5,372	5,131	5,163	5,426	6,572	14.4	13.4	13.6
35 to 44 years old	5,154	5,586	5,422	5,175	5,934	15.7	12.8	12.3
45 to 54 years old	3,237	4,110	4,910	5,323	4,998	11.6	13.2	10.3
55 to 64 years old	2,130	2,413	3,015	3,838	4,904	6.8	9.5	10.1
65 to 74 years old	1,625	1,690	1,804	2,070	4,041	4.8	5.1	8.4
75 to 84 years old	837	909	990	1,044	1,712	2.6	2.6	3.5
85 years old and over	278	333	382	439	635	0.9	1.1	1.3
Male	15,711	16,846	17,972	19,168	22,951	47.4	47.4	47.4
Female	17,436	18,680	19,936	21,261	25,437	52.6	52.6	52.6
Native American, total	2,247	2,409	2,583	2,772	3,386	100.0	100.0	100.0
Under 5 years old	220	224	242	264	308	9.3	9.5	9.1
5 to 13 years old	412	425	429	455	561	17.6	16.4	16.6
14 to 17 years old	174	193	208	204	254	8.0	7.4	7.5
18 to 24 years old	255	277	314	337	382	11.5	12.2	11.3
24 to 34 years old	362	356	367	407	481	14.8	14.7	14.2
35 to 44 years old	332	352	345	341	436	14.6	12.3	12.9
45 to 54 years old	219	262	298	318	320	10.9	11.5	9.5
55 to 64 years old	132	153	186	225	271	6.4	8.1	8.0
65 to 74 years old	85	93	104	123	210	3.9	4.4	6.2
75 to 84 years old	42	51	58	64	108	2.1	2.3	3.2
85 years old and over	15	22	28	35	56	0.9	1.3	1.7
Male	1,113	1,193	1,279	1,372	1,677	49.5	49.5	49.5
Female	1,133	1,216	1,304	1,400	1,709	50.5	50.5	50.5

Continued on next page

Table 1-7 provides information regarding the age, education, and income levels, employment status, and family type and residence of the Hispanic population. The term "Hispanic" is problematic because it includes many subcategories of people and because it overlaps considerably with other racial and ethnic groups. The *Statistical Abstract* (U.S. Bureau of the Census, 1993) calls for respondents to identify themselves as Mexican, Puerto Rican, Cuban, or Other Spanish/Hispanic origin (respondents could write in their entries for the Other category). The *Statistical Abstract* classifies as Hispanic those who report themselves to be Mexican American, Chicano, Mexican, Puerto Rican, Cuban, Central or South American from Spanish-speaking countries, or other Hispanic origin. As is noted throughout the book, data on Hispanics and other groups are not mutually exclusive, because Hispanics may be white, African American, Asian American, Native American, or members of any other group.

The whole issue of defining U.S. citizens according to ethnic or racial groups may become a controversial matter for the 2000 Census (Wright, 1994). Congressional hearings have been held because of concerns about classifying people with parents who fall under more than one of the official categories and even about the propriety of the government defining citizens racially or ethnically.

Figure 1-1 shows the percentage distribution of the population by race and Hispanic origin in 1990 and provides projections through 2050. The projected changes in the relative proportions of African American and Hispanic populations are noteworthy. Beginning in the year 2000, the size of the Hispanic population is expected to equal or surpass the African American population. However, it is important to note that many Hispanics are also African Americans, making it difficult to pinpoint this trend.

TABLE 1-6 **Continued**

Age, Race, and Gender	Population					Percent Distribution		
	1995	2000	2005	2010	2025	2000	2010	2025
Asian, Pacific Islander, total	9,849	12,287	14,840	17,496	26,017	100.0	100.0	100.0
Under 5 years old	836	1,006	1,163	1,320	1,824	8.2	7.5	7.0
5 to 13 years old	1,422	1,755	2,110	2,435	3,405	14.3	13.9	13.1
14 to 17 years old	623	801	956	1,136	1,608	6.5	6.5	6.2
18 to 24 years old	1,084	1,303	1,603	1,863	2,700	10.6	10.6	10.4
25 to 34 years old	1,813	2,104	2,361	2,722	3,952	17.1	15.6	15.2
35 to 44 years old	1,678	2,064	2,406	2,704	3,737	16.8	15.5	14.4
45 to 54 years old	1,079	1,479	1,866	2,236	3,101	12.0	12.8	11.9
55 to 64 years old	649	867	1,181	1,542	2,536	7.1	8.8	9.7
65 to 74 years old	439	568	717	907	1,806	4.6	5.2	6.9
75 to 84 years old	184	269	368	468	947	2.2	2.7	3.6
85 years old and over	46	72	108	165	402	0.6	0.9	1.5
Male	4,784	5,940	7,157	8,428	12,549	48.3	48.2	48.2
Female	5,066	6,347	7,684	9,068	13,468	51.7	51.8	51.8

Source: Reprinted from U.S. Bureau of the Census. (1993). *Statistical abstract of the United States: 1993* (113th ed., p. 24). Austin, TX: Reference Press.

TABLE 1-7 **Social and Economic Characteristics of the Hispanic Population: 1991 (Numbers in thousands)**

Characteristic	Number						Percent Distribution					
	Hispanic, Total	Mexican	Puerto Rican	Cuban	Central and South American	Other Hispanic	Hispanic, Total	Mexican	Puerto Rican	Cuban	Central and South American	Other Hispanic
Total persons	21,437	13,421	2,382	1,055	2,951	1,628	100.0	100.0	100.0	100.0	100.0	100.0
Under 5 years old	2,370	1,592	262	59	318	139	11.1	11.9	11.0	5.6	10.8	8.5
5 to 14 years old	4,006	2,698	478	91	497	242	18.7	20.1	20.1	8.6	16.8	14.9
15 to 44 years old	10,993	6,936	1,178	463	1,612	806	51.3	51.7	49.5	43.9	54.6	49.5
45 to 64 years old	2,976	1,608	352	287	435	295	13.9	12.0	14.8	27.2	14.7	18.1
65 years old and over	1,091	587	112	156	89	146	5.1	4.4	4.7	14.8	3.0	9.0
Years of school completed												
Persons 25 years old and over	11,208	6,518	1,261	784	1,658	986	100.0	100.0	100.0	100.0	100.0	100.0
Elementary: 0 to 8 years	3,761	2,609	306	223	456	166	33.6	40.0	24.3	28.4	27.5	16.8
High school: 1 to 3 years	1,695	1,067	224	83	201	119	15.1	16.4	17.8	10.6	12.1	12.1
High school: 4 years	3,285	1,747	416	220	533	370	29.3	26.8	33.0	28.1	32.1	37.5
College: 1 to 3 years	1,379	690	188	113	217	171	12.3	10.6	14.9	14.4	13.1	17.3
College: 4 years or more	1,089	405	127	145	251	160	9.7	6.2	10.1	18.5	15.1	16.2
Labor force status												
Civilians 16 years old and over	14,770	8,947	1,629	849	—	—	100.0	100.0	100.0	100.0	—	—
Civilian labor force	9,762	5,984	930	543	—	—	66.1	66.9	57.1	64.0	—	—
Employed	8,799	5,363	822	499	—	—	59.6	59.9	50.5	58.8	—	—
Unemployed	963	621	108	44	—	—	6.5	6.9	6.6	5.2	—	—
Unemployment rate	9.9	10.4	11.6	8.1	—	—	NA	NA	NA	NA	—	—
Not in labor force	5,008	2,963	699	306	—	—	33.9	33.1	42.9	36.0	—	—
Family type												
Total families	4,982	2,945	626	335	667	408	100.0	100.0	100.0	100.0	100.0	100.0
Married couple	3,454	2,164	328	255	441	266	69.3	73.5	52.4	76.1	66.1	65.1
Female householder, no spouse present	1,186	563	271	65	174	112	23.8	19.1	43.3	19.4	26.1	27.5
Male householder, no spouse present	342	218	27	15	52	30	6.9	7.4	4.3	4.5	7.8	7.3

Family income in 1990												
Total families	4,982	100.0	2,945	100.0	626	100.0	335	100.0	667	100.0	408	100.0
Less than $5,000	312	6.3	167	5.7	69	11.0	19	5.7	35	5.2	22	5.4
$5,000 to $9,999	614	12.3	340	11.5	142	22.7	27	8.1	61	9.1	44	10.8
$10,000 to $14,999	629	12.6	402	13.7	63	10.1	30	9.0	92	13.8	41	10.0
$15,000 to $24,999	1,082	21.7	659	22.4	118	18.8	59	17.6	170	25.4	76	18.6
$25,000 to $34,999	826	16.6	520	17.7	71	11.3	66	19.7	105	15.7	64	15.7
$35,000 to $49,999	784	15.7	498	16.9	76	12.1	54	16.1	92	13.8	65	15.9
$50,000 or more	734	14.7	359	12.2	88	14.1	80	23.9	111	16.6	96	23.5
Median income ($)	23,431	NA	23,240	NA	18,008	NA	31,439	NA	23,445	NA	27,382	NA
Families below poverty level[a]	1,244	25.0	736	25.0	235	37.5	46	13.8	148	22.2	79	19.4
Persons below poverty level[a]	6,006	28.1	3,764	28.1	966	40.6	178	16.9	748	25.4	350	21.5
Housing tenure												
Total occupied units	6,220	100.0	3,604	100.0	805	100.0	425	100.0	809	100.0	576	100.0
Owner-occupied	2,423	39.0	1,568	43.5	188	23.4	201	47.3	180	22.2	286	49.6
Renter-occupied	3,797	61.0	2,036	56.5	617	76.6	224	52.5	630	77.8	290	50.3

Notes: — = not available; NA = not applicable.

Source: Reprinted from U.S. Bureau of the Census. (1993). *Statistical abstract of the United States: 1993* (113th ed., p. 49). Austin, TX: Reference Press.

[a]Poverty levels are determined by family size and income. For example, in 1991 the poverty level for a family of four was $13,942 and for a family of eight was $23,605.

Table 1-8 provides information on the Asian and Pacific Islander population for the years 1990 and 1992. Information on the Native American (American Indian, Eskimo, and Aleut) population of the United States is provided in Tables 1-9 and 1-10. Table 1-9 shows the states in which many of them reside. It also provides information about the household composition of the Native American population.

Table 1-10 shows Native American trust lands and reservations with populations exceeding 5,000. (Nearly half the Native American population does not live on these trust lands or reservations.) Information is also provided on the various Indian nations or tribes.

The foreign-born population, various ancestry groups, and the percentage of adults who speak foreign languages are described in Table 1-11. Nationally, the major ancestry groups are German, Irish, and English. There are also large proportions of people of African American, Italian, Norwegian, Native American, Mexican, Polish, and (in the case of Hawaii) Japanese, Filipino, and Hawaiian ancestries. Table 1-12 provides more detail on the ancestry groups that make up the American population.

Metropolitan and Nonmetropolitan Areas

Another important index of the population is the distribution of the population in metropolitan areas. The U.S. Office of Management and Budget (OMB) divides the nation into 250 metropolitan statistical areas (MSAs), which it defines as cities or urbanized areas with 50,000 or more people. Demographers find it useful to use standardized units of measurement, such as MSAs, which are probably the most understandable and widely used divisions of the American population.

MSAs cross state and county lines. Former small towns or rural areas have become suburbs of major cities. The populations of many major cities have declined, although the MSAs they anchor have grown. Furthermore, state laws on what constitutes a city differ; thus, in some states, cities may readily annex adjacent small towns or unincorporated areas, whereas in others, constitutional and statutory provisions make it difficult for formerly separate rural areas to

FIGURE 1-1 **Percentage Distribution of the Population, by Race and Hispanic Origin: 1990 and Projections to 2050**

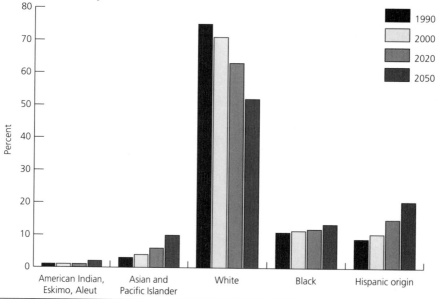

Note: People of Hispanic origin may be of any race.

Source: Reprinted from U.S. Bureau of the Census. (1993). *Statistical abstract of the United States: 1993* (113th ed., p. 7). Austin, TX: Reference Press.

be incorporated into cities. In many jurisdictions, the area to be incorporated must grant permission before it can be made part of a city. These issues have an impact on tax revenues, the organization and delivery of services, the duplication of efforts such as garbage collection, the enforcement of zoning and construction codes, and other government functions. Law enforcement agencies may overlap or duplicate their efforts by serving the same geographic areas and dealing with the same problems, although efforts to coordinate their work and to avoid such duplications are common.

TABLE 1-8 **Social and Economic Characteristics of the Asian and Pacific Islander Population: 1990 and 1992 (Numbers in thousands)**

Characteristic	Number		Percent Distribution	
	1990	1992	1990	1992
Total persons	6,679	7,193	100.0	100.0
Under 5 years old	602	589	9.0	8.2
5 to 14 years old	1,112	1,133	16.6	15.8
15 to 44 years old	3,345	3,609	50.1	50.2
45 to 64 years old	1,155	1,306	17.3	18.2
65 years old and over	465	555	7.0	7.7
Years of school completed				
Persons 25 years old and over	3,961	4,409	100.0	100.0
Elementary: 0 to 8 years	543	489	13.7	11.1
High school: 1 to 3 years	234	229	5.9	5.2
High school: 4 years	1,038	1,171	26.2	26.6
College: 1 to 3 years	568	784	14.3	17.8
College: 4 years or more	1,578	1,737	39.9	39.4
Labor force status				
Civilians 16 years old and over	4,849	5,342	100.0	100.0
Civilian labor force	3,216	3,473	66.3	65.0
Employed	3,079	3,255	63.5	60.9
Unemployed	136	218	2.8	4.1
Unemployment rate	4.2	6.3	NA	NA
Not in labor force	1,634	1,869	33.7	35.0
Family type				
Total families	1,531	1,624	100.0	100.0
Married couple	1,256	1,284	82.1	79.1
Female householder, no spouse present	188	237	12.3	14.6
Male householder, no spouse present	86	103	5.6	6.3
Family income in previous year in constant (1991) dollars				
Total families	1,531	1,624	100.0	100.0
Less than $5,000	—	69	—	4.2
$5,000 to $9,999	—	95	—	5.9
$10,000 to $14,999	—	108	—	6.7
$15,000 to $24,999	—	212	—	13.0
$25,000 to $34,999	—	219	—	13.5
$35,000 to $49,999	—	269	—	16.6
$50,000 or more	—	652	—	40.1
Median income ($)	44,320	42,661	NA	NA
Poverty				
Families below poverty level	182	210	11.9	13.0
Persons below poverty level	939	996	14.1	13.8
Housing tenure				
Total occupied units	1,988	2,094	100.0	100.0
Owner-occupied	977	1,068	49.1	51.0
Renter-occupied	982	997	49.4	47.6

Notes: — = not available; NA = not applicable.

Source: Reprinted from U.S. Bureau of the Census. (1993). *Statistical abstract of the United States: 1993* (113th ed., p. 47). Austin, TX: Reference Press.

The U.S. Bureau of the Census defines rural communities as those with 2,500 or fewer people. Metropolitan areas include over three-quarters of all American residents. Table 1-13 shows the metropolitan and nonmetropolitan composition of the states in 1980 and 1990 and illustrates the growth in metropolitan area population during the decade. As the table shows, the populations in both metropolitan and nonmetropolitan areas grew from 1980 to 1991. However, the growth of metropolitan areas was slightly greater. In 1990, 79.4 percent of the population lived in metropolitan areas, which means that only slightly more than one fifth of the population lived in nonmetropolitan areas. The most metropolitan states are New Jersey, California, and Massachusetts, in that order. The least metropolitan state is Montana.

TABLE 1-9 **Number of American Indians, Eskimos, and Aleuts Living inside and outside Identified Areas, and Households, by Type: 1990 (Numbers in thousands)**

Identified Area and Household Type	Total U.S.	Oklahoma	California	Arizona	New Mexico	Alaska	Washington
Total population	1,959	252	242	204	134	86	81
Inside identified areas	739	207	14	142	88	48	22
American Indian areas	692	207	14	142	88	1	22
Reservations[a]	411	6	13	142	68	1	21
Trust lands[b]	26	NA	c	c	19	NA	1
Tribal Jurisdiction Statistical Areas[d]	201	201	NA	NA	NA	NA	NA
Tribal Designated Statistical Areas[e]	54	NA	NA	NA	NA	NA	NA
Alaska Native Village Statistical Areas[f]	47	NA	NA	NA	NA	47	NA
Outside identified areas	1,220	45	229	61	47	37	60
Total households	591	78	79	50	33	22	25
Family households	442	59	56	41	28	16	18
Married couple family	284	43	37	24	16	10	11
With related children	179	25	21	18	13	7	6
With no related children	104	18	15	6	4	2	4
Male householder, no spouse present	37	3	5	4	3	2	2
With related children	25	2	3	3	2	1	1
With no related children	12	1	2	1	1	1	c
Female householder, no spouse present	121	13	15	13	8	5	6
With related children	94	9	11	10	6	4	5
With no related children	27	3	4	3	2	1	1
Nonfamily households	149	19	23	9	6	6	7
One-person households	116	16	16	7	5	5	5
Two- or more person households	33	2	7	2	1	1	2

Notes: Households are based on race of householder. NA = not applicable (area not located within this state).

Source: Reprinted from U.S. Bureau of the Census (1993). *Statistical abstract of the United States: 1993* (113th ed., p. 48). Austin, TX: Reference Press.

[a]Federal American Indian reservations are areas with boundaries established by treaty, statute, or executive or court order and recognized by the federal government as territory in which American Indian tribes have jurisdiction. State reservations are lands held in trust by state governments for the use and benefit of a given tribe.

[b]Property associated with a particular American Indian reservation or tribe, held in trust by the federal government. These lands are located outside of a reservation boundary.

[c]Fewer than 500.

[d]Areas delineated by federally recognized tribes in Oklahoma without a land base or associated trust lands to produce statistical areas for which the Census Bureau tabulates data.

[e]Areas delineated outside Oklahoma by federally and state-recognized tribes in Oklahoma without a land base or associated trust lands to provide statistical areas for which the Census Bureau tabulates data.

[f]Villages that constitute tribes, bands, clans, groups, villages, communities, or associations in Alaska that are recognized pursuant to the Alaska Native Claims Settlement Act of 1972.

Table 1-14 shows all the metropolitan areas of the United States and their sizes. It is important to note that metropolitan areas and cities or towns are not coterminous. That is, many metropolitan areas include several cities or towns, and some cross states lines. Table 1-15 shows the total population of the largest metropolitan areas and the percentages of various racial or ethnic groups.

Table 1-16 lists previous and projected population sizes for around the world. Many of the largest population centers are in Third World nations. The transition of many formerly predominantly rural nations to largely metropolitan nations has been a phenomenon of the past several decades. Many Third World nations have grown in population because of reductions in infant mortality rates, improved

TABLE 1-10 **Number of American Indians, Eskimos, and Aleuts Living on Selected Reservations and Trust Lands, and American Indian Tribes with 10,000 or More Members: 1990**

Reservation and Trust Lands with 5,000 or More American Indians, Eskimos, and Aleuts	Total Population	American Indians, Eskimos, Aleuts	
		Number	Percent of Total
All reservation and trust lands	808,163	437,431	54.1
Navajo and Trust Lands, AZ–NM–UT	148,451	143,405	96.6
Pine Ridge and Trust Lands, NE–SD	12,215	11,182	91.5
Fort Apache, AZ	10,394	9,825	94.5
Gila River, AZ	9,540	9,116	95.6
Papago, AZ	8,730	8,480	97.1
Rosebud and Trust Lands, SD	9,696	8,043	83.0
San Carlos, AZ	7,924	7,110	97.5
Zuni Pueblo, AZ–NM	7,412	7,073	95.4
Hopi and Trust Lands, AZ	7,360	7,061	95.9
Blackfeet, MT	8,549	7,025	82.2
Turtle Mountain and Trust Lands, ND–SD	7,106	6,772	95.3
Yakima and Trust Lands, WA	27,668	6,307	22.8
Osage, OK[a]	41,645	6,161	14.8
Fort Peck, MT	10,595	5,782	54.6
Wind River, WY	21,851	5,676	26.0
Eastern Cherokee, NC	6,527	5,388	82.5
Flathead, MT	21,259	5,130	24.1
Cheyenne River, SD	7,743	5,100	65.9

American Indian Tribe	Number	Percent Distribution
American Indian population, total	1,878,285	100.0
Cherokee	308,132	16.4
Navajo	219,198	11.7
Chippewa	103,826	5.5
Sioux[b]	103,255	5.5
Choctaw	82,299	4.4
Pueblo	52,939	2.8
Apache	50,051	2.7
Iroquois[c]	49,038	2.6
Lumbee	48,444	2.6
Creek	43,550	2.3
Blackfoot	32,234	1.7
Canadian and Latin American	22,379	1.2
Chickasaw	20,631	1.1
Potawatomi[c]	16,763	0.9
Tohono o'Odham	16,041	0.9
Pima	14,431	0.8
Tlingit	13,925	0.7
Seminole	13,797	0.7
Alaskan Athabaskans	13,738	0.7
Cheyenne	11,456	0.6
Comanche	11,322	0.6
Paiute	11,142	0.6
Puget Sound Salish	10,246	0.5

Source: Reprinted from U.S. Bureau of the Census. (1993). *Statistical abstract of the United States: 1993* (113th ed., p. 48). Austin, TX: Reference Press.
   [a]The Osage Reservation is coextensive with Osage County. Data shown for the reservation are for the entire reservation.
   [b]Any entry with the spelling "Siouan" was miscoded to Sioux in North Carolina.
   [c]Reporting and/or processing problems have affected the data for this tribe.

TABLE 1-11 Foreign-Born Population, Leading Ancestry Groups, and Numbers Speaking a Language Other Than English at Home, by State: 1990 (Numbers in thousands)

Region, Division, and State	Foreign-Born Population			Ancestry Groups						Persons 5 Years Old and Over Speaking Foreign Language	
	Number	Percent of Total Population	Year of Entry, 1980–90	Leading Ancestry Group Group	Number	Second Leading Group Group	Number	Third Leading Group Group	Number	Number	Percent of Total Population
United States	19,767	7.9	8,661	German	57,947	Irish	38,736	English	32,652	31,845	13.8
Northeast	5,321	10.3	2,059	German	9,929	Irish	9,420	Italian	7,504	7,824	16.5
Connecticut	279	8.5	90	Italian	628	Irish	614	English	463	466	15.2
Maine	36	3.0	7	English	372	Irish	224	English	217	105	9.2
Massachusetts	574	9.5	223	Irish	1,571	French	921	Irish	844	852	15.2
New Hampshire	41	3.7	10	English	266	English	232	Italian	205	89	8.7
New Jersey	967	12.5	385	Italian	1,457	Irish	1,415	French	1,408	1,406	19.5
New York	2,852	15.9	1,190	German	2,899	Italian	2,838	German	2,800	3,909	23.2
Pennsylvania	369	3.1	116	German	4,315	Irish	2,256	Irish	1,373	807	7.3
Rhode Island	95	9.5	35	Irish	214	Italian	199	Italian	161	159	17.0
Vermont	18	3.1	3	English	147	French	133	Irish	101	30	5.8
Midwest	2,131	3.6	754	German	22,477	Irish	9,643	English	7,294	3,921	7.1
Illinois	952	8.3	371	German	3,326	Irish	1,861	African American	1,426	1,499	14.2
Indiana	94	1.7	31	German	2,085	Irish	965	English	767	246	4.8
Iowa	43	1.6	19	German	1,395	Irish	527	English	389	100	3.9
Kansas	63	2.5	31	German	968	Irish	436	English	406	132	5.7
Michigan	355	3.8	94	German	2,666	Irish	1,320	English	1,315	570	6.6
Minnesota	113	2.6	51	German	2,021	Norwegian	757	Irish	574	227	5.6
Missouri	84	1.6	30	German	1,843	Irish	1,038	English	743	178	3.8
Nebraska	28	1.8	10	German	795	Irish	272	English	209	70	4.8
North Dakota	9	1.5	3	German	325	Norwegian	189	Irish	70	47	7.9
Ohio	260	2.4	71	German	4,068	Irish	1,896	English	1,449	546	5.4
South Dakota	8	1.1	2	German	355	Norwegian	106	Irish	88	42	6.5
Wisconsin	122	2.5	41	German	2,631	Irish	612	Polish	506	264	5.8
South	4,582	5.4	2,027	German	14,630	Irish	12,951	African American	12,936	8,670	10.9
Alabama	44	1.1	18	African American	839	American	687	Irish	617	108	2.9
Arkansas	25	1.1	10	Irish	464	German	400	African American	307	61	2.8
Delaware	22	3.3	4	Irish	139	German	138	English	123	42	6.9
District of Columbia	59	9.7	34	African American	315	German	39	Irish	34	71	12.5
Florida	1,663	12.9	660	German	2,410	Irish	1,899	English	1,846	2,098	17.3
Georgia	173	2.7	90	African American	1,421	Irish	971	English	890	285	4.8
Kentucky	34	0.9	14	German	798	Irish	696	American	586	86	2.5

State											
Louisiana	87	2.1	African American	35	French	1,097	Irish	550	518	392	10.1
Maryland	313	6.6	German	148	African American	1,218	Irish	966	769	395	8.9
Mississippi	20	0.8	African American	8	Irish	775	American	393	317	67	2.8
North Carolina	115	1.7	African American	52	German	1,228	English	1,111	987	241	3.9
Oklahoma	65	2.1	German	30	Irish	714	American Indian	642	469	146	5.0
South Carolina	50	1.4	African American	18	German	870	Irish	500	486	113	3.5
Tennessee	59	1.2	Irish	26	German	875	English	724	692	132	2.9
Texas	1,524	9.0	Mexican	718	German	3,403	Irish	2,950	2,369	3,970	25.4
Virginia	312	5.0	German	159	English	1,186	English	1,051	970	419	7.3
West Virginia	16	0.9	German	4	Irish	469	English	348	270	44	2.6
West	7,823	14.8	German	3,821	English	10,911	Irish	8,110	6,721	11,430	23.5
Alaska	25	4.5	German	11	English	127	Irish	77	74	60	12.1
Arizona	278	7.6	German	117	English	878	Irish	586	530	700	20.8
California	6,459	21.7	Mexican	3,256	German	5,322	English	4,935	3,646	8,619	31.5
Colorado	142	4.3	German	57	English	1,064	Irish	582	538	321	10.5
Hawaii	163	14.7	Japanese	67	Filipino	262	Hawaiian	176	157	255	24.8
Idaho	29	2.9	English	13	German	291	Irish	279	142	59	6.4
Montana	14	1.7	German	3	Irish	285	English	139	137	37	5.0
Nevada	105	8.7	German	48	English	280	Irish	207	200	146	13.2
New Mexico	81	5.3	German	31	Mexican	234	Spanish	216	191	494	35.5
Oregon	139	4.9	German	61	English	879	Irish	575	467	192	7.3
Utah	59	3.4	English	26	German	750	Danish	299	163	120	7.8
Washington	322	6.6	German	129	English	1,390	Irish	897	768	403	9.0
Wyoming	8	1.7	German	2	English	158	Irish	101	73	24	5.7

Note: Figures are based on a sample and subject to sampling variability.

Source: Reprinted from U.S. Bureau of the Census. (1993). *Statistical abstract of the United States: 1993* (113th ed., p. 52). Austin, TX: Reference Press.

TABLE 1-12 Population, by Selected Ancestry Group and Region: 1990 (Numbers in thousands)

Ancestry Group	Number	Northeast	Midwest	South	West
			Percent Distribution by Region		
Europe					
Austrian	865	38	21	19	22
British	1,119	17	18	39	26
Croatian	544	21	43	20	16
Czech	1,296	10	52	22	16
Danish	1,635	9	34	12	45
Dutch	6,227	16	34	29	21
English	32,652	18	22	35	25
European	467	14	17	31	39
Finnish	659	14	47	11	27
French	10,321	26	26	29	20
German	57,947	17	39	25	19
Greek	1,110	37	23	21	19
Hungarian	1,582	36	32	17	16
Irish	38,736	24	25	33	17
Italian	14,665	51	17	17	15
Lithuanian	812	43	28	16	13
Norwegian	3,869	6	52	10	33
Polish	9,366	37	37	15	11
Portuguese	1,153	49	3	8	41
Russian	2,953	44	16	18	22
Scandinavian	679	8	33	15	45
Scotch-Irish	5,618	14	19	47	20
Scottish	5,394	20	21	33	26
Slovak	1,883	40	34	14	11
Swedish	4,681	14	40	14	32
Swiss	1,045	16	36	17	30
Ukrainian	741	51	22	14	13
Welsh	2,034	22	24	27	27
Yugoslavian	258	23	28	12	37
Central and South America					
Cuban	860	18	3	69	9
Dominican	506	86	1	10	2
Hispanic	1,113	13	6	31	50
Mexican	11,587	1	9	33	57
Puerto Rican	1,955	66	11	15	8
Salvadoran	499	13	2	23	62
Spanish	2,024	16	8	30	45
West Indies					
Jamaican	435	59	5	31	6
Asia					
Asian Indian	570	32	19	26	24
Chinese	1,505	25	8	12	55
Filipino	1,451	10	9	13	68
Japanese	1,005	9	8	11	72
Korean	837	22	14	20	44
Vietnamese	536	9	8	28	54
North America					
Acadian	668	1	2	91	5
African American	23,777	15	21	54	10
American	12,396	10	18	61	11
American Indian	8,708	9	22	47	23
Canadian	550	34	18	21	28
French Canadian	2,167	45	20	20	15
United States	644	16	18	53	13
White	1,800	7	13	53	28

Notes: Information is based on a sample and subject to sampling variability. People who reported multiple ancestry groups may be included in more than one category. Major classifications of ancestry groups do not represent strict geographic or cultural definitions. The term "Europe" does not include any Hispanic groups.

Source: Reprinted from U.S. Bureau of the Census. (1993). *Statistical abstract of the United States: 1993* (113th ed., p. 51). Austin, TX: Reference Press.

TABLE 1-13 **Metropolitan and Nonmetropolitan Population, by State: 1980 and 1990 (Numbers in thousands)**

	Metropolitan Population						Nonmetropolitan Population					
	Total		Net Change, 1980–90		Percent of State		Total		Net Change, 1980–90		Percent of State	
Region and State	1980	1990	Number	Percent	1980	1990	1980	1990	Number	Percent	1980	1990
United States	176,663	197,467	20,804	11.8	78.0	79.4	49,879	51,243	1,364	2.7	22.0	20.6
Northeast	44,045	45,453	1,408	3.2	89.6	89.5	5,092	5,356	264	5.2	10.4	10.5
Connecticut	2,980	3,146	165	5.6	95.9	95.7	127	141	14	11.1	4.1	4.3
Maine	405	443	38	9.5	36.0	36.1	721	785	65	9.0	64.0	63.9
Massachusetts	5,530	5,788	258	4.7	96.4	96.2	207	229	22	10.5	3.6	3.8
New Hampshire	535	659	124	23.1	58.1	59.4	386	450	65	16.8	41.9	40.6
New Jersey	7,365	7,730	365	5.0	100.0	100.0	NA	NA	NA	NA	NA	NA
New York	16,144	16,515	371	2.3	91.9	91.8	1,414	1,475	61	4.3	8.1	8.2
Pennsylvania	10,067	10,083	16	0.2	84.8	84.9	1,798	1,799	1	a	15.2	15.1
Rhode Island	886	938	52	5.9	93.5	93.5	61	65	4	6.6	6.5	6.5
Vermont	133	152	18	13.8	26.0	26.9	378	411	33	8.7	74.0	73.1
Midwest	42,557	43,691	1,134	2.7	72.3	73.2	16,310	15,978	–332	–2.0	27.7	26.8
Illinois	9,461	9,574	113	1.2	82.8	83.8	1,967	1,857	–110	–5.6	17.2	16.2
Indiana	3,885	3,962	78	2.0	70.8	71.5	1,605	1,582	–24	–1.5	29.2	28.5
Iowa	1,198	1,200	2	0.1	41.1	43.2	1,716	1,577	–139	–8.1	58.9	56.8
Kansas	1,184	1,333	149	12.6	50.1	53.8	1,180	1,145	–36	–3.0	49.9	46.2
Michigan	7,719	7,698	–21	–0.3	83.3	82.8	1,543	1,598	54	3.5	16.7	17.2
Minnesota	2,674	3,011	337	12.6	65.6	68.8	1,402	1,364	–38	–2.7	34.4	31.2
Missouri	3,314	3,491	177	5.3	67.4	68.2	1,603	1,626	23	1.5	32.6	31.8
Nebraska	728	787	59	8.1	46.4	49.9	842	791	–50	–6.0	53.6	50.1
North Dakota	234	257	23	9.8	35.9	40.3	418	381	–37	–8.8	64.1	59.7
Ohio	8,791	8,826	35	0.4	81.4	81.4	2,007	2,021	14	0.7	18.6	18.6
South Dakota	194	221	27	13.9	28.0	31.7	497	475	–22	–4.3	72.0	68.3
Wisconsin	3,176	3,331	155	4.9	67.5	68.1	1,530	1,561	31	2.0	32.5	31.9
South	53,405	62,835	9,430	17.7	70.9	73.5	21,962	22,611	649	3.0	29.1	26.5
Alabama	2,560	2,710	150	5.8	65.7	67.1	1,334	1,331	–3	–0.2	34.3	32.9
Arkansas	963	1,040	77	8.0	42.1	44.2	1,323	1,311	–13	–0.9	57.9	55.8
Delaware	496	553	57	11.4	83.5	83.0	98	113	15	15.5	16.5	17.0
District of Columbia	638	607	–32	–4.9	100.0	100.0	NA	NA	NA	NA	NA	NA
Florida	9,039	12,023	2,985	33.0	92.7	92.9	708	915	206	29.1	7.3	7.1
Georgia	3,489	4,331	843	24.2	63.9	66.9	1,974	2,147	173	8.7	36.1	33.1
Kentucky	1,710	1,755	45	2.6	46.7	47.6	1,950	1,930	–20	–1.0	53.3	52.4
Louisiana	3,074	3,101	27	0.9	73.1	73.5	1,132	1,119	–13	–1.1	26.9	26.5
Maryland	3,920	4,439	519	13.2	93.0	92.8	297	343	46	15.3	7.0	7.2
Mississippi	716	776	60	8.3	28.4	30.1	1,805	1,798	–7	–0.4	71.6	69.9
North Carolina	3,713	4,325	612	16.5	63.2	65.2	2,167	2,304	137	6.3	36.8	34.8
Oklahoma	1,724	1,870	146	8.4	57.0	59.4	1,301	1,276	–26	–2.0	43.0	40.6
South Carolina	2,114	2,423	308	14.6	67.8	69.5	1,006	1,064	58	5.7	32.2	30.5
Tennessee	2,946	3,195	249	8.4	64.2	65.5	1,645	1,682	38	2.3	35.8	34.5
Texas	11,539	14,166	2,626	22.8	81.1	83.4	2,686	2,821	135	5.0	18.9	16.6
Virginia	3,966	4,773	807	20.4	74.2	77.1	1,381	1,414	33	2.4	25.8	22.9
West Virginia	796	748	–47	–6.0	40.8	41.7	1,155	1,045	–109	–9.5	59.2	58.3
West	36,655	45,487	8,832	24.1	84.9	86.2	6,516	7,299	783	12.0	15.1	13.8
Alaska	174	226	52	29.8	43.4	41.1	227	324	96	42.3	56.6	58.9
Arizona	2,264	3,106	842	37.2	83.3	84.7	453	559	107	23.5	16.7	15.3
California	22,907	28,799	5,891	25.7	96.8	96.8	760	961	201	26.4	3.2	3.2
Colorado	2,326	2,686	360	15.5	80.5	81.5	563	608	45	8.0	19.5	18.5
Hawaii	763	836	74	9.7	79.0	75.5	202	272	70	34.6	21.0	24.5
Idaho	257	296	39	15.2	27.2	29.4	687	711	24	3.4	72.8	70.6
Montana	189	191	2	1.3	24.0	23.9	598	608	10	1.7	76.0	76.1
Nevada	666	1,014	348	52.3	83.2	84.4	135	188	53	39.5	16.8	15.6
New Mexico	675	842	167	24.7	51.8	55.6	628	673	45	7.2	48.2	44.4
Oregon	1,799	1,985	186	10.3	68.3	69.8	834	858	23	2.8	31.7	30.2
Utah	1,128	1,336	207	18.4	77.2	77.5	333	387	54	16.3	22.8	22.5
Washington	3,366	4,036	670	19.9	81.5	82.9	766	830	64	8.4	18.5	17.1
Wyoming	141	134	–6	–4.4	29.9	29.6	329	319	–10	–3.0	70.1	70.4

Notes: *Metropolitan* refers to 250 metropolitan statistical areas and 18 consolidated metropolitan statistical areas as defined by the U.S. Office of Management and Budget; *nonmetropolitan* is outside metropolitan areas. NA = not applicable.

Source: Reprinted from U.S. Bureau of the Census. (1993). *Statistical abstract of the United States: 1993* (113th ed., p. 36). Austin, TX: Reference Press.

aLess than 0.05 percent.

TABLE 1-14 Population in Metropolitan Areas: 1980, 1990, and 1991 (Numbers in thousands)

Metropolitan Area	1980 Total	1990 Total	1990 Under 18 Years Old (percent)	1990 65 Years Old and Over (percent)	1991 Total	1991 Rank	Percent Change 1980–90	Percent Change 1990–91
Albany–Schenectady–Troy, NY MSA	825	861	23.3	14.1	869	52	4.4	0.9
Albuquerque, NM MSA	485	589	27.1	10.4	602	65	21.4	2.3
Allentown–Bethlehem–Easton, PA MSA	551	595	22.9	15.5	602	66	8.0	1.2
Appleton–Oshkosh–Neenah, WI MSA	291	315	26.7	11.9	320	113	8.0	1.5
Atlanta, GA MSA	2,233	2,960	25.9	8.0	3,051	13	32.5	3.1
Augusta–Aiken, GA–SC MSA	345	395	27.8	9.9	407	88	14.5	2.9
Austin–San Marcos, TX MSA	585	846	25.6	7.8	874	51	44.6	3.3
Bakersfield, CA MSA	403	543	31.5	9.7	567	70	34.8	4.3
Baton Rouge, LA MSA	444	470	28.2	9.0	478	77	5.8	1.8
Beaumont–Port Arthur, TX MSA	373	361	27.6	13.1	367	101	-3.2	1.6
Biloxi–Gulfport–Pascagoula, MS MSA	300	312	28.3	10.6	316	115	4.1	1.2
Binghamton, NY MSA	263	264	24.0	14.2	265	130	0.4	0.2
Birmingham, AL MSA	815	840	25.4	13.1	849	54	3.0	1.1
Boise City, ID MSA	257	296	29.1	11.4	310	116	15.2	4.7
Boston–Brockton–Nashua, MA–NH–ME–CT CMSA	5,122	5,455	22.6	12.7	5,432	7	6.5	-0.4
Boston, MA–NH–ME–CT PMSA	4,763	5,051	22.4	12.9	5,027	NA	6.0	-0.5
Brockton, MA PMSA	225	236	25.1	11.1	237	NA	5.1	0.4
Nashua, NH PMSA	134	168	26.5	8.3	168	NA	25.4	-0.1
Brownsville–Harlingen–San Benito, TX MSA	210	260	35.3	10.6	269	129	24.0	3.4
Buffalo–Niagara Falls, NY MSA	1,243	1,189	23.6	15.2	1,193	33	-4.3	0.3
Canton–Massillon, OH MSA	404	394	25.3	14.4	397	95	-2.6	0.7
Charleston–North Charleston, SC MSA	430	507	27.6	8.6	524	71	17.8	3.3
Charleston, WV MSA	270	250	23.8	14.9	252	135	-7.1	0.4
Charlotte–Gastonia–Rock Hill, NC–SC MSA	971	1,162	24.7	10.9	1,190	34	19.6	2.4
Chattanooga, TN–GA MSA	393	399	24.7	13.1	403	90	1.5	1.0
Chicago–Gary–Kenosha, IL–IN–WI CMSA	8,115	8,240	26.1	11.4	8,339	3	1.5	1.2
Chicago, IL PMSA	7,246	7,411	25.9	11.3	7,498	NA	2.3	1.2
Gary, IN PMSA	643	605	27.9	11.8	611	NA	-5.9	1.4
Kankakee, IL PMSA	103	96	28.1	13.7	98	NA	-6.5	2.9
Kenosha, WI PMSA	123	128	26.8	12.6	132	NA	4.1	1.4
Cincinnati–Hamilton, OH–KY–IN CMSA	1,726	1,818	26.8	11.8	1,843	23	5.3	1.4
Cincinnati, OH–KY–IN PMSA	1,468	1,526	26.9	12.1	1,544	NA	4.0	1.2
Hamilton–Middletown, OH PMSA	259	291	26.2	10.2	299	NA	12.6	2.5
Cleveland–Akron, OH CMSA	2,938	2,860	24.9	13.9	2,878	14	-2.7	0.6
Akron, OH PMSA	660	658	24.4	12.9	665	NA	-0.4	1.1
Cleveland–Lorain–Elyria, OH PMSA	2,278	2,202	25.1	14.2	2,213	NA	-3.3	0.5
Colorado Springs, CO MSA	309	397	27.6	8.0	404	89	28.3	1.9
Columbia, SC MSA	410	453	25.0	9.3	464	78	10.6	2.3

Columbus, GA–AL MSA	255	261	26.9	10.7	264	131	2.4	1.2
Columbus, OH MSA	1,214	1,345	25.1	10.0	1,370	29	10.8	1.8
Corpus Christi, TX MSA	326	350	30.8	10.2	356	103	7.3	1.9
Dallas–Forth Worth, TX CMSA	3,046	4,037	27.2	8.3	4,135	9	32.5	2.4
Dallas, TX PMSA	2,055	2,676	27.1	8.1	2,739	NA	30.2	2.3
Fort Worth–Arlington, TX PMSA	991	1,361	27.3	8.8	1,396	NA	37.4	2.5
Davenport–Moline–Rock Island, IA–IL MSA	385	351	26.7	13.7	354	104	-8.8	1.0
Dayton–Springfield, OH MSA	942	951	25.3	12.4	956	44	1.0	0.5
Daytona Beach, FL MSA	270	399	19.7	23.0	414	85	48.1	3.5
Denver–Boulder–Greeley, CO CMSA	1,742	1,980	25.7	9.2	2,034	21	13.7	2.7
Boulder–Longmont, CO PMSA	190	225	23.0	7.6	232	NA	18.8	3.0
Denver, CO PMSA	1,429	1,623	25.9	9.4	1,668	NA	13.6	2.8
Greeley, CO PMSA	123	132	28.1	10.2	134	NA	6.8	1.4
Des Moines, IA MSA	368	393	25.6	11.7	400	92	6.9	1.8
Detroit–Ann Arbor–Flint, MI CMSA	5,293	5,187	26.1	11.5	5,215	8	-2.0	0.5
Ann Arbor, MI PMSA	455	490	24.5	8.5	499	NA	7.7	1.7
Detroit, MI PMSA	4,388	4,267	26.0	11.9	4,285	NA	-2.8	0.4
Flint, MI PMSA	450	430	28.0	10.2	431	NA	-4.4	0.2
El Paso, TX MSA	480	592	32.6	8.2	612	63	23.3	3.4
Erie, PA MSA	280	276	25.9	13.8	278	125	-1.5	0.9
Eugene–Springfield, OR MSA	275	283	24.5	13.1	288	123	2.8	1.8
Evansville–Henderson, IN–KY MSA	276	279	25.4	14.0	281	124	1.0	0.7
Fayetteville, NC MSA	247	275	28.0	6.1	276	126	11.1	0.7
Fort Myers–Cape Coral, FL MSA	205	335	19.6	24.8	347	107	63.3	3.5
Fort Pierce–Port St. Lucie, FL MSA	151	251	20.9	23.6	260	134	66.1	3.5
Fort Wayne, IN MSA	445	456	28.2	12.0	460	79	2.6	0.9
Fresno, CA MSA	578	756	31.3	10.6	781	56	30.8	3.4
Grand Rapids–Muskegon–Holland, MI MSA	841	938	28.6	11.1	953	45	11.5	1.6
Greensboro–Winston-Salem–High Point, NC MSA	951	1,050	22.9	12.4	1,066	39	10.5	1.5
Greenville–Spartanburg–Anderson, SC MSA	744	831	24.5	12.4	843	55	11.6	1.5
Harrisburg–Lebanon–Carlisle, PA MSA	556	588	23.4	13.9	595	68	5.7	1.2
Hartford, CT MSA	1,081	1,158	22.6	13.2	1,159	35	5.7	0.1
Hickory–Morganton, NC MSA	270	292	23.8	12.2	296	119	7.1	1.1
Honolulu, HI MSA	763	836	24.5	11.0	851	53	8.1	1.7
Houston–Galveston–Brazoria, TX CMSA	3,118	3,731	28.9	7.3	3,859	10	9.7	3.4
Brazoria, TX PMSA	170	192	29.3	7.8	199	NA	19.6	3.9
Galveston–Texas City, TX PMSA	196	217	27.6	10.5	223	NA	13.0	2.5
Houston, TX PMSA	2,753	3,322	28.9	7.1	3,437	NA	11.1	3.5
Huntington–Ashland, WV–KY–OH MSA	311	288	24.3	14.5	289	122	20.7	0.3
Huntsville, AL MSA	243	293	24.7	9.4	300	117	-7.4	2.5
Indianapolis, IN MSA	1,306	1,380	26.2	11.4	1,406	28	20.6	1.8
Jackson, MS MSA	362	395	28.1	10.5	400	93	5.7	1.1
Jacksonville, FL MSA	722	907	26.0	10.9	934	46	9.2	3.0
Johnson City–Kingsport–Bristol, TN–VA MSA	434	436	22.3	14.6	441	80	25.5	1.1

Continued on next page

TABLE 1-14 **Continued**

Metropolitan Area	1980 Total	1990			1991		Percent Change	
		Total	Under 18 Years Old (percent)	65 Years Old and Over (percent)	Total	Rank	1980–90	1990–91
Kalamazoo–Battle Creek, MI MSA	421	429	25.9	11.8	433	82	2.1	0.8
Kansas City, MO–KS MSA	1,449	1,583	26.4	11.6	1,602	25	9.2	1.2
Knoxville, TN MSA	546	586	22.9	13.4	600	67	7.2	2.4
Lafayette, LA MSA	331	345	30.6	10.0	350	106	4.3	1.5
Lakeland–Winter Haven, FL MSA	322	405	24.1	18.6	413	86	26.0	1.9
Lancaster, PA MSA	362	423	26.5	13.1	430	83	16.7	1.8
Lansing–East Lansing, MI MSA	420	433	25.6	9.0	436	81	3.1	0.8
Las Vegas, NV–AZ MSA	528	853	24.3	11.6	925	47	61.5	8.5
Lexington, KY MSA	371	406	23.6	10.3	412	87	9.4	1.5
Little Rock–North Little Rock, AR MSA	474	513	26.5	11.4	519	72	8.1	1.1
Los Angeles–Riverside–Orange County, CA CMSA	11,498	14,532	26.6	9.8	14,818	2	26.4	2.0
Los Angeles–Long Beach, CA PMSA	7,477	8,863	26.2	9.7	8,978	NA	18.5	1.3
Orange County, CA PMSA	1,933	2,411	24.4	9.2	2,442	NA	24.7	1.3
Riverside–San Bernardino, CA PMSA	1,558	2,589	29.8	10.8	2,721	NA	66.1	5.1
Ventura, CA PMSA	529	669	27.4	9.4	677	NA	26.4	1.2
Louisville, KY–IN MSA	954	949	25.3	12.6	958	43	-0.5	1.0
Macon, GA MSA	273	291	27.4	10.8	295	120	6.6	1.4
Madison, WI MSA	324	367	22.7	9.3	376	97	13.5	2.3
McAllen–Edinburg–Mission, TX MSA	283	384	36.6	10.0	399	94	35.4	4.1
Melbourne–Titusville–Palm Bay, FL MSA	273	399	21.9	16.6	414	84	46.2	3.8
Memphis, TN–AR–MS MSA	939	1,007	27.9	10.4	1,020	40	7.3	1.3
Miami–Fort Lauderdale, FL CMSA	2,644	3,193	22.7	16.6	3,264	11	20.8	2.2
Fort Lauderdale, FL PMSA	1,018	1,255	20.4	20.8	1,287	NA	23.3	2.5
Miami, FL PMSA	1,626	1,937	24.2	14.0	1,977	NA	19.2	2.1
Milwaukee–Racine, WI CMSA	1,570	1,607	26.4	12.4	1,622	24	2.4	0.9
Milwaukee–Waukesha, WI PMSA	1,397	1,432	26.3	12.5	1,444	NA	2.5	0.9
Racine, WI PMSA	173	175	27.8	12.0	178	NA	1.1	1.7
Minneapolis–St. Paul, MN–WI MSA	2,198	2,539	26.4	9.8	2,583	15	15.5	1.7
Mobile, AL MSA	444	477	28.0	12.5	486	76	7.5	1.9
Modesto, CA MSA	266	371	30.6	10.8	387	96	39.3	4.4
Montgomery, AL MSA	273	293	27.4	11.4	298	118	7.3	1.7
Nashville, TN MSA	851	985	25.1	10.6	1,003	41	15.8	1.8
New London–Norwich, CT–RI MSA	273	291	23.6	12.5	290	121	6.5	-0.1
New Orleans, LA MSA	1,304	1,285	28.1	11.0	1,295	31	-1.5	0.8
New York–Northern New Jersey–Long Island, NY–NJ–CT–PA CMSA	18,713	19,342	23.1	13.1	19,384	1	3.4	0.2
Bridgeport, CT PMSA	439	444	23.2	14.7	443	NA	1.2	-0.1

Area								
Danbury, CT PMSA	188	208	24.0	11.3	209	NA	10.3	0.5
Dutchess County, NY PMSA	245	259	23.9	11.4	261	NA	5.9	0.6
New Haven, CT PMSA	500	530	22.6	14.1	530	NA	5.9	-0.1
New York–Newark, NY–NJ–PA PMSA	16,448	16,938	23.0	13.1	16,972	NA	3.0	0.2
Orange County, NY PMSA	260	308	27.6	10.4	312	NA	18.5	1.4
Stamford–Norwalk, CT PMSA	326	330	20.9	13.4	331	NA	1.3	0.2
Trenton, NJ PMSA	308	326	22.5	13.0	327	NA	5.8	0.2
Norfolk–Virginia Beach–Newport News, VA–NC MSA	1,201	1,443	26.4	9.2	1,465	27	20.2	1.5
Oklahoma City, OK MSA	861	959	26.6	11.0	971	42	11.4	1.3
Omaha, NE–IA MSA	605	640	27.9	10.7	649	60	5.6	1.5
Orlando, FL MSA	805	1,225	23.8	12.9	1,269	32	52.2	3.6
Pensacola, FL MSA	290	344	25.7	11.3	354	105	18.9	2.7
Peoria–Pekin, IL MSA	366	339	26.4	13.8	342	109	-7.3	0.9
Philadelphia–Wilmington–Atlantic City, PA–NJ–DE–MD CMSA	5,649	5,893	24.4	13.5	5,925	6	4.3	0.5
Atlantic–Cape May, NJ PMSA	276	319	22.7	16.2	323	NA	15.6	1.0
Philadelphia, PA–NJ PMSA	4,781	4,922	24.4	13.5	4,941	NA	2.9	0.4
Vineland–Millville–Bridgeton, NJ PMSA	133	138	26.0	13.5	139	NA	3.9	0.4
Wilmington–Newark, DE–MD PMSA	459	513	24.5	11.2	522	NA	11.9	1.7
Phoenix–Mesa, AZ MSA	1,600	2,238	26.4	12.6	2,287	19	39.9	2.2
Pittsburgh, PA MSA	2,571	2,395	22.0	17.1	2,404	18	-6.9	0.4
Portland–Salem, OR–WA CMSA	1,584	1,793	25.8	12.4	1,857	22	13.3	3.6
Portland–Vancouver, OR–WA PMSA	1,334	1,515	25.7	12.0	1,570	NA	13.6	3.6
Salem, OR PMSA	250	278	26.4	14.4	287	NA	11.3	3.3
Providence–Fall River–Warwick, RI–MA MSA	1,077	1,134	22.8	15.1	1,135	36	5.4	0.1
Provo–Orem, UT MSA	218	264	37.8	7.0	270	128	20.9	2.3
Raleigh–Durham–Chapel Hill, NC MSA	665	856	22.7	9.5	883	49	28.7	3.2
Reading, PA MSA	313	337	23.3	15.6	341	110	7.7	1.3
Reno, NV MSA	194	255	23.1	10.3	263	132	31.5	3.2
Richmond–Petersburg, VA MSA	761	866	24.3	11.3	881	50	13.7	1.8
Rochester, NY MSA	1,031	1,062	25.1	12.5	1,073	38	3.1	1.0
Rockford, IL MSA	326	330	26.5	12.8	336	111	1.2	1.9
Sacramento–Yolo, CA CMSA	1,100	1,481	26.2	10.8	1,532	26	34.7	3.4
Sacramento, CA PMSA	986	1,340	26.4	10.9	1,388	NA	35.8	3.6
Yolo, CA PMSA	113	141	24.1	9.5	144	NA	24.4	1.8
Saginaw–Bay City–Midland, MI MSA	422	399	27.5	12.1	401	91	-5.3	0.6
St. Louis, MO–IL MSA	2,414	2,493	26.3	12.8	2,507	17	3.3	0.6
Salinas, CA MSA	290	356	27.5	9.8	363	102	22.5	2.1
Salt Lake City–Ogden, UT MSA	910	1,072	35.6	8.4	1,103	37	17.8	2.9
San Antonio, TX MSA	1,089	1,325	29.0	10.3	1,348	30	21.7	1.8
San Diego, CA MSA	1,862	2,498	24.5	10.9	2,549	16	34.2	2.0
San Francisco–Oakland–San Jose, CA CMSA	5,368	6,253	23.1	11.1	6,332	5	16.5	1.3
Oakland, CA PMSA	1,762	2,083	24.3	10.7	2,112	NA	18.2	1.4

Continued on next page

TABLE 1-14 **Continued**

Metropolitan Area	1980 Total	1990 Total	1990 Under 18 Years Old (percent)	1990 65 Years Old and Over (percent)	1991 Total	1991 Rank	Percent Change 1980–90	Percent Change 1990–91
San Francisco, CA PMSA	1,489	1,604	18.9	13.3	1,622	NA	7.7	1.2
San Jose, CA PMSA	1,295	1,498	24.0	8.7	1,506	NA	15.6	0.5
Santa Cruz–Watsonville, CA PMSA	188	230	23.8	11.3	229	NA	22.1	-0.2
Santa Rosa, CA PMSA	300	388	24.7	13.4	396	NA	29.5	2.0
Vallejo–Fairfield–Napa, CA PMSA	334	451	27.4	10.2	466	NA	34.9	3.3
Santa Barbara–Santa Maria–Lompoc, CA MSA	299	370	23.2	12.3	374	99	23.7	1.2
Sarasota–Bradenton, FL MSA	351	489	17.2	30.4	501	73	39.6	2.4
Savannah, GA MSA	231	258	27.2	11.9	263	133	11.8	1.8
Scranton–Wilkes-Barre–Hazleton, PA MSA	659	638	21.9	19.0	641	61	-3.2	0.4
Seattle–Tacoma–Bremerton, WA CMSA	2,409	2,970	25.0	10.8	3,054	12	23.3	2.8
Bremerton, WA PMSA	147	190	27.9	10.7	201	NA	28.9	6.0
Olympia, WA PMSA	124	161	26.9	11.7	170	NA	29.8	5.2
Seattle–Bellevue–Everett, WA PMSA	1,652	2,033	23.9	10.8	2,078	NA	23.1	2.2
Tacoma, WA PMSA	486	586	27.2	10.5	605	NA	20.7	3.3
Shreveport–Bossier City, LA MSA	377	376	28.6	12.7	374	98	-0.1	-0.5
Spokane, WA MSA	342	361	26.4	13.3	374	100	5.7	3.5
Springfield, MA MSA	570	588	23.4	14.1	586	69	3.2	-0.3
Springfield, MO MSA	228	264	24.1	13.0	270	127	15.9	2.1
Stockton–Lodi, CA MSA	347	481	29.6	11.1	493	75	38.4	2.5
Syracuse, NY MSA	723	742	25.3	12.6	749	57	2.7	0.9
Tampa–St. Petersburg–Clearwater, FL MSA	1,614	2,068	20.4	21.6	2,101	20	28.2	1.6
Toledo, OH MSA	617	614	26.3	12.4	614	62	-0.4	0.0
Tucson, AZ MSA	531	667	24.9	13.7	677	59	25.5	1.5
Tulsa, OK MSA	657	709	26.8	11.6	723	58	7.9	1.9
Utica–Rome, NY MSA	320	317	24.5	15.7	318	114	-1.1	0.5
Visalia–Tulare–Porterville, CA MSA	246	312	33.1	10.8	323	112	26.9	3.7
Washington–Baltimore, DC–MD–VA–WV CMSA	5,791	6,727	23.9	9.9	6,830	4	16.2	1.5
Baltimore, MD PMSA	2,199	2,382	24.1	11.7	2,414	NA	8.3	1.3
Hagerstown, MD PMSA	113	121	22.7	13.8	123	NA	7.3	1.4
Washington, DC–MD–VA–WV PMSA	3,478	4,223	23.7	8.7	4,293	NA	21.4	1.6
West Palm Beach–Boca Raton, FL MSA	577	864	19.6	24.3	887	48	49.7	2.7
Wichita, KS MSA	442	485	27.8	11.9	493	74	9.7	1.6
York, PA MSA	313	340	24.2	13.1	346	108	8.5	1.8
Youngstown–Warren, OH MSA	645	601	25.1	15.6	603	64	-6.8	0.4

Notes: Data cover 18 consolidated metropolitan statistical areas (CMSAs), their 59 component primary metropolitan statistical areas (PMSAs), and the remaining 117 MSAs with a population of 250,000 or more in 1991 as defined by the U.S. Office of Management and Budget. Rank is based on rounded figures for CMSAs and MSAs only. NA = not applicable.

Source: Reprinted from U.S. Bureau of the Census. (1993). *Statistical abstract of the United States: 1993* (113th ed., pp. 37–39). Austin, TX: Reference Press.

TABLE 1-15 Percentage of Selected Races and Ethnicities in Largest Metropolitan Areas: 1990 (Numbers in thousands)

Metropolitan Area[a]	Total Population	Percent of Total Metropolitan Population			
		Black	American Indian, Eskimo, Aleut	Asian and Pacific Islander	Hispanic Origin[b]
New York–Northern New Jersey–Long Island, NY–NJ–CT–PA CMSA	19,342	17.8	0.2	4.6	14.7
Los Angeles–Riverside–Orange County, CA CMSA	14,532	8.5	0.6	9.2	32.9
Chicago–Gary–Kenosha, IL–IN–WI CMSA	8,240	19.0	0.2	3.1	10.9
Washington–Baltimore, DC–MD–VA–WV CMSA	6,727	25.2	0.3	3.7	3.9
San Francisco–Oakland–San Jose, CA CMSA	6,253	8.6	0.7	14.8	15.5
Philadelphia–Wilmington–Atlantic City, PA–NJ–DE–MD CMSA	5,893	18.4	0.2	2.0	3.8
Boston–Brockton–Nashua, MA–NH–ME–CT CMSA	5,455	4.8	0.2	2.5	4.4
Detroit–Ann Arbor–Flint, MI CMSA	5,187	20.5	0.4	1.4	2.0
Dallas–Fort Worth, TX CMSA	4,037	14.0	0.5	2.4	13.0
Houston–Galveston–Brazoria, TX CMSA	3,731	17.9	0.3	3.5	20.7
Miami–Fort Lauderdale, FL CMSA	3,193	18.5	0.2	1.4	33.3
Seattle–Tacoma–Bremerton, WA CMSA	2,970	4.5	1.3	6.1	3.0
Atlanta, GA MSA	2,960	25.2	0.2	1.8	2.0
Cleveland–Akron, OH CMSA	2,860	15.6	0.2	1.0	1.9
Minneapolis–St. Paul, MN–WI MSA	2,539	3.5	1.0	2.6	1.5
San Diego, CA MSA	2,498	6.4	0.8	7.9	20.4
St. Louis, MO–IL MSA	2,493	17.0	0.2	1.0	1.1
Pittsburgh, PA MSA	2,395	7.5	0.1	0.7	0.6
Phoenix–Mesa, AZ MSA	2,238	3.5	2.2	1.6	17.0
Tampa–St. Petersburg–Clearwater, FL MSA	2,068	9.0	0.3	1.1	6.7
Denver–Boulder–Greeley, CO CMSA	1,980	5.0	0.7	2.2	12.8
Cincinnati–Hamilton, OH–KY–IN CMSA	1,818	11.2	0.1	0.8	0.5
Portland–Salem, OR–WA CMSA	1,793	2.5	1.0	3.2	4.0
Milwaukee–Racine, WI CMSA	1,607	13.3	0.5	1.2	3.8
Kansas City, MO–KS MSA	1,583	12.7	0.5	1.1	2.9
Sacramento–Yolo, CA CMSA	1,481	6.9	1.1	7.7	11.6
Norfolk–Virginia Beach–Newport News, VA–NC MSA	1,443	28.3	0.3	2.4	2.3
Indianapolis, IN MSA	1,380	13.2	0.2	0.8	0.9
Columbus, OH MSA	1,345	12.1	0.2	1.6	0.8
San Antonio, TX MSA	1,325	6.7	0.4	1.2	47.4
New Orleans, LA MSA	1,285	34.8	0.3	1.7	4.2
Orlando, FL MSA	1,225	12.0	0.3	1.7	8.2
Buffalo–Niagara Falls, NY MSA	1,189	10.3	0.6	0.9	2.0
Charlotte–Gastonia–Rock Hill, NC–SC MSA	1,162	19.9	0.4	1.0	0.9
Hartford, CT MSA	1,158	8.3	0.2	1.5	6.9
Providence–Fall River–Warwick, RI–MA MSA	1,134	3.3	0.3	1.8	4.2
Salt Lake City–Ogden, UT MSA	1,072	1.0	0.8	2.4	5.8
Rochester, NY MSA	1,062	8.9	0.3	1.3	3.0
Greensboro–Winston Salem–High Point, NC MSA	1,050	19.3	0.3	0.7	0.7
Memphis, TN–AR–MS MSA	1,007	40.7	0.2	0.8	0.8
Nashville, TN MSA	985	15.5	0.2	1.0	0.8
Oklahoma City, OK MSA	959	10.5	4.8	1.9	3.6
Dayton–Springfield, OH MSA	951	13.3	0.2	1.0	0.8
Louisville, KY–IN MSA	949	12.9	0.2	0.6	0.6
Grand Rapids–Muskegon–Holland, MI MSA	938	6.9	0.6	0.9	3.1
Jacksonville, FL MSA	907	20.0	0.3	1.7	2.5
Richmond–Petersburg, VA MSA	866	29.2	0.3	1.4	1.1
West Palm Beach–Boca Raton, FL MSA	864	12.5	0.1	1.0	7.7
Albany–Schenectady–Troy, NY MSA	861	4.6	0.2	1.2	1.7
Raleigh–Durham–Chapel Hill, NC MSA	856	24.2	0.3	1.6	1.3
Las Vegas, NV–AZ NSA	853	8.4	1.1	3.1	10.4
Austin–San Marcos, TX MSA	846	9.4	0.4	2.2	20.9
Birmingham, AL MSA	840	28.7	0.2	0.5	0.4
Honolulu, HI MSA	836	3.1	0.4	63.0	6.8
Greenville–Spartanburg–Anderson, SC MSA	831	17.4	0.1	0.6	0.7

Continued on next page

public health practices, and better health care and nutrition, but better education about family planning and contraception has slowed their rates of growth (U.S. Bureau of the Census, 1993). Some scholars believe that technology and education will further reduce the birth rates of many countries.

Households

One important way to understand the U.S. population is through its household composition. As part of its study of the U.S. population in 1990, the U.S. Bureau of the Census calculated the number of households, the number of "family" or "nonfamily" house-

TABLE 1-15 **Continued**

Metropolitan Area[a]	Total Population	Percent of Total Metropolitan Population			
		Black	American Indian, Eskimo, Aleut	Asian and Pacific Islander	Hispanic Origin[b]
Fresno, CA MSA	756	4.8	1.1	7.7	35.3
Syracuse, NY MSA	742	5.7	0.6	1.1	1.4
Tulsa, OK MSA	709	8.2	6.8	0.9	2.1
Tucson, AZ MSA	667	3.1	3.0	1.8	24.5
Omaha, NE–IA MSA	640	8.0	0.5	1.0	2.6
Scranton–Wilkes-Barre–Hazleton, PA MSA	638	0.9	0.1	0.5	0.6
Toledo, OH MSA	614	11.4	0.2	1.0	3.3
Youngstown–Warren, OH MSA	601	9.4	0.2	0.4	1.3
Allentown–Bethlehem–Easton, PA MSA	595	2.0	0.1	1.1	4.6
El Paso, TX MSA	592	3.7	0.4	1.1	69.6
Albuquerque, NM MSA	589	2.5	5.1	1.4	37.1
Harrisburg–Lebanon–Carlisle, PA MSA	588	6.7	0.1	1.1	1.7
Springfield, MA MSA	588	6.3	0.2	1.4	8.5
Knoxville, TN MSA	586	6.1	0.2	0.8	0.5
Bakersfield, CA MSA	543	5.5	1.3	3.0	28.0
Little Rock–North Little Rock, AR MSA	513	19.9	0.4	0.7	0.8
Charleston–North Charleston, SC MSA	507	30.2	0.3	1.2	1.5
Sarasota–Bradenton, FL MSA	489	5.8	0.2	0.5	3.1
Wichita, KS MSA	485	7.6	1.1	1.9	4.1
Stockton–Lodi, CA MSA	481	5.6	1.1	12.4	23.4

Source: Reprinted from U.S. Bureau of the Census. (1993). *Statistical abstract of the United States: 1993* (113th ed., p. 41). Austin, TX: Reference Press.

[a]Metropolitan areas are shown in rank order of total population of consolidated metropolitan statistical areas (CMSAs) and metropolitan statistical areas (MSAs).

[b]People of Hispanic origin may be of any race.

TABLE 1-16 Population Figures for the World's Largest Urban Areas: Selected Years, 1950 to 1990, and Projections for 2000 (Numbers in millions)

Urban Area	Country	1950	1970	1990	2000
1. Mexico City	Mexico	3.1	9.4	20.2	25.6
2. Tokyo	Japan	6.7	14.9	18.1	19.0
3. São Paulo	Brazil	2.4	8.1	17.4	22.1
4. New York	United States	12.3	16.2	16.2	16.8
5. Shanghai	China	5.3	11.2	13.4	17.0
6. Los Angeles	United States	4.0	8.4	11.9	13.9
7. Calcutta	India	4.4	6.9	11.8	15.7
8. Buenos Aires	Argentina	5.0	8.4	11.5	12.9
9. Bombay	India	2.9	5.8	11.2	15.4
10. Seoul	South Korea	1.0	5.3	11.0	12.7
11. Beijing	China	3.9	8.1	10.8	14.0
12. Rio de Janeiro	Brazil	2.9	7.0	10.7	12.5
13. Tianjin	China	2.4	5.2	9.4	12.7
14. Jakarta	Indonesia	2.0	3.9	9.3	13.7
15. Cairo	Egypt	2.4	5.3	9.0	11.8
16. Moscow	Russia	4.8	7.1	8.8	9.0
17. Delhi	India	1.4	3.5	8.8	13.2
18. Metro Manila	Philippines	1.5	3.5	8.5	11.8
19. Osaka	Japan	3.8	7.6	8.5	8.6
20. Paris	France	5.4	8.3	8.5	8.6
21. Karachi	Pakistan	1.0	3.1	7.7	11.7
22. Lagos	Nigeria	0.3	2.0	7.7	12.9
23. London	United Kingdom	8.7	8.6	7.4	13.9
24. Bangkok	Thailand	1.4	3.1	7.2	10.3
25. Chicago	United States	4.9	6.7	7.0	7.3
26. Teheran	Iran	1.0	3.3	6.8	8.5
27. Istanbul	Turkey	1.1	2.8	6.7	9.5
28. Dhaka	Bangladesh	0.4	1.5	6.6	12.2
29. Lima	Peru	1.0	2.9	6.2	8.2
30. Madras	India	1.4	3.0	5.7	7.8
31. Hong Kong	Hong Kong	1.7	3.4	5.4	6.1
32. Milan	Italy	3.6	5.5	5.3	5.4
33. Madrid	Spain	1.6	3.4	5.2	5.9
34. St. Petersburg	Russia	2.6	4.0	5.1	5.4
35. Bangalore	India	0.8	1.6	5.0	8.2
36. Bogotá	Colombia	0.6	2.4	4.9	6.4
37. Shenyang	China	2.1	3.5	4.8	6.3
38. Philadelphia	United States	2.9	4.0	4.3	4.5
39. Caracas	Venezuela	0.7	2.0	4.1	5.2
40. Baghdad	Iraq	0.6	2.0	4.0	5.1
41. Lahore	Pakistan	0.8	2.0	4.1	6.0
42. Wuhan	China	1.2	2.7	3.9	5.3
43. Alexandria	Egypt	1.0	2.0	3.7	5.1
44. Detroit	United States	2.8	4.0	3.7	3.7
45. Guangzhou	China	1.3	3.0	3.7	4.8
46. San Francisco	United States	2.0	3.0	3.7	4.1
47. Ahmedabad	India	0.9	1.7	3.6	5.3
48. Belo Horizonte	Brazil	0.4	1.6	3.6	4.7
49. Naples	Italy	2.8	3.6	3.6	3.6
50. Hyderabad	India	1.1	1.7	3.5	5.0
51. Kinshasa	Zaire	0.2	1.4	3.5	5.5
52. Toronto	Canada	1.0	2.8	3.5	3.9
53. Athens	Greece	1.8	2.5	3.4	3.8
54. Barcelona	Spain	1.6	2.7	3.4	3.7
55. Dallas	United States	0.9	2.0	3.4	4.4
56. Katowice	Poland	1.7	2.8	3.4	3.7
57. Sydney	Australia	1.7	2.7	3.4	3.7
58. Yangon	Myanmar	0.7	1.4	3.3	4.7
59. Casablanca	Morocco	0.7	1.5	3.2	4.6
60. Guadalajara	Mexico	0.4	1.5	3.2	4.1
61. Ho Chi Minh City	Vietnam	0.9	2.0	3.2	4.1
62. Chongqing	China	1.7	2.3	3.1	4.2
63. Porto Alegre	Brazil	0.4	1.5	3.1	3.9
64. Rome	Italy	1.6	2.9	3.1	3.1

Continued on next page

holds (nonfamily households are those in which people are living alone or with non-relatives), the number of children, and the age structures of households. Table 1-17 presents the household composition of the United States broken down into family and nonfamily households from 1980 to 1992 and includes trends of relevance for social workers. For example, although most households grew in number, the only category that slightly declined was that of married couples living with their own children under age 18. That decline reflects the aging of the population, the growth in stepfamilies or "blended" families, and divorce. Although their numbers are small, males who were living without spouses and caring for their own children were the most rapidly growing group. The other important increase has been in the category of persons living alone and in nonfamily households.

Table 1-18 shows the living arrangements of people 15 years old and older. Patterns in the living arrangements of young adults are shown in Table 1-19. The data show that people are marrying later in life or are not marrying at all, and increasing numbers of young people are living with their parents.

Table 1-20 shows household arrangements by sizes of families with children. The table includes information about marital status (married-couple and female householders) and by race or ethnic origin (white, black, and Hispanic).

Some more general characteristics of American households in 1992 are depicted in Table 1-21. Information is provided on the ages of householders, sizes of households, marital status, and regional differences. Information is also included on ethnicity. The table also shows the proportions of households that own their dwellings and of those that rent.

The breakdown of households by state for the period 1970 through 1990 is shown in Table 1-22. The table shows that the number of people per household has declined nationally from 1980 to 1990.

TABLE 1-16 **Continued**

Urban Area	Country	1950	1970	1990	2000
65. Algiers	Algeria	0.4	1.3	3.0	4.5
66. Chengou	China	0.7	1.8	3.0	4.1
67. Harbin	China	1.0	2.1	3.0	3.9
68. Houston	United States	0.7	1.7	3.0	3.6
69. Monterrey	Mexico	0.4	1.2	3.0	3.9
70. Montreal	Canada	1.3	2.4	3.0	3.1
71. Taipei	Taiwan	0.6	1.8	3.0	4.2

Notes: An urban area is defined as a central city, or several cities, and the surrounding urbanized areas, also called a metropolitan area. Data are arranged according to urban areas that had populations of more than 3 million in 1990.

Source: THE UNIVERSAL ALMANAC copyright 1993 by John W. Wright. Reprinted with permission of Andrews & McMeel, Kansas City, MO. All rights reserved.

TABLE 1-17 **Households, by Type and Presence of Children: 1980, 1990, and 1992**

Type of Household and Presence of Children	Households Number (1,000) 1980	Households Number (1,000) 1990	Households Number (1,000) 1992	Percent Change, 1980–92	Percent Distribution 1980	Percent Distribution 1992	Persons in Households, 1992 Number (1,000)	Persons in Households, 1992 Percent Distribution	Persons per Household, 1992
Total households	80,776	93,347	95,669	18	100	100	250,984	100	2.62
Family households	59,550	66,090	67,173	13	74	70	216,054	86	3.22
With own children under 18	31,022	32,289	32,746	6	38	34	129,150	52	3.94
Without own children under 18	28,528	33,801	34,427	21	35	36	86,904	35	2.52
Married couple family	49,112	52,317	52,457	7	61	55	170,416	68	3.25
With own children under 18	24,961	24,537	24,420	–2	31	26	101,883	41	4.17
Without own children under 18	24,151	27,780	28,037	16	30	29	68,533	27	2.44
Male householder, no spouse present	1,733	2,884	3,025	75	2	3	9,329	4	3.08
With own children under 18	616	1,153	1,283	108	1	1	4,268	2	3.33
Without own children under 18	1,117	1,731	1,742	56	1	2	5,061	2	2.91
Female householder, no spouse present	8,705	10,890	11,692	34	11	12	36,309	15	3.11
With own children under 18	5,445	6,599	7,043	29	7	7	22,999	9	3.27
Without own children under 18	3,261	4,290	4,648	43	4	5	13,310	5	2.86
Nonfamily households	21,226	27,257	28,496	34	26	30	34,930	14	1.23
Living alone	18,296	22,999	23,974	31	23	25	23,974	10	1.00
Male householder	8,807	11,606	12,428	41	11	13	16,452	7	1.32
Living alone	6,966	9,049	9,613	38	9	10	9,613	4	1.00
Female householder	12,419	15,651	16,068	29	15	17	18,478	7	1.15
Living alone	11,330	13,950	14,361	27	14	15	14,361	6	1.00

Source: Reprinted from U.S. Bureau of the Census. (1993). *Statistical abstract of the United States: 1993* (113th ed., p. 59). Austin, TX: Reference Press.

TABLE 1-18 **Living Arrangements of People 15 Years Old and Older, by Selected Characteristics: 1992 (Numbers in thousands)**

| Age and Gender | Total | All Races[a] | | | | White Persons, Percent Living | | | Black Persons, Percent Living | | |
| | | Percent Living | | | | | | | | | |
		Alone	With Spouse	With Other Relatives	With Non-relatives	Alone	With Spouse	With Other Relatives	Alone	With Spouse	With Other Relatives
Total	195,243	12	55	26	7	12	58	23	13	32	48
15 to 19 years old	16,567	1	2	93	4	1	3	93	1	1	96
20 to 24 years old	17,848	6	23	56	15	6	25	52	5	12	74
25 to 34 years old	42,493	9	56	24	11	9	59	20	10	31	49
35 to 44 years old	39,571	9	70	16	5	9	73	14	10	46	38
45 to 54 years old	27,024	11	72	13	4	10	75	11	16	47	30
55 to 64 years old	21,150	14	72	11	3	14	76	8	20	46	27
65 years old and over	30,589	31	54	12	2	31	56	11	36	37	24
65 to 74 years old	18,440	25	63	10	2	24	65	9	34	43	20
75 years old and over	12,149	41	41	16	2	41	42	15	39	25	33
Male	93,760	10	57	24	8	10	60	22	13	36	40
15 to 19 years old	8,380	1	1	95	3	b	1	95	1	b	96
20 to 24 years old	8,800	6	17	60	17	6	19	57	5	9	75
25 to 34 years old	21,125	11	52	22	15	11	55	19	12	32	41
35 to 44 years old	19,506	11	70	12	7	11	72	10	13	52	25
45 to 54 years old	13,114	11	76	8	5	10	78	7	16	54	19
55 to 64 years old	10,036	11	79	6	4	10	82	5	19	53	16
65 years old and over	12,799	16	74	7	3	15	76	6	30	54	12
65 to 74 years old	8,266	13	77	6	3	12	79	6	28	58	9
75 years old and over	4,533	22	68	8	2	21	70	7	32	46	17
Female	101,483	14	53	28	5	15	56	24	13	29	54
15 to 19 years old	8,187	1	4	91	4	1	5	90	1	1	96
20 to 24 years old	9,048	6	29	52	14	6	31	48	5	14	74

Continued on next page

TABLE 1-18 Continued

Age and Gender	Total	All Races[a] Percent Living				White Persons, Percent Living			Black Persons, Percent Living		
		Alone	With Spouse	With Other Relatives	With Non-relatives	Alone	With Spouse	With Other Relatives	Alone	With Spouse	With Other Relatives
25 to 34 years old	21,368	8	59	25	8	8	64	20	8	31	56
35 to 44 years old	20,065	7	69	21	4	7	73	17	7	41	48
45 to 54 years old	13,910	11	69	17	3	10	72	14	15	41	39
55 to 64 years old	11,114	17	66	14	2	17	70	11	21	40	36
65 years old and over	17,790	42	40	16	2	42	41	14	40	25	33
65 to 74 years old	10,174	34	51	13	2	34	54	11	39	32	28
75 years old and over	7,616	52	24	21	2	53	25	19	43	14	41

Source: Reprinted from U.S. Bureau of the Census. (1993). *Statistical abstract of the United States: 1993* (113th ed., p. 59). Austin, TX: Reference Press.

[a]Includes other races not shown separately.

[b]Less than 0.5 percent.

TABLE 1-19 Living Arrangements of Young Adults: Selected Years, 1970 to 1990

Living Arrangements and Gender	Persons 18 to 24 Years Old					Persons 25 to 34 Years Old				
	1970	1980	1985	1990	1992	1970	1980	1985	1990	1992
Total (1,000)	22,357	29,122	27,844	25,310	24,434	24,566	36,796	40,857	43,240	42,493
Percent distribution										
Child of householder[a]	47	48	54	53	54	8	9	11	12	12
Family householder or spouse	38	29	24	22	21	83	72	68	65	63
Nonfamily householder	5	10	8	9	9	5	12	13	13	13
Other	10	13	14	16	16	4	7	9	11	12
Male (1,000)	10,398	14,278	13,695	12,450	12,083	11,929	18,107	20,184	21,462	21,125
Percent distribution										
Child of householder[a]	54	54	60	58	60	10	11	13	15	15
Family householder or spouse	30	21	16	15	14	79	66	60	56	54
Nonfamily householder	5	11	10	10	10	7	15	16	16	16
Other	10	13	14	17	16	5	8	11	13	15
Female (1,000)	11,959	14,844	14,149	12,860	12,351	12,637	18,689	20,673	21,779	21,368
Percent distribution										
Child of householder[a]	41	43	48	48	48	7	7	8	8	9
Family householder or spouse	45	36	32	30	23	86	78	76	73	72
Nonfamily householder	4	8	7	8	8	4	9	10	10	10
Other	10	13	13	15	16	4	6	7	9	9

Source: Reprinted from U.S. Bureau of the Census. (1993). *Statistical abstract of the United States: 1993* (113th ed., p. 60). Austin, TX: Reference Press.

[a]Includes unmarried college students living in dormitories.

TABLE 1-20 **Families, by Size and Presence of Children: 1980, 1990, and 1992 (Numbers in thousands)**

Characteristic	1980, Total	1990, Total	1992 All Races[a] Total[c]	Married Couple	Female Householder[d]	White Total[c]	Married Couple	Black Total[c]	Married Couple	Hispanic[b] Total[c]	Married Couple
Total	59,550	66,090	67,173	52,457	11,692	57,224	47,124	7,716	3,631	5,177	3,532
Size of family											
Two persons	23,461	27,606	28,202	20,838	5,527	24,828	19,360	2,680	1,026	1,266	696
Three persons	13,603	15,353	15,594	11,503	3,370	13,097	10,250	2,007	889	1,209	725
Four persons	12,372	14,026	14,162	12,219	1,656	11,997	10,840	1,582	886	1,238	927
Five persons	5,930	5,938	6,030	5,257	676	4,953	4,564	836	485	752	614
Six persons	2,461	1,997	1,986	1,709	230	1,534	1,333	341	219	387	314
Seven or more persons	1,723	1,170	1,200	931	234	815	717	272	126	324	255
Average per family	3.29	3.17	3.17	3.23	2.98	3.11	3.18	3.43	3.62	3.81	4.02
Own children under age 18											
None	28,528	33,801	34,427	28,037	4,648	30,178	25,607	3,271	1,705	1,843	1,210
One	12,443	13,530	13,615	9,520	3,327	11,204	8,355	1,870	766	1,160	754
Two	11,470	12,263	12,364	9,728	2,244	10,477	8,688	1,429	685	1,139	817
Three	4,674	4,650	4,836	3,757	980	3,925	3,297	740	332	655	481
Four or more	2,435	1,846	1,932	1,416	492	1,439	1,197	406	144	380	269
Own children under age 6											
None	46,063	50,905	51,769	40,532	8,721	44,612	36,643	5,557	2,706	3,388	2,210
One	9,441	10,304	10,642	8,153	2,097	8,722	7,135	1,471	661	1,174	871
Two or more	4,047	4,882	4,763	3,772	874	3,891	3,346	588	263	615	450
Percent distribution (total)	100	100	100	100	100	100	100	100	100	100	100
Size of family											
Two persons	39	42	42	40	47	43	41	35	28	24	20
Three persons	23	23	23	22	29	23	22	26	24	23	21
Four persons	21	21	21	23	14	21	23	21	24	24	26
Five persons	10	9	9	10	6	9	10	11	13	15	17
Six persons	4	3	3	3	2	3	3	4	6	7	9
Seven or more persons	3	2	2	2	2	1	2	4	3	6	7
Own children under age 18											
None	48	51	51	53	40	53	54	42	47	36	34
One	21	20	20	18	28	20	18	24	21	22	21
Two	19	19	18	19	19	18	18	19	19	22	23
Three	8	7	7	7	8	7	7	10	9	13	14
Four or more	4	3	3	3	4	3	3	5	4	7	8
Own children under age 6											
None	77	77	77	77	75	78	78	72	75	65	63
One	16	16	16	16	18	15	15	19	18	23	25
Two or more	7	7	7	7	7	7	7	9	7	12	13

Source: Reprinted from U.S. Bureau of the Census. (1993). Statistical abstract of the United States: 1993 (113th ed., p. 60). Austin, TX: Reference Press.

[a] Includes other races, not shown separately.

[b] Hispanic people may be of any race.

[c] Includes other types of families, not shown separately.

[d] No spouse present.

TABLE 1-21 **Household Characteristics, by Race or Ethnicity and Type: 1992**

	Number of Households (1,000)							Percent Distribution								Persons per Household		
				Family Households			Non-family House-holds				Family Households			Non-family House-holds				
Characteristic	Total	Black	Hispanic[a]	Total[b]	Married Couple	Female House-holder[c]		Total	Black	Hispanic[a]	Total[b]	Married Couple	Female House-holder[b]		Total	Black	Hispanic[a]
Total	95,669	11,083	6,379	67,173	52,457	11,692	28,496	100	100	100	100	100	100	100	2.62	2.81	3.45
Age of householder																	
15 to 24 years old	4,859	702	555	2,642	1,471	909	2,217	5	6	9	4	3	8	8	2.35	2.58	3.08
25 to 29 years old	8,810	1,203	785	5,859	4,205	1,285	2,951	9	11	12	9	8	11	10	2.68	2.98	3.56
30 to 34 years old	11,197	1,458	1,035	8,520	6,486	1,680	2,677	12	13	16	13	12	14	9	3.06	2.90	3.80
35 to 44 years old	21,774	2,636	1,640	17,533	13,519	3,230	4,241	23	24	26	26	26	28	15	3.26	3.34	3.94
45 to 54 years old	15,547	1,718	979	12,188	9,828	1,837	3,360	16	16	15	18	19	16	12	2.89	2.99	3.56
55 to 64 years old	12,559	1,418	728	9,296	7,758	1,203	3,263	13	13	11	14	15	10	11	2.34	2.62	2.98
65 to 74 years old	12,043	1,245	417	7,330	6,269	823	4,713	13	11	7	11	12	7	17	1.86	2.03	2.44
75 years old and over	8,878	703	238	3,805	2,919	724	5,073	9	6	4	6	6	6	18	1.57	1.84	2.05
Region																	
Northeast	19,314	1,907	1,135	13,428	10,399	2,422	5,886	20	17	18	20	20	21	21	2.63	2.84	3.03
Midwest	23,327	2,238	456	16,170	12,730	2,739	7,157	24	20	7	24	24	23	25	2.59	2.78	3.32
South	33,073	5,972	1,980	23,679	18,346	4,342	9,394	35	54	31	35	35	37	33	2.60	2.85	3.38
West	19,955	966	2,807	13,897	10,981	2,189	6,058	21	9	44	21	21	19	21	2.71	2.50	3.70
Size of household																	
One person	23,974	2,915	887	NA	NA	NA	23,974	25	26	14	NA	NA	NA	84	1.00	1.00	1.00
Two persons	30,734	2,887	1,364	27,119	20,702	4,967	3,615	32	26	21	40	39	42	13	2.00	2.00	2.00
Three persons	16,398	2,069	1,247	15,822	11,460	3,564	576	17	19	20	24	22	30	2	3.00	3.00	3.00
Four persons	14,710	1,661	1,272	14,459	12,197	1,813	251	15	15	20	22	23	16	1	4.00	4.00	4.00
Five persons	6,389	878	836	6,334	5,346	794	55	7	8	13	9	10	7	d	5.00	5.00	5.00
Six persons	2,126	368	406	2,107	1,742	284	19	2	3	6	3	3	2	d	6.00	6.00	6.00
Seven persons or more	1,338	304	367	1,332	1,011	270	6	1	3	6	2	2	2	d	—	—	—

Continued on next page

TABLE 1-21 Continued

Characteristic	Number of Households (1,000)							Percent Distribution									
				Family Households			Non-family Households				Family Households			Non-family Households	Persons per Household		
	Total	Black	Hispanic[a]	Total[b]	Married Couple	Female Householder[c]		Total	Black	Hispanic[a]	Total[b]	Married Couple	Female Householder[b]		Total	Black	Hispanic[a]
Marital status of householder																	
Never married (single)	14,461	2,931	1,118	3,935	NA	2,900	10,526	15	26	18	6	NA	25	37	—	—	—
Married, spouse present	52,457	3,631	3,532	52,457	52,457	NA	NA	55	33	55	78	100	NA	NA	—	—	—
Married, spouse absent	4,571	1,273	575	2,507	NA	2,049	2,064	5	11	9	4	NA	18	7	—	—	—
Widowed	11,895	1,527	444	2,938	NA	2,458	8,957	12	14	7	4	NA	21	31	—	—	—
Divorced	12,286	1,721	711	5,337	NA	4,285	6,949	13	16	11	8	NA	37	24	—	—	—
Housing tenure																	
Owner-occupied	61,310	4,683	2,547	47,819	41,102	5,040	13,491	64	42	40	71	78	43	47	2.73	3.01	3.58
Renter-occupied	34,359	6,400	3,832	19,354	11,355	6,651	15,005	36	58	60	29	22	57	53	2.43	2.66	3.37

Notes: — = not available; NA = not applicable.

Source: Reprinted from U.S. Bureau of the Census. (1993). *Statistical abstract of the United States: 1993* (113th ed., p. 57). Austin, TX: Reference Press.

[a]Hispanic people may be of any race.

[b]Includes male householder, no spouse present.

[c]No spouse present.

[d]Less than 0.5 percent.

TABLE 1-22 Households, by States: 1970, 1980, and 1990

Region and State	Households							Families, 1990 (1,000)				Nonfamily Households, 1990 (1,000)	
	Number (1,000)			Percent Change		Persons per Household		Total[a]	Married Couple		One-Parent[c]	Total[d]	One-Person
	1970	1980	1990	1970–80	1980–90	1980	1990		Total[b]	With Own Children			
United States	63,450	80,390	91,947	26.7	14.4	2.75	2.63	64,518	50,708	23,495	7,383	27,429	22,580
Northeast	15,483	17,471	18,873	12.8	8.0	2.74	2.61	13,071	10,089	4,505	1,421	5,802	4,828
Connecticut	933	1,094	1,230	17.2	12.5	2.76	2.59	864	685	299	87	366	297
Maine	303	395	465	30.5	17.7	2.75	2.56	329	271	126	35	137	108
Massachusetts	1,760	2,033	2,247	15.5	10.5	2.72	2.58	1,515	1,170	524	165	732	581
New Hampshire	225	323	411	43.5	27.1	2.75	2.62	293	245	119	27	119	90
New Jersey	2,218	2,549	2,795	14.9	9.7	2.84	2.70	2,021	1,579	708	195	773	646
New York	5,914	6,340	6,639	7.2	4.7	2.70	2.63	4,489	3,316	1,496	568	2,150	1,806
Pennsylvania	3,705	4,220	4,496	13.9	6.5	2.74	2.57	3,156	2,502	1,085	302	1,340	1,151
Rhode Island	292	339	378	16.0	11.6	2.70	2.55	259	202	89	28	119	99
Vermont	132	178	211	35.0	18.1	2.75	2.57	145	119	58	16	66	49
Midwest	17,537	20,859	22,317	18.9	7.0	2.75	2.60	15,675	12,574	5,875	1,740	6,642	5,588
Illinois	3,502	4,045	4,202	15.5	3.9	2.76	2.65	2,925	2,272	1,068	337	1,277	1,081
Indiana	1,609	1,927	2,065	19.7	7.2	2.77	2.61	1,480	1,202	563	160	585	497
Iowa	896	1,053	1,064	17.5	1.1	2.68	2.52	741	630	287	67	324	275
Kansas	727	872	945	19.9	8.3	2.62	2.53	659	552	260	65	286	245
Michigan	2,653	3,195	3,419	20.4	7.0	2.84	2.66	2,439	1,883	875	317	980	809
Minnesota	1,154	1,445	1,648	25.2	14.0	2.74	2.58	1,131	943	460	112	517	414
Missouri	1,521	1,793	1,961	17.9	9.4	2.67	2.54	1,368	1,105	502	149	593	511
Nebraska	474	571	602	20.6	5.4	2.66	2.54	415	351	168	39	187	160
North Dakota	182	228	241	25.4	5.8	2.75	2.55	166	142	71	14	75	64
Ohio	3,289	3,834	4,088	16.5	6.6	2.76	2.59	2,895	2,294	1,054	329	1,192	1,020
South Dakota	201	243	259	20.8	6.8	2.74	2.59	180	153	74	17	79	68
Wisconsin	1,329	1,652	1,822	24.3	10.3	2.77	2.61	1,275	1,048	493	133	547	444
South	19,258	26,486	31,822	37.5	20.1	2.77	2.61	22,722	17,786	8,181	2,647	9,101	7,641
Alabama	1,034	1,342	1,507	29.8	12.3	2.84	2.62	1,104	858	396	127	403	358
Arkansas	615	816	891	32.6	9.2	2.74	2.57	652	527	236	70	240	214
Delaware	165	207	247	25.7	19.5	2.79	2.61	176	138	62	20	72	57
District of Columbia	263	253	250	–3.6	–1.4	2.40	2.26	122	63	22	27	128	104
Florida	2,285	3,744	5,135	63.9	37.1	2.55	2.46	3,512	2,792	1,043	374	1,623	1,310
Georgia	1,389	1,872	2,367	36.7	26.4	2.84	2.66	1,713	1,307	633	222	654	538
Kentucky	984	1,263	1,380	28.4	9.2	2.82	2.60	1,016	817	391	108	364	321
Louisiana	1,052	1,412	1,499	34.2	6.2	2.91	2.74	1,090	803	403	162	409	356

Continued on next page

TABLE 1-22 **Continued**

Region and State	Households Number (1,000) 1970	1980	1990	Households Percent Change 1970–80	1980–90	Households Persons per Household 1980	1990	Families, 1990 (1,000) Total[a]	Married Couple Total[b]	Married Couple With Own Children	One-Parent[c]	Nonfamily Households, 1990 (1,000) Total[d]	One-Person
Maryland	1,175	1,461	1,749	24.3	19.7	2.82	2.67	1,246	949	437	149	503	395
Mississippi	637	827	911	29.9	10.2	2.97	2.75	674	498	242	99	237	213
North Carolina	1,510	2,043	2,517	35.4	23.2	2.78	2.54	1,812	1,424	634	202	705	597
Oklahoma	851	1,119	1,206	31.5	7.8	2.62	2.53	855	696	321	95	351	309
South Carolina	734	1,030	1,258	40.3	22.1	2.93	2.68	928	710	333	114	330	281
Tennessee	1,213	1,619	1,854	33.4	14.5	2.77	2.56	1,348	1,060	477	151	506	442
Texas	3,434	4,929	6,071	43.5	23.2	2.82	2.73	4,344	3,436	1,754	513	1,727	1,453
Virginia	1,391	1,863	2,291	34.0	23.0	2.77	2.61	1,629	1,302	611	167	662	524
West Virginia	547	686	689	25.4	0.3	2.79	2.55	500	406	187	47	188	169
West	11,172	15,574	18,935	39.4	21.6	2.71	2.72	13,050	10,260	4,934	1,575	5,885	4,523
Alaska	79	131	189	66.3	43.7	2.93	2.80	133	106	63	19	56	42
Arizona	539	957	1,369	77.5	43.0	2.79	2.62	940	748	332	114	429	338
California	6,574	8,630	10,381	31.3	20.3	2.68	2.79	7,139	5,470	2,656	889	3,242	2,430
Colorado	691	1,061	1,282	53.6	20.8	2.65	2.51	854	690	332	103	428	341
Hawaii	203	294	356	44.8	21.2	3.15	3.01	263	210	101	24	93	69
Idaho	219	324	361	48.0	11.3	2.85	2.73	263	224	111	25	98	81
Montana	217	284	306	30.6	7.9	2.70	2.53	212	177	84	23	94	80
Nevada	160	304	466	90.1	53.2	2.59	2.53	307	240	106	38	159	120
New Mexico	289	441	543	52.6	22.9	2.90	2.74	391	304	153	54	151	125
Oregon	692	992	1,103	43.4	11.3	2.60	2.52	751	613	269	85	352	279
Utah	298	449	537	50.6	19.8	3.20	3.15	411	348	202	41	126	102
Washington	1,106	1,541	1,872	39.3	21.5	2.61	2.53	1,265	1,029	475	148	607	476
Wyoming	105	166	169	58.3	1.9	2.78	2.63	120	101	52	13	49	41

Source: Reprinted from Ashcroft, J., & Strauss, A. (1993). *Families first: Report of the National Commission on America's Urban Families* (p. 58). Washington, DC: U.S. Government Printing Office.

[a]Includes other family types, not shown separately.

[b]Includes other married couple families, not shown separately.

[c]Comprises male family householders with no wife present and with own children and female family householders with no husband present and with own children.

[d]Includes nonfamily households with two or more people.

Marriage and Divorce

Another way to understand the U.S. population is through statistics on marriage and divorce, which are not specifically reflected in the data on households. The marital status of the U.S. population by gender and age in 1992 is detailed in Table 1-23. In that year, over 63 percent of men were married, some 26 percent were single, 7.6 percent were divorced, and less than 3 percent were widowed. For women, the percentages were smaller for every category except widowed and divorced, in which they exceeded men. One-month and six-month figures for marriages and divorces for each state in 1991 through 1993 are shown in Table 1-24.

TABLE 1-23 **Marital Status of the Population, by Gender and Age Group: 1992 (Numbers in thousands)**

Gender and Age	Number of Persons (1,000)					Percent Distribution				
	Total	Single	Married	Widowed	Divorced	Total	Single	Married	Widowed	Divorced
Male	88,663	23,220	56,162	2,529	6,752	100.0	26.2	63.3	2.9	7.6
18 to 19 years old	3,283	3,207	76	0	0	100.0	97.7	2.3	0.0	0.0
20 to 24 years old	8,800	7,067	1,612	2	119	100.0	80.3	18.3	0.0	1.4
25 to 29 years old	10,024	4,882	4,644	13	485	100.0	48.7	46.3	0.1	4.8
30 to 34 years old	11,101	3,262	6,991	10	837	100.0	29.4	63.0	0.1	7.5
35 to 39 years old	10,358	1,905	7,331	51	1,071	100.0	18.4	70.8	0.5	10.3
40 to 44 years old	9,148	839	7,117	57	1,134	100.0	9.2	77.8	0.6	12.4
45 to 54 years old	13,114	957	10,424	128	1,606	100.0	7.3	79.5	1.0	12.2
55 to 64 years old	10,036	559	8,249	351	877	100.0	5.6	82.2	3.5	8.7
65 to 74 years old	8,266	383	6,536	841	506	100.0	4.6	79.1	10.2	6.1
75 years old and over	4,533	159	3,180	1,076	118	100.0	3.5	70.2	23.7	2.6
Female	96,599	18,576	57,133	11,325	9,565	100.0	19.2	59.1	11.7	9.9
18 to 19 years old	3,303	2,974	308	0	21	100.0	90.0	9.3	0.0	0.6
20 to 24 years old	9,048	5,940	2,895	11	201	100.0	65.7	32.0	0.1	2.2
25 to 29 years old	10,108	3,356	5,916	26	811	100.0	33.2	58.5	0.3	8.0
30 to 34 years old	11,260	2,122	7,856	83	1,200	100.0	18.8	69.8	0.7	10.7
35 to 39 years old	10,595	1,334	7,808	115	1,337	100.0	12.6	73.7	1.1	12.6
40 to 44 years old	9,470	795	7,032	187	1,456	100.0	8.4	74.3	2.0	15.4
45 to 54 years old	13,910	744	10,238	642	2,285	100.0	5.3	73.6	4.6	16.4
55 to 64 years old	11,114	445	7,739	1,659	1,271	100.0	4.0	69.6	14.9	11.4
65 to 74 years old	10,174	451	5,395	3,468	681	100.0	4.4	53.0	35.9	6.7
75 years old and over	7,616	413	1,947	4,953	301	100.0	5.4	25.6	65.0	4.0

Source: Reprinted from U.S. Bureau of the Census. (1993). *Statistical abstract of the United States: 1993* (113th ed., p. 54). Austin, TX: Reference Press.

TABLE 1-24 Provisional Number of Marriages and Divorces by Division and State, June 1992 and 1993, and Six-Month Figures, 1991 to 1993

	Marriages					Divorces				
	June		January–June			June		January–June		
Area	1993	1992	1993	1992	1991	1993	1992	1993	1992	1991
Northeast										
Connecticut	—	2,858	—	10,127	10,659	—	975	—	5,764	6,832
Maine	1,705	1,368	4,090	4,251	4,016	451	621	2,788	3,070	2,458
Massachusetts	4,664	3,883	13,243	18,704	18,686	886	616	7,844	5,805	7,975
New Hampshire	621	427	2,698	3,155	3,517	453	973	2,383	3,101	2,558
New Jersey	5,506	5,900	22,754	24,152	24,243	2,648	2,534	13,188	13,687	13,527
New York[a]	16,546	14,668	64,699	64,624	67,423	4,506	3,918	26,970	28,260	27,881
Pennsylvania	8,436	9,673	32,130	34,188	33,694	3,649	3,602	19,641	19,863	19,747
Rhode Island	826	929	2,909	3,071	3,129	289	339	1,783	1,780	1,713
Vermont	541	578	1,957	1,927	1,975	293	188	1,413	1,494	1,289
Midwest										
Illinois	11,337	10,817	39,951	40,961	40,921	3,884	3,260	21,930	20,907	22,286
Indiana	6,508	5,535	22,209	22,607	22,287	—	—	—	—	—
Iowa	2,913	2,602	11,533	9,380	9,863	950	810	5,469	5,505	6,745
Kansas	882	2,237	8,025	9,518	9,182	615	273	5,433	6,108	7,023
Michigan	8,399	8,628	28,352	29,768	29,860	3,360	3,892	19,832	19,401	20,235
Minnesota	4,158	4,087	12,822	13,249	13,788	1,315	1,332	8,436	7,586	7,559
Missouri	5,960	5,854	20,430	21,015	21,215	2,322	2,241	13,325	13,380	13,533
Nebraska	1,576	1,443	5,708	6,053	6,203	463	561	3,116	3,301	3,268
North Dakota	820	760	2,139	2,092	1,986	180	193	1,078	1,154	1,080
Ohio	9,916	9,966	37,845	40,506	42,505	4,535	4,226	24,881	25,847	27,269
South Dakota	1,045	1,032	3,238	3,349	3,134	245	259	1,455	1,440	1,290
Wisconsin	3,919	3,984	17,055	17,677	17,963	1,572	1,680	8,891	9,266	9,124
South										
Alabama	3,104	5,295	18,341	20,192	20,014	1,973	2,358	13,545	13,712	13,768
Arkansas	4,096	3,877	18,023	17,509	19,008	1,875	1,347	8,975	8,885	9,732
Delaware	553	568	2,319	2,349	2,556	190	310	1,497	1,578	1,467
District of Columbia	763	499	1,226	1,381	1,911	193	220	887	1,272	979
Florida	15,030	12,818	73,836	70,758	68,872	7,002	9,264	43,302	43,556	41,446
Georgia	6,052	3,263	29,780	22,892	35,526	3,777	2,192	19,348	15,668	20,687
Kentucky	4,969	5,354	20,834	23,390	22,635	2,104	2,133	11,088	12,423	10,575
Louisiana	2,890	3,470	14,431	15,181	15,534	—	—	—	—	—
Maryland	4,787	4,104	18,724	18,827	18,759	1,178	1,575	8,220	8,747	8,065
Mississippi	2,636	2,329	11,644	11,059	11,490	890	1,067	6,009	7,715	6,914
North Carolina	5,557	5,747	22,719	23,852	23,810	3,110	3,026	17,642	18,037	16,370
Oklahoma	3,597	3,586	14,702	15,758	15,929	2,140	1,948	10,837	12,736	11,692
South Carolina	5,098	5,287	25,334	26,644	25,924	1,286	1,448	7,626	8,333	7,050
Tennessee	7,865	6,724	35,045	33,435	32,878	2,885	2,622	16,415	16,741	15,477
Texas[b]	14,507	16,757	92,450	94,516	96,992	8,176	8,168	52,562	52,555	46,870
Virginia	6,799	7,312	31,893	32,609	32,211	2,689	2,460	14,560	14,273	13,597
West Virginia	967	1,605	6,197	5,510	5,066	978	758	4,976	4,842	4,920
West										
Alaska	590	583	2,227	2,571	2,861	200	511	1,333	2,037	1,667
Arizona[a]	3,456	3,583	20,368	18,123	18,407	2,251	2,185	12,409	12,841	11,962
California	—	—	—	—	91,865	—	—	—	—	—
Colorado	—	3,987	—	15,175	15,506	1,549	1,836	9,474	9,705	9,378
Hawaii	1,528	1,519	8,532	8,736	8,514	354	456	2,433	2,576	2,566
Idaho	1,352	1,527	5,709	6,343	6,256	666	593	3,533	3,420	3,164
Montana	994	984	2,910	2,987	3,040	416	329	2,143	2,137	2,161
Nevada	10,339	11,247	59,688	56,825	56,373	—	—	—	—	—
New Mexico[c]	1,494	1,487	6,153	6,419	6,301	986	815	5,123	4,838	4,145
Oregon	1,654	2,571	9,336	9,509	9,012	1,064	1,474	7,631	7,821	7,419
Utah	1,993	1,932	8,900	8,848	7,863	727	916	4,535	4,877	4,273
Washington	3,605	4,622	13,772	18,765	23,401	1,311	2,980	10,346	14,248	14,679
Wyoming	602	467	1,996	2,011	2,040	204	300	1,431	1,570	1,572

Notes: Numbers of events reported. Divorces include reported annulments. — = not available.

Source: Adapted from Centers for Disease Control and Prevention. (1993, November 19). *Births, marriages, divorces, and deaths for June 1993* (p. 11). Hyattsville, MD: Public Health Service, National Center for Health Statistics.

[a]Figures for marriages are marriage licenses issued for some counties.

[b]Figures include adjustments for varying lengths of reporting periods.

[c]Figures for marriages are marriage licenses issued, and figures for divorces include estimates for some counties.

Characteristics of unmarried couples who live together are described in Table 1-25. The number of unmarried couples increased more than sixfold between 1970 and 1992 (from 523,000 to 3,308,000). Many of these households include children born to the partners before the current relationships, as well as children of those relationships. The largest group consists of couples between 25 and 44 years of age (2,026,000 in 1992, almost 20 times the number in 1970).

The shape of the American family has undergone dramatic changes between 1970 and 1994. Figures 1-2 and 1-3 show the living arrangements of children under 18. Less than 60 percent lived with their married biological parents in 1990; over 40 percent lived in other arrangements. In 1970, only 15 percent of

TABLE 1-25 **Unmarried Couples, by Age of Householder and Presence of Children: Selected Years, 1970 to 1992 (Numbers in thousands)**

Presence of Children and Age of Householder	1970	1980	1985	1990	1992
Unmarried couples, total	523	1,589	1,983	2,856	3,308
No children under 15 years old	327	1,159	1,380	1,966	2,187
Some children under 15 years old	196	431	603	891	1,121
Under 25 years old	55	411	425	596	661
25 to 44 years old	103	837	1,203	1,775	2,026
45 to 64 years old	186	221	239	358	475
65 years old and over	178	119	116	127	146

Note: An unmarried couple consists of two unrelated adults of the opposite sex sharing the same household.

Source: Reprinted from U.S. Bureau of the Census. (1993). *Statistical abstract of the United States: 1993* (113th ed., p. 54). Austin, TX: Reference Press.

FIGURE 1-2 **Living Arrangements of Children under 18 Years, All Races: 1970, 1980, and 1990**

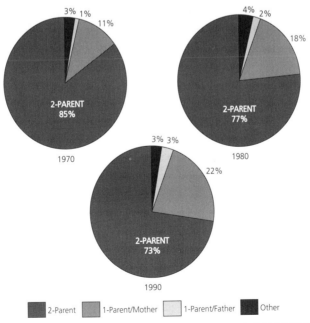

Source: Reprinted from Ashcroft, J., & Strauss, A. (1993). *Families first: Report of the National Commission on America's Urban Families* (p. 10). Washington, DC: U.S. Government Printing Office.

FIGURE 1-3 **Living Arrangements of Children under 18, by Marital Status of Parents: 1990**

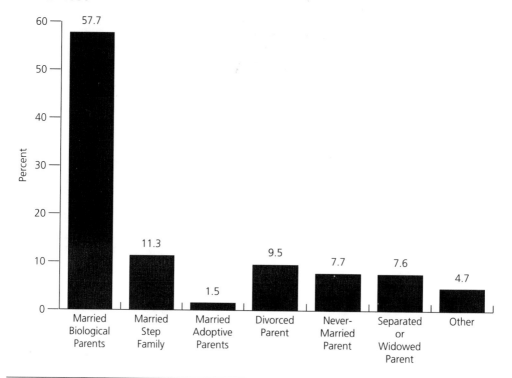

Source: Reprinted from Ashcroft, J., & Strauss, A. (1993). *Families first: Report of the National Commission on America's Urban Families* (p. 10). Washington, DC: U.S. Government Printing Office.

children did not live in a two-parent family, including 11 percent who lived with their mothers only, 3 percent who lived with their fathers only, and 1 percent who had some other arrangement. Figure 1-4 shows that rates of divorce and births to unmarried parents climbed steadily between 1970 and 1990.

The racial composition of married couples is outlined in Table 1-26. Although most couples are racially homogeneous, the number of interracial couples increased almost fourfold between 1970 and 1992 (from 310,000 to 1,161,000).

Statistics on marital status by gender and race or ethnicity, including Hispanic origin, from 1970 through 1992 are provided in Table 1-27. A slightly larger percentage of men are married than women; when age differences

FIGURE 1-4 **Rates of Divorce and Births to Unmarried Parents: 1970, 1980, and 1990**

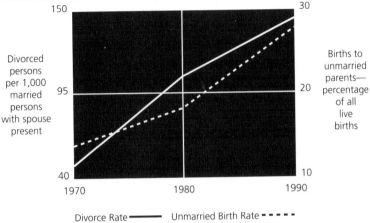

Divorced persons per 1,000 married persons with spouse present

Births to unmarried parents— percentage of all live births

Divorce Rate ——— Unmarried Birth Rate - - - - -

Source: Reprinted from Ashcroft, J., & Strauss, A. (1993). *Families first: Report of the National Commission on America's Urban Families* (p. 20). Washington, DC: U.S. Government Printing Office.

TABLE 1-26 **Married Couples of Same or Mixed Races or Origins: 1970, 1980, and 1992 (Numbers in thousands)**

Race and Origin of Spouses	1970	1980	1992
Married couples, total	44,598	49,714	53,512
Race			
Same-race couples	43,922	48,264	50,873
White/white	40,578	44,910	47,358
Black/black	3,344	3,354	3,515
Interracial couples	310	651	1,161
Black/white	65	167	246
Black husband/white wife	41	122	163
White husband/black wife	24	45	83
White/other race[a]	233	450	883
Black/other race[a]	12	34	32
All other couples[a]	366	799	1,478
Hispanic origin			
Hispanic/Hispanic	1,368	1,906	3,297
Hispanic/other origin (not Hispanic)	584	891	1,155
All other couples (not of Hispanic origin)	42,645	46,917	49,060

Note: Data include people age 15 years and older.

Source: Reprinted from U.S. Bureau of the Census. (1993). *Statistical abstract of the United States: 1993* (113th ed., p. 54). Austin, TX: Reference Press.

  [a]"Other" = excluding white and black people.

TABLE 1-27 **Marital Status of the Population, by Gender, Race, and Hispanic Origin: Selected Years, 1970 to 1992 (Numbers in millions)**

Marital Status, Race, and Hispanic Origin	Total				Male				Female			
	1970	1980	1990	1992	1970	1980	1990	1992	1970	1980	1990	1992
Total[a]	132.5	159.5	181.8	185.3	62.5	75.7	86.9	88.7	70.0	83.8	95.0	96.6
Never married	21.4	32.3	40.4	41.8	11.8	18.0	22.4	23.2	9.6	14.3	17.9	18.6
Married	95.0	104.6	112.6	113.3	47.1	51.8	55.8	56.2	47.9	52.8	56.7	57.1
Widowed	11.8	12.7	13.8	13.9	2.1	2.0	2.3	2.5	9.7	10.8	11.5	11.3
Divorced	4.3	9.9	15.1	16.3	1.6	3.9	6.3	6.8	2.7	6.0	8.8	9.6
Percentage of total	100.0	100.0	100.0	100.0	100.0	100.0	100.0	100.0	100.0	100.0	100.0	100.0
Never married	16.2	20.3	22.2	22.6	18.9	23.8	25.8	26.2	13.7	17.1	18.9	19.2
Married	71.7	65.5	61.9	61.1	75.3	68.4	64.3	63.3	68.5	63.0	59.7	59.1
Widowed	8.9	8.0	7.6	7.5	3.3	2.6	2.7	2.9	13.9	12.8	12.1	11.7
Divorced	3.2	6.2	8.3	8.8	2.5	5.2	7.2	7.6	3.9	7.1	9.3	9.9
Percentage standardized for age[b]												
Never married	14.1	16.5	20.6	21.7	16.5	18.7	23.3	24.4	12.1	14.5	18.2	19.2
Married	74.2	69.3	63.7	62.5	77.6	72.9	66.5	64.9	70.8	65.9	61.2	60.2
Widowed	8.3	7.6	6.9	6.7	3.3	2.7	2.7	2.8	13.0	12.1	10.8	10.3
Divorced	3.4	6.6	8.7	9.1	2.6	5.6	7.6	7.9	4.1	7.6	9.8	10.3
White												
Total	118.2	139.5	155.5	157.6	55.9	66.7	74.8	76.0	62.2	72.8	80.6	81.6
Never married	18.4	26.4	31.6	32.2	10.2	15.0	18.0	18.4	8.2	11.4	13.6	13.8
Married	85.8	93.8	99.5	100.1	42.7	46.7	49.5	50.0	43.1	47.1	49.9	50.3
Widowed	10.3	10.9	11.7	11.7	1.7	1.6	1.9	2.0	8.6	9.3	9.8	9.6
Divorced	3.7	8.3	12.6	13.6	1.3	3.4	5.4	5.8	2.3	5.0	7.3	7.9
Percentage of total	100.0	100.0	100.0	100.0	100.0	100.0	100.0	100.0	100.0	100.0	100.0	100.0
Never married	15.6	18.9	20.3	20.5	18.2	22.5	24.1	24.2	13.2	15.7	16.9	16.9
Married	72.6	67.2	64.0	63.5	76.3	70.0	66.2	65.5	69.3	64.7	61.9	61.6
Widowed	8.7	7.8	7.5	7.4	3.1	2.5	2.6	2.7	13.8	12.8	12.2	11.8
Divorced	3.1	6.0	8.1	8.6	2.4	5.0	7.2	7.6	3.8	6.8	9.0	9.6
Black												
Total	13.0	16.6	20.3	21.0	5.9	7.4	9.1	9.5	7.1	9.2	11.2	11.5
Never married	2.7	5.1	7.1	7.8	1.4	2.5	3.5	3.8	1.2	2.5	3.6	4.0
Married	8.3	8.5	9.3	9.0	3.9	4.1	4.5	4.4	4.4	4.5	4.8	4.7
Widowed	1.4	1.6	1.7	1.8	0.3	0.3	0.3	0.4	1.1	1.3	1.4	1.4
Divorced	0.6	1.4	2.1	2.3	0.2	0.5	0.8	0.9	0.4	0.9	1.3	1.4
Percentage of total	100.0	100.0	100.0	100.0	100.0	100.0	100.0	100.0	100.0	100.0	100.0	100.0
Never married	20.6	30.5	35.1	37.4	24.3	34.3	38.4	40.4	17.4	27.4	32.5	35.0
Married	64.1	51.4	45.8	43.0	66.9	54.6	49.2	46.0	61.7	48.7	43.0	40.6
Widowed	11.0	9.8	8.5	8.8	5.2	4.2	3.7	4.5	15.8	14.3	12.4	12.3
Divorced	4.4	8.4	10.6	10.8	3.6	7.0	8.8	9.1	5.0	9.5	12.0	12.2
Hispanic[c]												
Total	5.1	7.9	13.6	14.4	2.4	3.8	6.7	7.2	2.6	4.1	6.8	7.2
Never married	0.9	1.9	3.7	4.0	0.5	1.0	2.2	2.3	0.4	0.9	1.5	1.7
Married	3.6	5.2	8.4	8.7	1.8	2.5	4.1	4.3	1.8	2.6	4.3	4.4
Widowed	0.3	0.4	0.5	0.6	0.1	0.1	0.1	0.1	0.2	0.3	0.4	0.5
Divorced	0.2	0.5	1.0	1.1	0.1	0.2	0.4	0.4	0.1	0.3	0.6	0.6
Percentage of total	100.0	100.0	100.0	100.0	100.0	100.0	100.0	100.0	100.0	100.0	100.0	100.0
Never married	18.6	24.1	27.2	27.9	21.2	27.3	32.1	32.4	16.2	21.1	22.5	23.5
Married	71.8	65.6	61.7	60.3	73.8	67.1	60.9	60.0	70.0	64.3	62.4	60.7
Widowed	5.6	4.4	4.0	4.4	2.3	1.6	1.5	1.7	8.7	7.1	6.5	7.2
Divorced	3.9	5.8	7.0	7.3	2.7	4.0	5.5	5.9	5.1	7.6	8.5	8.7

Note: Data include people age 18 years and older.

Source: Reprinted from U.S. Bureau of the Census. (1993). *Statistical abstract of the United States: 1993* (113th ed., p. 53). Austin, TX: Reference Press.

[a]Includes people of other races, not shown separately.

[b]1960 age distribution used as standard; standardization improves comparability over time by removing effects of changes in age distribution of population.

[c]Hispanic people may be of any race.

are factored in, however, even that difference is reduced. For example, women live longer than men, and therefore there are more single older women than men. However, many of them would probably still be married if their husbands were alive (the percentages of both genders who are married are declining). Similarly, the numbers of both men and women who have never been married are increasing.

Income

Income is an important demographic indicator. The U.S. Bureau of the Census has calculated the median household incomes for all the states for 1989 (Table 1-28). The highest household incomes were in Connecticut (nearly $42,000 per year), and the lowest household incomes were in Mississippi (little more than $20,000 per year). Some people claim that Alaskans are the most prosperous people; Alaska's white households were at the top of the white earners, and Alaska's African Americans were second among African American earners. However, state and regional differences in living costs make a difference. Many jobs in Alaska pay a salary differential because of the unusually high cost of some goods and services in that state.

Since the era of the Great Society in the 1960s and the development of antipoverty programs, the federal government has maintained data about the extent of poverty in the nation. It is difficult, of course, to define such qualitative terms as "poverty" and "disadvantage." Needs, expectations, and experiences vary. There is a governmentally defined level of poverty reflecting the increased cost of living and the decreased value of the dollar. Thus, for example, families of four persons were considered impoverished in 1970 if they had incomes of $3,968 or less, whereas in 1992 the figure was $14,463 (Wright, 1993). Table 1-29 lists the poverty thresholds by family size for 1960 through 1992.

Analyses of the incomes of all families give a clearer picture of the economic status of the population as a whole. Income distribution has been described by dividing the population into fifths or tenths. Over a period of some 50 years, studies have calculated the poorest to the richest fifths, the wealthiest 5 percent and 1 percent, and the poorest tenth of the population. From 1950 to 1970, the differences between the top and the bottom income categories narrowed, so that there were smaller differences between the poorest and the wealthiest. In the 1970s, however, these differences began to increase, and in the 1980s they rose sharply.

Table 1-30 shows the average income of American families by quintiles (fifths) from 1969 to 1991. During 1989 to 1991, when the recession hit, there was an actual percentage drop in all family incomes. However, for the period as a whole, the incomes of the lowest earning families dropped, and those of the two highest income quintiles increased substantially.

In several states, the rich became richer and the poor poorer between 1979 and the late 1980s. Figure 1-5 and Table 1-31 show the states where those shifts occurred.

There were also major income discrepancies among the racial and ethnic groups. In 1991, the middle fifth of American white families earned $37,773. The middle fifth of Hispanic families earned $23,887 and of African American families, $21,585 (Brimhall-Vargas, 1993). Tables 1-28 and 1-32 provide information on the percentages of people of color who live in poverty and who receive social security and public aid. The incomes of 13.1 percent of all Americans were below the definition of poverty for 1989. Among African American households, 29.5 percent could be classified as poor. Mississippi ranked first both in its percentage of African Americans with earnings below the poverty level and in the percentage of its entire population who received public assistance or public aid. West Virginia ranked first in the percentage of its African American population who were social security recipients, and Florida, with its large retired population, was second. Alaska, with its relatively young and well-compensated wage earners, was 49th among the states in its proportion of African American population below the poverty line and 50th in its percentage of social security recipients. Idaho was last in public aid recipients. A large number of social security recipients sug-

TABLE 1-28 State Rankings on Median Household Income and Percentage of People below the Poverty Level: 1989

Region and State	Median Household Income						Persons below Poverty			
	All Races		White		Black		All Races		White	
	Dollars	Rank	Dollars	Rank	Dollars	Rank	Percent	Rank	Percent	Rank
United States	30,056	NA	31,435	NA	19,758	NA	13.1	NA	9.8	NA
Northeast	33,825	NA	35,461	NA	24,308	NA	10.6	NA	7.7	NA
Connecticut	41,721	1	43,407	2	28,011	6	6.8	49	4.6	50
Maine	27,854	26	27,901	32	26,250	8	10.8	35	10.7	19
Massachusetts	36,952	6	38,083	5	25,402	10	8.9	44	7.0	44
New Hampshire	36,329	7	36,379	9	31,657	1	6.4	50	6.3	45
New Jersey	40,927	3	42,740	3	29,145	4	7.6	48	5.0	49
New York	32,965	11	35,811	11	24,089	12	13.0	20	8.7	34
Pennsylvania	29,069	22	30,065	22	20,064	24	11.1	32	8.8	32
Rhode Island	32,181	13	33,103	13	20,377	22	9.6	42	8.0	40
Vermont	29,792	19	29,852	25	28,625	5	9.9	41	9.7	26
Midwest	29,334	NA	30,355	NA	19,012	NA	12.0	NA	9.4	NA
Illinois	32,252	12	34,358	12	20,990	19	11.9	26	7.8	42
Indiana	28,797	24	29,588	27	19,101	27	10.7	36	9.0	31
Iowa	26,229	36	26,427	39	16,010	43	11.5	29	10.8	18
Kansas	27,291	29	28,036	31	18,422	32	11.5	29	9.9	24
Michigan	31,020	15	32,463	14	18,851	29	13.1	19	9.4	27
Minnesota	30,909	17	31,322	18	18,878	28	10.2	38	8.7	34
Missouri	26,362	34	27,179	35	18,374	33	13.3	17	11.2	17
Nebraska	26,016	37	26,435	38	17,038	38	11.1	32	9.9	24
North Dakota	23,213	43	23,634	45	21,066	18	14.4	16	12.8	10
Ohio	28,706	25	30,026	23	17,716	37	12.5	23	10.0	22
South Dakota	22,503	46	23,220	47	20,890	20	15.9	11	12.6	11
Wisconsin	29,442	21	30,216	20	16,189	42	10.7	36	8.3	39
South	26,832	NA	29,185	NA	17,620	NA	15.7	NA	11.3	NA
Alabama	23,597	41	26,792	36	13,997	46	18.3	7	11.7	14
Arkansas	21,147	48	22,550	49	12,128	48	19.1	5	14.5	4
Delaware	34,875	9	36,660	8	24,286	11	8.7	45	5.7	47
District of Columbia	30,727	NA	45,991	NA	24,576	NA	16.9	NA	8.2	NA
Florida	27,483	28	28,981	30	18,055	34	12.7	22	9.4	27
Georgia	29,021	23	32,445	15	18,689	30	14.7	15	8.8	32
Kentucky	22,534	45	23,202	48	14,871	45	19.0	6	17.8	2
Louisiana	21,949	47	26,436	37	12,029	49	23.6	2	13.4	8
Maryland	39,386	4	41,964	4	30,746	3	8.3	46	5.3	48
Mississippi	20,136	50	24,940	43	11,625	50	25.2	1	13.2	9
North Carolina	26,647	33	29,300	28	17,979	35	13.0	20	8.6	36
Oklahoma	23,577	42	24,851	44	15,725	44	16.7	9	13.7	7
South Carolina	26,256	35	30,118	21	16,555	40	15.4	14	8.5	37
Tennessee	24,807	39	26,244	40	16,432	41	15.7	12	12.5	12
Texas	27,016	32	29,728	26	17,853	36	18.1	8	13.9	6
Virginia	33,328	10	36,039	10	21,987	15	10.2	38	7.4	43
West Virginia	20,795	49	21,034	50	13,174	47	19.7	4	19.1	1
West	32,270	NA	33,359	NA	25,229	NA	12.6	NA	9.9	NA
Alaska	41,408	2	44,998	1	31,474	2	9.0	43	6.1	46
Arizona	27,540	27	29,245	29	20,564	21	15.7	12	11.3	16
California	35,798	8	37,724	6	26,079	9	12.5	23	9.1	30
Colorado	30,140	18	31,024	19	21,676	17	11.7	28	10.0	22
Hawaii	38,829	5	37,406	7	27,215	7	8.3	46	7.9	41
Idaho	25,257	38	25,567	42	21,900	16	13.3	17	12.2	13
Montana	22,988	44	23,624	46	20,364	23	16.1	10	14.0	5
Nevada	31,011	16	31,813	16	22,528	14	10.2	38	8.4	38
New Mexico	24,087	40	25,872	41	19,561	26	20.6	3	16.1	3
Oregon	27,250	30	27,574	34	18,432	31	12.4	25	11.4	15
Utah	29,470	20	29,999	24	19,878	25	11.4	31	10.2	21
Washington	31,183	14	31,685	17	24,066	13	10.9	34	9.4	27
Wyoming	27,096	31	27,600	33	16,708	39	11.9	26	10.7	19

Notes: When states share the same rank, the next lower rank is omitted. Because of rounded data, states may have identical values shown, but different ranks. NA = not applicable.

Source: Reprinted from U.S. Bureau of the Census. (1993). *Statistical abstract of the United States: 1993* (113th ed., p. xix). Austin, TX: Reference Press.

gests an older population, but it is also an indicator of poverty, inasmuch as those who have only social security income are likely to be economically disadvantaged.

TABLE 1-29 **U.S. Poverty Thresholds, by Family Size: Selected Years, 1960 to 1992**

	Maximum Yearly Income by Family Size ($)						
Year	1 Person	2 Persons	3 Persons	4 Persons	5 Persons	6 Persons	7 Persons
1960	1,490	1,924	2,359	3,022	3,560	4,002	4,921
1965	1,582	2,048	2,514	3,223	3,797	4,264	5,248
1970	1,954	2,525	3,099	3,968	4,680	5,260	6,468
1975	2,724	3,506	4,293	5,500	6,499	7,316	9,022
1980	4,190	5,363	6,565	8,414	9,966	11,269	12,761
1985	5,469	6,998	8,573	10,989	13,007	14,696	16,656
1990	6,652	8,509	10,419	13,359	15,792	17,839	20,241
1991	6,942	8,880	10,873	13,942	16,481	18,617	21,124
1992	7,202	9,212	11,280	14,463	17,097	19,313	21,914

Source: THE UNIVERSAL ALMANAC copyright 1993 by John W. Wright. Reprinted with permission of Andrews & McMeel, Kansas City, MO. All rights reserved.

TABLE 1-30 **Average Family Income, by Quintiles, in 1991 Dollars, and Percentage Changes: Selected Years, 1969 to 1991**

Year	Lowest Fifth	Second Fifth	Middle Fifth	Fourth Fifth	Highest Fifth	Top 5%
Income						
1991	9,734	23,105	35,851	51,997	95,530	147,817
1990	10,247	23,900	36,808	52,935	98,377	154,357
1989	10,359	24,184	37,571	54,055	101,780	163,042
1979	10,765	23,750	35,870	49,395	85,589	129,585
1969	10,149	22,635	32,391	43,390	74,312	114,138
Percentage change						
1989–1991	−6.0	−4.5	−4.6	−3.8	−6.1	−9.3
1979–1991	−9.6	−2.7	−0.1	5.3	11.6	14.1
1979–1989	−3.8	1.8	4.7	9.4	18.9	25.8
1969–1979	6.1	4.9	10.7	13.8	15.2	13.5
1969–1991	−4.1	2.1	10.7	19.8	28.6	29.5
1969–1989	2.1	6.8	16.0	24.6	37.0	42.8

Source: Reprinted with permission from Brimhall-Vargas, M. (1993). *Poverty tables 1991* (p. 54). Washington, DC: Center on Budget and Policy Priorities.

FIGURE 1-5 Inequality between Top and Bottom Fifths: Most and Least Unequal States, Late 1980s

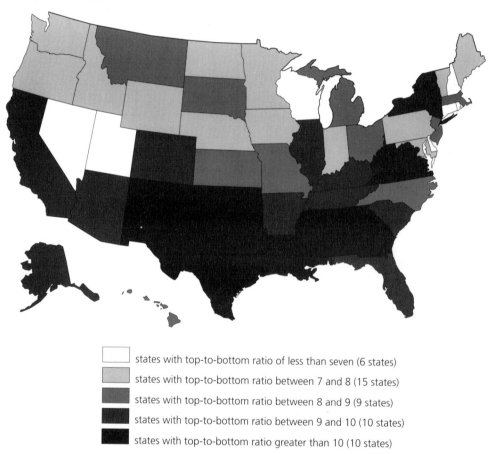

states with top-to-bottom ratio of less than seven (6 states)

states with top-to-bottom ratio between 7 and 8 (15 states)

states with top-to-bottom ratio between 8 and 9 (9 states)

states with top-to-bottom ratio between 9 and 10 (10 states)

states with top-to-bottom ratio greater than 10 (10 states)

Note: The top-to-bottom ratio shows the multiple of the bottom income that yields the top income. For example, Louisiana's bottom income of $6,225 multiplied by the top-to-bottom ratio is approximately the top income of $90,481.

Source: Reprinted with permission from Barancik, S., & Shapiro, I. (1992). *Where have all the dollars gone? A state-by-state analysis of income disparities over the 1980s* (p. 23). Washington, DC: Center for Budget and Policy Priorities.

Religious Affiliation

Religious bodies are the recipients of more voluntary financial contributions than any other beneficiaries. Religious groups sponsor large numbers of children's homes, nursing homes, shelters, youth organizations, and voluntary social services agencies of every kind. Religious organizations hire large numbers of social workers in many capacities. Figure 1-6 shows religious preferences in the United States and describes the religious affiliations of the population by Christian and "other" categories.

Table 1-33 provides data on U.S. religious bodies. It shows the number of churches, their memberships, and the numbers of their pastors and Sunday school enrollments. Table 1-34 shows the aggregate numbers of Christian adherents in 1990 and the Jewish population

TABLE 1-31 **States in Which the Top-to-Bottom Income Ratio Grew Most: 1979 and Late 1980s**

State	Top-to-Bottom Ratio, 1979	Top-to-Bottom Ratio, Late 1980s	Increase in Ratio
Louisiana	8.73	14.47	5.73
West Virginia	6.72	10.80	4.08
Virginia	7.16	10.44	3.28
Colorado	6.40	9.32	2.92
New York	8.07	10.75	2.68
Illinois	7.60	9.83	2.23
Kentucky	7.09	9.24	2.15
Indiana	5.79	7.92	2.13
Georgia	7.97	10.01	2.04
New Mexico	8.77	10.76	1.99

Note: The top-to-bottom ratio shows the multiple of the bottom income that yields the top income. For example, Louisiana's bottom income of $6,225 multiplied by the top-to-bottom ratio is approximately the top income of $90,481. The increase for Louisiana does not add exactly, due to rounding.

Source: Reprinted with permission from Barancik, S., & Shapiro, I. (1992). *Where have all the dollars gone? A state-by-state analysis of income disparities over the 1980s* (p. 25). Washington, DC: Center for Budget and Policy Priorities.

FIGURE 1-6 **Profile of Religious Identification by U.S. Adult Population: 1990**

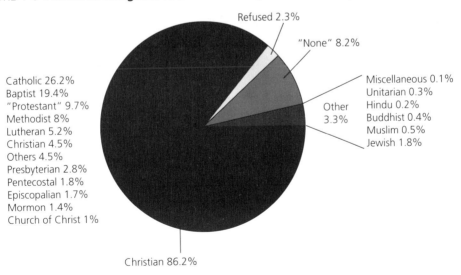

Source: Adapted with permission from Kosmin, B. A., & Lachman, S. P. (1993). *One nation under God: Religion in contemporary American society* (p. 3). New York: Harmony Books.

TABLE 1-32 State Rankings on Percentages of Black People below Poverty Level and Social Security and Public Aid Recipients: 1989 and 1991

Region and State	Black Persons below Poverty Level, 1989		Social Security Recipients, 1991		Public Aid Recipients, 1991	
	Percent	Rank	Percent	Rank	Percent	Rank
United States	29.5	NA	15.7	NA	7.0	NA
Northeast	24.3	NA	16.8	NA	7.0	NA
Connecticut	19.8	43	16.2	25	5.5	31
Maine	20.0	42	17.7	9	7.3	12
Massachusetts	23.0	35	16.5	22	7.0	15
New Hampshire	12.6	48	15.1	37	2.9	49
New Jersey	19.3	45	16.0	28	5.8	25
New York	25.0	32	15.9	29	8.3	7
Pennsylvania	29.0	25	18.9	4	6.4	21
Rhode Island	25.8	30	18.3	7	7.3	12
Vermont	21.0	41	15.9	29	6.6	18
Midwest	32.2	NA	16.5	NA	6.7	NA
Illinois	31.1	16	15.4	35	7.5	11
Indiana	29.0	25	16.4	24	4.3	42
Iowa	37.1	6	18.9	4	4.7	38
Kansas	30.0	22	16.6	21	4.2	44
Michigan	33.7	11	16.2	25	8.8	6
Minnesota	36.8	7	15.3	36	5.0	35
Missouri	29.9	23	17.9	8	6.2	24
Nebraska	31.1	16	17.1	17	3.9	45
North Dakota	15.5	47	17.6	13	3.8	46
Ohio	32.3	13	16.7	20	7.8	10
South Dakota	19.6	44	18.5	6	4.4	41
Wisconsin	40.8	4	17.2	16	6.7	16
South	31.6	NA	16.1	NA	6.6	NA
Alabama	37.7	5	17.7	9	6.6	17
Arkansas	43.0	3	19.9	3	6.4	20
Delaware	22.0	39	15.9	29	4.7	37
District of Columbia	20.2	NA	13.1	NA	12.3	NA
Florida	31.5	14	20.6	2	5.3	33
Georgia	30.3	21	13.7	42	7.9	9
Kentucky	35.2	9	17.7	9	9.1	4
Louisiana	45.7	2	15.6	33	9.7	3
Maryland	16.6	46	12.9	46	5.6	30
Mississippi	46.4	1	17.7	9	11.4	1
North Carolina	27.1	29	16.5	22	6.5	19
Oklahoma	34.6	10	17.0	19	5.8	26
South Carolina	31.4	15	15.7	32	6.3	23
Tennessee	32.4	12	17.1	17	7.9	8
Texas	31.0	18	13.0	45	5.8	27
Virginia	22.4	38	13.6	43	4.3	43
West Virginia	36.0	8	20.7	1	8.9	5
West	21.7	NA	13.3	NA	7.9	NA
Alaska	10.4	49	6.1	50	5.8	28
Arizona	27.5	28	16.2	25	5.4	32
California	21.1	40	12.3	48	10.1	2
Colorado	23.9	33	12.8	47	4.4	40
Hawaii	8.8	50	13.3	44	5.3	33
Idaho	22.8	36	15.5	34	2.8	50
Montana	31.0	18	17.6	13	5.7	29
Nevada	23.3	34	13.9	40	3.0	48
New Mexico	27.8	27	14.7	38	7.0	14
Oregon	29.8	24	17.4	15	4.9	36
Utah	30.5	20	11.2	49	3.5	47
Washington	22.8	36	14.5	39	6.4	22
Wyoming	25.2	31	13.9	40	4.7	39

Notes: When states share the same rank, the next lower rank is omitted. Because of rounded data, states may have identical values shown but different ranks. NA = not applicable.

Source: Reprinted from U.S. Bureau of the Census. (1993). *Statistical abstract of the United States: 1993* (113th ed., p. xx). Austin, TX: Reference Press.

TABLE 1-33 Religious Bodies: Selected Data, Various Years

Religious Body	Year Reported	Churches Reported	Membership (1,000)	Pastors Serving Parishes[a]	Sunday School Enrollment[b] (1,000)
African Methodist Episcopal Church	1981	6,200	2,210	6,050	—
African Methodist Episcopal Zion Church	1991	3,000	1,200	2,500	50
American Baptist Association	1986	1,705	250	1,740	—
American Baptist Churches in the U.S.A.	1990	5,808	1,536	5,351	300
Antiochian Orthodox Christian Archdiocese of North America, The	1989	160	350	250	—
Apostolic Catholic Assyrian Church of the East, N. American Diocese	1989	22	120	92	—
Armenian Apostolic Church of America	1991	28	150	22	1
Armenian Church of America, Diocese of the	1979	66	450	45	—
Assemblies of God	1990	11,353	2,182	16,336	1,403
Baptist Bible Fellowship, International	1986	3,449	1,406	3,400	—
Baptist General Conference	1991	799	135	1,200	79
Baptist Missionary Association of America	1990	1,372	229	1,232	98
Christian and Missionary Alliance, The	1990	1,856	279	1,596	194
Christian Brethren (a.k.a. Plymouth Brethren)	1984	1,150	98	—	—
Christian Church (Disciples of Christ)	1990	4,069	1,040	3,744	309
Christian Churches and Churches of Christ	1988	5,579	1,071	5,525	—
Christian Congregation, Inc., The	1990	1,453	110	1,451	48
Christian Methodist Episcopal Church	1983	2,340	719	2,340	—
Christian Reformed Church in North America	1990	715	226	634	—
Church of God, The	1978	2,035	76	1,910	—
Church of God (Anderson, IN)	1990	2,339	206	2,126	169
Church of God (Cleveland, TN)	1990	5,841	620	4,665	389
Church of God in Christ, The	1991	15,300	5,500	28,988	—
Church of God in Christ, International, The	1982	300	200	700	—
Church of God of Prophecy, The	1991	2,096	73	7,015	90
Church of Jesus Christ of Latter-Day Saints, The	1990	9,213	4,267	27,639	3,380
Church of the Brethren	1990	1,095	148	1,084	—
Church of the Nazarene	1991	5,172	574	4,416	860
Churches of Christ	1990	13,134	1,683	—	8
Community Churches, International Council of	1991	398	250	—	—
Congregational Christian Churches, National Association of	1991	400	90	550	—
Conservative Baptist Association of America	1989	1,126	210	1,126	—
Coptic Orthodox Church	1990	42	165	49	7
Cumberland Presbyterian Church	1990	796	99	571	45
Episcopal Church, The	1990	7,354	2,446	8,040	568
Evangelical Covenant Church, The	1990	590	90	824	77
Evangelical Free Church of America	1991	1,087	192	—	—
Evangelical Lutheran Church in America	1990	11,087	5,241	10,083	1,161
Free Methodist Church of North America	1990	1,096	74	—	98
Free Will Baptists, National Association of	1990	2,506	197	2,800	146
Full Gospel Fellowship of Churches and Ministers, International	1985	450	65	850	—
General Association of Regular Baptist Churches	1990	1,574	168	—	—
General Baptists (General Association of)	1990	876	74	1,384	—
Greek Orthodox Archdiocese of North and South America	1977	535	1,950	610	—
Independent Fundamental Churches of America	1991	700	78	745	75
International Church of the Foursquare Gospel	1990	1,451	199	—	—
Jehovah's Witnesses	1991	9,347	858	0	0
Jews[c]	1990	3,416	5,981	—	—

Continued on next page

in 1991 for each of the states. Table 1-35 details the religious populations of the world by region. Christianity is the largest religion worldwide, although it does not constitute a majority of all religious affiliations.

Some research has found basic demographic differences among religious groups, especially in income, full-time employment, education, and home ownership, as Figure 1-7 shows. For example, American Hindus led in full-time employment. Unitarians, Jews, and Hindus had the highest numbers of college graduates. More Congregationalists than any other group owned their own homes. Agnostics were only slightly behind Jews, Unitarians, and Episcopalians in median annual income.

Kosmin and Lachman (1993) surveyed 113,000 randomly selected households and

TABLE 1-33 **Continued**

Religious Body	Year Reported	Churches Reported	Membership (1,000)	Pastors Serving Parishes[a]	Sunday School Enrollment[b] (1,000)
Liberty Baptist Fellowship	1990	600	180	2,000	—
Lutheran Church—Missouri Synod, The	1990	5,296	2,603	5,347	673
Mennonite Church	1990	1,034	93	1,504	—
National Baptist Convention of America	*1956*	*11,398*	*2,669*	*7,598*	—
National Baptist Convention, U.S.A., Inc.	1991	30,000	7,800	30,000	—
National Primitive Baptist Convention, Inc.	*1975*	*616*	*250*	*460*	—
North American Old Roman Catholic Church	*1986*	*133*	*63*	*109*	—
Old Order Amish Church	*1989*	*785*	*71*	*3,140*	—
Orthodox Church in America	*1978*	*440*	*1,000*	*457*	—
Pentecostal Church of God	1990	1,174	91	—	74
Pentecostal Holiness Church, International	*1989*	*1,475*	*119*	*1,583*	—
Polish National Catholic Church of America	*1960*	*162*	*282*	*141*	—
Presbyterian Church in America	1990	1,167	224	1,204	112
Presbyterian Church (U.S.A.)	1990	11,501	3,788	10,308	1,144
Primitive Baptists	*1960*	*1,000*	*72*	—	—
Progressive National Baptist Convention, Inc.	1991	1,400	2,500	1,400	—
Reformed Church in America	1990	924	327	860	105
Reorganized Church of Jesus Christ of Latter-Day Saints	1990	1,025	190	16,666	—
Roman Catholic Church, The	1990	23,685	58,568	34,598	7,302
Romanian Orthodox Episcopate of America	1990	37	65	37	2
Salvation Army, The	1990	1,133	446	3,540	112
Serbian Eastern Orthodox Church in the U.S.A. and Canada	*1986*	*68*	*67*	*60*	—
Seventh-Day Adventist Church	1990	4,217	717	2,316	441
Southern Baptist Convention	1990	37,922	15,038	37,800	8,004
Ukrainian Orthodox Church in the U.S.A.	*1966*	*107*	*88*	*107*	—
Unitarian Universalist Association	1991	1,020	141	650	49
United Church of Christ	1990	6,260	1,599	4,813	426
United Methodist Church, The	*1989*	*37,407*	*8,905*	*20,774*	—
United Pentecostal Church, International	1991	3,626	500	—	—
Wesleyan Church, The	1990	1,628	111	1,857	121
Wisconsin Evangelical Lutheran Synod	1990	1,211	420	1,167	49

Notes: The figures were provided by religious bodies with memberships of 60,000 or more; a few groups gave no data and are excluded. Not all groups follow the same calendar year or count membership in the same way. Catholics count all baptized people, including infants; Jewish statistics are based on estimates of people living in the same household, which includes 7.4 percent non-Jews (due to intermarriage). Eastern Orthodox Churches include all people in a specific national or cultural group; most Protestant bodies count only people who have full membership (which tends to exclude most children under the age of 11). Figures in italics are older (that is, 1989 or earlier). — = not available.

Source: Reprinted from U.S. Bureau of the Census. (1993). *Statistical abstract of the United States: 1993* (113th ed., pp. 67–68). Austin, TX: Reference Press.

[a]Includes other pastors performing pastoral duties.

[b]Includes pupils, officers, and teachers.

[c]Estimates of size of Jewish community provided by *American Jewish Yearbook*. Estimates of the number of Jews holding membership in synagogues or temples of the four branches of Judaism amount to 4,750,000.

TABLE 1-34 Christian Church Adherents (1990) and Jewish Population (1991), by State (Numbers in thousands)

Region and State	Christian Adherents, 1990		Jewish Population, 1991	
	Number (1,000)	Percentage of Population	Number (1,000)	Percentage of Population
United States	137,065	55.1	5,798	2.3
Northeast	31,721	62.4	2,817	5.6
Connecticut	2,048	62.3	106	3.2
Maine	447	36.4	8	0.7
Massachusetts	3,942	65.5	275	4.6
New Hampshire	438	39.5	7	0.6
New Jersey	4,735	61.3	426	5.5
New York	11,813	65.7	1,644	9.1
Pennsylvania	7,291	61.4	330	2.8
Rhode Island	770	76.7	16	1.6
Vermont	237	42.1	5	0.8
Midwest	33,551	56.2	669	1.1
Illinois	6,848	59.9	257	2.2
Indiana	2,635	47.5	18	0.3
Iowa	1,681	60.5	6	0.2
Kansas	1,355	54.7	14	0.6
Michigan	4,687	50.4	107	1.2
Minnesota	2,837	64.9	30	0.7
Missouri	2,945	57.6	62	1.2
Nebraska	1,007	63.8	7	0.5
North Dakota	485	75.9	1	0.1
Ohio	5,438	50.1	131	1.2
South Dakota	474	68.1	a	0.1
Wisconsin	3,160	64.6	35	0.7
South	49,525	58.0	1,180	1.4
Alabama	2,867	71.0	9	0.2
Arkansas	1,425	60.6	2	0.1
Delaware	306	46.0	9	1.4
District of Columbia	374	61.7	25	4.2
Florida	5,673	43.8	593	4.6
Georgia	3,731	57.6	74	1.1
Kentucky	2,228	60.4	12	0.3
Louisiana	2,975	70.5	16	0.4
Maryland	2,312	48.3	211	4.4
Mississippi	1,806	70.2	2	0.1
North Carolina	3,978	60.0	16	0.2
Oklahoma	2,102	66.8	5	0.2
South Carolina	2,158	61.9	8	0.2
Tennessee	2,985	61.2	18	0.4
Texas	10,896	64.1	109	0.6
Virginia	2,966	47.9	68	1.1
West Virginia	742	41.4	2	0.1
West	22,268	42.2	1,133	2.1
Alaska	177	32.2	2	0.4
Arizona	1,577	43.0	72	2.0
California	12,585	42.3	923	3.1
Colorado	1,294	39.3	51	1.5
Hawaii	391	35.3	7	0.6
Idaho	507	50.4	a	0.1
Montana	341	42.7	a	0.1
Nevada	386	32.1	20	1.7
New Mexico	889	58.7	6	0.4
Oregon	915	32.2	15	0.5
Utah	1,374	79.8	3	0.2
Washington	1,613	33.1	33	0.7
Wyoming	216	47.7	a	0.1

Notes: Christian church adherents were defined as "all members, including full members, their children, and the estimated number of other church participants who are not considered as communicant, confirmed or full members." Data on Christian church adherents are based on reports of 133 church groupings and exclude 34 church bodies that reported more than 100,000 members to the *Yearbook of American and Canadian Churches*. Data on Jewish population are based primarily on a compilation of individual estimates made by local Jewish federations. Additionally, most large communities have completed Jewish demographic surveys from which the Jewish population can be determined. All percentages are based on U.S. Bureau of the Census estimates of July 1, 1991.

Source: Reprinted from U.S. Bureau of the Census. (1993). *Statistical abstract of the United States: 1993* (113th ed., p. 69). Austin, TX: Reference Press.

aFewer than 500.

reported their findings in a book entitled *One Nation under God*. According to Woodward (1993), they found that most of the United States population is secular. In fewer than half the states is most of the population committed in any degree to religion. Oregon is the most secular state and has the largest proportion of nonbelievers. Minnesota, North Dakota, and South Dakota are described as religiously committed, predominantly Lutheran. Idaho and Utah are referred to as modestly religious, the dominant sect being the Church of Jesus Christ of the Latter-Day Saints (Mormons). The nominally religious states are Alabama, Arkansas, Delaware, Florida, Georgia, Kentucky, Mississippi, Missouri, North Carolina, Oklahoma, South Carolina, Tennessee, Texas, Virginia, and West Virginia.

TABLE 1-35 **Religious Population of the World, by Region: 1992 (Numbers in thousands)**

Religion	Total	Percent Distribution	Africa	Asia	Latin America	Northern America	Europe	Eurasia[a]	Oceania
Total population	5,480,010	100.0	682,132	3,231,273	465,987	279,985	500,712	292,691	27,230
Christians	1,833,022	33.4	327,204	285,365	435,811	239,004	413,756	109,254	22,628
Roman Catholics	1,025,585	18.7	122,907	123,597	405,623	97,022	262,638	5,590	8,208
Protestants	373,698	6.8	87,332	81,476	17,263	96,312	73,939	9,858	7,518
Orthodox	170,422	3.1	28,549	3,655	1,764	6,008	36,165	93,705	576
Anglicans	74,883	1.4	26,863	707	1,300	7,338	32,956	b	5,719
Other Christians	188,434	3.4	61,553	75,930	9,861	32,324	8,058	101	607
Muslims	971,329	17.7	278,251	636,976	1,351	2,847	12,575	39,229	101
Nonreligious[c]	876,232	16.0	1,896	691,144	17,159	25,265	52,411	85,066	3,291
Hindus	732,812	13.4	1,475	728,118	884	1,269	704	2	360
Buddhists	314,939	5.7	21	313,114	541	558	272	407	26
Atheists	240,310	4.4	316	161,414	3,224	1,319	17,604	55,896	535
Chinese folk-religionists[d]	187,107	3.4	13	186,817	73	122	60	1	21
New-religionists[e]	143,415	2.6	21	141,382	530	1,421	50	1	10
Tribal religionists	96,581	1.8	70,588	24,948	936	41	1	0	67
Sikhs	18,801	0.3	26	18,272	8	254	231	1	9
Jews	17,822	0.3	337	5,587	1,092	7,003	1,469	2,236	98
Shamanists	10,493	0.2	1	10,233	1	1	2	254	1
Confucians	6,028	0.1	1	5,994	2	26	2	2	1
Baha'is	5,517	0.1	1,496	2,680	801	365	91	7	77
Jains	3,794	0.1	53	3,717	4	4	15	0	1
Shintoists	3,223	0.1	b	3,220	1	1	1	b	1
Other religionists	18,586	0.3	433	12,292	3,570	485	1,469	333	4

Source: Reprinted from U.S. Bureau of the Census. (1993). *Statistical abstract of the United States: 1993* (113th ed., p. 69). Austin, TX: Reference Press.

[a]"Eurasia" is the provisional new term for the former Soviet Union.

[b]Fewer than 500.

[c]People professing no religion, nonbelievers, agnostics, freethinkers, and dereligionized secularists indifferent to all religion.

[d]Followers of traditional Chinese religion (local deities, ancestor veneration, Confucian ethics, Taoism, etc.).

[e]Followers of Asiatic 20th-century New Religions, New Religious movements, radical new crisis religions, and non-Christian syncretistic mass religions.

Other interesting findings include the following: There were more members of the Church of Scientology (45,000) than people who identified themselves as fundamentalists (27,000), 8,000 people practiced witchcraft, and 20,000 people were devoted to New Age. Their findings about the association between ethnicity and religion contradict stereotypes: Most Arab Americans, they found, are not Muslims; most American Muslims are not of Arab origin; and most of those who identified themselves as Jewish had no religion.

U.S. Labor Force

According to the U.S. Department of Labor, Bureau of Labor Statistics (1993), there were about 127 million workers in the national labor force in 1992, an increase of 21 percent

FIGURE 1-7 **Socioeconomic Characteristics of Religious Groups: 1990**

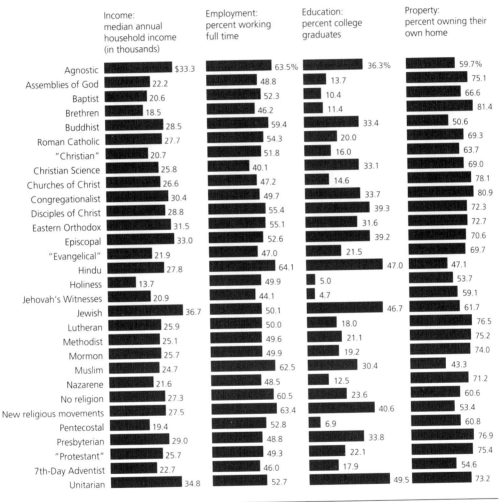

	Income: median annual household income (in thousands)	Employment: percent working full time	Education: percent college graduates	Property: percent owning their own home
Agnostic	$33.3	63.5%	36.3%	59.7%
Assemblies of God	22.2	48.8	13.7	75.1
Baptist	20.6	52.3	10.4	66.6
Brethren	18.5	46.2	11.4	81.4
Buddhist	28.5	59.4	33.4	50.6
Roman Catholic	27.7	54.3	20.0	69.3
"Christian"	20.7	51.8	16.0	63.7
Christian Science	25.8	40.1	33.1	69.0
Churches of Christ	26.6	47.2	14.6	78.1
Congregationalist	30.4	49.7	33.7	80.9
Disciples of Christ	28.8	55.4	39.3	72.3
Eastern Orthodox	31.5	55.1	31.6	72.7
Episcopal	33.0	52.6	39.2	70.6
"Evangelical"	21.9	47.0	21.5	69.7
Hindu	27.8	64.1	47.0	47.1
Holiness	13.7	49.9	5.0	53.7
Jehovah's Witnesses	20.9	44.1	4.7	59.1
Jewish	36.7	50.1	46.7	61.7
Lutheran	25.9	50.0	18.0	76.5
Methodist	25.1	49.6	21.1	75.2
Mormon	25.7	49.9	19.2	74.0
Muslim	24.7	62.5	30.4	43.3
Nazarene	21.6	48.5	12.5	71.2
No religion	27.3	60.5	23.6	60.6
New religious movements	27.5	63.4	40.6	53.4
Pentecostal	19.4	52.8	6.9	60.8
Presbyterian	29.0	48.8	33.8	76.9
"Protestant"	25.7	49.3	22.1	75.4
7th-Day Adventist	22.7	46.0	17.9	54.6
Unitarian	34.8	52.7	49.5	73.2

Source: Reprinted with permission from Woodward, K.L.C. (1993, November 29). The rites of Americans. *Newsweek*, p. 80.

TABLE 1-36 **State Rankings on Characteristics of Civilian Labor Force and Nonfarm Employment: 1992**

| | Civilian Labor Force, 1992 | | | | | | Nonfarm Employment, 1992 | | | |
| | Employment/ Population Ratio | | Female Participation Rate | | Unemployment Rate | | Services | | Manufacturing | |
Region and State	Ratio	Rank	Rate	Rank	Percent	Rank	Percent	Rank	Percent	Rank
United States	61.4	NA	57.8	NA	7.4	NA	26.7	NA	16.8	NA
Northeast	59.6	NA	56.2	NA	8.1	NA	29.6	NA	16.1	NA
Connecticut	66.0	14	63.8	8	7.5	12	27.6	14	20.1	12
Maine	63.7	24	61.7	18	7.1	23	25.2	27	18.0	20
Massachusetts	61.8	32	60.0	25	8.5	6	32.6	2	16.6	24
New Hampshire	66.6	8	64.9	4	7.5	12	26.6	18	20.0	13
New Jersey	60.8	35	57.0	35	8.4	8	28.2	9	15.3	30
New York	56.5	49	52.8	48	8.5	6	30.2	5	13.1	36
Pennsylvania	58.8	42	54.8	42	7.5	12	29.3	8	18.7	16
Rhode Island	62.1	30	60.6	23	8.9	4	30.2	5	21.4	11
Vermont	66.4	10	66.0	1	6.6	28	27.7	12	17.7	21
Midwest	63.7	NA	59.9	NA	6.5	NA	25.2	NA	20.0	NA
Illinois	63.1	27	59.8	27	7.5	12	26.7	16	17.7	21
Indiana	62.0	31	57.5	33	6.5	31	21.7	45	24.7	3
Iowa	68.2	3	63.5	9	4.6	46	24.5	33	18.4	17
Kansas	68.0	4	62.8	12	4.2	48	23.2	39	16.3	25
Michigan	59.7	38	56.8	36	8.8	5	24.8	30	22.9	8
Minnesota	68.9	1	65.7	2	5.1	42	27.1	15	18.1	19
Missouri	64.4	19	60.0	25	5.7	38	25.9	21	17.7	21
Nebraska	68.9	1	64.4	7	3.0	50	24.8	30	13.4	34
North Dakota	64.4	19	60.1	24	4.9	44	26.7	16	6.5	47
Ohio	61.1	34	57.1	34	7.2	21	25.5	24	21.7	10
South Dakota	67.3	6	62.4	15	3.1	49	25.4	25	12.1	38
Wisconsin	67.7	5	64.8	5	5.1	42	24.3	35	23.2	6
South	60.8	NA	57.3	NA	7.2	NA	25.2	NA	16.1	NA
Alabama	57.5	45	53.4	45	7.3	20	20.6	46	22.8	9
Arkansas	58.9	41	55.4	40	7.2	21	21.8	44	24.6	4
Delaware	65.5	17	62.3	16	5.3	41	25.0	28	19.8	14
District of Columbia	60.8	NA	61.7	NA	8.4	NA	37.8	NA	2.1	NA
Florida	56.8	47	54.8	42	8.2	9	31.6	3	9.0	42
Georgia	61.5	33	57.9	32	6.9	24	22.5	41	18.2	18
Kentucky	57.6	44	52.8	48	6.9	24	23.2	39	19.0	15
Louisiana	56.9	46	53.1	46	8.1	10	24.3	35	11.4	40
Maryland	66.4	10	64.8	5	6.6	28	30.3	4	8.8	43
Mississippi	56.6	48	53.1	46	8.1	10	18.4	50	26.1	2
North Carolina	64.0	22	60.8	21	5.9	36	20.4	48	26.6	1
Oklahoma	60.0	37	55.5	39	5.7	38	23.7	38	13.5	33
South Carolina	62.3	29	58.8	31	6.2	35	20.2	49	24.3	5
Tennessee	59.4	40	55.6	38	6.4	33	24.0	37	23.0	7
Texas	63.7	24	59.2	29	7.5	12	25.4	25	13.3	35
Virginia	66.4	10	63.0	10	6.4	33	26.6	18	14.4	31
West Virginia	48.3	50	43.7	50	11.3	1	24.7	32	12.8	37
West	61.5	NA	57.6	NA	8.1	NA	27.7	NA	13.8	NA
Alaska	66.1	13	65.7	2	9.1	2	21.9	42	7.3	44
Arizona	58.3	43	55.1	41	7.4	19	28.0	11	11.3	41
California	60.2	36	56.0	37	9.1	2	28.2	9	15.6	28
Colorado	65.9	15	62.6	13	5.9	36	27.7	12	11.6	39
Hawaii	65.7	16	61.9	17	4.5	47	29.9	7	3.7	50
Idaho	64.2	21	59.2	29	6.5	31	21.9	42	15.9	27
Montana	64.0	22	63.0	10	6.7	27	25.9	21	7.3	44
Nevada	65.2	18	61.7	18	6.6	28	44.3	1	4.1	49
New Mexico	59.5	39	53.6	44	6.8	26	26.6	18	6.7	46
Oregon	62.5	28	59.3	28	7.5	12	24.4	34	16.3	25
Utah	67.0	7	61.0	20	4.9	44	25.7	23	13.8	32
Washington	63.4	26	60.7	22	7.5	12	25.0	28	15.6	28
Wyoming	66.6	8	62.5	14	5.6	40	20.5	47	4.4	48

Note: NA = not applicable.

Source: Reprinted from U.S. Bureau of the Census. (1993). *Statistical abstract of the United States: 1993* (113th ed., p. xviii). Austin, TX: Reference Press.

since 1979. About 51.2 million workers were expected to enter the labor force between 1992 and 2005, 28 million as replacements for people who leave because of death, retirement, or other reasons and over 23 million as new workers.

Table 1-36 provides information on the 1992 civilian labor force by state, including women's participation, the unemployment rate, and nonfarm employment. Minnesota had the highest employment-to-population ratio, and West Virginia had the highest unemployment rate. North Carolina had the highest percentage of workers involved in manufacturing, whereas Nevada had the largest percentage of workers engaged in services.

Table 1-37 shows the gender and racial or ethnic composition of the 1992 labor force, the projected entrants and leavers through

TABLE 1-37 **Civilian Labor Force, by Gender and Racial or Ethnic Origin: 1992 Size and Projections to 2005 (Numbers in thousands)**

Group	Labor Force, 1992	Entrants, 1992–2005	Leavers, 1992–2005	Labor Force, 2005
Number				
Total	126,982	51,240	27,708	130,516
Men	89,184	25,058	15,524	78,718
Women	57,798	28,181	12,181	71,798
White, non-Hispanic	98,817	33,384	22,448	109,753
Men	53,995	16,107	12,884	57,218
Women	44,822	17,278	9,564	52,635
Black, non-Hispanic	13,694	6,096	3,160	16,630
Men	6,788	3,120	1,395	8,511
Women	6,908	2,976	1,765	8,119
Hispanic origin	10,131	7,801	1,352	16,581
Men	6,091	4,339	802	9,828
Women	4,040	3,462	550	6,953
Asian and other, non-Hispanic	4,340	3,958	746	7,552
Men	2,312	1,492	443	3,361
Women	2,028	2,468	303	4,181
Percentage share				
Total	100.0	100.0	100.0	100.0
Men	54.5	48.9	58.0	52.3
Women	45.5	51.1	44.0	47.7
White, non-Hispanic	77.8	65.2	81.0	72.9
Men	42.5	31.4	46.5	38.0
Women	35.3	33.7	34.5	34.9
Black, non-Hispanic	10.8	11.9	11.4	11.0
Men	5.3	6.1	5.0	5.7
Women	5.4	5.8	6.4	5.4
Hispanic origin	8.0	15.2	4.9	11.0
Men	4.8	8.5	2.9	6.4
Women	3.2	6.8	2.0	4.6
Asian and other, non-Hispanic	3.4	7.7	2.7	5.0
Men	1.8	2.9	1.6	2.2
Women	1.6	4.8	1.1	2.8

Source: Reprinted from U.S. Department of Labor, Bureau of Labor Statistics. (1993, November 24). *BLS releases new 1992–2005 employment projections* (Table 2). Washington, DC: Author.

2005, and the projected labor force in 2005. Whereas white non-Hispanics will constitute two-thirds of the labor force entrants through 2005, their percentage of the work force will decline because of the quick increase in the numbers of other groups. By 2005, the Hispanic proportion of the labor force will almost equal the African American non-Hispanic proportion.

Most of the employment growth will be in service industries. Manufacturing will remain stable; it will account for about one of every seven jobs. The greatest growth will be in health, business, and social services; eight of the 10 fastest growing industries fall into these categories. Table 1-38 shows the 10 fastest growing industries and the 10 fastest growing occupations. Many of those industries and occupations—residential care, health services, child day care, social services, home and personal aides, special education teachers, and human services workers—are central or closely related to social welfare and social work programs.

Table 1-39 shows the 1992 earnings of a variety of groups of workers, providing interesting comparisons with those of social workers, who had median weekly earnings of $489: Registered nurses earned $662 per week, higher education teachers earned $799, elementary and secondary teachers earned $561, and physical therapists earned $682.

Several studies show that even when workers are employed full-time or part-time, their income may still be at or near the poverty level. Table 1-40 shows the poverty status of workers who worked at some time during the year and those who worked full-time year-round.

TABLE 1-38 **Fastest Growing Industries and Occupations: Projected Change 1992 to 2005**

Jobs	Percentage Change, 1992–2005
Industry	
Residential care	150
Computer and data processing services	96
Health services	89
Child day care services	73
Business services	71
Management and public relations	69
Individual and miscellaneous social services	65
Passenger transportation arrangement	64
Miscellaneous equipment rental and leasing	59
Accounting, auditing, and services	51
Occupation	
Home health aides	138
Human services workers	136
Personal and home care aides	130
Computer engineers	112
System analysts	110
Physical therapy assistants	93
Physical therapists	88
Paralegals	86
Teachers, special education	74
Medical assistants	71

Source: Reprinted from U.S. Department of Labor, Bureau of Labor Statistics. (1993, November 24). *BLS releases new 1992–2005 employment projections* (Tables 5a and 5b). Washington, DC: Author.

TABLE 1-39 **Median Weekly Earnings of Full-Time Wage Earners, by Profession: 1992**

Occupation	Median Weekly Earnings ($)
Managerial and professional	655
Executive, administration and management	650
Administrators, education	772
Managers, medicine and health	716
Health assessment and training	666
Registered nurses	662
Dietitians	446
Therapists	646
Respiratory	617
Physical	682
Speech	693
Teachers, college and university	799
Teachers, except college and university	561
Counselors, education and vocational	577
Social scientists and urban planners	705
Economists	748
Psychologists	665
Social, recreation, and religious workers	479
Social workers	489
Recreation workers	287
Clergy	496
Protective services	486
Police and detectives	732
Firefighters	622

Source: Reprinted with permission from Gibelman, M., & Schervish, P. H. (1993). *What we earn: 1993 salary survey* (p. 32). Washington, DC: NASW Press.

Conclusion

This chapter provides some basic information and concepts that underlie all of the other chapters in this book. Basic demographic issues such as population and the distribution of age groups, genders, and ethnic groups all have a major impact on the other more specific social issues and social problems discussed in subsequent chapters.

TABLE 1-40 **Poverty Status of Workers: 1966 to 1991 (Numbers in thousands)**

Year	Persons Who Worked Some Time during the Year			Persons Who Worked Full-Time Year-Round		
	Total	Number in Poverty	Percentage in Poverty	Total	Number in Poverty	Percentage in Poverty
1991	132,571	9,175	6.9	79,574	2,076	2.6
1990	132,562	8,675	6.5	80,035	2,038	2.5
1989	132,730	8,419	6.3	80,223	1,887	2.4
1988	131,370	8,474	6.5	79,637	1,929	2.4
1987	129,181	8,347	6.5	77,030	1,821	2.4
1986	126,714	8,864	7.0	74,433	2,009	2.7
1985	124,443	9,112	7.3	72,422	1,972	2.7
1984	122,109	9,104	7.5	70,424	2,076	2.9
1983	118,629	9,440	8.0	66,836	2,066	3.1
1982	117,126	9,119	7.8	63,980	2,000	3.1
1981	117,866	8,631	7.3	65,300	1,883	2.9
1980	116,849	7,792	6.7	64,947	1,646	2.5
1979	113,937	6,545	5.7	63,621	1,365	2.1
1978	112,314	6,599	5.9	62,209	1,309	2.1
1977	109,292	6,459	5.9	58,869	1,458	2.5
1976	106,363	6,555	6.2	56,586	1,355	2.4
1975	103,233	6,697	6.5	55,054	1,316	2.4
1974	103,796	6,376	6.1	57,253	1,579	2.8
1973	102,651	6,186	6.0	57,190	1,433	2.5
1972	98,917	6,329	6.4	55,211	1,534	2.8
1971	97,212	6,836	7.0	53,221	1,682	3.2
1970	95,747	6,716	7.0	51,998	1,624	3.1
1969	94,760	6,469	6.8	52,430	1,671	3.2
1968	93,374	7,146	7.7	52,285	2,126	4.1
1967	91,383	7,929	8.7	51,705	2,370	4.6
1966	89,212	8,085	9.1	50,049	2,489	5.0

Note: "Workers" included people 14 years of age and older (1966 to 1978), 15 years of age and older (1979 to 1989), and 16 years of age (since 1990).

Source: Reprinted with permission from Brimhall-Vargas, M. (1993). *Poverty tables 1991* (p. 70). Washington, DC: Center on Budget and Policy Priorities.

2

CHILDREN

Few population groups have been as central to the study and practice of social work as have children. Children receive services from social workers in a wide variety of programs: personal growth–oriented group work, protective services for children who are abused or neglected, school social work, service to juvenile offenders, mental health services, income maintenance services, and family social work.

Population

As a nation, the United States is aging. In 1970, 34.1 percent of the population was under age 18. In 1990, that percentage had dropped to 25.6.

Table 2-1 shows the resident population of the United States by age group and state in 1992. Table 2-2 shows the projected population for 1995 through 2025, by age group and ethnicity; these figures are based on the U.S. Bureau of the Census (1993) middle-level estimates (assumptions reflecting neither minimal nor major changes in population growth rates). Although some growth is projected in absolute numbers, the proportion of young people in the total population is projected to decline. The declines are somewhat less for some groups than others, as the table shows, and there are isolated increases in certain age groups during some of the periods for which the projections are made.

The percentage of young people in the United States is lower than that in many other nations, as is shown in Table 2-3. Generally, the more developed and prosperous the nation, the lower its percentage of children as part of the total population. Factors that contribute to this phenomenon include the longer life expectancies for adults, lower birth rates, and access to resources (such as knowledge and money) necessary for effective family planning found in more-developed countries.

Living Arrangements of Children

Table 2-4 provides information about the living arrangements and socioeconomic status of U.S. children under age 18 in 1992. Of 64 million children, 46.6 million (73 percent) were living with two parents. This figure included almost 80 percent of white children, 66 percent of Hispanic children, and 38 percent of African American children (see Figure 2-1). Table 2-4 also shows that the greater the educational attainment of the parents, the greater the likelihood that children live with both parents. Income levels and home ownership also are positively correlated with two-parent households.

Table 2-5 provides additional information on parents of children under age 18 for 1980, 1985, and 1990. Comparative data are provided for white and African American children; information on Hispanic families was available only for 1990. It is interesting to note that the percentages of all children who were living with both biological parents declined during the decade and that there were significant percentage increases in children living with a biological parent and a stepparent, reflecting the increase in divorce and subsequent remarriage. The percentage of children living with an adoptive parent decreased, which may reflect a decline in the number of children available for adoption. There was a decline in the number of white children whose father or mother was unknown, but the number of African American children in that category increased.

Social Health of American Children

Marc L. Miringoff (1992), author of *The Index of Social Health,* found that the problems facing American children and youths in 1990 were more severe than they had been since 1970, when the *Index* was first devel-

TABLE 2-1 **Resident Population of Children and Youths, by Age Group and State: 1992 (Numbers in thousands)**

Region and State	Total (All Ages)	Under 5 Years	5 to 17 Years	18 to 24 Years
United States	255,082	19,512	46,655	25,919
Northeast	51,118	3,702	8,547	5,052
Connecticut	3,281	239	532	306
Maine	1,235	83	223	122
Massachusetts	5,998	434	950	632
New Hampshire	1,111	82	198	110
New Jersey	7,789	573	1,290	713
New York	18,119	1,366	3,056	1,810
Pennsylvania	12,009	813	2,031	1,185
Rhode Island	1,005	71	162	111
Vermont	570	40	104	63
Midwest	60,713	4,493	11,441	6,126
Illinois	11,631	899	2,130	1,167
Indiana	5,662	405	1,056	610
Iowa	2,812	194	541	281
Kansas	2,523	187	491	251
Michigan	9,437	724	1,785	978
Minnesota	4,480	335	871	425
Missouri	5,193	377	973	506
Nebraska	1,606	119	320	157
North Dakota	636	45	127	67
Ohio	11,016	793	2,027	1,119
South Dakota	711	54	150	69
Wisconsin	5,007	360	970	497
South	88,143	6,633	16,226	9,164
Alabama	4,136	298	778	449
Arkansas	2,399	171	458	244
Delaware	689	52	12	72
District of Columbia	589	41	76	70
Florida	13,488	943	2,163	1,173
Georgia	6,751	530	1,270	732
Kentucky	3,755	258	706	402
Louisiana	4,287	340	898	462
Maryland	4,908	383	843	465
Mississippi	2,614	203	545	302
North Carolina	6,843	491	1,171	767
Oklahoma	3,212	232	626	330
South Carolina	3,603	273	672	409
Tennessee	5,024	353	893	529
Texas	17,656	1,489	3,583	1,881
Virginia	6,377	468	1,094	688
West Virginia	1,812	108	330	191
West	55,108	4,684	10,442	5,577
Alaska	587	57	128	57
Arizona	3,832	320	727	384
California	30,867	2,763	5,660	3,195
Colorado	3,470	262	647	341
Hawaii	1,160	91	202	119
Idaho	1,067	83	241	108
Montana	824	58	168	75
Nevada	1,327	106	232	118
New Mexico	1,581	133	336	156
Oregon	2,977	211	555	274
Utah	1,813	176	478	215
Washington	5,136	390	965	488
Wyoming	466	34	104	46

Source: Adapted from U.S. Bureau of the Census. (1993). *Statistical abstract of the United States: 1993* (113th ed., p. 33). Austin, TX: Reference Press.

oped. Miringoff's index measures social health of children and youths in eight areas: infant mortality, child abuse, children in poverty, high school dropouts, SAT (scholastic achievement test) scores, drug abuse, teen suicide, and deaths by homicide. Figure 2-2 shows the children and youth social health index for the years 1970 through 1990.

Child Mortality

Table 2-6 lists the numbers and causes of child deaths by age group in 1990. (This topic is covered more thoroughly in chapter 5.)

Child Abuse

Official statistics on child maltreatment are collected from the states by the federal gov-

TABLE 2-2 **Projections of Hispanic and Non-Hispanic Children and Youth Populations, by Age Group: Selected Years, 1995 to 2025 (Numbers in thousands)**

Racial and Ethnic Origin and Age	Population					Percent Distribution		
	1995	2000	2005	2010	2025	2000	2010	2025
Hispanic origin, total	26,522	30,602	34,842	39,312	54,018	100.0	100.0	100.0
Under 5 years old	2,804	3,055	3,338	3,683	4,746	10.0	9.4	8.8
5 to 13 years old	4,535	5,226	5,720	6,212	8,133	17.1	15.8	15.1
14 to 17 years old	1,816	2,097	2,486	2,698	3,464	6.9	6.9	6.4
18 to 24 years old	3,224	3,544	4,059	4,676	5,919	11.6	11.9	11.0
Non-Hispanic white, total	193,307	196,701	199,274	201,668	207,439	100.0	100.0	100.0
Under 5 years old	12,753	11,706	11,214	11,270	11,155	6.0	5.6	5.4
5 to 13 years old	23,083	23,290	22,097	20,815	21,007	11.8	10.3	10.1
14 to 17 years old	10,008	10,423	10,821	10,318	9,480	5.3	5.1	4.6
18 to 24 years old	16,915	17,385	18,317	18,871	16,475	8.8	9.4	7.9
Non-Hispanic black, total	31,702	33,834	35,957	38,201	45,237	100.0	100.0	100.0
Under 5 years old	3,024	3,014	3,111	3,316	3,807	8.9	8.7	8.4
5 to 13 years old	5,083	5,531	5,615	5,723	6,731	16.3	15.0	14.9
14 to 17 years old	2,198	2,298	2,638	2,647	2,977	6.8	6.9	6.6
18 to 24 years old	3,533	3,729	3,966	4,424	4,743	11.0	11.6	10.5
Non-Hispanic American Indian, Eskimo, Aleut, total	1,956	2,096	2,245	2,407	2,942	100.0	100.0	100.0
Under 5 years old	193	196	212	230	273	9.4	9.6	9.3
5 to 13 years old	351	369	375	398	492	17.6	16.5	16.7
14 to 17 years old	150	165	179	178	221	7.9	7.4	7.5
18 to 24 years old	220	238	268	288	332	11.4	12.0	11.3
Non-Hispanic Asian, Pacific Islander, total	9,266	11,582	14,005	16,522	24,580	100.0	100.0	100.0
Under 5 years old	778	938	1,084	1,230	1,701	8.1	7.4	6.9
5 to 13 years old	1,319	1,634	1,974	2,276	3,183	14.1	13.8	12.9
14 to 17 years old	582	750	895	1,066	1,506	6.5	6.5	6.1
18 to 24 years old	1,013	1,220	1,504	1,747	2,536	10.5	10.6	10.3

Notes: Data are for middle series. People of Hispanic origin may be of any race.

Source: Adapted from U.S. Bureau of the Census. (1993). *Statistical abstract of the United States: 1993* (113th ed., p. 25). Austin, TX: Reference Press.

ernment and some voluntary organizations, often with support from federal funds. Miringoff (1992) noted that child abuse has worsened significantly and that the 1990 rate of child abuse reports was four times the 1970 rate. Although part of that increase may be due to reporting practices that changed during the 1980s, he believes that the absolute incidence of child abuse is also increasing.

In 1992, almost 3 million children were reported to public child protective and social services agencies as abused or neglected. The 3 million represented an increase of nearly 8 percent over the previous year, part of an overall increase of nearly 50 percent since 1985 (McCurdy & Daro, 1993). Not all of these reports were substantiated. In some cases reports cover behavior not officially classified

TABLE 2-3 **Percentages of People under Age 15 in the United States and Selected Nations: Projections for 2000**

Nation	Percentage under 15 Years
Syria	47.5
Nigeria	44.7
Mexico	34.7
Brazil	28.5
China	25.0
United States	21.4
Russia	20.1
Canada	20.0
United Kingdom	19.4
France	19.0
Germany	16.3

Source: Adapted from U.S. Bureau of the Census. (1993). *Statistical abstract of the United States: 1993* (113th ed., p. 843). Austin, TX: Reference Press.

FIGURE 2-1 **Percentage Distribution of Children, by Presence of Parents and Race or Ethnic Origin: 1980 and 1992**

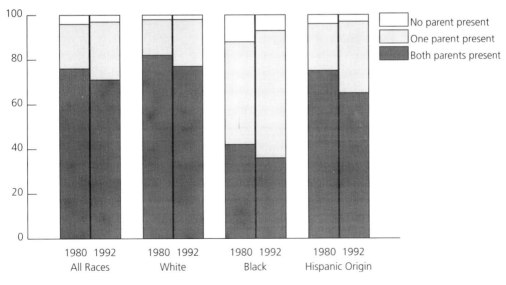

Note: Persons of Hispanic origin may be of any race.

Source: Adapted from U.S. Bureau of the Census. (1993). *Statistical abstract of the United States: 1993* (113th ed., p. 8). Austin, TX: Reference Press.

TABLE 2-4 **Living Arrangements of Children under Age 18, by Selected Characteristics of Parent: 1992 (Numbers in thousands)**

| | Children of All Races[a] | | | | White Children | | | | Black Children | | | | Hispanic Children[b] | | | |
| | | Living with | | | | Living with | | | | Living with | | | | Living with | | |
Characteristic	Total	Both Parents	Mother Only	Father Only	Total	Both Parents	Mother Only	Father Only	Total	Both Parents	Mother Only	Father Only	Total	Both Parents	Mother Only	Father Only
Children under 18 years old	64,216	46,638	15,396	2,182	51,606	40,635	9,250	1,721	9,648	3,714	5,607	327	7,382	4,935	2,168	279
Parent age																
15 to 24 years old	3,709	1,345	2,188	176	2,417	1,144	1,139	133	1,163	149	984	31	594	296	274	25
25 to 29 years old	8,466	5,010	3,132	325	6,337	4,328	1,761	249	1,858	527	1,266	65	1,192	731	422	39
30 to 34 years old	14,771	10,559	3,785	427	12,061	9,385	2,331	344	2,105	701	1,353	51	1,853	1,181	605	68
35 to 39 years old	15,733	12,140	3,152	440	13,045	10,739	1,951	355	2,038	905	1,074	59	1,542	1,067	448	38
40 to 44 years old	12,213	9,905	1,915	393	10,080	8,482	1,270	329	1,387	780	558	48	1,189	909	231	49
45 to 54 years old	7,904	6,516	1,090	299	6,609	5,670	712	228	851	481	332	38	833	617	171	46
55 to 64 years old	1,233	1,043	104	87	922	807	64	52	203	138	33	32	159	124	23	12
65 years old and over	186	121	30	36	134	80	22	32	43	34	6	4	19	11	4	4
Parent educational attainment																
Less than 9th grade	4,138	2,765	1,182	191	3,504	2,406	929	169	399	173	214	12	2,414	1,663	653	98
9th to 12th grade, no diploma	7,947	4,061	3,548	337	5,471	3,372	1,836	264	2,188	506	1,618	64	1,556	869	651	36
High school graduate	22,858	16,122	5,905	831	17,996	14,055	3,282	659	4,016	1,447	2,431	138	1,911	1,284	556	71
Some college, no degree or associate degree	15,480	11,360	3,594	527	12,712	10,008	2,301	403	2,128	919	1,141	68	1,007	697	260	50
Bachelor's degree	8,652	7,573	857	222	7,442	6,611	652	179	618	440	150	28	301	257	24	20
Graduate or professional degree	5,141	4,757	310	74	4,480	4,184	250	46	299	229	52	18	193	165	23	4
Parent employment status[c]																
In the civilian labor force	53,634	42,385	9,345	1,904	44,882	37,376	5,965	1,542	6,442	3,100	3,083	259	5,568	4,313	1,026	229
Employed	49,539	39,819	8,009	1,711	41,890	35,191	5,300	1,398	5,502	2,844	2,441	217	4,911	3,861	850	200
Both parents employed	25,692	25,692	NA	NA	22,435	22,435	NA	NA	2,107	2,107	NA	NA	2,023	2,023	NA	NA
Unemployed	4,095	2,566	1,335	193	2,992	2,185	664	143	941	256	642	43	658	452	176	29
Not in the labor force	9,552	3,251	6,046	254	5,961	2,519	3,280	162	3,003	415	2,524	64	1,731	542	1,142	46

Family income															
Under $5,000	3,789	717	2,901	171	2,113	587	1,439	88	1,526	94	1,367	65	626	167	434	26
$5,000 to $9,999	5,403	1,338	3,850	215	3,223	1,035	2,022	166	1,874	165	1,671	37	1,071	374	660	37
$10,000 to $14,999	4,774	2,431	2,124	219	3,460	1,993	1,294	173	1,069	271	767	33	1,025	648	350	28
$15,000 to $24,999	9,469	6,045	2,904	519	7,289	4,993	1,831	466	1,684	684	956	44	1,657	1,216	368	72
$25,000 to $29,999	4,886	3,783	893	210	4,043	3,226	657	160	621	360	224	38	639	518	84	37
$30,000 to $39,999	9,333	7,714	1,283	336	7,957	6,813	910	234	1,027	623	333	71	972	811	143	18
$40,000 to $49,999	8,149	7,313	634	202	7,173	6,496	496	181	671	546	112	12	587	504	52	30
$50,000 and over	18,414	17,296	808	310	16,348	15,491	602	255	1,176	972	176	27	804	697	77	31
Housing tenure[d]															
Owner[d]	39,702	33,703	4,885	1,114	34,612	30,180	3,497	935	3,432	2,104	1,200	128	2,593	2,112	387	94
Renter[d]	24,514	12,935	10,511	1,068	16,994	10,455	5,753	786	6,215	1,609	4,407	199	4,789	2,822	1,781	185

Notes: Figures cover only those persons under age 18 who are living with one or both parents. NA = not applicable.

Source: Adapted from U.S. Bureau of the Census. (1993). *Statistical abstract of the United States: 1993* (113th ed., p. 63). Austin, TX: Reference Press.

[a]Includes other races, not shown separately.

[b]Persons of Hispanic origin may be of any race.

[c]Excludes children whose parent is in the Armed Forces.

[d]Householder may or may not be the child's parent.

as abuse or neglect. In other cases, angry estranged partners, relatives, and neighbors use the child protective services reporting system to retaliate against caretakers of children.

In 1992, 1.16 million of the reports were substantiated, representing a 10 percent increase over 1991 and an overall substantiation rate of 40 percent, the same rate as for 1991. Figure 2-3 depicts the growth in the number of reports of child maltreatment from 1980 to 1991.

Tables 2-7 through 2-11 provide various types of information about abused and neglected children. Table 2-7 shows the numbers of victims by age (from infancy to 18 years) by state, and Figure 2-4 shows the number and percentage of victims in each age group for the country as a whole. The inci-

TABLE 2-5 **Number of Children under Age 18 Who Live with Biological Parents, Step Parents, and Adoptive Married-Couple Parents, by Race and Hispanic Origin of Mother: 1980, 1985, and 1990**

Type of Parent	All Races[a]			White			Black			Hispanic[b]
	1980	1985	1990	1980	1985	1990	1980	1985	1990	1990
Number of children under 18 years, in thousands	47,248	45,347	45,448	42,329	39,942	39,732	3,775	3,816	3,671	4,568
Biological mother and father	39,523	37,213	37,026	35,852	33,202	32,975	2,698	2,661	2,336	3,703
Biological mother–stepfather	5,355	6,049	6,643	4,362	4,918	5,258	877	952	1,149	699
Stepmother–biological father	727	740	608	664	676	549	46	50	38	38
Adoptive mother and father	1,350	866	974	1,209	754	815	119	76	97	101
Unknown mother or father	293	479	197	242	391	135	35	77	51	27
Percent distribution										
Biological mother and father	83.7	82.1	81.5	84.7	83.1	83.0	71.5	69.7	63.6	81.1
Biological mother–stepfather	11.3	13.3	14.6	10.3	12.3	13.2	23.2	24.9	31.3	15.3
Stepmother–biological father	1.5	1.6	1.3	1.6	1.7	1.4	1.2	1.3	1.0	0.8
Adoptive mother and father	2.9	1.9	2.1	2.9	1.9	2.1	3.1	2.0	2.6	2.2
Unknown mother or father	0.6	1.1	0.4	0.6	1.0	0.3	0.9	2.0	1.4	0.6

Source: Adapted from U.S. Bureau of the Census. (1993). *Statistical abstract of the United States: 1993* (113th ed., p. 62). Austin, TX: Reference Press.

[a]Includes other races, not shown separately.

[b]People of Hispanic origin may be of any race.

dence of maltreatment is high for young children and declines steadily among latency age children (seven to 12 years) and more slowly for young teenagers (13 to 14 years). For children 15 years and older, the incidence drops rapidly. The patterns of increase and decrease in the incidence of child maltreatment may be related to child behavioral development and family interactions. Figure 2-5 provides details on the race and ethnicity of the victims.

The numbers of children who were victims of specific types of abuse are provided in Table 2-8 and Figure 2-6. Thirty-five states provided information on the perpetrators of child abuse; this is presented in Table 2-9. The vast majority were parents or other relatives. However, a substantial 30,000 were noncaretakers, which includes neighbors and strangers.

FIGURE 2-2 **Index of Social Health for Children and Youth: 1970 to 1990**

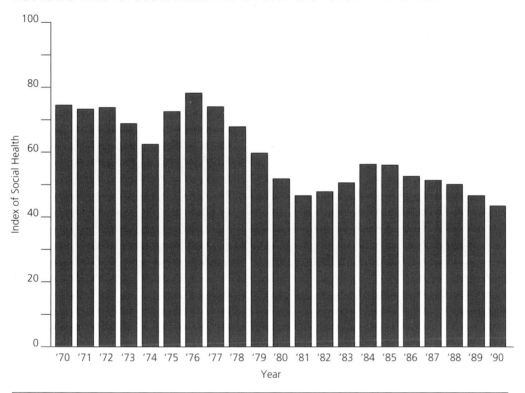

Source: Reprinted with permission from Miringoff, M. L. (1992). *The index of social health: Monitoring the social well-being of the nation* (p. 5). Tarrytown, NY: Fordham Institute for Innovation in Social Policy.

TABLE 2-6 **Number of Deaths and Death Rate per 100,000 for Leading Causes of Child Death, by Age Group: 1990**

Cause of Death	Number of Deaths	Death Rate
Under 1 year		
All causes	38,351	922.3
Congenital anomalies (birth defects)	8,239	198.1
Sudden infant death syndrome	5,417	130.3
Disorders relating to short gestation and low birthweight	4,013	96.5
Respiratory distress syndrome	2,850	68.5
Newborn affected by maternal complications of pregnancy	1,655	39.8
Newborn affected by complications of placenta, cord, and membranes	975	23.4
Accidents and adverse effects	930	22.4
Infections specific to the perinatal period	875	21.0
Intrauterine hypoxia and birth asphyxia	762	18.3
Pneumonia and influenza	634	15.2
All other causes	12,001	288.6
1 to 4 years		
All causes	6,931	46.8
Accidents and adverse effects	2,566	17.3
Motor vehicle accidents	928	6.3
All other accidents and adverse effects	1,638	11.1
Congenital anomalies	896	6.0
Malignant neoplasms, including neoplasms of lymphatic and hematopoietic tissues	513	3.5
Homicide and legal intervention	378	2.6
Diseases of heart	282	1.9
Pneumonia and influenza	171	1.2
Certain conditions originating in the perinatal period	134	0.9
Human immunodeficiency virus infection	123	0.8
Septicemia	100	0.7
Meningitis	81	0.5
All other causes	1,687	11.4
5 to 14 years		
All causes	8,436	24.0
Accidents and adverse effects	3,650	10.4
Motor vehicle accidents	2,059	5.9
All other accidents and adverse effects	1,591	4.5
Malignant neoplasms, including neoplasms of lymphatic and hematopoietic tissues	1,094	3.1
Homicide and legal intervention	512	1.5
Congenital anomalies	468	1.3
Diseases of heart	308	0.9
Suicide	264	0.8
Pneumonia and influenza	134	0.4
Chronic obstructive pulmonary diseases and allied conditions	115	0.3
Benign neoplasms, carcinoma in situ, and neoplasms of uncertain behavior and of unspecified nature	100	0.3
Human immunodeficiency virus infection	84	0.2
All other causes	1,707	4.9
15 to 24 years		
All causes	36,733	99.2
Accidents and adverse effects	16,241	43.9
Motor vehicle accidents	12,607	34.1
All other accidents and adverse effects	3,634	9.8
Homicide and legal intervention	7,354	19.9
Suicide	4,869	13.2
Malignant neoplasms, including neoplasms of lymphatic and hematopoietic tissues	1,819	4.9
Diseases of heart	917	2.5
Human immunodeficiency virus infection	541	1.5
Congenital anomalies	491	1.3
Cerebrovascular diseases	234	0.6
Pneumonia and influenza	231	0.6
Chronic obstructive pulmonary diseases and allied conditions	178	0.5
All other causes	3,858	10.4

Notes: Rates shown for children under age 1 year are actually infant mortality rates (deaths per 100,000 live births). Death rates for other age groups are deaths per 100,000 population in the age group.

Source: Reprinted from Committee on Ways and Means, U.S. House of Representatives. (1993). *Overview of entitlement programs: 1993 greenbook* (pp. 1178–1179). Washington, DC: U.S. Government Printing Office.

Table 2-10 shows the reports of child abuse and neglect by state and source of report in 1991. The last two reporting entities listed are the armed services in the continental United States (CONUS) and outside the continental United States (OCONUS). The armed services have extensive child abuse and neglect programs that employ both uniformed and civilian social workers.

Schools are the largest reporters of abuse and neglect, followed by social services; legal organizations, including law enforcement agencies; and medical organizations, including emergency rooms and their staffs, who were among the first to identify physical child abuse (Figure 2-7). A significant number of reporters of child maltreatment were anonymous, and the states generally protect those

FIGURE 2-3 **National Estimates of Child Abuse Cases Reported by Selected Children's Welfare Organizations: 1980 to 1991**

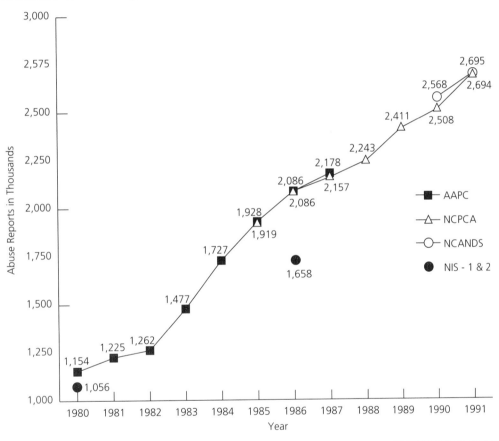

Notes: AAPC = American Association for Protecting Children; NCPCA = National Committee for the Prevention of Child Abuse; NCANDS = National Child Abuse and Neglect Data System; NIS = National Incidence Study.

Source: Adapted from U.S. Department of Health and Human Services, National Center on Child Abuse and Neglect. (1993). *National child abuse and neglect data system working paper 2: 1991 summary data component* (p. 26). Gaithersburg, MD: Author.

TABLE 2-7 Number of Child Abuse Victims, by State and Age of Victims: 1991

State	Age in Years									
	<1	1	2	3	4	5	6	7	8	9
Alabama	1,482	1,271	1,352	1,312	1,216	1,351	1,338	1,271	1,232	1,197
Alaska	410	377	449	410	397	401	445	413	378	381
Arizona	2,212	2,005	2,136	2,043	1,924	1,877	1,809	1,651	1,628	1,464
Arkansas	845	500	591	569	512	542	507	482	437	446
California	1,971	1,971	4,082	4,082	4,082	4,082	4,607	4,606	4,606	4,606
Colorado	738	532	520	576	562	625	523	580	559	527
Connecticut	502	916	905	991	935	890	911	905	794	757
Delaware	131	139	119	134	118	106	124	125	96	124
District of Columbia	100	121	82	81	62	63	62	53	53	52
Florida	9,080	5,198	5,233	4,862	4,588	4,424	4,410	4,101	3,995	3,857
Georgia	1,593	2,105	3,178	2,952	3,060	2,897	2,756	2,679	2,570	2,370
Hawaii	165	155	153	127	115	94	130	113	117	120
Idaho	57	282	344	360	402	373	459	417	405	416
Illinois	6,650	3,074	3,031	2,750	2,591	2,458	2,380	2,215	2,074	1,964
Indiana	2,380	1,845	2,144	2,067	2,041	1,960	2,040	1,848	1,784	1,742
Iowa	515	557	558	554	539	481	499	440	425	382
Kansas	—	—	—	—	—	—	—	—	—	—
Kentucky	1,707	1,685	1,740	1,681	1,682	1,576	1,467	1,301	1,417	1,316
Louisiana	791	791	791	791	932	932	932	884	884	884
Maine	254	254	254	254	254	298	298	298	298	236
Maryland	—	—	—	—	—	—	—	—	—	—
Massachusetts	3,066	2,014	2,095	2,180	2,022	1,861	1,720	1,577	1,468	1,381
Michigan	3,245	1,815	1,726	1,573	1,557	1,545	1,486	1,455	1,395	1,331
Minnesota	678	696	713	668	634	692	608	588	565	577
Mississippi	1,039	426	418	384	375	430	433	379	402	360
Missouri	—	—	—	—	—	—	—	—	—	—
Montana	—	—	—	—	—	—	—	—	—	—
Nebraska	4	786	437	406	362	401	376	355	338	323
Nevada	707	590	590	473	473	473	443	443	442	442
New Hampshire	—	—	—	—	—	—	—	—	—	—
New Jersey	1,563	1,110	1,129	1,041	1,020	931	1,086	1,014	1,020	926
New Mexico	245	312	312	310	310	324	324	299	299	296
New York	5,017	3,652	3,652	3,262	3,225	3,083	3,083	3,083	3,084	3,083
North Carolina	933	2,042	2,030	1,938	1,754	1,679	1,740	1,541	1,444	1,355
North Dakota	155	170	226	234	213	213	253	219	208	182
Ohio	2,490	2,967	3,075	3,161	3,110	3,060	3,056	2,929	2,745	2,645
Oklahoma	307	438	438	538	538	538	538	507	507	507
Oregon	750	427	487	507	478	479	502	459	478	470
Pennsylvania	211	293	274	393	456	538	487	446	448	443
Rhode Island	542	374	419	420	435	416	359	346	305	294
South Carolina	460	1,466	759	697	633	668	625	612	558	548
South Dakota	117	117	117	272	272	271	238	238	238	238
Tennessee	705	629	682	707	660	632	655	603	578	562
Texas	5,607	3,807	4,001	3,997	3,907	3,994	4,006	3,613	3,668	3,320
Utah	400	537	669	701	692	679	671	631	644	610
Vermont	62	46	71	78	101	91	87	92	89	70
Virginia	1,152	968	968	926	853	963	920	901	832	765
Washington	—	—	—	—	—	—	—	—	—	—
West Virginia	—	—	—	—	—	—	—	—	—	—
Wisconsin	836	889	952	1,077	1,080	1,083	1,047	992	943	868
Wyoming	—	—	—	—	—	—	—	—	—	—
Total	61,881	50,356	53,927	52,574	51,186	50,496	50,469	47,731	46,465	44,458
No. reporting	44	44	44	44	44	44	44	44	44	44
CONUS	351	517	783	761	757	667	663	586	571	489
OCONUS	85	124	192	180	141	139	157	143	130	133

Notes: CONUS = Armed services in the continental United States; OCONUS = Armed services outside the continental United States; — = not available.

Source: Adapted from U.S. Department of Health and Human Services, National Center on Child Abuse and Neglect. (1993). *National child abuse and neglect data system working paper 2: 1991 summary data component* (pp. 11–12). Gaithersburg, MD: Author.

Age in Years

10	11	12	13	14	15	16	17	18+	Unknown	Total
1,144	1,079	1,092	1,198	1,135	1,046	658	388	—	572	21,334
309	355	301	297	313	251	235	130	—	—	6,252
1,468	1,435	1,290	1,323	1,150	1,017	780	359	—	520	28,091
426	411	389	362	382	390	234	110	—	—	8,135
3,234	4,233	4,233	4,233	3,625	3,625	2,624	3,624	820	24	68,970
432	428	411	435	428	381	257	164	6	4	8,688
680	687	672	745	757	704	499	326	247	705	14,528
110	98	96	108	111	107	104	75	39	145	2,209
53	53	33	33	33	34	34	33	—	—	1,035
3,590	3,367	3,209	3,186	3,123	2,861	2,296	1,308	1	24	72,713
2,254	2,270	2,031	2,066	1,988	1,851	1,577	1,167	1,114	2,272	44,750
103	105	100	115	138	130	138	63	36	49	2,266
422	431	413	410	404	382	378	294	454	—	7,103
1,759	1,684	1,589	1,437	1,353	1,148	900	476	—	39	39,572
1,746	1,721	1,751	1,872	2,115	2,072	1,383	813	—	5	33,329
395	403	372	384	371	347	240	—	—	692	8,154
—	—	—	—	—	—	—	—	—	—	—
1,287	1,218	1,233	1,323	1,274	1,093	887	582	—	—	24,469
797	797	798	798	797	798	797	797	—	—	14,991
236	237	237	234	234	235	135	135	—	—	4,381
—	—	—	—	—	—	—	—	—	—	—
1,350	1,311	1,178	1,261	1,179	1,068	827	469	—	21	28,048
1,267	1,266	1,298	1,387	1,424	1,218	948	430	—	—	26,366
524	536	474	492	492	431	330	194	—	56	9,948
393	364	325	346	287	284	189	109	14	—	6,957
—	—	—	—	—	—	—	—	—	—	—
—	—	—	—	—	—	—	—	—	—	—
323	306	254	298	292	243	210	127	—	—	5,841
354	354	354	354	288	287	173	173	—	—	7,413
—	—	—	—	—	—	—	—	—	—	—
929	922	897	893	879	843	678	520	209	1,879	19,489
296	285	285	302	302	221	222	50	45	78	5,117
2,799	2,799	2,798	2,798	2,798	1,540	1,540	1,540	1,540	1,163	55,539
1,225	1,199	1,079	1,086	1,035	1,003	805	471	277	—	24,636
191	158	142	172	163	181	110	72	—	—	3,262
2,549	2,479	2,390	2,418	2,573	2,397	2,185	1,744	765	3,233	51,971
506	506	345	346	345	346	345	346	346	—	8,287
442	388	459	432	418	357	273	155	—	—	7,961
433	461	428	511	575	567	492	383	147	—	7,986
268	279	238	261	245	279	219	137	17	66	5,919
601	502	514	530	513	447	331	179	—	—	10,643
238	238	176	176	176	176	176	176	175	—	3,825
527	545	603	532	516	464	439	328	—	—	10,367
3,170	2,997	2,819	2,711	2,503	2,046	1,500	533	—	—	58,199
604	600	565	564	563	452	351	185	61	—	10,179
79	81	81	81	100	96	76	48	3	5	1,437
721	637	622	636	624	512	424	275	3	—	13,702
—	—	—	—	—	—	—	—	—	—	—
926	871	903	1,079	1,286	1,324	886	602	3	—	17,647
—	—	—	—	—	—	—	—	—	—	—
41,179	41,126	39,485	40,232	39,317	35,254	27,885	20,090	6,322	11,552	811,985
44	44	44	44	44	43	43	42	22	20	44
419	385	365	335	341	317	261	188	90	—	8,846
112	93	72	71	91	64	61	37	17	55	2,097

who report child maltreatment from civil suits by alleged perpetrators. Neighbors and relatives also report child abuse and neglect.

Table 2-11 shows how some states responded to cases of child abuse. Cases of abuse and neglect are handled in a variety of ways. In most cases, more than one action was taken per case. Casework counseling is provided, usually by a child protective services worker, who maintains regular contact with the family and attempts to help them overcome the causes of the neglect or abuse. Court action, which could lead to the punishment of perpetrators, the temporary or permanent severing of ties between caretakers and their children, or other judicial action, may be initiated. In a small percentage of cases, immediate or short-term crisis services such as emergency, medical care, or emergency shelter

FIGURE 2-4 **Number and Percentages of Child Abuse Victims, by Age: 1991**

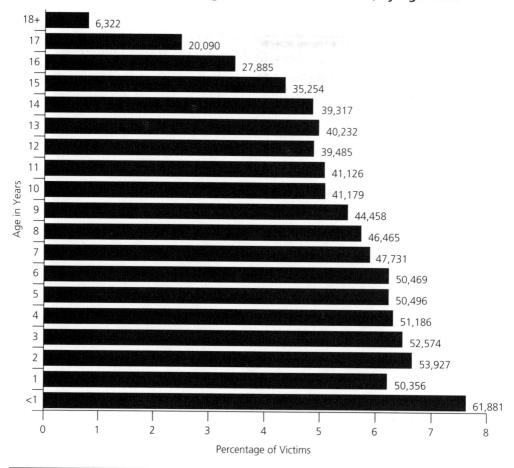

Note: Total number of victims (44 states reporting) = 811,985; the ages of 11,552 victims were not known.

Source: Adapted from U.S. Department of Health and Human Services, National Center on Child Abuse and Neglect. (1993). *National child abuse and neglect data system working paper 2: 1991 summary data component* (p. 30). Gaithersburg, MD: Author.

care were provided. Long-term or support services, including foster care and homemaker and day care services, may be provided. Other kinds of services are often provided, such as referral to mental health facilities, special educational help, and other services appropriate to the case.

Sometimes child abuse results in the death of a child. Table 2-12 shows a state-by-state breakdown of child abuse and neglect fatali-

ties from 1985 to 1992. Table 2-13 shows that in 1990, 1991, and 1992, almost all fatalities involved children under age five, and nearly half were children under age one. Over half of all the deaths resulted from abuse, but a substantial proportion were the consequence of neglect. Nearly one in five of the deaths also involved parental substance abuse. Families whose children died due to abuse or ne-

FIGURE 2-5 **Number and Percentages of Child Abuse Victims, by Race or Ethnic Group: 1991**

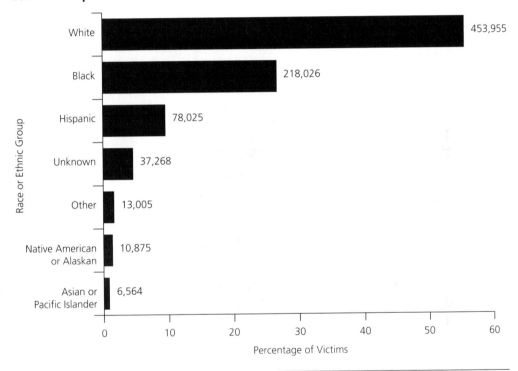

Note: Total number of reports (42 states reporting) = 817,718.

Source: Adapted from U.S. Department of Health and Human Services, National Center on Child Abuse and Neglect. (1993). *National child abuse and neglect data system working paper 2: 1991 summary data component* (p. 34). Gaithersburg, MD: Author.

TABLE 2-8 Number of Child Abuse Victims, by State and Type of Abuse: 1991

State	Physical Abuse	Neglect	Medical Neglect	Sexual Abuse	Emotional Maltreatment	Other	Unknown	Total
Alabama	6,344	12,128	—	3,816	1,879	—	—	24,167
Alaska	2,404	2,888	—	1,252	116	44	—	6,704
Arizona	2,941	6,824	—	3,562	503	14,261	—	28,091
Arkansas	2,874	4,437	358	2,089	594	—	—	10,352
California	38,236	3,332	—	25,055	4,347	—	256	71,226
Colorado	2,587	3,233	469	2,056	932	—	632	9,909
Connecticut	2,337	11,445	—	979	—	—	—	14,761
Delaware	377	773	57	209	220	544	29	2,209
District of Columbia	841	11,467	—	52	—	—	—	12,360
Florida	13,651	38,816	3,415	8,348	3,924	30,996	—	99,150
Georgia	6,160	11,476	1,888	4,131	1,590	729	—	25,974
Hawaii	992	513	151	279	242	725	34	2,936
Idaho	2,096	3,361	193	1,445	—	237	50	7,382
Illinois	4,378	22,796	1,743	5,086	496	11,457	—	45,956
Indiana	8,301	17,878	—	7,150	—	—	—	33,329
Iowa	2,641	3,911	—	1,167	—	335	—	8,054
Kansas	—	—	—	—	—	—	—	—
Kentucky	6,314	14,893	—	2,189	1,073	—	—	24,469
Louisiana	4,044	9,494	—	1,199	79	181	—	14,997
Maine	997	1,255	—	696	1,425	—	—	4,373
Maryland	—	—	—	—	—	—	—	—
Massachusetts	7,630	20,763	—	2,538	3,728	172	—	34,831
Michigan	5,789	10,539	606	2,533	7,587	334	—	27,388
Minnesota	3,959	4,889	647	1,248	941	—	33	11,717
Mississippi	1,972	4,426	—	1,201	183	—	—	7,782
Missouri	3,171	5,885	1,456	2,285	447	771	—	14,015
Montana	—	—	—	—	—	—	—	—
Nebraska	1,870	3,584	—	717	—	—	—	6,171
Nevada	—	—	—	—	—	—	—	—
New Hampshire	288	530	—	392	1	—	—	1,211
New Jersey	7,515	9,149	923	1,663	239	—	—	19,489
New Mexico	1,359	3,165	—	593	—	—	—	5,117
New York	—	—	—	—	—	—	—	—
North Carolina	1,117	21,391	706	1,315	84	23	—	24,636
North Dakota	999	1,692	—	214	—	357	—	3,262
Ohio	15,017	31,907	—	10,146	5,559	24	—	62,653
Oklahoma	2,918	3,840	402	1,351	660	1,754	—	10,925
Oregon	2,394	2,776	276	2,784	2,325	13	—	10,568
Pennsylvania	3,628	414	—	4,348	167	—	—	8,557
Rhode Island	1,936	3,328	—	655	—	—	—	5,919
South Carolina	2,104	6,073	710	1,669	249	3,536	202	14,543
South Dakota	815	2,346	—	551	783	—	—	4,495
Tennessee	2,403	4,256	227	2,658	309	514	—	10,367
Texas	17,151	24,593	2,137	8,590	3,775	1,938	15	58,199
Utah	2,269	3,921	228	2,316	1,445	—	—	10,179
Vermont	416	413	37	734	19	—	—	1,619
Virginia	3,497	8,233	566	1,869	2,279	246	—	16,690
Washington	—	—	—	—	—	—	—	—
West Virginia	—	—	—	—	—	—	—	—
Wisconsin	5,083	6,850	—	6,135	650	—	—	18,718
Wyoming	520	1,187	58	390	247	82	—	2,484
Total	204,404	367,200	17,266	129,697	49,124	69,290	1,251	838,232
No. reporting	45	45	23	45	36	24	8	45
CONUS	3,553	3,345	—	1,586	938	9	—	9,431
OCONUS	911	792	—	196	231	—	—	2,130

Notes: CONUS = Armed services in the continental United States; OCONUS = Armed services outside the continental United States; — = not available.

Source: Adapted from U.S. Department of Health and Human Services, National Center on Child Abuse and Neglect. (1993). *National child abuse and neglect data system working paper 2: 1991 summary data component* (p. 15). Gaithersburg, MD: Author.

FIGURE 2-6 **Number and Percentages of Child Abuse Reports, by Type of Maltreatment: 1991**

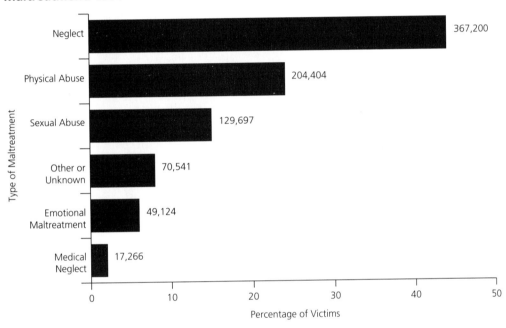

Note: Total number of maltreatment types (45 states reporting) = 838,232.

Source: Adapted from U.S. Department of Health and Human Services, National Center on Child Abuse and Neglect. (1993). *National child abuse and neglect data system working paper 2: 1991 summary data component* (p. 29). Gaithersburg, MD: Author.

TABLE 2-9 Number of Child Abuse Victims, by State and Relationship to Abuser: 1991

State	Parents	Other Relatives	Foster Parents	Facility Staff	Child Care	Non-caretakers	Unknown or Missing Data	Total
Alabama	—	—	—	—	—	—	—	—
Alaska	5,267	662	—	—	79	146	71	6,225
Arizona	—	—	—	—	—	—	—	—
Arkansas	—	—	—	—	—	—	—	—
California	—	—	—	—	—	—	—	—
Colorado	—	—	—	—	—	—	—	—
Connecticut	12,267	1,290	—	—	—	608	448	14,613
Delaware	1,688	232	2	—	8	74	14	2,018
District of Columbia	—	—	—	—	—	—	—	—
Florida	11,656	1,726	53	211	374	696	35	14,751
Georgia	30,258	2,399	158	—	355	1,340	682	35,192
Hawaii	2,375	206	4	—	9	—	204	2,798
Idaho	4,031	570	9	1	90	470	75	5,246
Illinois	20,812	3,933	112	36	790	1,701	—	27,384
Indiana	33,055	3,740	46	11	362	5,344	584	43,142
Iowa	5,334	431	26	13	431	—	606	6,235
Kansas	3,088	225	—	208	346	—	213	4,080
Kentucky	22,576	2,610	109	—	341	705	249	26,590
Louisiana	10,740	—	68	76	28	476	—	11,388
Maine	—	—	—	—	—	—	—	—
Maryland	—	—	—	—	—	—	—	—
Massachusetts	—	—	—	—	—	—	—	—
Michigan	17,432	727	51	3	17	790	725	19,745
Minnesota	6,411	1,145	27	13	87	86	19	7,788
Mississippi	4,004	731	20	10	20	200	20	5,005
Missouri	16,671	1,168	97	76	344	509	903	19,768
Montana	4,120	—	—	35	—	896	—	5,051
Nebraska	4,050	654	17	6	96	445	92	5,360
Nevada	8,972	289	62	45	16	484	33	9,901
New Hampshire	560	118	4	—	1	90	48	821
New Jersey	15,840	2,207	180	116	300	78	768	19,489
New Mexico	—	—	—	—	—	—	—	—
New York	47,397	13,687	765	74	101	1,176	685	63,885
North Carolina	26,483	894	83	52	315	865	—	28,692
North Dakota	—	—	—	—	—	—	—	—
Ohio	—	—	—	—	—	—	—	—
Oklahoma	—	—	—	—	—	—	—	—
Oregon	4,827	906	54	4	114	1,443	140	7,488
Pennsylvania	4,404	1,997	64	61	786	1,435	—	8,747
Rhode Island	5,881	410	98	80	192	465	24	7,150
South Carolina	17,249	1,432	131	10	105	82	106	19,115
South Dakota	3,697	437	12	5	7	300	35	4,493
Tennessee	7,623	1,572	58	10	46	1,000	334	10,643
Texas	36,819	5,442	72	31	104	3,369	90	45,927
Utah	5,448	1,162	14	—	69	5	1,005	7,703
Vermont	969	344	6	16	4	389	145	1,873
Virginia	13,566	1,803	53	25	410	68	180	16,105
Washington	—	—	—	—	—	—	—	—
West Virginia	—	—	—	—	—	—	—	—
Wisconsin	12,489	1,855	142	126	278	4,263	317	19,470
Wyoming	—	—	—	—	—	—	—	—
Total	428,145	57,029	2,597	1,354	6,635	30,013	8,850	534,623
No. reporting	36	34	31	27	34	33	30	36
CONUS	6,735	287	—	—	154	389	266	7,831
OCONUS	1,781	29	—	—	45	73	44	1,972

Notes: CONUS = Armed services in the continental United States; OCONUS = Armed services outside the continental United States; — = not available.

Source: Adapted from U.S. Department of Health and Human Services, National Center on Child Abuse and Neglect. (1993). *National child abuse and neglect data system working paper 2: 1991 summary data component* (p. 20). Gaithersburg, MD: Author.

TABLE 2-10 **Number of Child Abuse Reports, by State and Source of Report: 1991**

State	Social Services	Medical	Legal Justice	Education	Child Care Providers	Victims	Parents
Alabama	2,756	2,378	3,577	4,419	271	525	3,238
Alaska	1,132	729	1,126	1,783	160	582	—
Arizona	4,145	3,006	3,984	4,297	483	—	1,660
Arkansas	1,468	1,975	1,496	2,095	360	394	1,457
California	—	—	—	—	—	—	—
Colorado	—	—	—	—	—	—	—
Connecticut	1,097	2,808	2,145	2,967	146	166	945
Delaware	316	503	562	584	71	118	545
District of Columbia	452	738	871	425	14	52	352
Florida	15,528	11,892	12,530	13,196	1,234	2,337	10,798
Georgia	3,135	2,814	3,837	5,154	250	1,034	2,408
Hawaii	579	497	597	764	17	45	213
Idaho	2,971	593	671	884	781	225	762
Illinois	10,063	11,884	7,732	8,800	847	438	5,361
Indiana	—	—	—	—	—	—	—
Iowa	3,476	1,720	1,562	2,691	—	—	—
Kansas	692	1,029	865	1,804	276	126	861
Kentucky	3,381	2,411	3,291	4,406	588	846	3,498
Louisiana	4,320	2,236	3,217	3,695	—	9,903	—
Maine	473	440	441	917	80	120	120
Maryland	—	—	—	—	—	—	—
Massachusetts	6,724	8,690	7,109	5,938	1,133	505	3,430
Michigan	9,386	3,307	5,185	8,344	1,219	636	3,950
Minnesota	2,389	1,705	2,829	3,472	909	418	1,400
Mississippi	1,150	1,725	2,732	2,588	72	288	719
Missouri	6,956	3,168	4,588	4,982	725	—	4,223
Montana	406	516	803	1,224	216	194	680
Nebraska	521	520	1,327	1,031	288	240	551
Nevada	1,335	823	2,341	2,669	258	195	1,119
New Hampshire	—	—	—	—	—	—	—
New Jersey	7,088	5,400	5,836	8,934	—	996	4,257
New Mexico	1,164	1,645	2,784	3,433	1,099	233	1,582
New York	17,722	18,166	13,590	24,554	375	—	—
North Carolina	5,819	3,811	3,266	7,266	750	647	3,686
North Dakota	913	166	586	635	99	44	405
Ohio	10,682	8,875	9,511	12,308	1,448	1,507	—
Oklahoma	—	—	—	—	—	—	—
Oregon	2,023	1,943	4,366	4,161	447	1,592	794
Pennsylvania	3,175	4,435	1,472	4,784	845	1,048	2,820
Rhode Island	2,520	1,351	1,324	1,683	434	814	1,659
South Carolina	1,621	2,085	1,826	2,965	186	317	1,086
South Dakota	396	602	2,371	1,860	174	289	858
Tennessee	1,270	2,569	4,253	2,950	431	678	3,439
Texas	9,518	19,480	11,163	20,804	1,595	977	7,595
Utah	1,780	1,309	2,053	1,634	176	198	—
Vermont	365	213	333	558	108	97	358
Virginia	3,349	3,035	3,634	6,281	448	616	3,166
Washington	4,969	4,275	3,137	7,237	936	934	3,323
West Virginia	—	—	—	—	—	—	—
Wisconsin	7,459	2,658	6,962	7,693	1,201	748	5,034
Wyoming	—	—	—	—	—	—	—
Total	166,704	141,136	153,899	208,903	21,155	31,134	88,376
No. reporting	44	44	44	44	41	40	38
CONUS	3,143	2,669	2,032	—	—	141	—
OCONUS	81	404	879	—	—	46	—

Notes: CONUS = Armed services in the continental United States; OCONUS = Armed services outside the continental United States; — = not available.

Source: Adapted from U.S. Department of Health and Human Services, National Center on Child Abuse and Neglect. (1993). *National child abuse and neglect data system working paper 2: 1991 summary data component* (pp. 11–12). Gaithersburg, MD: Author.

Continued on next page

TABLE 2-10 **Continued**

State	Other Relatives	Friends or Neighbors	Perpetrators	Other	Anonymous Reporters	Total
Alabama	3,635	1,457	—	2,702	3,504	28,462
Alaska	1,134	1,435	—	215	687	8,983
Arizona	1,796	3,017	766	1,339	2,038	26,531
Arkansas	1,743	1,823	—	613	1,786	15,210
California	—	—	—	—	—	—
Colorado	—	—	—	—	—	—
Connecticut	883	589	—	77	2,012	13,835
Delaware	392	445	216	218	397	4,367
District of Columbia	923	746	—	78	468	5,119
Florida	10,168	13,391	784	4,938	21,090	117,886
Georgia	3,322	2,523	—	13,097	2,568	40,142
Hawaii	329	329	13	209	1,425	5,017
Idaho	370	945	—	614	661	9,477
Illinois	7,115	5,135	—	2,150	8,226	67,751
Indiana	—	—	—	—	—	—
owa	—	—	—	7,926	1,650	19,025
Kansas	857	853	91	605	888	8,947
Kentucky	4,335	4,017	—	—	6,732	33,505
Louisiana	—	—	—	146	2,356	25,873
Maine	366	399	—	244	484	4,084
Maryland	—	—	—	—	—	—
Massachusetts	2,713	6,619	—	4,521	10,836	58,218
Michigan	5,379	6,072	—	1,876	3,720	49,074
Minnesota	1,433	1,955	159	193	618	17,480
Mississippi	2,013	1,006	—	790	1,294	14,377
Missouri	3,430	—	473	8,646	9,152	46,343
Montana	543	772	—	1,882	—	7,236
Nebraska	639	831	278	248	1,519	7,993
Nevada	797	1,840	—	687	794	12,858
New Hampshire	—	—	—	—	—	—
New Jersey	4,373	7,427	—	—	9,439	53,750
New Mexico	1,307	2,252	—	116	2,619	18,234
New York	15,897	8,010	—	26,769	6,393	131,476
North Carolina	6,747	7,482	—	—	5,841	45,315
North Dakota	220	420	6	210	221	3,925
Ohio	15,923	11,012	3,222	4,491	9,146	88,125
Oklahoma	—	—	—	—	—	—
Oregon	1,303	2,124	—	3,268	1,509	23,530
Pennsylvania	1,435	1,495	90	1,477	786	23,862
Rhode Island	1,070	2,156	—	190	1,142	14,343
South Carolina	1,841	2,271	21	562	1,557	16,338
South Dakota	1,201	1,043	—	1,452	959	11,205
Tennessee	3,853	4,501	150	1,418	4,203	29,715
Texas	10,657	11,796	—	6,884	6,207	97,676
Utah	2,837	2,051	137	1,668	691	14,534
Vermont	175	173	25	172	58	2,635
Virginia	3,097	4,340	413	1,565	4,062	34,006
Washington	2,383	5,134	—	4,473	2,266	39,067
West Virginia	—	—	—	—	—	—
Wisconsin	4,069	3,697	163	2,494	4,727	46,905
Wyoming	—	—	—	—	—	—
Total	132,717	133,613	7,007	111,230	146,764	1,342,638
No. reporting	42	41	17	41	43	44
CONUS	—	—	222	4,233	185	12,625
OCONUS	—	—	35	1,259	19	2,723

FIGURE 2-7 **Number and Percentages of Child Abuse Reports, by Source of Report: 1991**

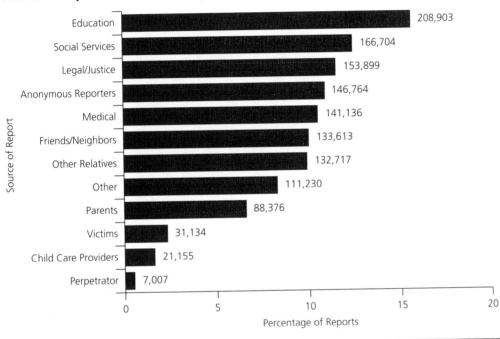

Note: Total number of reports (44 states reporting) = 1,342,638.

Source: Adapted from U.S. Department of Health and Human Services, National Center on Child Abuse and Neglect. (1993). *National child abuse and neglect data system working paper 2: 1991 summary data component* (p. 27). Gaithersburg, MD: Author.

TABLE 2-11 Number of Child Abuse Victims, by State and Response to Abuse: 1991

State	Victims Removed from Home	Court Action Initiated	Receiving Additional Services Number of Victims	Receiving Additional Services Number of Families	Died from Abuse or Neglect
Alabama	426	—	—	5,011	17
Alaska	826	740	1,489	—	1
Arizona	—	—	4,003	2,405	14
Arkansas	—	1,264	9,551	4,145	7
California	—	—	—	—	100
Colorado	—	—	—	—	28
Connecticut	2,213	—	—	—	11
Delaware	—	—	—	2,183	5
District of Columbia	665	502	—	—	—
Florida	9,441	18,338	41,490	24,052	65
Georgia	—	6,147	—	9,192	6
Hawaii	—	—	—	—	5
Idaho	630	2,651	3,276	766	5
Illinois	7,320	—	—	—	74
Indiana	7,809	5,826	—	—	50
Iowa	633	1,842	—	3,712	9
Kansas	—	—	765	419	4
Kentucky	1,928	4,560	—	31,605	22
Louisiana	2,615	2,615	—	3,607	35
Maine	834	—	—	1,237	1
Maryland	—	—	—	5,011	38
Massachusetts	3,596	—	25,864	15,229	9
Michigan	3,798	8,700	9,500	5,750	—
Minnesota	2,364	2,497	8,707	5,627	10
Mississippi	1,436	2,337	—	6,595	25
Missouri	3,432	4,189	13,360	9,918	31
Montana	731	—	—	—	9
Nebraska	1,560	—	—	—	4
Nevada	—	737	—	3,588	7
New Hampshire	—	583	564	345	—
New Jersey	467	—	13,376	—	18
New Mexico	—	—	—	—	6
New York	—	—	101,555	67,703	72
North Carolina	1,895	2,391	—	—	13
North Dakota	—	264	—	5,552	—
Ohio	1,867	5,074	93,012	—	76
Oklahoma	—	1,682	—	—	38
Oregon	2,620	—	—	—	13
Pennsylvania	4,459	259	6,824	5,165	60
Rhode Island	840	—	—	—	8
South Carolina	2,250	—	—	7,927	22
South Dakota	1,127	411	—	—	1
Tennessee	—	—	—	—	—
Texas	5,232	6,070	24,942	15,483	93
Utah	1,163	1,257	—	—	12
Vermont	302	855	823	652	2
Virginia	1,834	3,349	648	—	34
Washington	—	—	—	—	—
West Virginia	—	—	—	2,401	—
Wisconsin	2,302	4,386	8,865	—	17
Wyoming	—	—	—	—	3
Total	78,666	89,626	368,641	245,307	1,081
No. reporting	33	28	20	28	45
CONUS	—	1,149	9,079	—	31
OCONUS	—	51	2,005	—	3

Notes: CONUS = Armed services in the continental United States; OCONUS = Armed services outside the continental United States; — = not available.

Source: Adapted from U.S. Department of Health and Human Services, National Center on Child Abuse and Neglect. (1993). *National child abuse and neglect data system working paper 2: 1991 summary data component* (p. 19). Gaithersburg, MD: Author.

TABLE 2-12 Child Abuse and Neglect-Related Fatalities, by State: 1985 to 1992

State	1985	1986	1987	1988	1989	1990	1991	1992
Alabama[a]	—	—	—	—	—	14	17	—
Alaska	—	—	1	1	1	0	2	0
Arizona[a]	—	—	—	13	14	14	12	13
Arkansas	9	6	5	10	14	9	7	10
California	18	27	83	120	97	78	100	69[b]
Colorado	12	18	18	26	23	31	30	32[b]
Connecticut	6	9	—	6	6	17	11	10
Delaware	2	1	—	1	4	1	3	—
District of Columbia	—	2	5	9	—	—	—	—
Florida[a]	—	47	43	48	47	53	50	44
Georgia	—	—	—	4	5	12	13	—
Hawaii	1	1	2	2	7	2	5	3
Idaho	5	3	6	3	6	4	6	3
Illinois	53	79	54	98	102	75	92	75[b]
Indiana	29	38	17	27	29	52	48	49
Iowa	9	7	14	13	9	9	15	9[b]
Kansas	9	12	12	7	6	10	4	6
Kentucky	10	9	16	15	8	20	17	24
Louisiana	50	57	30	31	20	28	36	25[b]
Maine	0	1	3	1	—	6	6	5
Maryland	8	17	23	20	29	16	38	31
Massachusetts	13	15	13	25	13	16	9	—
Michigan	11	15	—	—	—	—	—	—
Minnesota	6	10	7	9	13	14	13	—
Mississippi	—	7	14	10	14	12	24	13[b]
Missouri	25	18	19	28	20	26	40	46
Montana[a]	2	3	7	2	6	7	8	5
Nebraska	2	2	2	5	1	2	4	2
Nevada	6	4	7	5	—	1	7	—
New Hampshire	—	—	—	—	—	—	—	—
New Jersey	21	12	26	34	30	38	17	17[b]
New Mexico[a]	10	7	11	8	13	8	6	4
New York[a]	63[b]	126[b]	102[b]	125	106	105[b]	106[b]	—
North Carolina	4	3	6	6	7	30	30	51
North Dakota	0	0	1	0	1	0	0	0
Ohio	37	50	75	—	61	52	76	81
Oklahoma	16	24	31	23	25	18	38	20
Oregon	8	18	24	17	19	14	14	27
Pennsylvania[a]	34	44	44	40	55	58	60	—
Rhode Island	5	4	4	0	—	4	8	7
South Carolina	21	25	13	11	14	21	21	28[b]
South Dakota	4	2	10	2	1	2	1	2
Tennessee	—	—	—	—	—	—	—	—
Texas	113	129	97	77	94	112	97	103
Utah	8	3	4	5	12	12	10	17
Vermont	1	1	2	0	0	0	2	0
Virginia	14	14	27	25	34	28	34	32
Washington	27	37	24	21	8	8	16	—
West Virginia	—	—	—	—	3	1	3	—
Wisconsin	10	9	18	11	23	16	17	—
Wyoming	3	3	0	5	3	4	2	6
Total fatalities	685	919	920	949	1003	1060	1176	869
Total projected fatalities nationwide	805	1014	1074	1093	1103	1143	1255	1261
Rate per 100,000 children	1.3	1.6	1.68	1.71	1.72	1.78	1.93	1.94
Percentage change from previous year	—	23.1	5.0	1.8	0.6	3.5	8.4	0.5

Note: — = not available.

Source: Adapted with permission from McCurdy, K., & Daro, D. (1993). *Current trends in child abuse reporting and fatalities: The results of the 1992 annual fifty state survey* (pp. 14–15). Chicago: National Committee for the Prevention of Child Abuse.

[a]States collect data on deaths due only to abuse.

[b]Some cases pending; numbers not final.

glect were no strangers to the public authorities. Over one-third had had contact with child protective services agencies.

Poverty, Educational Achievement, and Substance Abuse

Tables 2-14 through 2-20 provide historical information on a number of factors involved in assessing "the state of the child." The number of children living with one parent or with a never-married parent increased steadily (Table 2-14). Out-of-wedlock births (Table 2-15) and teenage pregnancy (Table 2-16) have also increased over the years. The percentage of children living in poverty has increased since 1974, although not greatly (Table 2-17). Their numbers, however, are high and are the basis for the commonly held

TABLE 2-13 **Characteristics of Child Abuse Fatalities: 1990 to 1992**

Characteristic	1990		1991		1992		Total
	n	%	n	%	n	%	%
Prior or current contact with child protective services	25	33	26	35	24	38	35
Deaths due to neglect	32	38	32	37	23	36	37
Deaths due to abuse	32	57	32	60	23	58	58
Deaths due to neglect and abuse	32	5	32	3	23	6	5
Deaths of children under five years	32	88	33	90	26	84	87
Deaths of children under one year	30	45	33	50	25	43	46
Deaths involving parental substance abuse	13	15	13	17	11	25	19

Source: Adapted with permission from McCurdy, K., & Daro, D. (1993). *Current trends in child abuse reporting and fatalities: The results of the 1992 annual fifty state survey* (p. 17). Chicago: National Committee for the Prevention of Child Abuse.

TABLE 2-14 **Living Arrangements of Children under Age 18: Selected Years, 1960 to 1991 (Numbers in thousands)**

Arrangement	1960	1970	1980	1990	1991
Total in population	63,727	69,162	63,427	64,137	65,093
Living with one parent	5,829	8,199	12,466	15,867	16,624
Percent of all children	9.1	11.9	19.7	24.7	25.5
Living with never-married parent	243	557	1,820	4,853	5,568
Percent of all children	0.4	0.8	2.9	7.6	8.6

Source: Adapted from Committee on Ways and Means, U.S. House of Representatives. (1993). *Overview of entitlement programs: 1993 greenbook* (p. 1110). Washington, DC: U.S. Government Printing Office.

belief that children are the most disadvantaged segment of American society.

Calculating the U.S. infant mortality rate by race leads to two different conclusions: The rate for white children is comparable to those of industrialized countries with the best social services systems, but the rate for black children is comparable to that of a former Eastern bloc country—Hungary (Table 2-18). The high school dropout rate has increased modestly but steadily (Table 2-19) and average SAT scores have dropped (Table 2-20) since the late 1960s.

Suicide and Homicide

Another significant indicator of children's well-being is suicide. Wright (1993) noted that the suicide rate among 15- to 24-year-olds almost tripled between 1950 and 1990, from 4.5 per 100,000 in 1950 to 13.2 per 100,000, or almost 31,000, in 1990. During the same period, the rates for most age groups either declined or stayed approximately the same. Only the rate for young adults ages 25 to 34 increased as significantly. Homicide rates for various age groups are provided in Table 2-6.

TABLE 2-15 Out-of-Wedlock Births per 1,000 Population: 1980 and 1990

Age	1980	1990	Percent Change, 1980–90
Under 15	9,024	10,675	18.3
15 to 19	262,777	349,970	33.2
20 to 24	237,265	403,873	70.2
25 to 29	99,583	229,991	131.0
30 to 34	40,984	118,200	188.4
35 to 39	13,187	44,149	234.8
40 and over	2,927	8,526	191.3

Source: Adapted from Committee on Ways and Means, U.S. House of Representatives. (1993). *Overview of entitlement programs: 1993 greenbook* (p. 1110). Washington, DC: U.S. Government Printing Office.

TABLE 2-16 Teenage Pregnancies and Outcomes: Selected Years, 1973 to 1990

Pregnancies and Outcomes	1973	1980	1985	1989	1990
Female population (ages 15 to 19)	10,193,000	10,413,000	9,174,000	8,840,000	8,709,000
Pregnancies	980,600	1,145,941	980,685	—	—
Births	604,096	552,161	467,485	506,503	521,826
Legal abortions	232,440	444,780	399,200	—	—
Estimated miscarriages	144,060	149,000	114,000	—	—

Note: — = not available.

Source: Adapted from Committee on Ways and Means, U.S. House of Representatives. (1993). *Overview of entitlement programs: 1993 greenbook* (p. 1110). Washington, DC: U.S. Government Printing Office.

TABLE 2-17 **Children Living below the Poverty Level: Selected Years, 1974 to 1991 (Numbers in thousands)**

Race	1974 No.	1974 Rate	1979 No.	1979 Rate	1989 No.	1989 Rate	1990 No.	1990 Rate	1991 No.	1991 Rate
Total	10,156	15.4	10,377	16.4	12,590	19.6	13,431	20.6	14,341	21.8
Black	3,755	39.8	3,833	41.2	4,375	43.7	4,550	44.8	4,755	45.9
White	6,223	11.2	6,193	11.8	7,599	14.8	8,232	15.9	8,848	16.8
Hispanic	—	—	1,535	28.0	2,603	36.2	2,865	38.4	3,944	40.4

Note: — = not available.

Source: Adapted from Committee on Ways and Means, U.S. House of Representatives. (1993). *Overview of entitlement programs: 1993 greenbook* (p. 1110). Washington, DC: U.S. Government Printing Office.

TABLE 2-18 **International Infant Mortality Rates per 1,000 Live Births: Selected Years, 1950–52 to 1986–88**

Country	1950–52	1970–72	1980–82	1986–88
Japan	55.9	12.4	7.1	5.0
Sweden	20.9	11.0	6.9	6.0
Canada	39.4	17.8	9.7	7.5
United States (white)	26.0	17.1	10.5	8.7
England and Wales	29.1	17.7	11.3	9.3
United States (total)	28.7	19.2	12.0	10.1
Hungary	77.0	34.7	21.4	17.4
United States (black)	45.1	30.9	20.3	17.8

Source: Adapted from Committee on Ways and Means, U.S. House of Representatives. (1993). *Overview of entitlement programs: 1993 greenbook* (p. 1110). Washington, DC: U.S. Government Printing Office.

TABLE 2-19 **Percentage of High School Dropouts Ages 18–24, by Race: Selected Years, 1968 to 1992**

Race	1968	1980	1985	1990	1992
Total	19.1	15.6	13.9	13.6	14.2
White	17.3	14.4	13.5	13.5	14.2
Black	33.0	23.5	17.6	15.1	15.6

Source: Adapted from Committee on Ways and Means, U.S. House of Representatives. (1993). *Overview of entitlement programs: 1993 greenbook* (p. 1110). Washington, DC: U.S. Government Printing Office.

TABLE 2-20 **Average SAT (Scholastic Aptitude Test) Scores: Selected Years, 1967 to 1992**

Test	1967	1975	1985	1991	1992
Verbal	468	434	431	422	423
Math	492	472	475	474	478

Source: Adapted from Committee on Ways and Means, U.S. House of Representatives. (1993). *Overview of entitlement programs: 1993 greenbook* (p. 1110). Washington, DC: U.S. Government Printing Office.

Children with Special Needs

Social workers provide services for children with activity limitations, delays in growth or development, and severe behavioral problems. Children who have been involved in special education programs also have special needs that social workers, among other professionals, address. Table 2-21 shows the percentage of children with delays in growth or development, learning disabilities, or severe emotional problems. Table 2-22 shows the numbers of children who were treated for or received special education for disabilities in federally supported programs for disabled people.

Substitute Care

One of the most important services provided to children in need of protection is foster care.

TABLE 2-21 **Percentages of Children Who Ever Had a Delay in Growth or Development, a Learning Disability, or an Emotional Problem that Lasted Three or More Months or Required Psychological Help, by Age and Selected Characteristics: 1988**

Characteristic	All Ages 3–17 Years	3–5 Years	6–11 Years	12–17 Years
All children	19.5	9.5	19.1	25.2
Sex				
Male	22.9	10.5	22.8	29.2
Female	16.0	8.5	15.4	20.8
Race				
White	20.7	10.0	20.3	26.7
Black	14.9	5.0	14.8	19.5
Hispanic origin				
Hispanic	17.2	8.5	19.6	19.2
Non-Hispanic	19.9	9.7	19.1	25.8
Family income				
Less than $10,000	22.8	11.5	23.8	28.6
$10,000–$24,999	21.0	10.1	21.3	27.3
$25,000–$39,999	19.5	11.3	17.6	26.0
$40,000 or more	18.6	6.8	18.0	24.1
Place of residence				
Metropolitan statistical area	19.6	8.5	19.5	25.4
Central city	18.7	8.0	19.2	24.1
Not central city	20.1	8.9	19.6	26.1
Not metropolitan statistical area	19.4	12.3	17.9	24.6
Assessed health status				
Excellent, very good, or good	19.1	8.9	18.7	24.8
Fair or poor	35.3	25.7	35.7	39.3
Mother's education				
Less than 12 years	20.3	10.2	18.4	26.2
12 years	19.0	11.2	18.8	23.2
More than 12 years	19.3	7.3	19.4	26.3
Family structure				
Biological mother and father	14.6	8.1	14.4	19.2
Biological mother and stepfather	29.6	14.4	27.0	34.5
Biological mother only	24.8	11.7	24.5	31.4
All other	28.2	13.5	29.7	31.4

Source: Reprinted from Zill, N., & Schoenborn, C. A. (1990). Developmental, learning, and emotional problems. In *Health of our nation's children, United States, 1988: Advance data* (No. 190, p. 15). Washington, DC: U.S. Government Printing Office.

TABLE 2-22 Children Ages 0 to 21 Served in Federally Supported Programs for Disabled People, by Type of Disability: 1976–77 to 1990–91

Type of Disability	1976–77	1979–80	1980–81	1981–82	1982–83	1983–84	1984–85	1985–86	1986–87	1987–88	1988–89	1989–90	1990–91
Number Served, in Thousands[a]													
All disabilities	3,692	4,005	4,142	4,198	4,255	4,298	4,315	4,317	4,374	4,447	4,544	4,641	4,771
Specific learning disabilities	796	1,276	1,462	1,622	1,741	1,806	1,832	1,862	1,914	1,928	1,987	2,050	2,130
Speech or language impairments	1,302	1,186	1,168	1,135	1,131	1,128	1,126	1,125	1,136	953	967	973	987
Mental retardation	959	869	829	786	757	727	694	660	643	582	564	548	536
Serious emotional disturbance	283	329	346	339	352	361	372	375	383	373	376	381	391
Hearing impairments	87	80	79	75	73	72	69	66	65	56	56	57	58
Orthopedic impairments	87	66	58	58	57	56	56	57	57	47	47	48	58
Other health impairments	141	106	98	79	50	53	68	57	52	45	43	52	49
Visual impairments	38	31	31	29	28	29	28	27	26	22	23	22	23
Multiple disabilities	—	60	68	71	63	65	69	86	97	77	85	86	96
Deaf–blindness	—	2	3	2	2	2	2	2	2	1	2	2	1
Preschool disabled[b]	c	c	c	c	c	c	c	c	c	363	394	422	445
Percentage Distribution of Children Served													
All disabilities	100.0	100.0	100.0	100.0	100.0	100.0	100.0	100.0	100.0	100.0	100.0	100.0	100.0
Specific learning disabilities	21.6	31.9	35.3	38.6	40.9	42.0	42.4	43.1	43.8	43.4	43.6	44.2	44.6
Speech or language impairments	35.3	29.6	28.2	27.0	26.6	26.2	26.1	26.1	26.0	21.4	21.1	21.0	20.7
Mental retardation	26.0	21.7	20.0	18.7	17.8	16.9	16.1	15.3	14.7	13.1	12.7	11.8	11.2
Serious emotional disturbance	7.7	8.2	8.4	8.1	8.3	8.4	8.6	8.7	8.8	8.4	8.3	8.2	8.2
Hearing impairments	2.4	2.0	1.9	1.8	1.7	1.7	1.6	1.5	1.5	1.3	1.3	1.2	1.2
Orthopedic impairments	2.4	1.6	1.4	1.4	1.3	1.3	1.3	1.3	1.3	1.1	1.0	1.2	1.2
Other health impairments	3.8	2.6	2.4	1.9	1.2	1.2	1.6	1.3	1.2	1.0	1.0	1.1	1.0
Visual impairments	1.0	0.8	0.7	0.7	0.7	0.7	0.7	0.6	0.6	0.5	0.5	0.5	0.5
Multiple disabilities	—	1.5	1.6	1.7	1.5	1.5	1.6	2.0	2.2	1.7	1.8	1.9	2.0
Deaf–blindness	—	d	d	d	d	d	d	d	d	d	d	d	d
Preschool disabled[b]	c	c	c	c	c	c	c	c	c	8.2	8.7	9.1	9.3
Percentage of Total Enrollment[e]													
All disabilities	8.33	9.62	10.13	10.47	10.75	10.95	11.00	10.95	11.00	11.11	11.30	11.44	11.57
Specific learning disabilities	1.80	3.06	3.58	4.05	4.40	4.60	4.67	4.72	4.81	4.82	4.94	5.06	5.17
Speech or language impairments	2.94	2.85	2.86	2.83	2.86	2.87	2.87	2.85	2.86	2.38	2.41	2.40	2.39
Mental retardation	2.16	2.09	2.03	1.96	1.91	1.85	1.77	1.68	1.62	1.45	1.40	1.35	1.30

Serious emotional disturbance	0.64	0.79	0.85	0.85	0.89	0.92	0.95	0.95	0.96	0.93	0.94	0.94	0.95
Hearing impairments	0.20	0.19	0.19	0.19	0.18	0.18	0.18	0.17	0.16	0.14	0.14	0.14	0.14
Orthopedic impairments	0.20	0.16	0.14	0.14	0.14	0.14	0.14	0.14	0.14	0.12	0.11	0.12	0.12
Other health impairments	0.32	0.25	0.24	0.20	0.13	0.13	0.17	0.14	0.13	0.11	0.11	0.13	0.13
Visual impairments	0.09	0.08	0.08	0.07	0.07	0.07	0.07	0.07	0.07	0.05	0.06	0.06	0.06
Multiple disabilities	—	0.14	0.17	0.18	0.16	0.17	0.17	0.22	0.24	0.19	0.21	0.21	0.23
Deaf-blindness	c	0.01	c	f	0.01	0.01	f	0.01	f	f	f	f	f
Preschool disabled[b]	c	c	c	c	c	c	c	c	c	0.91	0.98	1.04	1.08

Notes: Increases since 1987–88 are due in part to new legislation enacted in fall 1986 that mandates public school special education services for all handicapped children ages 3 through 5. Because of rounding, details may not add to totals. — = not available.

Source: Adapted from U.S. Department of Education, National Center for Education Statistics. (1993). *Digest of education statistics* (p. 65). Washington, DC: Author.

[a] Includes students served under Chapter 1 and Individuals with Disabilities Education Act (IDEA), formerly the Education of the Handicapped Act.
[b] Includes preschool children aged 3–5 years and 0–5 years served under Chapter 1 and IDEA, respectively.
[c] Prior to 1987–88, states are no longer required to report preschool handicapped children by handicapping condition. Beginning in 1987–88, these students were included in the counts by handicapping condition.
[d] Less than 0.05.
[e] Figures are based on the enrollment in public schools, kindergarten through 12th grade, including a relatively small number of prekindergarten students.
[f] Less than 0.005.

Figure 2-8 shows the foster care population per 1,000 children from 1982 to 1992. The data, reported by Tatara (1993b), come from the U.S. Bureau of the Census and the American Public Welfare Association. The historical reason for the "substitute care" of children, a term that encompasses foster care, institutional care, and adoptions, was the fact that many children were orphans. This is no longer the case. According to the U.S. Bureau of the Census (1990), only 3.3 percent of the child population, or 221,300 children, were orphans in 1988, and less than one-tenth of 1 percent of all children had lost both parents. Therefore, the reasons for substitute care are more typically the inability or unsuitability of parents to care for their children or the adoption of children by relatives or by one biological parent's spouse.

FIGURE 2-8 **Trends in the U.S. Child Substitute Care Population, 1982 to 1992 (Numbers in thousands)**

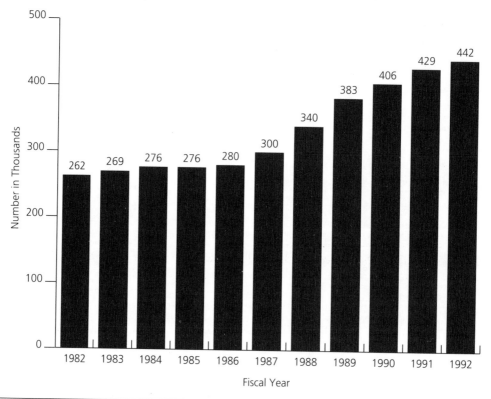

Notes: Figures for fiscal years 1982 through 1990 are final; figures for fiscal years 1991 and 1992 are tentative.

Source: Adapted with permission from Tatara, T. (1993). *Voluntary cooperative information system research notes no. 9* (p. 3). Washington, DC: American Public Welfare Association.

According to Tatara (1993b), the substitute care population did not change appreciably from 1982 through 1986. However, between 1986 and 1990, there were significant increases. Although there was continued growth from 1990 through 1992, the rate of increase declined. Table 2-23 and Figure 2-9 show the numbers of children entering and leaving the substitute care system from 1982 to 1992, and

Table 2-24 and Figure 2-10 show entry and exit rates in the same years. The substitute care entry rate is the proportion of children who entered care as part of the total number served by the substitute care system. The exit rate is the proportion who left substitute care as part of the total number served by the substitute care system. The entry rate is calculated by dividing the number who entered care by the

TABLE 2-23 **Number of Children Entering and Leaving the Substitute Care System: 1982 to 1992 (Numbers in thousands)**

Fiscal Year	Substitute Care Entries	Substitute Care Exits	Difference
1982	161	172	−11
1983	184	178	+ 6
1984	184	180	+ 4
1985	190	184	+ 6
1986	183	176	+ 6
1987	222	202	+20
1988	199	171	+28
1989	222	182	+40
1990	245	202	+43
1991	224	207	+17
1992	238	217	+21

Source: Adapted with permission from Tatara, T. (1993). *Voluntary cooperative information system research notes no. 9* (p. 5). Washington, DC: American Public Welfare Association.

FIGURE 2-9 **Trends in National Child Substitute Care Entries and Exits, 1982 to 1992**

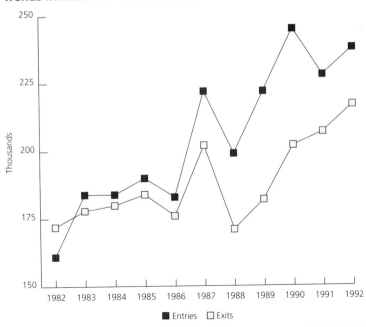

Notes: Figures for fiscal years 1982 through 1990 are final; figures for fiscal years 1991 and 1992 are tentative.
Source: Adapted with permission from Tatara, T. (1993). *Voluntary cooperative information system research notes no. 9* (p. 4). Washington, DC: American Public Welfare Association.

total number at the beginning of the fiscal year plus the number who entered care. For the exit rate, the number who left care is divided by the number in care when the fiscal year began plus the number who entered care. Tatara attributed the increases to child abuse, substance abuse, poverty, and parental unemployment. It is clear that for recent years, the numbers leaving have not kept pace with those entering the system, increasing the overall numbers in substitute care.

Financing Children's Services

Adequate funding for children's services is a priority for social workers and other groups that advocate improving services for children. However, identifying the specific expenditures for children is difficult, because they come

TABLE 2-24 **Entry and Exit Rates of Children in the Substitute Care System: 1982 to 1992**

Fiscal Year	Entry Rate	Exit Rate
1982	0.371	0.396
1983	0.412	0.398
1984	0.404	0.395
1985	0.413	0.400
1986	0.401	0.386
1987	0.442	0.402
1988	0.389	0.335
1989	0.393	0.322
1990	0.403	0.332
1991	0.352	0.325
1992	0.361	0.329

Source: Adapted with permission from Tatara, T. (1993). *Voluntary cooperative information system research notes no. 9* (p. 9). Washington, DC: American Public Welfare Association.

FIGURE 2-10 **Trends in National Child Substitute Care Entry and Exit Rates, 1982 to 1992**

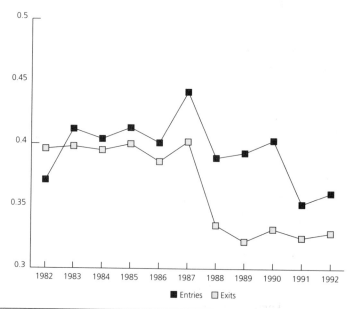

■ Entries □ Exits

Notes: Explanation of rates. Figures for fiscal years 1982 through 1990 are final; figures for fiscal years 1991 and 1992 are tentative.
Source: Adapted with permission from Tatara, T. (1993). *Voluntary cooperative information system research notes no. 9* (p. 7). Washington, DC: American Public Welfare Association.

from a variety of programs that provide other services and that benefit other age groups as well.

Elementary and secondary education is typically the largest single expenditure for state and local governments. Major proportions of all nonfederal taxes are spent on children through the education process. Federal outlays have steadily increased, but the percentage of the federal budget devoted to education declined from 5.39 percent in 1980 to 3.55 percent in 1993. Social services, many of which are devoted to children, declined from 1.04 of the federal budget to 0.93 percent of the federal budget during the same period (U.S. Bureau of the Census, 1993).

Federal expenditures for income security, which also benefit children, declined from 14.64 percent in 1980 to 14.06 percent in 1993. The U.S. Department of Health and Human Services, however, which has a significant role in serving children, grew from 12.92 percent of the budget in 1980 to 19.84 percent in 1993.

It seems clear that there is greater support for children's programs under the Clinton presidency than in other recent administrations. The Child Welfare League of America (Pizzigatti, 1994) reported that the President's budget continued the Child Welfare Services Program at its current level, in addition to adding a $150 million program for family preservation and family support services. Several other child-oriented programs were also created, maintained, or enhanced in the budget proposal.

Child Welfare Organizations

Several organizations work as advocates for children in the United States. Some are sources of the data presented here. The federal and state documents used also rely on these organizations. The most visible organizations are the American Humane Association (and its American Association for Protecting Children), the Children's Defense Fund, the National Committee for the Prevention of Child Abuse, and the Child Welfare League of America. There is also the National Committee for Adoption, as well as a variety of other specialized children's advocacy groups for preschool children; for training child welfare workers; for developmentally disabled children and their families; for children with other special conditions, such as autism, cerebral palsy, and physical handicaps; and for education. Statistical and other kinds of information is often available from the state and national offices of such groups. Several members of the Clinton administration, including First Lady Hillary Clinton, have been involved in child advocacy organizations, especially the Children's Defense Fund.

Conclusion

The plight of children, perhaps the most disadvantaged Americans, will become increasingly severe as the development of services continues to lag behind the development of social problems and needs. As other chapters in this book indicate, welfare programs have declined in recent years when calculated in constant dollars. The consequence is that children who are on the edge of disadvantage go over because the services they require are not available. Statistics on children in the United States point to the need for much stronger efforts if the social health of children is to improve.

3

CRIME, CORRECTIONS, AND DELINQUENCY

Among the social issues of increasing concern in the United States are crime and delinquency and the societal approaches for dealing with them. This chapter includes detailed information on the crime rate, which has fluctuated over the years and is currently lower than it has been in recent years, and on the kinds of offenses defined as part of the crime index.

The chapter includes information on victims of crime, another growing concern of U.S. society. Many states have been developing and operating programs to assist crime victims.

Issues related to crime are important to social workers and other human services professionals for a number of reasons. As chapter 9 shows, many social workers are employed in the criminal justice system in prisons, as probation and parole officers, as employees of family and juvenile courts, as juvenile workers in public agencies, and as corrections planners and administrators. Clinical social workers are often hired to evaluate people facing trial and may testify at those trials. Social workers are also engaged in the operation of community residential facilities that include adult and youth offenders and parolees. Clinical social workers routinely treat clients affected by such crimes as illegal drug use, drunk driving, and domestic violence. As criminal justice issues become more important in the United States, it is likely that increasing numbers of social workers will be employed directly or indirectly in this field.

Crime in the United States

The Federal Bureau of Investigation (FBI) defines the extent of crime through its index crimes, which are analyzed by its Uniform Crime Reporting Program. This program re-

ceives monthly and annual reports from law enforcement agencies throughout the United States representing 98 percent of the population. The index crimes are murder and nonnegligent manslaughter, forcible rape, robbery, burglary, larceny, and motor vehicle theft. The rates reflect the occurrences of these crimes per 100,000 people. Crime statistics are also developed through the National Crime Survey, which surveys crime victims and is conducted by the Bureau of Justice Statistics. The National Crime Survey obtains information on both reported and unreported crimes.

Table 3-1 shows historical trends in the crime index from 1973, when the crime rate was 4,154.4 per 100,000 people, through 1992, when the rate was 5,660.2. From 1991 to 1992, the total number of crimes dropped 2.9 percent and the crime rate dropped 4.0 percent. From 1988 until 1992, the number of crimes committed increased 3.7 percent, but the crime rate fell 0.1 percent during the same period. During the 20-year period, there was a percentage increase of 19.2 and a rate increase of 9.4 percent.

Figure 3-1 shows the percentage distribution of crime index offenses for 1992. The occurrence of larceny and theft, by far the largest category, has remained constant since the 1989 data, published in the first edition of the *Almanac*, so have aggravated assault, motor vehicle theft, and forcible rape. During the same period, the percentage distribution of murder declined from 1 percent to less than 0.2 percent. Robbery grew by nearly 1 percent, and burglary declined by 1 percent.

In late 1993 the FBI reported a 5 percent drop in violent crime during the first half of that year compared with the same period in 1992 (Bayles, 1993). However, the incidence

TABLE 3-1 **Crime Index Offenses: 1973 to 1992**

Year	Population[a]	Crime Index Total[b]	Violent Crime[c]	Property Crime[d]	Murder and Nonnegligent Manslaughter	Forcible Rape	Robbery	Aggravated Assault	Burglary	Larceny–Theft	Motor Vehicle Theft
				Number of Offenses							
1973	209,851,000	8,718,100	875,910	7,842,200	19,640	51,400	384,220	420,650	2,565,500	4,347,900	928,800
1974	211,392,000	10,253,400	974,720	9,278,700	20,710	55,400	442,400	456,210	3,039,200	5,262,500	977,100
1975	213,124,000	11,292,400	1,039,710	10,252,700	20,510	56,090	470,500	492,620	3,265,300	5,977,700	1,009,600
1976	214,659,000	11,349,700	1,004,210	10,345,500	18,780	57,080	427,810	500,530	3,108,700	6,270,800	966,000
1977	216,332,000	10,984,500	1,029,580	9,955,000	19,120	63,500	412,610	534,350	3,071,500	5,905,700	977,700
1978	218,059,000	11,209,000	1,085,550	10,123,400	19,560	67,610	426,930	571,460	3,128,300	5,991,000	1,004,100
1979	220,099,000	12,249,500	1,208,030	11,041,500	21,460	76,390	480,700	629,480	3,327,700	6,601,000	1,112,800
1980	225,349,264	13,408,300	1,344,520	12,063,700	23,040	82,990	565,840	672,650	3,795,200	7,136,900	1,131,700
1981	229,146,000	13,423,800	1,361,820	12,061,900	22,520	82,500	592,910	663,900	3,779,700	7,194,400	1,087,800
1982	231,534,000	12,974,400	1,322,390	11,652,000	21,010	78,770	553,130	669,480	3,447,100	7,142,500	1,062,400
1983	233,981,000	12,108,600	1,258,090	10,850,500	19,310	78,920	506,570	653,290	3,129,900	6,712,800	1,007,900
1984	236,158,000	11,881,800	1,273,280	10,608,500	18,690	84,230	485,010	685,350	2,984,400	6,591,900	1,032,200
1985	238,740,000	12,431,400	1,328,800	11,102,600	18,980	88,670	497,870	723,250	3,073,300	6,926,400	1,102,900
1986	241,077,000	13,211,900	1,489,170	11,722,700	20,610	91,460	542,780	834,320	3,241,400	7,257,200	1,224,100
1987	243,400,000	13,508,700	1,484,000	12,024,700	20,100	91,110	517,700	855,090	3,236,200	7,499,900	1,288,700
1988	245,807,000	13,923,100	1,566,220	12,356,900	20,680	92,490	542,970	910,090	3,218,100	7,705,900	1,432,900
1989	248,239,000	14,251,400	1,646,040	12,605,400	21,500	94,500	578,330	951,710	3,168,200	7,872,400	1,564,800
1990	248,709,873	14,475,600	1,820,130	12,655,500	23,440	102,560	639,270	1,054,860	3,073,900	7,945,700	1,635,900
1991	252,177,000	14,872,900	1,911,770	12,961,100	24,700	106,590	687,730	1,092,740	3,157,200	8,142,200	1,661,700
1992	255,082,000	14,438,200	1,932,270	12,505,900	23,760	109,060	672,480	1,126,970	2,979,900	7,915,200	1,610,800
1991–1992, percent change		−2.9	+1.1	−3.5	−3.8	+2.3	−2.2	+3.1	−5.6	−2.8	−3.1
1988–1992, percent change		+3.7	+23.4	+1.2	+14.9	+17.9	+23.9	+23.8	−7.4	+2.7	+12.4
1983–1992, percent change		+19.2	+53.6	+15.3	+23.0	+38.2	+32.8	+72.5	−4.8	+17.9	+59.8
				Rate per 100,000 Inhabitants							
1973		4,154.4	417.4	3,737.0	9.4	24.5	183.1	200.5	1,222.5	2,071.9	442.6
1974		4,850.4	461.1	4,389.3	9.8	26.2	209.3	215.8	1,437.7	2,489.5	462.2
1975		5,298.5	487.8	4,810.7	9.6	26.3	220.8	231.1	1,532.1	2,804.8	473.7
1976		5,287.3	467.8	4,819.5	8.8	26.6	199.3	233.2	1,448.2	2,921.3	450.0
1977		5,077.6	475.9	4,601.7	8.8	29.4	190.7	247.0	1,419.8	2,729.9	451.9
1978		5,140.3	497.8	4,642.5	9.0	31.0	195.8	262.1	1,434.6	2,747.4	460.5
1979		5,565.5	548.9	5,016.6	9.7	34.7	218.4	286.0	1,511.9	2,999.1	505.6
1980		5,950.0	596.6	5,353.3	10.2	36.8	251.1	298.5	1,684.1	3,167.0	502.2
1981		5,858.2	594.3	5,263.9	9.8	36.0	258.7	289.7	1,649.5	3,139.7	474.7

Continued on next page

TABLE 3-1 Continued

Year	Population[a]	Crime Index Total[b]	Violent Crime[c]	Property Crime[d]	Murder and Nonnegligent Manslaughter	Forcible Rape	Robbery	Aggravated Assault	Burglary	Larceny–Theft	Motor Vehicle Theft
1982		5,603.6	571.1	5,032.5	9.1	34.0	238.9	289.2	1,488.8	3,084.8	458.8
1983		5,175.0	537.7	4,637.4	8.3	33.7	216.5	279.2	1,337.7	2,868.9	430.8
1984		5,031.3	539.2	4,492.1	7.9	35.7	205.4	290.2	1,263.7	2,791.3	437.1
1985		5,207.1	556.6	4,650.5	7.9	37.1	208.5	302.9	1,287.3	2,901.2	462.0
1986		5,480.4	617.7	4,862.6	8.6	37.9	225.1	346.1	1,344.6	3,010.3	507.8
1987		5,550.0	609.7	4,940.3	8.3	37.4	212.7	351.3	1,329.6	3,081.3	529.4
1988		5,664.2	637.2	5,027.1	8.4	37.6	220.9	370.2	1,309.2	3,134.9	582.9
1989		5,741.0	663.1	5,077.9	8.7	38.1	233.0	383.4	1,276.3	3,171.3	630.4
1990		5,820.3	731.8	5,088.5	9.4	41.2	257.0	424.1	1,235.9	3,194.8	657.8
1991		5,897.8	758.1	5,139.7	9.8	42.3	272.7	433.3	1,252.0	3,228.8	659.0
1992		5,660.2	757.5	4,902.7	9.3	42.8	263.6	441.8	1,168.2	3,103.0	631.5
1991–1992, percent change		-4.0	-.1	-4.6	-5.1	+1.2	-3.3	+2.0	-6.7	-3.9	-4.2
1988–1992, percent change		-.1	+18.9	-2.5	+10.7	+13.8	+19.3	+19.3	-10.8	-1.0	+8.3
1983–1992, percent change		+9.4	+40.9	+5.7	+12.0	+27.0	+21.8	+58.2	-12.7	+8.2	+46.6

Note: Although arson data are included in the trend and clearance tables, sufficient data are not available to estimate totals for this offense.

Source: Reprinted from Federal Bureau of Investigation. (1993). *Crime in the United States, 1992* (p. 58). Washington, DC: Author.

[a] U.S. Bureau of the Census provisional estimates as of July 1, except 1980 and 1990 (the decennial census counts).

[b] Because of rounding, the offenses may not add to totals.

[c] Violent crimes are offenses of murder, forcible rape, robbery, and aggravated assault.

[d] Property crimes are offenses of burglary, larceny–theft, and motor vehicle theft.

of violent crime, especially the youth murder rate, is the subject of much public concern, as is discussed later in this chapter.

Federal government statisticians (Federal Bureau of Investigation, 1993) estimated a "crime clock" for 1992:

- one crime index offense every two seconds
- one violent crime every 22 seconds
- one murder every 22 minutes
- one forcible rape every five minutes
- one robbery every 47 seconds
- one aggravated assault every 28 seconds
- one property crime every three seconds
- one burglary every 11 seconds
- one larceny–theft every four seconds
- one motor vehicle theft every 20 seconds (p. 4).

These estimates do not imply that crimes occur at regular intervals; rather, they indicate the ratio of the occurrence of certain crimes to fixed periods of time.

Table 3-2 shows the crime rates for 1992 by state. In 1992, Washington, DC, had the highest crime rate in the nation: 11,407 crimes per 100,000 people. West Virginia had the lowest overall crime rate (2,609.7 crimes per 100,000 people), although North Dakota had the lowest rate of violent crime. As a region, the Midwest has the lowest rate of violent crimes, such as aggravated assault, forcible rape, murder, and robbery; the largest rate of such crimes occurs in the West.

Although the statistics do not show dramatic yearly increases in the crime rate (in some years it has declined), there is greater public attention to crime, partly because of coverage by newspapers, radio, and television. Violent crimes make good stories, particularly for the electronic media. Coverage of crime has been expanded in recent years because of the increase in television "magazine" programs such as *20–20* and *Dateline*. Television has extensively covered certain murder cases, such as that of media personality and athlete O. J. Simpson's alleged murder of his former wife and her friend. The number and sales of tabloid newspapers, which often feature crimes, have increased.

The absolute number of crimes has certainly increased over the years. There are more crimes to report, more criminals to arrest, more people in prisons, and more victims. Even so, the rate of crime, which allows for the increase in population, has remained steady.

FIGURE 3-1 **Percentage Distribution of Crime Index Offenses: 1992**

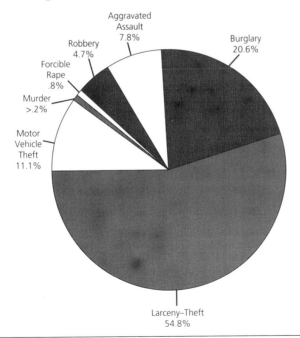

Note: Arson, also an index offense, is not included, so the percentages do not total 100.

Source: Adapted from Federal Bureau of Investigation. (1993). *Crime in the United States, 1992* (p. 8). Washington, DC: Author.

TABLE 3-2 **Crime Index, by State: 1992**

State	Population	Crime Index Total	Violent Crime[a]	Property Crime[b]	Murder and Nonnegligent Manslaughter	Forcible Rape	Robbery	Aggravated Assault	Burglary	Larceny–Theft	Motor Vehicle Theft
Alabama											
Metropolitan statistical areas	2,774,796	175,698	28,816	146,882	373	1,359	6,140	20,944	38,797	94,859	13,226
Cities outside metropolitan areas	572,282	31,821	5,639	26,182	45	208	573	4,813	6,237	18,773	1,172
Rural	788,922	10,370	1,597	8,773	37	137	106	1,317	4,019	4,169	585
Total	4,136,000	217,889	36,052	181,837	455	1,704	6,819	27,074	49,053	117,801	14,983
Rate per 100,000 inhabitants		5,268.1	871.7	4,396.4	11.0	41.2	164.9	654.6	1,186.0	2,848.2	362.3
Alaska											
Metropolitan statistical areas	241,565	17,045	1,971	15,074	17	253	484	1,217	2,650	10,813	1,611
Cities outside metropolitan areas	153,096	8,369	1,016	7,353	9	140	113	754	853	5,789	711
Rural	192,339	7,279	890	6,389	18	186	43	643	1,667	4,126	596
Total	587,000	32,693	3,877	28,816	44	579	640	2,614	5,170	20,728	2,918
Rate per 100,000 inhabitants		5,569.5	660.5	4,909.0	7.5	98.6	109.0	445.3	880.7	3,531.2	497.1
Arizona											
Metropolitan statistical areas	3,250,143	246,754	23,660	223,094	288	1,516	5,632	16,224	49,686	143,200	30,208
Cities outside metropolitan areas	293,000	17,718	1,319	16,399	11	85	218	1,005	2,905	12,531	963
Rural	288,857	4,863	727	4,136	13	46	17	651	1,504	2,322	310
Total	3,832,000	269,335	25,706	243,629	312	1,647	5,867	17,880	54,095	158,053	31,481
Rate per 100,000 inhabitants		7,028.6	670.8	6,357.8	8.1	43.0	153.1	466.6	1,411.7	4,124.6	821.5
Arkansas											
Metropolitan statistical areas	1,061,493	72,946	9,718	63,228	119	655	2,284	6,660	15,303	42,120	5,805
Cities outside metropolitan areas	520,832	29,277	3,004	26,273	69	192	635	2,108	6,878	18,039	1,356
Rural	816,675	12,010	1,109	10,901	71	143	92	803	4,033	6,129	739
Total	2,399,000	114,233	13,831	100,402	259	990	3,011	9,571	26,214	66,288	7,900
Rate per 100,000 inhabitants		4,761.7	576.5	4,185.2	10.8	41.3	125.5	399.0	1,092.7	2,763.2	329.3
California											
Metropolitan statistical areas	29,630,870	2,006,065	339,310	1,666,755	3,848	12,305	130,191	192,966	413,103	936,659	316,993
Cities outside metropolitan areas	538,451	34,580	3,597	30,983	33	243	516	2,805	7,408	21,507	2,068
Rural	697,679	21,116	2,717	18,399	40	213	190	2,274	6,980	10,368	1,051
Total	30,867,000	2,061,761	345,624	1,716,137	3,921	12,761	130,897	198,045	427,491	968,534	320,112
Rate per 100,000 inhabitants		6,679.5	1,119.7	5,559.8	12.7	41.3	424.1	641.6	1,384.9	3,137.8	1,037.1
Colorado											
Metropolitan statistical areas	2,821,939	175,610	18,110	157,500	182	1,485	4,038	12,405	32,915	108,027	16,558
Cities outside metropolitan areas	299,462	21,148	1,289	19,859	15	127	103	1,044	2,851	16,303	705
Rural	348,599	10,012	687	9,325	19	29	39	600	2,087	6,839	399
Total	3,470,000	206,770	20,086	186,684	216	1,641	4,180	14,049	37,853	131,169	17,662
Rate per 100,000 inhabitants		5,958.8	578.8	5,379.9	6.2	47.3	120.5	404.9	1,090.9	3,780.1	509.0
Connecticut											
Metropolitan statistical areas	3,026,682	159,736	15,651	144,085	160	834	6,847	7,810	34,797	86,038	23,250
Cities outside metropolitan areas	66,274	2,518	98	2,420	3	12	30	53	549	1,718	153
Rural	188,044	3,533	503	3,030	3	38	41	421	1,026	1,707	297

State/Area	Population	Crime Index total	Violent crime	Property crime	Murder and nonnegligent manslaughter	Forcible rape	Robbery	Aggravated assault	Burglary	Larceny-theft	Motor vehicle theft
Total	3,281,000	165,787	16,252	149,535	166	884	6,918	8,284	36,372	89,463	23,700
Rate per 100,000 inhabitants		5,052.9	495.3	4,557.6	5.1	26.9	210.9	252.5	1,108.6	2,726.7	722.3
Delaware											
Metropolitan statistical areas	575,611	28,211	3,453	24,758	26	455	959	2,013	5,327	17,434	1,997
Cities outside metropolitan areas	28,013	2,095	263	1,832	4	26	45	188	289	1,501	42
Rural	85,376	3,100	564	2,536	2	110	38	414	982	1,484	70
Total	689,000	33,406	4,280	29,126	32	591	1,042	2,615	6,598	20,419	2,109
Rate per 100,000 inhabitants		4,848.5	621.2	4,227.3	4.6	85.8	151.2	379.5	957.6	2,963.6	306.1
District of Columbia[c]											
Metropolitan statistical area	589,000	67,187	16,685	50,502	443	215	7,459	8,568	10,721	30,663	9,118
Cities outside metropolitan area	NA										
Rural	NA										
Total	589,000	67,187	16,685	50,502	443	215	7,459	8,568	10,721	30,663	9,118
Rate per 100,000 inhabitants		11,407.0	2,832.8	8,574.2	75.2	36.5	1,266.4	1,454.7	1,820.2	5,205.9	1,548.0
Florida											
Metropolitan statistical areas	12,418,935	1,075,004	155,451	919,553	1,140	6,801	48,347	99,163	240,810	569,904	108,839
Cities outside metropolitan areas	232,573	19,071	2,463	16,608	18	93	552	1,800	4,047	11,586	975
Rural	836,492	33,285	4,913	28,372	50	416	583	3,864	9,898	16,603	1,871
Total	13,488,000	1,127,360	162,827	964,533	1,208	7,310	49,482	104,827	254,755	598,093	111,685
Rate per 100,000 inhabitants		8,358.2	1,207.2	7,151.0	9.0	54.2	366.9	777.2	1,888.8	4,434.3	828.0
Georgia											
Metropolitan statistical areas	4,554,910	339,851	37,941	301,910	564	2,422	14,861	20,094	74,104	193,330	34,476
Cities outside metropolitan areas	829,275	57,073	7,143	49,930	76	347	1,550	5,170	11,862	35,860	2,208
Rural	1,366,815	35,506	4,412	31,094	101	288	452	3,571	11,436	17,429	2,229
Total	6,751,000	432,430	49,496	382,934	741	3,057	16,863	28,835	97,402	246,619	38,913
Rate per 100,000 inhabitants		6,405.4	733.2	5,672.3	11.0	45.3	249.8	427.1	1,442.8	3,653.1	576.4
Hawaii											
Metropolitan statistical areas	875,297	53,558	2,382	51,176	31	326	1,013	1,012	9,106	38,563	3,507
Cities outside metropolitan areas	38,785	2,757	109	2,648	1	18	23	67	569	1,960	119
Rural	245,918	14,584	507	14,077	10	96	115	286	3,331	10,021	725
Total	1,160,000	70,899	2,998	67,901	42	440	1,151	1,365	13,006	50,544	4,351
Rate per 100,000 inhabitants		6,112.0	258.4	5,853.5	3.6	37.9	99.2	117.7	1,121.2	4,357.2	375.1
Idaho											
Metropolitan statistical areas	313,650	15,103	1,040	14,063	10	144	126	760	2,754	10,698	611
Cities outside metropolitan areas	364,198	19,967	1,309	18,658	13	115	73	1,108	3,092	14,845	721
Rural	389,152	7,569	654	6,915	14	80	30	530	2,088	4,480	347
Total	1,067,000	42,639	3,003	39,636	37	339	229	2,398	7,934	30,023	1,679
Rate per 100,000 inhabitants		3,996.2	281.4	3,714.7	3.5	31.8	21.5	224.7	743.6	2,813.8	157.4
Illinois[d]											
Metropolitan statistical areas	9,753,210			508,237	1,279		47,398	57,857	112,917	324,986	70,334
Cities outside metropolitan areas	948,182			37,163	24		512	1,725	8,108	27,916	1,139
Rural	929,608			11,500	19		63	475	4,281	6,716	503
Total	11,631,000	670,564	113,664	556,900	1,322	4,312	47,973	60,057	125,306	359,618	71,976
Rate per 100,000 inhabitants		5,765.3	977.3	4,788.1	11.4	37.1	412.5	516.4	1,077.3	3,091.9	618.8

Continued on next page

TABLE 3-2 Continued

State	Population	Crime Index Total	Violent Crime[a]	Property Crime[b]	Murder and Nonnegligent Manslaughter	Forcible Rape	Robbery	Aggravated Assault	Burglary	Larceny–Theft	Motor Vehicle Theft
Indiana											
Metropolitan statistical areas	4,047,261	217,137	24,007	193,130	342	1,997	6,366	15,302	42,814	127,351	22,965
Cities outside metropolitan areas	564,780	28,552	2,270	26,282	24	186	433	1,627	5,153	19,717	1,412
Rural	1,049,959	19,686	2,514	17,172	98	215	122	2,079	5,940	10,113	1,119
Total	5,662,000	265,375	28,791	236,584	454	2,398	6,921	19,008	53,907	157,181	25,496
Rate per 100,000 inhabitants		4,686.9	508.5	4,178.5	8.2	42.4	122.2	335.7	952.1	2,776.1	450.3
Iowa											
Metropolitan statistical areas	1,215,362	70,263	5,815	64,448	28	378	962	4,447	12,995	48,560	2,893
Cities outside metropolitan areas	691,763	29,862	1,468	28,394	5	81	132	1,250	4,948	22,385	1,061
Rural	904,875	11,150	533	10,617	11	69	19	434	3,254	6,843	520
Total	2,812,000	111,275	7,816	103,459	44	528	1,113	6,131	21,197	77,788	4,474
Rate per 100,000 inhabitants		3,957.1	278.0	3,679.2	1.6	18.8	39.6	218.0	753.8	2,766.3	159.1
Kansas											
Metropolitan statistical areas	1,359,013	89,826	9,511	80,315	123	729	2,984	5,675	21,969	51,643	6,703
Cities outside metropolitan areas	699,606	35,845	2,602	33,243	21	235	253	2,093	7,628	24,478	1,137
Rural	464,381	8,551	775	7,776	7	78	40	650	3,042	4,405	329
Total	2,523,000	134,222	12,888	121,334	151	1,042	3,277	8,418	32,639	80,526	8,169
Rate per 100,000 inhabitants		5,319.9	510.8	4,809.1	6.0	41.3	129.9	333.7	1,293.7	3,191.7	323.8
Kentucky											
Metropolitan statistical areas	1,730,279	80,684	11,592	69,092	96	628	2,672	8,196	16,759	46,618	5,715
Cities outside metropolitan areas	613,298	24,540	3,974	20,566	26	164	449	3,335	4,712	14,709	1,145
Rural	1,411,423	19,575	4,541	15,034	94	417	152	3,878	5,907	7,859	1,268
Total	3,755,000	124,799	20,107	104,692	216	1,209	3,273	15,409	27,378	69,186	8,128
Rate per 100,000 inhabitants		3,323.5	535.5	2,788.1	5.8	32.2	87.2	410.4	729.1	1,842.5	216.5
Louisiana											
Metropolitan statistical areas	3,103,502	240,845	35,971	204,874	617	1,514	11,230	22,610	49,653	129,547	25,674
Cities outside metropolitan areas	368,742	22,249	2,813	19,436	64	111	276	2,362	4,762	14,034	640
Rural	814,756	17,553	3,425	14,128	66	188	130	3,041	4,159	9,357	612
Total	4,287,000	280,647	42,209	238,438	747	1,813	11,636	28,013	58,574	152,938	26,926
Rate per 100,000 inhabitants		6,546.5	984.6	5,561.9	17.4	42.3	271.4	653.4	1,366.3	3,567.5	628.1
Maine											
Metropolitan statistical areas	455,621	20,638	884	19,754	10	131	207	536	4,599	14,239	916
Cities outside metropolitan areas	447,012	16,484	443	16,041	5	92	49	297	2,893	12,583	565
Rural	332,367	6,394	289	6,105	6	71	32	180	2,664	3,144	297
Total	1,235,000	43,516	1,616	41,900	21	294	288	1,013	10,156	29,966	1,778
Rate per 100,000 inhabitants		3,523.6	130.9	3,392.7	1.7	23.8	23.3	82.0	822.3	2,426.4	144.0
Maryland											
Metropolitan statistical areas	4,556,384	289,457	46,833	242,624	577	2,118	20,713	23,425	51,834	155,737	35,053
Cities outside metropolitan areas	87,892	9,096	1,136	7,960	10	63	233	830	1,770	5,913	277

	Population	Crime Index total	Violent crime	Property crime	Murder and nonnegligent manslaughter	Forcible rape	Robbery	Aggravated assault	Burglary	Larceny-theft	Motor vehicle theft
Rural	263,724	6,950	1,116	5,834	9	97	108	902	1,916	3,594	324
Total	4,908,000	305,503	49,085	256,418	596	2,278	21,054	25,157	55,520	165,244	35,654
Rate per 100,000 inhabitants		6,224.6	1,000.1	5,224.5	12.1	46.4	429.0	512.6	1,131.2	3,366.8	726.4
Massachusetts											
Metropolitan statistical areas	5,711,721	286,162	44,892	241,270	209	2,042	10,967	31,674	61,251	133,576	46,443
Cities outside metropolitan areas	274,132	13,792	1,805	11,987	4	122	90	1,589	3,039	7,995	953
Rural	12,147	117	30	87	1	2	2	25	28	39	20
Total	5,998,000	300,071	46,727	253,344	214	2,166	11,059	33,288	64,318	141,610	47,416
Rate per 100,000 inhabitants		5,002.9	779.0	4,223.8	3.6	36.1	184.4	555.0	1,072.3	2,361.0	790.5
Michigan											
Metropolitan statistical areas	7,814,215	477,389	68,496	408,893	902	6,063	20,703	40,828	85,290	266,334	57,269
Cities outside metropolitan areas	609,655	23,778	1,512	22,266	6	394	105	1,007	3,184	18,349	733
Rural	1,013,130	28,305	2,664	25,641	30	1,093	94	1,447	9,783	14,803	1,055
Total	9,437,000	529,472	72,672	456,800	938	7,550	20,902	43,282	98,257	299,486	59,057
Rate per 100,000 inhabitants		5,610.6	770.1	4,840.5	9.9	80.0	221.5	458.6	1,041.2	3,173.5	625.8
Minnesota											
Metropolitan statistical areas	3,084,463	163,193	13,371	149,822	122	1,527	4,819	6,903	30,890	105,427	13,505
Cities outside metropolitan areas	521,812	24,319	889	23,430	9	159	63	658	3,163	19,089	1,178
Rural	873,725	18,152	884	17,268	19	154	24	687	5,806	10,234	1,228
Total	4,480,000	205,664	15,144	190,520	150	1,840	4,906	8,248	39,859	134,750	15,911
Rate per 100,000 inhabitants		4,590.7	338.0	4,252.7	3.3	41.1	109.5	184.1	889.7	3,007.8	355.2
Mississippi											
Metropolitan statistical areas	788,148	53,952	5,090	48,862	132	631	1,993	2,334	15,715	27,207	5,940
Cities outside metropolitan areas	677,944	46,886	4,120	42,766	122	334	1,066	2,598	13,188	27,374	2,204
Rural	1,147,908	11,106	1,553	9,553	66	201	195	1,091	4,630	4,270	653
Total	2,614,000	111,944	10,763	101,181	320	1,166	3,254	6,023	33,533	58,851	8,797
Rate per 100,000 inhabitants		4,282.5	411.7	3,870.7	12.2	44.6	124.5	230.4	1,282.8	2,251.4	336.5
Missouri											
Metropolitan statistical areas	3,542,676	227,766	34,968	192,798	487	1,591	11,454	21,436	47,602	120,774	24,422
Cities outside metropolitan areas	481,073	23,854	1,933	21,921	24	146	262	1,501	4,355	16,696	870
Rural	1,169,251	13,074	1,547	11,527	36	158	67	1,286	5,170	5,818	539
Total	5,193,000	264,694	38,448	226,246	547	1,895	11,783	24,223	57,127	143,288	25,831
Rate per 100,000 inhabitants		5,097.1	740.4	4,356.7	10.5	36.5	226.9	466.5	1,100.1	2,759.3	497.4
Montana											
Metropolitan statistical areas	197,220	12,898	330	12,568	2	60	131	137	1,910	9,962	696
Cities outside metropolitan areas	202,389	13,497	468	13,029	4	73	60	331	1,199	11,321	509
Rural	424,391	11,477	602	10,875	18	77	31	476	2,197	7,960	718
Total	824,000	37,872	1,400	36,472	24	210	222	944	5,306	29,243	1,923
Rate per 100,000 inhabitants		4,596.1	169.9	4,426.2	2.9	25.5	26.9	114.6	643.9	3,548.9	233.4
Nebraska											
Metropolitan statistical areas	801,259	46,465	4,767	41,698	52	354	825	3,536	7,317	31,957	2,424
Cities outside metropolitan areas	383,075	16,629	557	16,072	11	91	74	381	2,518	13,019	535
Rural	421,666	6,350	274	6,076	5	59	12	198	1,642	4,168	266
Total	1,606,000	69,444	5,598	63,846	68	504	911	4,115	11,477	49,144	3,225

Continued on next page

TABLE 3-2 Continued

State	Population	Crime Index Total	Violent Crime[a]	Property Crime[b]	Murder and Nonnegligent Manslaughter	Forcible Rape	Robbery	Aggravated Assault	Burglary	Larceny–Theft	Motor Vehicle Theft
Rate per 100,000 inhabitants		4,324.0	348.6	3,975.5	4.2	31.4	56.7	256.2	714.6	3,060.0	200.8
Nevada											
Metropolitan statistical areas	1,119,523	74,494	8,286	66,208	135	760	4,324	3,067	15,123	42,183	8,902
Cities outside metropolitan areas	40,106	2,808	187	2,621	4	34	28	121	784	1,682	155
Rural	167,371	5,022	774	4,248	6	39	45	684	1,201	2,849	198
Total	1,327,000	82,324	9,247	73,077	145	833	4,397	3,872	17,108	46,714	9,255
Rate per 100,000 inhabitants		6,203.8	696.8	5,506.9	10.9	62.8	331.3	291.8	1,289.2	3,520.3	697.4
New Hampshire											
Metropolitan statistical areas	656,359	21,729	791	20,938	14	209	290	278	4,518	14,636	1,784
Cities outside metropolitan areas	323,835	11,626	510	11,116	1	181	72	254	2,054	8,710	352
Rural	130,806	870	96	774	1	34	5	56	337	408	29
Total	1,111,000	34,225	1,397	32,828	18	424	367	588	6,909	23,754	2,165
Rate per 100,000 inhabitants		3,080.6	125.7	2,954.8	1.6	38.2	33.0	52.9	621.9	2,138.1	194.9
New Jersey											
Metropolitan statistical areas	7,789,000	394,463	48,745	345,718	397	2,392	22,216	23,740	75,508	206,686	63,524
Cities outside metropolitan areas	NA										
Rural	NA										
Total	7,789,000	394,463	48,745	345,718	397	2,392	22,216	23,740	75,508	206,686	63,524
Rate per 100,000 inhabitants		5,064.4	625.8	4,438.5	5.1	30.7	285.2	304.8	969.4	2,653.6	815.6
New Mexico											
Metropolitan statistical areas	878,392	61,279	8,860	52,419	69	484	1,749	6,558	14,491	33,664	4,264
Cities outside metropolitan areas	411,631	30,923	4,037	26,886	31	292	314	3,400	6,341	19,446	1,099
Rural	290,977	9,521	1,884	7,637	41	214	139	1,490	3,064	3,962	611
Total	1,581,000	101,723	14,781	86,942	141	990	2,202	11,448	23,896	57,072	5,974
Rate per 100,000 inhabitants		6,434.1	934.9	5,499.2	8.9	62.6	139.3	724.1	1,511.4	3,609.9	377.9
New York											
Metropolitan statistical areas	16,634,346	1,014,910	199,122	815,788	2,355	4,814	107,791	84,162	182,436	465,550	167,802
Cities outside metropolitan areas	649,460	26,287	2,216	24,071	16	164	266	1,770	4,469	19,019	583
Rural	835,194	20,292	1,973	18,319	26	174	97	1,676	6,643	11,139	537
Total	18,119,000	1,061,489	203,311	858,178	2,397	5,152	108,154	87,608	193,548	495,708	168,922
Rate per 100,000 inhabitants		5,858.4	1,122.1	4,736.3	13.2	28.4	596.9	483.5	1,068.2	2,735.8	932.3
North Carolina											
Metropolitan statistical areas	4,463,505	296,062	35,611	260,451	486	1,936	10,967	22,222	81,027	164,659	14,765
Cities outside metropolitan areas	701,605	59,848	7,064	52,784	84	247	1,392	5,341	14,422	35,922	2,440
Rural	1,677,890	41,137	3,925	37,212	153	272	425	3,075	17,668	17,136	2,408
Total	6,843,000	397,047	46,600	350,447	723	2,455	12,784	30,638	113,117	217,717	19,613
Rate per 100,000 inhabitants		5,802.2	681.0	5,121.2	10.6	35.9	186.8	447.7	1,653.0	3,181.6	286.6
North Dakota											
Metropolitan statistical areas	256,342	11,147	393	10,754	9	94	42	248	1,298	8,863	593
Cities outside metropolitan areas	146,416	5,033	87	4,946	1	34	6	46	563	4,185	198

	Population	Violent crime	Property crime	Murder	Forcible rape	Robbery	Aggravated assault	Burglary	Larceny-theft	Motor vehicle theft
Rural	233,242	2,285	2,235	2	20	2	26	626	1,450	159
Total	636,000	18,465	17,935	12	148	50	320	2,487	14,498	950
Rate per 100,000 inhabitants		2,903.3	2,820.0	1.9	23.3	7.9	50.3	391.0	2,279.6	149.4
Ohio										
Metropolitan statistical areas	8,963,351	459,625	405,529	662	5,212	21,403	26,819	93,443	262,591	49,495
Cities outside metropolitan areas	744,925	35,659	33,183	35	323	412	1,706	5,368	26,418	1,397
Rural	1,307,724	18,668	17,305	27	204	110	1,022	5,546	10,765	994
Total	11,016,000	513,952	456,017	724	5,739	21,925	29,547	104,357	299,774	51,886
Rate per 100,000 inhabitants		4,665.5	4,139.6	6.6	52.1	199.0	268.2	947.3	2,721.3	471.0
Oklahoma										
Metropolitan statistical areas	1,909,683	129,471	114,055	133	1,197	3,897	10,189	30,890	68,829	14,336
Cities outside metropolitan areas	669,873	34,554	30,892	42	279	429	2,912	8,670	20,559	1,663
Rural	632,444	10,439	9,512	35	80	50	762	4,118	4,792	602
Total	3,212,000	174,464	154,459	210	1,556	4,376	13,863	43,678	94,180	16,601
Rate per 100,000 inhabitants		5,431.6	4,808.8	6.5	48.4	136.2	431.6	1,359.8	2,932.1	516.8
Oregon										
Metropolitan statistical areas	2,078,296	132,743	119,661	105	1,215	4,136	7,626	24,635	81,198	13,828
Cities outside metropolitan areas	414,028	28,079	26,857	16	168	293	745	4,529	21,090	1,238
Rural	484,676	12,467	11,582	18	197	78	592	3,781	6,986	815
Total	2,977,000	173,289	158,100	139	1,580	4,507	8,963	32,945	109,274	15,881
Rate per 100,000 inhabitants		5,820.9	5,310.7	4.7	53.1	151.4	301.1	1,106.7	3,670.6	533.5
Pennsylvania										
Metropolitan statistical areas	10,199,167	369,358	321,201	687	2,929	21,370	23,171	65,792	201,405	54,004
Cities outside metropolitan areas	761,568	21,909	19,940	15	145	213	1,596	3,500	15,446	994
Rural	1,048,265	16,164	15,014	44	250	118	738	6,542	7,299	1,173
Total	12,009,000	407,431	356,155	746	3,324	21,701	25,505	75,834	224,150	56,171
Rate per 100,000 inhabitants		3,392.7	2,965.7	6.2	27.7	180.7	212.4	631.5	1,866.5	467.7
Rhode Island										
Metropolitan statistical areas	922,685	42,147	38,573	35	293	909	2,337	9,688	21,624	7,261
Cities outside metropolitan areas	82,315	3,836	3,451	1	18	41	325	837	2,413	201
Rural	—	26	20	0	0	0	6	4	15	1
Total	1,005,000	46,009	42,044	36	311	950	2,668	10,529	24,052	7,463
Rate per 100,000 inhabitants		4,578.0	4,183.5	3.6	30.9	94.5	265.5	1,047.7	2,393.2	742.6
South Carolina										
Metropolitan statistical areas	2,504,995	157,022	133,081	245	1,536	4,805	17,335	35,507	87,645	9,929
Cities outside metropolitan areas	311,957	24,258	19,365	42	169	749	3,933	4,877	13,576	912
Rural	786,048	31,047	25,852	86	367	594	4,148	9,285	14,965	1,602
Total	3,603,000	212,327	178,298	373	2,072	6,148	25,436	49,669	116,186	12,443
Rate per 100,000 inhabitants		5,893.1	4,948.6	10.4	57.5	170.6	706.0	1,378.5	3,224.7	345.4
South Dakota										
Metropolitan statistical areas	226,940	10,022	9,133	0	220	84	585	1,496	7,313	324
Cities outside metropolitan areas	190,433	7,824	7,570	0	62	20	172	1,321	5,997	252
Rural	293,627	3,476	3,236	4	86	16	134	1,032	2,061	143
Total	711,000	21,322	19,939	4	368	120	891	15,371	15,371	719
Rate per 100,000 inhabitants		2,998.9	2,804.4	0.6	51.8	16.9	125.3	541.4	2,161.9	101.1

Continued on next page

TABLE 3-2 **Continued**

State	Population	Crime Index Total	Violent Crime[a]	Property Crime[b]	Murder and Nonnegligent Manslaughter	Forcible Rape	Robbery	Aggravated Assault	Burglary	Larceny–Theft	Motor Vehicle Theft
Tennessee											
Metropolitan statistical areas	3,312,984	211,710	32,349	179,361	423	2,120	10,467	19,339	50,655	102,795	25,911
Cities outside metropolitan areas	590,449	28,405	3,164	25,241	34	128	387	2,615	5,893	17,799	1,549
Rural	1,120,567	17,906	1,974	15,932	63	129	110	1,672	7,117	7,340	1,475
Total	5,024,000	258,021	37,487	220,534	520	2,377	10,964	23,626	63,665	127,934	28,935
Rate per 100,000 inhabitants		5,135.8	746.2	4,389.6	10.4	47.3	218.2	470.3	1,267.2	2,546.5	575.9
Texas											
Metropolitan statistical areas	14,719,612	1,142,157	129,867	1,012,290	2,020	8,618	43,510	75,719	240,573	630,902	140,815
Cities outside metropolitan areas	1,320,218	71,314	8,837	62,477	95	480	859	7,403	15,947	43,814	2,716
Rural	1,616,170	32,677	3,665	29,012	124	339	219	2,983	12,408	15,064	1,540
Total	17,656,000	1,246,148	142,369	1,103,779	2,239	9,437	44,588	86,105	268,928	689,780	145,071
Rate per 100,000 inhabitants		7,057.9	806.3	6,251.6	12.7	53.4	252.5	487.7	1,523.2	3,906.8	821.7
Utah											
Metropolitan statistical areas	1,405,774	87,069	4,623	82,446	43	705	959	2,916	13,463	65,299	3,684
Cities outside metropolitan areas	204,306	11,092	325	10,767	1	53	39	232	1,529	8,822	416
Rural	202,920	4,428	319	4,109	10	65	16	228	1,053	2,843	213
Total	1,813,000	102,589	5,267	97,322	54	823	1,014	3,376	16,045	76,964	4,313
Rate per 100,000 inhabitants		5,658.5	290.5	5,368.0	3.0	45.4	55.9	186.2	885.0	4,245.1	237.9
Vermont											
Metropolitan statistical areas	114,157	7,198	171	7,027	5	51	24	91	1,276	5,513	238
Cities outside metropolitan areas	198,438	6,826	228	6,598	1	45	18	164	1,275	5,127	196
Rural	257,405	5,413	225	5,188	6	46	9	164	2,155	2,867	166
Total	570,000	19,437	624	18,813	12	142	51	419	4,706	13,507	600
Rate per 100,000 inhabitants		3,410.0	109.5	3,300.5	2.1	24.9	8.9	73.5	825.6	2,369.6	105.3
Virginia											
Metropolitan statistical areas	4,919,458	240,181	20,926	219,255	474	1,708	8,448	10,296	37,967	163,239	18,049
Cities outside metropolitan areas	412,205	17,311	1,334	15,977	18	101	187	1,028	2,604	12,789	584
Rural	1,045,337	16,626	1,647	14,979	72	199	152	1,224	4,646	9,478	855
Total	6,377,000	274,118	23,907	250,211	564	2,008	8,787	12,548	45,217	185,506	19,488
Rate per 100,000 inhabitants		4,298.5	374.9	3,923.6	8.8	31.5	137.8	196.8	709.1	2,909.0	305.6
Washington											
Metropolitan statistical areas	4,170,036	265,000	23,903	241,097	214	2,902	6,682	14,105	47,301	172,392	21,404
Cities outside metropolitan areas	491,452	37,617	2,444	35,173	20	512	430	1,482	5,844	27,254	2,075
Rural	474,512	14,418	1,107	13,311	24	283	66	734	4,467	8,109	735
Total	5,136,000	317,035	27,454	289,581	258	3,697	7,178	16,321	57,612	207,755	24,214
Rate per 100,000 inhabitants		6,172.8	534.5	5,638.3	5.0	72.0	139.8	317.8	1,121.7	4,045.1	471.5
West Virginia											
Metropolitan statistical areas	755,237	26,951	2,294	24,657	56	237	607	1,394	6,006	17,030	1,621
Cities outside metropolitan areas	277,769	9,028	497	8,531	18	52	98	329	1,543	6,673	315

Rural	778,994	11,309	1,042	10,267	41	104	83	814	3,738	5,497	1,032
Total	1,812,000	47,288	3,833	43,455	115	393	788	2,537	11,287	29,200	2,968
Rate per 100,000 inhabitants		2,609.7	211.5	2,398.2	6.3	21.7	43.5	140.0	622.9	1,611.5	163.8
Wisconsin											
Metropolitan statistical areas	3,410,573	169,869	11,825	158,044	191	1,076	5,848	4,710	25,730	112,438	19,876
Cities outside metropolitan areas	599,604	29,239	1,006	28,233	8	130	121	747	3,184	24,147	902
Rural	996,823	17,146	975	16,171	19	109	28	819	5,731	9,613	827
Total	5,007,000	216,254	13,806	202,448	218	1,315	5,997	6,276	34,645	146,198	21,605
Rate per 100,000 inhabitants		4,319.0	275.7	4,043.3	4.4	26.3	119.8	125.3	691.9	2,919.9	431.5
Wyoming											
Metropolitan statistical areas	138,105	7,743	531	7,212	6	63	32	430	1,136	5,817	259
Cities outside metropolitan areas	203,811	10,899	680	10,219	6	75	41	558	1,336	8,544	339
Rural	124,084	2,678	278	2,400	5	25	11	237	655	1,642	103
Total	466,000	21,320	1,489	19,831	17	163	84	1,225	3,127	16,003	701
Rate per 100,000 inhabitants		4,575.1	319.5	4,255.6	3.6	35.0	18.0	262.9	671.0	3,434.1	150.4

Notes: Totals are based on estimates extrapolated from areas actually reporting, which vary by state. Although arson data were included in the trend and clearance tables, sufficient data are not available to estimate totals for this offense. — = not available.

Source: Reprinted from U.S. Department of Justice. (1993). *Sourcebook of criminal justice statistics, 1992* (pp. 68–78). Washington, DC: U.S. Government Printing Office.

[a]Violent crimes are offenses of murder, forcible rape, robbery, and aggravated assault.

[b]Property crimes are offenses of burglary, larceny–theft, and motor vehicle theft.

[c]Includes offenses reported by the Zoological Police.

[d]Forcible rape figures furnished by the state-level Uniform Crime Reporting (UCR) Program administered by the Illinois Department of State Police were not in accordance with national UCR guidelines. The 1992 forcible rape totals for Illinois were estimated using the national rate of forcible rapes when grouped by like agencies. Therefore, only the state total is shown.

Unfortunately, crimes are underreported to law enforcement authorities, perhaps in part because victims believe that the crimes are too small to pursue or that they will not be compensated. The National Crime Survey found in 1991 that only 59 percent of rapes, 55 percent of robberies, 47 percent of assaults, 28 percent of personal robberies without contact, 50 percent of household burglaries, and 74 percent of motor vehicle thefts were reported to police (U.S. Bureau of the Census, 1993). It is also possible that police agencies do not pursue the investigation or prosecution of smaller (especially nonviolent) crimes. Therefore, the crime rate may well be rising, but the increase may not be reflected in the crime-index statistics.

Criminal Justice Expenditures

Figure 3-2 shows the breakdown of the $74 billion spent on criminal justice in 1990. Thirty-four percent of the funds were spent on corrections, over 43 percent went for police protection, and 13 percent was spent on the court system. The balance was for legal services (7 percent), public defense (2 percent), and other justice activities (1 percent).

Metropolitan and Nonmetropolitan Crime

Crime is not as common in rural areas as it is in metropolitan areas, and the crime rate is not as high. Statistics reflect this fact in a number of ways. First, crime rates are lower in states that have large nonmetropolitan populations than in those that are largely metropolitan. The crime rate in Washington, DC, is so high partly because it is totally metropolitan; there are no rural areas to dilute its crime rate. Rural states such as West Virginia, North Dakota, and South Dakota have low crime rates.

Second, crime rates in nonmetropolitan areas are lower than their proportion of the population. For example, some 4 percent of California's population lives in nonmetropolitan areas, but only 3 percent of all crimes in the state were committed in those areas in 1992. Florida's nonmetropolitan population was 10 percent, but its nonmetropolitan crime rate in 1992 was 6 percent. Likewise, New York had a nonmetropolitan population of 10 percent and a nonmetropolitan crime rate of 5 percent.

Table 3-3 shows the crime rates in cities with populations over 250,000 in 1991. The table also shows firearm-related robberies and assaults in those cities.

FIGURE 3-2 **Criminal Justice System Public Expenditures: 1990**

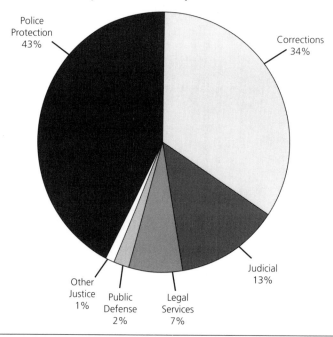

Police Protection 43%

Corrections 34%

Judicial 13%

Other Justice 1%

Public Defense 2%

Legal Services 7%

Note: Total expenditures were $74 billion.

Source: Reprinted from Federal Bureau of Investigation. (1993). *Crime in the United States, 1992* (p. 188). Washington, DC: Author.

TABLE 3-3 Rate per 100,000 Population of Selected Offenses in Cities with a Population of More than 250,000: 1991

City	Violent Crime Rate	Homicide Rate	Rape Rate	Robbery Rate	Robbery Firearm-Related Rate	Assault Rate	Assault Firearm-Related Rate
Albuquerque, NM	1,422.1	13.0	66.4	332.4	162.3	1,010.3	220.3
Anaheim, CA	714.1	9.2	40.8	361.5	119.1	302.6	99.3
Arlington, TX	788.6	9.7	62.1	261.9	104.0	454.9	116.0
Atlanta, GA	4,041.1	50.9	158.3	1,607.4	774.5	2,224.6	707.5
Austin, TX	624.1	10.3	58.0	327.0	103.0	228.8	60.8
Baltimore, MD	2,544.0	40.6	93.7	1,439.6	754.6	970.1	354.8
Birmingham, AL[a]	2,565.0	51.6	103.6	691.0	—	1,718.8	—
Boston, MA	2,066.4	19.7	84.9	835.7	219.2	1,126.0	207.7
Buffalo, NY	1,834.5	15.2	96.9	821.3	169.1	901.2	95.0
Charlotte, NC	2,176.3	28.3	101.6	720.0	309.2	1,326.3	534.0
Chicago, IL[a]	—	32.9	—	1,557.3	—	1,502.3	—
Cincinnati, OH	1,578.2	14.7	130.2	630.6	122.3	802.7	204.8
Cleveland, OH	1,831.9	34.3	179.1	1,006.5	389.7	612.1	216.5
Colorado Springs, CO	480.6	8.7	80.2	134.3	44.4	257.5	138.5
Columbus, OH	1,130.9	21.6	101.8	586.8	275.2	420.7	182.9
Corpus Christi, TX	824.5	12.2	77.6	226.3	53.6	508.5	66.6
Dallas, TX	2,568.3	48.6	117.5	1,094.4	525.8	1,307.8	659.6
Denver, CO	1,049.9	18.4	89.1	341.0	88.0	601.5	224.4
Detroit, MI	2,727.3	59.3	137.7	1,309.4	680.7	1,220.8	539.9
El Paso, TX	1,067.0	9.3	50.3	281.9	73.1	725.4	169.5
Fort Worth, TX	1,949.8	42.7	96.7	749.4	282.6	1,061.1	417.6
Fresno, CA	1,274.4	14.4	78.0	603.5	253.1	578.6	121.7
Honolulu, HA	240.3	3.4	32.1	100.4	6.5	104.4	13.4
Houston, TX	1,599.9	36.5	72.8	833.4	446.0	657.2	245.5
Indianapolis, IN	1,445.1	19.4	114.6	408.9	188.4	902.1	265.8
Jacksonville, FL	1,760.5	19.6	122.1	632.1	333.9	986.7	327.8
Kansas City, MO	2,832.8	30.8	108.9	1,130.8	559.6	1,562.3	825.4
Las Vegas, NV	862.4	15.7	66.0	486.4	218.5	294.3	70.2
Long Beach, CA	2,100.7	21.4	64.8	928.7	325.7	1,085.8	293.6
Los Angeles, CA	2,525.8	28.9	55.3	1,117.9	469.9	1,323.8	360.1
Louisville, KY[a]	827.7	15.9	57.9	459.4	—	294.6	—
Memphis, TN	1,422.3	27.3	105.3	726.5	377.8	563.2	268.6
Mesa, AZ	698.2	5.1	52.9	132.0	55.3	508.2	116.7
Miami, FL	4,252.0	36.4	68.8	2,321.5	609.6	1,825.3	545.2
Milwaukee, WI	978.7	25.6	78.9	668.2	420.7	206.0	146.5
Minneapolis, MN	1,577.5	17.1	199.3	699.2	426.7	661.9	51.4
Nashville, TN	1,574.7	17.3	101.3	522.0	312.8	934.1	325.6
Newark, NJ	3,400.2	31.8	88.2	1,880.9	797.8	1,399.2	298.4
New Orleans, LA	2,190.3	68.9	60.3	1,191.9	789.2	869.2	401.8
New York, NY	2,318.2	29.3	39.3	1,340.3	568.7	909.3	208.3
Norfolk, VA	1,158.3	32.4	77.2	576.5	241.5	472.1	200.1
Oakland, CA	2,495.8	39.2	121.1	1,035.0	360.8	1,300.5	172.4
Oklahoma City, OK	1,128.2	12.5	105.3	333.8	125.2	676.6	305.8
Omaha, NE	956.4	10.3	61.1	187.0	67.0	698.0	205.6
Philadelphia, PA	1,408.0	27.6	56.6	871.9	368.7	451.9	164.7
Phoenix, AZ	1,105.5	12.9	48.2	346.2	122.3	698.3	266.1
Pittsburgh, PA	1,153.2	9.7	80.6	726.2	186.9	336.8	60.4
Portland, OR	1,806.0	11.8	103.2	605.6	174.8	1,085.5	215.0
Sacramento, CA	1,298.5	17.5	58.6	604.7	177.2	617.7	269.7
St. Louis, MO	3,520.2	65.0	85.5	1,324.0	584.2	2,045.7	891.6
St. Paul, MN[a]	990.3	4.4	103.7	308.2	—	574.0	—
San Antonio, TX	792.2	21.8	73.0	395.2	173.7	302.2	142.2
San Diego, CA	1,219.9	14.7	41.6	470.2	124.5	693.3	112.6

Continued on next page

Households Experiencing Crime

Another set of data useful for understanding the distribution and nature of crime in the United States describes the households that experienced crimes in 1992 and some of their characteristics. Table 3-4 shows the percentages of those households by income, region, place of residence, and kind of crime experienced. Urban residents, of course, were most vulnerable to crime. More than one-fourth of all urban households experienced crime in 1992. Household income did not appear to be a significant factor; the percentage of households experiencing crime was roughly the same for all income groups. However, there were differences among income groups in type of crime experienced. For example, families with annual incomes of $50,000 or more were more likely to experience property crimes than were families with annual incomes of less than $25,000. However, high-income families had the lowest percentage of serious violent crimes (rape, robbery, or aggravated assault) and the second lowest percentage (after families with incomes of $15,000 to $24,999) of crimes of high concern (rape, robbery, or assault by a stranger or burglary).

Low-income families face some special problems. They are more likely than other incomes groups to be the victims of violent crimes. They may lose a greater proportion of what they own through property crimes, may have more difficulty replacing stolen vehicles or personal articles, and may not be able to afford insurance coverage.

The larger the household, the greater the probability that it experienced crime in 1992, as Table 3-5 shows, because there are more people against whom a crime can be committed.

In 1992, African American households were more vulnerable to crime than white households. Nearly 10 percent experienced crimes in 1992, compared to some 6 percent of white and other ethnic-group households. African American families were also more likely to have experienced a crime of high concern (rape, robbery, or assault by a stranger or burglary): Some 17 percent of African Americans who were crime victims encountered one of those crimes, compared to 10 percent of white people (Rand, 1993). However, overall, crimes of high concern have declined as a percentage of all crime, from 11 percent in 1981 to 7

TABLE 3-3 **Continued**

City	Violent Crime Rate	Homicide Rate	Rape Rate	Robbery		Assault	
				Rate	Firearm-Related Rate	Rate	Firearm-Related Rate
San Francisco, CA	1,645.4	12.9	54.1	949.9	210.7	628.5	87.0
San Jose, CA	658.5	6.6	55.7	166.3	55.0	429.8	47.8
Santa Ana, CA	1,102.5	19.7	25.3	649.0	263.8	408.5	183.8
Seattle, WA	1,356.3	8.1	74.8	518.6	126.6	754.9	97.7
Tampa, FL	3,606.0	22.3	120.8	1,076.7	451.4	2,386.3	447.9
Toledo, OH	1,038.2	10.7	124.5	538.2	134.0	364.8	104.8
Tucson, AZ	939.3	5.8	80.0	214.3	85.8	639.2	242.3
Tulsa, OK	1,327.9	11.3	111.7	396.2	185.6	808.7	249.5
Virginia Beach, VA	272.2	6.8	31.8	128.2	64.4	105.4	22.8
Washington, DC	2,452.3	80.6	35.8	1,214.9	520.4	1,121.1	311.0
Wichita, KS	872.2	7.8	92.7	458.3	194.2	313.4	110.0

Notes: Firearm-related figures are projections that are based on Uniform Crime Reports supplemental data showing incomplete reports from the cities. — = not available.

Source: Reprinted from U.S. Department of Justice. (1993). *Sourcebook of ciminal justice statistics, 1992* (p. 372). Washington, DC: U.S. Government Printing Office.

[a]Incomplete reports were filed; therefore, certain data were omitted by the source.

TABLE 3-4 **Percentages of Households Experiencing Crime, by Selected Characteristics: 1992**

Crime	Annual Household Income					Place of Residence[a]			Region			
	Under $7,500	$7,500–$14,999	$15,000–$24,999	$25,000–$49,999	$50,000 or more	Urban	Suburban	Rural	Northeast	Midwest	South	West
Any NCVS crime	23.6	21.0	21.6	23.6	25.2	28.1	21.4	16.9	18.0	20.9	23.4	28.5
Violent crime	7.0	5.3	5.1	4.8	4.3	6.4	4.6	3.8	3.8	4.4	5.1	6.9
Rape	.2	.1	.2	.1	.1	.2	.1	.1	.2	.1	.1	.2
Robbery	1.4	1.1	1.0	1.0	.8	1.8	.7	.4	1.0	.7	1.0	1.4
Assault	5.7	4.2	4.2	3.9	3.5	4.7	3.9	3.5	2.9	3.7	4.1	5.8
Aggravated	2.5	1.7	1.5	1.2	1.0	1.9	1.2	1.3	.9	1.2	1.6	2.2
Simple	3.7	2.8	3.1	2.9	2.7	3.1	2.9	2.5	2.2	2.7	2.8	4.0
Total theft	14.8	13.5	14.9	17.3	18.5	19.5	15.0	11.4	11.8	14.3	16.2	21.0
Personal	8.6	7.3	8.5	10.8	13.1	11.4	9.8	6.9	7.7	9.1	9.6	12.7
Household	7.6	7.3	7.6	7.8	6.6	9.7	6.3	5.2	4.8	6.1	7.8	10.1
Burglary	6.1	5.5	3.9	3.4	3.8	5.0	3.8	3.7	2.6	4.2	4.7	5.0
Motor vehicle theft	1.5	1.9	1.9	2.0	2.2	3.2	1.8	.6	2.5	1.5	1.9	2.2
Serious violent crime[b]	3.9	2.9	2.6	2.2	1.9	3.7	2.0	1.8	1.9	2.0	2.7	3.6
Crimes of high concern[c]	9.3	7.8	6.5	6.0	6.4	8.8	6.1	5.3	4.7	6.3	7.2	9.1

Notes: Detail does not add to total because of overlap in households experiencing various crimes. NCVS = National Crime Victimization Survey.

Source: Reprinted from Rand, M. R. (1993). *Crime and the nation's households, 1992: Bureau of Justice Statistics bulletin* (p. 4). Washington, DC: U.S. Department of Justice, Bureau of Justice Statistics.

[a] These estimates are not comparable to estimates for place of residence prior to 1986 because of changes in geographic classification.

[b] Rape, robbery, or aggravated assault.

[c] A rape, robbery, or assault by a stranger or a burglary.

percent in 1989, a figure that held steady through 1991 and 1992 (Rand, 1993).

Victims of Crime

An October 1993 U.S. Department of Justice study (Zawitz et al., 1993) of crime victims from 1973 to 1992 reported that 59 percent of all violent crimes—52 percent of rapes, 84 percent of robberies, and 54 percent of assaults—were committed by strangers. Women were as likely to be the victim of a violent crime by an intimate such as a husband or boyfriend as by an acquaintance or stranger. Men were much more likely to be the victim of crime by an acquaintance or stranger. People who live in cities or suburbs are more likely to be the victims of crimes committed by strangers than are rural residents. Rural dwellers are much more likely to be the victims of crimes committed by a relative or an acquaintance.

Selected Offenses

Forcible Rape and Murder

The number of incidents of forcible rape and the rate per 1,000 people grew significantly from 1990 to 1991, as is shown in Table 3-6. Table 3-7 provides information on the age, gender, and race of murder victims in 1992. Men were more than three times as likely to be murdered as women. African Americans constitute only 13 percent of the population, but more African Americans than white people were murdered in 1992.

Although the overall murder rate is declining, a serious social problem is associated with the rise in the murders of and by youths (Bayles, 1993). Bayles reported that the 465 homicides in Washington, DC, in 1993 represented an increase of only 3 percent over 1992 but that the murders committed by people under 17 years of age had increased 17 percent. There was a drop in murders in Richmond, Virginia, from 120 to 110 from 1992 to 1993. However, the average age of murder suspects dropped from 24 to 20. Although there may be drops in the national murder rate, the increases among young people, especially in the larger cities, are especially disturbing.

TABLE 3-5 **Percentages of Households Touched by Selected Crimes, by Size of Household: 1992**

Crime	Number of People in Household			
	1	2–3	4–5	6+
Any NCVS crime	15.3	21.7	31.6	36.8
Violent crime	2.9	4.4	7.9	12.0
Total theft	9.9	15.1	22.5	26.9
Personal	6.0	9.2	14.3	16.9
Household	4.5	7.0	10.2	12.9
Burglary	3.8	4.0	4.8	6.4
Motor vehicle theft	0.9	2.1	2.9	2.8

Note: NCVS = National Crime Victimization Survey.

Source: Reprinted from Rand, M. R. (1993). *Crime and the nation's households, 1992: Bureau of Justice Statistics bulletin* (p. 5). Washington, DC: U.S. Department of Justice, Bureau of Justice Statistics.

TABLE 3-6 **Increase in Incidents of Forcible Rape: 1990 and 1991**

Criterion	1990	1991	Percentage Increase
No. of victims	130,000	173,000	33.0
Rate of victimization	17.6	19.4	9.7

Note: Increases were statistically significant.

Source: Adapted from Bastian, L. D. (1992). *Criminal victimization 1991: Bureau of Justice Statistics bulletin* (p. 3). Washington, DC: U.S. Department of Justice, Bureau of Justice Statistics.

Drunk Driving

A growing concern in the United States is drunk driving, technically referred to as driving under the influence (DUI) or driving while intoxicated (DWI), which are defined as the operation of a motor vehicle by a driver who has a blood alcohol level above a certain limit. Each state defines the specific concentration of intoxicants in the blood above which a driver may be accused of violating state law.

Many states passed new laws against drunk driving after a federal highway law in 1983 imposed sanctions on states that had legal drinking ages of less than 21 years. By 1989 laws in all states made it illegal for anyone under age 21 to purchase an alcoholic drink, although the age at which people may consume or possess alcohol varies by state.

Table 3-8 shows the numbers of licensed drivers and arrests for drunk driving and the rates of arrest per 100,000 drivers from 1981 through 1989. Although the numbers in all categories fluctuated within a slow growth trend, the percentage increase in arrests is significantly larger than the percentage increase in licensed drivers.

Table 3-9 compares DUI figures in 1980, before the 1983 federal highway law was in effect, and in 1989, when its impact was universal. It shows, among other facts, a significant decline in DUI arrests of young drivers. Part of the reason for raising the minimum drinking age, which had been 18 in several states before the law changed, was to increase the average age of underage drinkers: With a minimum age of 21, underage drinkers tend to be 18 to 20 years old, rather than 16 and 17 as with a drinking age of 18. The data in Table 3-9 appear to support that assumption.

Table 3-10 shows the type and amount of alcohol consumed by those who were convicted of drunk driving in 1989. Those arrested and convicted appear to have consumed large quantities of alcohol. More than three-quarters of those who consumed more than one type of alcohol had consumed seven ounces or more.

Table 3-11 shows the estimated mean blood alcohol concentration at the time of arrest of 29,223 jail inmates. The federal government recommended to the states in 1983 that a concentration of 0.08 be considered

TABLE 3-7 **Age, Gender, and Race of Murder Victims: 1992**

Age (Years)	Total	Gender			Race			
		Male	Female	Unknown	White	Black	Other	Unknown
Total	22,540	17,576	4,936	28	10,647	11,175	548	170
Percent distribution	100.0	78.0	21.9	0.1	47.2	49.6	2.4	0.8
Under 18[a]	2,428	1,748	679	1	1,103	1,240	72	13
18 and over[a]	19,803	15,608	4,193	2	9,409	9,820	469	105
Infant (under 1)	254	137	116	1	147	99	3	5
1 to 4	408	237	171	0	204	192	12	0
5 to 9	126	64	62	0	60	56	10	0
10 to 14	351	230	121	0	163	171	14	3
15 to 19	2,851	2,444	407	0	1,114	1,664	60	13
20 to 24	4,181	3,551	630	0	1,614	2,451	97	19
25 to 29	3,455	2,749	706	0	1,479	1,891	69	16
30 to 34	3,045	2,382	662	1	1,420	1,530	76	19
35 to 39	2,231	1,706	525	0	1,145	1,027	51	8
40 to 44	1,650	1,262	388	0	858	731	47	14
45 to 49	1,072	819	253	0	634	396	35	7
50 to 54	695	519	175	1	406	265	21	3
55 to 59	449	356	93	0	281	146	18	4
60 to 64	412	307	105	0	283	120	6	3
65 to 69	315	205	110	0	187	120	7	1
70 to 74	262	159	103	0	177	80	4	1
75 and over	474	229	245	0	340	121	11	2
Unknown	309	220	64	25	135	115	7	52

Source: Reprinted from Federal Bureau of Investigation. (1993). *Crime in the United States, 1992* (p. 16). Washington, DC: Author.

[a]Does not include unknown ages.

TABLE 3-8 **Number of Licensed Drivers and Arrests for Driving under the Influence (DUI) and Rate of Arrest for DUI: 1980 to 1989**

Year	Number of Licensed Drivers	Number of Arrests for DUI	Rate of Arrest per 100,000 Drivers
1980	145,295	1,426,700	982
1981	147,075	1,531,400	1,041
1982	150,234	1,778,400	1,184
1983	154,389	1,921,100	1,244
1984	155,424	1,779,400	1,145
1985	156,868	1,788,400	1,140
1986	159,487	1,793,300	1,124
1987	161,818	1,727,200	1,067
1988	162,853	1,792,500	1,101
1989	165,555	1,736,200	1,049
Percent change, 1980–1989	13.9	21.7	6.8

Source: Reprinted from Cohen, R. L. (1992). *Drunk driving: Bureau of Justice Statistics special report, 1989 survey of inmates of local jails* (p. 2). Washington, DC: U.S. Department of Justice, Bureau of Justice Statistics.

TABLE 3-9 **Licensed Drivers and Arrests for Driving under the Influence (DUI), by Age: 1980 and 1989**

	1980			1989			Percent Change in Rate, 1980–89
	Percent of		Arrests per 100,000 Drivers	Percent of		Arrests per 100,000 Drivers	
Age	Drivers	Arrests		Drivers	Arrests		
Total	100	100	981	100	100	1,048	6.8
16–17	3.2	2.2	668	2.3	1.1	503	−24.7
18–20	7.2	12.9	1,757	5.4	8.3	1,607	−8.5
21–24	10.6	19.3	1,784	8.3	17.3	2,183	22.4
25–29	13.0	17.9	1,347	12.4	22.2	1,869	38.8
30–34	12.0	13.1	1,076	12.4	17.6	1,486	38.1
35–39	9.4	9.6	996	11.2	12.0	1,123	12.8
40–44	7.7	7.4	944	9.7	8.1	872	−7.6
45–49	6.9	5.9	837	7.6	5.3	725	−13.4
50–54	6.9	4.9	686	6.2	3.3	558	−18.7
55–59	6.7	3.5	509	5.7	2.2	400	−21.4
60–64	5.7	1.9	335	5.6	1.4	262	−21.8
65 and older	10.7	1.5	140	13.0	1.2	100	−28.6

Notes: Percentages may not add to 100 because of rounding. Table excludes licensed drivers and arrests for those less than 16 years old. For those 16 or older, there were 145,207,000 licensed drivers in 1980 and 165,517,596 in 1989; there were 1,424,736 DUI arrests in 1980 and 1,734,909 in 1989. The number of arrests for each age group was obtained by applying the age distribution of known arrests for DUI to the total number of estimated DUI arrests.

Source: Reprinted from Cohen, R. L. (1992). *Drunk driving: Bureau of Justice Statistics special report, 1989 survey of inmates of local jails* (p. 3). Washington, DC: U.S. Department of Justice, Bureau of Justice Statistics.

TABLE 3-10 Type of Alcoholic Beverage and Amount of Ethanol Consumed prior to Arrest of Jail Inmates Convicted of Driving while Intoxicated: 1989

Ounces of Ethanol Consumed	Percent of Inmates Who Drank		
	Beer Only	Liquor Only	More than One Type
Total no. of inmates	16,322	4,489	5,100
Less than 1 oz.	1.0	1.8	0
1–1.9	6.7	8.2	1.7
2–2.9	16.4	12.2	3.2
3–3.9	15.2	6.4	0
4–4.9	9.7	11.4	6.6
5–5.9	3.1	1.8	5.6
6–6.9	25.2	1.8	3.5
7–10.9	7.0	17.4	13.9
11–14.9	12.5	9.6	29.7
15 or more	3.2	29.5	35.8

Notes: Percentages may not add to 100 because of rounding. Figures exclude an estimated 576 inmates serving time in jail who reported drinking only wine and an estimated 2,736 inmates for whom information on drinking was not reported.

Source: Adapted from Cohen, R. L. (1992). *Drunk driving: Bureau of Justice Statistics special report, 1989 survey of inmates of local jails* (p. 6). Washington, DC: U.S. Department of Justice, Bureau of Justice Statistics.

TABLE 3-11 Estimated Mean Blood Alcohol Concentration (BAC) at Arrest of Jail Inmates Convicted of Driving while Intoxicated: 1989

Characteristic	Estimated BAC
Age	
17–24 years	0.20
25–29	0.21
30–34	0.20
35–39	0.25
40–44	0.21
45–49	0.16
50 or more	0.24
Number of prior DWI sentences to jail or prison	
None	0.21
1	0.23
2	0.18
3 or more	0.21
Number of hours spent drinking before arrest	
1 hour or less	0.11
2	0.16
3	0.20
4	0.23
5	0.20
6	0.23
7	0.27
8	0.32
Beverage consumed prior to arrest	
Beer	0.18
Wine	0.17
Liquor	0.25
More than one type	0.32

Notes: Figures apply to 29,223 inmates and exclude an estimated 8,062 jail inmates who were drinking at the time of the offense but did not report one or more of the following: amount of ethanol consumed, the number of hours spent drinking prior to the arrest, or their weight. BAC is estimated for those who reported drinking for up to eight hours before their arrest. Because of too few cases, reliable estimates could not be obtained for those who reported drinking for more than eight hours.

Source: Adapted from Cohen, R. L. (1992). *Drunk driving: Bureau of Justice Statistics special report, 1989 survey of inmates of local jails* (p. 8). Washington, DC: U.S. Department of Justice, Bureau of Justice Statistics.

sufficient for charging a person with drunk driving. However, the National Institute on Alcohol Abuse and Alcoholism (a federal agency) recommended an even lower level of 0.05. As the table makes clear, those arrested and convicted for drunk driving exceeded both standards by large margins. The usual drinking behavior of jail inmates convicted of drunk driving in 1989 is shown in Table

3-12. Nearly three-quarters were daily or weekly drinkers.

Table 3-13 lists the lengths of sentences for drunk driving offenders and indicates the proportions of those sentenced with prior sentences for the same crime. Those with the most prior convictions served longer sentences than those with no more than one previous conviction.

TABLE 3-12 **Usual Drinking Behavior of Jail Inmates Convicted of Driving while Intoxicated, by Amount of Ethanol Consumed prior to Arrest: 1989**

| Frequency of Usual Drinking | Percent of Inmates, by Amount of Ethanol Consumed prior to Arrest | | | | |
	All Convicted Inmates	Less than 2 Ounces	2–4.9 Ounces	5–9.9 Ounces	10 or More Ounces
Total no. of inmates	26,021	1,807	8,687	7,610	7,916
Daily	35.5	18.2	26.7	40.4	44.5
Once a week	36.1	36.8	40.1	35.0	32.8
Less than once a week	6.6	14.6	4.6	5.3	8.3
Once a month	9.7	21.1	10.6	9.7	6.2
Less than once per month	11.9	9.4	17.9	9.6	8.2

Notes: Percentages may not add to 100 because of rounding. Figures exclude an estimated 3,202 inmates with unknown data on drinking at the time of the offense, drinking during the previous year, the frequency of their usual drinking sessions, or the amount of alcoholic beverages consumed.

Source: Reprinted from Cohen, R. L. (1992). *Drunk driving: Bureau of Justice Statistics special report, 1989 survey of inmates of local jails* (p. 6). Washington, DC: U.S. Department of Justice, Bureau of Justice Statistics.

TABLE 3-13 **Length of Sentence Imposed on Convicted Driving while Intoxicated (DWI) Offenders, by Number of Prior DWI Sentences: 1989**

| Sentence Length | All Offenders | Percent of Offenders, by Prior DWI Sentences | | |
		None	One	Two or More
Total no. of inmates	23,061	10,549	5,212	7,299
30 days or less	13.6	16.3	20.4	4.8
31–90 days	23.1	31.7	20.4	12.6
91–120 days	6.6	6.5	6.4	6.9
121–240 days	27.8	20.1	28.3	38.5
241–365 days	17.3	12.6	17.6	23.7
More than 1 year	11.6	12.7	7.0	13.4
Mean no. of days	258	228	194	346
Median no. of days	180	115	134	181

Note: Percentages may not add to 100 because of rounding.

Source: Reprinted from Cohen, R. L. (1992). *Drunk driving: Bureau of Justice Statistics special report, 1989 survey of inmates of local jails* (p. 6). Washington, DC: U.S. Department of Justice, Bureau of Justice Statistics.

Family Violence

"Family violence is difficult to measure; no consensus exists as to what constitutes family violence, it most often occurs in private, and victims are often reluctant to report incidents of family violence to anyone because of shame or from fear of reprisal" (Zawitz et al., 1993, p. 24). The scope of the family violence problem is difficult to determine; reluctance to publicly acknowledge domestic violence results in no more than estimates of rapes, robberies, or assaults that were committed by intimates and relatives such as spouses and former spouses, children, parents, and boyfriends and girlfriends. The estimates do not include crimes against children under 12, which are discussed in chapter 2.

Family violence may actually be more dangerous to the victims than violence committed by strangers, according to Zawitz et al. (1993). Half of the victims of intimates were injured, compared to one-fourth of those victimized by strangers. One-fourth of those experiencing violence by an intimate received medical care in a hospital, emergency room, doctor's office, or another medical facility.

Data from the National Crime Victimization Survey show that 85 percent of family violence crimes are assaults (Zawitz et al., 1993). Over one-third of all domestic or family assaults are committed by boyfriends or girlfriends, as Table 3-14 shows. Most of the victims are women. Nationally, women are victims of family violence at a rate of six crimes per 1,000 women compared to two crimes per 1,000 men. Domestic violence and the imprisonment of women may be related; 41 percent of women inmates in 1966 (the most recent data available) reported that they had experienced physical or sexual abuse at some time prior to their imprisonment (Greenfeld & Minor-Harper, 1991).

Zawitz et al. (1993) found that three of every 1,000 white women who were victims of family violence had been assaulted by current or former spouses, whereas four of every 1,000 African American women had been assaulted by current or former boyfriends. There are no apparent differences in family violence rates between Hispanic and non-Hispanic women. With regard to age, victims of current or former spouses are likely to be older (20 to 34 years old) than victims of boyfriends (16 to 24 years old). Those who are victims of other family members are more likely to be under age 25. Women in families with annual incomes of less than $20,000 are four times more likely to be domestic violence victims than are women in families with incomes over $50,000 (Zawitz et al., 1993).

Arrests

The FBI estimated that in 1983 11.7 million people were arrested; their estimates for 1992 were 14 million people, an increase of about 20 percent (FBI, 1993). Of these arrests, crime index arrests were up 22 percent, violent crime arrests were up 51 percent, property crime arrests were up 14 percent, and drug abuse arrests were up 57 percent. Six percent of those arrested were under age 15, 16 percent were under 18, and 29 percent were under 21.

The tables in this section that detail arrests for 1992 have smaller totals than the 14 million estimate. The total estimate is based on actual reports plus estimates for the agencies not reporting; the tables report only actual received reports.

Although people ages 14 to 24 years are only 15.6 percent of the population, they constitute a disproportionately large share of all those arrested (5.3 million of the 11.9 million total in 1992, or 44.6 percent). Table 3-15 shows the number of people under ages 15, 18, 21, and 25 who were arrested in 1992 and the percentage of the total arrests for each category.

Many more men than women are arrested. In 1992, 19.0 percent of those who were arrested were women (up from 18.1 percent in 1989). Table 3-16 shows the number of men and women arrested for selected offenses in 1992.

Arrests are also reported by ethnicity. Table 3-17 shows the arrest data for 1992 by race and ethnicity.

Jails

In 1992 about 441,000 people (or 174 of every 100,000 Americans) were held in jails. Jails are local facilities used to detain people when they are arrested, to hold people awaiting trial, and to house people serving short sentences (usually a year or less). As Tables 3-18 and 3-19 show, there were increases in the one-day counts between 1991 and 1992 and in the average daily populations. These increases continue the dramatic long-term growth in jail populations; the average populations were 157,930 in 1978; 227,541 in 1983; 336,017 in 1988; 386,845 in 1989; and 405,320 in 1990 (Snell, 1993).

Many people who are jailed are quickly released; more than 10.25 million people were admitted to jails in 1991 (Snell, 1993), but the average daily count was fewer than 450,000.

On a typical day, slightly more than half of all people in jail have been convicted of a crime, and the others are awaiting trials or other legal proceedings (Beck et al., 1993). Juveniles were a very small percentage of all

TABLE 3-14 **Family Violence: Number of Incidents and Percentages of Female Victims, by Relationship of the Offender to the Victim: 1987 to 1991**

Relationship of Offender to Victim	Average Annual Incidents	Percentage of All Family Victimizations	Percentage of Female Victims
Boyfriend or girlfriend	315,956	37	91
Spouse	211,872	25	93
Ex-spouse	93,134	10	89
Other relative	71,788	8	57
Brother or sister	54,436	7	59
Parent	31,991	4	52
Child	34,571	4	78
Unspecified	33,052	5	28
Other known offender			38
Stranger			32

Source: Adapted from Zawitz, M. W., et al. (1993). *Highlights from 20 years of surveying crime victims: The National Crime Victimization Survey, 1973–92* (p. 25). Washington, DC: U.S. Department of Justice, Bureau of Justice Statistics.

TABLE 3-15 Total Number of Arrests of People under the Ages of 15, 18, 21, and 25: 1992

Offense Charged	Total All Ages	Number of People Arrested				Percent of Total All Ages			
		Under 15	Under 18	Under 21	Under 25	Under 15	Under 18	Under 21	Under 25
Total	11,893,153	689,877	1,943,138	3,474,226	5,300,253	5.8	16.3	29.2	44.6
Violent crime[a]	641,250	34,233	112,409	200,843	304,365	5.3	17.5	31.3	47.5
Property crime[b]	1,839,274	259,974	608,401	861,703	1,082,552	14.1	33.1	46.9	58.9
Crime index total[c]	2,480,524	294,207	720,810	1,062,546	1,386,917	11.9	29.1	42.8	55.9
Murder and nonnegligent manslaughter	19,491	304	2,829	6,857	10,729	1.6	14.5	35.2	55.0
Forcible rape	33,385	2,049	5,369	9,519	14,616	6.1	16.1	28.5	43.8
Robbery	153,456	11,514	40,434	68,541	94,666	7.5	26.3	44.7	61.7
Aggravated assault	434,918	20,366	63,777	115,926	184,354	4.7	14.7	26.7	42.4
Burglary	359,699	50,131	122,567	181,932	229,919	13.9	34.1	50.6	63.9
Larceny–theft	1,291,984	182,623	402,066	564,883	714,795	14.1	31.1	43.7	55.3
Motor vehicle theft	171,269	22,010	75,800	105,361	126,915	12.9	44.3	61.5	74.1
Arson	16,322	5,210	7,968	9,527	10,923	31.9	48.8	58.4	66.9
Other assaults	912,517	60,280	143,797	236,829	377,897	6.6	15.8	26.0	41.4
Forgery and counterfeiting	88,649	1,218	7,024	20,471	36,713	1.4	7.9	23.1	41.4
Fraud	346,314	4,234	15,027	47,930	108,996	1.2	4.3	13.8	31.5
Embezzlement	11,707	100	671	2,291	4,548	.9	5.7	19.6	38.8
Stolen property (buying, receiving, possessing)	136,765	10,668	36,325	62,918	84,283	7.8	26.6	46.0	61.6
Vandalism	262,477	58,742	118,027	152,816	184,161	22.4	45.0	58.2	70.2
Weapons (carrying, possessing, etc.)	204,116	13,893	46,256	83,075	118,894	6.8	22.7	40.7	58.2
Prostitution and commercialized vice	86,988	165	1,095	7,563	23,876	.2	1.3	8.7	27.4
Sex offenses (except forcible rape and prostitution)	91,560	8,496	16,632	24,125	34,408	9.3	18.2	26.3	37.6
Drug abuse violations	920,424	10,800	73,981	201,587	369,164	1.2	8.0	21.9	40.1
Gambling	15,029	199	1,088	2,524	4,058	1.3	7.2	16.8	27.0
Offenses against family and children	84,328	1,361	3,940	10,868	23,215	1.6	4.7	12.9	27.5
Driving under the influence	1,319,583	365	11,956	101,014	319,034	d	.9	7.7	24.2
Liquor laws	442,985	9,541	97,443	285,273	332,795	2.2	22.0	64.4	75.1
Drunkenness	664,236	1,898	15,114	66,571	160,369	.3	2.3	10.0	24.1
Disorderly conduct	605,367	37,483	109,684	196,174	303,624	6.2	18.1	32.4	50.2
Vagrancy	29,004	1,150	3,436	6,168	9,033	4.0	11.8	21.3	31.1
All other liquor-law offenses (except traffic)	2,954,440	85,541	295,075	676,103	1,188,973	2.9	10.0	22.9	40.2
Suspicion	15,351	1,877	4,968	6,591	8,506	12.2	32.4	42.9	55.4
Curfew and loitering law violations	74,619	22,529	74,619	74,619	74,619	30.2	100.0	100.0	100.0
Runaways	146,170	65,130	146,170	146,170	146,170	44.6	100.0	100.0	100.0

Note: As reported by 10,962 agencies.

Source: Reprinted from Federal Bureau of Investigation. (1993). Crime in the United States, 1992 (p. 233). Washington, DC: Author.

[a]Violent crimes are offenses of murder, forcible rape, robbery, and aggravated assault.

[b]Property crimes are offenses of burglary, larceny–theft, motor vehicle theft, and arson.

[c]Includes arson.

[d]Less than 0.1 percent.

jail inmates in 1991 and 1992. Most juveniles are treated differently from adult offenders, as discussed later in this chapter.

Prisons

The incarceration rates per 100,000 people for the total nation, each region, and each state are provided in Table 3-20. The figures include both federal and state prisoners. Less than 10 percent of all prisoners are housed in federal facilities. Most prisoners are violators of state laws and are under state jurisdiction. For most states *incarceration* means under supervision, which includes imprisonment, parole, and probation. States that use "custody" (a prison or residential facility) and "jurisdiction" (house arrest, electronic monitoring, probation, or parole) synonymously have the

TABLE 3-16 **Total Arrests, by Offense and Gender: 1992**

Offense Charged	Number of People Arrested			Percent Male	Percent Female	Percent Distribution[a]		
	Total	Male	Female			Total	Male	Female
Total	11,893,153	9,633,809	2,259,344	81.0	19.0	100.0	100.0	100.0
Violent crime[c]	641,250	561,310	79,940	87.5	12.5	5.4	5.8	3.5
Property crime[d]	1,839,274	1,370,198	469,076	74.5	25.5	15.5	14.2	20.8
Crime index total[e]	2,480,524	1,931,508	549,016	77.9	22.1	20.9	20.0	24.3
Murder and nonnegligent manslaughter	19,491	17,592	1,899	90.3	9.7	.2	.2	.1
Forcible rape	33,385	32,965	420	98.7	1.3	.3	.3	[b]
Robbery	153,456	140,374	13,082	91.5	8.5	1.3	1.5	.6
Aggravated assault	434,918	370,379	64,539	85.2	14.8	3.7	3.8	2.9
Burglary	359,699	326,570	33,129	90.8	9.2	3.0	3.4	1.5
Larceny–theft	1,291,984	876,736	415,248	67.9	32.1	10.9	9.1	18.4
Motor vehicle theft	171,269	152,753	18,516	89.2	10.8	1.4	1.6	.8
Arson	16,322	14,139	2,183	86.6	13.4	.1	.1	.1
Other assaults	912,517	755,933	156,584	82.8	17.2	7.7	7.8	6.9
Forgery and counterfeiting	88,649	57,849	30,800	65.3	34.7	.7	.6	1.4
Fraud	346,314	200,366	145,948	57.9	42.1	2.9	2.1	6.5
Embezzlement	11,707	7,147	4,560	61.0	39.0	.1	.1	.2
Stolen property (buying, receiving, possessing)	136,765	119,688	17,077	87.5	12.5	1.1	1.2	.8
Vandalism	262,477	232,852	29,625	88.7	11.3	2.2	2.4	1.3
Weapons (carrying, possessing, etc.)	204,116	188,797	15,319	92.5	7.5	1.7	2.0	.7
Prostitution and commercialized vice	86,988	30,180	56,808	34.7	65.3	.7	.3	2.5
Sex offenses (except forcible rape and prostitution)	91,560	84,540	7,020	92.3	7.7	.8	.9	.3
Drug abuse violations	920,424	769,080	151,344	83.6	16.4	7.7	8.0	6.7
Gambling	15,029	12,942	2,087	86.1	13.9	.1	.1	.1
Offenses against family and children	84,328	69,115	15,213	82.0	18.0	.7	.7	.7
Driving under the influence	1,319,583	1,137,542	182,041	86.2	13.8	11.1	11.8	8.1
Liquor laws	442,985	357,669	85,316	80.7	19.3	3.7	3.7	3.8
Drunkenness	664,236	592,324	71,912	89.2	10.8	5.6	6.1	3.2
Disorderly conduct	605,367	480,677	124,690	79.4	20.6	5.1	5.0	5.5
Vagrancy	29,004	26,170	2,834	90.2	9.8	.2	.3	.1
All other liquor-law offenses (except traffic)	2,954,440	2,448,952	505,488	82.9	17.1	24.8	25.4	22.4
Suspicion	15,351	12,678	2,673	82.6	17.4	.1	.1	.1
Curfew and loitering law violations	74,619	54,622	19,997	73.2	26.8	.6	.6	.9
Runaways	146,170	63,178	82,992	43.2	56.8	1.2	.7	3.7

Notes: As reported by 10,962 agencies.

Source: Reprinted from Federal Bureau of Investigation. (1993). *Crime in the United States, 1992* (p. 234). Washington, DC: Author.

[a]Because of rounding, the percentages may not add to total.

[b]Less than 0.1 percent.

[c]Violent crimes are offenses of murder, forcible rape, robbery, and aggravated assault.

[d]Property crimes are offenses of burglary, larceny–theft, motor vehicle theft, and arson.

[e]Includes arson.

TABLE 3-17 Total Arrests, by Offense and Race and Ethnicity: 1992

Offense Charged	Total Arrests					Percent Distribution[a]				
	Total	White	Black	American Indian or Alaskan Native	Asian or Pacific Islander	Total	White	Black	American Indian or Alaskan Native	Asian or Pacific Islander
Total	11,876,204	8,030,171	3,598,259	130,770	117,004	100.0	67.6	30.3	1.1	1.0
Violent crime[b]	640,512	343,338	287,122	4,635	5,417	100.0	53.6	44.8	.7	.8
Property crime[c]	1,836,995	1,209,499	584,925	18,623	23,948	100.0	65.8	31.8	1.0	1.3
Crime index total[d]	2,477,507	1,552,837	872,047	23,258	29,365	100.0	62.7	35.2	.9	1.2
Murder and nonnegligent manslaughter	19,463	8,466	10,728	107	162	100.0	43.5	55.1	.5	.8
Forcible rape	33,332	18,490	14,258	291	293	100.0	55.5	42.8	.9	.9
Robbery	153,246	57,837	93,392	608	1,409	100.0	37.7	60.9	.4	.9
Aggravated assault	434,471	258,545	168,744	3,629	3,553	100.0	59.5	38.8	.8	.8
Burglary	359,306	243,637	109,165	2,840	3,664	100.0	67.8	30.4	.8	1.0
Larceny–theft	1,290,278	853,558	404,707	14,293	17,720	100.0	66.2	31.4	1.1	1.4
Motor vehicle theft	171,136	99,874	67,481	1,355	2,426	100.0	58.4	39.4	.8	1.4
Arson	16,275	12,430	3,572	135	138	100.0	76.4	21.9	.8	.8
Other assaults	911,374	584,668	308,170	10,567	7,969	100.0	64.2	33.8	1.2	.9
Forgery and counterfeiting	88,573	57,377	29,804	492	900	100.0	64.8	33.6	.6	1.0
Fraud	345,768	223,483	118,931	1,531	1,823	100.0	64.6	34.4	.4	.5
Embezzlement	11,699	8,022	3,476	52	149	100.0	68.6	29.7	.4	1.3
Stolen property (buying, receiving, possessing)	136,411	77,622	56,817	755	1,217	100.0	56.9	41.7	.6	.9
Vandalism	262,084	199,657	57,295	2,707	2,425	100.0	76.2	21.9	1.0	.9
Weapons (carrying, possessing, etc.)	203,739	115,377	85,072	1,055	2,235	100.0	56.6	41.8	.5	1.1
Prostitution and commercialized vice	86,932	53,922	31,541	485	984	100.0	62.0	36.3	.6	1.1
Sex offenses (except forcible rape and prostitution)	91,454	72,366	17,280	861	947	100.0	79.1	18.9	.9	1.0
Drug abuse violations	919,561	546,430	364,546	3,500	5,085	100.0	59.4	39.6	.4	.6
Gambling	15,021	7,194	6,756	59	1,012	100.0	47.9	45.0	.4	6.7
Offenses against family and children	83,770	56,124	24,437	1,044	2,165	100.0	67.0	29.2	1.2	2.6
Driving under the influence	1,317,968	1,155,884	132,894	17,797	11,393	100.0	87.7	10.1	1.4	.9
Liquor laws	441,781	378,288	47,388	12,147	3,958	100.0	85.6	10.7	2.7	.9
Drunkenness	663,573	534,629	113,496	13,627	1,821	100.0	80.6	17.1	2.1	.3
Disorderly conduct	604,612	394,210	199,055	7,788	3,559	100.0	65.2	32.9	1.3	.6
Vagrancy	28,611	14,563	13,588	359	101	100.0	50.9	47.5	1.3	.4
All other liquor-law offenses (except traffic)	2,950,424	1,818,980	1,067,226	30,326	33,892	100.0	61.7	36.2	1.0	1.1
Suspicion	15,336	7,572	7,634	24	106	100.0	49.4	49.8	.2	.7
Curfew and loitering law violations	74,428	56,752	15,607	703	1,366	100.0	76.3	21.0	.9	1.8
Runaways	145,578	114,214	25,199	1,633	4,532	100.0	78.5	17.3	1.1	3.1

Note: As reported by 10,950 agencies.

Source: Reprinted from Federal Bureau of Investigation. (1993). *Crime in the United States, 1992* (p. 235). Washington, DC: Author.

[a]Because of rounding, the percentages may not add to total. [b]Violent crimes are offenses of murder, forcible rape, robbery, and aggravated assault. [c]Property crimes are offenses of burglary, larceny–theft, motor vehicle theft, and arson. [d]Includes arson.

same rates for people under supervision and people in custody. Most states also separate jail sentences from prison sentences.

Final overall figures for state and federal prisoners in 1991 and estimated totals for 1992 are reported in Table 3-21. The table also shows the percentage change from 1991 to 1992 and federal, regional, and state incarceration rates for 1992.

State Prison Inmates

In 1992 more than 803,000 inmates were held in state prisons (penitentiaries, which typically hold prisoners sentenced to terms of one year or more), and another 80,000 were held in federal prisons (Gilliard, 1993). The tables that follow provide differing totals, because the data come from censuses made at different times and because certain details,

---

TABLE 3-18 **One-Day Count and Average Daily Jail Population, by Legal Status and Gender: 1991 and 1992**

Status and Gender	Number of Jail Inmates		Percent Change, 1991–92
	1991	1992	
One-day count			
All inmates	426,479	444,584	4.2
Adults	424,129	441,781	4.2
Male	384,628	401,106	4.3
Female	39,501	40,674	3.0
Juveniles[a]	2,350	2,804	19.3
Average daily population			
All inmates	422,609	441,889	4.6
Adults	420,276	439,362	4.5
Male	381,458	399,528	4.7
Female	38,818	39,834	2.8

Note: Data for one-day counts are for June 28, 1991, and June 30, 1992.

Source: Adapted from Beck, A. J., Bonczar, T. P., & Gilliard, D. K. (1993). *Jail inmates 1992* (p. 2). Washington, DC: U.S. Department of Justice, Bureau of Justice Statistics.

[a]Juveniles are people defined by state statute as being under a certain age, usually 18, and subject initially to juvenile court authority even if tried as adults in criminal court. Because less than 1 percent of the jail population were juveniles, caution must be used.

TABLE 3-19 **Average Daily Jail Population and One-Day Count in 25 Largest Jurisdictions: 1991 and 1992**

Jurisdiction	Number of Jails in Jurisdiction		Average Daily Population		One-Day Count	
	1991	1992	1991	1992	June 28, 1991	June 30, 1992
Los Angeles County, CA	9	9	20,779	22,220	20,885	22,289
New York City, NY	17	16	20,419	18,673	20,563	18,427
Harris County, TX	3	4	6,751	8,086	6,808	11,727
Cook County, IL	a	a	7,257	7,621	8,356	9,089
Shelby County, TN	2	2	5,008	6,108	5,755	6,096
Dade County, FL	7	7	5,343	5,965	5,493	5,733
Dallas County, TX	4	4	5,247	5,502	4,686	5,881
Philadelphia County, PA	7	6	4,897	4,878	4,589	4,422
Maricopa County, AZ	6	7	4,312	4,829	4,480	4,934
Orleans Parish, LA	a	a	3,677	4,737	4,481	4,737
Orange County, CA	3	3	4,378	4,688	4,390	4,690
San Diego County, CA	12	11	4,660	4,543	4,303	5,039
Santa Clara County, CA	7	7	4,072	4,368	4,166	4,369
Tarrant County, TX	4	4	3,779	4,321	4,000	4,858
Orange County, FL	2	2	3,267	3,582	3,225	3,536
Sacramento County, CA	3	3	3,170	3,265	2,980	3,165
Alameda County, CA	3	3	2,912	3,250	2,891	3,550
Broward County, FL	3	3	3,502	3,173	3,584	3,069
Baltimore City, MD	4	4	2,828	2,900	2,894	3,006
San Bernardino County, CA	2	2	2,735	2,855	2,929	2,860
Fresno County, CA	3	3	2,061	2,572	1,980	2,286
Fulton County, GA	4	4	2,983	2,545	2,969	2,590
Bexar County, TX	1	1	2,313	2,377	1,981	2,626
Hillsborough County, FL	3	3	2,051	2,328	1,944	2,268
Riverside County, CA	4	4	2,240	2,180	2,174	2,181

Source: Adapted from Beck, A. J., Bonczar, T. P., & Gilliard, D. K. (1993). *Jail inmates 1992* (p. 4). Washington, DC: U.S. Department of Justice, Bureau of Justice Statistics.

[a]Jurisdictions that provided a single report covering all of their jail facilities.

TABLE 3-20 Incarceration Rates for Prisoners under State or Federal Jurisdiction or in State or Federal Custody, by Sentence Lengths: 1991

Number of Prisoners per 100,000 Resident Population

Region and State	Total		More than a Year		Year or Less or Unsentenced	
	Under Federal or State Jurisdiction	In Federal or State Custody	Under Federal or State Jurisdiction	In Federal or State Custody	Under Federal or State Jurisdiction	In Federal or State Custody
United States total	323	311	310	299	14	12
Federal	28	25	22	20	6	5
State	295	286	287	278	8	8
Northeast	257	247	248	239	9	9
Connecticut[a]	337	324	263	253	73	71
Maine	125	124	123	122	2	2
Massachusetts	153	153	143	143	10	10
New Hampshire	132	130	132	126	NA	4
New Jersey	301	245	301	245	0	0
New York	320	320	320	320	NA	0
Pennsylvania	192	192	192	192	0	0
Rhode Island[a]	274	275	173	169	101	105
Vermont[a]	189	184	124	119	65	65
Midwest	256	255	255	255	1	1
Illinois[b]	247	247	247	247	0	0
Indiana	229	229	226	226	3	3
Iowa	144	144	144	144	NA	NA
Kansas	231	231	231	231	NA	0
Michigan	388	388	388	388	NA	0
Minnesota	78	79	78	78	NA	1
Missouri	305	305	305	305	NA	0
Nebraska	153	158	145	151	7	8
North Dakota	76	86	68	78	8	8
Ohio[b]	324	321	324	321	—	0
South Dakota	191	193	191	193	0	0
Wisconsin	158	155	157	154	1	1
South	343	322	333	312	11	10
Alabama	402	395	394	386	9	9
Arkansas	319	307	317	305	2	2
Delaware[a]	526	469	344	319	182	150
District of Columbia[a,b]	1,796	1,478	1,221	1,006	575	472
Florida	344	343	344	343	0	0
Georgia	353	353	342	342	11	11
Kentucky	262	239	262	239	NA	0
Louisiana[b]	462	346	462	346	—	0
Maryland	396	389	366	360	30	30
Mississippi	339	310	330	304	8	6
North Carolina	278	282	269	269	9	12
Oklahoma[b]	416	346	416	346	—	—
South Carolina	502	442	473	414	29	28
Tennessee[b]	227	187	227	187	—	0
Texas	297	297	297	297	NA	0
Virginia	314	268	311	268	3	0
West Virginia	83	87	83	83	0	4
West	298	297	287	287	11	11
Alaska[a]	508	466	345	319	162	147
Arizona	411	411	396	396	15	15
California	329	329	318	318	11	11
Colorado[b]	249	247	249	247	—	—
Hawaii[a]	234	212	153	137	81	74
Idaho	205	197	205	197	NA	0
Montana	183	178	183	178	0	0
Nevada	439	466	439	455	NA	11
New Mexico	198	199	191	190	7	9
Oregon[b]	228	223	228	223	—	0
Utah	150	160	149	154	1	6
Washington	182	182	182	181	NA	1
Wyoming	237	237	237	237	0	0

Notes: All data from Arizona, California, Florida, Georgia, Illinois, Indiana, Iowa, Massachusetts, Michigan, Texas, and Wyoming are custody rather than jurisdiction counts. Most, but not all, states reserve prisons for offenders sentenced to one year or more. NA = not applicable; — = not available.

Source: Reprinted from Snell, T. L. (1993). *Correctional populations in the United States, 1991* (p. 55). Washington, DC: U.S. Department of Justice, Bureau of Justice Statistics.

[a]Figures include both jail and prison inmates; jails and prisons are combined in one system.

[b]Counts of inmates by sentence length may be slightly incorrect.

TABLE 3-21 Prisoners under the Jurisdiction of State or Federal Correctional Authorities, by Region and State: 1991 and 1992

Region and State	Total Advance 1992	Total Final 1991	Total Percent Change, 1991–92	Sentenced Advance 1992	Sentenced Final 1991	Sentenced Percent Change, 1991–92	Incarceration Rate, 1992[a]
United States total	883,593	824,133	7.2	846,695	789,349	7.3	329
Federal	80,259	71,608	12.1	65,706	56,696	15.9	26
State	803,334	752,525	6.8	780,989	732,653	6.6	303
Northeast	138,156	131,866	4.8	133,372	127,450	4.7	259
Connecticut	11,403	10,977	3.9	8,794	8,585	2.4	269
Maine	1,515	1,579	-4.1	1,488	1,558	-4.5	116
Massachusetts	10,056	9,155	9.8	9,382	8,561	9.6	156
New Hampshire	1,777	1,533	15.9	1,777	1,533	15.9	150
New Jersey	22,653	23,483	-3.5	22,653	23,483	-3.5	289
New York	61,736	57,862	6.7	61,736	57,862	6.7	340
Pennsylvania	24,974	23,388	6.8	24,966	23,386	6.8	204
Rhode Island	2,775	2,771	.1	1,709	1,749	-2.3	168
Vermont	1,267	1,118	13.3	867	733	18.3	144
Midwest	166,339	155,917	6.7	166,042	155,573	6.7	271
Illinois	31,640	29,115	8.7	31,640	29,115	8.7	267
Indiana	13,166	13,008	1.2	13,012	12,865	1.1	227
Iowa	4,518	4,145	9.0	4,518	4,145	9.0	157
Kansas	6,028	5,903	2.1	6,028	5,903	2.1	234
Michigan	39,019	36,423	7.1	39,019	36,423	7.1	414
Minnesota	3,822	3,472	10.1	3,822	3,472	10.1	84
Missouri	16,198	15,897	1.9	16,198	15,897	1.9	309
Nebraska	2,565	2,495	2.8	2,492	2,375	4.9	152
North Dakota	464	492	-5.7	415	441	-5.9	65
Ohio	38,378	35,744	7.4	38,378	35,744	7.4	346
South Dakota	1,487	1,374	8.2	1,487	1,374	8.2	206
Wisconsin	9,054	7,849	15.4	9,033	7,819	15.5	180
South	324,454	301,866	7.5	315,280	292,542	7.8	355
Alabama	17,453	16,760	4.1	16,938	16,400	3.3	404
Arkansas	8,433	7,766	8.6	8,129	7,722	5.3	332
Delaware	3,977	3,717	7.0	2,665	2,430	9.7	371
District of Columbia	10,875	10,455	4.0	7,528	7,106	5.9	1,312
Florida	48,302	46,533	3.8	48,302	46,533	3.8	348
Georgia	25,290	23,644	7.0	24,848	22,910	8.5	366
Kentucky	10,364	9,799	5.8	10,364	9,799	5.8	277
Louisiana	20,810	20,003	4.0	20,603	20,003	3.0	478
Maryland	19,977	19,291	3.6	18,808	17,824	5.5	380
Mississippi	9,083	8,904	2.0	8,877	8,682	2.3	337
North Carolina	20,455	18,903	8.2	20,024	18,272	9.6	291
Oklahoma	14,821	13,340	11.1	14,821	13,340	11.1	463
South Carolina	18,643	18,269	2.0	17,612	17,208	2.4	477
Tennessee	11,849	11,474	3.3	11,849	11,474	3.3	232
Texas	61,178	51,677	18.4	61,178	51,677	18.4	348
Virginia	21,199	19,829	6.9	20,989	19,660	6.8	327
West Virginia	1,745	1,502	16.2	1,745	1,502	16.2	97
West	174,385	162,876	7.1	166,295	157,088	5.9	298
Alaska	2,865	2,706	5.9	1,944	1,840	5.7	363
Arizona	16,477	15,415	6.9	15,850	14,843	6.8	415
California	109,496	101,808	7.6	105,467	98,515	7.1	332
Colorado	8,997	8,392	7.2	8,997	8,392	7.2	266
Hawaii	2,926	2,700	8.4	1,922	1,766	8.8	164
Idaho	2,475	2,143	15.5	2,475	2,143	15.5	234
Montana	1,553	1,478	5.1	1,553	1,478	5.1	192
Nevada	6,049	5,503	9.9	6,049	5,503	9.9	461
New Mexico	3,271	3,119	4.9	3,154	3,016	4.6	197
Oregon[b]	6,596	6,732	-2.0	5,216	6,732	NA	173
Utah	2,699	2,625	2.8	2,687	2,605	3.2	152
Washington	9,959	9,156	8.8	9,959	9,156	8.8	193
Wyoming	1,022	1,099	-7.0	1,022	1,099	-7.0	223

Notes: The advance count of prisoners is conducted immediately after the calendar year ends. Prisoner counts for 1991 may differ from those reported in previous publications. Counts for 1992 are subject to revision as updated figures become available. NA = not applicable.

Source: Reprinted from Gilliard, D. K. (1993). *Prisoners in 1992* (p. 2). Washington, DC: U.S. Department of Justice, Bureau of Justice Statistics.

[a]The number of prisoners with sentences of more than one year per 100,000 resident population.

[b]Before 1992, because of its sentencing guidelines, Oregon reported all prisoners as having a sentence of more than one year. Comparing the number of prisoners sentenced to more than one year in 1992 with the counts from previous years would be inappropriate.

such as ethnicity, offenses, and special sentencing considerations, were available for 1991 but not for 1992.

Gender. The characteristics of state prison inmates by gender are detailed in Table 3-22. The five-year period from 1986 to 1991 shows a startling increase in the prison population of 261,227 people: More than a quarter million more people were incarcerated in 1991 than in 1986. Only a small portion of state prison inmates (5 percent) were women in 1991, a large percentage increase from 1986, when 4 percent were women. In 1992 the number of women inmates increased by 5.9 percent from 1991, but women remained about 6 percent of the total prison population (Gilliard, 1993).

Women in prison pose some special issues for the criminal justice system. Brinson (1993)

TABLE 3-22 **Characteristics of State Prison Inmates, by Gender: 1986 and 1991**

Characteristic	Percent of Prison Inmates in 1986			Percent of Prison Inmates in 1991		
	Total	Male	Female	Total	Male	Female
Race or Hispanic origin						
White non-Hispanic	39.6	39.6	39.7	35.4	35.4	36.2
Black non-Hispanic	45.3	45.3	46.0	45.6	45.5	46.0
Hispanic	12.6	12.7	11.7	16.7	16.8	14.2
Other[a]	2.5	2.5	2.5	2.4	2.3	3.6
Age (years)						
17 or younger	0.5	0.5	0.2	0.6	0.7	0.1
18–24	26.7	26.9	22.3	21.3	21.6	16.3
25–29	26.2	26.1	28.1	24.2	24.1	26.1
30–34	19.5	19.3	22.4	21.5	21.3	24.2
35–39	13.0	13.0	13.6	14.1	14.0	16.6
40–44	6.4	6.5	5.9	8.6	8.6	8.9
45–49	3.4	3.4	3.6	4.3	4.4	4.0
50–54	1.8	1.8	1.9	2.2	2.2	2.1
55–59	1.2	1.2	1.0	1.4	1.5	0.9
60–64	0.7	0.7	0.5	1.0	1.0	0.4
65 or older	0.6	0.6	0.4	0.7	0.8	0.4
Marital status						
Married	20.3	20.4	20.1	18.1	18.1	17.3
Widowed	1.9	1.6	6.7	1.9	1.6	5.9
Divorced	18.1	18.0	20.5	18.5	18.4	19.1
Separated	6.0	5.8	11.0	6.3	5.9	12.5
Never married	53.7	54.3	41.7	55.3	55.9	45.1
Education						
8th grade or less	20.8	20.9	16.5	14.3	14.4	12.1
9th to 11th grade	40.8	40.8	40.4	26.9	26.7	29.5
High school graduate	27.5	27.4	28.4	46.3	46.5	42.9
Some college or more	10.9	10.8	14.8	12.5	12.3	15.5
Military service						
Veteran	20.2	21.0	2.0	16.4	17.2	1.9
Vietnam era	4.5	4.7	0.2	2.7	2.9	0.1
Other	15.7	16.3	1.8	13.6	14.3	1.7
Nonveteran	79.8	79.0	98.0	83.6	82.8	98.1
No. of inmates	450,416	430,604	19,812	711,643	672,847	38,796

Notes: Data were missing for marital status on 1.1 percent of the inmates; for education, 0.8 percent of the inmates; and for military service, 0.2 percent. Detail may not add to total because of rounding.

Source: Reprinted from Snell, T. L. (1993). *Correctional populations in the United States, 1991* (p. 26). Washington, DC: U.S. Department of Justice, Bureau of Justice Statistics.

[a]Includes Asians, Pacific Islanders, American Indians, Alaska Natives, and other racial groups.

cited U.S. Department of Justice data that show that 80 percent of the women imprisoned in the United States are mothers who altogether have left behind 167,000 children. In addition, 10 percent of women who enter prison are pregnant, and 15 percent have recently given birth. In many prisons special arrangements are made to provide prenatal care and childbirth services and, in some cases, nurseries for newborns. Although children are eventually placed in foster care or with family members while their mothers complete their sentences, some prisons provide for the mother and child to remain together during the early months of the child's life.

Age and Education. Table 3-22 demonstrates that the state prison population, like the population of those arrested, is skewed toward young people. In 1991 inmates had completed more years of school than in 1986. Close to one-half (46.3 percent) had graduated from high school, and 12.5 percent had some college education, compared to the 1986 figures of 27.5 percent and 10.9 percent, respectively.

Race and Ethnicity. Table 3-22 shows that African Americans and Hispanics were overrepresented in the prison population. The race and ethnicity of prisoners under federal or state jurisdiction in 1991 is detailed in Table 3-23. Table 3-24 provides a state-by-state breakdown of prisoners by gender and Hispanic origin.

Family Background. Significant family characteristics of state prison inmates are presented in Table 3-25. In 1991 most inmates had not lived with both parents while growing up, and more than one-quarter of inmates' parents had abused drugs or alcohol. Thirty-one percent of inmates had a brother with a jail or prison record.

Sentence Lengths and Conditions. Sentence lengths and special sentencing conditions (other than incarceration, including fines, community service, substance abuse treatment, and so forth) for state prison inmates are described in Table 3-26. The mean sentence length for all offenses was 12.5 years, and the median sentence was nine years. Despite increasing publicity about long sentences for drug offenses, they remain no longer than

those given to committers of violent and property offenses. Twenty-six percent of prisoners were held in maximum security, most for violent offenses; medium security was used for 49 percent, and 23 percent were in minimum security (Beck et al., 1993).

Drug Use. Drugs remained an important factor in crime. When they committed the offenses for which they were imprisoned, 18 percent of inmates were under the influence of alcohol, 17 percent were under the influence of drugs, and 14 percent were under the influence of both alcohol and drugs. Table 3-27 shows the breakdown by type of offense. There have been some slight decreases in the use of marijuana by prisoners and an increase in the use of cocaine or crack. In 1991, 79 percent of prisoners had used some drug at some time. Seventy-four percent had used marijuana; 50 percent, cocaine or crack; and 25 percent, heroin or opiates (Beck et al., 1993).

Kramer (1993), writing in *Time* magazine, stated that heroin and cocaine prices had dropped because there was a worldwide glut (evidence, perhaps, of a general decline in drug use, as described in chapter 5, Health and Mortality Statistics) but added that 2 million Americans are regular drug users: "At least 60% of violent crime is associated with drug use. Addicts commit 15 times as many robberies and 20 times as many burglaries as criminals not on drugs. Approximately 70% of the nation's 1.4 million prisoners have drug problems, but only 1% of federal inmates and about 15% of state prisoners receive adequate treatment" (p. 35). He added that providing treatment adds only $3,000 per year to the cost of $28,000 to house one inmate, whereas community care costs $18,000 per year.

Inequities of the System
According to the Edna McConnell Clark Foundation (1993), several states have doubled their prison populations since the mid-1980s. In 1992 the U.S. government and the states spent nearly $25 billion to build, operate, and maintain their prisons and jails. The construction of new prisons alone cost $6.8 billion in 1992. Housing for one state prisoner cost $54,209 to build and for a fed-

TABLE 3-23 Prisoners under State or Federal Jurisdiction, by Race and Ethnicity: 1991

Region and State	Prisoner Population 12/31/91	White	Black	American Indian/ Alaska Native	Asian/ Pacific Islander	Not Known
United States total	824,133	385,347	395,245	7,407	3,423	32,711
Federal	71,608	46,868	22,727	1,222	791	0
State	752,525	338,479	372,518	6,185	2,632	32,711
Northeast	131,866	56,815	66,442	214	338	8,057
Connecticut[a,b]	10,977	3,053	5,144	7	26	2,747
Maine	1,579	1,522	37	16	4	0
Massachusetts[b]	9,155	4,410	3,036	14	51	1,644
New Hampshire	1,533	1,443	80	5	5	0
New Jersey[b]	23,483	6,762	15,005	4	41	1,671
New York[c]	57,862	28,181	29,151	135	155	240
Pennsylvania[b]	23,388	8,470	13,090	28	45	1,755
Rhode Island[a]	2,771	1,856	899	5	11	0
Vermont[a,d]	1,118	1,118	—	—	—	0
Midwest	155,917	71,227	79,217	1,394	130	3,949
Illinois[b]	29,115	8,055	18,306	49	28	2,677
Indiana	13,008	8,000	4,971	30	7	0
Iowa	4,145	3,089	940	69	15	32
Kansas[b]	5,903	3,329	2,145	81	33	315
Michigan[b]	36,423	14,586	20,985	137	25	690
Minnesota[b]	3,472	1,960	1,051	287	1	173
Missouri	15,897	8,547	7,317	30	3	0
Nebraska	2,495	1,564	830	95	0	6
North Dakota	492	397	4	88	3	0
Ohio[d]	35,744	16,433	19,311	0	0	0
South Dakota	1,374	992	32	350	—	0
Wisconsin	7,849	4,275	3,325	178	15	56
South	301,866	104,969	181,341	1,249	374	13,933
Alabama[b]	16,760	5,958	10,793	6	2	1
Arkansas[b]	7,766	3,302	4,437	3	1	23
Delaware[a,b]	3,717	1,175	2,449	2	3	88
District of Columbia[a,d]	10,455	218	10,237	0	0	0
Florida[b]	46,533	18,383	27,185	0	105	860
Georgia	23,644	7,613	15,931	20	6	74
Kentucky	9,799	6,672	3,123	2	0	2
Louisiana[e]	20,003	5,168	14,834	—	—	1
Maryland	19,291	4,581	14,638	6	0	66
Mississippi[b]	8,904	2,437	6,410	7	9	41
North Carolina	18,903	6,747	11,522	421	11	202
Oklahoma[b]	13,340	7,522	4,652	760	0	406
South Carolina	18,269	6,099	12,120	13	2	35
Tennessee[e]	11,474	5,857	5,503	—	—	114
Texas[b]	51,677	15,013	24,520	6	193	11,945
Virginia[b]	19,829	6,942	12,769	2	41	75
West Virginia	1,502	1,282	218	1	1	0
West	162,876	105,468	45,518	3,328	1,790	6,772
Alaska[a,d]	2,706	1,488	339	847	32	0
Arizona	15,415	12,271	2,633	498	12	1
California	101,808	61,594	35,205	662	—	4,347
Colorado[d]	8,392	5,990	1,937	108	27	330
Hawaii[a,b,d]	2,700	642	155	34	1,470	399
Idaho[d]	2,143	1,997	32	94	15	5
Montana	1,478	1,189	20	269	0	0
Nevada[b]	5,503	3,141	1,719	77	50	516
New Mexico	3,119	2,680	316	97	4	22
Oregon	6,732	4,994	923	147	51	617
Utah	2,625	2,264	222	67	36	36
Washington	9,156	6,345	1,966	372	91	382
Wyoming[b]	1,099	873	51	56	2	117

Notes: All data for Arizona, California, Florida, Georgia, Illinois, Indiana, Iowa, Massachusetts, Michigan, Texas, and Wyoming are custody rather than jurisdiction counts. — = not available.

Source: Reprinted from Snell, T. L. (1993). *Correctional populations in the United States, 1991* (p. 57). Washington, DC: U.S. Department of Justice, Bureau of Justice Statistics.

[a]Figures include both jail and prison inmates; jails and prisons are combined in one system. [b]Hispanic prisoners reported under "unknown race." [c]New York includes all Hispanic inmates under "white." [d]Race was estimated. [e]Louisiana and Tennessee reported people whose race was neither black nor white under "other race." These people are here reported under "unknown race."

TABLE 3-24 Prisoners under State or Federal Jurisdiction, by Gender and Hispanic Origin: 1991

Region and State	Prisoner Population 12/31/91	Total			Male				Female			
		Hispanic	Non-Hispanic	Not Known	Total	Hispanic	Non-Hispanic	Not Known	Total	Hispanic	Non-Hispanic	Not Known
United States total	824,133	112,520	520,952	190,661	776,550	106,979	489,128	180,443	47,583	5,541	31,824	10,218
Federal	71,608	19,086	52,522	0	65,954	17,805	48,149	0	5,654	1,281	4,373	0
State	752,525	93,434	468,430	190,661	710,596	89,174	440,979	180,443	41,929	4,260	27,451	10,218
Northeast	131,866	29,174	78,529	24,163	124,646	27,444	74,177	23,025	7,220	1,730	4,352	1,138
Connecticut[a]	10,977	2,747	8,230	0	10,317	2,618	7,699	0	660	129	531	0
Maine	1,579	16	1,563	0	1,517	16	1,501	0	62	0	62	0
Massachusetts	9,155	1,702	7,102	351	8,525	1,574	6,682	269	630	128	420	82
New Hampshire	1,533	103	1,430	0	1,460	98	1,362	0	73	5	68	0
New Jersey	23,483	3,699	18,963	821	22,376	3,556	17,999	821	1,107	143	964	0
New York	57,862	18,723	38,899	240	54,494	17,491	36,770	233	3,368	1,232	2,129	7
Pennsylvania	23,388	1,755		21,633	22,300	1,679		20,621	1,088	76		1,012
Rhode Island[a]	2,771	429	2,342	0	2,576	412	2,164	0	195	17	178	0
Vermont[a]	1,118	—	—	1,118	1,081	—	—	1,081	37	—	—	37
Midwest	155,917	4,830	113,755	37,332	147,852	4,698	108,211	34,943	8,065	132	5,544	2,389
Illinois	29,115	2,675	26,438	2	27,858	2,605	25,251	2	1,257	70	1,187	0
Indiana	13,008	260	12,748	0	12,302	254	12,048	0	706	6	700	0
Iowa	4,145	100	3,935	110	3,949	98	3,752	99	196	2	183	11
Kansas	5,903	311	5,588	4	5,610	304	5,303	3	293	7	285	1
Michigan[b]	36,423	569	35,854	0	34,689	542	34,147	0	1,734	27	1,707	0
Minnesota	3,472	143	3,299	30	3,299	142	3,129	28	173	1	170	2
Missouri	15,897	143	15,754	0	15,076	136	14,940	0	821	7	814	0
Nebraska	2,495	141	2,354	0	2,357	137	2,220	0	138	4	134	0
North Dakota	492	11	481	0	461	11	450	0	31	0	31	0
Ohio	35,744	—	—	35,744	33,451	—	—	33,451	2,293	—	—	2,293
South Dakota	1,374	—	—	1,374	1,294	—	—	1,294	80	—	—	80
Wisconsin	7,849	477	7,304	68	7,506	469	6,971	66	343	8	333	2
South	301,866	15,924	162,354	123,588	285,126	15,463	152,349	117,314	16,740	461	10,005	6,274
Alabama	16,760	2	16,758	0	15,705	2	15,703	0	1,055	0	1,055	0
Arkansas	7,766	23	7,743	0	7,329	22	7,307	0	437	1	436	0
Delaware[a]	3,717	148	3,554	15	3,477	143	3,320	14	240	5	234	1
District of Columbia[a]	10,455	0	10,455	0	9,701	0	9,701	0	754	0	754	0
Florida	46,533	3,138	43,395	0	43,895	3,083	40,812	0	2,638	55	2,583	0
Georgia	23,644	172		23,472	22,253	164		22,089	1,391	8	0	1,383
Kentucky	9,799	—	—	9,799	9,286	—	—	9,286	513	—	—	513
Louisiana[c]	20,003	—	—	20,003	19,092	—	—	19,092	911	—	—	911
Maryland	19,291	—	—	19,291	18,360	—	—	18,360	931	—	—	931

Mississippi	8,904	37	8,863	4	8,396	34	8,358	4	508	3	505	0
North Carolina	18,903	—	—	18,903	17,882	—	—	17,882	1,021	—	—	1,021
Oklahoma	13,340	351	12,935	54	12,104	332	11,720	52	1,236	19	1,215	2
South Carolina	18,269	43	17,419	807	17,224	40	16,390	794	1,045	3	1,029	13
Tennessee[c]	11,474	—	—	11,474	11,015	—	—	11,015	459	—	—	459
Texas	51,677	11,945	39,732	0	49,186	11,578	37,608	0	2,491	367	2,124	0
Virginia	19,829	63	0	19,766	18,789	63	0	18,726	1,040	0	0	1,040
West Virginia	1,502	2	1,500	0	1,432	2	1,430	0	70	0	70	0
West	162,876	43,506	113,792	5,578	152,972	41,569	106,242	5,161	9,904	1,937	7,550	417
Alaska[a,d]	2,706	77	2,629	0	2,574	76	2,498	0	132	1	131	0
Arizona	15,415	4,351	11,064	0	14,476	4,140	10,336	0	939	211	728	0
California[b]	101,808	31,824	64,975	5,009	95,506	30,400	60,461	4,645	6,302	1,424	4,514	364
Colorado[d]	8,392	2,122	6,052	218	7,939	2,028	5,709	202	453	94	343	16
Hawaii[a,d]	2,700	100	2,586	14	2,533	94	2,430	9	167	6	156	5
Idaho[d]	2,143	263	1,863	17	2,022	249	1,758	15	121	14	105	2
Montana	1,478	30	1,448	0	1,405	29	1,376	0	73	1	72	0
Nevada	5,503	511	4,992	0	5,071	492	4,579	0	432	19	413	0
New Mexico	3,119	1,794	1,303	22	2,959	1,711	1,235	13	160	83	68	9
Oregon	6,732	540	6,118	74	6,323	531	5,722	70	409	9	396	9
Utah	2,625	435	2,154	36	2,505	414	2,056	35	120	21	98	4
Washington	9,156	1,342	7,626	188	8,617	1,293	7,152	172	539	49	474	16
Wyoming	1,099	117	982	0	1,042	112	930	0	57	5	52	0

Notes: All data for Arizona, California, Florida, Georgia, Illinois, Indiana, Iowa, Massachusetts, Michigan, Texas, and Wyoming are custody rather than jurisdiction counts. — = not available.

Source: Reprinted from Snell, T. L. (1993). *Correctional populations in the United States, 1991* (p. 60). Washington, DC: U.S. Department of Justice, Bureau of Justice Statistics.

[a]Figures include both jail and prison inmates; jails and prisons are combined in one system.

[b]Michigan and California reported only Mexican Americans as Hispanic prisoners and reported other Hispanic inmates as non-Hispanic.

[c]Louisiana and Tennessee do not distinguish Hispanic ethnicity of prisoners.

[d]Alaska, Colorado, Hawaii, and Idaho estimated the number of Hispanic prisoners.

eral prisoner some $78,000. Operating costs vary among the states, with the range between $9,500 and $32,000 per prisoner per year. Probation and parole have also become more costly.

Incarceration rates are rising more rapidly than crime rates. Much of the increase in incarceration may be attributed to antidrug efforts; two-thirds of the annual federal expen-

ditures of $12 billion on such efforts goes to law enforcement, leaving little for education, prevention, and treatment. The number of adults in prison for drug offenses tripled from 1986 to 1991. Their sentences are also longer than in the past, and many states have adopted long mandatory sentences for drug offenses. These efforts discriminate against African Americans and Hispanics; for example, only

TABLE 3-25 **Family Characteristics of State Prison Inmates, by Gender, Race, and Hispanic Origin: 1991**

Characteristic	All Inmates	Gender		Hispanic Origin			
		Male	Female	White Non-Hispanic	Black Non-Hispanic	Hispanic	Other
Person(s) lived with most of time while growing up							
Both parents	43.1	43.1	42.0	56.2	31.9	46.1	41.1
Mother only	39.2	39.2	38.9	27.6	49.7	36.1	31.1
Father only	3.9	4.0	3.4	4.9	3.0	4.0	5.9
Grandparents	7.7	7.6	9.3	5.2	10.0	6.8	5.3
Other relatives	3.0	3.0	3.0	1.7	3.5	3.8	5.5
Other[a]	3.2	3.2	3.5	4.5	1.7	3.2	11.0
Ever lived in a foster home, agency, or institution while growing up							
No	82.7	82.7	82.8	76.9	86.9	85.8	65.8
Yes	17.3	17.3	17.2	23.1	13.1	14.2	34.2
Family member ever incarcerated							
No	62.6	63.1	53.4	66.9	58.4	65.3	59.8
Yes	37.4	36.9	46.6	33.1	41.6	34.7	40.2
Mother	1.6	1.5	4.0	1.9	1.5	1.1	2.9
Father	6.4	6.3	7.8	8.4	5.0	5.3	10.6
Brother	31.2	30.9	35.1	25.8	36.0	29.1	33.3
Sister	4.5	4.2	10.0	3.6	5.1	4.3	8.1
Child	0.3	0.2	1.6	0.3	0.3	0.5	0.1
Parent or guardian abused alcohol or drugs while inmate was growing up							
No	73.1	73.5	66.4	63.2	79.9	77.8	57.8
Yes	26.9	26.5	33.6	36.8	20.1	22.2	42.2
Alcohol	22.2	21.9	26.3	30.5	16.7	17.5	36.1
Drugs	0.8	0.8	1.6	0.7	0.7	1.3	0.2
Both	3.7	3.6	5.7	5.3	2.5	3.2	5.9

Source: Reprinted from Snell, T. L. (1993). *Correctional populations in the United States, 1991* (p. 30). Washington, DC: U.S. Department of Justice, Bureau of Justice Statistics.

[a]Includes friends, foster home, agency, or institution.

TABLE 3-26 **Sentence Length and Special Sentencing Conditions of State Prison Inmates, by Most Serious Offense: 1991**

Most Serious Offense	Number of Inmates	Maximum Sentence Length (months)		Special Conditions of Sentence (%)							
		Median	Mean	Fines	Court Costs	Victim Restitution	Community Service	Drug Treatment	Drug Testing	Alcohol Treatment	Psychiatric or Psychological Counseling[a]
All offenses	690,721	108	150	10.6	12.1	10.5	1.0	6.2	5.2	3.2	2.5
Violent offenses	323,064	180	216	7.5	10.0	9.7	0.7	3.7	2.6	2.6	4.1
Murder	73,838	Life	381	4.7	6.9	4.7	0.2	1.9	1.0	1.4	1.3
Negligent manslaughter	12,642	156	185	8.2	8.4	9.1	2.4	4.0	2.3	5.3	1.0
Kidnapping	8,092	360	293	12.7	11.1	11.5	0	3.3	4.1	2.6	3.2
Rape	24,477	240	277	6.1	11.0	10.3	0.5	3.0	2.0	3.9	12.6
Other sexual assault	41,352	120	175	11.4	12.0	6.7	0.9	3.8	1.5	3.7	14.8
Robbery	102,642	144	200	6.8	10.1	13.2	0.7	4.8	3.7	2.1	1.4
Assault	56,313	114	158	9.8	11.8	11.8	0.9	4.4	3.5	3.1	1.9
Other violent offenses	3,708	72	103	2.1	18.4	9.7	2.0	1.7	5.5	6.1	2.0
Property offenses	171,446	60	114	10.7	14.3	18.7	1.5	6.6	5.3	4.0	1.2
Burglary	86,237	96	140	10.8	12.9	17.6	1.4	6.7	5.5	3.9	1.5
Larceny–theft	33,265	48	72	9.2	16.3	17.5	0.4	6.3	5.1	3.1	0.5
Motor vehicle theft	15,217	54	80	9.2	10.5	12.6	1.5	4.0	5.1	5.3	1.2
Arson	4,652	120	197	11.7	10.6	22.0	1.3	4.4	3.7	5.2	8.0
Fraud	19,496	60	98	11.1	18.5	28.6	3.9	8.7	4.6	3.2	0.4
Stolen property	9,554	60	79	16.5	19.6	21.4	1.2	5.6	8.0	4.8	0
Other property offenses	3,025	48	76	11.6	14.4	17.5	0.6	10.9	1.7	9.0	0
Drug offenses	146,803	60	95	15.8	13.2	4.1	1.2	11.2	10.6	2.2	0.5
Possession	51,925	54	81	12.1	11.9	3.5	1.1	10.4	11.9	2.4	0.4
Trafficking	91,690	72	104	18.1	13.8	4.3	1.4	11.4	9.9	2.1	0.5
Other or unspecified	3,188	48	70	12.7	17.2	6.6	0	15.9	10.3	2.3	1.9
Public-order offenses	46,590	48	82	14.7	13.2	6.0	1.2	6.3	5.8	7.2	2.8
Weapons	12,595	54	74	9.2	11.5	3.9	0.5	4.4	4.9	1.4	1.8
DWI[b]	9,985	30	40	26.4	14.9	7.2	1.9	3.2	7.1	15.5	0.6
Other public-order offenses	24,010	60	104	12.8	13.1	6.6	1.2	8.5	5.7	6.8	4.1

Notes: Figures exclude an estimated 20,922 inmates for whom current offense and sentencing information were unknown. Detail may add to more than total because inmates may have been given more than one special sentencing condition. DWI = driving while intoxicated.

Source: Reprinted from Snell, T. L. (1993). Correctional populations in the United States, 1991 (p. 29). Washington, DC: U.S. Department of Justice, Bureau of Justice Statistics.

[a]Includes participation in sex offender treatment programs.

[b]Includes driving while intoxicated and driving under the influence of drugs or alcohol.

7 percent of incarcerated drug offenders in New York in 1989 were white, although most drug users are white. Laws call for stricter enforcement of prohibitions governing the use of drugs favored by people of color (such as crack cocaine) than for those more often used by white people (such as powdered cocaine) (Edna McConnell Clark Foundation, 1993).

The Edna McConnell Clark Foundation (1993) describes the incarcerated population as socioeconomically disadvantaged. Only one-third were employed full-time at the time of their arrest. Half of all inmates had reported annual incomes of less than $10,000 before their arrests.

White offenders are more likely to be sentenced to probation than offenders of color. Although less than one-half the inmate population is white, they are 65 percent of the probationary population. The Edna McConnell Clark Foundation (1993) quoted a report by the Sentencing Project stating that one-fourth of all African American men ages 20 to 29 were under the criminal justice system's supervision in 1990 and that in two cities, Baltimore and Washington, DC, about half of

young African American men were under criminal justice supervision.

Incarcerated Juveniles

In the 1970s and 1980s there were major conceptual and programmatic changes in the handling of juveniles who are in conflict with the law. As a result, many young violators considered in need of supervision were dealt with through the child welfare and mental health systems. Efforts were made to help them remain in their communities and with their families. Many were placed in foster care, if they were placed at all; provided with services through community education and mental health treatment programs, which often included their families; or otherwise diverted from corrections programs.

Through some of its juvenile justice grant programs, the federal government imposes penalties on states that jail children. Most states hold children in emergency shelters, juvenile detention centers, and other specialized facilities.

At the same time, most states have provisions for treating juveniles of varying ages as

TABLE 3-27 **Inmates under the Influence of Alcohol, Drugs, or Both at the Time of Their Arrest, by Type of Offense: 1991**

Current Offense	Percentage of Inmates under the Influence		
	Alcohol Only	Drugs Only	Both
All offenses	18	17	14
Violent offenses	21	12	16
Homicide	25	10	17
Sexual assault	22	5	14
Robbery	15	19	18
Assault	27	8	14
Property offenses	18	21	14
Drug offenses	8	26	10
Public-order offenses	31	10	9
DWI	70	3	8
Other public-order offenses	20	11	10

Note: DWI = driving while intoxicated.

Source: Reprinted from Beck, A., et al. (1993). *Survey of state prison inmates, 1991* (p. 26). Washington, DC: U.S. Department of Justice, Bureau of Justice Statistics.

adult offenders for crimes such as murder and rape. Some states even permit imposition of death sentences for juveniles. It remains to be seen whether increased public fear of crime will lead to a rise in severe punishments for juveniles.

Because the practices are so mixed, the data on juvenile custody are not as complete or current as they are for adults. However, some trends can be identified. Delinquency cases often are handled by juvenile courts (U.S. Bureau of the Census, 1993). In 1990, 1.27 million juvenile delinquency cases were disposed of by juvenile courts, up from 1.21 million in 1989 and 1.07 million in 1982. In the 1990 figures, 95,000 cases were violent offenses; 535,000 cases were property crimes; and 635,000 cases were for delinquency offenses such as vandalism, simple assault, obstruction of justice, drug violations, sex offenses, trespassing, and liquor law violations.

In 1994 the Associated Press reported that the U.S. Department of Justice found a 68 percent increase from 1988 to 1992 of juvenile court cases involving serious offenses such as murder and aggravated assault. There were 118,700 serious crimes committed by young people. Aggravated assault increased the most, by 80 percent; there were 77,900 cases in 1992. Homicides increased 55 percent, to 2,500; robberies increased 52 percent, to 32,999; and forcible rape increased 27 percent, to 5,400. Juvenile court cases increased to almost 1.5 million, a 26 percent increase. Professor Wesley Skogan of Northwestern University was quoted in the article as saying that some of the increase in court cases is attributable to a greater willingness to prosecute young people.

Private facilities are increasingly used for holding juveniles (Maguire, Pastore, & Flanagan, 1993). These may include children's homes and detention facilities operated by private organizations under contract with the state government. In the 10-year period 1979 to 1989, admissions to such facilities more than doubled, whereas the increase in public facilities was less than 10 percent. This trend reflects the federal government's effort, which many states support, to keep juveniles out of corrections facilities. Following residence in such facilities, many young people commit adult crimes and become inmates of adult corrections facilities. Many in the field of juvenile delinquency—including social workers—have sought to divert young offenders away from the classic reformatories and to keep them in their own families, with foster families, in group homes, and in other noncustodial settings. Maintaining young people in community settings enhances the possibilities of rehabilitation and avoidance of future offenses. Some states have closed their public juvenile facilities, and others have substantially reduced them.

Table 3-28 shows the numbers of juvenile offenders in custody and Table 3-29 shows the custody rate per 100,000 juveniles on a state-by-state basis. The total rate for the United States in 1991 was 221 per 100,000, the same as in 1989. Many states have dramatically lower figures. The variations in state rates are almost totally a function of public policy. Some state laws discourage the incarceration of young people in correctional facilities such as reformatories. Others believe that such facilities are the appropriate solution to youth misbehavior. Many states have ceased treating "status offenders"—those who engage in behaviors that would not be subject to government intervention if they were adults, such as alcohol use, truancy, and sexual activity—as delinquents, and consequently they are handled by child welfare agencies rather than the juvenile justice system. So acts that would in some states be defined as juvenile delinquency and punished by incarceration are defined in others as behavior requiring the intervention and assistance of child welfare workers.

Capital Punishment

Seventeen states have the death penalty for people under 18. Two set 14 as the minimum age; one, Virginia, sets the minimum age as 15; nine specify 16; and four use 17. South Dakota sets the minimum age at 10 but only after a transfer hearing for a juvenile to be tried as an adult (Greenfeld, 1992).

From 1977 to 1991, there were 157 executions—90 by electrocution, 61 by lethal injection, five by lethal gas, and one by firing

TABLE 3-28 **Juvenile Offenders in Custody, by Selected Characteristics and State: 1991**

State	Number of Juveniles in Custody		Age Limits of Juvenile Offenders		Number of Staff	Average Length of Stay (in Months)
	Male	Female	Lower	Upper		
Alabama	689	39	0	18	400	8.5
Alaska	217[a]	—	11	17	260	—
Arizona	514	45	8	Up to 18th birthday	573	90 days
Arkansas	200	11	8	18	354	4.5
California	8,475	299	11	25	5,033[b]	22.3
Colorado	543	23	12	18	535	9.2
Connecticut	203	24	None	16[c]	350	4 to 18
Delaware	79	8	13/14	18[d]	138	18 weeks
District of Columbia	524	43	7	21	419	6 to 8
Florida	1,057[a]	—	9	18	696[e]	45 days to 18 months
Georgia	1,908	378	None	17	786	8.1
Hawaii	50	3	12	19	67	27 days to 9 months
Idaho	185[f]	46[f]	None	17[g]	156	9
Illinois	1,268	67	13	21	950	10.7
Indiana	635	164	12	21	766	5.2[h]
Iowa	171	41	12	18	325	4 to 6
Kansas	420	84	10	18	520	8
Kentucky	518	95	12	18	650	6.5
Louisiana	1,919	343	1[i]	16	756	12
Maine	195	28	11	18[j]	243.5	6.5
Maryland	1,259	230	12	18	371	k
Massachusetts	1,507	142	7	17	266	8 to 10
Michigan	700[h]	70	12	19[l]	980	16
Minnesota	124	1	10	19[m]	167	5.1
Mississippi	376[a]	—	10	17	282	Varies
Missouri	404	62	12	17	273	6
Montana	133	61	10	19	182	7
Nebraska	185	40	12	18	191	5 to 7
Nevada	279	67	12	18[n]	201	7.6
New Hampshire	130	37	11	18	197	6
New Jersey	704[o]	18[o]	12	NA	1,254[p]	NA
New York	2,518	395	7	21	2,450	4.9
North Carolina	3,759[q]	1,739[q]	10	15	834	9
North Dakota	181	61	12	18	81	5.7
Ohio	2,155	103	12	18	1,875	7.8
Oklahoma	1,141	127	10[r]	18[s]	356	6
Oregon	452	42	12	18	320	232 days
Pennsylvania	563	32	12	21[t]	925	9.5
Rhode Island	164	8	0	21	198	261 days
South Carolina	723	59	12	u	524	—
South Dakota	144	37	10	20	120	8
Tennessee	1,185	152	12	21	515	v
Texas	1,786	118	10	w	1,570	6.5
Utah	400	83	10	18[x]	91	8.4
Vermont	372	58	10	17	20	21
Virginia	751	85	11	17	450	5.7
Washington	877	60	10	20	644	8.1
West Virginia	99	11	10	18	94	7 to 8
Wisconsin	597	38	12	18[y]	593	7.9
Wyoming	70	56	12	21	128	z

Source: Reprinted from Maguire, K., Pastore, A. L., & Flanagan, T. J. (1993). *Sourcebook of criminal justice statistics, 1992* (p. 585). Washington, DC: U.S. Department of Justice, Bureau of Justice Statistics.

[a]Includes both males and females. [b]Departmentwide. [c]Offense committed prior to 16th birthday. [d]If in custody youth can remain until age 19. [e]State-operated programs only. [f]Residential placements. [g]Can be retained in custody until age 21. [h]Approximation. [i]Legal. [j]Can be up to age 21. [k]Four to six months if committed; 23 days if detained. [l]Up to age 21 for various offenses. [m]Offense must be committed prior to 18th birthday. [n]Up to age 21 for offenses committed prior to 18th birthday. [o]Includes probation. [p]Includes nonsupervisory officers. [q]Includes training schools and detention. [r]Although there are not statutory limits, age 10 is generally the lowest. [s]New laws may enforce up to age 19. [t]Those over age 18 would have committed acts prior to turning 18. [u]Must have committed the offense prior to 17th birthday. [v]6.5 months if indeterminate sentence; 18 months if determinate sentence. [w]Delinquent acts committed prior to age 17; agency retains jurisdiction until age 21. [x]With continuing jurisdiction until age 21. [y]Youths can be retained for murder until age 25 and other serious offenses until age 21. All others are a maximum of age 19. [z]Approximately four months for males; approximately nine months for females.

squad. An average of nearly 10 years elapses between a death sentence and execution, persuading some analysts that the legal costs of imposing a death sentence are greater than the overall costs of a life sentence.

In 1991 there were 14 executions (seven white prisoners and seven African Americans) in the following states: five in Texas; two each in Florida and Virginia; and one each in Georgia, Louisi-ana, Missouri, North Carolina, and South Carolina. There were 2,482 prisoners under sentence of death (Greenfeld, 1992). Table 3-30 shows the number of prisoners under death sentence, those removed from death row, and those executed, by race for states with the death penalty and the federal government.

Table 3-31 shows the number of Hispanic and women prisoners under death sentence

TABLE 3-29 **Custody Rate of Juveniles Held in Public Juvenile Facilities, by Region and State: 1987, 1989, and 1991**

Region and State	Custody Rate per 100,000 Juveniles			Region and State	Custody Rate per 100,000 Juveniles		
	1987	1989	1991		1987	1989	1991
United States total	208	221	221	District of Columbia	779	808	826
Northeast	133	143	—	Florida	198	193	161
Connecticut	94	124	123	Georgia	197	233	235
Maine	155	194	185	Kentucky	133	138	151
Massachusetts	42	48	37	Louisiana	214	231	251
New Hampshire	107	114	95	Maryland	211	166	172
New Jersey	239	247	222	Mississippi	100	132	123
New York	161	171	192	North Carolina	150	164	168
Pennsylvania	85	90	106	Oklahoma	117	89	90
Rhode Island	103	131	168	South Carolina	194	209	257
Vermont	24	39	28	Tennessee	180	171	138
Midwest	184	198	—	Texas	133	133	144
Illinois	169	165	181	Virginia	226	258	264
Indiana	197	203	214	West Virginia	60	76	77
Iowa	133	143	128	West	364	385	—
Kansas	250	264	232	Alaska	283	324	312
Michigan	188	208	209	Arizona	270	279	226
Minnesota	124	136	128	California	498	529	492
Missouri	166	207	206	Colorado	140	164	186
Nebraska	152	166	155	Hawaii	130	79	71
North Dakota	91	124	99	Idaho	90	85	98
Ohio	246	273	300	Montana	240	223	230
South Dakota	285	269	246	Nevada	463	510	427
Wisconsin	124	130	157	New Mexico	265	283	268
South	168	174	—	Oregon	199	208	220
Alabama	157	178	174	Utah	88	85	95
Arkansas	85	91	100	Washington	229	236	256
Delaware	238	206	187	Wyoming	262	217	164

Notes: Juvenile custody rates are calculated by dividing the number of juveniles in public facilities on the census date by the number of people from 10 years of age up to the statutorily defined maximum age of original juvenile court jurisdiction in each state. — = not available.

Source: Reprinted from Maguire, K., Pastore, A. L., & Flanagan, T. J. (1993). *Sourcebook of criminal justice statistics, 1992* (p. 585). Washington, DC: U.S. Department of Justice, Bureau of Justice Statistics.

TABLE 3-30 Prisoners under Sentence of Death, by Region, State, and Race: 1990 and 1991

Region and State	Prisoners under Sentence of Death, 12/31/90			Received under Sentence of Death			Removed from Death Row (excluding executions)[a]			Executed			Prisoners under Sentence of Death, 12/31/91		
	Total[b]	White	Black	Total[b]	White	Black	Total[b]	White	Black	Total[b]	White	Black	Total[b]	White	Black
United States total	2,346	1,368	940	266	163	101	116	60	52	14	7	7	2,482	1,464	982
Federal[c]	0	0	0	1	1	0	0	0	0	0	0	0	1	1	0
State	2,346	1,368	940	265	162	101	116	60	52	14	7	7	2,481	1,463	982
Northeast	134	53	80	21	6	14	10	2	8	0	0	0	145	57	86
Connecticut	2	2	0	2	2	0	0	0	0	0	0	0	4	2	2
New Hampshire	0	0	0	0	0	0	0	0	0	0	0	0	0	0	0
New Jersey	10	4	6	0	0	0	6	2	4	0	0	0	4	2	2
Pennsylvania	122	47	74	19	6	12	4	0	4	0	0	0	137	53	82
Midwest	362	169	191	37	21	16	17	5	12	1	0	1	381	185	194
Illinois	128	47	81	7	1	6	3	0	3	0	0	0	132	48	84
Indiana	48	32	16	3	2	1	2	1	1	0	0	0	49	33	16
Missouri	71	39	32	13	9	4	6	3	3	1	0	1	77	45	32
Nebraska	11	7	3	1	1	0	0	0	0	0	0	0	12	8	3
Ohio	104	44	59	13	8	5	6	1	5	0	0	0	111	51	59
South Dakota	0	0	0	0	0	0	0	0	0	0	0	0	0	0	0
South	1,362	801	540	158	104	53	73	40	31	13	7	6	1,434	858	556
Alabama	117	58	58	6	4	2	4	2	2	0	0	0	119	60	58
Arkansas	33	21	12	2	1	1	1	0	1	0	0	0	34	22	12
Delaware	6	2	4	1	1	0	0	0	0	0	0	0	7	3	4
Florida	291	188	103	45	29	16	23	12	11	2	1	1	311	204	107
Georgia	99	53	46	7	2	5	4	1	3	1	1	0	101	54	47
Kentucky	27	21	6	3	3	0	0	0	0	0	0	0	30	24	6
Louisiana	32	14	18	7	3	4	1	0	1	1	1	0	37	17	20
Maryland	17	2	15	1	1	0	2	2	0	0	0	0	16	1	15
Mississippi	46	18	28	5	3	2	2	2	0	0	0	0	51	21	30
North Carolina	84	45	35	17	10	7	26	13	11	1	1	0	74	41	31
Oklahoma	117	80	28	12	6	5	4	3	1	0	0	0	125	83	32
South Carolina	40	17	23	8	7	1	2	2	0	1	1	0	45	21	24
Tennessee	85	57	23	12	10	2	0	0	0	0	0	0	97	67	28
Texas	323	201	117	26	19	7	4	3	1	5	3	2	340	214	121
Virginia	45	24	21	6	5	1	2	2	0	2	1	1	47	26	21

State													
West	488	330	122	49	31	18	16	13	1	0	0	521	383	146
Arizona	87	77	7	13	11	2	3	3	0	0	0	97	85	9
California	280	173	99	24	11	13	3	2	0	0	0	301	182	112
Colorado	3	3	0	1	1	0	1	1	0	0	0	3	3	0
Idaho	19	19	0	2	2	0	0	0	0	0	0	21	21	0
Montana	6	4	4	0	0	2	0	0	0	0	0	6	4	0
Nevada	59	42	17	4	2	0	3	3	0	0	0	60	41	19
New Mexico	1	1	1	0	0	0	0	0	1	0	0	1	1	0
Oregon	10	8	2	3	3	0	4	3	0	0	0	9	8	1
Utah	11	8	3	1	1	1	0	0	0	0	0	12	9	3
Washington	10	8	1	1	0	0	1	0	0	0	0	10	8	2
Wyoming	2	2	0	0	0	0	1	1	0	0	0	1	1	0

Notes: States not listed and the District of Columbia did not authorize the death penalty as of December 31, 1990. Some figures shown for year end 1990 are revised.

Source: Reprinted from Greenfeld, L. A. (1992). *Capital punishment 1991* (p. 8). Washington, DC: U.S. Department of Justice, Bureau of Justice Statistics.

aIncludes six deaths due to natural causes (two each in Pennsylvania and Florida and one each in Missouri and California) and one suicide in Nevada.

bTotals include people of other races.

cExcludes five males held under Armed Forces jurisdiction with a military death sentence for murder.

in 1990 and 1991. One Hispanic was executed in 1991; no women have been executed in the United States since 1977.

According to Greenfeld (1992), the median education level of those under death sentence in 1991 was about 12 years. The mean age of the group was 35 years and the median age was 34 years, although there were 192 prisoners under age 25 under sentence of death. Fourteen of them were under age 20. Of those for whom the information was available, over two-thirds had prior felony convictions.

Conclusion

Crime and delinquency issues are the subject matter of political campaigns and frequent public policy discussions. Crime in all its manifestations is probably the most popular subject of true as well as fictional presentations on television and the most frequent theme of American fiction, including films. Criminal episodes and trials are among the most-watched television programs. Crime is also a constant preoccupation of most Americans, especially elderly people and parents.

Knowing the facts about the extent and nature of crime, criminals, delinquents, and the justice system is indispensable for social workers—not only the many who work directly in the corrections and justice systems, but also those who work in and with communities that are more susceptible to crime than others. Social workers who have realistic, accurate knowledge about these often inflammatory and emotionally charged issues can be more effective in working with their clients—all of whom are potential victims of crime—and with the communities they serve. American communities need help in identifying and coping effectively with issues of crime and delinquency, which may receive more attention than they deserve and treatments that may not be the most appropriate for the circumstances.

TABLE 3-31 **Hispanics and Women under Sentence of Death, by State: 1990 and 1991**

	Under Sentence of Death, 12/31/90		Received under Sentence of Death		Death Sentence Removed[a]		Under Sentence of Death, 12/31/91	
	Hispanics	Women	Hispanics	Women	Hispanics	Women	Hispanics	Women
United States total	171	32	20	4	7	2	184	34
Alabama	0	5	0	0	0	0	0	5
Arizona	19	0	2	1	2	0	19	1
Arkansas	1	0	0	0	0	0	1	0
California	37	1	2	0	1	0	38	1
Colorado	1	0	0	0	0	0	1	0
Florida	27	2	5	0	1	0	31	2
Georgia	1	0	0	0	0	0	1	0
Idaho	1	0	0	0	0	0	1	0
Illinois	8	0	0	0	0	0	8	0
Indiana	2	0	0	0	0	0	2	0
Kentucky	0	1	0	0	0	0	0	1
Mississippi	1	2	0	0	0	0	1	2
Nevada	6	1	1	0	0	0	7	1
Missouri	0	1	1	2	0	1	1	2
North Carolina	1	5	1	1	0	0	2	6
Ohio	5	4	1	0	1	1	5	3
Oklahoma	5	4	0	0	0	0	5	4
Oregon	0	0	0	0	0	0	0	0
Pennsylvania	3	1	0	0	1	0	2	1
South Carolina	0	1	0	0	0	0	0	1
Tennessee	0	1	1	0	0	0	1	1
Texas	51	3	6	0	1	0	56	3
Utah	2	0	0	0	0	0	2	0

Source: Reprinted from Greenfeld, L. A. (1992). *Capital punishment 1991* (p. 9). Washington, DC: U.S. Department of Justice, Bureau of Justice Statistics.

[a]No women were executed during 1991. One Hispanic was executed during 1991 in Texas.

4

EDUCATION

Education is among the most important elements that contribute to human well-being—especially in modern industrial societies. Few factors are more crucial in determining the ability of individuals to be self-supporting and to support others. For example, there is a clear relationship between the earnings of "prime-age" men and their level of education. Although discrimination in employment is also a factor, Table 4-1 shows that wages appear to be closely correlated with educational attainment: The greater the educational attainment, the greater the earnings. In 1989 more than 40 percent of African American and Hispanic men with no more than an 8th grade education had low earnings. Table 4-2 gives the actual dollar earnings in 1989 dollars for 1979 and 1989 by years of schooling completed.

School-Age Population

The numbers and proportions of school-age people in the United States vary from decade to decade. Although the population has shown a steady increase over the years, the number of young people who are considered school age (5 to 17 years old) has declined since the 1970s, contributing to the aging of the U.S. population: The median age of the population in 1970 was 28 years; in 1990, it was 33 years (Wright, 1993).

In 1970 there were 205 million residents, and 52.5 million of them were school age (about 26 percent). In 1990 the total population had increased to 250 million people, but only 45.5 million of them (about 18.2 percent) were school age. These dramatic changes help to explain the recent public policy emphasis on elderly people rather than children—older people are a growing population,

and children are a declining population. The declining school-age population explains why many public schools are totally or partially abandoned. Of course, the changes are not equally distributed. Some rapidly growing areas with younger populations, including California, Florida, and Texas, have overcrowded schools.

School Enrollment

Figure 4-1 shows the trends in school enrollments beginning in 1970, with projections to the year 2000 in elementary and secondary school and at the college level. Table 4-3 shows elementary, secondary, and college enrollments for 1980 and projected through 2000, further divided into public and private enrollments.

Table 4-4 shows school enrollment by age, from preprimary through college, in 1970 through 1991. In addition to absolute numbers, the percentage of children of each age group who are enrolled is shown. Almost all children ages 7 to 13 were enrolled, but less than 10 percent of young adults (ages 25 to 34) were. Information is also provided on the ethnicity of enrolled students; a separate category is reserved for Mexican Americans, the largest group of Hispanics in the United States.

Public Schools

The overwhelming majority of American young people are students in public schools. Historically, the public schools have been one of the most important institutions in the nation. They are a major influence on American family structures, values, employment patterns, and economy. Furthermore, they are typically the largest single item of appropriation in the budgets of most state and local governments. Public schools have also become a major employer of social workers, as chapter 9 demonstrates. Issues of health, family relations, juvenile delinquency, and economic self-sufficiency are typically addressed, at least in part, through the school systems by school social workers and related personnel. Table 4-5 shows the total enrollments in public elementary and secondary schools by state in 1980 and 1990.

Projected enrollments for 1991 through 1993 are presented in Table 4-6.

Private Schools

Not all school-age children are enrolled in public schools. Nearly 5 million were enrolled in private schools in 1991, as Table 4-7 shows. More than half of them were in Roman Catholic schools; the rest were enrolled in

TABLE 4-1 **Percentage of Employed Men with Low Earnings, by Race and Ethnicity and Years of Education: 1979 and 1989**

Ethnicity	Years of Schooling Completed						
	0–8	9–11	12	13–15	16	17+	All
All							
1979	20.9	13.1	8.3	7.8	5.9	4.9	9.0
1989	36.2	30.1	15.2	9.3	6.6	6.2	13.9
White, non-Hispanic							
1979	12.8	10.5	7.0	6.5	5.3	4.4	7.0
1989	33.0	25.4	12.3	8.0	5.5	5.9	10.9
Black, non-Hispanic							
1979	38.4	25.2	15.9	15.0	9.5	15.2	20.2
1989	42.4	41.2	25.5	18.3	14.8	7.7	24.8
Hispanic							
1979	28.4	18.7	11.0	9.6	9.1	8.1	17.4
1989	42.2	41.0	25.4	16.4	13.1	5.1	30.0

Note: The figures reported are the weighted percentages of employed men in each age group with earnings of less than $11,662 per year (1989 dollars).

Source: Reprinted from Committee on Ways and Means, U.S. House of Representatives. (1993). *Overview of entitlement programs: 1993 greenbook* (p. 259). Washington, DC: U.S. Government Printing Office.

TABLE 4-2 **Mean Earnings in 1989 Dollars of Employed Men, by Race and Ethnicity and Years of Education: 1979 and 1989**

Ethnicity	Years of Schooling Completed						
	0–8	9–11	12	13–15	16	17+	All
All							
1979	20,199	23,921	28,446	30,665	35,775	39,933	30,105
1989	16,195	18,434	25,018	29,806	38,306	43,458	29,222
Percent change	−19.8	−22.9	−12.1	−2.8	+7.1	+8.8	−2.9
White, non-Hispanic							
1979	22,946	25,732	29,694	31,584	36,744	40,173	31,706
1989	19,164	19,780	26,509	31,116	39,331	44,396	31,344
Percent change	−16.5	−23.1	−10.7	−1.5	+7.0	+10.5	−1.2
Black, non-Hispanic							
1979	15,348	17,916	21,642	23,989	27,763	35,329	21,394
1989	13,800	15,180	19,020	23,119	28,287	34,344	20,930
Percent change	−10.1	−15.3	−12.1	−3.6	+1.9	−2.8	−2.2
Hispanic							
1979	17,566	20,441	24,022	27,027	31,412	36,440	22,800
1989	14,255	15,413	19,942	24,811	31,297	36,863	19,593
Percent change	−18.8	−24.6	−17.0	−8.2	−0.0	+1.2	−14.1

Note: Only employed men between the ages of 25 and 54 are included in the samples.

Source: Reprinted from Committee on Ways and Means, U.S. House of Representatives. (1993). *Overview of entitlement programs: 1993 greenbook* (p. 259). Washington, DC: U.S. Government Printing Office.

other religious schools or in nonsectarian private schools. Table 4-7 also shows the number of schools and tuition costs. In addition, about 36 percent of private schools had minority enrollments of less than 5 percent in 1991, but in 14.4 percent minority students constituted more than half the student body (U.S. Bureau of the Census, 1993).

High-School Graduation Rates

Figure 4-2 shows the percentage of people age 25 years and older who had completed four years of high school or more, by ethnicity, in 1970 and 1992. Over the two decades, the percentages of those graduating from high school or achieving higher education has increased for all ethnic groups. Figure 4-3 shows

FIGURE 4-1 **School Enrollment from 1970 Onward, with Projections from 1995 to the Year 2000**

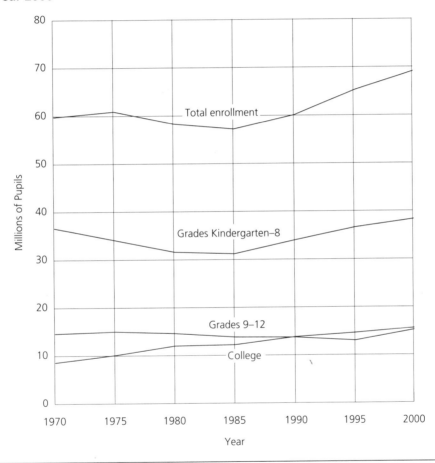

Source: Reprinted from U.S. Bureau of the Census. (1993). *Statistical abstract of the United States: 1993* (113th ed., p. 144). Austin, TX: Reference Press.

TABLE 4-3 **Enrollment in Educational Institutions, by Level and Control of Institution: Selected Years, Fall 1980 to Fall 2000 (Numbers in thousands)**

Level of Instruction and Type of Control	Fall 1980	Fall 1985	Fall 1986	Fall 1987	Fall 1988	Fall 1989	Fall 1990	Fall 1991[a]	Fall 1992[b]	Projected, Fall 1993	Projected, Fall 1995	Projected, Fall 2000
All levels	58,305	57,226	57,709	58,254	58,485	59,436	60,268	61,558	62,429	63,919	65,655	69,874
Public	50,335	48,901	49,467	49,981	50,350	51,121	52,061	53,310	53,966	55,298	56,744	60,453
Private	7,971	8,325	8,242	8,273	8,135	8,316	8,206	8,248	8,463	8,621	8,911	9,421
Elementary and secondary education[c]	46,208	44,979	45,205	45,488	45,430	45,898	46,448	47,199	47,870	48,925	50,709	54,412
Public	40,877	39,422	39,753	40,008	40,189	40,543	41,217	42,000	42,496	43,454	45,049	48,345
Private	5,331	5,557	5,452[d]	5,479	5,241	5,355	5,232	5,199	5,375	5,471	5,660	6,067
Grades K–8[e]	31,639	31,229	31,536	32,165	32,537	33,314	33,973	34,544	35,031	35,727	36,668	39,129
Public	27,647	27,034	27,420	27,933	28,501	29,152	29,878	30,470	30,819	31,447	32,275	34,441
Private	3,992	4,195	4,116[d]	4,232	4,036	4,162	4,095	4,074	4,212	4,280	4,393	4,688
Grades 9–12	14,570	13,750	13,669	13,323	12,893	12,583	12,475	12,655	12,841	13,198	14,041	15,283
Public	13,231	12,388	12,333	12,076	11,687	11,390	11,338	11,530	11,678	12,007	12,774	13,904
Private	1,339	1,362	1,336[d]	1,247	1,206	1,193	1,137	1,125	1,163	1,191	1,267	1,379
Higher education[f]	12,097	12,247	12,504	12,767	13,055	13,539	13,820	14,359	14,558	14,994	14,946	15,462
Public	9,457	9,479	9,714	9,973	10,161	10,578	10,845	11,310	11,470	11,844	11,695	12,108
Undergraduate[g]	8,442	8,477	8,661	8,919	9,103	9,488	9,710	10,148	10,190	10,525	10,367	10,797
First-professional	114	112	112	110	109	113	112	111	128	132	131	125
Graduate[h]	901	890	941	945	949	978	1,023	1,050	1,152	1,187	1,197	1,186
Private	2,640	2,768	2,790	2,793	2,894	2,961	2,975	3,049	3,088	3,150	3,251	3,354
Undergraduate[g]	2,033	2,120	2,137	2,128	2,213	2,255	2,250	2,291	2,295	2,325	2,394	2,512
First-professional	163	162	158	158	158	162	162	169	180	188	195	187
Graduate[h]	443	486	494	507	522	544	563	589	613	637	662	655

Notes: Higher education enrollment projections are based on the middle alternative projections published by the National Center for Education Statistics. Because of rounding, details may not add to totals. Some data have been revised from previously published figures.

Source: Reprinted from U.S. Department of Education, National Center for Education Statistics. (1993). *Digest of education statistics* (p. 11). Washington, DC: Author.

[a]Preliminary.

[b]Based on "early estimates" surveys for public and private elementary and secondary schools.

[c]Includes enrollments in local public school systems and in most private schools (religiously affiliated and nonsectarian). Excludes subcollegiate departments of institutions of higher education, residential schools for exceptional children, and federal schools. Excludes preprimary pupils in schools that do not offer first grade or above.

[d]Estimated.

[e]Includes kindergarten and some nursery school pupils.

[f]Includes full-time and part-time students enrolled in degree-credit and nondegree-credit programs in universities and 2-year and 4-year colleges.

[g]Includes unclassified students below the baccalaureate level.

[h]Includes unclassified postbaccalaureate students.

TABLE 4-4 **School Enrollment, by Age, Race, and Hispanic Origin: Selected Years, 1970 to 1991 (Numbers in thousands)**

Age and Ethnicity	Enrollment						Rate					
	1970	1980	1985	1989	1990	1991	1970	1980	1985	1989	1990	1991
Total 3 to 34 years old[a]	60,357	57,348	58,013	59,235	60,588	61,276	56.4	49.7	48.3	49.1	50.2	50.7
3 and 4 years old	1,461	2,280	2,801	2,898	3,292	3,068	20.5	36.7	38.9	39.1	44.4	40.5
5 and 6 years old	7,000	5,853	6,697	6,990	7,207	7,178	89.5	95.7	96.1	95.2	96.5	95.4
7 to 13 years old	28,943	23,751	22,849	24,431	25,016	25,445	99.2	99.3	99.2	99.3	99.6	99.7
14 and 15 years old	7,869	7,282	7,362	6,493	6,555	6,634	98.1	98.2	98.1	98.8	99.0	98.8
16 and 17 years old	6,927	7,129	6,654	6,254	6,098	6,155	90.0	89.0	91.7	92.7	92.5	93.3
18 and 19 years old	3,322	3,788	3,716	4,125	4,044	3,969	47.7	46.4	51.6	56.0	57.3	59.6
20 and 21 years old	1,949	2,515	2,708	2,630	2,852	3,041	31.9	31.0	35.3	38.5	39.7	42.0
22 to 24 years old	1,410	1,931	2,068	2,207	2,231	2,365	14.9	16.3	16.9	19.9	21.0	22.2
25 to 29 years old	1,011	1,714	1,942	1,960	2,013	2,045	7.5	9.3	9.2	9.3	9.7	10.2
30 to 34 years old	466	1,105	1,218	1,248	1,281	1,377	4.2	6.4	6.1	5.7	5.8	6.2
35 years old and over	—	1,290	1,766	2,230	2,439	2,620	—	1.4	2.1	2.0	2.1	2.2
White: Total 3 to 34 years old	51,719	47,673	47,452	47,923	48,899	49,156	56.2	48.9	47.8	48.4	49.5	50.0
3 and 4 years old	1,181	1,844	2,250	2,370	2,700	2,502	19.9	36.3	38.6	39.4	44.9	41.3
5 and 6 years old	5,899	4,781	5,437	5,598	5,750	5,727	90.3	95.8	96.4	95.2	96.5	95.3
7 to 13 years old	24,564	19,585	18,464	19,638	20,076	20,325	99.2	99.2	99.3	99.3	99.6	99.6
14 and 15 years old	6,761	6,038	6,007	5,197	5,265	5,311	98.2	98.3	98.1	98.8	99.1	98.7
16 and 17 years old	6,008	5,937	5,449	4,993	4,858	4,902	90.6	88.6	91.6	92.3	92.5	93.3
18 and 19 years old	2,924	3,199	3,105	3,392	3,271	3,197	48.7	46.3	52.4	56.4	57.1	59.7
20 and 21 years old	1,750	2,206	2,318	2,208	2,402	2,517	33.1	31.9	36.1	39.5	41.0	43.2
22 to 24 years old	1,305	1,669	1,744	1,841	1,781	1,910	15.7	16.4	17.0	20.0	20.2	21.7
25 to 29 years old	910	1,473	1,635	1,659	1,706	1,646	7.7	9.2	9.2	9.9	9.9	9.9
30 to 34 years old	416	942	1,043	1,028	1,090	1,119	4.2	6.3	6.2	5.6	5.9	6.0
35 years old and over	—	1,104	1,533	1,956	2,096	2,219	—	1.3	1.7	2.0	2.1	2.2
Black: Total 3 to 34 years old	7,829	8,251	8,444	8,707	8,854	9,031	57.4	53.9	50.9	51.3	51.9	52.5
3 and 4 years old	250	371	469	407	452	428	22.7	38.2	42.7	38.9	41.6	37.2
5 and 6 years old	999	904	1,030	1,084	1,129	1,108	84.9	95.4	95.7	94.9	96.3	95.8
7 to 13 years old	3,998	3,598	3,549	3,761	3,832	3,941	99.3	99.4	99.1	99.2	99.8	99.8
14 and 15 years old	1,025	1,088	1,106	1,023	1,023	1,032	97.6	97.9	97.9	99.4	99.2	99.1
16 and 17 years old	837	1,047	994	1,033	962	959	85.7	90.6	91.7	93.7	91.7	91.7
18 and 19 years old	352	494	472	541	596	578	40.1	45.7	44.1	50.2	55.2	55.6
20 and 21 years old	174	242	298	309	305	329	22.8	23.4	27.7	30.7	28.4	30.0
22 to 24 years old	84	196	215	253	274	249	8.0	13.6	13.7	17.2	20.0	18.2
25 to 29 years old	68	187	192	168	162	229	4.8	8.8	7.4	6.4	6.1	8.7
30 to 34 years old	41	124	119	130	119	177	3.4	6.8	5.1	4.9	4.4	6.5
35 years old and over	—	186	233	167	238	289	—	1.8	1.9	1.5	2.1	2.5
Hispanic[b]: Total 3 to 34 years old	—	4,263	5,070	5,722	6,073	6,306	—	49.8	47.7	45.8	47.4	47.9
3 and 4 years old	—	172	213	202	249	299	—	28.5	27.0	23.8	29.8	30.6
5 and 6 years old	—	491	662	785	835	850	—	94.5	94.5	92.8	94.8	92.4

Continued on next page

TABLE 4-4 Continued

Age and Ethnicity	Enrollment						Rate					
	1970	1980	1985	1989	1990	1991	1970	1980	1985	1989	1990	1991
7 to 13 years old	—	2,009	2,322	2,637	2,794	2,909	—	99.2	99.0	98.7	99.4	99.7
14 and 15 years old	—	568	606	706	739	732	—	94.3	96.1	96.5	99.0	97.2
16 and 17 years old	—	454	562	554	592	532	—	81.8	84.5	86.4	85.4	82.6
18 and 19 years old	—	226	238	327	329	394	—	37.8	41.8	44.6	44.1	47.9
20 and 21 years old	—	111	137	152	213	215	—	19.5	24.0	18.8	27.2	26.4
22 to 24 years old	—	93	125	153	121	144	—	11.7	11.6	12.0	9.9	11.6
25 to 29 years old	—	84	120	129	130	140	—	6.9	6.6	6.6	6.3	6.9
30 to 34 years old	—	54	83	76	72	93	—	5.1	5.7	3.8	3.6	4.5
35 years old and over	—	—	—	136	145	148	—	—	—	2.1	2.1	2.0
Mexican American: Total 3 to 34 years old	—	2,698	3,180	3,743	4,017	4,171	—	49.0	47.5	44.7	46.8	47.7
3 and 4 years old	—	104	137	148	165	215	—	27.0	26.0	22.7	27.4	32.3
5 and 6 years old	—	327	458	553	619	581	—	93.2	95.3	91.8	94.7	92.1
7 to 13 years old	—	1,378	1,526	1,768	1,815	1,957	—	99.5	99.2	98.9	99.7	99.7
14 and 15 years old	—	361	367	481	499	475	—	92.1	97.7	95.7	99.5	97.6
16 and 17 years old	—	257	358	356	403	351	—	76.1	83.8	85.3	83.8	81.0
18 and 19 years old	—	113	127	176	213	282	—	32.0	35.2	36.9	40.9	47.0
20 and 21 years old	—	55	61	79	121	132	—	15.6	16.4	14.6	23.6	24.8
22 to 24 years old	—	40	55	77	70	70	—	7.5	7.8	8.9	8.3	8.2
25 to 29 years old	—	41	56	64	64	61	—	5.4	5.0	5.0	4.9	4.8
30 to 34 years old	—	22	36	41	47	48	—	3.3	4.5	3.3	3.6	3.7
35 years old and over	—	—	—	73	81	89	—	—	—	2.0	2.1	2.2

Notes: Covers civilian noninstitutional population enrolled in nursery school and above. — = not available.

Source: Reprinted from U.S. Bureau of the Census. (1993). *Statistical abstract of the United States: 1993* (113th ed., p. 151). Austin, TX: Reference Press.

[a]Includes other races, not shown separately.
[b]People of Hispanic origin may be of any race.

TABLE 4-5 **Public Elementary and Secondary School Enrollment, by State: 1980 and 1990 (Numbers in thousands)**

	Enrollment				Enrollment Rate[a]	
	K through Grade 8		Grades 9–12			
State	1980	1990	1980	1990	1980	1990
United States	27,647	29,888	13,231	11,336	86.5	91.3
Alabama	528	527	231	195	87.6	93.3
Alaska	60	85	26	29	94.0	97.3
Arizona	357	479	157	161	88.9	93.3
Arkansas	310	314	138	123	90.3	95.9
California	2,730	3,615	1,347	1,336	88.0	92.8
Colorado	374	420	172	154	92.2	94.6
Connecticut	364	347	168	122	83.3	90.2
Delaware	62	73	37	27	79.5	87.4
District of Columbia	71	61	29	19	91.8	100.0
Florida	1,042	1,370	468	492	84.4	92.6
Georgia	742	849	327	303	86.9	93.6
Hawaii	110	123	55	49	83.4	87.6
Idaho	144	160	59	61	95.4	96.9
Illinois	1,335	1,310	649	512	82.6	86.9
Indiana	708	676	347	279	88.0	90.4
Iowa	351	345	183	139	88.4	92.1
Kansas	283	320	133	117	88.7	92.6
Kentucky	464	459	206	177	83.7	90.5
Louisiana	544	586	234	199	80.3	88.2
Maine	153	155	70	60	91.5	96.5
Maryland	493	527	258	188	83.9	89.1
Massachusetts	676	604	346	230	88.6	88.8
Michigan	1,227	1,146	570	436	90.1	90.2
Minnesota	482	546	272	211	87.2	91.3
Mississippi	330	372	147	131	79.6	91.3
Missouri	567	585	277	227	83.8	86.0
Montana	106	111	50	42	92.9	93.8
Nebraska	189	198	91	76	86.6	88.7
Nevada	101	150	49	51	93.4	98.7
New Hampshire	112	126	55	46	85.3	89.1
New Jersey	820	784	426	306	81.5	86.1
New Mexico	186	208	85	94	89.5	94.3
New York	1,838	1,828	1,033	770	80.8	86.6
North Carolina	786	783	343	304	90.0	94.8
North Dakota	77	85	40	33	85.9	92.8
Ohio	1,312	1,258	645	514	84.8	88.0
Oklahoma	399	425	179	154	92.9	95.1
Oregon	319	351	145	134	88.5	93.0
Pennsylvania	1,231	1,172	678	496	80.4	83.6
Rhode Island	98	102	51	37	79.7	87.3
South Carolina	426	452	193	170	88.1	93.8
South Dakota	86	95	42	34	87.4	89.7
Tennessee	602	598	252	226	87.8	93.5
Texas	2,049	2,511	851	872	92.4	98.4
Utah	250	326	93	122	98.2	98.0
Vermont	66	71	29	25	87.9	93.9
Virginia	703	728	307	270	90.7	94.2
Washington	515	613	242	227	91.0	94.0
West Virginia	270	224	113	98	92.6	95.7
Wisconsin	528	566	303	232	82.1	86.0
Wyoming	70	71	28	27	97.3	97.3

Notes: Includes unclassified students. K = kindergarten.

Source: Reprinted from U.S. Bureau of the Census. (1993). *Statistical abstract of the United States: 1993* (113th ed., p. 159). Austin, TX: Reference Press.

[a]Percent of people ages 5 to 17 years.

TABLE 4-6 Public Elementary and Secondary School Enrollment Projections: 1991 to 1993 (Numbers in thousands)

State	Kindergarten through Grade 8			Grades 9–12		
	1991	1992	1993	1991	1992	1993
United States	30,186	30,663	31,091	11,389	11,587	11,880
Alabama	531	533	536	195	197	199
Alaska	84	84	86	28	29	30
Arizona	495	513	530	165	172	179
Arkansas	315	316	316	123	125	127
California	3,728	3,850	3,967	1,373	1,410	1,449
Colorado	421	428	432	155	159	163
Connecticut	357	367	378	120	120	122
Delaware	76	76	79	27	29	29
District of Columbia	61	62	64	20	19	20
Florida	1,426	1,488	1,545	467	479	504
Georgia	875	898	920	304	310	319
Hawaii	129	133	138	47	49	52
Idaho	155	152	149	60	62	65
Illinois	1,294	1,305	1,318	517	521	531
Indiana	682	682	680	280	285	290
Iowa	336	330	323	141	145	148
Kansas	322	323	324	120	125	128
Kentucky	445	440	434	177	181	184
Louisiana	573	570	567	194	197	203
Maine	157	160	163	60	60	63
Maryland	549	571	594	190	196	203
Massachusetts	621	637	655	225	226	230
Michigan	1,153	1,161	1,166	436	440	449
Minnesota	552	558	559	215	222	230
Mississippi	364	362	361	132	135	136
Missouri	594	601	606	232	237	244
Montana	108	108	106	43	42	43
Nebraska	197	196	195	77	78	79
Nevada	151	158	162	54	56	60
New Hampshire	136	141	147	46	48	50
New Jersey	800	824	852	300	302	309
New Mexico	212	216	221	93	95	97
New York	1,831	1,854	1,881	768	779	793
North Carolina	796	815	836	302	306	314
North Dakota	84	83	82	33	34	35
Ohio	1,262	1,268	1,269	514	519	529
Oklahoma	418	415	408	156	158	162
Oregon	345	347	347	137	141	144
Pennsylvania	1,188	1,201	1,213	493	500	509
Rhode Island	102	105	106	37	37	38
South Carolina	456	462	467	171	174	179
South Dakota	96	96	96	35	36	37
Tennessee	602	608	612	225	227	233
Texas	2,493	2,516	2,532	887	892	902
Utah	319	316	311	126	133	140
Vermont	71	72	74	26	26	26
Virginia	755	782	812	269	274	283
Washington	620	632	639	232	240	250
West Virginia	216	210	204	97	95	96
Wisconsin	567	569	566	235	241	248
Wyoming	67	66	64	27	27	28

Notes: Includes unclassified students. Data will not agree with national level projections presented in other tables due to revised projections at the national level.

Source: Reprinted from U.S. Bureau of the Census. (1993). *Statistical abstract of the United States: 1993* (113th ed., p. 159). Austin, TX: Reference Press.

TABLE 4-7 Private Elementary and Secondary Enrollment, Schools, and Tuition Paid, by Orientation and Tuition Levels: 1991

Orientation and Tuition Level	Enrollment (1,000)				Schools				Average Annual Tuition			
	Total	Elementary	Secondary	Combined	Total	Elementary	Secondary	Combined	Total	Elementary	Secondary	Combined
Total	4,912	2,850	889	1,173	24,690	15,701	2,467	6,522	2,593	1,745	3,650	3,850
Catholic schools[a]	2,631	1,884	679	[b]	8,731	7,205	1,322	[b]	1,765	1,263	3,008	[b]
Less than $1,000	713	688	[b]	[b]	3,003	2,864	[b]	[b]	NA	NA	NA	NA
$1,000–$2,499	1,478	1,137	325	[b]	4,802	4,134	629	[b]	NA	NA	NA	NA
$2,500–$4,999	401	[b]	320	[b]	793	[b]	572	[b]	NA	NA	NA	NA
$5,000 or more	[b]	[b]	[b]	[b]	[b]	[b]	[b]	[b]	NA	NA	NA	NA
Other religious schools[a]	1,568	704	123	741	11,476	6,225	568	4,683	2,615	2,258	4,070	2,713
Less than $1,000	136	85	[b]	51	2,989	1,694	[b]	1,213	NA	NA	NA	NA
$1,000–$2,499	858	458	[b]	377	6,490	3,731	[b]	2,644	NA	NA	NA	NA
$2,500–$4,999	419	124	71	224	1,550	670	323	557	NA	NA	NA	NA
$5,000 or more	152	37	28	87	514	128	121	265	NA	NA	NA	NA
Nonsectarian schools[a]	713	262	87	364	4,483	2,271	577	1,634	5,599	3,837	8,061	6,279
Less than $1,000	76	[b]	[b]	40	610	[b]	[b]	288	NA	NA	NA	NA
$1,000–$2,499	82	41	[b]	[b]	569	435	[b]	[b]	NA	NA	NA	NA
$2,500–$4,999	213	125	[b]	76	1,666	1,225	[b]	392	NA	NA	NA	NA
$5,000 or more	340	67	66	207	1,600	417	353	830	NA	NA	NA	NA

Notes: Data are based on survey and subject to sampling error. NA = not applicable.

Source: Reprinted from U.S. Bureau of the Census. (1993). *Statistical abstract of the United States: 1993* (113th ed., p. 168). Austin, TX: Reference Press.

[a]Includes schools not reporting.

[b]Base figure too small to meet statistical standards for a derived figure.

the projected change in the number of high school graduates from 1993–94 to 2003–04.

Table 4-8 shows the state-by-state educational attainments and dropout rates for 1990. Over 75 percent of the population had completed high school, and another 18.7 percent had some college education. The national dropout rate was 11.2 percent. Of course, there are large variations in all categories among states. Alaska had the smallest percentage of people who had not finished high school. Washington, DC, had both a relatively high percentage of people who had not graduated from high school and the largest percentage of people with advanced degrees.

Table 4-9 shows high school dropouts by age and ethnicity from 1970 through 1991. Table 4-10 shows the place of high school dropouts

FIGURE 4-2 **Percentage of People Age 25 Years and Older Who Completed at Least Four Years of High School, by Race and Ethnicity: 1970 and 1992**

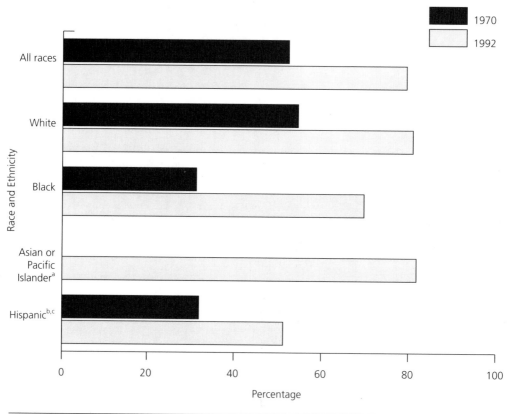

Source: Reprinted from U.S. Bureau of the Census. (1993). *Statistical abstract of the United States: 1993* (113th ed., p. 144). Austin, TX: Reference Press.
[a]Data are from 1991 rather than 1992. No 1970 data are available.
[b]Data are from 1991 rather than 1992.
[c]People of Hispanic origin may be of any race.

FIGURE 4-3 **Projected Change in the Number of High School Graduates, 1993–94 to 2003–04**

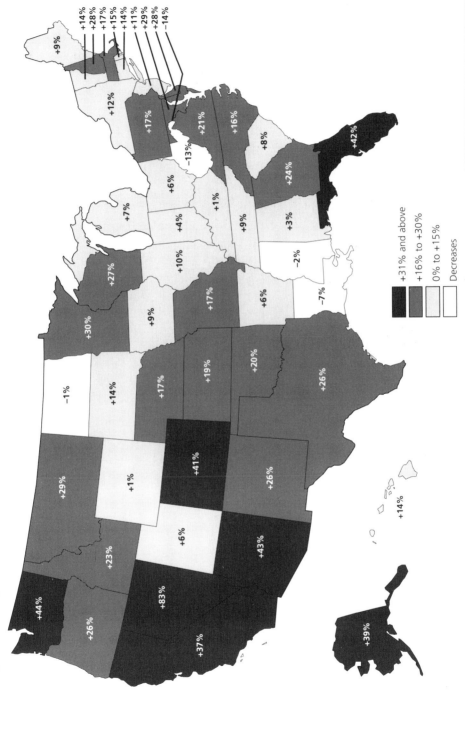

+31% and above
+16% to +30%
0% to +15%
Decreases

Source: Adapted with permission from Western Interstate Commission for Higher Education. (1993). *High school graduates: Projections by state, 1992–2009.* Boulder, CO: Author.

TABLE 4-8 Educational Attainment, by State: 1990

State	Population (1,000)	Not a High School Graduate	High School Graduate	With Some College, but No Degree	With an Associate's Degree	With a Bachelor's Degree	With an Advanced Degree	Dropouts[a]
United States	158,868	24.8	30.0	18.7	6.2	13.1	7.2	11.2
Alabama	2,546	33.1	29.4	16.8	5.0	10.1	5.5	12.6
Alaska	323	13.4	28.7	27.6	7.2	15.0	8.0	10.9
Arizona	2,301	21.3	26.1	25.4	6.8	13.3	7.0	14.4
Arkansas	1,496	33.7	32.7	16.6	3.7	8.9	4.5	11.4
California	18,695	23.8	22.3	22.6	7.9	15.3	8.1	14.2
Colorado	2,107	15.6	26.5	24.0	6.9	18.0	9.0	9.8
Connecticut	2,199	20.8	29.5	15.9	6.6	16.2	11.0	9.0
Delaware	428	22.5	32.7	16.9	6.5	13.7	7.7	10.4
District of Columbia	409	26.9	21.2	15.6	3.1	16.1	17.2	13.9
Florida	8,887	25.6	30.1	19.4	6.6	12.0	6.3	14.3
Georgia	4,023	29.1	29.6	17.0	5.0	12.9	6.4	14.1
Hawaii	710	19.9	28.7	20.1	8.3	15.8	7.1	7.5
Idaho	601	20.3	30.4	24.2	7.5	12.4	5.3	10.4
Illinois	7,294	23.8	30.0	19.4	5.8	13.6	7.5	10.6
Indiana	3,489	24.4	38.2	16.6	5.3	9.2	6.4	11.4
Iowa	1,777	19.9	38.5	17.0	7.7	11.7	5.2	6.6
Kansas	1,566	18.7	32.8	21.9	5.4	14.1	7.0	8.7
Kentucky	2,334	35.4	31.8	15.2	4.1	8.1	5.5	13.3
Louisiana	2,537	31.7	31.7	17.2	3.3	10.5	5.6	12.5
Maine	796	21.2	37.1	16.1	6.9	12.7	6.1	8.3
Maryland	3,123	21.6	28.1	18.6	5.2	15.6	10.9	10.9
Massachusetts	3,962	20.0	29.7	15.8	7.2	16.6	10.6	8.5
Michigan	5,843	23.2	32.3	20.4	6.7	10.9	6.4	10.0
Minnesota	2,771	17.6	33.0	19.0	8.6	15.6	6.3	6.4
Mississippi	1,539	35.7	27.5	16.9	5.2	9.7	5.1	11.8
Missouri	3,292	26.1	33.1	18.4	4.5	11.7	6.1	11.4
Montana	508	19.0	33.5	22.1	5.6	14.1	5.7	8.1
Nebraska	996	18.2	34.7	21.1	7.1	13.1	5.9	7.0
Nevada	790	21.2	31.5	25.8	6.2	10.1	5.2	15.2
New Hampshire	714	17.8	31.7	18.0	8.1	16.4	7.9	9.4
New Jersey	5,166	23.3	31.1	15.5	5.2	16.0	8.8	9.6
New Mexico	923	24.9	28.7	20.9	5.0	12.1	8.3	11.7
New York	11,819	25.2	29.5	15.7	6.5	13.2	9.9	9.9
North Carolina	4,253	30.0	29.0	16.8	6.8	12.0	5.4	12.5
North Dakota	397	23.3	28.0	20.5	10.0	13.5	4.5	4.6
Ohio	6,925	24.3	36.3	17.0	5.3	11.1	5.9	8.9
Oklahoma	1,995	25.4	30.5	21.3	5.0	11.8	6.0	10.4
Oregon	1,855	18.5	28.9	25.0	6.9	13.6	7.0	11.8
Pennsylvania	7,873	25.3	38.6	12.9	5.2	11.3	6.6	9.1
Rhode Island	659	28.0	29.5	15.0	6.3	13.5	7.8	11.1
South Carolina	2,168	31.7	29.5	15.8	6.3	11.2	5.4	11.7
South Dakota	431	22.9	33.7	18.8	7.4	12.3	4.9	7.7
Tennessee	3,139	32.9	30.0	16.9	4.2	10.5	5.4	13.4
Texas	10,311	27.9	25.6	21.1	5.2	13.9	6.5	12.9
Utah	897	14.9	27.2	27.9	7.8	15.4	6.8	8.7
Vermont	357	19.2	34.6	14.7	7.2	15.4	8.9	8.0
Virginia	3,975	24.8	26.6	18.5	5.5	15.4	9.1	10.0
Washington	3,126	16.2	27.9	25.0	7.9	15.9	7.0	10.6
West Virginia	1,172	34.0	36.6	13.2	3.8	7.5	4.8	10.9
Wisconsin	3,094	21.4	37.1	16.7	7.1	12.1	5.6	7.1
Wyoming	278	17.0	33.2	24.2	6.9	13.1	5.7	6.9

Note: Data are for people 25 years old and older, except as indicated.

Source: Reprinted from U.S. Bureau of the Census. (1993). *Statistical abstract of the United States: 1993* (113th ed., p. 155). Austin, TX: Reference Press.

[a]For people 16 to 19 years old. A dropout is a person who is not in regular school and who has not completed the 12th grade or received a general equivalency degree.

and high school graduates in the labor force. A much larger percentage of dropouts are outside the labor force than high school graduates.

Special Education Programs

Numerous students are involved in programs of special education. Such programs enable students to learn English as a second language if they are recent immigrants from non–English-speaking countries or to participate in specialized programs for exceptional students, including those who are handicapped, gifted, or deficient in a specific area such as mathematics or reading. Some schools also have special programs for bilingual children, especially Spanish-speaking children.

TABLE 4-9 **High School Dropouts by Age, Race, and Hispanic Origin: Selected Years, 1970 to 1991 (Numbers in thousands)**

Age and Ethnicity	Number of Dropouts								Percentage of Population			
	1970	1980	1985	1987	1988	1989	1990	1991	1970	1980	1985	1991
Total dropouts[a,b]	4,670	5,212	4,456	4,349	4,300	4,109	3,854	3,964	12.2	12.0	10.6	10.5
16–17 years	617	709	505	500	482	395	418	395	8.0	8.8	7.0	6.0
18–21 years	2,138	2,578	2,095	1,966	2,081	2,128	1,921	1,960	16.4	15.8	14.1	14.1
22–24 years	1,770	1,798	1,724	1,785	1,668	1,516	1,458	1,526	18.7	15.2	14.1	14.3
White[b]	3,577	4,169	3,583	3,522	3,480	3,314	3,127	3,229	10.8	11.3	10.3	10.5
16–17 years	485	619	424	401	411	328	334	312	7.3	9.2	7.1	5.9
18–21 years	1,618	2,032	1,678	1,577	1,670	1,690	1,516	1,558	14.3	14.7	13.6	13.9
22–24 years	1,356	1,416	1,372	1,465	1,342	1,236	1,235	1,287	16.3	14.0	13.3	14.6
Black[b]	1,047	934	748	706	709	648	611	631	22.2	16.0	12.6	11.3
16–17 years	125	80	70	77	67	61	73	77	12.8	6.9	6.5	7.4
18–21 years	500	486	376	338	368	363	345	354	30.5	23.0	17.5	16.6
22–24 years	397	346	279	273	263	220	185	191	37.8	24.0	17.8	14.0
Hispanic[b,c]	—	919	820	941	1,177	1,168	1,122	1,262	—	29.5	23.3	29.5
16–17 years	—	92	97	76	123	80	89	102	—	16.6	14.6	15.8
18–21 years	—	470	335	410	552	538	502	574	—	40.3	29.3	35.1
22–24 years	—	323	365	439	494	524	523	565	—	40.6	33.9	45.7

Notes: Data are for people 14 to 24 years old. — = not available.

Source: Reprinted from U.S. Bureau of the Census. (1993). *Statistical abstract of the United States: 1993* (113th ed., p. 169). Austin, TX: Reference Press.

[a]Includes other groups not shown separately.

[b]Includes people 14 to 15 years old, not shown separately.

[c]People of Hispanic origin may be of any race.

Table 4-11 lists the number and percentage of children enrolled in special programs in both public and private schools in 1990–91. Table 4-12 shows the proportion of children with disabilities who were ever treated and the proportion receiving special education for delays in growth or development, learning disabilities, and emotional or behavioral problems in 1980 to 1991. Some 4.3 million children were enrolled in such programs in 1991, nearly half of whom were classified as having learning disabilities. The next largest number had speech impairments, and the third largest group had mental retardation. Nine percent were classified as emotionally disturbed.

TABLE 4-10 **Employment Status of High School Graduates Not Enrolled in College and School Dropouts, by Gender and Race: Selected Years, 1980 to 1991 (Numbers in thousands)**

Employment Status, Gender, and Race	Graduates					Dropouts				
	1980	1985	1989	1990	1991	1980	1985	1989	1990	1991
Civilian population	11,622	10,381	8,645	8,370	7,804	5,254	4,323	4,042	3,800	3,884
In labor force	9,795	8,825	7,266	7,107	6,444	3,549	2,920	2,703	2,506	2,464
Percent of population	84.3	85.0	84.1	84.9	82.6	67.5	67.5	66.9	66.0	63.4
Employed[a]	8,567	7,707	6,552	6,279	5,641	2,651	2,165	2,147	1,993	1,849
Percent of labor force	87.5	87.3	90.2	88.3	87.5	74.7	74.1	79.4	79.5	75.0
Male	4,462	4,001	3,534	3,435	3,123	1,780	1,475	1,491	1,304	1,288
Female	4,105	3,706	3,018	2,845	2,518	871	690	656	689	561
White	7,638	6,732	5,543	5,334	4,724	2,310	1,888	1,861	1,761	1,631
Black	817	865	853	794	766	305	226	223	178	167
Unemployed[a]	1,228	1,118	714	828	803	898	755	555	513	614
Percent of labor force	12.5	12.7	9.8	11.7	12.5	25.3	25.9	20.6	20.5	24.9
Male	695	569	364	428	441	548	462	343	301	362
Female	532	549	350	400	362	350	293	213	212	253
White	924	729	478	526	506	636	582	397	361	447
Black	289	360	224	279	273	239	160	148	136	153
Not in labor force	1,827	1,556	1,379	1,262	1,360	1,705	1,403	1,339	1,294	1,420
Percent of population	15.7	15.0	16.0	15.1	17.4	32.5	32.5	33.1	34.1	36.6

Notes: Data are for civilian noninstitutional population 16 to 24 years old. High school graduates are defined as people who are not enrolled in college who have completed four years of high school only; dropouts are defined as people who are not in regular school and who have not completed the 12th grade or received a general equivalency degree.

Source: Reprinted from U.S. Bureau of the Census. (1993). *Statistical abstract of the United States: 1993* (113th ed., p. 169). Austin, TX: Reference Press.

[a]Includes other races not shown separately.

TABLE 4-11 **Student Participation in School Programs and Services, by Level of School and Type of Community: 1990–91**

Level and Community Type	Total Students		Percentage of Students Participating in Program or Service							
	Number	Percent Distribution	Bilingual Education	English as a Second Language	Remedial Reading	Remedial Mathematics	Programs for the Handicapped	Programs for the Gifted and Talented	Diagnostic and Prescriptive	Extended Day
Public total	40,103,700	100.0	2.80	3.37	10.82	7.14	7.07	6.86	8.81	2.20
School level[a]										
Elementary	25,071,464	62.5	3.55	3.70	12.85	7.63	6.69	6.61	8.92	3.14
Secondary	13,652,193	34.0	1.48	2.82	6.99	6.13	7.02	7.50	8.12	0.52
Combined	1,380,043	3.4	2.33	2.79	11.71	8.35	14.29	5.01	13.63	1.89
Community type										
Central city	11,892,503	29.7	5.37	6.12	12.79	9.02	6.91	7.56	9.15	3.33
Urban fringe or large town	12,515,609	31.2	2.34	3.42	9.16	6.10	6.84	7.01	8.95	2.45
Rural or small town	15,695,586	39.1	1.23	1.24	10.64	6.55	7.36	6.20	8.45	1.15
Private total	4,673,878	100.0	1.50	1.42	6.17	4.38	2.09	6.58	4.57	8.40
School level[a]										
Elementary	2,653,599	56.8	1.22	0.93	6.17	4.12	0.92	4.77	3.48	10.84
Secondary	888,944	19.0	0.82	2.26	4.29	3.35	1.64	8.81	2.86	0.70
Combined	1,131,335	24.2	2.71	1.91	7.66	5.82	5.18	9.09	8.47	8.71
Community type										
Central city	2,299,025	49.2	1.51	1.30	6.09	4.10	1.85	6.66	4.15	9.39
Urban fringe or large town	1,553,338	33.2	1.48	1.20	5.91	4.77	2.51	6.30	5.24	8.20
Rural or small town	821,515	17.6	1.51	2.18	6.90	4.46	1.97	6.90	4.48	6.00

Notes: Students may participate in more than one program or service. Includes only kindergarten students who attend schools that offer at least first grade; excludes prekindergarten students.

Source: Reprinted from U.S. Department of Education, National Center for Education Statistics. (1993). *Digest of education statistics* (p. 70). Washington, DC: Author.

[a]Elementary schools have grade 6 or lower or a low grade of ungraded and no grade higher than 8. Secondary schools have no grade lower than grade 7. Combined schools have grades lower than 7 and higher than 8.

Home Schooling

According to the National Home Education Research Institute (Ray, 1993), 300,000 to 500,000 U.S. students in kindergarten through grade 12 are being taught at home. Generally, home schooling is designed to make it possible for students to be taught specific religious or philosophical values, to control social interactions, to develop closer families, and to pursue high levels of academics. Home schooling advocates report that the achievement of such students is well above average. One study of a random sample of 1,516 families showed the students' average achievement to be at the 80th percentile (the national average being the 50th percentile) (Ray, 1993).

Head Start

Head Start—a child development program for preschool children who are economically disadvantaged—began in the 1960s as part of President Lyndon B. Johnson's Great Society program, part of which was called the War on Poverty. Table 4-13 presents the state-by-state allocations and enrollments for Head Start in 1990, 1991, and 1992. The size of Head Start reflects the amount of money available for it, because the program has never had enough resources to reach all eligible children. According to the National Commission on Children (1991), fewer than one-fourth of the children who are eligible for Head Start are enrolled. In 1990, 575,802 of the 2,475,000 eligible children were enrolled, as Table 4-14 shows. The commission's report acknowledged that enrollment may be low because of competing early childhood programs and because all states have public kindergarten programs for five-year-olds.

Table 4-15 shows the preprimary enrollment in 1978 and 1991 and the labor force status of the mothers of the children, by ethnic group. Table 4-16 shows the enrollment in public and private nursery schools and kindergartens, as well as the enrollment rates, from 1970 to 1991.

Standardized Test Scores

A commonly used indicator of educational achievement is the scores earned by students on standardized tests. Some states periodically test all students at various grade levels to moni-

---

TABLE 4-12 **Children and Youths with Disabilities in Educational Programs, by Type of Disability: Selected Years, 1980 to 1991**

Disability	1980	1983	1984	1985	1986	1987	1988[a]	1989[a]	1990[a]	1991[a]
All conditions (1,000)	4,005	4,255	4,298	4,315	4,317	4,374	4,128	4,173	4,219	4,326
Percent distribution										
Learning disability	31.9	40.9	42.0	42.4	43.1	43.6	47.0	47.8	48.6	49.2
Speech impairment	29.6	26.6	26.2	26.1	26.1	25.8	23.2	23.1	23.1	22.8
Mental retardation	21.7	17.8	16.9	16.1	15.3	15.0	14.6	13.8	13.0	12.4
Emotional disturbance	8.2	8.3	8.4	8.6	8.7	8.7	9.1	8.9	9.0	9.0
Hearing impairment	2.0	1.7	1.7	1.6	1.5	1.5	1.4	1.4	1.3	1.3
Orthopedic disability	1.6	1.3	1.3	1.3	1.3	1.3	1.1	1.1	1.1	1.1
Other health impairment	2.6	1.2	1.2	1.6	1.3	1.2	1.1	1.2	1.2	1.3
Visual disability	0.8	0.7	0.7	0.7	0.6	0.6	0.6	0.5	0.5	0.5
Multiple disabilities	1.5	1.5	1.5	1.6	2.0	2.2	1.9	2.0	2.0	2.2
Deaf-blindness	0.1	0.1	0.1	0.1	[b]	[b]	[b]	[b]	[b]	[b]

Notes: For people under 22 years old, except as noted. Represents children under age 20 served under Chapter 1 of the Elementary and Secondary Education Act, State Operated Programs, and children 3 to 21 years old served under the Individuals with Disabilities Education Act, Part B. Excludes outlying areas.

Source: Reprinted from U.S. Bureau of the Census. (1993). *Statistical abstract of the United States: 1993* (113th ed., p. 166). Austin, TX: Reference Press.

[a]For children 6 to 21 years old; total number of children served under 22 years old was 4,494,280 in school year 1987–88; 4,568,118 in school year 1988–89; 4,640,969 in 1989–90; and 4,771,398 in 1990–91.

[b]Less than 0.05 percent.

TABLE 4-13 **Allocations for and Enrollment in Head Start, by State: Fiscal Years 1990 to 1992**

State	1990 Head Start Allocations (in thousands of dollars)	Enrollment	1991 Head Start Allocations (in thousands of dollars)	Enrollment	1992 Head Start Allocations (in thousands of dollars)	Enrollment
Total	1,517,240	540,934	1,951,775	583,471	2,120,862	621,078
Alabama	29,935	11,587	36,102	12,463	40,021	13,012
Alaska	2,840	800	3,887	970	4,434	1,067
Arizona	13,745	4,730	17,695	5,344	20,729	6,179
Arkansas	16,026	7,284	19,778	7,761	22,297	8,213
California	152,094	45,135	192,555	49,945	219,423	52,658
Colorado	13,674	5,625	17,043	6,124	19,353	6,604
Connecticut	13,609	4,726	16,813	5,051	18,694	5,311
Delaware	3,147	1,113	3,771	1,199	4,454	1,333
District of Columbia	7,747	2,493	9,108	2,560	9,673	2,639
Florida	45,381	16,975	58,817	19,034	67,552	20,567
Georgia	37,304	13,792	46,208	14,978	52,225	16,080
Hawaii	5,547	1,703	6,739	1,846	7,547	1,974
Idaho	4,452	1,369	5,834	1,502	6,745	1,658
Illinois	73,839	25,857	88,580	27,184	99,852	28,802
Indiana	21,890	8,689	27,371	9,543	31,054	10,213
Iowa	11,558	4,580	14,563	4,971	16,484	5,266
Kansas	9,778	3,938	11,958	4,332	14,175	4,705
Kentucky	27,793	11,292	34,165	11,772	38,053	12,467
Louisiana	34,383	13,686	42,049	14,558	48,205	15,804
Maine	6,239	2,724	8,037	2,928	9,476	3,132
Maryland	19,894	6,641	24,435	7,234	27,043	7,594
Massachusetts	30,731	9,257	37,634	9,624	42,348	10,159
Michigan	60,674	23,411	73,505	24,914	82,321	26,174
Minnesota	16,468	6,129	21,155	6,654	24,373	7,136
Mississippi	57,176	21,026	66,198	21,511	71,861	22,343
Missouri	26,207	10,726	31,661	11,348	35,641	11,972
Montana	3,874	1,535	5,366	1,786	6,436	1,961
Nebraska	6,254	2,535	8,901	2,820	10,284	3,154
Nevada	2,384	801	3,566	911	4,000	1,073
New Hampshire	2,746	865	3,595	945	4,080	1,016
New Jersey	41,481	10,765	48,996	11,051	54,532	11,688
New Mexico	9,408	4,381	11,960	4,647	13,655	4,958
New York	111,997	30,050	137,040	32,492	153,858	34,688
North Carolina	31,971	12,426	39,459	13,438	44,259	14,083
North Dakota	2,129	985	3,501	1,208	4,283	1,458
Ohio	62,438	26,250	76,276	27,794	84,964	29,132
Oklahoma	17,743	8,200	21,587	8,562	24,078	8,977
Oregon	12,223	3,436	15,623	3,634	17,760	3,885
Pennsylvania	61,536	20,061	75,220	21,247	82,449	22,414
Rhode Island	4,833	2,085	6,152	2,197	6,964	2,293
South Carolina	19,871	7,930	24,556	8,544	27,716	9,025
South Dakota	3,694	1,382	4,750	1,569	5,421	1,691
Tennessee	28,016	10,846	34,272	11,546	39,271	12,481
Texas	77,069	30,573	98,971	33,615	113,612	36,394
Utah	7,020	2,702	9,295	3,097	10,669	3,403
Vermont	2,821	973	3,814	1,041	4,556	1,129
Virginia	22,098	7,380	28,719	8,345	33,134	9,455
Washington	18,767	5,378	24,005	5,923	27,533	6,361
West Virginia	12,958	4,937	16,273	5,386	18,959	5,842
Wisconsin	22,931	8,612	27,651	9,161	31,052	9,665
Wyoming	1,876	826	2,777	990	3,371	1,128
Migrant programs[a]	111,096	39,076	141,140	42,769	153,755	44,770
Special projects	2,711	NA	69,656	NA	NA	NA

Notes: Allocations are from Department of Health and Human Services. Because of rounding, details may not add to totals. In 1990, 1991, and 1992, the distribution of enrollment by age was as follows: 7 percent were five years old and above; 63 percent were four years old; 27 percent were three years old; and 3 percent were under age three. Children with disabilities accounted for 13.9 percent of Head Start enrollees in 1990, 13.1 percent in 1991, and 13.4 percent in 1992. The racial and ethnic composition during the three years was as follows: Native American, 4 percent; Hispanic, 22 percent (23 percent in 1992); African American, 38 percent (37 percent in 1992); white, 33 percent; and Asian, 3 percent. NA = not applicable.

Source: Reprinted from U.S. Department of Education, National Center for Education Statistics. (1993). *Digest of education statistics* (p. 382). Washington, DC: Author.

[a]Includes Native Americans and migrant programs.

tor their achievement. Other states require "exit exams" before students graduate from high school to guarantee that they have achieved an appropriate level of learning, even if they have also completed all of the required courses for graduation.

The Scholastic Aptitude Test (SAT) is taken by high school students who plan to go to college. The number of students who take the test varies by state. In some states, fewer students aspire to postsecondary education than in others, and in some admission to most of the colleges and universities requires completion of the American College Testing exam (ACT) rather than the SAT. Some community colleges and vocational or technical schools, as well as some four-year colleges and universities, have open admissions for their state residents and do not require the completion of standardized tests.

Scores on the SAT do not provide conclusive evidence of the achievements or abilities of a state's students. For example, in states where the ACT is the more common requirement, the ACT scores may be relatively low but the SAT scores high because only high-achieving students who want to attend institutions outside their states or prestigious private institutions take the SAT.

Table 4-17 shows the SAT scores from 1967 through 1992, along with some other characteristics of those who completed it. There are two parts to the test—verbal and math. The minimum score on each is 200, and the maximum is 800. Therefore, no one who takes the test would have a combined score of less than 400 or more than 1600. The table also shows the high school rank related to the scores of students who took the SAT.

Table 4-18 describes the results of students who took the ACT exam from 1967 through 1992. The scores are not comparable from 1990 on because a new version of the test was introduced in that year. Also, the data are based on a sample of those who took the test through 1985 but on the entire population of those who took it in 1986 and after.

Other proficiency test scores are shown in Table 4-19. Information is provided in the table about scores in reading, writing, mathematics, and science, with additional information on gender, ethnicity, and parental education.

TABLE 4-14 **Number of Children Enrolled in Head Start Programs and Eligible on the Basis of Income, by Age: 1990**

Age	Children Enrolled	Income-Eligible Children
3 years	146,051	825,000
4 years	391,886	825,000
5 years	37,865	825,000
Total	575,802	2,475,000

Source: Reprinted from National Commission on Children. (1991). *Beyond rhetoric: A new American agenda for children and families* (p. 191). Washington, DC: U.S. Government Printing Office.

TABLE 4-15 Preprimary School Enrollment, by Level of Enrollment and Labor Force Status of Mother: 1978 and 1991

Ethnicity and Mother's Labor Force Status	All Children (1,000)		Percentage Enrolled in							Percent not Enrolled	
			Nursery School				Kindergarten				
			Total		Full Day		Total		Full Day		
	1978	1991	1978	1991	1978	1991	1978	1991	1991	1978	1991
Total[a]											
Children 3 to 5 years old	9,110	11,370	20.0	24.8	6.9	8.2	30.3	30.9	13.0	49.7	44.3
Living with mother	8,883	10,602	19.8	25.3	6.8	8.3	30.4	30.8	12.8	49.8	43.9
Mother in labor force	4,097	6,146	22.1	28.5	11.4	11.8	31.0	31.6	14.1	47.0	39.9
Employed	3,737	5,568	22.5	29.2	11.7	12.2	31.0	31.8	14.1	46.5	39.0
Full-time	2,446	3,860	22.3	27.3	15.2	14.2	31.2	31.7	14.8	46.4	41.0
Part-time	1,291	1,709	23.0	33.5	5.2	7.7	30.5	31.9	12.3	45.7	34.6
Unemployed	360	578	17.4	21.6	7.8	8.0	30.6	30.1	14.2	52.0	48.3
Mother not in labor force	4,786	4,456	17.9	20.9	2.9	3.5	29.9	29.8	11.1	52.2	49.3
White											
Children 3 to 5 years old	7,460	9,083	19.5	26.0	5.2	7.4	30.1	30.0	11.3	50.5	44.0
Living with mother	7,301	8,574	19.4	26.5	5.1	7.5	30.1	30.2	11.3	50.5	43.3
Mother in labor force	3,235	4,939	21.1	27.9	9.2	10.7	30.4	30.8	12.4	48.5	41.3
Employed	3,014	4,578	21.3	29.9	9.4	11.0	30.7	30.8	12.4	48.0	39.3
Full-time	1,877	3,037	20.1	27.9	12.6	13.1	31.0	30.7	13.1	48.9	41.4
Part-time	1,137	1,541	23.3	33.8	4.1	6.7	30.2	31.0	11.1	46.5	35.2
Unemployed	220	360	17.9	21.9	6.4	6.7	27.1	30.8	12.2	55.0	47.3
Mother not in labor force	4,067	3,635	18.0	22.6	1.9	3.3	29.8	29.4	9.8	52.2	48.0
Black											
Children 3 to 5 years old	1,410	1,747	22.1	19.3	15.3	12.0	31.0	33.8	21.2	46.9	46.9
Living with mother	1,347	1,529	21.7	19.7	15.5	12.4	31.3	33.8	20.9	47.1	46.5
Mother in labor force	731	933	25.9	24.4	20.6	17.0	32.5	35.7	22.6	41.6	39.9
Employed	598	750	28.0	24.7	22.8	18.4	31.7	37.3	23.6	40.3	38.0
Full-time	469	641	29.6	24.0	24.8	19.0	32.0	35.7	22.9	38.4	40.3
Part-time	128	111	22.3	27.9	15.8	14.4	30.7	45.9	27.0	47.0	26.2
Unemployed	133	182	16.7	24.2	10.6	11.5	35.7	29.1	18.7	47.6	46.7
Mother not in labor force	616	596	16.6	12.2	9.4	5.2	29.8	31.0	18.3	53.5	56.8
Hispanic[b]											
Children 3 to 5 years old	720	1,456	11.8	14.2	5.0	5.7	29.1	32.1	12.4	59.1	53.7
Living with mother	713	1,348	11.7	22.8	5.0	8.8	28.9	52.2	20.2	59.4	25.0
Mother in labor force	296	573	16.3	17.8	7.1	10.1	27.5	33.2	13.6	56.2	49.0
Employed	263	494	17.1	19.4	6.7	10.5	26.0	32.6	13.4	56.9	48.0
Full-time	196	395	16.9	18.0	7.5	10.1	25.9	32.4	12.2	57.2	49.6
Part-time	67	99	c	25.3	c	12.1	c	32.3	18.2	c	42.4
Unemployed	33	79	c	7.6	c	7.6	c	38.0	15.2	c	54.4
Mother not in labor force	417	776	8.4	11.1	3.5	1.9	29.9	31.1	11.5	61.7	57.8

Source: Reprinted from U.S. Bureau of the Census. (1993). *Statistical abstract of the United States: 1993* (113th ed., p. 156). Austin, TX: Reference Press.

[a] Includes races not shown separately.
[b] People of Hispanic origin may be of any race.
[c] Estimate does not meet standards of reliability.

Enrollment in Institutions of Higher Education

An important measure of educational achievement and quality is enrollment in colleges and universities. Table 4-20 shows state-by-state educational attainment rates in 1990 (measured in terms of high school graduate and dropout rates, bachelor's degree rates, and so on); information also is provided regarding state population, per capita income, and the poverty rate. The percentage of adults in each state with at least a bachelor's degree in 1990 is shown in Figure 4-4.

The number of college students enrolled in each state in 1991 is shown in Table 4-21. Minority enrollment rates and either ACT or SAT scores (depending on the test most commonly taken in the state) also are given. Table

TABLE 4-16 **Preprimary School Enrollment, by Type of Program, Age, and Race: Selected Years, 1970 to 1991**

Item	1970	1975	1980	1985	1986	1987	1988	1989	1990	1991
Number of children (1,000) Population,										
3 to 5 years old	10,949	10,183	9,284	10,733	10,866	10,872	10,994	11,038	11,207	11,370
Total enrolled[a]	4,104	4,954	4,878	5,865	5,971	5,932	5,977	6,026	6,659	6,334
Nursery	1,094	1,745	1,981	2,477	2,545	2,555	2,621	2,825	3,378	2,824
Public	332	570	628	846	829	819	852	930	1,202	996
Private	762	1,174	1,353	1,631	1,715	1,736	1,770	1,894	2,177	1,827
Kindergarten	3,010	3,211	2,897	3,388	3,426	3,377	3,356	3,201	3,281	3,510
Public	2,498	2,682	2,438	2,847	2,859	2,842	2,875	2,704	2,767	2,968
Private	511	528	459	541	567	535	481	496	513	543
White	3,443	4,105	3,994	4,757	4,851	4,748	4,891	4,911	5,389	5,104
Black	586	731	725	919	892	893	814	872	964	928
Hispanic[b]	—	—	370	496	593	587	544	520	642	675
3 years old	454	683	857	1,035	1,041	1,022	1,028	1,005	1,205	1,075
4 years old	1,007	1,418	1,423	1,765	1,772	1,717	1,768	1,882	2,086	1,993
5 years old	2,643	2,852	2,598	3,065	3,157	3,192	3,183	3,139	3,367	3,266
Enrollment rate										
Total enrolled[a]	37.5	48.6	52.5	54.6	55.0	54.6	54.4	54.6	59.4	55.7
White	37.8	48.6	52.7	54.7	55.2	54.1	55.4	55.0	59.7	56.2
Black	34.9	48.1	51.8	55.8	54.1	54.2	48.2	54.2	57.8	53.1
Hispanic[b]	—	—	43.3	43.3	47.8	45.5	44.2	41.6	49.0	46.4
3 years old	12.9	21.5	27.3	28.8	28.9	28.6	27.6	27.1	32.6	28.2
4 years old	27.8	40.5	46.3	49.1	49.0	47.7	49.1	51.0	56.0	53.0
5 years old	69.3	81.3	84.7	86.5	86.7	86.1	86.6	86.4	88.8	86.0

Notes: Data are for civilian noninstitutional population and include public and nonpublic nursery school and kindergarten programs; five-year-olds enrolled in elementary schools are excluded. — = not available.

Source: Reprinted from U.S. Bureau of the Census. (1993). *Statistical abstract of the United States: 1993* (113th ed., p. 156). Austin, TX: Reference Press.

[a]Includes races not shown separately.

[b]People of Hispanic origin may be of any race. The method of identifying Hispanic children was changed in 1980 from allocation on the basis of the mother's status to status reported for each child. The number of Hispanic children using the new method is larger.

4-22 shows the number of students enrolled in 1993 and projected enrollments in public and private institutions of higher education for 1994 through 2003. The projections of degrees to be awarded (as well as the figures on high school graduation) are also provided. The table shows that total enrollments, particularly part-time enrollments, are expected to increase. The great increase in the number of part-time students reflects the pattern of the 1980s, when many students combined careers and family responsibilities with part-time study.

Table 4-22 reflects another major change in higher education: the increased enrollment of women. In 1960 only 37.9 percent of the high school graduates who enrolled in college were women, but by 1993 that percentage had

TABLE 4-17 **Scholastic Aptitude Test (SAT) Scores and Characteristics of College-Bound Seniors: Selected Years, 1967 to 1992**

Type of Test and Characteristic	Unit	1967	1970	1975	1980	1985	1987	1988	1989	1990	1991	1992
Test scores[a]												
Verbal, total[b]	Point	466	460	434	424	431	430	428	427	424	422	423
Male	Point	463	459	437	428	437	435	435	434	429	426	428
Female	Point	468	461	431	420	425	425	422	421	419	418	419
Math, total[b]	Point	492	488	472	466	475	476	476	476	476	474	476
Male	Point	514	509	495	491	499	500	498	500	499	497	499
Female	Point	467	465	449	443	452	453	455	454	455	453	456
Participants												
Total	1,000	—	—	996	992	977	1,080	1,134	1,088	1,026	1,033	1,034
Male	Percent	—	—	49.9	48.2	48.3	48.2	47.0	47.9	47.8	47.7	47.6
White	Percent	—	—	86.0	82.1	81.0	78.2	77.0	74.7	73.0	72.0	71.5
Black	Percent	—	—	7.9	9.1	7.5	8.7	9.2	9.6	10.0	10.0	10.4
Scores[a]												
600 or above												
Verbal	Percent	—	—	7.9	7.2	7.9	8.1	7.3	7.8	7.4	7.2	7.3
Math	Percent	—	—	15.6	15.1	17.1	18.3	17.6	18.0	18.4	17.8	18.1
Below 400												
Verbal	Percent	—	—	37.8	41.8	39.4	39.8	39.4	40.4	41.2	42.4	41.3
Math	Percent	—	—	28.5	30.2	28.2	28.3	27.8	28.0	28.4	29.1	28.2
Selected intended area of study												
Business and commerce	Percent	—	—	11.5	18.6	21.0	23.1	23.0	22.3	21.0	19.0	16.8
Engineering	Percent	—	—	6.7	11 1	11.7	11.1	10.1	10.1	10.0	10.0	10.5
Social Science	Percent	—	—	7.7	7.8	7.5	10.9	11.7	12.6	13.0	12.0	12.1
Education	Percent	—	—	9.1	6.1	4.7	6.0	6.6	7.1	7.0	8.0	8.1
SAT average[a] by high school rank												
Top tenth	Point	—	—	—	539	547	552	550	550	549	548	549
Second tenth	Point	—	—	—	470	482	484	483	483	481	480	480
Second fifth	Point	—	—	—	431	442	440	440	440	438	437	438
Third fifth	Point	—	—	—	386	396	395	395	394	392	391	392

Note: — = not available.

Source: Reprinted from U.S. Bureau of the Census. (1993). *Statistical abstract of the United States: 1993* (113th ed., p. 170). Austin, TX: Reference Press.

[a]Minimum score is 200; maximum score is 800.

[b]1967 and 1970 figures are estimates that are based on the total number of people taking the SAT.

risen to 55.6. Women received 54 percent of all bachelor's degrees and 53 percent of all master's degrees in 1993 but only about 38 percent of all doctoral degrees.

Table 4-23 shows college enrollment among 18- to 24-year-olds from 1981 through 1991. The percentage of high school graduates and of all 18- to 24-year-olds enrolled in college increased steadily during the 10-year period.

However, from 1990 to 1991 the percentage of African American youths enrolled in college declined, an alarming setback in a decade-long trend.

Table 4-24 shows degrees awarded from 1950 to 1990, with projections through 2003. It is notable that the majority of degrees are now awarded to women, a major and steady shift since the mid-20th century. Men con-

TABLE 4-18 American College Testing (ACT) Program Scores and Characteristics of College-Bound Students: Selected Years, 1967 to 1992

Type of Test and Characteristic	Unit	1967	1970	1975	1980	1985	1987	1988	1989	1990[a]	1991[a]	1992[a]
Test scores[b]												
Composite	Point	19.9	18.6	18.5	18.5	18.6	18.7	18.8	18.6	20.6	20.6	20.6
Male	Point	20.3	19.5	19.3	19.3	19.4	19.5	19.6	19.3	21.0	20.9	20.9
Female	Point	19.4	17.8	17.9	17.8	17.9	18.1	18.1	18.0	20.3	20.4	20.5
English	Point	18.5	17.7	17.9	17.8	18.1	18.4	18.5	18.4	20.5	20.3	20.2
Male	Point	17.6	17.1	17.3	17.3	17.6	17.9	18.0	17.8	20.1	19.8	19.8
Female	Point	19.4	18.3	18.3	18.2	18.6	18.9	18.9	19.0	20.9	20.7	20.6
Math	Point	20.0	17.6	17.4	17.3	17.2	17.2	17.2	17.1	19.9	20.0	20.0
Male	Point	21.1	19.3	18.9	18.9	18.6	18.6	18.4	18.3	20.7	20.6	20.7
Female	Point	18.8	16.2	16.2	16.0	16.0	16.1	16.1	16.1	19.3	19.4	19.5
Reading[c]	Point	19.7	17.4	17.2	17.2	17.4	17.5	17.4	17.2	—	21.2	21.1
Male	Point	20.3	18.7	18.2	18.3	18.3	18.4	18.4	18.1	—	21.3	21.1
Female	Point	19.0	16.4	16.4	16.4	16.6	16.7	16.6	16.4	—	21.1	21.1
Science reasoning[d]	Point	20.8	21.1	21.1	21.0	21.2	21.4	21.4	21.2	—	20.7	20.7
Male	Point	21.6	22.4	22.4	22.3	22.6	22.8	22.8	22.6	—	21.3	21.4
Female	Point	20.0	20.0	20.0	20.0	20.0	20.1	20.2	20.0	—	20.1	20.1
Participants[e]												
Total	1,000	788	714	822	836	739	777	842	855	817	796	832
Male	Percent	52	46	45	45	46	46	46	46	46	45	45
White	Percent	—	77	83	83	82	81	81	80	79	79	80
Black	Percent	4	7	8	8	8	8	9	9	9	9	9
Composite scores[f]												
27 or above	Percent	14	14	13	13	14	14	14	14	12	11	12
18 or below	Percent	21	33	33	33	32	31	31	32	35	35	35
Planned educational major												
Business[g]	Percent	18	21	20	19	21	23	23	22	20	18	17
Engineering	Percent	8	6	8	10	9	8	9	9	9	10	11
Social science[h]	Percent	10	9	6	6	7	9	10	11	10	10	10
Education	Percent	16	12	9	7	6	8	8	8	8	10	9

Notes: Except as indicated, test scores and characteristic data are for college-bound students. Through 1985, data are based on a 10 percent sample; thereafter, data are based on all ACT-tested seniors. — = not available.

Source: Reprinted from U.S. Bureau of the Census. (1993). *Statistical abstract of the United States: 1993* (113th ed., p. 170). Austin, TX: Reference Press.

[a] Beginning in 1990, data are not comparable with previous years because a new version of the ACT was introduced. The estimated average composite scores for prior years are as follows: in 1989, 20.6; in 1988, 1987, and 1986, 20.8.

[b] Minimum score = 1; maximum score = 36.

[c] Prior to 1990, social studies data were not comparable with previous years.

[d] Prior to 1990, natural sciences data were not comparable with previous years.

[e] Beginning in 1985, data are for seniors who graduated in the year shown and had taken the ACT in their junior or senior years.

[f] Prior to 1990, 26 or above and 15 or below.

[g] Includes political and persuasive (for example, sales) fields through 1975; thereafter, business and commerce.

[h] Includes religion through 1975.

TABLE 4-19 **Proficiency Test Scores for Selected Subjects, by Students' Gender, Race and Ethnicity, and Level of Parental Education: Selected School Years, 1976–77 to 1989–90**

| | | Gender | | Ethnicity | | | Parental Education | | | | |
| | | | | | | | Less than High School | High School | More than High School | | |
Test and Year	Total	Male	Female	White[a]	Black[a]	Hispanic			Total	Some College	College Graduate
Reading											
9-year-olds											
1979–80	215	210	220	221	189	190	194	213	226	—	—
1983–84	211	208	214	218	186	187	195	209	223	—	—
1987–88	212	208	216	218	189	194	193	211	220	—	—
1989–90	209	204	215	217	182	189	193	209	218	—	—
13-year-olds											
1979–80	259	254	263	264	232	237	239	254	271	—	—
1983–84	257	253	262	263	236	240	240	253	268	—	—
1987–88	258	252	263	261	243	240	247	253	265	—	—
1989–90	257	251	263	262	242	238	241	251	267	—	—
17-year-olds											
1979–80	286	282	290	293	243	261	262	277	299	—	—
1983–84	289	284	294	296	264	268	269	281	301	—	—
1987–88	290	286	294	295	274	271	267	282	300	—	—
1989–90	290	284	297	297	267	275	270	283	300	—	—
Writing											
4th graders											
1983–84	179	176	184	186	154	163	157	171	187	—	193
1987–88	186	176	195	193	154	169	158	183	179	—	195
1989–90	183	174	193	191	155	168	169	183	195	—	191
8th graders											
1983–84	206	199	214	210	190	191	196	203	210	—	215
1987–88	203	193	213	207	190	188	195	198	213	—	208
1989–90	198	187	208	202	182	189	191	195	207	—	203
11th graders											
1983–84	212	201	223	218	195	188	200	207	218	—	220
1987–88	214	204	223	219	200	199	202	211	217	—	220
1989–90	212	200	224	217	194	198	190	204	215	—	221
Mathematics											
9-year-olds											
1977–78	219	217	220	224	192	203	200	219	—	230	231
1981–82	219	217	221	224	195	204	199	218	—	225	229
1985–86	222	222	222	227	202	205	201	218	—	229	231
1989–90	230	229	230	235	208	214	210	226	—	236	238
13-year-olds											
1977–78	264	264	265	272	230	238	245	263	—	273	284
1981–82	269	269	268	274	240	252	251	263	—	275	282
1985–86	269	270	268	274	249	254	252	263	—	274	280
1989–90	270	271	270	276	249	255	253	263	—	277	280
17-year-olds											
1977–78	300	304	297	306	268	276	280	294	—	305	317
1981–82	299	302	296	304	272	277	279	293	—	304	312
1985–86	302	305	299	308	279	283	279	293	—	305	314
1989–90	305	306	303	310	289	284	285	294	—	308	316
Science											
9-year-olds											
1976–77	220	222	218	230	192	175	199	223	—	237	232
1981–82	221	221	221	229	189	187	198	218	—	229	231
1985–86	224	227	221	232	199	196	204	220	—	236	235
1989–90	229	230	227	238	196	206	210	226	—	238	236
13-year-olds											
1976–77	247	251	244	256	208	213	224	245	—	260	267
1981–82	250	256	245	257	217	226	225	243	—	259	264
1985–86	251	256	247	259	222	226	229	245	—	258	264
1989–90	255	259	252	264	226	232	233	247	—	263	268
17-year-olds											
1976–77	290	297	282	298	262	240	265	284	—	296	309
1981–82	283	292	275	293	249	235	259	275	—	290	300
1985–86	289	295	282	298	259	253	258	277	—	295	304
1989–90	290	296	285	301	253	262	261	276	—	297	306

Notes: Data are based on the National Assessment of Educational Progress Tests, which are administered to a representative sample of students in public and private schools. Test scores can range from 0 to 500, except for writing, which ranges from 0 to 400. — = not available.

Source: Reprinted from U.S. Bureau of the Census. (1993). *Statistical abstract of the United States: 1993* (113th ed., p. 171). Austin, TX: Reference Press.

[a]Non-Hispanic.

TABLE 4-20 **Education Attainment Rates of Adults, by State: 1990**

State	1992 Population	Rank	Educational Attainment of Adults in 1990 (Highest Level, %)							1992 Per Capita Income ($)	1990 Poverty Rate (%)	1993–94 High School Graduates	High School Dropout Rate in 1990 (%)
			8th Grade or Less	Some High School, No Diploma	High School Diploma	Some College, No Degree	Associate Degree	Bachelor's Degree	Graduate Degree				
United States	255,082,000		10.4	14.4	30.0	18.7	6.2	13.1	7.2	19,841	13.1	2,490,832	11.2
Alabama	4,136,000	22	13.7	19.4	29.4	16.8	5.0	10.1	5.5	16,220	18.3	42,120	12.6
Alaska	587,000	49	5.1	8.2	28.7	27.6	7.2	15.0	8.0	21,603	9.0	5,871	10.9
Arizona	3,832,000	23	9.0	12.3	26.1	25.4	6.8	13.3	7.0	17,119	15.7	36,788	14.4
Arkansas	2,399,000	33	15.2	18.4	32.7	16.6	3.7	8.9	4.5	15,439	19.1	26,385	11.4
California	30,867,000	1	11.2	12.6	22.3	22.6	7.9	15.3	8.1	21,278	12.5	275,543	14.2
Colorado	3,470,000	26	5.6	10.0	26.5	24.0	6.9	18.0	9.0	20,124	11.7	33,902	9.8
Connecticut	3,281,000	27	8.4	12.4	29.5	15.9	6.6	16.2	11.0	26,979	6.8	31,822	9.0
Delaware	689,000	46	7.2	15.3	32.7	16.9	6.5	13.7	7.7	21,451	8.7	6,853	10.4
District of Columbia	589,000	48	9.6	17.3	21.2	15.6	3.1	16.1	17.2	26,360	16.9	5,392	13.9
Florida	13,488,000	4	9.5	16.1	30.1	19.4	6.6	12.0	6.3	19,397	12.7	102,274	14.3
Georgia	6,751,000	11	12.0	17.1	29.6	17.0	5.0	12.9	6.4	18,130	14.7	63,852	14.1
Hawaii	1,160,000	40	10.1	9.8	28.7	20.1	8.3	15.8	7.1	21,218	8.3	11,713	7.5
Idaho	1,067,000	42	7.4	12.9	30.4	24.2	7.5	12.4	5.3	16,067	13.3	14,230	10.4
Illinois	11,631,000	6	10.3	13.5	30.0	19.4	5.8	13.6	7.5	21,608	11.9	118,145	10.6
Indiana	5,662,000	14	8.5	15.8	38.2	16.6	5.3	9.2	6.4	18,043	10.7	60,642	11.4
Iowa	2,812,000	30	9.2	10.7	38.5	17.0	7.7	11.7	5.2	18,287	11.5	33,607	6.6
Kansas	2,523,000	32	7.7	11.0	32.8	21.9	5.4	14.1	7.0	19,376	11.5	26,473	8.7
Kentucky	3,755,000	24	19.0	16.4	31.8	15.2	4.1	8.1	5.5	16,534	19.0	39,144	13.3
Louisiana	4,287,000	21	14.7	17.0	31.7	17.2	3.3	10.5	5.6	15,712	23.6	41,321	12.5
Maine	1,235,000	39	8.8	12.4	37.1	16.1	6.9	12.7	6.1	18,226	10.8	13,597	8.3
Maryland	4,908,000	19	7.9	13.7	28.1	18.6	5.2	15.6	10.9	22,974	8.3	44,602	10.9
Massachusetts	5,998,000	13	8.0	12.0	29.7	15.8	7.2	16.6	10.6	24,059	8.9	55,256	8.5
Michigan	9,437,000	8	7.8	15.5	32.3	20.4	6.7	10.9	6.4	19,508	13.1	96,116	10.0
Minnesota	4,480,000	20	8.6	9.0	33.0	19.0	8.6	15.6	6.3	20,049	10.2	51,745	6.4
Mississippi	2,614,000	31	15.6	20.1	27.5	16.9	5.2	9.7	5.1	14,088	25.2	26,843	11.8
Missouri	5,193,000	15	11.6	14.5	33.1	18.4	4.5	11.7	6.1	18,835	13.3	53,119	11.4
Montana	824,000	44	8.1	10.9	33.5	22.1	5.6	14.1	5.7	16,062	16.1	10,350	8.1
Nebraska	1,606,000	36	8.0	10.2	34.7	21.1	7.1	13.1	5.9	19,084	11.1	18,980	7.0
Nevada	1,327,000	38	6.0	15.2	31.5	25.8	6.2	10.1	5.2	20,266	10.2	10,623	15.2
New Hampshire	1,111,000	41	6.7	11.2	31.7	18.0	8.1	16.4	7.9	22,934	6.4	12,120	9.4
New Jersey	7,789,000	9	9.4	13.9	31.1	15.5	5.2	16.0	8.8	26,457	7.6	82,871	9.6
New Mexico	1,581,000	37	11.4	13.5	28.7	20.9	5.0	12.1	8.3	15,353	20.6	16,019	11.7
New York	18,119,000	2	10.2	15.0	29.5	15.7	6.5	13.2	9.9	23,534	13.0	158,177	9.9
North Carolina	6,843,000	10	12.7	17.3	29.0	16.8	6.8	12.0	5.4	17,667	13.0	60,733	12.5

State													
North Dakota	636,000	47	15.0	8.3	28.0	20.5	10.0	13.5	4.5	16,854	14.4	8,099	4.6
Ohio	11,016,000	7	7.9	16.4	36.3	17.0	5.3	11.1	5.9	18,624	12.5	114,143	8.9
Oklahoma	3,212,000	28	9.8	15.6	30.5	21.3	5.0	11.8	6.0	16,198	16.7	33,284	10.4
Oregon	2,977,000	29	6.2	12.3	28.9	25.0	6.9	13.6	7.0	18,202	12.4	28,816	11.8
Pennsylvania	12,009,000	5	9.4	15.9	38.6	12.9	5.2	11.3	6.6	20,253	11.1	118,200	9.1
Rhode Island	1,005,000	43	11.1	16.9	29.5	15.0	6.3	13.5	7.8	20,299	9.6	9,001	11.1
South Carolina	3,603,000	25	13.6	18.1	29.5	15.8	6.3	11.2	5.4	15,989	15.4	35,222	11.7
South Dakota	711,000	45	13.4	9.5	33.7	18.8	7.4	12.3	4.9	16,558	15.9	8,855	7.7
Tennessee	5,024,000	17	16.0	17.0	30.0	16.9	4.2	10.5	5.4	17,341	15.7	46,361	13.4
Texas	17,656,000	3	13.5	14.4	25.6	21.1	5.2	13.9	6.5	17,892	18.1	174,456	12.9
Utah	1,813,000	34	3.4	11.5	27.2	27.9	7.8	15.4	6.8	15,325	11.4	28,964	8.7
Vermont	570,000	50	8.7	10.6	34.6	14.7	7.2	15.4	8.9	18,834	9.9	6,461	8.0
Virginia	6,377,000	12	11.2	13.7	26.6	18.5	5.5	15.4	9.1	20,629	10.2	62,175	10.0
Washington	5,136,000	16	5.5	10.7	27.9	25.0	7.9	15.9	7.0	20,398	10.9	49,140	10.6
West Virginia	1,812,000	35	16.8	17.3	36.6	13.2	3.8	7.5	4.8	15,065	19.7	20,802	10.9
Wisconsin	5,007,000	18	9.5	11.9	37.1	16.7	7.1	12.1	5.6	18,727	10.7	53,643	7.1
Wyoming	466,000	51	5.7	11.2	33.2	24.2	6.9	13.1	5.7	17,423	11.9	5,982	6.9

Source: Adapted with permission from Evangelauf, J. (Ed.). (1993, August 25). *The Chronicle of Higher Education almanac* (p. 6). Washington, DC: Chronicle of Higher Education. © 1993, Chronicle of Higher Education.

FIGURE 4-4 **Percentages of Adults with a Bachelor's Degree or Higher, by State: 1990**

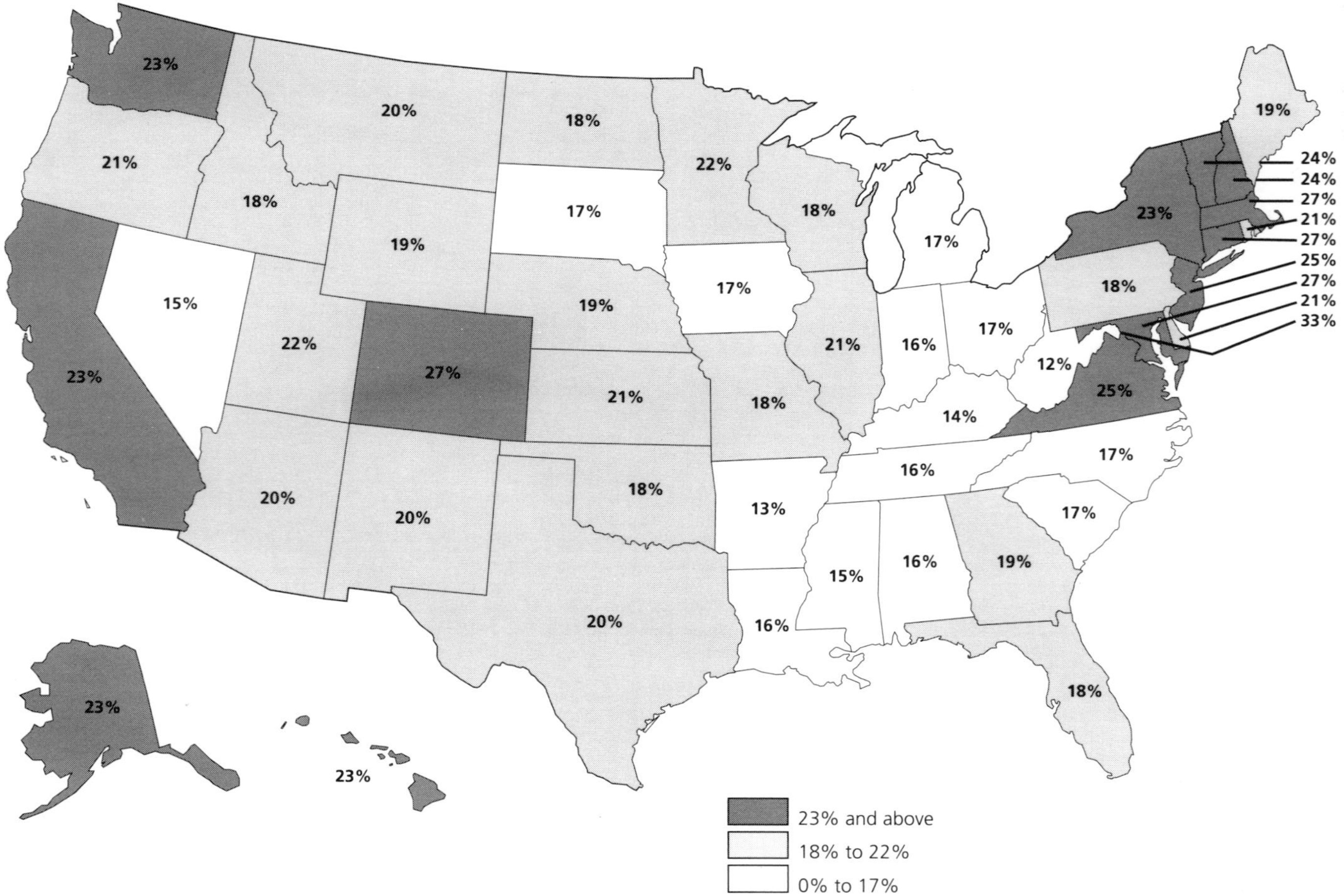

24%
24%
27%
21%
27%
25%
27%
21%
21%
33%

19%

23%

18%

25%

17%

12%

17%

17%

18%

17%

16%

14%

16%

19%

16%

18%

21%

18%

13%

15%

16%

22%

17%

18%

17%

19%

21%

18%

20%

18%

27%

20%

20%

19%

22%

20%

18%

21%

15%

23%

23%

23%

23%

23% and above
18% to 22%
0% to 17%

Source: Adapted with permission from Evangelauf, J. (Ed.). (1993, August 25). *The Chronicle of Higher Education almanac* (p. 6). Washington, DC: Chronicle of Higher Education. © 1993, Chronicle of Higher Education.

TABLE 4-21 Enrollment in Institutions of Higher Education, Minority Enrollment Rates, and Average Student Test Scores, by State: 1991

State	Enrollment, Fall 1991								Minority Enrollment, Fall 1991 (%)				Test Scores	
	Public 4-Year	Public 2-Year	Private 4-Year	Private 2-Year	Under-graduate	Graduate	Professional	Total	Public 4-Year	Public 2-Year	Private 4-Year	Private 2-Year	Test Taken	Score
United States	5,904,748	5,404,815	2,802,305	247,085	12,439,287	1,639,135	280,531	14,358,953	19.3	24.6	17.7	28.5	ACT / SAT	20.6 / 902
Alabama	127,754	74,557	18,788	3,232	200,342	20,924	3,065	224,331	19.6	21.0	45.5	38.6	ACT	19.8
Alaska	29,019	0	1,432	342	29,450	1,343	0	30,793	17.1	—	21.6	39.2	SAT	915
Arizona	95,514	158,117	17,761	1,579	242,478	28,975	1,518	272,971	16.1	23.6	21.5	37.4	ACT	21.0
Arkansas	63,464	18,688	10,070	2,118	85,742	6,985	1,613	94,340	16.1	14.8	15.7	36.2	ACT	20.0
California	530,942	1,273,712	207,568	12,052	1,808,267	183,443	32,564	2,024,274	38.8	35.6	26.6	44.1	SAT	899
Colorado	131,564	75,081	23,158	5,305	196,759	35,283	3,066	235,108	13.2	18.1	13.6	24.2	ACT	21.3
Connecticut	63,557	43,764	57,170	1,369	130,809	31,752	3,263	165,824	9.9	18.1	12.7	12.6	SAT	904
Delaware	23,745	11,566	7,677	0	37,398	3,460	2,130	42,988	14.7	20.4	12.4	—	SAT	894
District of Columbia	12,033	0	65,931	0	46,235	23,236	8,493	77,964	90.8	—	33.2	—	SAT	846
Florida	183,117	323,225	98,099	7,340	547,717	55,839	8,225	611,781	24.6	25.9	27.1	38.2	SAT	882
Georgia	151,218	67,706	49,783	8,316	237,260	31,838	7,925	277,023	19.7	25.4	39.0	29.2	SAT	844
Hawaii	22,656	23,026	11,620	0	49,599	7,264	439	57,302	71.1	75.3	49.8	—	SAT	879
Idaho	37,936	6,213	2,897	8,351	47,912	6,929	556	55,397	6.0	4.5	4.4	3.0	ACT	21.0
Illinois	202,006	369,243	172,498	9,550	641,614	94,641	17,042	753,297	21.4	28.1	19.9	55.0	ACT	20.9
Indiana	190,444	37,934	58,215	3,708	253,051	31,836	5,414	290,301	9.1	10.2	9.3	16.8	SAT	869
Iowa	68,088	52,272	48,390	2,274	146,801	17,999	6,224	171,024	6.4	4.7	5.9	4.9	ACT	21.6
Kansas	89,572	62,777	14,462	888	146,387	19,162	2,150	167,699	8.7	11.4	10.7	32.5	ACT	21.1
Kentucky	109,780	45,993	26,941	5,244	164,420	18,983	4,555	187,958	7.9	8.0	6.0	16.2	ACT	20.0
Louisiana	143,219	25,603	26,624	1,992	169,207	22,288	5,943	197,438	28.3	30.9	32.0	42.7	ACT	19.4
Maine	34,038	6,890	14,675	1,575	51,430	5,114	634	57,178	2.0	2.8	3.8	10.3	SAT	885
Maryland	113,096	115,542	38,438	855	226,154	37,939	3,838	267,931	29.3	25.7	15.2	17.4	SAT	909
Massachusetts	105,884	74,675	225,175	13,647	332,752	73,496	13,133	419,381	9.2	14.1	15.0	15.8	SAT	903
Michigan	259,113	227,188	79,129	3,061	497,367	61,300	9,824	568,491	13.7	13.9	18.5	19.1	ACT	
Minnesota	130,665	69,088	51,150	4,151	223,446	24,273	6,835	255,054	5.6	6.2	6.2	13.2	ACT	21.5
Mississippi	60,187	51,199	10,996	2,968	112,737	10,492	2,121	125,350	31.5	26.2	33.9	47.2	ACT	18.8
Missouri	126,104	77,021	90,721	3,308	252,568	36,321	8,265	297,154	10.2	13.9	12.7	14.5	ACT	21.0
Montana	29,520	3,933	3,126	1,242	34,120	3,474	227	37,821	4.7	24.4	5.8	79.2	ACT	21.7
Nebraska	60,695	33,997	18,477	479	98,398	12,271	2,979	113,648	5.1	6.7	7.5	6.3	ACT	21.2
Nevada	30,851	31,134	329	350	56,754	5,714	196	62,664	15.5	19.5	1.9	36.0	ACT	21.1
New Hampshire	25,956	8,562	25,611	3,589	54,685	8,343	690	63,718	2.2	5.2	6.8	5.5	SAT	929
New Jersey	138,129	132,599	59,893	4,020	285,281	43,039	6,321	334,641	23.7	24.6	19.9	37.9	SAT	892
New Mexico	49,323	40,530	3,034	620	82,656	10,221	630	93,507	34.2	45.0	26.1	37.9	ACT	20.0
New York	346,305	259,593	417,112	33,477	860,227	169,427	26,833	1,056,487	32.4	26.2	19.9	38.7	SAT	887
North Carolina	152,320	153,153	62,053	4,442	335,109	30,682	6,177	371,968	21.7	21.4	21.4	25.5	SAT	859

Continued on next page

TABLE 4-21 **Continued**

State	Enrollment, Fall 1991								Minority Enrollment, Fall 1991 (%)				Test Scores	
	Public 4-Year	Public 2-Year	Private 4-Year	Private 2-Year	Under-graduate	Graduate	Professional	Total	Public 4-Year	Public 2-Year	Private 4-Year	Private 2-Year	Test Taken	Score
North Dakota	27,559	7,659	3,297	224	35,844	2,392	503	38,739	3.7	17.2	4.7	100.0	ACT	20.7
Ohio	290,742	145,550	113,972	19,062	491,277	65,775	12,274	569,326	10.7	12.5	11.8	18.1	ACT	20.9
Oklahoma	95,426	64,740	19,616	3,754	158,210	21,892	3,434	183,536	17.0	16.8	15.1	33.4	ACT	20.0
Oregon	65,169	79,282	22,369	287	147,139	16,230	3,738	167,107	11.6	9.1	9.0	6.4	SAT	933
Pennsylvania	236,644	117,791	218,144	47,457	526,549	78,635	14,852	620,036	10.5	14.2	9.2	27.6	SAT	878
Rhode Island	25,173	17,330	36,609	0	69,165	9,631	316	79,112	6.0	11.9	10.2	—	SAT	883
South Carolina	85,518	51,494	25,268	2,627	143,494	18,864	2,549	164,907	17.9	26.1	25.1	44.6	SAT	838
South Dakota	28,737	151	7,191	253	32,079	3,769	484	36,332	5.8	85.4	12.2	0.4	ACT	21.0
Tennessee	112,789	73,652	46,848	4,753	209,991	22,775	5,276	238,042	15.9	17.5	18.1	19.6	ACT	20.2
Texas	420,161	396,393	95,897	4,992	804,194	96,426	16,823	917,443	28.7	34.5	23.8	39.5	SAT	885
Utah	61,782	33,020	34,592	1,025	119,343	9,848	1,228	130,419	5.8	8.1	2.8	5.7	ACT	21.1
Vermont	16,287	5,198	15,808	143	32,276	4,308	852	37,436	3.9	0.9	5.2	2.9	SAT	893
Virginia	163,232	134,875	54,270	3,948	305,280	44,624	6,421	356,325	20.7	18.7	22.7	41.5	SAT	894
Washington	81,189	157,156	34,266	2,149	250,598	20,922	3,240	274,760	15.4	14.2	12.1	16.7	SAT	921
West Virginia	70,937	7,278	7,815	2,572	76,059	11,225	1,318	88,602	5.2	3.8	6.2	6.1	ACT	19.8
Wisconsin	154,316	105,766	47,376	1,528	274,389	31,152	3,445	308,986	6.4	10.3	8.6	25.7	ACT	21.6
Wyoming	12,646	18,605	0	867	28,909	2,990	219	32,118	5.9	6.1	—	4.7	ACT	21.2

Notes: SAT = Scholastic Aptitude Test (scores range from 400 to 1,600); ACT = American College Testing (scores range from 1 to 36). — = not available.

Source: Adapted with permission from Evangelauf, J. (Ed.). (1993, August 25). *The Chronicle of Higher Education almanac* (p. 8). Washington, DC: Chronicle of Higher Education. © 1993, Chronicle of Higher Education.

TABLE 4-22 Students Enrolled in College, Degrees Conferred, and High School Graduates: Annual Projections, 1993 to 2003

	1993	1994	1995	1996	1997	1998	1999	2000	2001	2002	2003
College enrollment											
Total	14,431,000	14,373,000	14,591,000	14,739,000	14,922,000	15,167,000	15,431,000	15,634,000	15,814,000	15,993,000	16,124,000
Men											
Total	6,400,000	6,355,000	6,471,000	6,551,000	6,658,000	6,794,000	6,956,000	7,071,000	7,194,000	7,300,000	7,386,000
Full-time	3,826,000	3,762,000	3,851,000	3,903,000	3,973,000	4,069,000	4,194,000	4,275,000	4,369,000	4,447,000	4,507,000
Part-time	2,574,000	2,593,000	2,620,000	2,648,000	2,685,000	2,725,000	2,762,000	2,796,000	2,825,000	2,853,000	2,879,000
Women											
Total	8,031,000	8,018,000	8,120,000	8,188,000	8,264,000	8,373,000	8,475,000	8,563,000	8,620,000	8,693,000	8,738,000
Full-time	4,271,000	4,199,000	4,280,000	4,321,000	4,382,000	4,473,000	4,561,000	4,641,000	4,718,000	4,771,000	4,820,000
Part-time	3,760,000	3,819,000	3,840,000	3,867,000	3,882,000	3,900,000	3,914,000	3,922,000	3,902,000	3,922,000	3,918,000
Public institutions	11,242,000	11,206,000	11,376,000	11,494,000	11,637,000	11,826,000	12,029,000	12,186,000	12,320,000	12,457,000	12,555,000
Private institutions	3,189,000	3,167,000	3,215,000	3,245,000	3,285,000	3,341,000	3,402,000	3,448,000	3,494,000	3,536,000	3,569,000
Full-time equivalent[a]											
Total	10,386,000	10,277,000	10,465,000	10,578,000	10,727,000	10,934,000	11,165,000	11,342,000	11,515,000	11,664,000	11,780,000
Public	7,799,000	7,722,000	7,865,000	7,953,000	8,066,000	8,223,000	8,397,000	8,528,000	8,658,000	8,767,000	8,852,000
Private	2,585,000	2,556,000	2,600,000	2,624,000	2,661,000	2,712,000	2,769,000	2,813,000	2,858,000	2,897,000	2,928,000
Four-year institutions											
Total	9,048,000	8,984,000	9,117,000	9,203,000	9,320,000	9,481,000	9,662,000	9,800,000	9,935,000	10,058,000	10,155,000
Public	6,130,000	6,085,000	6,177,000	6,235,000	6,317,000	6,428,000	6,552,000	6,649,000	6,742,000	6,825,000	6,891,000
Private	2,918,000	2,899,000	2,940,000	2,968,000	3,003,000	3,053,000	3,110,000	3,151,000	3,193,000	3,233,000	3,264,000
Two-year institutions											
Total	5,383,000	5,389,000	5,474,000	5,536,000	5,602,000	5,686,000	5,769,000	5,834,000	5,879,000	5,935,000	5,969,000
Public	5,112,000	5,121,000	5,199,000	5,259,000	5,320,000	5,398,000	5,477,000	5,537,000	5,578,000	5,632,000	5,664,000
Private	271,000	268,000	275,000	277,000	282,000	288,000	292,000	297,000	301,000	303,000	305,000
Undergraduate											
Total	12,307,000	12,230,000	12,443,000	12,582,000	12,755,000	12,992,000	13,245,000	13,447,000	13,623,000	13,787,000	13,909,000
Public	9,947,000	9,898,000	10,065,000	10,178,000	10,315,000	10,499,000	10,696,000	10,852,000	10,984,000	11,113,000	11,206,000
Private	2,360,000	2,332,000	2,378,000	2,404,000	2,440,000	2,493,000	2,549,000	2,595,000	2,639,000	2,674,000	2,703,000
Graduate											
Total	1,796,000	1,817,000	1,822,000	1,831,000	1,839,000	1,847,000	1,856,000	1,857,000	1,859,000	1,871,000	1,877,000
Public	1,160,000	1,174,000	1,177,000	1,181,000	1,187,000	1,192,000	1,197,000	1,198,000	1,199,000	1,206,000	1,211,000
Private	636,000	643,000	645,000	650,000	652,000	655,000	659,000	659,000	660,000	665,000	666,000
First professional											
Total	328,000	326,000	326,000	326,000	328,000	328,000	330,000	330,000	332,000	335,000	338,000
Public	135,000	134,000	134,000	135,000	135,000	135,000	136,000	136,000	137,000	138,000	138,000
Private	193,000	192,000	192,000	191,000	193,000	193,000	194,000	194,000	195,000	197,000	200,000

Continued on next page

TABLE 4-22 Continued

	1993	1994	1995	1996	1997	1998	1999	2000	2001	2002	2003
Degrees											
Associate											
Total	490,000	492,000	497,000	489,000	502,000	510,000	517,000	528,000	540,000	548,000	557,000
Men	203,000	201,000	200,000	197,000	202,000	206,000	209,000	214,000	220,000	224,000	228,000
Women	287,000	291,000	297,000	292,000	300,000	304,000	308,000	314,000	320,000	324,000	329,000
Bachelor's											
Total	1,131,000	1,166,000	1,166,000	1,170,000	1,146,000	1,173,000	1,186,000	1,208,000	1,239,000	1,275,000	1,303,000
Men	520,000	539,000	535,000	532,000	524,000	538,000	547,000	559,000	574,000	594,000	607,000
Women	611,000	627,000	631,000	638,000	622,000	635,000	639,000	649,000	665,000	681,000	696,000
Master's											
Total	345,000	350,000	354,000	354,000	350,000	350,000	351,000	353,000	358,000	361,000	365,000
Men	160,000	162,000	166,000	166,000	163,000	163,000	165,000	167,000	173,000	175,000	179,000
Women	185,000	188,000	188,000	188,000	187,000	187,000	186,000	186,000	185,000	186,000	186,000
Doctorate											
Total	40,500	40,900	40,900	41,100	41,300	41,400	41,900	41,600	41,600	41,700	41,800
Men	24,800	24,700	24,200	23,900	23,700	23,400	23,400	22,700	22,300	22,000	21,700
Women	15,700	16,200	16,700	17,200	17,600	18,000	18,500	18,900	19,300	19,700	20,100
First professional											
Total	81,000	84,600	85,700	85,200	85,700	85,400	86,200	86,600	87,300	87,300	88,000
Men	46,700	48,000	49,100	49,100	49,800	49,800	50,400	50,800	51,500	51,500	52,200
Women	34,300	36,600	36,600	36,100	35,900	35,600	35,800	35,800	35,800	35,800	35,800
High school graduates											
Total	2,480,000	2,506,000	2,601,000	2,631,000	2,748,000	2,863,000	2,921,000	2,978,000	3,009,000	3,010,000	3,011,000
Public	2,236,000	2,259,000	2,345,000	2,372,000	2,478,000	2,581,000	2,634,000	2,685,000	2,713,000	2,714,000	2,715,000
Private	244,000	247,000	256,000	259,000	270,000	282,000	287,000	293,000	296,000	296,000	296,000

Source: Adapted with permission from Evangelauf, J. (Ed.). (1993, August 25). *The Chronicle of Higher Education almanac* (p. 14). Washington, DC: Chronicle of Higher Education. © 1993, Chronicle of Higher Education.

[a]Estimate based on full-time enrollment plus full-time equivalent of part-time enrollment as reported by institutions.

tinue to complete more doctoral degrees than women, but the gap is projected to narrow. Table 4-25 shows the number and types of higher education institutions by state, the numbers of full-time faculty members and their average salaries, and the numbers and kinds of degrees awarded.

Table 4-26 provides a summary of educational attainment in the United States, cor-related with such demographic factors as age, gender, race and ethnicity, region, marital status, and employment. The South lags behind other regions in educational attainment. Women are as likely to have had some college education as men, but more men complete bachelor's and advanced degrees.

TABLE 4-23 **Percentages of 18- to 24-Year-Olds Enrolled in College, by High School Graduation Status and Race and Ethnicity: 1981 to 1991**

	All Youths		White		Black		Hispanic	
Year	All Youths	High School Graduates	All Youths	High School Graduates	All Youths	High School Graduates	All Youths	High School Graduates
1981	26.2	32.5	26.7	32.5	19.9	28.0	16.7	29.9
1982	26.6	33.0	27.2	33.1	19.8	28.0	16.8	29.2
1983	26.2	32.5	27.0	32.9	19.2	27.0	17.2	31.4
1984	27.1	33.2	28.0	33.7	20.4	27.2	17.9	29.9
1985	27.8	33.7	28.7	34.4	19.8	26.1	16.9	26.9
1986	28.2	34.3	28.6	34.5	22.2	29.1	18.2	30.4
1987	29.6	36.4	30.2	36.6	22.8	30.0	17.6	28.5
1988	30.3	37.3	31.3	38.1	21.1	28.1	17.0	30.9
1989	30.9	38.1	31.8	38.8	23.5	30.8	16.1	28.7
1990	32.0	39.2	23.5	39.4	25.4	33.0	15.8	29.0
1991	33.3	41.1	34.1	41.7	23.6	31.5	18.0	34.4

Notes: The figures are based on annual Census Bureau surveys of 60,000 households. The survey defined high school graduates as those who had completed four years of high school or more. Hispanics may be of any race.

Source: Adapted with permission from Evangelauf, J. (Ed.). (1993, August 25). *The Chronicle of Higher Education almanac* (p. 14). Washington, DC: Chronicle of Higher Education. © 1993, Chronicle of Higher Education.

Reading Proficiency

Figure 4-5 presents information on reading proficiency levels, perhaps a better measure of educational attainment than literacy. Literacy, which simply means the ability to read and write, is difficult to measure. In 1979 the Bureau of the Census suggested that 99.5 percent of the U.S. population was literate, but the U.S. Office of Vocational and Adult Education reported in 1983 that 74 million adult Americans were marginally functionally illiterate. In 1984 the U.S. Office of Education estimated that one-third of American adults were illiterate (Harris & Bradford, 1987). Reading proficiency, on the other hand, provides a specific measure of achievement in reading standardized materials. More than half of all students have basic reading

TABLE 4-24 **Earned Degrees Conferred, by Level of Degree and Gender: Selected Years, 1950 to 1990, and Projections, 1995 to 2003 (Numbers in thousands)**

Year	Degrees Total	Percent Male	Associate Male	Associate Female	Bachelor's Male	Bachelor's Female	Master's Male	Master's Female	First Professional Male	First Professional Female	Doctorate Male	Doctorate Female
1950[a]	497	75.7	—	—	329	103	41	17	—	—	6	1
1960[a]	477	65.8	—	—	254	138	51	24	—	—	9	1
1965	664	61.6	—	—	289	213	78	40	27	1	15	2
1970	1,271	59.2	117	89	451	341	126	83	33	2	26	4
1971	1,393	59.0	144	108	476	364	138	92	36	2	28	5
1972	1,509	58.7	166	126	501	387	150	102	41	3	28	5
1973	1,586	58.1	175	141	518	404	154	109	46	4	29	6
1974	1,653	57.5	189	155	527	418	158	119	49	5	27	6
1975	1,666	56.1	191	169	505	418	162	131	49	7	27	7
1976	1,726	55.7	210	181	505	421	167	145	53	10	26	8
1977	1,741	54.7	211	196	496	424	168	149	52	12	25	8
1978	1,744	53.3	205	208	487	434	161	150	52	14	24	8
1979	1,727	52.1	192	211	477	444	153	148	53	16	24	9
1980	1,731	51.1	184	217	474	456	151	147	53	17	23	10
1981	1,752	50.3	189	228	470	465	147	149	53	19	23	10
1982	1,788	49.8	197	238	473	480	146	150	52	20	22	10
1983	1,822	49.6	207	249	479	490	145	145	51	22	22	11
1984	1,819	49.6	203	250	482	492	144	141	51	23	22	11
1985	1,828	49.3	203	252	483	497	143	143	50	25	22	11
1986	1,830	49.0	196	250	486	502	144	145	49	25	22	12
1987	1,825	48.4	192	246	481	510	141	148	47	25	22	12
1988	1,835	48.0	190	245	477	518	145	154	45	25	23	12
1989	1,873	47.3	186	250	483	535	149	161	45	26	23	13
1990	1,937	46.7	191	264	491	558	154	170	44	27	24	14
1995, projected	2,144	45.4	200	297	535	631	166	188	49	37	24	17
2000, projected	2,218	45.7	214	314	559	649	167	186	51	36	23	19
2003, projected	2,355	46.2	228	329	607	696	179	186	52	36	22	20

Notes: Includes Alaska and Hawaii, beginning in 1960. — = not available.

Source: Reprinted from U.S. Bureau of the Census. (1993). *Statistical abstract of the United States: 1993* (113th ed., p. 183). Austin, TX: Reference Press.

[a]First professional degrees are included with bachelor's degrees.

TABLE 4-25 **Number of Institutions of Higher Education, 1991–92, Number and Average Salary of Full-Time Faculty Members and Degrees Awarded, 1990–91, by State**

State	Number of Institutions, 1991–92					Full-Time Faculty Members, 1990–91	Average Pay of Full-Time Faculty Members, 1990–91 ($)			Degrees Awarded, 1990–91				
	Public 4-Year	Public 2-Year	Private 4-Year	Private 2-Year	Total		Public 4-Year	Public 2-Year	Private 4-Year	Associate	Bachelor's	Master's	Doctorate	Professional
United States	599	999	1,558	445	3,601	379,373	44,497	37,064	42,183	481,720	1,094,538	337,168	39,294	71,948
Alabama	18	37	18	13	86	5,942	38,481	33,240	30,947	6,584	18,308	5,162	392	850
Alaska	3	0	3	1	7	757	44,567	NA	29,948	636	1,148	294	10	0
Arizona	3	18	15	3	39	4,823	45,918	40,478	32,438	6,066	18,068	7,597	668	425
Arkansas	10	10	10	5	35	2,957	34,960	26,811	31,410	2,741	7,729	1,649	123	354
California	31	108	147	32	318	37,763	55,380	47,122	48,804	56,943	100,484	34,419	4,540	7,685
Colorado	13	15	21	10	59	5,391	43,262	29,606	42,974	6,163	16,728	5,241	715	772
Connecticut	7	17	19	2	45	5,594	51,222	43,335	49,717	4,758	14,630	6,281	610	980
Delaware	2	3	5	0	10	1,288	44,231	37,175	40,069	1,304	4,008	809	133	418
District of Columbia	2	0	15	0	17	3,352	45,057	NA	48,393	325	7,614	5,228	456	2,310
Florida	9	29	50	16	104	13,038	43,855	32,294	35,881	35,876	38,927	11,295	1,249	2,303
Georgia	20	46	30	15	111	7,648	39,909	31,709	36,501	7,938	22,322	6,566	827	1,952
Hawaii	3	7	7	0	17	1,829	47,053	38,436	26,068	2,317	3,711	1,086	144	118
Idaho	4	2	3	2	11	1,517	36,649	30,532	27,890	3,117	3,136	778	76	122
Illinois	12	47	90	18	167	17,811	42,447	40,239	44,388	24,464	50,508	19,948	2,449	4,476
Indiana	14	14	40	11	79	8,985	41,975	27,169	40,268	8,851	28,886	6,843	1,028	1,384
Iowa	3	18	35	5	61	5,255	47,944	30,745	34,196	8,079	16,996	3,168	694	1,462
Kansas	8	20	21	2	51	4,659	39,869	31,337	25,263	5,821	13,035	3,402	369	629
Kentucky	8	14	26	16	64	5,249	38,818	28,463	30,086	5,759	12,973	3,968	324	1,130
Louisiana	14	6	12	4	36	6,006	36,705	29,878	41,362	2,866	16,309	4,100	417	1,640
Maine	8	6	12	5	31	1,923	40,122	31,775	39,463	2,118	5,227	854	33	173
Maryland	13	19	21	3	56	6,613	46,028	40,313	42,484	7,656	19,235	6,924	838	997
Massachusetts	14	17	72	13	116	15,571	46,965	35,873	51,004	13,330	44,487	19,014	2,172	3,674
Michigan	15	30	49	7	101	14,193	46,407	32,793	34,078	22,422	44,213	14,139	1,487	2,536
Minnesota	10	27	34	10	81	7,286	44,975	39,536	37,351	8,008	23,619	4,585	823	1,454
Mississippi	9	20	12	5	46	3,920	33,717	28,195	34,888	5,119	9,106	2,511	340	452
Missouri	13	14	54	12	93	7,215	39,031	34,915	36,860	7,563	24,917	8,790	643	2,186
Montana	6	7	3	3	19	1,342	34,404	24,641	26,680	890	3,872	753	56	61
Nebraska	7	13	15	1	36	2,767	41,233	27,393	32,879	2,965	8,945	1,691	219	736
Nevada	2	4	1	2	9	1,128	43,777	36,434	31,445	1,013	2,373	613	36	38
New Hampshire	5	7	13	4	29	1,918	41,977	30,582	42,839	2,657	7,128	2,029	89	184
New Jersey	14	19	22	5	60	8,485	50,329	42,030	47,557	10,703	23,624	7,538	816	1,648
New Mexico	6	17	6	1	30	2,222	39,437	27,768	30,949	2,479	5,242	1,916	232	167
New York	42	46	184	49	321	34,459	50,914	43,373	46,120	50,865	92,629	39,079	4,019	7,468

Continued on next page

TABLE 4-25 **Continued**

State	Number of Institutions, 1991–92					Full-Time Faculty Members, 1990–91	Average Pay of Full-Time Faculty Members, 1990–91 ($)			Degrees Awarded, 1990–91				
	Public 4-Year	Public 2-Year	Private 4-Year	Private 2-Year	Total		Public 4-Year	Public 2-Year	Private 4-Year	Associate	Bachelor's	Master's	Doctorate	Professional
North Carolina	16	58	37	11	122	9,675	43,035	26,141	35,798	11,469	28,795	6,185	872	1,625
North Dakota	6	9	4	1	20	1,381	34,391	29,438	26,250	1,784	4,487	587	63	133
Ohio	25	36	67	31	159	15,569	47,142	34,951	36,832	18,446	48,799	13,436	1,751	3,148
Oklahoma	14	15	12	6	47	4,460	37,921	30,342	37,535	6,375	14,067	3,717	380	909
Oregon	8	13	24	1	46	4,652	37,147	33,724	35,983	4,844	12,963	3,397	436	942
Pennsylvania	44	20	101	56	221	20,665	44,618	38,392	43,805	19,884	62,184	15,611	2,120	3,382
Rhode Island	2	1	9	0	12	2,697	46,351	37,706	49,161	3,930	9,153	1,984	270	80
South Carolina	12	21	22	6	61	5,520	40,541	27,649	31,510	5,097	14,250	3,935	370	591
South Dakota	7	1	10	1	19	1,135	33,607	18,628	27,442	906	3,680	781	49	113
Tennessee	10	14	42	15	81	7,270	41,089	30,509	35,883	6,717	18,063	4,716	642	1,268
Texas	40	65	57	13	175	22,095	41,351	33,439	40,273	21,521	65,112	18,794	2,304	4,208
Utah	4	5	3	3	15	3,337	38,483	28,606	41,157	4,099	11,340	2,452	356	383
Vermont	4	2	14	2	22	1,504	42,272	27,546	36,154	1,227	4,553	1,066	48	227
Virginia	15	24	33	11	83	9,974	47,650	35,361	36,269	8,883	28,960	7,913	874	1,739
Washington	8	28	20	5	61	6,847	43,780	33,156	36,647	15,246	19,201	5,200	656	832
West Virginia	13	3	9	3	28	2,552	35,610	27,610	28,904	2,632	7,533	1,707	110	353
Wisconsin	13	19	29	4	65	10,112	43,894	37,699	36,320	9,049	26,343	5,977	872	1,012
Wyoming	1	7	0	1	9	1,022	42,133	28,930	NA	1,633	1,641	304	67	70

Note: NA = not applicable.

Source: Adapted with permission from Evangelauf, J. (Ed.). (1993, August 25). *The Chronicle of Higher Education almanac* (p. 14). Washington, DC: Chronicle of Higher Education. © 1993, Chronicle of Higher Education.

proficiency, as shown in Figure 4-5, and a significant percentage have advanced reading skills. However, many others lack basic reading skills. Children who live with neither their fathers nor their mothers appear to be at a disadvantage, and children who live with both parents appear to be more likely than those in other living situations to have advanced skills in reading.

Table 4-27 provides information on literacy in selected nations. In general, the more developed a nation, the higher its literacy rate. However, as the table indicates, there are many exceptions. Some of the variations in rates may relate to the importance of reading and writing in the nation. There are greater survival needs associated with literacy in some cultures

TABLE 4-26 **Years of School Completed, by Selected Characteristics: 1992**

Characteristic	Population (1,000)	Percentage of Population					
		Not a High School Graduate	High School Graduate	With Some College, but No Degree	With an Associate's Degree[a]	With a Bachelor's Degree	With an Advanced Degree
Total people	160,827	20.6	36.0	16.2	5.9	14.2	7.2
Age							
25 to 34 years old	42,493	13.5	37.7	18.6	7.0	17.9	5.3
35 to 44 years old	39,571	11.8	34.2	19.1	8.0	17.4	9.5
45 to 54 years old	27,023	17.3	36.7	16.3	5.6	13.9	10.3
55 to 64 years old	21,150	26.9	38.0	13.3	4.2	10.5	7.2
65 to 74 years old	18,440	35.0	37.2	11.8	3.3	8.3	4.5
75 years old or over	12,149	48.4	28.9	9.9	2.6	6.6	3.6
Gender							
Male	76,579	20.3	33.7	16.4	5.4	15.3	9.0
Female	84,248	20.8	38.1	16.0	6.4	13.1	5.6
Race							
White	137,646	19.1	36.4	16.4	6.1	14.6	7.5
Black	17,445	32.3	35.7	15.5	4.6	8.3	3.6
Other	5,736	19.7	27.8	13.9	5.3	22.1	11.2
Hispanic origin							
Hispanic	11,623	47.4	27.3	11.7	4.2	6.3	3.0
Non-Hispanic	149,204	18.5	36.7	16.5	6.0	14.8	7.5
Region							
Northeast	33,361	19.2	38.3	12.4	6.3	14.9	8.9
Midwest	38,376	18.7	40.2	16.1	5.3	13.2	6.4
South	55,054	24.2	35.2	16.1	5.3	12.7	6.5
West	34,036	18.2	30.2	20.1	7.0	16.8	7.6
Marital status							
Never married	22,606	17.8	33.0	16.2	5.8	18.8	8.3
Married spouse present	102,536	17.5	37.1	16.3	6.3	15.0	7.9
Married spouse absent	5,868	32.9	32.9	16.6	4.5	9.0	4.2
Separated	4,478	31.9	34.6	17.8	4.5	8.1	3.2
Widowed	13,840	45.5	33.2	10.5	2.9	5.6	2.4
Divorced	15,977	18.4	36.6	20.4	6.7	11.6	6.3
Civilian labor force status							
Employed	99,072	11.9	35.6	17.9	7.2	17.7	9.6
Unemployed	6,954	24.8	41.4	17.3	4.9	8.7	2.9
Not in the labor force	54,090	36.2	35.9	12.6	3.5	8.3	3.3

Note: For people 25 years and older.

Source: Reprinted from U.S. Bureau of the Census. (1993). *Statistical abstract of the United States: 1993* (113th ed., p. 153). Austin, TX: Reference Press.

[a]Includes vocational degrees.

than in others. Nations also vary in their commitments to promoting literacy among their citizens and in the quantity of the resources they devote to education. There are also varying definitions and ways of estimating literacy, which is reported by the nations themselves rather than an outside entity.

Conclusion

Education in the United States is a major human services effort—the preparation of citizens for work and family responsibilities. Readers may want to compare the extent and quality of education in the nation and in individual states with other data on matters such

FIGURE 4-5 **Percentage of Students Performing at Each Reading Proficiency Level, by Parents Living in Household: 1988**

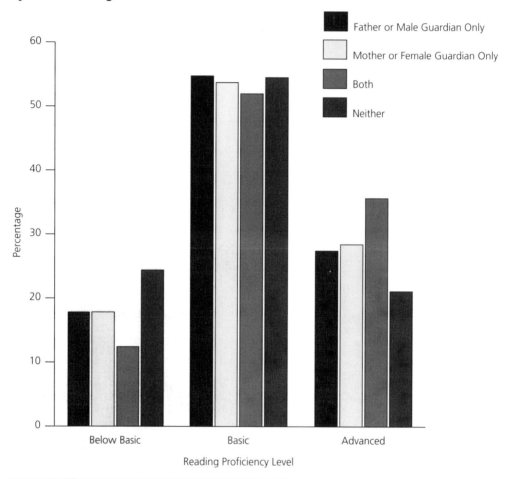

Source: Reprinted from Ashcroft, J., & Strauss, J. (1993). *Families first: Report of the National Commission on America's Urban Families* (p. 27). Washington, DC: U.S. Government Printing Office.

as entitlement programs, health problems, and income distribution. It is almost an article of faith in the United States that education is the source of all kinds of other achievement. It is difficult to directly and reliably correlate such phenomena, but if it were possible to do so, education would probably be only one factor among many in determining, for example, the per capita income, health status, crime rates, and other measures of the success or problems of a city or state. In its own way, however, education is an important factor in social as well as economic well-being. For most Americans, it is an effort worth pursuing and enhancing; this shared value is reflected in the allotment of the single largest chunk of state budgets to education.

TABLE 4-27 **Literacy Rates in Selected Nations: 1994**

Nation	Literacy Rate (%)	Nation	Literacy Rate (%)
Austria	98	Laos	85
Bahrain	80	Lebanon	80
Bangladesh	36	Libya	64
Barbados	99	Malaysia	78
Bolivia	78	Mexico	88
Brazil	81	Morocco	50
Bulgaria	95	Nepal	36
Cambodia	35	Netherlands	99
Canada	99	New Zealand	99
Chile	94	Nicaragua	57
China	73	Nigeria	51
Colombia	87	Norway	100
Congo	57	Pakistan	35
Costa Rica	93	Panama	88
Cuba	94	Paraguay	90
Czech Republic	99	Peru	80
Denmark	99	Phillipines	90
Dominican Republic	83	Poland	98
Ecuador	92	Portugal	85
Egypt	50	Romania	98
El Salvador	73	Russia	—
Ethiopia	62	Saudi Arabia	62
Finland	100	Singapore	91
France	99	Somalia	24
Germany	99	South Africa	76
Greece	93	Spain	97
Grenada	98	Sweden	99
Guatemala	55	Switzerland	99
Haiti	53	Taiwan	94
Hungary	99	Tanzania	46
India	52	Turkey	91
Indonesia	86	Uganda	48
Iran	48	United Kingdom	99
Iraq	55–65	United States	97
Ireland	99	Uruguay	94
Israel	92	Venezuela	86
Jamaica	98	Vietnam	88
Japan	100	Yugoslavia	91
Jordan	82	Zaire	72
Kenya	69	Zambia	76
Korea, South	96	Zimbabwe	74
Kuwait	74		

Note: — = not available.

Source: Compiled from Johnson, O. (Ed.). (1993). *The 1994 information please almanac*. New York: Houghton-Mifflin. © 1993 by Houghton Mifflin Company. Reprinted by permission of Houghton Mifflin Company. All rights reserved.

CHAPTER

5

HEALTH AND MORTALITY STATISTICS

Health services are the second largest employer of social workers in the United States. When one includes related programs for older adults, children, people with developmental disabilities, and services to those who are dying and their families in programs such as hospices, the health field may be the single largest field employing social workers. In addition, health concerns are typically involved in all the needs of social work clients and the communities in which they live. This chapter provides information on a number of health issues, such as life expectancy, infant mortality, and several causes of death such as cardiovascular disease, cancer, and AIDS.

Life Expectancy

United States

Life expectancy is an important indicator of the physical health of a society or nation. Table 5-1 shows the average remaining life expectancy for men and women in the United States on the basis of their ages in 1990. Life expectancy differs for each age. For example, as Table 5-1 shows, a 70-year-old white man has an expected 12.0 years of life remaining. However, if he reaches age 80, he does not have only an expected two years of life remaining. By age 80, he has survived the diseases that might have ended his life during his 70s and would, at age 80, have 7.1 years of life expectancy. Five years later, at age 85, he could expect another 5.2 years of life. In other words, life expectancy is recalculated for each additional year one lives.

In the early years of life, the differences between males and females in life expectancy are great. As life goes on, the differences shrink, although women always have longer life expectancies than do men. As people age,

the large differences between white people and those of other races decrease.

International Comparisons

International perspectives on life expectancy are provided in Table 5-2. The table gives actual and projected world population figures for 1992 and 2025 and compares birth and death rates per 1,000 population, life expectancies, and the fertility rate for women from 1990 to 1995. The table also shows the percentage of the population of each nation that is urban.

Table 5-2 allows one to compare nations on specific indicators. Life expectancy generally correlates with the proportion of urban residents; in most nations, urban people have better access to health care than do rural people. Life expectancy may also be correlated with economic prosperity. The better developed nations tend to have longer life expectancies than do the developing nations. It is important to note that life expectancy rates do not indicate how long people survive in each nation. Infant mortality rates, which are also discussed in this chapter, affect the statistical computations of average aggregate life expectancy, not the expectancy for each individual life.

It is interesting to note that in many cases, nations with high death rates also have high birth and fertility rates: It is an axiom in demographic studies that societies with high death rates attempt to compensate with high birth rates. In general, nations with low death rates also tend toward low birth rates.

Mortality

Table 5-3 shows the numbers of deaths, the death rates, and selected causes of death in the United States in 1991 and 1992. Cardiovascular diseases were the leading cause of death. Although the total number of deaths from such diseases increased from 1991 to 1992, the rate decreased, reflecting the increased size of the population. Strokes or cerebrovascular diseases declined absolutely and by rate. Cancer deaths and rates increased slightly.

Figure 5-1 shows death rates from 14 leading causes beginning in 1960, with projections to 1995. The rates are "age adjusted," which means that they have been adjusted to control for changes and variations in the age composition of the population, making them better indicators of causes of death than the crude or actual rates (Centers for Disease Control and Prevention, 1993a). A population that is in the aggregate growing older, as in the United States, will normally experience

TABLE 5-1 **Average Remaining Life Expectancy in Years, by Race: 1990**

Age in 1990	All Races		White		Other Race		Age in 1990	All Races		White		Other Race	
	Male	Female	Male	Female	Male	Female		Male	Female	Male	Female	Male	Female
Birth	71.8	78.8	72.7	79.4	67.0	75.2	43	32.4	37.8	32.9	38.1	29.4	35.3
1	71.6	78.4	72.3	78.9	67.2	75.3	44	31.5	36.8	32.0	37.2	28.6	34.4
2	70.6	77.5	71.4	78.0	66.2	74.4	45	30.7	35.9	31.1	36.2	27.8	33.6
3	69.7	76.5	70.4	77.0	65.3	73.4	46	29.8	35.0	30.2	35.3	27.0	32.7
4	68.7	75.5	69.4	76.0	64.3	72.5	47	28.9	34.1	29.3	34.4	26.3	31.8
5	67.7	74.5	68.5	75.0	63.4	71.5	48	28.1	33.1	28.4	33.5	25.5	30.9
6	66.8	73.6	67.5	74.1	62.4	70.5	49	27.2	32.2	27.6	32.5	24.7	30.1
7	65.8	72.6	66.5	73.1	61.4	69.5	50	26.4	31.3	26.7	31.6	23.9	29.2
8	64.8	71.6	65.5	72.1	60.4	68.5	51	25.5	30.5	25.8	30.7	23.2	28.4
9	63.8	70.6	64.5	71.1	59.4	67.6	52	24.7	29.6	25.0	29.8	22.4	27.6
10	62.8	69.6	63.5	70.1	58.5	66.6	53	23.9	28.7	24.2	29.0	21.7	26.7
11	61.8	68.6	62.6	69.1	57.5	65.6	54	23.1	27.8	23.3	28.1	21.0	25.9
12	60.8	67.6	61.6	68.1	56.5	64.6	55	22.3	27.0	22.5	27.2	20.3	25.1
13	59.8	66.6	60.6	67.1	55.5	63.6	56	21.5	26.1	21.7	26.4	19.6	24.3
14	58.9	65.7	59.6	66.2	54.5	62.6	57	20.7	25.3	21.0	25.5	18.9	23.6
15	57.9	64.7	58.6	65.2	53.6	61.7	58	20.0	24.4	20.2	24.7	18.3	22.8
16	57.0	63.7	57.7	64.2	52.6	60.7	59	19.2	23.6	19.4	23.8	17.6	22.0
17	56.0	62.7	56.7	63.2	51.7	59.7	60	18.5	22.8	18.7	23.0	17.0	21.3
18	55.1	61.8	55.8	62.3	50.8	58.7	61	17.8	22.0	18.0	22.2	16.4	20.6
19	54.2	60.8	54.9	61.3	49.9	57.8	62	17.1	21.2	17.3	21.4	15.8	19.9
20	53.3	59.8	54.0	60.3	49.0	56.8	63	16.4	20.4	16.6	20.6	15.2	19.1
21	52.3	58.8	53.0	59.3	48.1	55.8	64	15.8	19.7	15.9	19.8	14.6	18.5
22	51.4	57.9	52.1	58.4	47.3	54.9	65	15.1	18.9	15.2	19.1	14.0	17.8
23	50.5	56.9	51.2	57.4	46.4	53.9	66	14.5	18.2	14.6	18.3	13.5	17.1
24	49.6	55.9	50.3	56.4	45.5	53.0	67	13.8	17.4	13.9	17.5	12.9	16.4
25	48.7	55.0	49.3	55.4	44.6	52.0	68	13.2	16.7	13.3	16.8	12.4	15.8
26	47.8	54.0	48.4	54.5	43.8	51.0	69	12.6	16.0	12.7	16.1	11.9	15.2
27	46.9	53.0	47.5	53.5	42.9	50.1	70	12.0	15.3	12.1	15.4	11.4	14.5
28	45.9	52.1	46.6	52.5	42.0	49.2	71	11.5	14.6	11.5	14.7	10.9	13.9
29	45.0	51.1	45.6	51.6	41.2	48.2	72	10.9	13.9	11.0	14.0	10.5	13.3
30	44.1	50.1	44.7	50.6	40.3	47.3	73	10.4	13.3	10.4	13.3	10.0	12.7
31	43.2	49.2	43.8	49.6	39.4	46.3	74	9.9	12.6	9.9	12.6	9.5	12.1
32	42.3	48.2	42.9	48.7	38.6	45.4	75	9.4	12.0	9.4	12.0	9.1	11.5
33	41.4	47.2	41.9	47.7	37.7	44.5	76	8.9	11.3	8.9	11.4	8.7	10.9
34	40.5	46.3	41.0	46.7	36.9	43.5	77	8.4	10.7	8.4	10.8	8.3	10.4
35	39.6	45.3	40.1	45.8	36.0	42.6	78	7.9	10.1	7.9	10.2	7.8	9.8
36	38.7	44.4	39.2	44.8	35.2	41.7	79	7.5	9.5	7.5	9.6	7.4	9.3
37	37.8	43.4	38.3	43.8	34.4	40.8	80	7.1	9.0	7.1	9.0	7.0	8.8
38	36.9	42.5	37.4	42.9	33.5	39.9	81	6.7	8.4	6.7	8.4	6.7	8.2
39	36.0	41.5	36.5	41.9	32.7	39.0	82	6.3	7.9	6.3	7.9	6.3	7.7
40	35.1	40.6	35.6	41.0	31.9	38.1	83	5.9	7.4	5.9	7.4	6.9	7.3
41	34.2	39.6	34.7	40.0	31.1	37.1	84	5.6	6.9	5.5	6.9	5.6	6.8
42	33.3	38.7	33.8	39.1	30.3	36.2	85+	5.2	6.4	5.2	6.4	5.3	6.4

TABLE 5-2 Projected Population, 1992 and 2025, and Population Indicators by Region and Nation, 1990 to 1995

Region and Country	Population Estimate (1,000) 1992	Population Estimate (1,000) 2025	Birth Rate, 1990–95	Death Rate, 1990–95	Life Expectancy, 1990–95	Percent Urban, 1990	Fertility Rate per Woman, 1990–95
World total	5,479,000	8,472,400	26	9	65	44	3.3
More developed regions	1,224,700	1,403,300	14	10	75	73	1.9
Less developed regions	4,254,300	7,069,200	29	9	62	35	3.6
Africa	681,700	1,582,500	43	14	53	33	6.0
Eastern Africa	207,400	516,000	48	16	49	20	6.8
Burundi	5,800	13,400	46	17	48	6	6.8
Ethiopia	53,000	130,700	49	18	47	13	7.0
Kenya	25,200	63,800	44	10	59	25	6.3
Madagascar	12,800	33,700	45	13	55	25	6.6
Malawi	10,400	24,900	54	21	44	12	7.6
Mauritius	1,100	1,400	18	7	70	41	2.0
Mozambique	14,900	36,300	45	18	47	30	6.5
Rwanda	7,500	20,600	52	18	46	6	8.5
Somalia	9,200	23,400	50	19	47	25	7.0
Tanzania	27,800	74,200	48	15	51	22	6.8
Uganda	18,700	45,900	51	21	42	12	7.3
Zambia	8,600	21,000	46	18	44	42	6.3
Zimbabwe	10,600	22,900	41	11	56	30	5.3
Middle Africa	75,100	190,000	46	15	51	33	6.5
Angola	9,900	26,600	51	19	46	30	7.2
Cameroon	12,200	29,300	41	12	56	42	5.7
Central African Republic	3,200	7,000	44	18	47	48	6.2
Chad	5,800	12,900	44	18	48	34	5.9
Congo	2,400	5,800	45	15	52	42	6.3
Gabon	1,200	2,900	43	16	54	47	5.3
Zaire	39,900	104,500	47	15	52	28	6.7
Northern Africa	147,700	280,400	34	9	61	45	4.7
Algeria	26,300	51,800	34	7	66	53	4.9
Egypt	54,800	93,500	31	9	62	44	4.1
Libya	4,900	12,900	42	8	63	84	6.4
Morocco	26,300	47,500	32	8	63	47	4.4
Sudan	26,700	60,600	42	14	52	23	6.0
Tunisia	8,400	13,400	27	6	68	57	3.4
Southern Africa	45,300	85,300	32	9	63	47	4.2
Botswana	1,300	2,900	38	9	61	27	5.1
Lesotho	1,800	3,800	34	10	61	21	4.7
Namibia	1,500	3,800	43	11	59	29	6.0
South Africa	39,800	73,200	31	9	63	50	4.1
Western Africa	206,200	510,800	46	15	51	35	6.5
Benin	4,900	12,400	49	18	46	40	7.1
Burkina Faso	9,500	22,600	47	18	48	17	6.5
Ghana	16,000	38,000	42	12	56	35	6.0
Guinea	6,100	15,100	51	20	45	27	7.0
Guinea–Bissau	1,000	2,000	43	21	44	21	5.8
Ivory Coast	12,900	37,900	50	15	52	42	7.4
Liberia	2,800	7,200	47	14	55	47	6.8
Mali	9,800	24,600	51	19	46	25	7.1
Mauritania	2,100	5,000	46	18	48	49	6.5
Niger	8,300	21,300	51	19	47	21	7.1
Nigeria	115,700	285,800	45	14	53	37	6.4
Senegal	7,700	17,100	43	16	49	41	6.1
Sierra Leone	4,400	9,800	48	22	43	34	6.5
Togo	3,800	9,400	45	13	55	29	6.6
Latin America	457,700	701,600	26	7	68	73	3.1
Caribbean	34,600	50,400	24	8	69	60	2.8
Cuba	10,800	13,000	17	7	76	74	1.9
Dominican Republic	7,500	11,400	28	6	68	62	3.3
Haiti	6,800	13,100	35	12	57	30	4.8
Jamaica	2,500	3,500	22	6	74	54	2.4
Puerto Rico	3,600	4,700	18	7	75	75	2.2

Continued on next page

TABLE 5-2 **Continued**

Region and Country	Population Estimate (1,000) 1992	Population Estimate (1,000) 2025	Birth Rate, 1990–95	Death Rate, 1990–95	Life Expectancy, 1990–95	Percent Urban, 1990	Fertility Rate per Woman, 1990–95
Trinidad and Tobago	1,300	1,800	23	6	71	65	2.7
Central America	118,600	199,200	30	6	69	67	3.5
Costa Rica	3,200	5,600	26	4	76	48	3.1
El Salvador	5,400	9,700	33	7	66	45	4.0
Guatemala	9,700	21,700	39	8	65	40	5.4
Honduras	5,500	11,500	37	7	66	45	4.9
Mexico	88,200	137,500	28	5	70	74	3.2
Nicaragua	4,000	9,100	40	7	67	61	5.0
Panama	2,500	3,900	25	5	73	54	2.9
South America	304,500	451,900	24	7	67	76	2.9
Argentina	33,100	45,500	20	9	71	87	2.8
Bolivia	7,500	14,100	34	9	61	52	4.6
Brazil	154,100	219,700	23	7	66	76	2.7
Chile	13,600	19,800	23	6	72	85	2.7
Colombia	33,400	49,400	24	6	69	71	2.7
Ecuador	11,100	18,600	30	7	67	58	3.6
Guyana	800	1,200	24	7	65	35	2.4
Paraguay	4,500	9,200	33	6	67	49	4.3
Peru	22,500	37,400	29	8	65	71	3.6
Uruguay	3,100	3,700	17	10	72	89	2.3
Venezuela	20,200	32,700	26	5	70	91	3.1
North America	282,700	360,500	16	9	76	76	2.0
Canada	27,400	38,400	14	8	77	78	1.8
United States	255,200	322,000	16	9	76	76	2.1
Asia	3,233,000	4,900,300	26	8	65	32	3.2
Southern Asia	1,387,900	1,762,200	20	7	72	35	2.1
China	1,188,000	1,539,800	21	7	71	28	2.2
Hong Kong	5,800	6,400	13	6	78	94	1.4
Japan	124,500	127,000	11	7	79	77	1.7
Korea, North	22,600	33,300	24	5	71	60	2.4
Korea, South	44,200	50,300	16	6	71	74	1.8
Mongolia	2,300	4,600	34	8	64	59	4.6
Southeastern Asia	461,500	715,600	28	8	63	30	3.4
Cambodia	8,800	16,700	39	14	51	12	4.5
Indonesia	191,200	283,300	27	8	63	30	3.1
Laos	4,500	9,400	45	15	51	20	6.7
Malaysia	18,800	31,300	29	5	71	45	3.6
Myanmar	43,700	75,600	33	11	58	25	4.2
Philippines	65,200	105,100	30	7	65	44	3.9
Singapore	2,800	3,300	16	6	74	100	1.7
Thailand	56,100	72,300	21	6	69	23	2.2
Vietnam	69,500	117,000	29	9	64	20	3.9
Southwestern Asia	1,244,300	2,135,800	32	10	59	27	4.3
Afghanistan	19,100	45,800	53	22	43	19	6.9
Bangladesh	119,300	223,300	38	14	53	18	4.7
Bhutan	1,600	3,400	40	17	48	6	5.9
India	879,500	1,393,900	29	10	60	26	3.9
Iran	61,600	144,600	40	7	67	58	6.0
Nepal	20,600	40,100	37	13	54	12	5.5
Pakistan	124,800	259,600	41	10	59	33	6.2
Sri Lanka	17,700	24,700	21	6	72	22	2.5
Western Asia	139,300	286,600	34	7	66	65	4.7
Iraq	19,300	46,300	39	7	66	73	5.7
Israel	5,100	8,100	21	7	77	92	2.9
Jordan	4,300	10,800	40	5	68	69	5.7
Kuwait	2,000	2,800	28	2	75	93	3.7
Lebanon	2,800	4,500	27	7	69	86	3.1
Oman	1,600	4,700	40	5	70	12	6.7
Saudi Arabia	15,900	40,400	36	5	69	78	6.4
Syria	13,300	35,300	42	6	67	51	6.1
Turkey	58,400	92,900	28	7	67	64	3.5
United Arab Emirates	1,700	2,800	21	4	71	82	4.5

Continued on next page

increases in deaths from conditions such as cancer (malignant neoplasms), heart diseases, and strokes (cerebrovascular diseases). However, the age-adjusted figures show that the rates of heart diseases and strokes are actually declining. Malignant neoplasms, which also have more young victims, are remaining steady or slightly increasing. Similar phenomena such as the larger incidence of deaths from accidents and homicides among younger people are also considered in the age-adjustment process.

As Figure 5-1 shows, most causes of death are declining, as are death rates in general. However, some are increasing, especially human immunodeficiency virus (HIV) infection, which causes acquired immune deficiency syndrome (AIDS), and septicemia,

TABLE 5-2 **Continued**

Region and Country	Population Estimate (1,000)		Birth Rate, 1990–95	Death Rate, 1990–95	Life Expectancy, 1990–95	Percent Urban, 1990	Fertility Rate per Woman, 1990–95
	1992	2025					
Yemen, Republic of	12,500	34,200	48	14	53	31	7.2
Europe	512,000	541,800	13	11	75	74	1.7
Eastern Europe	96,900	107,200	14	11	71	64	2.0
Bulgaria	9,000	8,800	13	12	72	69	1.8
Czechoslovakia	15,700	17,900	14	11	73	79	2.0
Hungary	10,500	10,400	12	14	70	66	1.8
Poland	38,400	43,800	14	10	72	63	2.1
Romania	23,300	26,300	16	11	70	55	2.1
Northern Europe	92,800	97,800	14	11	76	83	1.9
Denmark	5,200	5,100	12	12	76	85	1.7
Estonia	1,600	1,700	14	12	71	72	2.0
Finland	5,000	5,200	13	10	76	60	1.8
Ireland	3,500	3,600	14	9	75	58	2.1
Latvia	2,700	2,800	14	12	71	72	2.0
Lithuania	3,800	4,100	15	10	73	70	2.0
Norway	4,300	4,900	15	11	77	76	2.0
Sweden	8,700	9,500	14	11	78	84	2.1
United Kingdom	57,700	60,300	14	11	76	89	1.9
Southern Europe	144,600	148,200	11	10	76	67	1.5
Albania	3,300	4,500	23	5	73	36	2.7
Greece	10,200	10,100	10	10	78	63	1.5
Italy	57,800	56,200	10	10	77	70	1.3
Portugal	9,900	10,100	12	10	75	35	1.5
Spain	39,100	40,600	11	9	78	79	1.4
Yugoslavia (former)	23,900	26,100	14	10	72	58	1.9
Western Europe	177,600	188,700	12	11	76	80	1.6
Austria	7,800	8,300	12	11	76	59	1.5
Belgium	10,000	9,900	12	11	76	96	1.7
France	57,200	60,800	13	10	77	73	1.8
Germany	80,300	83,900	11	11	76	86	1.5
Netherlands	15,200	17,700	14	9	77	89	1.7
Switzerland	6,800	7,700	13	10	78	62	1.7
Oceania	27,500	41,300	19	8	73	71	2.5
Australia– New Zealand	21,100	29,500	15	8	77	85	1.9
Australia	17,600	25,200	15	8	77	85	1.9
New Zealand	3,500	4,300	17	8	76	84	2.1
Melanesia	5,500	10,200	32	9	59	21	4.6
Papua New Guinea	4,100	7,800	33	11	56	17	4.9
Former Soviet Union	284,500	344,500	16	10	70	67	2.3

Note: Birth and death rates are per 1,000 population.

Source: THE UNIVERSAL ALMANAC copyright 1993 by John W. Wright. Reprinted with permission of Andrews & McMeel, Kansas City, MO. All rights reserved.

TABLE 5-3 Deaths and Death Rates for 72 Selected Causes: 1991 and 1992

Cause of Death	Number 1991	Number 1992	Rate 1991	Rate 1992
All causes	2,165,000	2,177,000	858.5	853.3
Shigellosis and amebiasis	20	a	b	b
Certain other intestinal infections	660	760	0.3	0.3
Tuberculosis	1,740	1,360	0.7	0.5
Tuberculosis of respiratory system	1,210	1,060	0.5	0.4
Other tuberculosis	530	300	0.2	0.1
Whooping cough	a	10	b	b
Streptococcal sore throat, scarlatina, and erysipelas	10	a	b	b
Meningococcal infection	260	230	0.1	0.1
Septicemia	19,450	19,910	7.7	7.8
Acute poliomyelitis	10	a	b	b
Measles	20	a	b	b
Viral hepatitis	1,920	1,940	0.8	0.8
Syphilis	130	70	0.1	b
All other infectious and parasitic diseases[c]	36,870	40,410	14.6	15.8
Malignant neoplasms, including neoplasms of lymphatic and hematopoietic tissues	514,310	521,090	204.0	204.3
Malignant neoplasms of lip, oral cavity, and pharynx	7,550	8,380	3.0	3.3
Malignant neoplasms of digestive organs and peritoneum	120,410	121,430	47.8	47.6
Malignant neoplasms of respiratory and intra-thoracic organs	148,830	154,960	59.0	60.7
Malignant neoplasms of breast	44,450	44,170	17.6	17.3
Malignant neoplasms of genital organs	59,380	58,620	23.5	23.0
Malignant neoplasms of urinary organs	20,960	22,210	8.3	8.7
Malignant neoplasms of all other and unspecified sites	62,470	61,140	24.8	24.0
Leukemia	19,630	19,190	7.8	7.5
Other malignant neoplasms of lymphatic and hematopoietic tissues	30,630	31,000	12.1	12.2
Benign neoplasms, carcinoma in situ, and neoplasms of uncertain behavior and of unspecified nature	6,970	6,480	2.8	2.5
Diabetes mellitus	49,980	50,180	19.8	19.7
Nutritional deficiencies	3,160	3,100	1.3	1.2
Anemias	4,150	3,970	1.6	1.6
Meningitis	730	730	0.3	0.3
Major cardiovascular diseases	913,350	915,360	362.2	358.8
Diseases of heart	718,090	720,480	284.8	282.5
Rheumatic fever and rheumatic heart disease	6,020	5,960	2.4	2.3
Hypertensive heart disease	22,020	22,340	8.7	8.8
Hypertensive heart and renal disease	2,040	2,980	0.8	1.2
Ischemic heart disease	478,530	480,170	189.8	188.2
Acute myocardial infarction	233,600	229,250	92.6	89.9
Other acute and subacute forms of ischemic heart disease	3,060	2,840	1.2	1.1
Angina pectoris	900	1,290	0.4	0.5
Old myocardial infarction and other forms of chronic ischemic heart disease	240,970	246,790	95.6	96.7
Other diseases of endocardium	14,150	15,760	5.6	6.2
All other forms of heart disease	195,320	193,270	77.5	75.8
Hypertension with or without renal disease	9,220	10,510	3.7	4.1
Cerebrovascular diseases	144,070	143,640	57.1	56.3
Intracerebral and other intracranial hemorrhage	21,000	21,010	8.3	8.2
Cerebral thrombosis and unspecified occlusion of cerebral arteries	17,950	15,720	7.1	6.2
Cerebral embolism	690	680	0.3	0.3
All other and late effects of cerebrovascular diseases	104,420	106,240	41.4	41.6
Atherosclerosis	17,060	16,100	6.8	6.3
Other diseases of arteries, arterioles, and capillaries	24,910	24,630	9.9	9.7
Acute bronchitis and bronchiolitis	580	500	0.2	0.2
Pneumonia and influenza	74,980	76,120	29.7	29.8
Pneumonia	73,990	74,860	29.3	29.3
Influenza	990	1,260	0.4	0.5
Chronic obstructive pulmonary diseases and allied conditions	89,130	91,440	35.3	35.8
Bronchitis, chronic and unspecified	3,970	4,180	1.6	1.6
Emphysema	16,550	16,630	6.6	6.5

Continued on next page

which is the rapid release of bacteria and their toxins in the blood and is commonly called "blood poisoning" (Clayman, 1989). Septicemia may be increasing because of the increase in AIDS, and the increase may also be related to such current social problems as homelessness and intravenous drug use.

Figure 5-2 shows the seasonality of death in the United States. Deaths increase in the winter and decrease in the spring and summer. Cold weather illnesses such as influenza and pneumonia may contribute to the higher winter death rates.

Age and Mortality

Some causes of death cluster in people of a certain age group. As Table 5-4 demonstrates, heart disease, cerebrovascular diseases, and

TABLE 5-3 **Continued**

Cause of Death	Number		Rate	
	1991	1992	1991	1992
Asthma	4,520	4,650	1.8	1.8
Other chronic obstructive pulmonary diseases and allied conditions	64,090	65,980	25.4	25.9
Ulcer of stomach and duodenum	6,410	5,770	2.5	2.3
Appendicitis	470	300	0.2	0.1
Hernia of abdominal cavity and intestinal obstruction without mention of hernia	5,800	6,230	2.3	2.4
Chronic liver disease and cirrhosis	24,740	24,830	9.8	9.7
Cholelithiasis and other disorders of gallbladder	3,030	2,990	1.2	1.2
Nephritis, nephrotic syndrome, and nephrosis	22,020	22,400	8.7	8.8
Acute glomerulonephritis and nephrotic syndrome	300	270	0.1	0.1
Chronic glomerulonephritis, nephritis, and nephropathy, not specified as acute or chronic, and renal sclerosis, unspecified	1,460	1,660	0.6	0.7
Renal failure, disorders resulting from impaired renal function, and small kidney of unknown cause	20,250	20,470	8.0	8.0
Infections of kidney	1,260	1,220	0.5	0.5
Hyperplasia of prostate	340	380	0.1	0.1
Complications of pregnancy, childbirth, and the puerperium	300	270	0.1	0.1
Pregnancy with abortive outcome	60	30	b	b
Other complications of pregnancy, childbirth, and the puerperium	240	240	0.1	0.1
Congenital anomalies	11,810	12,440	4.7	4.9
Certain conditions originating in the perinatal period	16,620	15,790	6.6	6.2
Birth trauma, intrauterine hypoxia, birth asphyxia, and respiratory distress syndrome	3,250	3,340	1.3	1.3
Other conditions originating in the perinatal period	13,370	12,450	5.3	4.9
Symptoms, signs, and ill-defined conditions	23,550	24,170	9.3	9.5
All other diseases	178,300	180,960	70.7	70.9
Accidents and adverse effects	91,700	86,310	36.4	33.8
Motor vehicle accidents	45,240	41,710	17.9	16.4
All other accidents and adverse effects	46,460	44,600	18.4	17.5
Suicide	30,200	29,760	12.0	11.7
Homicide and legal intervention	27,440	26,570	10.9	10.4
All other external causes	2,320	2,590	0.9	1.0

Notes: Rates are per 100,000 population. Data are provisional, estimated from a 10 percent sample of deaths. Due to rounding of estimates, figures may not add to totals.

Source: Adapted from Centers for Disease Control and Prevention. (1993, September). *Annual summary of births, marriages, divorces, and deaths: United States, 1992* (pp. 25–26). Hyattsville, MD: U.S. Public Health Service, National Center for Health Statistics.

[a]Estimate does not meet standards of reliability.

[b]Numbers too small to compute a rate.

[c]Includes data for human immunodeficiency virus infection.

FIGURE 5-1 Age-Adjusted Death Rates for 14 of the 15 Leading Causes of Death in the United States: 1958 to 1992

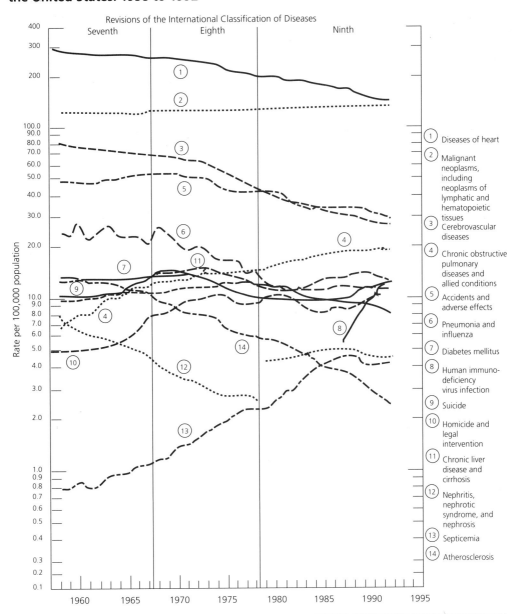

Source: Reprinted from Centers for Disease Control and Prevention. (1993, September). *Annual summary of births, marriages, divorces, and deaths: United States, 1992* (p. 8). Hyattsville, MD: U.S. Public Health Service, National Center for Health Statistics.

malignancies (cancer) are primarily diseases of older people. Among young people, accidents are a leading cause of death; homicide (including being killed in law enforcement situations) is highest among young people and insignificant among elderly people. Likewise, AIDS is a leading cause of death among young people but almost nonexistent among the elderly population. The suicide rate is fairly consistent for teenagers, young adults, and middle-aged people, but it increases among people above age 75, a fact of aging that has not received the attention it deserves.

Infant Mortality

Infant deaths are another important indicator of a nation's health. Figure 5-3 shows the U.S. infant mortality rates in 1992, 1993,

FIGURE 5-2 **U.S. Death Rates, by Month: 1992 to 1994**

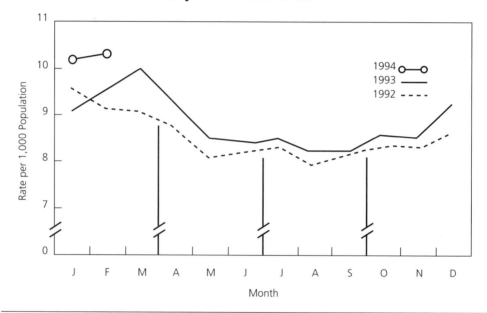

Source: Reprinted from Centers for Disease Control and Prevention. (1994, July 21). *Monthly vital statistics report* (p. 3). Hyattsville, MD: U.S. Public Health Service, National Center for Health Statistics.

TABLE 5-4 Age-Specific and Age-Adjusted Death Rates for the 15 Leading Causes of Death in 1992 and Selected Components: 1991 and 1992

Cause of Death	Year	All Ages[a]	Under 1 Year	1–14 Years	15–24 Years	25–34 Years	35–44 Years	45–54 Years	55–64 Years	65–74 Years	75–84 Years	85 Years and Over	Age-Adjusted Rate
All causes	1992	853.3	864.5	28.6	97.4	135.0	233.0	452.2	1,161.0	2,580.1	5,794.2	14,909.1	504.9
	1991	858.5	908.6	31.1	104.4	139.0	223.2	464.6	1,179.9	2,620.8	5,854.2	15,057.4	513.1
Diseases of heart	1992	282.5	14.8	1.1	2.7	7.3	31.8	112.7	344.9	852.2	2,175.3	6,513.2	144.5
	1991	284.8	20.4	1.1	2.9	7.3	30.1	120.3	359.6	867.8	2,199.9	6,596.4	147.9
Rheumatic fever and rheumatic heart disease	1992	2.3	b	b	b	0.3	0.5	1.3	3.7	8.5	18.0	30.7	1.4
	1991	2.4	b	b	b	b	0.5	1.5	3.8	9.0	18.6	31.1	1.4
Hypertensive heart disease	1992	8.8	b	b	b	0.6	1.5	5.4	14.6	26.5	61.2	170.7	4.9
	1991	8.7	b	b	b	0.5	1.5	5.8	13.8	27.1	59.8	180.4	4.9
Hypertensive heart and renal disease	1992	1.2	b	b	b	b	b	b	1.2	3.8	9.5	27.3	0.6
	1991	0.8	b	b	b	b	b	0.4	b	2.3	7.7	17.8	0.4
Ischemic heart disease	1992	188.2	b	b	0.3	2.4	17.4	72.1	229.6	585.6	1,481.4	4,285.5	95.6
	1991	189.8	b	b	b	2.5	16.3	76.1	243.6	598.6	1,510.9	4,266.6	98.2
Acute myocardial infarction	1992	89.9	b	b	b	1.3	9.6	42.5	130.9	313.1	711.8	1,618.2	49.0
	1991	92.6	b	b	b	1.5	9.9	46.5	140.3	320.6	750.4	1,629.7	51.4
Other acute and subacute forms of ischemic heart disease	1992	1.1	b	b	b	b	0.3	0.9	2.3	3.8	7.3	15.7	0.7
	1991	1.2	b	b	b	b	b	0.7	2.0	4.8	6.8	23.8	0.7
Angina pectoris	1992	0.5	b	b	b	b	b	b	b	1.0	5.5	12.9	0.2
	1991	0.4	b	b	b	b	b	b	b	1.0	3.0	7.9	0.2
Old myocardial infarction and other forms of chronic ischemic heart disease	1992	96.7	b	b	b	1.1	7.4	28.7	96.0	267.8	756.8	2,639.0	45.7
	1991	95.6	b	b	b	1.0	6.2	28.7	100.8	272.2	750.8	2,605.3	45.9
Other diseases of endocardium	1992	6.2	b	b	b	b	0.5	1.7	4.9	13.5	54.6	173.7	2.8
	1991	5.6	b	b	b	0.3	0.6	1.6	3.6	12.6	47.6	169.3	2.5
All other forms of heart disease	1992	75.8	14.3	1.0	2.3	4.0	11.8	32.0	90.8	214.2	550.6	1,825.4	39.2
	1991	77.5	19.7	1.1	2.3	3.9	11.3	34.9	94.4	218.1	555.2	1,930.9	40.4
Malignant neoplasms, including neoplasms of lymphatic and hematopoietic tissues	1992	204.3	b	2.9	4.5	12.4	44.0	148.6	441.6	870.3	1,359.1	1,768.3	133.2
	1991	204.0	b	3.3	5.7	12.4	43.3	156.3	439.7	872.4	1,349.3	1,795.5	134.2
Malignant neoplasms of lip, oral cavity, and pharynx	1992	3.3	b	b	b	b	0.7	3.5	9.2	14.1	18.0	21.2	2.3
	1991	3.0	b	b	b	b	0.8	3.8	8.9	12.0	14.4	18.7	2.2
Malignant neoplasms of digestive organs and peritoneum	1992	47.6	b	b	0.4	1.6	7.7	28.0	94.7	197.5	341.1	536.8	29.3
	1991	47.8	b	b	0.4	1.4	7.6	31.0	93.5	198.7	339.9	555.5	29.6
Malignant neoplasms of respiratory and intrathoracic organs	1992	60.7	b	b	b	0.8	7.0	46.6	163.8	307.6	368.0	278.7	41.8
	1991	59.0	b	b	b	0.8	7.2	46.1	158.0	301.7	355.7	272.0	40.8

Continued on next page

TABLE 5-4 Continued

Cause of Death	Year	All Ages[a]	Under 1 Year	1-14 Years	15-24 Years	25-34 Years	35-44 Years	45-54 Years	55-64 Years	65-74 Years	75-84 Years	85 Years and Over	Age-Adjusted Rate
Malignant neoplasms of breast	1992	17.3	b	b	b	1.5	9.2	21.9	39.2	62.8	87.2	147.6	12.2
	1991	17.6	b	b	b	1.6	8.6	22.3	43.0	62.7	90.3	152.2	12.6
Malignant neoplasms of genital organs	1992	23.0	b	b	b	1.2	4.1	10.4	31.4	91.0	195.1	292.8	13.2
	1991	23.5	b	b	b	1.2	3.9	10.9	33.7	93.9	197.1	310.1	13.6
Malignant neoplasms of urinary organs	1992	8.7	b	b	b	b	0.9	5.7	16.8	33.3	67.4	103.7	5.3
	1991	8.3	b	b	b	b	1.0	4.9	14.2	32.5	67.0	105.3	4.9
Malignant neoplasms of all other and unspecified sites	1992	24.0	b	1.3	1.9	3.7	8.2	20.0	51.8	89.5	144.0	208.1	16.3
	1991	24.8	b	1.8	1.9	3.3	8.0	23.4	53.7	95.5	149.2	193.4	17.2
Leukemia	1992	7.5	b	1.2	1.2	1.2	1.8	3.9	12.8	27.1	52.5	79.5	4.9
	1991	7.8	b	1.2	1.7	1.6	2.0	4.5	12.5	27.0	53.6	84.7	5.1
Other malignant neoplasms of lymphatic and hematopoietic tissues	1992	12.2	b	b	0.7	2.2	4.3	8.5	22.0	47.4	85.8	99.8	8.0
	1991	12.1	b	b	0.9	2.3	4.1	9.3	22.4	48.1	82.3	103.4	8.1
Cerebrovascular diseases	1992	56.3	b	0.3	0.3	1.8	7.2	16.9	46.5	134.5	465.7	1,575.2	26.1
	1991	57.1	b	0.3	0.5	1.8	6.7	16.9	47.5	141.8	480.2	1,596.1	26.8
Chronic obstructive pulmonary diseases and allied conditions	1992	35.8	b	0.4	0.5	0.6	2.0	8.9	48.2	156.1	323.6	443.5	19.9
	1991	35.3	b	0.4	0.6	0.8	1.8	7.5	47.1	155.2	319.6	456.2	19.6
Accidents and adverse effects	1992	33.8	21.3	11.3	38.5	31.8	28.0	26.1	31.7	44.6	95.8	267.3	29.2
	1991	36.4	22.2	12.6	44.0	35.8	28.7	27.9	31.4	49.2	104.4	255.2	31.8
Motor vehicle accidents	1992	16.4	5.3	5.2	29.0	20.4	14.7	13.1	15.0	16.5	27.2	33.8	16.0
	1991	17.9	4.7	6.0	33.1	23.3	15.3	14.4	13.9	18.5	27.9	32.0	17.7
All other accidents	1992	17.5	16.1	6.0	9.5	11.5	13.3	13.1	16.8	28.1	68.5	233.6	13.2
	1991	18.4	17.2	6.6	10.9	12.5	13.4	13.5	17.5	30.8	76.5	223.2	14.1
Pneumonia and influenza	1992	29.8	18.1	0.7	0.7	1.1	3.1	5.4	17.3	55.7	227.1	1,034.1	12.7
	1991	29.7	15.2	0.6	0.7	1.7	3.5	5.6	17.3	53.0	230.6	1,049.1	12.8
Diabetes mellitus	1992	19.7	b	b	b	1.4	3.9	12.1	35.6	76.6	144.4	239.1	12.0
	1991	19.8	b	b	0.4	1.2	4.1	11.6	35.9	76.1	149.6	244.1	12.1
Human immunodeficiency virus infection	1992	13.2	0.6[b,c]	b	1.3	23.4	36.3	21.3		4.7[d]			12.4
	1991	11.8	0.7[b,c]	b	1.8	22.4	31.7	18.3		3.9[d]			11.3
Suicide	1992	11.7	NA	0.6	12.9	14.2	14.4	14.5	14.5	14.2	26.3	18.4	10.9
	1991	12.0	NA	0.5	13.4	14.3	14.6	14.2	14.5	16.6	24.2	28.9	11.0
Homicide and legal intervention	1992	10.4	8.8	1.8	22.8	17.9	12.6	7.6	5.4	3.3	4.1	b	10.9
	1991	10.9	8.2	1.9	23.5	19.1	11.8	8.0	5.7	4.6	4.1	b	11.3
Chronic liver disease and cirrhosis	1992	9.7	b	b	b	1.9	9.7	15.6	28.0	31.6	31.1	24.6	7.9
	1991	9.8	b	b	b	1.6	9.1	16.0	30.8	31.6	31.6	20.6	8.1
Nephritis, nephrotic syndrome, and nephrosis	1992	8.8	6.0	b	b	0.4	1.1	2.8	8.7	23.7	71.8	211.5	4.4
	1991	8.7	6.2	b	b	0.5	1.3	2.4	8.5	24.9	67.1	222.9	4.4

Septicemia	1992	7.8	5.8	0.2	b	0.7	1.5	3.0	7.5	20.9	60.9	181.7	4.0
	1991	7.7	8.0	0.3	b	0.6	1.6	3.4	8.0	20.6	58.1	179.8	4.1
Atherosclerosis	1992	6.3	b	b	b	b	b	0.7	3.0	10.8	43.4	266.1	2.3
	1991	6.8	b	b	b	b	b	0.7	2.6	11.7	50.8	282.8	2.5
Certain conditions originating in the perinatal period	1992	6.2	391.8	0.3	b	b	b	b	b	b	b	b	NA
	1991	6.6	409.1	0.3	b	b	b	b	b	b	b	b	NA

Notes: Rates are per 100,000 population in specified group. Data are estimated from a 10 percent sample of deaths. NA = not applicable.

Source: Adapted from Centers for Disease Control and Prevention. (1993, September). Annual summary of births, marriages, divorces, and deaths: United States, 1992 (pp. 23–24). Hyattsville, MD: U.S. Public Health Service, National Center for Health Statistics.

aIncludes those whose ages were not known.

bNumbers too small to compute a rate.

cFigures for under 1 year old and 1–14 years are combined.

dFigures for 55 and older are combined.

and part of 1994; Table 5-5 provides the numbers and rates for each state. In general, southern states and the District of Columbia have the highest rates and the northeastern states the lowest. Figure 5-4 shows the changes in the infant mortality rates from 1989 through 1993. Over the years the rate has been decreasing, but the estimated or provisional 1993 figures indicate an increase during the early part of the year, which may indicate some real changes in the national infant mortality picture.

FIGURE 5-3 **Infant Mortality Rates, by Month: 1992 to 1994**

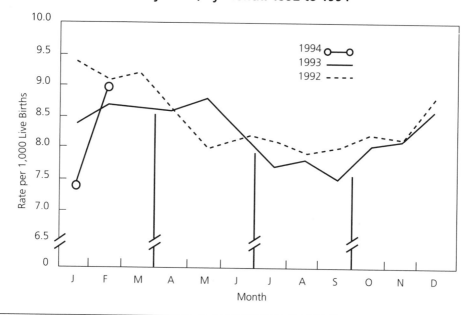

Source: Reprinted from Centers for Disease Control and Prevention. (1994, July 21). *Monthly vital statistics report* (p. 3). Hyattsville, MD: U.S. Public Health Service, National Center for Health Statistics.

TABLE 5-5 **Deaths of Infants under One Year of Age and Infant Mortality Rates, by Region and State: 1992 and 1993**

Region and State	1992 Number	1992 Rate	1993 Number	1993 Rate
Northeast	1,285	6.8	881	6.5
Connecticut	364	7.6	—	—
Maine	107	6.5	83	5.4
Massachusetts	566	6.5	545	6.5
New Hampshire	85	5.4	76	5.2
New Jersey	1,034	8.8	1,016	8.3
New York	2,411	8.3	2,533	9.1
Pennsylvania	1,481	8.9	1,413	8.7
Rhode Island	111	7.6	131	9.0
Vermont	52	6.8	46	6.0
Midwest	6,289	9.5	6,033	9.2
Illinois	1,989	10.3	1,890	9.8
Indiana	798	9.7	828	9.7
Iowa	306	8.2	250	6.7
Kansas	337	9.0	318	8.7
Michigan	1,483	9.9	1,407	9.9
Minnesota	482	7.2	481	7.5
Missouri	716	9.2	690	9.2
Nebraska	194	8.2	168	7.5
North Dakota	75	8.4	59	6.7
Ohio	1,475	8.9	1,380	8.3
South Dakota	110	9.9	113	10.1
Wisconsin	544	7.6	528	7.6
South	6,643	9.7	6,561	9.7
Alabama	690	11.0	640	10.1
Arkansas	364	10.3	312	9.1
Delaware	125	11.4	91	8.5
District of Columbia	195	19.7	180	18.1
Florida	1,734	9.0	1,691	8.8
Georgia	1,183	10.7	1,116	10.0
Kentucky	446	8.2	471	8.9
Louisiana	728	9.6	672	9.7
Maryland	650	8.0	702	9.2
Mississippi	478	11.1	512	11.8
North Carolina	1,090	10.6	1,069	10.6
Oklahoma	451	9.5	440	9.3
South Carolina	623	10.9	554	10.0
Tennessee	740	10.3	698	9.5
Texas	2,522	7.8	2,388	7.4
Virginia	846	8.7	934	9.7
West Virginia	197	8.9	224	10.0
West	1,917	7.8	1,917	7.7
Alaska	89	7.9	86	8.0
Arizona	566	8.3	575	8.3
California	4,406	7.2	3,923	6.7
Colorado	429	7.7	429	7.9
Hawaii	131	6.6	136	6.9
Idaho	126	7.3	154	8.7
Montana	103	8.7	83	7.4
Nevada	159	6.8	142	6.3
New Mexico	270	9.7	218	7.7
Oregon	302	7.1	312	7.5
Utah	216	5.9	246	6.7
Washington	538	7.4	—	—
Wyoming	48	7.1	70	10.6

Notes: Data are for 12 months ending in June of each year. — = not available.

Source: Adapted from Centers for Disease Control and Prevention. (1993, November). *Births, marriages, divorces, and deaths for June 1993* (p. 3). Hyattsville, MD: U.S. Public Health Service, National Center for Health Statistics.

Leading Causes of Death

The following sections provide information on several leading causes of death and illness in the United States.

Cardiovascular Disease

As Table 5-4 indicates, cardiovascular disease is the leading cause of death in the United States for both men and women. Table 5-6 presents the state-by-state death rates from cardiovascular disease, coronary heart disease, and stroke and the rankings of states from low to high in 1989.

Table 5-7 lists heart disease death rates in 1960, 1970, 1980, and 1989 by age group. Although the absolute numbers of such deaths have risen, the rates have declined.

FIGURE 5-4 **Infant Mortality Rates for Successive 12-Month Periods, 1990 to 1994**

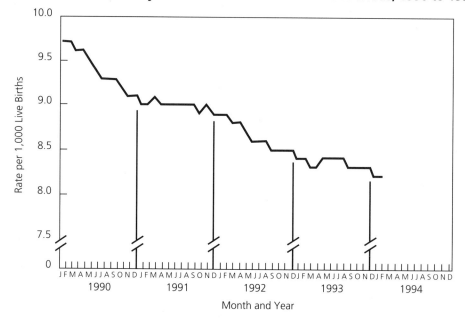

Source: Reprinted from Centers for Disease Control and Prevention. (1994, July21). *Monthly vital statistics report* (p. 5). Hyattsville, MD: U.S. Public Health Service, National Center for Health Statistics.

TABLE 5-6 **Age-Adjusted Death Rates per 100,000 Population for Total Cardiovascular Disease, Heart Attack, and Stroke, by State: 1989**

State	Total Cardiovascular Disease		Coronary Heart Disease		Stroke	
	Rank (Lowest to Highest)	Death Rate	Rank (Lowest to Highest)	Death Rate	Rank (Lowest to Highest)	Death Rate
Total		195.4		105.2		28.0
Alabama	47	225.3	21	95.7	45	35.0
Alaska	17	175.0	12	90.0	33	28.1
Arizona	8	166.8	27	97.3	3	22.3
Arkansas	40	208.5	43	116.3	46	35.1
California	24	182.9	19	95.0	37	29.7
Colorado	3	154.0	8	84.7	6	22.8
Connecticut	14	174.0	9	88.3	7	23.2
Delaware	32	201.5	18	94.7	22	25.7
District of Columbia	51	245.2	3	62.2	51	41.6
Florida	13	173.7	24	96.8	12	23.9
Georgia	46	223.1	32	104.1	48	36.3
Hawaii	1	145.4	1	60.2	28	27.0
Idaho	11	170.3	25	96.8	27	26.9
Illinois	35	204.5	37	111.1	34	28.5
Indiana	34	204.0	41	115.3	40	30.8
Iowa	19	175.6	15	93.3	17	25.1
Kansas	12	172.7	20	95.7	20	25.5
Kentucky	45	222.2	50	123.6	42	31.6
Louisiana	50	237.1	49	122.4	44	34.7
Maine	26	185.8	31	103.1	13	24.2
Maryland	28	195.0	5	79.1	30	27.3
Massachusetts	20	175.6	23	96.8	8	23.5
Michigan	42	212.4	48	120.3	35	29.0
Minnesota	5	157.0	10	88.4	19	25.4
Mississippi	52	259.0	42	115.9	50	38.5
Missouri	30	195.3	40	112.8	31	27.4
Montana	6	160.9	11	88.5	9	23.5
Nebraska	18	175.5	17	94.2	18	25.2
Nevada	37	206.6	6	83.0	29	27.1
New Hampshire	22	180.1	22	96.8	21	25.6
New Jersey	27	188.9	36	108.9	14	24.8
New Mexico	2	153.8	2	60.7	1	20.7
New York	39	207.3	52	129.4	11	23.7
North Carolina	44	215.6	46	118.2	47	36.1
North Dakota	7	163.7	14	93.1	4	22.4
Ohio	38	207.0	47	119.2	26	26.8
Oklahoma	41	210.7	44	116.7	41	31.3
Oregon	15	174.5	26	96.9	38	29.7
Pennsylvania	36	205.0	38	111.7	23	26.1
Rhode Island	25	183.1	33	106.0	10	23.6
South Carolina	49	235.0	45	117.8	52	43.2
South Dakota	16	174.6	28	98.9	15	24.8
Tennessee	43	214.9	39	111.9	43	34.3
Texas	29	195.1	16	94.0	36	29.0
Utah	4	155.3	4	68.7	16	25.1
Vermont	9	167.4	13	91.3	5	22.4
Virginia	33	202.1	29	99.8	39	30.3
Washington	10	167.6	7	83.7	25	26.7
West Virginia	48	234.5	51	125.8	32	27.6
Wisconsin	21	179.2	35	108.5	24	26.5
Wyoming	23	182.0	30	101.1	2	22.3

Source: Reprinted with permission from American Heart Association. (1992). *1993 heart and stroke facts* (p. 6). Dallas: Author. Copyright American Heart Association.

Cancer

Cancer is the second leading cause of death in the United States. Figure 5-5 shows a map of the United States and the estimated number of new cancer cases in 1993. Tables 5-8 and 5-9 show deaths and rates by state and the estimated number of new cancer cases (by type of cancer) in 1993.

Because cancer occurs in a variety of sites in the body, it is difficult to describe generally. There are cancers with high recovery rates (meaning the patient is free of symptoms, usually for five years, after developing the illness) and others with very low recovery or survival rates. Figures 5-6 and 5-7 show cancer death rates by site per 100,000 people for men and women from 1930 to 1989. Cancer incidence is either remaining steady or declining, with the exception of lung cancer, which exceeds all other types of cancer and is the major cause of cancer deaths in men and women. Table 5-10 shows the 30-year trend for new cases of cancer and percentage changes for 1957–59 to 1987–89.

The American Cancer Society (1993) estimated that 46,000 women died of breast cancer and 35,000 men died of prostate cancer in 1993. The two cancers received extensive publicity, although the increases in incidence have not been as substantial as those for other cancers—especially lung cancer. But between the two of them, breast and prostate cancer strike more than twice as many people as lung cancer does. For that reason, many Americans know or have heard of patients with one or the other. Because not all fatal conditions are fully diagnosed before death, it is possible that deaths from these cancers may be even greater when one considers those who die with neither a diagnosis nor an autopsy.

There are ethnic differences among cancer patients and cancer deaths. For example, more African American men than white men develop oral and pharynx cancer. Table 5-11 shows the number of deaths for several nonwhite ethnic groups in 1989.

TABLE 5-7 **Heart Disease Death Rates, by Age: Selected Years, 1960 to 1989**

Age	1960[a]	1970	1980	1989
All ages				
Age adjusted	286.2	253.6	202.2	155.9
Crude	369.0	362.0	336.0	295.6
Under 1 year	6.6	13.1	22.8	19.7
1–4 years	1.3	1.7	2.6	1.9
5–14 years	1.3	0.8	0.9	0.8
15–24 years	4.0	3.0	2.9	2.6
25–34 years	15.6	11.4	8.3	7.9
35–44 years	74.6	66.7	44.6	32.3
45–54 years	271.8	238.4	180.2	124.2
55–64 years	737.9	652.3	494.1	376.7
65–74 years	1,740.5	1,558.2	1,218.6	911.8
75–84 years	4,089.4	3,683.8	2,993.1	2,400.6
85 and older	9,317.8	7,891.3	7,777.1	6,701.6

Source: THE UNIVERSAL ALMANAC copyright 1993 by John W. Wright. Reprinted with permission of Andrews & McMeel, Kansas City, MO. All rights reserved.

[a]Includes nonresidents of the United States.

FIGURE 5-5 **New Cancer Cases, by State: 1993**

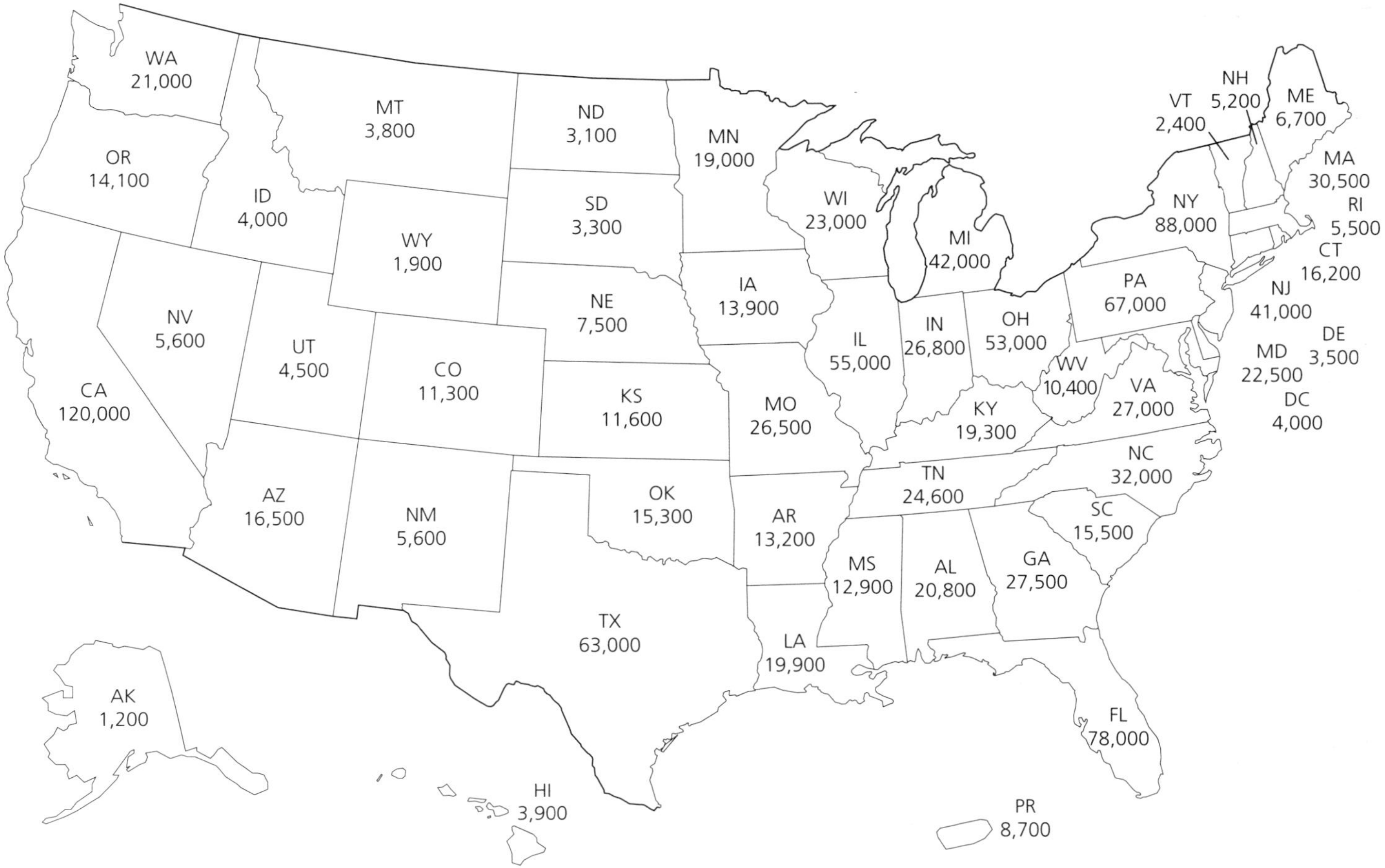

State	Cases
VT	2,400
NH	5,200
ME	6,700
MA	30,500
RI	5,500
CT	16,200
NJ	41,000
DE	3,500
MD	22,500
DC	4,000
NY	88,000
PA	67,000
VA	27,000
NC	32,000
SC	15,500
FL	78,000
WV	10,400
OH	53,000
KY	19,300
GA	27,500
MI	42,000
IN	26,800
TN	24,600
AL	20,800
WI	23,000
IL	55,000
MS	12,900
IA	13,900
MO	26,500
AR	13,200
LA	19,900
MN	19,000
KS	11,600
OK	15,300
TX	63,000
ND	3,100
SD	3,300
NE	7,500
HI	3,900
MT	3,800
WY	1,900
CO	11,300
NM	5,600
UT	4,500
AZ	16,500
ID	4,000
NV	5,600
WA	21,000
OR	14,100
CA	120,000
AK	1,200
PR	8,700

Source: Reprinted with permission from American Cancer Society. (1993). *Cancer facts and figures—1993* (cover). Atlanta: Author.

State	Reported Death Rate per 100,000[a]	Number of Deaths									
		All Sites	Female Breast	Colon and Rectum	Lung	Oral	Uterus	Prostate	Skin Melanoma	Pancreas	Leukemia
United States	172	526,000	46,000	57,000	149,000	7,700	10,100	35,000	6,800	25,000	18,600
Alabama	179	9,300	700	850	2,800	150	225	600	125	425	300
Alaska	165	500	50	50	175	10	10	25	10	25	20
Arizona	155	7,500	600	750	2,200	80	100	500	125	350	300
Arkansas	173	5,900	450	600	2,000	60	125	400	70	300	225
California	168	52,000	4,500	5,400	14,200	850	1,000	3,500	850	2,700	1,900
Colorado	140	5,000	450	550	1,200	70	80	400	100	275	175
Connecticut	172	7,300	650	900	1,900	100	125	400	80	350	250
Delaware	195	1,600	175	175	475	40	30	100	25	60	50
District of Columbia	228	1,800	150	225	450	50	60	175	20	80	60
Florida	165	36,000	2,900	3,800	11,000	650	600	2,700	500	1,700	1,200
Georgia	176	12,400	1,100	1,100	3,700	225	225	850	175	550	425
Hawaii	139	1,700	100	200	425	25	30	100	20	90	50
Idaho	146	1,800	150	200	450	20	40	150	30	100	80
Illinois	179	24,600	2,200	2,900	6,800	350	500	1,600	250	1,200	850
Indiana	179	12,100	1,100	1,300	3,700	125	225	750	125	500	425
Iowa	161	6,300	600	800	1,700	80	90	475	100	300	250
Kansas	155	5,200	475	600	1,500	70	100	325	70	250	225
Kentucky	185	8,700	650	900	3,000	100	175	475	100	350	250
Louisiana	187	9,000	700	850	2,800	150	200	550	80	500	300
Maine	185	3,000	225	325	900	50	50	200	40	150	90
Maryland	194	10,100	850	1,100	2,900	150	175	650	125	475	325
Massachusetts	179	13,700	1,300	1,700	3,700	250	225	800	200	650	450
Michigan	177	19,100	1,700	2,000	5,300	275	400	1,300	175	900	700
Minnesota	156	8,500	800	1,000	1,900	90	150	700	100	475	350
Mississippi	174	5,800	425	550	1,800	90	125	400	60	300	200
Missouri	173	11,900	1,000	1,200	3,700	125	225	750	125	500	425
Montana	157	1,700	125	200	450	30	30	150	30	75	50
Nebraska	158	3,400	325	350	900	40	60	250	60	150	125
Nevada	184	2,500	200	225	850	20	50	150	25	125	80
New Hampshire	183	2,400	225	250	650	40	60	175	30	100	60
New Jersey	185	18,300	1,800	2,200	4,800	275	375	1,100	250	800	600
New Mexico	144	2,500	225	250	600	30	50	175	30	125	100
New York	177	39,500	4,000	4,800	10,000	650	850	2,400	500	1,900	1,300
North Carolina	171	14,400	1,300	1,500	4,400	225	300	1,000	225	700	500
North Dakota	151	1,400	100	150	300	20	25	150	10	70	70

Ohio	181	24,000	2,200	2,700	7,000	300	475	1,500	275	1,100	900
Oklahoma	164	6,900	550	700	2,100	100	150	450	90	275	250
Oregon	168	6,300	500	650	1,900	90	125	450	90	300	250
Pennsylvania	180	30,300	2,700	3,600	8,200	375	600	2,100	375	1,400	1,100
Rhode Island	182	2,500	250	300	700	40	40	150	25	100	75
South Carolina	172	7,000	550	700	2,200	150	150	475	80	350	250
South Dakota	153	1,500	150	175	375	20	25	125	10	70	60
Tennessee	176	11,000	900	1,200	3,600	125	225	700	150	550	375
Texas	158	29,200	2,300	2,800	8,300	400	500	1,600	325	1,400	1,100
Utah	121	2,000	200	200	325	20	50	200	40	100	90
Vermont	174	1,100	125	100	275	10	20	100	20	50	50
Virginia	180	12,200	1,100	1,200	3,600	150	225	850	150	550	400
Washington	165	9,300	850	950	2,700	125	125	700	125	425	350
West Virginia	178	4,700	350	500	1,500	70	80	300	70	200	150
Wisconsin	164	10,300	900	1,200	2,400	150	200	800	125	500	400
Wyoming	147	800	75	75	200	10	20	75	10	30	40

Note: Figures are estimates based on data collected by the Surveillance, Epidemiology and End Results (SEER) program, which collects data from nine population-based cancer registries covering about 10 percent of the population.

Source: Reprinted with permission from American Cancer Society. (1993). *Cancer facts and figures—1993* (p. 9). Atlanta: Author.

[a] Average annual mortality rate for 1985–89, adjusted to the age distribution on the 1970 U.S. census population.

TABLE 5-9 New Cancer Cases and Deaths, by Type of Cancer and Gender: 1993

Site	Estimated New Cases			Estimated Deaths		
	Both Sexes	Male	Female	Both Sexes	Male	Female
All sites	1,170,000	600,000	570,000	526,000	277,000	249,000
Buccal cavity and pharynx (oral)	29,800	20,300	9,500	7,700	4,975	2,725
Lip	3,500	3,000	500	100	75	25
Tongue	5,900	3,800	2,100	1,750	1,100	650
Mouth	11,200	6,800	4,400	2,050	1,200	850
Pharynx	9,200	6,700	2,500	3,800	2,600	1,200
Digestive organs	236,900	125,200	111,700	120,325	64,350	55,975
Esophagus	11,300	8,100	3,200	10,200	7,600	2,600
Stomach	24,000	14,800	9,200	13,600	8,200	5,400
Small intestine	3,600	2,000	1,600	925	500	425
Large intestine } (Colon–	109,000	53,000	56,000	50,000	25,000	25,000
Rectum } Rectum)	43,000	24,000	19,000	7,000	3,800	3,200
Liver and biliary passages	15,800	8,500	7,300	12,600	6,800	5,800
Pancreas	27,700	13,500	14,200	25,000	12,000	13,000
Other and unspecified digestive	2,500	1,300	1,200	1,000	450	550
Respiratory system	187,100	113,000	74,100	154,200	96,900	57,300
Larynx	12,600	10,000	2,600	3,800	3,000	800
Lung	170,000	100,000	70,000	149,000	93,000	56,000
Other and unspecified respiratory	4,500	3,000	1,500	1,400	900	500
Bone	2,000	1,100	900	1,050	600	450
Connective tissue	6,000	3,300	2,700	3,100	1,500	1,600
Melanoma of skin	32,000	17,000	15,000	6,800	4,200	2,600
Breast	183,000	1,000	182,000	46,300	300	46,000
Genital organs	244,400	172,900	71,500	59,950	35,550	24,400
Cervix uteri	13,500	NA	13,500	4,400	NA	4,400
Corpus and } (Uterus) unspecified	31,000	NA	31,000	5,700	NA	5,700
Ovary	22,000	NA	22,000	13,300	NA	13,300
Other and unspecified genital, female	5,000	NA	5,000	1,000	NA	1,000
Prostate	165,000	165,000	NA	35,000	35,000	NA
Testis	6,600	6,600	NA	350	350	NA
Other and unspecified genital, male	1,300	1,300	NA	200	200	NA
Urinary organs	79,500	55,800	23,700	20,800	13,000	7,800
Bladder	52,300	39,000	13,300	9,900	6,500	3,400
Kidney and other urinary	27,200	16,800	10,400	10,900	6,500	4,400
Eye	1,750	950	800	250	125	125
Brain and central nervous system	17,500	9,600	7,900	12,100	6,600	5,500
Endocrine glands	14,050	4,150	9,900	1,725	800	925
Thyroid	12,700	3,400	9,300	1,050	450	600
Other endocrine	1,350	750	600	675	350	325
Leukemia	29,300	16,700	12,600	18,600	10,100	8,500
Lymphocytic leukemia	12,600	7,500	5,100	5,400	3,100	2,300
Granulocytic leukemia	11,700	6,400	5,300	7,300	3,900	3,400
Other and unspecified leukemia	5,000	2,800	2,200	5,900	3,100	2,800
Other blood and lymph tissues	63,700	35,000	28,700	31,400	16,300	15,100
Hodgkin's disease	7,900	4,500	3,400	1,500	900	600
Non-Hodgkin's disease lymphoma	43,000	24,000	19,000	20,500	10,600	9,900
Multiple myeloma	12,800	6,500	6,300	9,400	4,800	4,600
All other and unspecified sites	43,000	24,000	19,000	41,700	21,700	20,000

Notes: Figures are estimates based on data collected by the Surveillance, Epidemiology and End Results (SEER) program, which collects data from nine population-based cancer registries covering about 10 percent of the population. Carcinoma in situ and basal and squamous cell skin cancers are not included in totals. Overall, about 100,000 new cases of carcinoma in situ of all sites of cancer are diagnosed each year. Basal cell and squamous cell skin cancers account for more than 700,000 new cases annually. About 2,300 nonmelanoma skin cancer deaths will occur in 1993. Incidence estimates are based on rates from the National Cancer Institute's SEER program, 1987–89. NA = not applicable.

Source: Reprinted with permission from American Cancer Society. (1993). *Cancer facts and figures—1993* (p. 7). Atlanta: Author.

FIGURE 5-6 **Cancer Death Rates in Males, by Type of Cancer: 1930 to 1989**

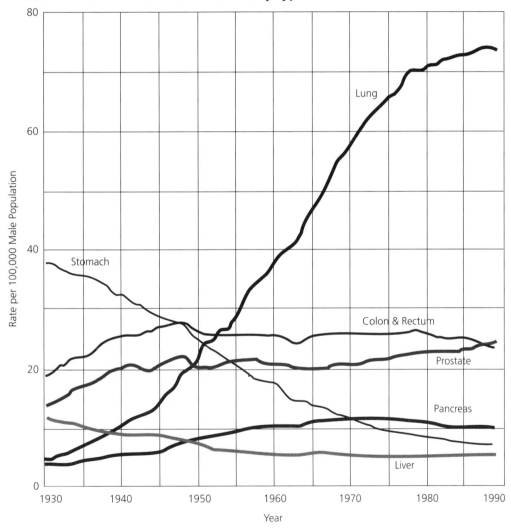

Note: Rates are adjusted to the 1970 U.S. census population.
Source: Reprinted with permission from American Cancer Society. (1993). *Cancer facts and figures—1993* (p. 4). Atlanta: Author.

FIGURE 5-7 Cancer Death Rates in Females, by Type of Cancer: 1930 to 1989

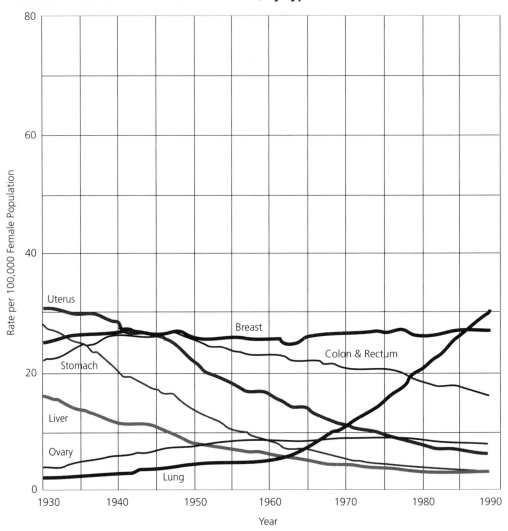

Note: Rates are adjusted to the 1970 U.S. census population.
Source: Reprinted with permission from American Cancer Society. (1993). *Cancer facts and figures—1993* (p. 5). Atlanta: Author.

TABLE 5-10 **30-Year Trends in Cancer Death Rates, by Type of Cancer and Gender: 1957–59 and 1987–89**

Site	Gender	Death Rate 1957–59	Death Rate 1987–89	Percent Change	Number of Deaths, 1959	Number of Deaths, 1989
All sites	Male	180.4	216.2	20	139,078	263,309
	Female	138.2	139.8	a	120,969	232,843
Oral	Male	6.1	4.6	−24	4,710	5,340
	Female	1.5	1.7	11	1,343	2,764
Esophagus	Male	4.8	5.8	21	3,722	7,154
	Female	1.2	1.5	25	1,097	2,483
Stomach	Male	18.0	6.9	−62	13,271	8,520
	Female	9.3	3.1	−66	7,753	5,666
Colon and rectum	Male	25.2	23.6	−6	18,741	28,248
	Female	23.1	16.4	−29	19,748	29,134
Colon	Male	17.0	20.2	19	12,633	24,152
	Female	17.5	14.3	−18	15,116	25,581
Rectum	Male	8.3	3.5	−58	6,108	4,096
	Female	5.6	2.1	−63	4,632	3,553
Liver[b]	Male	5.8	5.1	−12	4,292	6,383
	Female	6.1	3.2	−48	5,216	5,636
Pancreas	Male	10.0	9.8	a	7,854	11,965
	Female	6.2	7.1	16	5,462	12,578
Larynx	Male	2.6	2.5	a	2,021	2,961
	Female	0.3	0.5	87	238	768
Lung	Male	34.9	73.7	111	29,335	89,052
	Female	5.4	29.4	440	4,967	48,098
Melanoma of skin	Male	1.3	3.0	122	1,098	3,736
	Female	1.0	1.5	50	954	2,425
Other skin	Male	1.7	1.3	−25	1,214	1,532
	Female	0.9	0.4	−56	680	657
Breast	Male	0.3	0.2	−22	214	301
	Female	25.8	27.2	6	22,871	42,837
Cervix uteri	Female	9.6	3.0	−69	8,383	4,487
Other uterus	Female	7.2	3.5	−52	6,005	5,867
Ovary	Female	8.8	7.8	−11	7,901	12,431
Prostate	Male	20.9	24.4	17	14,037	30,520
Bladder	Male	7.2	5.6	−22	5,288	6,843
	Female	2.8	1.7	−40	2,352	3,278
Kidney	Male	3.7	5.0	35	3,065	6,133
	Female	2.0	2.4	20	1,788	3,979
Brain	Male	4.0	5.0	25	3,593	6,046
	Female	2.7	3.4	26	2,439	5,084
Non-Hodgkin's lymphoma	Male	4.7	7.4	56	3,842	9,420
	Female	3.1	4.9	57	2,837	8,777
Hodgkin's disease	Male	2.3	0.8	−66	1,920	1,007
	Female	1.3	0.5	−65	1,131	714
Multiple myeloma	Male	1.9	3.6	91	1,515	4,335
	Female	1.3	2.4	80	1,226	4,252
Leukemia	Male	8.8	8.1	−8	7,123	10,039
	Female	5.7	4.8	−16	5,147	8,207

Note: Cancer death rates were adjusted to the age distribution of the 1970 U.S. census population.

Source: Reprinted with permission from American Cancer Society. (1993). *Cancer facts and figures—1993* (p. 6). Atlanta: Author.

[a]Less than a 6 percent change.

[b]Primary and nonspecified.

Deaths Involving Firearms

Murders by firearms have been a serious problem in the United States, especially among young people of color. In 1990 firearm injury resulted in the deaths of 19,722 people ages 1 to 34 years (Fingerhut, 1993). In early 1994, African American leaders held a summit conference in Washington, DC, to focus attention on the fact that murder was the leading cause of death among African Americans ages 15 to 24 (Montgomery, 1994).

Figure 5-8 shows the percentages of deaths due to firearms for people ages 1 to 34 by age, race and ethnicity, and gender in 1990. The figure graphically shows a disproportionate death rate from firearms for African American males age 10 and above.

TABLE 5-11 **Cancer Deaths for Black Males and Females, American Indians, Chinese, Japanese, and Hispanics, by Type of Cancer: 1993**

Site	Black Males	Black Females	American Indians	Chinese	Japanese	Hispanics[a]
All sites	31,452	24,112	1,318	1,425	1,124	13,538
Oral cavity	939	312	23	62	14	209
Esophagus	1,524	523	20	28	29	257
Stomach	1,390	859	54	86	139	793
Colon and rectum	2,765	3,080	131	169	164	1,327
Liver and other biliary	791	568	85	153	53	754
Pancreas	1,403	1,551	74	68	84	690
Lung (male)	10,457	NA	221	239	139	1,789
Lung (female)	NA	4,246	118	134	78	800
Breast (female)	NA	4,403	90	62	78	1,115
Cervix uteri	NA	1,049	31	19	10	274
Other uterus	NA	873	12	22	9	159
Ovary	NA	901	26	31	34	365
Prostate	4,785	NA	71	40	36	689
Bladder	484	369	14	8	26	224
Kidney	525	363	46	14	18	334
Brain and central nervous system	335	299	30	22	10	373
Lymphoma	750	558	40	45	52	722
Leukemia	868	672	45	50	37	645
Multiple myeloma	684	703	30	13	8	271

Note: NA = not applicable.

Source: Reprinted with permission from American Cancer Society. (1993). *Cancer facts and figures—1993* (p. 19). Atlanta: Author.

[a]People classified as Hispanic on death certificates may be of any race. Hispanic deaths in Connecticut, Louisiana, Maryland, New Hampshire, Oklahoma, and Virginia are not included. Caution should be exercised in generalizing these mortality data to the entire U.S. Hispanic population.

Figure 5-9 shows a comparison of deaths by natural causes and by firearms for African American and white male teenagers, ages 15 to 19, from 1985 to 1990. The death rate from firearms for African American youths began high in 1985 and increased steadily. The firearms death rate for white youths increased slightly. Deaths from natural causes for white young males were relatively steady, but deaths from natural causes for African American male youths actually declined slightly (Fingerhut, 1993).

The magnitude of the problem of death by firearms (which includes homicides, suicides, and accidental shootings) can be understood more fully when compared with deaths from motor vehicle accidents. Motor vehicle accidents have been implicated in a much larger

FIGURE 5-8 **Percentages of Deaths due to Firearms for People Ages 1 to 34, by Age, Race and Ethnicity, and Gender: 1990**

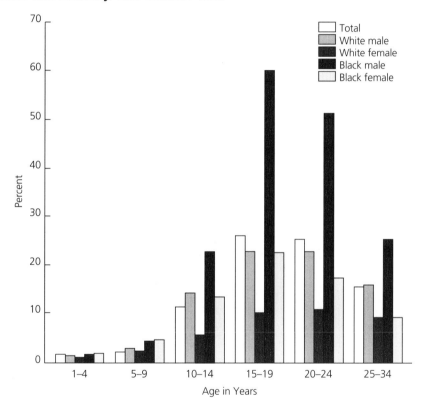

Source: Adapted from Fingerhut, L. A. (1993, March). *Firearm mortality among children, youth, and young adults 1–34 years of age, trends and current status: United States, 1985–90* (p. 2). Hyattsville, MD: U.S. Public Health Service, National Center for Health Statistics.

number of deaths of Americans than firearms. However, auto safety measures and education have decreased the automobile-related deaths over the years, whereas continuing increases in urban violence have increased the firearms deaths of young people (Fingerhut, Jones, & Makuc, 1994).

In 1990–91, there were 24.4 deaths by firearms and 27.3 deaths by motor vehicle accident per 100,000 population. The death by firearms rates were heavily weighted toward some minority groups and the large urban areas. For example, among African Americans, the death rate per 100,000 from firearms was 70.7 and from motor vehicle accidents, 23.0. Among Hispanics, the firearm death rate was 29.6 and the motor vehicle death rate, 28.7. For non-Hispanic whites, however, the fire-

FIGURE 5-9 **Death Rates for Natural Causes and Firearm Injuries for Males Ages 15 to 19: 1985 to 1990**

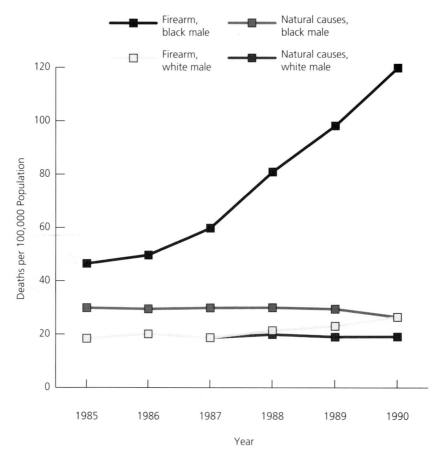

Source: Reprinted from Fingerhut, L. A. (1993). *Firearm mortality among children, youth, and young adults 1–34 years of age, trends and current status: United States, 1985–90* (p. 3). Hyattsville, MD: U.S. Public Health Service, National Center for Health Statistics.

arm death rate was 15.2 and the motor vehicle death rate was 28.4; for Asian and Pacific Islanders, the death rates were 10.7 for firearms and 13.7 for motor vehicle accidents; and for American Indians and Alaskan Natives, the rates were 24.1 for firearms and 50.6 for motor vehicle accidents (Fingerhut, Jones, & Makuc, 1994).

Accidents

A significant number of deaths each year are caused by accidents, as Table 5-12 indicates. Motor vehicle accidents, which affect people of all ages, are the leading cause of accidental deaths, followed by falls, which primarily affect elderly people.

Table 5-13 lists the numbers of deaths due to accidents for several nations. The United

TABLE 5-12 Accidental Deaths, by Type and Age Group: 1991

Type	Number of Deaths	Age Group (Years)						
		0–4	5–14	15–24	25–44	45–64	65–74	75+
All accidents	88,000	3,600	3,700	15,100	26,300	13,300	8,600	17,400
Motor vehicle	43,500	1,100	2,000	11,800	15,300	6,400	3,300	3,600
Falls	12,200	100	60	240	1,100	1,400	1,700	7,600
Poisoning by solids and liquids[a]	5,600	100	30	400	3,600	750	270	450
Drowning	4,600	700	450	850	1,500	550	300	250
Fires and burns	4,200	800	450	300	950	600	450	650
Suffocation	2,900	270	60	60	260	500	450	1,300
Firearms	1,400	50	180	500	400	160	60	50
Poisoning by gases	800	30	20	150	290	140	70	100
All other[b]	12,800	450	450	800	2,900	2,800	2,000	3,400

Source: THE UNIVERSAL ALMANAC copyright 1993 by John W. Wright. Reprinted with permission of Andrews & McMeel, Kansas City, MO. All rights reserved.

[a]Deaths from poisons, drugs, medicines, mushrooms, and shellfish. Excludes poisonings from spoiled foods, salmonella, and so forth, which are classified as disease deaths.

[b]Medical complications, air and water transport, machinery, excessive cold, and so forth.

TABLE 5-13 Accidental Deaths and Death Rates, by Nation: 1989–90

Nation	Year Reported	Accidental Deaths	Rate per 100,000 Population
Austria	1990	3,584	46.4
Bulgaria	1990	3,881	43.2
Canada	1989	9,436	36.0
Czechoslovakia	1990	9,280	59.3
Denmark	1990	2,301	44.8
Finland	1990	2,815	56.5
France	1990	33,933	59.8
Greece	1989	4,448	44.3
Hong Kong	1989	825	14.3
Hungary	1990	8,760	84.5
Iceland	1990	85	33.4
Ireland	1989	1,108	31.5
Israel	1989	1,345	29.8
Japan	1990	32,122	26.2
Netherlands	1990	3,629	24.3
Norway	1989	2,053	48.6
Poland	1990	21,857	57.3
Portugal	1990	4,560	46.2
Singapore	1989	392	14.6
Switzerland	1990	3,505	52.2
United Kingdom	1990	14,008	24.4
United States	1989	95,028	38.3
Uruguay	1989	1,485	47.8
West Germany	1990	20,653	32.3

Note: Accidental deaths are classified on the basis of a World Health Organization standard. However, differences in reporting among nations affect comparisons.

Source: THE UNIVERSAL ALMANAC copyright 1993 by John W. Wright. Reprinted with permission of Andrews & McMeel, Kansas City, MO. All rights reserved.

States has the highest number of accident-related deaths, followed by France and Japan. Hungary, France, and Czechoslovakia have the highest rates.

Many product-related accidents lead to death. Table 5-14 lists products associated with injuries that were treated in emergency rooms.

Other factors may also contribute to accidents and deaths from them. One of those may be left-handedness. According to Sloan (1993), 10 percent of people are left-handed, and left-handed men outnumber left-handed women three to one. Sloan found that left-handers' chances of being accidentally injured are 20 percent greater while playing a sport, 25 percent greater while working, 49 percent greater while in the home, and 85 percent greater while driving.

Accidents have costs for society. Table 5-15 shows the total costs in billions of dollars in 1991. Medical expenses resulting from accidents alone totaled $29.6 billion. In addition, workers lost $45.8 billion in wages.

Suicide

The numbers of suicides in 1991 and 1992 are listed in Table 5-3. Some researchers believe that the incidence of suicide may be underestimated. David P. Phillips, a sociologist at the University of California at San Diego, studied death rates of people at the decennial milestone ages of 30, 40, 50, and so on (cited in Rensberger, 1993). California death certificates showed that death rates from suicide rose when people reached each of those ages, a result, he believed, of depressed people killing themselves at symbolically important ages. He also found that deaths from other causes (accidental poisoning, drug overdoses, single-car crashes, and pedestrian accidents) peaked at those same ages and were especially high for women and African Americans. Deaths from natural causes and multiple-car crashes did not have similar peaks at those ages. He concluded that African Americans and women may commit suicide more often than official records show by using methods that appear to be accidental. He believed that suicide rates for African Americans could be as much as 15 percent higher than the official reports state

and that rates for women could be 6 percent higher (Rensberger, 1993).

Many firearm deaths are suicides. The states with the highest percentage of suicide firearm deaths in 1990–91 were as follows: In Nevada 80 percent of firearm deaths were suicides; in Arizona, New Mexico, and Wyoming about 75 percent were suicides; and in Texas about 66 percent were suicides. In 1990 the

---

TABLE 5-14 **Estimated Number of Injuries Caused by Selected Products: 1992**

Product	Estimated Injuries
Stairs, steps	1,058,787
Bicycles, accessories	649,536
Knives	468,644
Tables	346,874
Chairs	307,800
Nails, screws, tacks	239,711
Bathtubs, showers	150,995
Ladders	139,595
Drinking glasses	130,201
Fences, fence posts	123,014
Drugs, medications	115,338
Bottles, jars	106,629
Carpets, rugs	104,039
Metal containers	104,026
Footwear	90,130
Lawnmowers	83,132
Sinks, toilets	61,832
Wheelchairs	55,514
Hammers	50,683
Jewelry	50,337
Skateboards	44,068
Trampolines	43,665
Bunk beds	43,513
Razors, shavers	42,964
Hot water	41,773
Chainsaws	38,692
Sleds	38,211
Television	36,735
Shopping carts	35,813
Scissors	34,558
Contact lenses	32,692
Pens, pencils	32,197
Paper money, coins	30,274
Refrigerators	30,095
Pins, needles	22,551
Gasoline	18,895
Telephones, accessories	18,880
Irons	16,421
Baby strollers	15,578

Notes: These national estimates are based on injuries treated in hospital emergency rooms participating in the National Electronic Injury Surveillance System. Patients said their injuries were related to the products; this does not necessarily mean that the injuries were caused by the products.

Source: THE UNIVERSAL ALMANAC copyright 1993 by John W. Wright. Reprinted with permission of Andrews & McMeel, Kansas City, MO. All rights reserved.

rates per 100,000 population of firearm suicide among young people were 0.8 for people ages 10 to 14, 7.5 for people ages 15 to 19, 9.6 for people ages 20 to 24, and 8.7 for people ages 25 to 34 (Fingerhut, Jones, & Makuc, 1994).

AIDS

Acquired immune deficiency syndrome (AIDS) is "a deficiency of the immune system due to infection with . . . human immunodeficiency virus [HIV], which belongs to the class of retroviruses" (Clayman, 1989, pp. 76, 541). It has been a persistent and growing global health problem and cause of death since the early 1980s. Because the disease is so lethal and because it is so widespread, it is important to know both the scope of this health epidemic and the extent of the public's awareness of how the disease is transmitted. Social work is especially concerned with AIDS because so many of those who develop it are disadvantaged people—young people, gay men, homeless people, and ethnic minorities—and because social workers are so likely to encounter people with AIDS in their work.

The U.S. government has been tracking the AIDS epidemic since the condition began to be recognized. The Centers for Disease Control and Prevention periodically publishes a surveillance report on AIDS. The tables in this section are taken from the October 1993 report. Table 5-16 shows that as of September 1993 there were 334,344 diagnosed cases of adults and adolescents with AIDS and that over 60 percent (nearly 202,000) of these adults and adolescents had died. During the same period, there had been 4,906 cases of AIDS among children under 13. Over half of them had died.

Table 5-17 shows the adult and adolescent and pediatric cases by gender both for the most recent periods and for the whole history of tracking the disease. It demonstrates that AIDS is overwhelmingly a disease of adult and adolescent males. The primary means of transmission is sexual contact with someone who has the disease, and the second most common means is injecting drugs with needles that have been contaminated with HIV-contaminated blood. The largest percentage of people with the disease are men who have sex with other men and men who inject drugs. Those who

TABLE 5-15 **Costs of Accidents: 1991**

Cost	Amount (in billions of dollars)					Percent Distribution				
	Total[a]	Motor Vehicle	Work	Home	Other	Total[a]	Motor Vehicle	Work	Home	Other
Total	177.2	96.1	63.3	22.0	13.9	100.0	100.0	100.0	100.0	100.0
Wage loss[b]	45.8	24.5	10.0	7.4	6.3	25.8	25.5	15.8	33.6	45.3
Medical expense	29.6	6.7	8.7	9.3	5.6	16.7	7.0	13.7	42.3	40.3
Insurance administration[c]	35.4	27.7	11.0	1.0	0.8	20.0	28.8	17.4	4.5	5.8
Fire loss	7.7	—	2.2	4.3	1.2	4.3	—	3.5	19.5	8.6
Motor vehicle property damage	29.0	29.0	1.7	—	—	16.4	30.2	2.7	—	—
Uninsured work loss[d]	29.7	8.2	29.7	—	—	16.8	8.5	46.9	—	—

Notes: Covers costs for accidents in which deaths or disabling injuries occurred beyond the day of the accident, together with vehicle accidents and fires. — = not available.

Source: Reprinted from U.S. Bureau of the Census. (1993). *Statistical abstract of the United States: 1993* (113th ed., p. 132). Austin, TX: Reference Press.

[a]Excludes duplication between work and motor vehicle ($18.1 billion).

[b]Actual wage losses, the present value of future earnings lost, and the replacement-cost value of household services of employed people and householders.

[c]The difference between premiums paid to companies and the claims paid by them.

[d]The value of time lost by noninjured workers (for example, giving first aid).

contracted AIDS through heterosexual contact most often had that contact with an injecting drug user or with someone whose risk factor was not known. In children, the disease is typically transmitted through the mother. To a lesser extent, blood transfusions remain a risk factor.

Table 5-17 identifies as a risk factor being born in or having sex with someone born in a "Pattern II" country, a term developed by the World Health Organization for sub-Saharan Africa and some Caribbean countries in which AIDS affects primarily heterosexuals and in which drug injection and homosexual transmissions are rare. According to Conover (1993), "of the fourteen million people with H.I.V. worldwide, more than eight million of them are in sub-Saharan Africa" (p. 57).

TABLE 5-16 **AIDS Cases, Case Fatality Rates, and Deaths in the United States, by Half-Year and Age Group: 1981 to September 1993**

Half-Year		Adults and Adolescents			Children under 13 Years Old		
		Cases Diagnosed during Interval	Case Fatality Rate	Deaths Occurring during Interval	Cases Diagnosed during Interval	Case Fatality Rate	Deaths Occurring during Interval
Total[a]		334,344	60.3	201,775	4,906	53.3	2,615
Before 1981		92	81.5	30	6	66.7	1
1981	January–June	98	89.8	37	11	81.8	2
	July–December	208	91.3	87	5	100.0	6
1982	January–June	407	92.6	155	13	84.6	9
	July–December	707	91.1	290	16	81.3	5
1983	January–June	1,312	93.2	526	32	100.0	13
	July–December	1,654	93.2	939	42	90.5	16
1984	January–June	2,581	92.8	1,406	51	84.3	26
	July–December	3,408	92.8	1,981	62	87.1	22
1985	January–June	4,970	92.0	2,825	99	76.8	45
	July–December	6,379	91.6	3,904	128	82.8	69
1986	January–June	8,413	90.4	5,109	138	81.9	65
	July–December	10,026	88.3	6,568	189	70.9	91
1987	January–June	13,115	88.6	7,613	218	72.0	117
	July–December	14,574	85.7	8,013	257	67.7	168
1988	January–June	16,836	83.4	9,397	258	64.7	134
	July–December	17,425	83.1	10,764	338	61.2	174
1989	January–June	20,096	78.7	12,379	352	60.2	171
	July–December	20,434	76.5	14,231	333	57.4	184
1990	January–June	22,629	70.8	14,404	357	52.9	191
	July–December	22,128	66.3	15,265	377	43.0	190
1991	January–June	25,769	58.7	15,902	357	42.3	163
	July–December	27,410	49.4	17,497	325	35.7	199
1992	January–June	30,925	36.1	17,431	384	32.3	168
	July–December	31,177	23.4	17,555	318	27.0	197
1993	January–June	27,847	11.4	14,787	213	18.3	161
	July–September	3,724	5.5	2,410	27	7.4	26

Notes: Case fatality rates are calculated for each half-year by date of diagnosis. Each six-month case fatality rate is the number of deaths ever reported among cases diagnosed in that period (regardless of the year of death), divided by the number of total cases diagnosed in that period, multiplied by 100. For example, during the interval January through June 1982, AIDS was diagnosed in 407 adults and adolescents. Through September 1993, 377 of these 407 were reported as dead. Therefore, the case fatality rate is 92.6 (377 divided by 407, multiplied by 100). The case fatality rates shown here may be underestimates because of incomplete reporting of deaths. Reported deaths are not necessarily caused by HIV-related disease.

Source: Reprinted from Centers for Disease Control and Prevention. (1993). *HIV/AIDS Surveillance Report, 5*(3), 12.

[a]Death totals include 270 adults and adolescents and two children known to have died but whose dates of death are unknown.

TABLE 5-17 **AIDS Cases in the United States by Age Group, Exposure Category, and Gender: 1992 and 1993**

Exposure Category	Males 1992 Number	Males 1992 %	Males 1993 Number	Males 1993 %	Females 1992 Number	Females 1992 %	Females 1993 Number	Females 1993 %	Total 1992 Number	Total 1992 %	Total 1993 Number	Total 1993 %	Cumulative Totals Number	Cumulative Totals %
Total	40,202		82,144		6,514		15,224		46,716		97,368		339,250	
Adult and adolescent														
Men who have sex with men	24,334	61	46,025	56	NA		NA		24,334	53	46,025	48	183,344	55
Injecting drug use	8,621	22	19,142	23	2,815	46	6,891	47	11,436	25	26,033	27	80,713	24
Men who have sex with men and inject drugs	2,638	7	5,353	7	NA		NA		2,638	6	5,353	6	21,142	6
Hemophilia or coagulation disorder	317	1	990	1	6	0	27	0	323	1	1,017	1	2,963	1
Heterosexual contact	1,613	4	3,328	4	2,588	42	5,545	37	4,201	9	8,873	9	24,358	7
Sex with injecting drug user	703		1,102		1,474		2,474		2,177		3,576		11,750	
Sex with bisexual male	NA		NA		177		423		177		423		1,250	
Sex with person with hemophilia	3		10		20		61		23		71		193	
Born in Pattern II country	271		607		165		324		436		931		3,758	
Sex with person born in Pattern II country	14		43		15		31		29		74		279	
Sex with transfusion recipient with HIV infection	18		59		49		101		67		160		456	
Sex with HIV-infected person, risk not specified	604		1,507		688		2,131		1,292		3,638		6,672	
Receipt of blood transfusion, blood components, or tissue	385	1	695	1	278	5	496	3	663	1	1,191	1	5,984	2
Other or risk not identified[a]	1,925	5	6,174	8	466	8	1,833	12	2,391	5	8,007	8	15,840	5
Adult and adolescent total	39,833	100	81,707	100	6,153	100	14,792	100	45,986	100	96,499	100	334,344	100
Pediatric (under 13 years old)														
Hemophilia or coagulation disorder	23	6	18	4	6		0		23	3	18	2	202	4
Mother with or at risk for HIV infection	329	89	397	91	347	96	417	97	676	93	814	94	4,328	88
Injecting drug use	114		126		144		138		258		264		1,920	
Sex with injecting drug user	54		68		62		65		116		133		846	
Sex with bisexual male	7		5		8		4		15		9		88	
Sex with person with hemophilia	5		1		2		2		7		3		21	
Born in Pattern II country	19		22		12		15		31		37		305	
Sex with person born in Pattern II country	3		3		2		2		5		5		23	
Sex with transfusion recipient with HIV infection	1		1		3		2		4		3		19	
Sex with HIV-infected person, risk not specified	31		45		21		51		52		96		275	
Receipt of blood transfusion, blood components, or tissue	12		16		10		7		22		23		98	
Has HIV infection, risk not specified	83		110		83		131		166		241		733	
Receipt of blood transfusion, blood components, or tissue	12	3	15	3	6	2	9	2	18	2	24	3	327	7
Risk not identified[a]	5	1	7	2	8	2	6	1	13	2	13	1	49	1
Pediatric total	369	100	437	100	361	100	432	100	730	100	869	100	4,906	100

Notes: Figures are for 12 months ending in September of each year. In Pattern II countries, designated as such by the World Health Organization, transmission is primarily through heterosexual contact, and the male-to-female ratio is about 1:1. NA = not applicable.

Source: Reprinted from Centers for Disease Control and Prevention. (1993). *HIV/AIDS Surveillance Report, 5*(3). 8.

[a] "Other" refers to 11 health care workers who developed AIDS after occupational exposure to HIV-infected blood, as documented by evidence of seroconversion; to four patients who developed AIDS after exposure to HIV within the health care setting, as documented by laboratory studies; to one person who acquired HIV perinatally and was diagnosed with AIDS after age 13; and to one person with intentional self-inoculation of blood from an HIV-infected person. "Risk not identified" refers to people whose mode of exposure to HIV is unknown. This includes people under investigation; people who died, were lost to follow-up, or declined interview; and people whose mode of exposure to HIV remains unidentified after investigation.

Table 5-18 shows the AIDS incidence for adult and adolescent males by race and ethnicity, and Table 5-19 shows the same information for women. Although most of those who develop AIDS are white, a disproportionately large percentage (in terms of overall population) are African American and Hispanic.

The state-by-state breakdown of AIDS cases is shown in Table 5-20. Although the largest states have the largest numbers of cases, there is some evidence that the more metropolitan the state, the higher the incidence of AIDS. In North Dakota and South Dakota, for example, the disease is barely present. Alaska, Idaho, Montana, New Hampshire, Vermont, West Virginia, and Wyoming have had very few cases, even taking into consideration their small populations. Other largely rural states

TABLE 5-18 **Male Adult and Adolescent AIDS Cases in the United States, by Exposure Category and Race or Ethnicity: 1993**

	White, not Hispanic				Black, not Hispanic				Hispanic			
	1993		Cumulative		1993		Cumulative		1993		Cumulative	
Exposure Category	Number	%	Number	%	Number	%	Number	%	Number	%	Number	%
Total	41,244	100	160,923	100	26,048	100	82,174	100	13,407	100	47,351	100
Men who have sex with men	30,094	73	125,392	78	9,614	37	34,166	42	5,638	42	21,475	45
Injecting drug use	4,285	10	12,670	8	9,667	37	29,762	36	5,094	38	18,143	38
Men who have sex with men and inject drugs	3,001	7	11,959	7	1,568	6	5,974	7	712	5	3,021	6
Hemophilia or coagulation disorder	794	2	2,349	1	110	0	260	0	68	1	224	0
Heterosexual contact	607	1	1,654	1	2,125	8	6,279	8	570	4	1,375	3
Sex with injecting drug user	227		804		682		2,118		185		599	
Sex with person with hemophilia	6		13		1		4		2		4	
Born in Pattern II country	1		8		605		2,571		0		10	
Sex with person born in Pattern II country	10		52		31		86		2		11	
Sex with transfusion recipient with HIV infection	25		72		26		51		6		28	
Sex with HIV-infected person, risk not specified	338		705		780		1,449		375		723	
Receipt of blood transfusion, blood components, or tissue	431	1	2,519	2	157	1	606	1	91	1	385	1
Risk not identified[b]	2,032	5	4,380	3	2,807	11	5,127	6	1,234	9	2,728	6

Notes: Figures are for 12 months ending September 1993. In Pattern II countries, designated as such by the World Health Organization, transmission is primarily through heterosexual contact, and the male-to-female ratio is about 1:1.

Source: Reprinted from Centers for Disease Control and Prevention. (1993). *HIV/AIDS Surveillance Report, 5*(3), 7.

[a]Includes 573 men whose race or ethnicity is unknown.

[b]"Risk not identified" refers to people whose mode of exposure to HIV is unknown. This includes people under investigation; people who died, were lost to follow-up, or declined interview; and people whose mode of exposure to HIV remains unidentified after investigation.

such as Iowa have rates that are in the single digits. The larger metropolitan incidence is shown in Table 5-21. The disease appears to be concentrated on the coasts, with low rates and incidences in the middle of nation. The AIDS rate in metropolitan areas with 500,000 people or more is twice that of smaller metropolitan areas, which, in turn, is twice that of nonmetropolitan communities.

International Conference on AIDS

The tenth International Conference on AIDS was held in Yokohama, Japan, in August 1994 and reviewed the extent and changing nature of the disease. There were some 10,000 participants from 128 nations. According to a World Health Organization report discussed at the conference (Radin, 1994), nearly 17 million people have been

Asian or Pacific Islander				American Indian/Alaska Native				Cumulative Totals[a]			
1993		Cumulative		1993		Cumulative		1993		Cumulative	
Number	%	Number	%	Number	%	Number	%	Number	%	Number	%
603	100	2,007	100	249	100	614	100	81,707	100	293,642	100
445	74	1,583	79	158	63	388	63	46,025	56	183,344	62
28	5	79	4	23	9	62	10	19,142	23	60,835	21
22	4	57	3	42	17	107	17	5,353	7	21,142	7
12	2	35	2	6	2	16	3	990	1	2,890	1
15	2	29	1	4	2	10	2	3,328	4	9,361	3
6		12		1		5		1,102		3,539	
0		0		0		0		10		22	
0		3		0		0		607		2,597	
0		1		0		0		43		150	
2		2		0		0		59		154	
7		11		3		5		1,507		2,899	
12	2	72	4	1	0	5	1	695	1	3,596	1
69	11	152	8	15	6	26	4	6,174	8	12,474	4

infected with AIDS since 1981, including 50,000 each in East Asia and the Pacific region, 50,000 in Eastern Europe/Central Asia, 25,000 in Australia/Oceania, 100,000 in North Africa and the Middle East, 2.5 million in South and Southeast Asia, 500,000 in Western Europe, 2 million in Latin America and the Caribbean, 1 million in North America, and 10 million in sub-Saharan Af-

rica. Although there is no vaccine or cure in the offing, maintenance of the health of the immune system seems to prolong the lives of AIDS patients as long as 25 years (Radin, 1994). The understanding of AIDS and its course is also changing. For example, not all HIV-infected people develop AIDS. A study of gay men infected with HIV found that 7 percent of them had not developed AIDS af-

TABLE 5-19 **Female Adult and Adolescent AIDS Cases in the United States, by Exposure Category and Race and Ethnicity: 1993**

| Exposure Category | White, not Hispanic | | | | Black, not Hispanic | | | | Hispanic | | | |
| | 1993 | | Cumulative | | 1993 | | Cumulative | | 1993 | | Cumulative | |
	Number	%	Number	%	Number	%	Number	%	Number	%	Number	%
Total	3,740	100	10,293	100	8,008	100	21,728	100	2,877	100	8,273	100
Injecting drug use	1,718	46	4,459	43	3,861	48	11,386	52	1,265	44	3,907	47
Hemophilia or coagulation disorder	14	0	48	0	7	0	15	0	5	0	9	0
Heterosexual contact	1,387	37	3,595	35	2,884	36	7,864	36	1,192	41	3,377	41
Sex with injecting drug user	586		1,703		1,191		4,101		667		2,337	
Sex with bisexual male	199		627		150		428		60		162	
Sex with person with hemophilia	50		140		9		21		1		7	
Born in Pattern II country	3		5		316		1,143		4		11	
Sex with person born in Pattern II country	4		15		26		110		1		4	
Sex with transfusion recipient with HIV infection	49		176		27		63		17		51	
Sex with HIV-infected person, risk not specified	496		929		1,165		1,998		442		805	
Receipt of blood transfusion, blood components, or tissue	223	6	1,398	14	167	2	571	3	88	3	349	4
Risk not identified[b]	398	11	793	8	1,089	14	1,892	9	327	11	631	8

Notes: Figures are for 12 months ending September 1993. In Pattern II countries, designated as such by the World Health Organization, transmission is primarily through heterosexual contact, and the male-to-female ratio is about 1:1.

Source: Reprinted from Centers for Disease Control and Prevention. (1993). *HIV/AIDS Surveillance Report, 5*(3), 8.

[a]Includes 75 women whose race or ethnicity is unknown.

[b]"Risk not identified" refers to people whose mode of exposure to HIV is unknown. This includes people under investigation; people who died, were lost to follow-up, or declined interview; and people whose mode of exposure to HIV remains unidentified after investigation.

ter 15 years and that their immune systems were near normal (Levy, 1994).

Table 5-22 shows information on government appropriations for AIDS since 1984. Although the figures are not comprehensive, they provide some information on the magnitude of the costs of serving people with AIDS.

Asian or Pacific Islander				American Indian/Alaska Native				Cumulative Totals[a]			
1993		Cumulative		1993		Cumulative		1993		Cumulative	
Number	%	Number	%	Number	%	Number	%	Number	%	Number	%
99	100	230	100	46	100	103	100	14,792	100	40,702	100
15	15	34	15	17	37	52	50	6,891	47	19,878	49
1	1	1	0	0		0		27	0	73	0
57	58	104	45	20	43	32	31	5,545	37	14,997	37
15		31		12		21		2,474		8,211	
13		28		1		3		423		1,250	
0		2		1		1		61		171	
1		1		0		0		324		1,161	
0		0		0		0		31		129	
8		11		0		0		101		302	
20		31		6		7		2,131		3,773	
16	16	59	26	2	4	8	8	496	3	2,388	6
10	10	32	14	7	15	11	11	1,833	12	3,366	8

TABLE 5-20 AIDS Cases and Annual Rates, by State: 1992 and 1993

State	1992 Number	1992 Rate	1993 Number	1993 Rate	Cumulative Totals: Adults and Adolescents	Cumulative Totals: Children under 13 Years Old	Total
Total	44,900	17.8	94,703	37.0	323,747	4,645	328,392
Alabama	465	11.4	705	17.0	2,275	43	2,318
Alaska	18	3.2	60	10.2	154	2	156
Arizona	408	10.9	1,202	31.3	3,059	14	3,073
Arkansas	237	10.0	420	17.5	1,239	21	1,260
California	8,641	28.4	17,474	56.4	62,201	356	62,557
Colorado	415	12.3	1,193	34.5	3,516	18	3,534
Connecticut	538	16.3	1,693	51.4	4,415	98	4,513
Delaware	126	18.5	346	49.9	830	7	837
District of Columbia	724	121.0	1,370	232.3	5,231	78	5,309
Florida	5,007	37.7	9,613	70.6	32,008	751	32,759
Georgia	1,348	20.4	2,597	38.4	9,255	87	9,342
Hawaii	175	15.4	324	27.9	1,250	10	1,260
Idaho	36	3.5	71	6.6	203	2	205
Illinois	1,842	16.0	3,005	25.8	10,522	140	10,662
Indiana	370	6.6	831	14.6	2,443	17	2,460
Iowa	86	3.1	196	7.0	577	6	583
Kansas	188	7.5	335	13.3	1,031	5	1,036
Kentucky	207	5.6	316	8.4	1,148	13	1,161
Louisiana	829	19.5	1,172	27.4	4,811	67	4,878
Maine	50	4.0	126	10.2	427	4	431
Maryland	1,096	22.6	2,353	47.6	7,187	152	7,339
Massachusetts	767	12.8	2,532	42.4	7,238	132	7,370
Michigan	784	8.4	1,752	18.6	4,904	62	4,966
Minnesota	237	5.3	624	13.9	1,829	13	1,842
Mississippi	231	8.9	468	17.9	1,483	20	1,503
Missouri	650	12.6	1,679	32.3	4,626	33	4,659
Montana	22	2.7	35	4.3	134	2	136
Nebraska	68	4.3	179	11.1	469	4	473
Nevada	235	18.3	601	44.0	1,641	15	1,656
New Hampshire	48	4.3	99	9.0	368	6	374
New Jersey	2,051	26.4	4,390	56.3	18,106	423	18,529
New Mexico	90	5.8	307	19.4	831	2	833
New York	8,232	45.6	16,031	88.4	63,660	1,321	64,981
North Carolina	648	9.6	1,059	15.5	3,735	75	3,810
North Dakota	4	0.6	4	0.6	32	0	32
Ohio	696	6.4	1,490	13.5	4,944	68	5,012
Oklahoma	228	7.2	716	22.3	1,795	15	1,810
Oregon	283	9.7	732	24.4	2,233	9	2,242
Pennsylvania	1,338	11.2	2,556	21.2	9,086	120	9,206
Rhode Island	102	10.2	305	30.3	842	9	851
South Carolina	347	9.7	1,395	38.4	3,022	38	3,060
South Dakota	8	1.1	23	3.2	57	2	59
Tennessee	442	8.9	967	19.2	2,734	26	2,760
Texas	2,944	17.0	7,164	40.4	23,572	213	23,785
Utah	145	8.2	270	14.9	818	20	838
Vermont	26	4.6	60	10.5	176	2	178
Virginia	606	9.6	1,590	24.9	4,710	82	4,792
Washington	573	11.4	1,459	28.2	4,765	18	4,783
West Virginia	61	3.4	78	4.3	359	5	364
Wisconsin	224	4.5	700	13.9	1,705	19	1,724
Wyoming	4	0.9	36	7.7	91	0	91

Note: Figures are for 12 months ending in September of each year.

Source: Reprinted from Centers for Disease Control and Prevention. (1993). *HIV/AIDS Surveillance Report, 5*(3), 3.

TABLE 5-21 AIDS Cases and Annual Rates, by Metropolitan Area: 1992 and 1993

Metropolitan Area	1992 Number	1992 Rate	1993 Number	1993 Rate	Cumulative Totals Adults and Adolescents	Cumulative Totals Children under 13 Years Old	Total
Akron, OH	36	5.4	46	6.9	214	0	214
Albany–Schenectady, NY	106	12.2	217	24.7	672	14	686
Albuquerque, NM	58	9.6	186	30.2	490	1	491
Allentown, PA	32	5.3	122	20.0	314	4	318
Ann Arbor, MI	29	5.8	63	12.4	194	4	198
Atlanta, GA	956	31.3	1,773	56.4	6,836	43	6,879
Austin, TX	241	27.6	586	65.0	1,705	14	1,719
Bakersfield, CA	50	8.8	161	27.3	357	3	360
Baltimore, MD	669	27.7	1,628	66.6	4,548	113	4,661
Baton Rouge, LA	92	17.1	135	24.7	469	7	476
Bergen–Passaic, NJ	267	20.9	677	52.8	2,425	51	2,476
Birmingham, AL	116	13.7	259	30.2	716	11	727
Boston, MA	659	11.6	2,268	40.2	6,510	117	6,627
Buffalo, NY	69	5.8	198	16.5	653	8	661
Charleston, SC	70	13.4	259	47.9	611	5	616
Charlotte, NC	118	9.9	245	20.1	747	10	757
Chicago, IL	1,614	21.5	2,619	34.5	9,251	125	9,376
Cincinnati, OH	112	7.3	230	14.7	768	11	779
Cleveland, OH	199	9.0	458	20.6	1,414	27	1,441
Columbus, OH	158	11.5	336	24.1	1,085	6	1,091
Dallas, TX	759	27.7	1,805	64.4	5,867	24	5,891
Dayton, OH	67	7.0	132	13.7	481	8	489
Denver, CO	335	20.1	1,010	58.9	2,918	13	2,931
Detroit, MI	606	14.1	1,233	28.7	3,484	45	3,529
El Paso, TX	46	7.5	116	18.3	303	1	304
Fort Lauderdale, FL	848	65.9	1,165	88.4	5,114	109	5,223
Fort Worth, TX	160	11.5	404	28.2	1,350	15	1,365
Fresno, CA	99	12.7	173	21.5	519	4	523
Gary, IN	47	7.7	78	12.6	240	2	242
Grand Rapids, MI	37	3.9	126	13.0	326	3	329
Greensboro, NC	128	12.0	151	14.0	631	11	642
Greenville, SC	62	7.4	255	29.8	521	2	523
Harrisburg, PA	46	7.7	78	12.9	313	6	319
Hartford, CT	167	14.8	565	50.2	1,397	17	1,414
Honolulu, HI	124	14.6	256	29.6	946	6	952
Houston, TX	1,023	29.8	2,587	72.8	9,225	87	9,312
Indianapolis, IN	170	12.1	397	27.7	1,178	5	1,183
Jacksonville, FL	327	35.0	910	94.7	2,140	49	2,189
Jersey City, NJ	313	56.6	619	111.8	2,933	68	3,001
Kansas City, MO	314	19.6	736	45.4	2,197	9	2,206
Knoxville, TN	35	5.8	78	12.7	238	2	240
Las Vegas, NV	180	19.5	468	46.9	1,260	14	1,274
Little Rock, AR	82	15.8	171	32.6	485	9	494
Los Angeles, CA	3,327	37.1	5,557	61.1	21,704	146	21,850
Louisville, KY	90	9.4	166	17.2	509	8	517
Memphis, TN	174	17.1	414	40.1	1,007	9	1,016
Miami, FL	1,324	67.0	2,423	120.1	9,303	260	9,563
Middlesex, NJ	217	21.1	354	34.2	1,515	33	1,548
Milwaukee, WI	127	8.8	361	24.8	914	12	926
Minneapolis–Saint Paul, MN	204	7.9	550	20.9	1,619	10	1,629
Monmouth–Ocean City, NJ	111	11.1	366	36.4	1,253	35	1,288
Nashville, TN	125	12.5	269	26.3	844	10	854
Nassau–Suffolk, NY	370	14.1	1,010	38.4	3,200	66	3,266
New Haven, CT	318	19.5	987	60.4	2,654	77	2,731
New Orleans, LA	476	36.8	612	46.9	2,868	37	2,905
New York, NY	7,163	83.8	13,288	155.3	54,716	1,183	55,899
Newark, NJ	838	43.8	1,540	80.6	7,229	184	7,413
Norfolk, VA	105	7.2	325	21.9	1,006	22	1,028
Oakland, CA	563	26.7	1,225	57.2	4,138	26	4,164

Continued on next page

TABLE 5-21 Continued

Metropolitan Area	1992 Number	1992 Rate	1993 Number	1993 Rate	Cumulative Totals Adults and Adolescents	Cumulative Totals Children under 13 Years Old	Cumulative Totals Total
Oklahoma City, OK	113	11.6	310	31.5	825	1	826
Omaha, NE	49	7.5	136	20.6	343	1	344
Orange County, CA	553	22.6	717	29.0	2,811	21	2,832
Orlando, FL	331	26.1	870	66.3	2,249	42	2,291
Philadelphia, PA	1,005	20.3	2,110	42.5	7,082	87	7,169
Phoenix, AZ	292	12.8	863	36.9	2,236	9	2,245
Pittsburgh, PA	148	6.2	214	8.9	1,026	6	1,032
Portland, OR	249	15.9	655	40.3	1,943	6	1,949
Providence, RI	96	10.5	285	31.1	791	8	799
Raleigh–Durham, NC	128	14.5	189	20.8	787	18	805
Richmond, VA	140	15.9	385	42.9	1,006	13	1,019
Riverside–San Bernardino, CA	435	16.0	1,045	36.6	2,727	27	2,754
Rochester, NY	76	7.1	243	22.4	742	8	750
Sacramento, CA	287	20.7	453	31.5	1,490	14	1,504
Saint Louis, MO	290	11.6	841	33.3	2,224	21	2,245
Salt Lake City, UT	129	11.7	241	21.3	726	14	740
San Antonio, TX	217	16.1	426	31.1	1,591	14	1,605
San Diego, CA	631	24.8	1,474	56.7	4,877	32	4,909
San Francisco, CA	1,896	116.9	4,592	279.8	17,397	27	17,424
San Jose, CA	183	12.2	502	33.2	1,514	11	1,525
Sarasota, FL	90	18.0	148	28.9	570	12	582
Scranton, PA	26	4.1	54	8.4	188	3	191
Seattle, WA	424	20.4	1,043	49.1	3,536	10	3,546
Springfield, MA	92	15.3	210	35.0	574	15	589
Stockton, CA	34	6.9	109	21.6	307	8	315
Syracuse, NY	71	9.5	168	22.2	497	6	503
Tacoma, WA	38	6.3	137	21.9	360	7	367
Tampa–Saint Petersburg, FL	535	25.5	1,421	66.6	3,781	53	3,834
Toledo, OH	33	5.4	90	14.6	271	4	275
Tucson, AZ	93	13.7	258	37.6	619	5	624
Tulsa, OK	70	9.7	236	32.1	549	5	554
Ventura, CA	73	10.8	130	19.0	378	1	379
Washington, DC	1,345	31.3	2,560	58.7	9,366	138	9,504
West Palm Beach, FL	529	59.7	787	86.5	2,916	107	3,023
Wichita, KS	62	12.6	96	19.2	276	2	278
Wilmington, DE	93	17.8	261	49.1	617	6	623
Youngstown, OH	23	3.8	29	4.8	148	0	148
Metropolitan areas with 500,000 or more population	39,112	24.8	81,352	50.9	284,441	4,131	288,572
Metropolitan areas with 50,000 to 500,000 population	4,821	10.5	10,306	22.0	31,977	485	32,462
Nonmetropolitan areas	2,587	4.9	5,288	10.0	16,621	268	16,889
Total[a]	46,716	18.2	97,368	37.5	334,344	4,906	339,250

Note: Figures are for 12 months ending in September of each year.

Source: Reprinted from Centers for Disease Control and Prevention. (1993). *HIV/AIDS Surveillance Report, 5*(3), 4–5.

[a]Totals include 1,327 people whose area of residence is unknown.

Public Awareness

In 1992 a federal government survey of 20,974 American adults assessed their knowledge levels about AIDS. Table 5-23 reports on the survey. Although there are some misconceptions about AIDS and HIV, knowledge levels appear to be relatively high. The aggressive information campaigns to teach people about AIDS seem to have had a major impact on this new and growing epidemic. This table is one of the best sources of information about public knowledge of AIDS and the issues associated with it. Information campaigns will be an important component of the effort to reduce the spread of AIDS, especially in the absence of a cure or preventive vaccine.

TABLE 5-22 **Appropriations for AIDS, by Category and Leading States: 1984 to 1992**

Appropriation Characteristic	Unit	1984–92 Total	1986	1987	1988	1989	1990	1991	1992
U.S. Public Health Service expenditures	Millions of dollars	8,606.3	233.8	502.5	962.0	1,301.0	1,588.6	1,888.2	1,960.1
State government appropriations[a]	Millions of dollars	1,519.9	26.3	65.0	149.2	249.1	278.9	330.7	401.9
Number of states	Number	NA	21	28	37	47	51	51	51
Appropriations for									
Education and information	Percent	—	25	19	21	26	28	25	27
Patient care[b]	Percent	—	4	15	16	25	45[c]	51[c]	50[c]
Support services[b]	Percent	—	12	11	19	13	c	c	c
Research	Percent	—	41	27	17	8	1	2	4
Testing and counseling	Percent	—	3	11	12	18	14	12	11
Leading areas by appropriations									
California	$1,000	377,010	16,020	31,515	58,033	76,877	46,649	47,738	92,684
New York	$1,000	375,152	4,500	9,500	39,920	52,884	68,576	90,493	101,229
Florida	$1,000	100,200	576	5,557	12,539	17,765	19,432	20,994	23,280
Massachusetts	$1,000	84,995	1,604	4,073	7,591	14,754	18,517	18,242	18,714
New Jersey	$1,000	86,780	1,969	4,963	7,907	13,012	15,469	14,446	27,564
Percent of total	Percent	67.0	89.6	83.3	80.6	71.0	60.5	58.0	65.6

Notes: NA = not applicable; — = not available.

Source: Reprinted from U.S. Bureau of the Census. (1993). *Statistical abstract of the United States: 1993* (113th ed., p. 134). Austin, TX: Reference Press.

[a]Includes appropriations from state governments' direct general revenue funds only; excludes Medicaid expenditures. Includes appropriations for other activities not shown separately.

[b]Beginning in 1989, hospice care included inpatient care rather than support services.

[c]Beginning in 1990, patient care and support services were combined.

TABLE 5-23 **AIDS Knowledge and Attitudes of People 18 Years of Age and Older, by Selected Characteristics: 1992 (Percent distribution)**

AIDS Knowledge or Attitude	Total	Age			Sex		Ethnicity			Education		
		18–29 Years	30–49 Years	50 Years and Over	Male	Female	Non-Hispanic White	Non-Hispanic Black	Hispanic	Less than 12 Years	12 Years	More than 12 Years
Total	100	100	100	100	100	100	100	100	100	100	100	100
1. How much would you say you know about AIDS?												
A lot	26	31	31	18	26	27	27	25	25	14	23	36
Some	45	50	50	37	45	45	47	39	40	32	48	49
A little	21	17	17	29	22	20	20	23	27	32	24	13
Nothing	7	2	3	16	7	7	6	13	8	22	5	2
Don't know	0	0	0	0	0	0	0	—	—	0	0	0
2. In the past month have you—												
2a. Seen any Public Service Announcements about AIDS on television?												
Yes	84	85	87	80	84	84	84	86	81	77	86	86
No	14	14	12	18	15	14	14	13	18	21	13	13
Don't know	2	1	1	3	2	2	2	1	1	3	1	1
2b. Heard any Public Service Announcements about AIDS on the radio?												
Yes	49	57	54	37	52	46	47	57	57	37	48	55
No	48	40	43	60	45	52	50	42	40	60	49	42
Don't know	3	3	3	3	3	3	3	2	2	3	3	3
2c. Seen any Public Service Posters in airports about AIDS?												
Yes	10	11	11	8	11	10	9	14	15	7	8	13
No	88	87	87	90	87	89	90	84	82	91	90	85
Don't know	2	2	2	2	2	2	2	2	4	2	2	2
3. In the past month, have you received information about AIDS from any of these sources?[a]												
Television programs	75	77	77	71	75	74	74	76	75	69	75	77
Radio programs	38	45	41	29	42	34	36	44	46	28	37	43
Magazine articles	44	49	47	37	41	47	44	44	41	26	42	55
Newspaper articles	52	48	56	51	53	51	53	49	49	35	51	62
Street signs/billboards	19	27	21	12	21	18	18	25	25	12	18	24
Store displays/store distributed brochures	9	12	9	6	9	8	7	12	14	7	9	9
Bus/streetcar/subway displays	7	12	8	4	8	7	5	14	13	6	6	9
Health department brochures	16	23	17	10	14	18	14	24	22	13	15	18
Workplace distributed brochures	12	13	16	6	12	13	11	17	12	5	11	17
School distributed brochures	10	18	11	3	9	11	9	13	12	7	9	12
Church distributed brochures	5	5	5	5	5	6	4	11	8	4	5	6

Community organization	5	6	6	4	5	5	4	9	5	4	4	7
Friend/acquaintance	10	15	11	6	10	11	9	15	13	8	10	12
AIDS hotline	1	2	2	1	1	2	1	3	3	1	1	1
Other	3	3	4	2	3	4	3	4	3	2	2	5
Don't know	1	0	0	1	1	1	1	1	0	1	1	0
Received no AIDS information in past month	13	9	11	17	12	13	13	13	12	21	13	8
4. Have you heard the AIDS virus called by the name "HIV"?												
Yes	95	97	97	91	95	95	96	94	84	85	96	98
No	4	3	3	7	4	4	3	4	14	12	3	1
Don't know	1	0	0	2	1	1	1	1	2	3	1	0
5. Tell me whether you think the following statements are true or false or if you don't know if they are true or false.												
5a. AIDS can reduce the body's natural protection against disease.												
True	87	90	92	79	88	86	90	76	79	68	87	96
False	3	3	3	4	3	4	3	8	5	6	4	2
Don't know	10	7	6	17	9	10	8	17	16	26	9	3
5b. AIDS can damage the brain.												
True	54	46	55	59	54	54	53	59	59	55	54	54
False	15	24	17	7	16	14	16	11	14	8	14	20
Don't know	30	30	27	34	30	31	31	30	27	37	32	26
5c. AIDS is an infectious disease caused by a virus.												
True	85	92	90	75	87	83	85	88	86	75	85	91
False	4	3	4	6	4	5	5	2	4	4	5	4
Don't know	10	5	6	19	9	12	10	10	10	21	10	5
5d. A person can be infected with the AIDS virus and not have the disease AIDS.												
True	84	88	89	75	84	84	86	80	77	68	84	92
False	4	5	4	4	4	4	3	6	7	6	4	3
Don't know	12	7	7	21	12	12	11	14	16	26	11	5
5e. Any person with the AIDS virus can pass it on to someone else through sexual intercourse.												
True	96	98	98	93	96	96	96	95	96	91	97	98
False	1	1	1	0	1	0	1	1	1	1	1	1
Don't know	3	2	2	6	3	3	3	4	3	8	3	1
5f. A pregnant woman who has the AIDS virus can give it to her baby.												
True	94	96	96	91	93	95	95	92	94	89	94	96
False	1	1	1	1	1	1	1	1	1	1	1	1
Don't know	5	3	4	9	6	4	5	8	6	10	5	3

Continued on next page

TABLE 5-23 Continued

AIDS Knowledge or Attitude	Total	Age			Sex		Ethnicity			Education		
		18–29 Years	30–49 Years	50 Years and Over	Male	Female	Non-Hispanic White	Non-Hispanic Black	Hispanic	Less than 12 Years	12 Years	More than 12 Years
5g. A person who has the AIDS virus can look and feel well and healthy.												
True	86	91	91	77	87	85	88	84	75	69	87	94
False	5	4	4	7	4	6	4	5	11	10	5	3
Don't know	9	5	5	16	9	9	8	11	14	22	8	3
5h. There are drugs available that can lengthen the life of a person infected with the AIDS virus.												
True	71	71	75	65	71	71	73	67	60	54	68	81
False	7	9	7	6	8	7	6	9	12	8	8	6
Don't know	22	20	18	29	22	22	21	24	27	37	24	13
5i. Early treatment of the AIDS virus infection can reduce symptoms in an infected person.												
True	60	61	65	53	61	59	61	59	54	46	57	70
False	10	12	10	8	10	10	9	11	12	10	11	9
Don't know	30	27	25	39	30	31	30	31	34	45	33	21
5j. There is a vaccine available to the public that protects a person from getting the AIDS virus.												
True	3	4	2	4	3	3	2	6	6	6	3	2
False	83	85	88	75	84	82	86	74	73	66	83	91
Don't know	14	11	9	21	13	15	12	19	22	28	14	7
5k. There is no cure for AIDS at present.												
True	93	93	95	90	93	93	95	90	84	83	94	96
False	2	3	2	3	3	2	2	3	6	4	2	2
Don't know	5	4	3	7	5	5	4	7	10	12	4	2
6. How likely do you think it is that a person will get AIDS or the AIDS virus infection from—												
6a. Working near someone with the AIDS virus?												
Very likely	2	2	2	3	2	2	2	4	6	4	2	1
Somewhat likely	5	4	5	5	5	5	4	6	6	6	6	4
Somewhat unlikely	7	7	7	7	7	7	7	7	9	8	8	6
Very unlikely	44	45	44	44	46	43	46	43	32	38	45	47
Definitely not possible	36	39	39	31	35	37	37	32	40	29	35	40
Don't know	6	3	3	11	5	6	5	8	7	15	4	2
6b. Eating in a restaurant where the cook has the AIDS virus?												
Very likely	7	5	6	8	6	7	5	10	10	10	7	4
Somewhat likely	17	18	16	17	17	17	17	19	16	20	19	13

	Col1	Col2	Col3	Col4	Col5	Col6	Col7	Col8	Col9	Col10	Col11	Col12
Somewhat unlikely	13	15	14	11	13	13	13	13	12	11	13	14
Very unlikely	35	37	37	32	37	34	37	30	28	25	33	42
Definitely not possible	19	19	21	15	18	19	19	16	23	15	17	22
Don't know	10	5	7	17	9	11	9	13	10	19	10	5
6c. Sharing plates, forks, or glasses with someone who has the AIDS virus?												
Very likely	9	7	9	11	9	9	9	12	12	14	11	6
Somewhat likely	18	15	17	20	18	17	18	19	15	19	19	16
Somewhat unlikely	13	15	14	11	13	13	14	11	13	10	13	15
Very unlikely	32	36	34	27	33	32	33	28	29	24	31	37
Definitely not possible	18	22	19	14	17	19	18	16	22	14	17	21
Don't know	10	5	7	16	9	10	9	13	10	20	10	5
6d. Using public toilets?												
Very likely	6	5	5	7	5	6	4	10	9	10	6	3
Somewhat likely	11	11	9	14	11	12	11	12	14	16	12	8
Somewhat unlikely	11	13	11	10	11	11	11	11	11	9	12	11
Very unlikely	38	39	40	35	39	37	40	33	29	29	37	43
Definitely not possible	26	28	29	21	25	26	26	22	27	18	24	31
Don't know	9	4	6	15	8	9	8	12	9	19	8	4
6e. Sharing needles for drug use with someone who has the AIDS virus?												
Very likely	96	97	97	92	96	95	96	94	94	90	96	98
Somewhat likely	1	1	1	2	1	1	1	2	1	2	1	1
Somewhat unlikely	0	0	0	0	0	0	0	0	1	0	0	0
Very unlikely	0	1	0	0	0	0	0	0	1	1	0	0
Definitely not possible	0	0	0	0	0	0	0	0	0	0	0	0
Don't know	2	1	1	5	2	2	2	4	2	7	2	1
6f. Being coughed or sneezed on by someone who has the AIDS virus?												
Very likely	9	5	8	12	9	9	8	12	10	13	10	5
Somewhat likely	18	15	17	21	17	19	18	18	20	21	19	16
Somewhat unlikely	15	16	16	13	15	15	15	15	13	11	15	16
Very unlikely	32	36	36	25	33	31	33	28	26	21	31	39
Definitely not possible	15	20	16	11	15	16	15	14	20	13	14	17
Don't know	11	7	7	18	10	11	10	13	11	21	11	6
6g. Attending school with a child who has the AIDS virus?												
Very likely	2	1	2	2	2	2	1	3	3	4	2	1
Somewhat likely	5	4	5	6	5	5	4	6	5	7	5	3
Somewhat unlikely	7	7	7	7	7	7	7	8	8	7	8	7
Very unlikely	44	43	46	43	46	43	46	42	32	36	45	48
Definitely not possible	35	43	37	29	34	37	35	31	43	30	34	38
Don't know	7	3	4	13	7	7	6	10	8	17	6	3
6h. Mosquitoes or other insects?												
Very likely	9	9	9	9	9	9	8	12	12	13	10	6

Continued on next page

TABLE 5-23 Continued

AIDS Knowledge or Attitude	Total	Age			Sex		Ethnicity			Education		
							Non-Hispanic					
		18–29 Years	30–49 Years	50 Years and Over	Male	Female	White	Black	Hispanic	Less than 12 Years	12 Years	More than 12 Years
Somewhat likely	16	18	16	15	17	16	15	21	18	19	17	14
Somewhat unlikely	9	11	9	6	10	8	9	7	10	7	9	10
Very unlikely	25	25	27	23	26	25	27	22	18	17	24	30
Definitely not possible	20	20	22	17	19	21	21	14	21	14	18	24
Don't know	21	16	17	29	20	22	21	23	21	31	22	16
6i. Being cared for by a nurse, doctor, dentist, or other health care worker who has the AIDS virus?												
Very likely	26	22	24	30	24	27	24	33	30	33	29	19
Somewhat likely	36	38	36	34	35	36	37	33	32	30	37	37
Somewhat unlikely	15	17	17	11	16	14	15	12	13	9	13	19
Very unlikely	15	16	16	12	17	13	16	9	12	10	12	20
Definitely not possible	3	3	3	3	3	3	3	3	6	4	2	3
Don't know	6	4	4	10	6	7	5	9	7	14	5	3
7. Can a person get AIDS or the AIDS virus infection while giving or donating blood for use by others?												
Yes	29	31	28	30	30	28	26	43	36	39	31	23
No	62	61	66	56	61	62	66	45	51	42	60	72
Don't know	9	8	6	14	9	10	8	12	13	19	9	5
10. Have you ever discussed AIDS with any of your children aged 10–17?[b]												
Yes	75	55	76	68	64	84	77	75	67	64	74	79
No	25	43	23	30	35	16	23	25	33	36	25	20
Don't know	0	0	0	—	0	0	0	0	—	0	0	0
11. Have any or all of your children aged 10–17 had instruction at school about AIDS?[b]												
Yes	76	64	77	77	72	80	77	74	75	72	77	78
No	8	20	8	5	7	10	8	8	8	9	8	8
Don't know	15	15	15	16	20	10	14	17	16	19	15	14
12. Have you ever given or donated blood?												
Yes	42	34	45	44	53	32	45	34	28	27	39	52
No	58	66	55	55	47	67	54	66	72	72	61	48
Don't know	0	0	0	1	0	0	0	1	0	1	0	0
13a. Have you donated blood since March 1985?												
Yes	19	26	23	9	23	16	20	14	14	7	16	27
No	80	73	76	90	76	84	79	85	85	92	83	72
Don't know	1	1	1	1	1	1	1	1	1	1	1	1
13b. Have you donated blood in the past 12 months?												
Yes	6	8	8	3	7	5	7	4	4	2	5	9

No	90	94	97	95	95	92	94	91	96	91	91	93
Don't know	1	1	1	1	1	1	1	1	1	1	1	1
14. How many times in the past 12 months have you dontated blood?												
Once	5	3	1	3	2	3	3	4	1	4	5	3
Twice	2	1	1	1	1	2	1	2	1	2	2	2
Three times or more	2	1	0	1	0	1	1	2	1	2	1	1
Don't know	0	0	0	—	—	0	0	0	0	0	0	0
Did not donate blood in past 12 months[c]	91	95	98	96	96	93	95	93	97	92	92	94
15. To the best of your knowledge, are blood donations routinely tested for the AIDS virus infection?												
Yes	87	79	62	68	68	82	80	79	72	84	82	79
No	5	7	10	9	12	6	7	7	8	6	6	7
Don't know	7	14	28	23	19	12	13	15	20	10	12	14
16. Was one of your reasons for donating blood because you wanted to be tested for the AIDS virus infection?[d]												
Yes	2	3	4	3	7	2	2	3	1	2	4	3
No	89	88	81	85	88	89	88	89	90	89	87	88
Don't know	—	—	—	—	—	—	—	—	—	—	—	—
17a. Except for blood donations since 1985, have you had your blood tested for the AIDS virus infection?												
Yes	22	17	14	28	29	16	17	20	8	22	27	18
No	74	77	78	67	64	78	77	74	83	73	69	76
Don't know	5	6	8	5	7	6	6	6	9	5	4	6
17b. Why haven't you been tested?[a,e]												
Don't consider myself at risk of AIDS	84	81	76	76	73	83	83	79	86	82	71	81
Don't believe anything can be done if I am positive	0	1	0	1	1	0	0	1	0	0	1	0
Don't like needles	1	1	1	1	3	1	1	1	0	1	2	1
Afraid of losing job, insurance, housing, friends, family if people knew I was positive	0	0	0	0	0	0	0	0	0	0	0	0
Don't trust medical clinics/hospitals to keep test results confidential	0	0	0	1	0	0	0	0	0	0	0	0
Already know whether I have the AIDS virus infection	1	1	0	0	1	1	1	1	0	1	1	1
Don't know where to go for a test	0	1	1	1	0	0	1	1	0	1	2	1
Other	9	8	9	11	11	8	9	9	7	9	12	9
Don't know	6	9	13	9	12	8	7	10	7	8	13	9
18. How many times have you had your blood tested for the AIDS virus infection, not including blood donations?												
Once	14	10	9	20	15	10	11	11	5	14	16	11
Twice	4	3	2	5	7	3	3	3	1	4	5	3

Continued on next page

TABLE 5-23 Continued

AIDS Knowledge or Attitude	Total	Age			Sex		Ethnicity			Education		
							Non-Hispanic					
		18–29 Years	30–49 Years	50 Years and Over	Male	Female	White	Black	Hispanic	Less than 12 Years	12 Years	More than 12 Years
Three times or more	3	4	3	1	4	2	2	6	3	2	2	3
Don't know	0	0	0	1	1	0	0	6	0	1	0	0
Never had test[f]	82	73	78	93	81	84	85	71	72	86	84	79
19. How many times in the past 12 months have you had your blood tested for the AIDS virus infection, not including blood donations?												
None	9	12	11	3	10	8	8	11	15	6	8	11
Once	8	12	8	3	8	7	6	14	11	6	7	9
Twice	1	2	1	0	1	1	1	3	1	1	1	1
Three times or more	0	0	0	0	0	0	0	1	1	0	0	0
Don't know	0	0	0	0	0	0	0	0	0	0	0	0
Never had test[f]	82	73	78	93	81	84	85	71	73	86	84	79
20. Did you have any of the AIDS blood tests—[a,g]												
For hospitalization or a surgical procedure?	13	12	12	23	10	17	14	14	10	20	15	10
To apply for health insurance?	5	3	6	4	6	3	5	4	2	2	4	6
To apply for life insurance?	12	6	17	10	16	8	15	7	5	2	9	17
For employment?	6	7	7	3	8	5	5	7	10	5	7	6
To apply for a marriage license?	4	7	3	2	4	5	5	3	5	3	6	4
For military induction or military service?	7	11	5	1	11	2	7	8	3	2	8	7
For immigration?	5	5	5	3	4	5	1	2	23	13	2	3
Just to find out if you were infected?	30	35	28	23	28	32	28	39	27	28	33	29
Because of referral by the doctor?	5	5	4	7	4	5	4	8	4	6	5	3
Because of referral by the Health Department?	1	1	1	0	1	1	0	2	0	1	1	1
Referred by your sex partner?	1	2	1	0	1	1	0	1	1	1	1	1
Other	20	22	18	22	14	25	21	19	12	22	21	18
Don't know	0	—	0	1	0	0	0	0		0	—	0
21. When was your last AIDS blood test for the AIDS virus infection, not including blood donation?[g]												
1992	26	29	24	24	26	26	25	30	23	24	27	25
1991	29	31	28	30	28	31	28	37	24	29	30	30
1990	13	12	13	11	13	12	14	9	14	10	13	14
1989	9	8	10	10	9	9	10	7	9	8	9	9
1988	7	8	7	5	7	7	6	7	11	8	7	6
1987	3	3	4	3	3	3	4	4	3	3	3	3
1986	2	1	2	2	2	1	2	1	3	3	1	2
1985	1	1	1	2	1	1	1	1	0	1	1	1
Don't know	6	6	6	8	6	7	5	7	8	9	6	5

22. Did you have your last AIDS blood test—[a,g]												
For hospitalization or a surgical procedure?	12	10	11	22	9	16	13	12	11	18	14	10
To apply for health insurance?	4	3	6	4	6	3	5	3	2	1	3	6
To apply for life insurance?	12	6	16	10	16	7	15	6	5	5	8	17
For employment?	6	7	7	4	8	5	5	7	10	5	7	6
To apply for a marriage license?	3	5	3	2	3	3	4	2	4	2	4	3
For military induction or military service?	6	9	5	2	10	2	7	7	3	13	7	7
For immigration?	4	5	4	3	4	5	1	1	23	29	2	3
Just to find out if you were infected?	30	34	29	23	27	32	28	38	27	6	31	28
Because of referral by the doctor?	5	4	4	7	4	5	4	9	4	1	5	3
Because of referral by the Health Department?	1	1	1	0	1	0	0	1	0	0	1	0
Referred by your sex partner?	1	1	0	0	1	0	1	1	1	21	1	1
Other	20	22	18	23	15	25	22	17	12	0	21	19
Don't know	0	0	0	1	0	0	0	0	0		0	0
23. Not including a blood donation, where did you have your last blood test for the AIDS virus?[g]												
AIDS clinic/counseling/testing site	1	2	2	0	1	1	1	1	2	1	1	1
Community health clinic	8	10	7	6	7	8	6	13	11	10	8	7
Clinic run by employer	2	2	2	2	2	2	2	2	3	2	2	2
Doctor/HMO	28	28	27	31	24	32	29	28	22	24	29	28
Hospital/emergency room/outpatient clinic	24	22	23	31	21	27	23	26	23	31	24	22
STD clinic	0	0	0	0	0	0	0	0	—	0	0	0
Family planning clinic	1	2	1	—	1	2	1	1	1	1	2	1
Prenatal clinic	0	0	0	—	0	1	0	1	0	1	0	0
Tuberculosis clinic	0	1	0	—	0	0	0	0	0	0	0	—
Public clinic	5	7	4	1	5	5	3	7	11	9	6	3
Other clinic	4	3	4	3	4	3	3	2	6	5	3	4
Drug treatment facility	0	0	0	0	1	0	0	0	0	0	1	0
Military induction/service site	6	9	5	2	10	2	7	7	3	2	7	7
Immigration site	1	0	1	1	1	1	0	0	4	2	1	1
Other	10	8	11	10	12	8	11	6	8	7	9	12
Don't know	1	0	1	1	1	0	0	0	0	0	0	1
25. Did you get the results of your last test?[g]												
Yes	80	83	79	78	78	82	78	85	84	80	83	78
No	19	16	21	20	21	17	21	15	15	18	17	21
Don't know	1	1	1	1	1	1	1	0	1	2	0	1
26. Was this because you decided you didn't want the results, or was it because you were unable to get the results?[h]												
Didn't want	9	10	8	10	9	8	7	10	17	8	7	10
Unable to get	21	20	24	12	26	15	18	28	34	26	24	18
Both	1	1	1	—	1	1	1	1	—	1	1	1
Other	56	57	55	54	52	60	61	44	35	49	51	60
Don't know	13	12	10	23	11	15	12	16	10	17	15	10

Continued on next page

TABLE 5-23 Continued

AIDS Knowledge or Attitude	Total	Age			Sex		Ethnicity			Education		
		18–29 Years	30–49 Years	50 Years and Over	Male	Female	Non-Hispanic White	Black	Hispanic	Less than 12 Years	12 Years	More than 12 Years
28. Were the results given in person, by telephone, by mail, or in some other way?												
In person	58	62	55	59	54	63	52	68	74	75	61	51
By telephone	17	14	19	18	17	18	20	14	10	12	18	19
By mail	16	13	17	16	20	12	18	13	12	9	14	20
Other	8	9	7	6	9	6	9	5	4	4	7	10
Don't know	0	0	0	1	0	0	1	0	—	0	0	1
29. Do you believe the results of your last test were accurate?												
Yes	97	97	98	97	97	98	98	97	97	96	97	98
No	1	1	1	—	1	1	1	1	0	0	1	1
Don't know	2	2	1	3	2	1	1	2	3	4	2	1
30. Do you feel that the confidentiality of the results of your last test for the AIDS virus infection was handled properly?												
Yes	94	94	94	92	94	94	94	95	91	92	95	93
No	2	4	2	1	2	3	2	2	2	2	2	3
Don't know	4	2	4	6	4	3	3	3	6	6	2	3
31. Do you expect to have a blood test for the AIDS virus infection in the next 12 months?												
Yes	11	22	11	4	13	10	9	26	17	11	11	12
No	81	68	81	89	79	82	85	59	70	78	81	81
Don't know	8	11	8	7	8	8	6	15	12	11	8	7
32. Tell me if each of these statements explains why you expect to have the blood test in the next 12 months.												
Because it will be part of a blood donation	17	15	18	18	18	15	21	10	8	10	15	21
Because it will be part of hospitalization or surgery you expect to have	6	6	6	8	5	8	5	7	9	12	6	4
Because you expect to apply for life or health insurance	9	10	9	4	11	6	7	10	12	8	9	9
Because you expect to apply for a job	7	10	7	2	9	6	4	11	12	9	9	6
Because you expect to join the military	2	3	1	2	3	1	1	3	4	4	1	2
Because you expect to apply for a marriage license	7	11	5	1	8	6	8	7	7	10	6	7
Because you want to know the results	72	76	69	66	68	76	65	82	78	80	73	67

33. Where will you go to have a blood test for the AIDS virus infection? (and related questions)

	20	19	20	21	22	18	18	24	21	22	22	18
Because it will be a required part of some other activity that includes automatic AIDS testing — AIDS testing												
33. Where will you go to have a blood test for the AIDS virus infection?												
AIDS clinic/counseling/testing site	2	2	2	1	2	2	2	1	3	2	2	2
Community health clinic	10	12	10	9	9	12	8	17	9	13	11	9
Clinic run by employer	2	2	2	2	3	2	2	2	4	1	3	2
Doctor/HMO	36	32	38	46	35	38	38	36	32	31	36	39
Hospital/emergency room/outpatient clinic	17	17	16	20	18	16	15	19	15	21	18	14
STD clinic	0	0	0	0	0	0	0	0	—	0	0	0
Family planning clinic	1	0	1	—	1	2	2	0	1	1	2	1
Prenatal clinic	0	0	—	—	—	—	—	—	0	—	0	—
Tuberculosis clinic	0	—	0	—	—	—	—	—	—	—	—	—
Public clinic	6	7	6	2	6	6	5	8	8	9	7	4
Other clinic	3	3	2	3	2	3	2	2	5	4	3	2
Drug treatment facility	—	—	—	—	—	—	—	—	—	—	—	—
Military induction/service site	3	3	3	1	5	1	4	3	2	1	3	4
Immigration site	0	0	0	—	0	0	0	—	0	—	0	0
Other	1	1	2	2	1	2	2	1	1	1	1	2
Don't know	7	9	5	3	7	6	6	6	13	9	7	5
34. Tell me whether you think the following statements about the blood test for the AIDS virus infection are true or false or if you do not know whether they are true or false.												
34a. Sometimes the results of a blood test for the AIDS virus infection can be wrong.												
True	76	76	79	73	76	76	78	74	65	62	75	83
False	6	8	7	3	6	6	6	6	10	7	6	6
Don't know	18	16	14	24	18	18	17	20	25	32	18	11
34b. After a person becomes infected with the AIDS virus, there can be a period of time before the test shows the infection.												
True	79	85	83	70	79	80	81	80	70	63	79	88
False	2	3	3	2	3	2	2	2	3	3	3	2
Don't know	18	12	14	28	19	18	17	18	27	35	18	10
37. Have you ever heard of a drug called AZT, also known as zidovudine or Retrovir?												
Yes	58	56	68	48	59	57	62	52	36	30	54	76
No	38	42	30	46	37	39	34	43	61	65	42	22
Don't know	4	2	3	5	4	4	3	5	3	5	4	2
38. Tell me whether you think the following statements about AZT are true or false or if you don't know whether they are true or false.[k]												

Continued on next page

TABLE 5-23 **Continued**

AIDS Knowledge or Attitude	Total	Age			Sex		Ethnicity			Education		
							Non-Hispanic					
		18–29 Years	30–49 Years	50 Years and Over	Male	Female	White	Black	Hispanic	Less than 12 Years	12 Years	More than 12 Years
38a. AZT can delay or slow down the symptoms of AIDS virus infection.												
True	83	86	85	77	83	82	83	79	82	70	78	88
False	2	1	2	2	2	2	1	2	2	3	2	1
Don't know	15	12	13	22	15	16	15	19	16	27	20	11
38b. AZT cures people with AIDS.												
True	1	1	1	1	1	1	1	1	1	1	1	1
False	92	94	93	88	92	91	92	88	91	82	90	94
Don't know	7	5	6	11	7	8	7	10	8	16	9	5
38c. AZT has no known side effects.												
True	4	4	4	5	4	4	3	7	6	5	4	4
False	61	65	65	51	61	61	62	57	56	45	54	69
Don't know	35	30	31	44	35	35	34	36	37	51	42	27
38d. AZT is appropriate for a person with the AIDS virus infection only at certain times during the illness.												
True	35	40	37	27	35	35	34	36	41	25	30	40
False	12	12	13	10	12	12	11	15	15	12	12	12
Don't know	53	48	50	63	52	54	54	49	43	63	58	48
38e. There are other drugs available to treat AIDS-related illnesses.												
True	55	54	60	50	59	52	57	49	47	39	47	63
False	12	14	11	11	11	13	11	15	19	15	13	10
Don't know	32	32	29	39	30	35	32	36	33	46	39	26
39. Did you have a blood transfusion at any time between 1977 and 1985?												
Yes	5	2	5	7	5	5	5	5	4	5	5	5
No	94	97	94	91	93	94	94	93	95	92	94	94
Don't know	1	1	1	2	1	1	1	1	1	2	1	1
40. Do you have frequent blood transfusions because of sickle cell or chronic anemia?												
Yes	0	0	0	0	0	0	0	0	0	0	0	0
No	100	100	100	100	100	100	100	100	100	100	100	100
Don't know	0	0	0	0	0	0	0	0	0	0	0	0
41. How effective do you think the use of a condom is to prevent getting the AIDS virus through sexual activity?	0 100 0	0 100 0	0 100 0	0 100 0	0 100 0	0 100 0	0 100 0	0 100 0	0 100 0	0 100 0	0 100 0	0 100 0

Very effective	26	32	28	18	30	22	25	26	27	19	24	30
Somewhat effective	54	56	57	49	52	56	56	47	46	42	56	58
Not at all effective	4	7	4	5	3	5	4	5	5	6	4	3
Don't know how effective	14	7	10	24	13	15	13	20	16	28	14	7
Don't know method	2	1	1	3	1	2	1	2	6	5	2	1

42. Tell me whether you think the following statements are true or false or whether you don't know whether they are true or false.

42a. Latex condoms and natural-membrane condoms are equally good at preventing transmission of the AIDS virus.

True	16	23	17	11	19	14	15	21	19	15	18	15
False	27	34	33	15	30	25	29	20	21	13	22	39
Don't know	55	42	49	71	50	59	55	56	54	68	58	45
Don't know method	2	1	1	3	1	2	1	2	6	5	2	1

42b. Oil-based lubricants can cause latex condoms to break.

True	33	44	38	19	36	30	34	34	28	21	29	42
False	5	7	6	4	7	4	5	6	7	4	6	6
Don't know	60	47	55	74	56	63	60	58	59	70	63	51
Don't know method	2	1	1	3	1	2	1	2	6	5	2	1

43. What are your chances of having the AIDS virus?

High	0	1	1	0	0	1	0	1	1	1	0	0
Medium	2	3	2	1	2	2	2	3	3	2	2	2
Low	22	32	25	12	23	21	23	22	17	13	20	28
None	73	62	71	83	72	74	74	67	74	78	75	68
Don't know	2	2	2	3	2	2	2	6	5	5	2	1

44. What are your chances of getting the AIDS virus?

High	1	1	1	0	1	0	0	1	1	1	1	1
Medium	3	5	3	1	3	3	3	4	4	3	3	3
Low	29	38	33	18	31	27	30	27	22	17	26	37
None	64	53	60	77	62	67	65	60	67	72	68	57
Don't know	3	2	3	4	3	3	2	6	1	6	3	2
High change of already having the AIDS virus	0	1	1	0	0	1	0	1	1	1	0	0

45. Have you ever had a coworker who had AIDS or the AIDS virus?

Yes	5	5	8	3	6	5	5	6	5	2	4	9
No	86	86	83	89	84	87	86	84	83	90	89	82
Never worked, never had a coworker	1	1	0	1	0	1	1	1	3	2	1	0
Don't know	8	8	9	7	10	6	8	9	8	7	7	9

46. Besides a coworker, have you ever had a friend or relative who had AIDS or the AIDS virus?

Yes	12	13	15	8	11	13	12	17	14	7	10	16
No	84	83	81	89	85	84	85	78	81	89	86	80
Don't know	4	4	4	3	4	3	3	5	4	4	4	4

Continued on next page

TABLE 5-23 **Continued**

AIDS Knowledge or Attitude	Total	Age			Sex		Ethnicity			Education		
		18–29 Years	30–49 Years	50 Years and Over	Male	Female	Non-Hispanic White	Non-Hispanic Black	Hispanic	Less than 12 Years	12 Years	More than 12 Years
47. Are any of these statements true for you?												
a. You have hemophilia or another clotting disorder and have received clotting factor concentrations since 1977.												
b. You are a man who has had sex with another man at some time since 1977, even one time.												
c. You have taken illegal drugs by needle at any time since 1977.												
d. You have had sex for money or drugs at any time since 1977.												
e. Since 1977, you are or have been the sex partner of any peson who would answer yes to any of the items above (a–d)												
Yes to at least one statement	4	6	5	1	4	3	4	5	5	3	4	4
No to all statements	96	94	95	99	95	97	96	95	95	97	96	96
Don't know	0	0	0	0	0	0	0	1	0	0	0	0

Notes: Data are based on the National Health Interview Survey comprising household interviews of the civilian noninstitutionalized population. HMO = health maintenance organization; STD = sexually transmitted disease; — = no responses in this category.

Source: Reprinted from Schoenborn, C. A., Marsh, S. L., & Hardy, A. M. (1994). *AIDS knowledge and attitudes for 1992: Data from the National Health Interview Survey* (pp. 7–14). Hyattsville, MD: U.S. Public Health Service, National Center for Health Statistics.

[a] Multiple responses may add to more than 100 percent.

[b] Question asked of those responding "yes" to question 8, "Do you have any children aged 10 through 17?"

[c] Estimates were based on people answering "no" or "don't know" to questions 12, 13a, or 13b.

[d] Question was asked of people answering "yes" to questions 13a and 15.

[e] Question asked of people answering "no" to question 17a.

[f] Estimates were based on people answering "no" or "don't know" to question 17a.

[g] Question asked of people answering "yes" to question 17a.

[h] Question asked of people answering "no" or "don't know" to question 25.

[i] Question asked of people answering "yes" to question 25.

[j] Question asked of people answering "yes" to question 31.

[k] Question asked of people answering "yes" to question 37.

Chronic Conditions

Although this chapter has focused thus far on serious health problems that often lead to death, even greater social concerns may arise from chronic health problems that limit the activities of those who have them. Chronic conditions, which include life-threatening as well as rarely fatal but frequently disabling conditions, may cause social problems as distressing as those caused by fatal illnesses and may also be a greater burden, overall, on health and social services.

The Centers for Disease Control and Prevention collects and distributes information on the impact of the chronic conditions. In most cases, the information is based on interviews with households and not on official reports from health departments or hospitals. The interviews were conducted in 1986, 1987, and 1988 with a national sample of 124,328 households that included 307,221 people. When possible, all adult family members in the household were interviewed. The findings were published in 1993, so the information is the most current available. (Information collected from large numbers of people who responded to many questions does not change very much from year to year.) The data presented here deal with two issues—the prevalence of chronic conditions and the impact of those chronic conditions on activity outside the house. AIDS and mental illnesses were not covered in this study.

Table 5-24 ranks the most common chronic conditions by gender, race, and age. Chronic sinusitis is the most prevalent chronic condition for all people. When men and women are considered separately, deformities or orthopedic impairments are the most common chronic condition among men; the most common among women is arthritis. However, Figure 5-10 shows that more women than men suffer from the three most prevalent conditions—chronic sinusitis, deformities and orthopedic impairments, and arthritis. For African Americans, high blood pressure is the most prevalent chronic condition, and chronic sinusitis ranks third (Table 5-24).

Some conditions are more common among certain age groups. Older people have difficulties with conditions that do not trouble many younger people, such as cataracts, constipation, and tinnitus. Deafness and other forms of hearing impairment are the most prevalent impairments. Acne, on the other hand, is a common problem among young people but not for any other age group. Children and adolescents only rarely have arthritis; older people are the group least bothered by chronic sinusitis (see Table 5-24). Figure 5-11 shows the rates of the most common chronic conditions per 1,000 people by age group. The incidences of some other chronic conditions are listed in Table 5-25.

Another critical issue in analyzing chronic conditions is determining the impact they have on the activities of those who experience them. Table 5-26 shows the chronic conditions that limited major or outside activities by at least 30 percent. In the table,

TABLE 5-24 **Selected Chronic Conditions with Highest Prevalence in Rank Order, by Gender, Race, and Age: 1986–88**

Chronic Condition	All Persons[a]	Gender Male	Gender Female	Race White	Race Black	Age Under 18 Years	Age 18–44 Years	Age 45–64 Years	Age 65–74 Years	Age 75 Years and Over
Chronic sinusitis	1	2	2	1	3	2	1	3	6	7
Deformities or orthopedic impairments	2	1	3	2	4	6	2	4	5	6
Arthritis	3	5	1	3	2	b	7	1	1	1
High blood pressure	4	3	4	4	1	b	4	2	2	2
Hay fever or allergic rhinitis without asthma	5	6	5	5	6	1	3	7	10	b
Deafness and other hearing impairments	6	4	7	6	8	b	6	5	4	3
Heart disease	7	7	6	7	5	9	b	6	3	4
Chronic bronchitis	8	9	8	8	10	3	b	b	b	b
Hemorrhoids	9	8	b	9	b	b	9	8	b	b
Asthma	10	b	b	10	7	4	b	b	b	b
Blindness and other visual impairments	b	10	b	b	b	b	b	b	b	8
Migraine headache	b	b	9	b	b	b	5	b	b	b
Other headache (excludes tension headache)	b	b	10	b	b	b	8	b	b	b
Diabetes	b	b	b	b	9	b	b	9	8	9
Dermatitis	b	b	b	b	b	5	10	b	b	b
Chronic disease of tonsils and adenoids	b	b	b	b	b	7	b	b	b	b
Acne	b	b	b	b	b	8	b	b	b	b
Speech impairments	b	b	b	b	b	10	b	b	b	b
Varicose veins of lower extremities	b	b	b	b	b	b	b	10	b	b
Cataracts	b	b	b	b	b	b	b	b	7	5
Tinnitus	b	b	b	b	b	b	b	b	9	b
Constipation	b	b	b	b	b	b	b	b	b	10

Notes: This table shows rank by condition prevalence, not person prevalence. A person may have more than one condition in some groupings such as deformities, orthopedic impairments, or heart conditions.

Source: Reprinted from Centers for Disease Control and Prevention. (1993, February). *Prevalence of selected chronic conditions: United States, 1986–88* (p. 10). Hyattsville, MD: U.S. Public Health Service, National Center for Health Statistics.

[a]Includes races other than white and black.

[b]Indicated rank is not in top 10.

limitation in activity refers to "a long-term reduction in a person's capacity to perform the average kind or amount of activities associated with his or her age group" and refers to what a person is generally capable of doing (Centers for Disease Control and Prevention, 1993e, p. 73).

The conditions listed in the table are the most disabling but not usually the most prevalent. For example, mental retardation, which affects relatively few people, causes 83.6 percent of those who have it to experience severe activity limitations. Respiratory neoplasms—lung cancer and related cancers—are the next most limiting. Multiple sclerosis, blindness, various forms of paralysis, heart disease, diabetes, and other conditions affect relatively few people but affect them very severely.

FIGURE 5-10 **Rate of Chronic Conditions with Highest Prevalence, by Age: 1986–88**

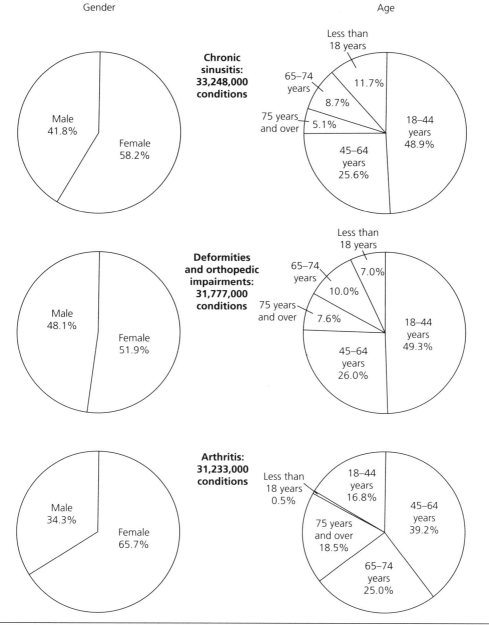

Source: Reprinted from Centers for Disease Control and Prevention. (1993, February). *Prevalence of selected chronic conditions: United States, 1986–88* (p. 13). Hyattsville, MD: U.S. Public Health Service, National Center for Health Statistics.

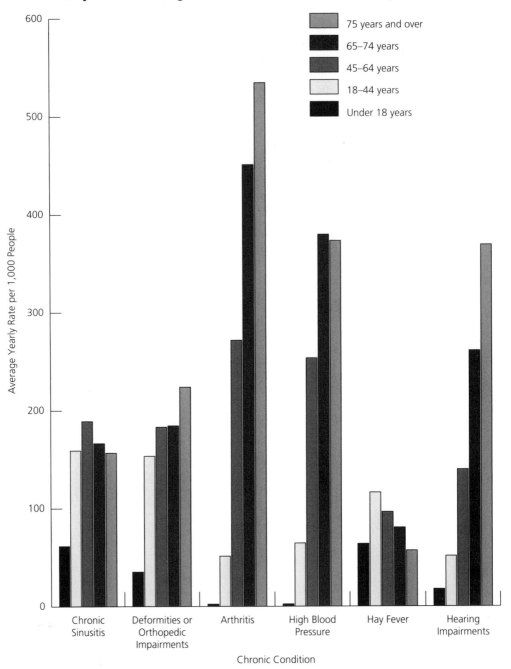

FIGURE 5-11 **Percentage Distribution of Selected Chronic Conditions with Highest Prevalence, by Gender and Age: 1986–88**

Legend:
- 75 years and over
- 65–74 years
- 45–64 years
- 18–44 years
- Under 18 years

Y-axis: Average Yearly Rate per 1,000 People

X-axis (Chronic Condition): Chronic Sinusitis, Deformities or Orthopedic Impairments, Arthritis, High Blood Pressure, Hay Fever, Hearing Impairments

Source: Adapted from Centers for Disease Control and Prevention. (1993, February). *Prevalence of selected chronic conditions: United States, 1986–88* (p. 12). Hyattsville, MD: U.S. Public Health Service, National Center for Health Statistics.

TABLE 5-25 **Incidence of Selected Birth Defects and Health Conditions**

Condition	Incidence	Source[a]
Achondroplasia	One in 10,000 births	March of Dimes Birth Defects Foundation, 1987
Alzheimer's disease	4 million	Blue Ribbon Task Force, 1993
Aphasia	1 million	National Aphasia Association, 1993
Autism	Five in 10,000 births	Autism Society of America, no date
Brain tumors	41,200 new cases per year, including malignant and benign, primary, and metastatic	Association for Brain Tumor Research, 1991
Cleft lip and palate	One in 700 births	March of Dimes Birth Defects Foundation, 1988a
Clubfoot	One in 9,000 births	March of Dimes Birth Defects Foundation, 1986a
Congenital heart defects	One in 175 births	March of Dimes Birth Defects Foundation, 1988b
Cystic fibrosis	30,000 cases—one of every 2,500 live births. 1,300 new cases each year. Five percent of population are unknowing carriers.	Cystic Fibrosis Foundation, 1993
Diabetes	13 million to 14 million cases, 7.2 million diagnosed, 6.35 million (adults) undiagnosed. 90 percent to 95 percent of cases are adult onset. 128,000 cases are children under 18. African Americans have 1 million diagnosed cases and 1 million undiagnosed; Hispanics have 1.3 million diagnosed cases. Rate is 6.1 percent in whites; 9.9 percent among African Americans. There are 500,000 to 731,000 new cases each year.	National Diabetes Information Clearing House, 1993
Dyslexia	10 percent to 15 percent of population	Hardman & Morton, 1991
Marfan syndrome	One in 10,000 births	March of Dimes Birth Defects Foundation, 1993
Multiple sclerosis	One per 1,000 people. Female to male ratio of 3:2.	Clayman, 1989
Neurofibromatoses		
NF–1	One in 3,500 births	March of Dimes Birth
NF–2	One in 50,000 births	Defects Foundation, 1992a
Parkinson's disease	1 percent of population over 65 0.4 percent of population over 40	Berkow, 1992
Phenylketonuria	One in 8,000 births	March of Dimes Birth Defects Foundation, 1986b
Rh disease	6,000 cases per year	March of Dimes Birth Defects Foundation, 1986c
Sickle cell disease	One in every 400 to 600 African Americans inherits it. Also affects people of Arab, Greek, Maltese, Italian, Sardinian, Turkish, and southern Asian ancestry.	March of Dimes Birth Defects Foundation, 1992b
Spina bifida	One in 2,000 births	March of Dimes Birth Defects Foundation, 1992c
Thalassemia	2,500 people hospitalized each year	March of Dimes Birth Defects Foundation, no date

[a]Full reference information is found in the reference list at the end of the book.

Conditions involving the respiratory system are the most prevalent group of chronic conditions. Tables 5-27 and 5-28 provide details on those who experience respiratory conditions by family income and geographic region, respectively. For most respiratory conditions, the lowest-income families have the most problems. (An exception is hay fever, which more commonly affects people with higher incomes.) People in the Northeast have fewer chronic respiratory problems than those in other parts of the United States.

Table 5-29 shows the prevalence and limitations caused by various endocrine, nutritional, and metabolic diseases, as well as the percentage of those disorders that cause limitations of activity, one or more hospitalizations, and one or more physician visits. Table 5-30 shows the number of days of restricted activity arising from several chronic conditions by age and gender of those who experience them. *Restriction of activity* is a long-term or short-term, but temporary, reduction in a person's activity below his or her normal capacity (Centers for Disease Control and Prevention, 1993e). Lung cancer, a growing American health problem, causes the most restriction on activity; heart disease, cerebrovascular disease, and emphysema also cause significant limitations. Because these diseases are related to cigarette smoking, these data serve as a reminder that the use of cigarettes is a significant national public health and economic problem. Other serious problems are orthopedic or related to the skeletal structure or the limbs, including back problems and paralysis.

TABLE 5-26 **People with Selected Chronic Conditions Who Experience Limitations in Activity: 1986–88**

Chronic Condition	Percent with Limitation in Activity
Mental retardation	83.6
Malignant neoplasms of the lung, bronchus, and other respiratory sites	75.0
Multiple sclerosis	70.2
Blindness—both eyes	61.2
Paralysis of extremities—complete or partial	57.4
Paralysis of extremities—complete	47.5
Paralysis of extremities—partial	62.8
Cerebral palsy	69.8
Other deformities or orthopedic impairments	50.0
Other selected diseases of the heart (excludes hypertension)	47.4
Emphysema	46.6
Intervertebral disc disorders	46.6
Paralysis of other sites—complete or partial	45.5
Disorders of bone or cartilage	41.1
Malignant neoplasms of stomach, intestines, colon, and rectum	39.5
Cerebrovascular disease	39.2
Malignant neoplasm of prostate	38.5
Epilepsy	35.8
Absence of lower extremities or parts of lower extremities	35.4
Orthopedic impairment of shoulder	34.7
Diabetes	33.3
Pneumoconiosis and asbestosis	32.5
Ischemic heart disease	32.2

Source: Reprinted from U.S. Bureau of the Census. (1993). *Statistical abstract of the United States: 1993* (113th ed., p. 15). Austin, TX: Reference Press.

TABLE 5-27 **Average Annual Number of Selected Chronic Respiratory Conditions and Rates, by Family Income: 1986–88**

Chronic Respiratory Condition	Annual Number (1,000)					Rate per 1,000 People				
	All Incomes	Less Than $10,000	$10,000–$19,999	$20,000–$34,999	$35,000 or More	All Incomes	Less Than $10,000	$10,000–$19,999	$20,000–$34,999	$35,000 or More
Chronic bronchitis	12,014	2,110	2,198	2,970	3,369	50.4	68.0	50.1	48.4	48.6
Emphysema	1,981	628	482	374	273	8.3	20.2	11.0	6.1	3.9
Asthma	9,736	1,775	1,704	2,241	2,815	40.8	57.2	38.8	36.6	40.6
Hay fever or allergic rhinitis without asthma	22,280	2,414	3,298	6,038	8,286	93.4	77.8	75.1	98.5	119.6
Nasal polyps	636	106	128	161	168	2.7	3.4	2.9	2.6	2.4
Chronic sinusitis	33,248	4,647	5,974	8,805	9,829	139.3	149.7	136.1	143.6	141.9
Deviated nasal septum	1,398	103	120	413	642	5.9	3.3	2.7	6.7	9.3
Chronic disease of tonsils and adenoids	3,323	524	581	977	952	13.9	16.9	13.2	15.9	13.7
Chronic laryngitis	1,493	316	250	368	462	6.3	10.2	5.7	6.0	6.7
Pleurisy	730	220	153	161	128	3.1	7.1	3.5	2.6	1.8
Pneumoconiosis and asbestosis	345	71	115	86	41[a]	1.4	2.3	2.6	1.4	0.6[a]
Malignant neoplasms of lung, bronchus, and other respiratory sites	188	79	38[a]	23[a]	20[a]	0.8	2.5	0.9[a]	0.4[a]	0.3[a]
Other diseases of the lung	1,200	232	313	336	189	5.0	7.5	7.1	5.5	2.7

Source: Reprinted from Centers for Disease Control and Prevention. (1993, February). *Prevalence of selected chronic conditions: United States, 1986–88* (p. 30). Hyattsville, MD: U.S. Public Health Service, National Center for Health Statistics.

[a]Estimate does not meet standards of reliability.

TABLE 5-28 **Average Annual Number of Selected Chronic Respiratory Conditions and Rates, by Geographic Region: 1986–88**

Chronic Respiratory Condition	Annual Number (1,000)					Rate per 1,000 People				
	All Regions	Northeast	Midwest	South	West	All Regions	Northeast	Midwest	South	West
Chronic bronchitis	12,014	2,168	3,127	4,500	2,219	50.4	43.4	53.7	55.2	45.5
Emphysema	1,981	419	491	755	316	8.3	8.4	8.4	9.3	6.5
Asthma	9,736	2,015	2,327	3,374	2,020	40.8	40.3	40.0	41.4	41.4
Hay fever or allergic rhinitis without asthma	22,280	3,921	4,745	8,079	5,535	93.4	78.4	81.5	99.1	113.4
Nasal polyps	636	88	173	225	150	2.7	1.8	3.0	2.8	3.1
Chronic sinusitis	33,248	4,507	9,900	14,109	4,731	139.3	90.1	170.0	173.0	96.9
Deviated nasal septum	1,398	391	231	449	327	5.9	7.8	4.0	5.5	6.7
Chronic disease of tonsils and adenoids	3,323	461	1,147	1,219	497	13.9	9.2	19.7	14.9	10.2
Chronic laryngitis	1,493	347	416	486	244	6.3	6.9	7.1	6.0	5.0
Pleurisy	730	82	246	289	114	3.1	1.6	4.2	3.5	2.3
Pneumoconiosis and asbestosis	345	82	64	104	94	1.4	1.6	1.1	1.3	1.9
Malignant neoplasms of lung, bronchus, and other respiratory sites	188	45[a]	50[a]	70	23[a]	0.8	0.9[a]	0.9[a]	0.9	0.5[a]
Other diseases of the lung	1,200	158	339	465	238	5.0	3.2	5.8	5.7	4.9

Source: Reprinted from Centers for Disease Control and Prevention. (1993, February). *Prevalence of selected chronic conditions: United States, 1986–88* (p. 31). Hyattsville, MD: U.S. Public Health Service, National Center for Health Statistics.

[a]Estimate does not meet standards of reliability.

TABLE 5-29 **Average Annual Number of Selected Chronic Endocrine, Nutritional, and Metabolic Diseases and Immunity Disorders; Diseases of the Blood and Blood-Forming Organs; and Genitourinary Conditions; Rates per 1,000 People, by Age; and Percentage of Conditions Causing Activity Limitation, Hospitalization, and Physician Visits: 1986–88**

Condition	Number (1,000)	Rate per 1,000 People						Percent Experiencing		
		All Ages	Under 18 Years	18–44 Years	45–64 Years	65–74 Years	75 Years and Over	Limitation of Activity	1 or More Hospitalizations	1 or More Physician Visits
Endocrine, nutritional, and metabolic diseases and immunity disorders										
Gout	2,193	9.2	a,b	2.8	22.5	31.8	31.4	10.0	6.4	92.6
Goiter	415	1.7	0.3a	1.3	3.1	3.5a	5.3a	8.7b	14.5b	97.6
Other diseases of the thyroid	2,905	12.2	1.0	8.6	25.3	30.1	28.3	8.2	12.9	99.3
Diabetes	6,486	27.2	2.2	9.9	58.2	95.2	98.1	33.3	29.9	100.0
Diseases of the blood and blood-forming organs										
Anemias	3,460	14.5	8.4	17.3	11.8	18.1	29.3	4.5	11.4	98.2
Genitourinary conditions										
Kidney stones	1,213	5.1	0.4a	5.3	8.4	10.8	7.2	4.3b	60.5	97.6
Kidney infections	1,559	6.5	2.2	8.1	7.3	7.5	12.1	4.4	30.5	98.8
Other kidney trouble, not elsewhere classified	762	3.2	1.0	2.1	4.6	7.5	12.9	24.3	40.6	97.5
Bladder infections	1,692	7.1	1.9	8.0	9.8	10.8	11.7	2.0b	14.4	99.0
Other disorders of bladder	1,742	7.3	1.6	5.2	9.9	17.3	33.7	5.4	20.8	94.7
Diseases of prostate	1,411	5.9	a,b	2.1	10.5	28.0	22.1	5.5	38.8	98.1
Inflammatory disease of female genital organs	367	1.5	0.1a	3.2	0.4a	0.5a	0.3a	2.5b	28.1	98.9
Noninflammatory disease of female genital organs	1,038	4.4	0.3a	7.8	4.4	0.9a	0.4a	3.0b	38.0	100.0
Menstrual disorders	1,972	8.3	2.5	15.9	4.1	0.2a	a,b	0.5b	10.7	87.1
Other diseases of female genital organs	1,971	8.3	2.5	12.8	8.3	5.0	3.8a	5.1	23.2	90.7
Female trouble, not otherwise specified	136	0.6	a,b	0.9	0.6a	0.7a	0.4a	14.0b	27.9b	97.1
Malignant neoplasm of breast	623	2.6	a,b	0.8	5.0	9.3	14.2	16.1	82.5	100.0
Malignant neoplasm of female genital organs	222	0.9	a,b	1.1	1.5	2.1a	0.4a	27.9	45.9	100.0
Malignant neoplasm of prostate	205	0.9	a,b	a,b	1.4	5.4	4.6a	38.5	69.3	100.0
Benign neoplasm of breast	86	0.4	a,b	0.4a	0.3a	1.2a	0.7a	a,b	33.7b	100.0
Benign neoplasm of female genital organs	658	2.8	a,b	4.2	4.5	1.1a	0.8a	2.1b	45.0	100.0

Source: Reprinted from Centers for Disease Control and Prevention. (1993, February). *Prevalence of selected chronic conditions: United States, 1986–88* (p. 52). Hyattsville, MD: U.S. Public Health Service, National Center for Health Statistics.

aNumbers too small to compute a rate.

bEstimate does not meet standards of reliability.

Chronic Condition	All Persons		Age				Gender			
			Under 65 Years		65 Years and Over		Male		Female	
	Number of Days (1,000)	Days per Condition	Number of Days (1,000)	Days per Condition	Number of Days (1,000)	Days per Condition	Number of Days (1,000)	Days per Condition	Number of Days (1,000)	Days per Condition
Circulatory condition										
Heart disease	338,541	17.4	157,624	14.0	180,917	22.1	173,602	19.4	164,939	15.7
Ischemic heart disease	173,129	24.1	100,161	30.3	72,968	18.8	101,959	24.1	71,170	24.0
Heart rhythm disorders	29,777	3.9	17,083	3.0	12,694[a]	6.1[a]	4,622[a]	1.7[a]	25,155	5.1
Other selected diseases of the heart (excludes hypertension)	127,871	33.0	37,664	21.0	90,208	43.4	62,403	38.5	65,468	29.1
Rheumatic fever with or without heart disease	15,487	8.9	10,111[a]	7.5[a]	5,376[a]	13.6[a]	4,139[a]	7.8[a]	11,349[a]	9.3[a]
High blood pressure (hypertension)	116,934	4.1	66,347	3.6	50,587	4.7	48,905	3.9	68,030	4.2
Cerebrovascular disease	98,261	36.7	25,644	24.4	72,617	44.6	49,384	39.5	48,877	34.2
Hardening of the arteries	42,155	16.4	12,644[a]	14.5[a]	29,512	17.3	25,769	19.2	16,386	13.2
Poor circulation	18,099	19.1	4,851[a]	12.1[a]	13,248[a]	24.3	6,000[a]	16.9[a]	12,099[a]	20.5[a]
Respiratory condition										
Chronic bronchitis	58,725	4.9	42,976	4.2	15,750	8.4	22,999	4.7	35,726	5.0
Emphysema	55,010	27.8	22,674	26.3	32,336	28.9	33,894	26.9	21,116	29.2
Asthma	88,742	9.1	65,029	7.6	23,713	20.6	36,783	7.9	51,959	10.2
Hay fever or allergic rhinitis without asthma	30,000	1.3	24,865	1.2	5,135[a]	2.6[a]	11,298[a]	1.1[a]	18,701	1.6
Chronic sinusitis	51,651	1.6	46,411	1.6	5,240[a]	1.1[a]	13,284[a]	1.0[a]	38,367	2.0
Malignant neoplasms of lung, bronchus, and other respiratory sites	16,563	88.1	6,782[a]	92.9[a]	9,781[a]	85.1[a]	12,964[a]	111.8[a]	3,599[a]	50.0[a]
Other diseases of the lung	27,902	23.3	15,985	17.9	11,916[a]	39.2[a]	10,652[a]	21.8	17,249	24.2
Digestive condition										
Ulcer, gastric, duodenal, and/or peptic	29,224	6.8	23,372	6.7	5,852[a]	6.9[a]	13,205[a]	6.7[a]	16,019	6.9
Hernia of abdominal cavity	36,786	7.9	28,122	9.6	8,664[a]	5.1[a]	22,754	9.7	14,032	6.1
Gastritis and duodenitis	14,328	5.1	12,918[a]	5.8[a]	1,410[a]	2.3[a]	6,436[a]	5.9[a]	7,892[a]	4.5[a]
Enteritis and colitis	19,135	8.3	14,042	8.0	5,093[a]	9.4[a]	2,954[a]	4.2[a]	16,181	10.1
Impairment										
Blindness and other visual impairments	34,986	4.3	22,248	3.9	12,739[a]	5.2[a]	11,938[a]	2.4[a]	23,048	6.9
Absence of extremities or parts of extremities (excluding absence of tips of fingers or toes only)	21,086	12.7	10,764[a]	10.3[a]	10,322[a]	16.7[a]	14,669	11.2	6,417[a]	18.0[a]
Absence of bone, joint, muscle of extremity	14,274	23.6	3,537[a]	11.0[a]	10,737[a]	38.3[a]	3,024[a]	9.9[a]	11,250[a]	37.5[a]
Paralysis of extremities, complete or partial	42,778	31.2	27,741	29.6	15,038	34.6	23,332	30.6	19,446	31.9

Condition										
Paralysis of extremities, complete	18,901	39.2	16,234	45.1	2,668[a]	21.9[a]	14,472	54.6	4,430[a]	20.3[a]
Paralysis of extremities, partial	23,877	26.9	11,507[a]	20.0[a]	12,370[a]	39.5[a]	8,861[a]	17.8[a]	15,016	38.4
Deformities or orthopedic impairments, total	416,479	13.1	329,094	12.6	87,385	15.6	200,533	13.1	215,946	13.1
Deformities or orthopedic impairments of back	195,289	12.3	156,433	11.7	38,856	15.5	87,910	12.9	107,380	11.8
Curvature or other deformity of back or spine	39,152	8.2	36,530	9.4	2,621[a]	3.0[a]	16,268	11.1	22,884	6.9
Deformities or orthopedic impairments of upper extremities	62,292	19.5	54,342	20.7	7,950[a]	14.1[a]	36,533	20.6	25,759	18.2
Orthopedic impairment of shoulder	48,358	22.4	42,406	23.3	5,952[a]	17.8[a]	30,573	24.4	17,785	19.7
Deformities or orthopedic impairments of lower extremities	153,541	12.5	114,285	11.6	39,256	16.0	73,209	11.2	80,333	13.9
Condition of nervous system and sense organs										
Cataracts	24,510	4.4	7,466[a]	6.5[a]	17,044	3.9	10,298[a]	5.6[a]	14,213	3.8
Epilepsy	20,048	17.4	20,048	18.9		[a]	11,631[a]	22.8[a]	8,418[a]	13.1[a]
Migraine headache	46,758	5.3	42,046	5.1	4,712[a]	9.1[a]	12,747[a]	5.7[a]	34,011	5.2
Other headache (excludes tension headache)	34,493	3.9	31,439	4.0	3,054[a]	3.3[a]	11,857[a]	4.5[a]	22,636	3.7

Source: Reprinted from Centers for Disease Control and Prevention. (1993, February). *Prevalence of selected chronic conditions: United States, 1986–88* (p. 60). Hyattsville, MD: U.S. Public Health Service, National Center for Health Statistics.

[a]Numbers too small to compute a rate.

Additional information on the social costs of disabilities is provided in Table 5-31. It shows the numbers of days of disability by characteristics of those who are disabled from 1970 through 1990. Women, in general, had more days of disability than men; older people more than younger; Southerners more than people in other regions; and African Americans more than white people. Disability is also associated with income. Those with lower incomes appear to have more days of disability than those with higher incomes. Part of the explanation for the differences may be the nature of low-income work, which in some cases is more potentially disabling than white collar or technical work.

Tables 5-32 and 5-33 provide some historical information on acute and chronic condi-

TABLE 5-31 Days of Disability, by Selected Characteristics: Selected Years, 1970 to 1990

Characteristic	Total Days of Disability (millions)						Days per Person					
	1970	1980	1985	1988	1989	1990	1970	1980	1985	1988	1989	1990
Restricted-activity days[a]	2,913	4,165	3,453	3,536	3,693	3,669	14.6	19.1	14.8	14.7	15.2	14.9
Male	1,273	1,802	1,442	1,487	1,558	1,558	13.2	17.1	12.8	12.7	13.2	13.1
Female	1,640	2,363	2,011	2,049	2,135	2,111	15.8	21.0	16.6	16.5	17.0	16.7
White[b]	2,526	3,518	2,899	2,969	3,087	3,057	14.4	18.7	14.5	14.6	15.0	14.8
Black[b]	365	580	489	487	511	536	16.2	22.7	17.4	16.6	17.1	17.7
Hispanic[c]	—	—	228	253	278	—	—	—	13.2	13.0	13.2	—
Under 65 years	2,331	3,228	2,557	2,657	2,774	2,734	12.9	16.6	12.4	12.5	12.9	12.6
65 years and over	582	937	895	879	919	936	30.7	39.2	33.1	30.6	31.5	31.4
Northeast	709	862	689	667	669	656	14.5	17.9	13.8	13.5	13.7	13.2
Midwest	691	989	744	762	812	836	12.4	17.2	12.7	12.8	13.6	14.0
South	996	1,415	1,308	1,328	1,392	1,404	15.9	19.8	16.3	16.1	16.7	16.7
West	518	899	712	779	820	773	15.6	22.0	15.7	15.6	15.8	14.8
Family income												
Under $10,000	—	—	893	754	694	662	—	—	25.8	26.6	26.5	27.3
$10,000 to $19,999	—	—	781	751	768	758	—	—	16.7	17.8	18.7	19.1
$20,000 to $34,999	—	—	791	734	752	715	—	—	12.1	12.3	13.3	13.5
$35,000 or more	—	—	568	726	798	912	—	—	9.9	9.7	9.9	10.3
Bed-disability days[d]	1,222	1,520	1,436	1,519	1,579	1,521	6.1	7.0	6.1	6.3	6.5	6.2
Male	503	616	583	607	652	625	5.2	5.9	5.2	5.2	5.5	5.2
Female	720	904	852	912	927	896	6.9	8.0	7.1	7.3	7.4	7.1
Under 65 years	959	1,190	1,064	1,107	1,164	1,115	5.3	6.1	5.1	5.2	5.4	5.2
65 years and over	263	330	371	412	415	406	13.8	13.8	13.7	14.4	14.2	13.6
Work-loss days[e]	417	485	575	609	659	621	5.4	5.0	5.3	5.3	5.6	5.3
Male	243	271	287	307	322	303	5.0	4.9	4.8	4.8	5.0	4.7
Female	175	215	288	302	337	319	5.9	5.1	6.0	5.8	6.4	5.9
School-loss days[f]	222	204	217	222	260	212	4.9	5.3	4.8	4.9	5.7	4.6
Male	108	95	100	107	129	100	4.7	4.8	4.4	4.6	5.6	4.3
Female	114	109	117	115	131	112	5.1	5.7	5.3	5.2	5.9	5.0

Notes: Beginning in 1985, the levels of estimates may not be comparable to estimates for 1970–80 because the later data are based on a revised questionnaire and field procedures. Data are based on the National Health Interview Survey. — = not available.

Source: Reprinted from U.S. Bureau of the Census. (1993). *Statistical abstract of the United States: 1993* (113th ed., p. 132). Austin, TX: Reference Press.

[a]A day when a person cuts down on his or her activities for more than half a day because of illness or injury; includes bed-disability, work-loss, and school-loss days. Total includes other races and unknown income, not shown separately.

[b]Beginning in 1980, race was determined by asking the household respondent to report his or her race. In earlier years the racial classification of respondents was determined by interviewer observation.

[c]People of Hispanic origin may be of any race.

[d]A day when a person stayed in bed more than half a day because of illness or injury; includes those work loss and school loss days actually spent in bed.

[e]A day when a person lost more than half a workday because of illness or injury. Computed for people 17 years of age and over (beginning in 1985, 18 years of age and older) in the currently employed population, defined as those who were working or had a job or business from which they were not on layoff during the two-week period preceding the week of interview.

[f]Child's loss of more than half a school day because of illness or injury. Computed for children 6 to 16 years old and, beginning in 1985, children 5 to 17 years old.

TABLE 5-32 Acute Conditions, by Type, Selected Years, 1970 to 1990, and by Selected Characteristics, 1990

Year and Characteristic	Number of Conditions (million)					Rate per 100 Population				
	Infective and Parasitic	Respiratory		Digestive System	Injuries	Infective and Parasitic	Respiratory		Digestive System	Injuries
		Common Cold	Influenza				Common Cold	Influenza		
1970	48.2	—	—	23.0	59.2	24.1	—	—	11.5	29.6
1975	47.6	—	—	21.6	76.2	22.8	—	—	10.3	36.4
1980	53.6	—	—	24.9	72.7	24.6	—	—	11.4	33.4
1985	47.8	—	—	16.3	64.0	20.5	—	—	7.0	27.4
1990, total[a]	51.7	61.5	106.8	13.0	60.1	21.0	25.0	43.4	5.3	24.4
Under 5 years old	10.5	12.6	11.5	0.8	5.3	54.8	65.8	60.3	4.2	27.6
5 to 17 years old	19.7	14.7	28.2	3.3	13.5	43.3	32.2	61.8	7.3	29.7
18 to 24 years old	5.3	6.8	11.6	1.7	7.2	21.2	27.2	46.3	6.6	28.8
25 to 44 years old	10.2	16.3	34.5	3.9	20.1	12.7	20.3	43.0	4.9	25.2
45 to 64 years old	3.8	6.5	15.4	2.0	9.3	8.2	14.0	33.0	4.3	19.9
65 years old and over	2.1	4.6	5.7	1.3	4.7	7.2	15.4	19.3	4.4	15.9
Male	22.1	26.9	46.4	5.4	33.6	18.5	22.5	38.9	4.6	28.1
Female	29.6	34.6	60.4	7.6	26.6	23.3	27.3	47.7	6.0	21.0
White	44.4	51.2	95.8	10.4	52.8	21.4	24.7	46.3	5.0	25.5
Black	6.1	8.1	7.3	2.1	5.9	20.2	26.8	24.1	6.8	19.5
Northeast	10.2	13.9	15.2	2.0	10.3	20.5	27.8	30.5	4.1	20.6
Midwest	10.3	13.3	32.7	3.2	15.5	17.2	22.3	54.7	5.4	26.0
South	23.2	18.3	25.4	4.7	21.6	27.5	21.7	30.2	5.6	25.7
West	8.0	16.0	33.4	3.1	12.7	15.3	30.6	64.1	5.9	24.3
Family income										
Under $10,000	5.6	7.9	10.8	1.6	6.7	23.0	32.5	44.4	6.8	27.4
$10,000 to $19,999	7.9	10.3	18.0	2.0	9.8	19.8	25.9	45.3	5.1	24.6
$20,000 to $34,999	10.3	12.4	23.5	2.7	13.5	19.4	23.3	44.3	5.2	25.5
$35,000 or more	21.0	23.3	40.3	5.0	21.2	23.7	26.4	45.5	5.6	23.9

Notes: Estimates include only acute conditions that were medically attended or caused at least one day of restricted activity. Figures are based on the National Health Interview Survey. — = not available.

Source: Reprinted from U.S. Bureau of the Census. (1993). *Statistical abstract of the United States: 1993* (113th ed., p. 135). Austin, TX: Reference Press.

[a]Includes other races and unknown income not shown separately.

TABLE 5-33 **Prevalence of Selected Reported Chronic Conditions, by Age and Gender: 1980 and 1990**

Chronic Condition	1980 Conditions (1,000)	1980 Rate[a]	1990, Conditions (1,000)	Male Under 45 Years	Male 45–64 Years	Male 65–74 Years	Male 75 Years and Over	Female Under 45 Years	Female 45–64 Years	Female 65–74 Years	Female 75 Years and Over
Arthritis	27,773	127.4	30,833	25.8	204.9	373.3	376.8	35.8	289.7	472.2	628.6
Dermatitis, including eczema	9,139	41.9	8,681	28.2	21.9	22.7	24.4[b]	42.1	50.9	41.6	38.2
Trouble with											
Dry (itching) skin	3,698[c]	16.3[c]	5,045	12.9	19.7	30.6	30.4[b]	20.7	25.3	46.4	39.5
Ingrown nails	4,503[c]	19.8[c]	6,040	20.1	33.0	34.3	45.7	14.9	35.0	56.2	61.6
Corns and calluses	4,811[c]	21.2[c]	4,931	10.0	22.7	23.0	28.6[b]	13.7	41.9	65.1	59.9
Visual impairments	7,984	36.6	7,525	30.3	49.5	73.3	109.8	11.7	28.4	33.9	104.5
Cataracts	5,124[c]	22.6[c]	5,927	1.2[b]	17.4	81.2	129.4	2.5	26.3	137.2	271.0
Hearing impairments	17,370	79.7	23,296	49.7	197.8	350.1	480.2	29.6	106.0	194.9	370.3
Tinnitus	5,130[c]	22.6[c]	7,149	12.6	59.6	101.3	92.3	9.8	48.2	88.4	87.2
Deformities or orthopedic impairments	18,504	84.9	28,899	92.4	151.4	152.3	121.1	98.2	170.8	181.0	220.9
Ulcer	3,891[c]	17.1[c]	4,466	11.0	31.6	38.3	38.1	14.3	25.8	29.2	29.9
Hernia of abdominal cavity	4,970[c]	21.9[c]	4,179	6.7	35.1	42.7	79.3	6.4	24.0	56.5	60.4
Frequent indigestion	5,360[c]	23.6[c]	5,770	16.6	36.5	29.2	46.4	18.9	29.1	57.0	30.6
Frequent constipation	4,431[c]	19.5[c]	3,991	4.9	5.6[b]	17.3[b]	55.1	15.5	22.3	47.3	100.2
Diabetes	5,665	26.0	6,232	5.6	48.6	102.0	86.3	7.4	52.1	102.3	75.9
Migraine	5,630	25.8	9,790	20.9	23.9	4.7[b]	0.7[b]	55.8	87.3	37.0	28.9
Heart conditions	16,434	75.4	19,307	27.3	137.4	275.2	404.8	34.2	101.5	242.5	292.3
High blood pressure (hypertension)	24,919	114.3	27,129	38.1	221.9	285.0	304.2	32.3	215.1	409.8	444.1
Varicose veins of lower extremities	5,930	27.2	6,976	4.8	27.5	27.5	59.7	25.8	73.6	99.5	98.7
Hemorrhoids	8,616	39.5	9,446	22.7	71.1	53.4	32.7[b]	28.9	70.8	73.4	60.8
Chronic bronchitis	7,869	36.1	12,584	40.4	31.6	62.0	50.5	51.7	81.1	87.8	67.8
Asthma	6,803	31.2	10,311	43.4	28.8	28.6	44.3	44.1	47.7	35.6	41.2
Hay fever, allergic rhinitis without asthma	17,433	80.0	22,187	89.1	80.6	65.1	67.6	96.3	108.4	83.5	49.0
Chronic sinusitis	31,956	145.0	32,314	99.9	162.7	132.2	145.5	127.7	199.5	171.7	149.6

Note: Data are based on the National Health Interview Survey.

Source: Reprinted from U.S. Bureau of the Census. (1993). *Statistical abstract of the United States: 1993* (113th ed., p. 135). Austin, TX: Reference Press.

[a]Conditions per 1,000 people.

[b]Figure does not meet standards of reliability or precision.

[c]1982 data.

tions. Increases in the incidence of many of the conditions result in part from the older average age of the population in 1990 than in 1980.

Other Health Issues

Tobacco

The American Cancer Society (1993) called smoking the most preventable cause of death in the United States. It is associated with 400,000 deaths each year and is responsible for 87 percent of lung cancers. Other forms of tobacco such as snuff and chewing tobacco, which are used by 12 million Americans, also dramatically increase the risk of cancer and other diseases.

Table 5-34 shows changes in cigarette use from 1965 through 1991. Smoking rates ap-

TABLE 5-34 **Percentages of Current Cigarette Smokers, by Gender, Age, and Race: Selected Years, 1965 to 1991**

Gender, Age, and Race	1965	1974	1979	1983	1985	1987	1988	1990	1991
Total smokers, 18 years old and over	42.4	37.1	33.5	32.1	30.1	28.8	28.1	25.5	25.6
Male, total	51.9	43.1	37.5	35.1	32.6	31.2	30.8	28.4	28.1
18 to 24 years	54.1	42.1	35.0	32.9	28.0	28.2	25.5	26.6	23.5
25 to 34 years	60.7	50.5	43.9	38.8	38.2	34.8	36.2	31.6	32.8
35 to 44 years	58.2	51.0	41.8	41.0	37.6	36.6	36.5	34.5	33.1
45 to 64 years	51.9	42.6	39.3	35.9	33.4	33.5	31.3	29.3	29.3
65 years and over	28.5	24.8	20.9	22.0	19.6	17.2	18.0	14.6	15.1
White, total	51.1	41.9	36.8	34.5	31.7	30.5	30.1	28.0	27.4
18 to 24 years	53.0	40.8	34.3	32.5	28.4	29.2	26.7	27.4	25.1
25 to 34 years	60.1	49.5	43.6	38.6	37.3	33.8	35.4	31.6	32.1
35 to 44 years	57.3	50.1	41.3	40.8	36.6	36.2	35.8	33.5	32.1
45 to 64 years	51.3	41.2	38.3	35.0	32.1	32.4	30.0	28.7	28.0
65 years and over	27.7	24.3	20.5	20.6	18.9	16.0	16.9	13.7	13.7
Black, total	60.4	54.3	44.1	40.6	39.9	39.0	36.5	32.5	35.0
18 to 24 years	62.8	54.9	40.2	34.2	27.2	24.9	18.6	21.3	15.0
25 to 34 years	68.4	58.5	47.5	39.9	45.6	44.9	41.6	33.8	39.4
35 to 44 years	67.3	61.5	48.6	45.5	45.0	44.0	42.5	42.0	44.4
45 to 64 years	57.9	57.8	50.0	44.8	46.1	44.3	43.2	36.7	42.0
65 years and over	36.4	29.7	26.2	38.9	27.7	30.3	29.8	21.5	24.3
Female, total	33.9	32.1	29.9	29.5	27.9	26.5	25.7	22.8	23.5
18 to 24 years	38.1	34.1	33.8	35.5	30.4	26.1	26.3	22.5	22.4
25 to 34 years	43.7	38.8	33.7	32.6	32.0	31.8	31.3	28.2	28.4
35 to 44 years	43.7	39.8	37.0	33.8	31.5	29.6	27.8	24.8	27.6
45 to 64 years	32.0	33.4	30.7	31.0	29.9	28.6	27.7	24.8	24.6
65 years and over	9.6	12.0	13.2	13.1	13.5	13.7	12.8	11.5	12.0
White, total	34.0	31.7	30.1	29.4	27.7	26.7	25.7	23.4	23.7
18 to 24 years	38.4	34.0	34.5	36.5	31.8	27.8	27.5	25.4	25.1
25 to 34 years	43.4	38.6	34.1	32.2	32.0	31.9	31.0	28.5	28.4
35 to 44 years	43.9	39.3	37.2	34.8	31.0	29.2	28.3	25.0	27.0
45 to 64 years	32.7	33.0	30.6	30.6	29.7	29.0	27.7	25.4	25.3
65 years and over	9.8	12.3	13.8	13.2	13.3	13.9	12.6	11.5	12.1
Black, total	33.7	36.4	31.1	32.2	31.0	28.0	27.8	21.2	24.4
18 to 24 years	37.1	35.6	31.8	32.0	23.7	20.4	21.8	10.0	11.8
25 to 34 years	47.8	42.2	35.2	38.0	36.2	35.8	37.2	29.1	32.4
35 to 44 years	42.8	46.4	37.7	32.7	40.2	35.3	27.6	25.5	35.3
45 to 64 years	25.7	38.9	34.2	36.3	33.4	28.4	29.5	22.6	23.4
65 years and over	7.1	8.9	8.5	13.1	14.5	11.7	14.8	11.1	9.6

Notes: A current smoker is a person who has smoked at least 100 cigarettes and who now smokes; includes occasional smokers and excludes unknown smoking status.

Source: Reprinted from U.S. Bureau of the Census. (1993). *Statistical abstract of the United States: 1993* (113th ed., p. 138). Austin, TX: Reference Press.

pear to have decreased over the years, except in 1991. In some age groups, smoking rates among African Americans have increased. The smoking rate among women has not declined as much as for other groups.

Reportable Diseases

Federal and state laws require the reporting of certain health conditions, which are listed in Table 5-35. Rabies and tuberculosis have shown significant recent increases. Chicken pox and measles have declined dramatically. The incidence of sexually transmitted diseases is of special importance because it is associated with AIDS; the increase in conditions such as gonorrhea and syphilis may be related to the increases in HIV infection and AIDS.

TABLE 5-35 **Cases of Specified Reportable Diseases: Selected Years, 1970 to 1991**

Disease	1970	1980	1984	1985	1986	1987	1988	1989	1990	1991
AIDS[a]	—	—	4,445	8,249	13,166	21,070	31,001	33,722	41,595	43,672
Amebiasis	2,888	5,271	5,252	4,433	3,532	3,123	2,860	3,217	3,328	2,989
Aseptic meningitis	6,480	8,028	8,326	10,619	11,374	11,487	7,234	10,274	11,852	14,526
Chickenpox (1,000)	[b]	190.9	222.0	178.2	183.2	213.2	192.9	185.4	173.1	147.1
Encephalitis										
Primary infectious[c]	1,580	1,362	1,257	1,376	1,302	1,418	882	981	1,341	1,021
Post infectious[c]	370	40	108	161	124	121	121	88	105	82
Haemophilius influenza	[b]	[b]	[b]	[b]	[b]	[b]	[b]	[b]	[b]	2,764
Hepatitis										
B (serum) (1,000)	8.3	19.0	26.1	26.6	26.1	25.9	23.2	23.4	21.1	18.0
A (infectious) (1,000)	56.8	29.1	22.0	23.2	23.4	25.3	28.5	35.8	31.4	24.4
Unspecified (1,000)	[b]	11.9	5.5	5.5	3.9	3.1	2.5	2.3	1.7	1.3
Non-A, non-B (1,000)	[b]	[b]	3.9	4.2	3.6	3.0	2.6	2.5	2.6	3.6
Legionellosis	[b]	[b]	750	830	948	1,038	1,085	1,190	1,370	1,317
Lyme disease	[b]	[b]	[b]	[b]	[b]	[b]	[b]	[b]	[b]	9,465
Malaria	3,051	2,062	1,007	1,049	1,123	944	1,099	1,277	1,292	1,278
Measles (1,000)	47.4	13.5	2.6	2.8	6.3	3.7	3.4	18.2	27.8	9.6
Meningococcal infections	2,505	2,840	2,746	2,479	2,594	2,930	2,964	2,727	2,451	2,130
Mumps (1,000)	105.0	8.6	3.0	3.0	7.8	12.8	4.9	5.7	5.3	4.3
Pertussis (1,000)	4.2	1.7	2.3	3.6	4.2	2.8	3.5	4.2	4.6	2.7
Rabies, animal	3,224	6,421	5,567	5,565	5,504	4,658	4,651	4,724	4,826	6,910
Rubella (1,000)	56.6	3.9	1.0	0.6	0.6	0.3	0.2	0.4	1.1	1.4
Salmonellosis[d] (1,000)	22.1	33.7	40.9	65.3	50.0	50.9	48.9	47.8	48.6	48.2
Shigellosis (1,000)	13.8	19.0	17.4	17.1	17.1	23.9	30.6	25.0	27.1	23.5
Tuberculosis[e] (1,000)	37.1	27.7	22.3	22.2	22.8	22.5	22.4	23.5	25.7	26.3
Venereal diseases (civilian cases)										
Gonorrhea (1,000)	600	1,004	879	911	901	781	720	733	690	620
Syphilis (1,000)	91	69	70	68	68	87	103	111	134	129
Other (1,000)	2.2	1.0	1.0	2.3	4.2	5.3	5.2	4.9	4.6	4.0

Notes: For diseases with 1,000 or more cases reported in 1991. Figures should be interpreted with caution. Although reporting of some of these diseases is incomplete, the figures are of value in indicating trends of disease incidence. Includes cases imported from outside the United States. — = not available.

Source: Reprinted from U.S. Bureau of the Census. (1993). *Statistical abstract of the United States: 1993* (113th ed., p. 137). Austin, TX: Reference Press.

[a]AIDS (acquired immune deficiency syndrome) was not a notifiable disease until 1984. Figures are shown for years in which cases were reported to the Centers for Disease Control and Prevention.

[b]Disease was not notifiable.

[c]Beginning in 1980, reported data reflect new diagnostic categories.

[d]Excludes typhoid fever.

[e]Newly reported active cases. New diagnostic standards were introduced in 1980.

Sexuality-Related Health Issues

In addition to sexually transmitted diseases, other issues related to sexuality are of concern to social workers. According to the Alan Guttmacher Institute (1993), 50 percent of unmarried women and 60 percent of unmarried men between the ages of 15 and 19 have had sexual intercourse. By age 19, 75 percent of women and 86 percent of men have had intercourse. Sexual activity is becoming more common in younger age groups than it was even 12 years ago. In 1982, for example, 19 percent of unmarried women age 15 had had intercourse; by 1988, the figure was 27 percent. About 56 percent of 17-year-old men had had intercourse in 1979; in 1988, 72 percent had. Although African Americans and Hispanics are sexually active at a younger age than white Americans, most of the increase in sexual activity among female teenagers was in white, upper-income families, so the ethnic and socioeconomic differences are narrowing (Alan Guttmacher Institute, 1993).

Contraception. Condoms are used as a means of contraception primarily by the sexual partners of teenagers and unmarried women. Birth control pills are most commonly used by women who hope to have children in the future, by unmarried women, and by women under age 25. Married women and white women are more likely than other groups to rely on their partners' vasectomies. Table 5-36 lists contraceptive methods used by women in the United States (Alan Guttmacher Institute, 1993).

Abortion. The Alan Guttmacher Institute (1993) reported that about 27 abortions per 1,000 women are performed in the United States each year. Three percent of women in the childbearing years (ages 15 to 44) have abortions each year. About 40 percent of teen pregnancies end in abortion; one-quarter of abortions are provided to women under age 20. Although white women have about 65 percent of all abortions, the nonwhite abortion rate is more than twice that of the white rate. Hispanic women are 60 percent more likely to have abortions than non-Hispanic women. Roman Catholic women are 30 percent more likely to have abortions than Protestant women; Jewish women are less likely to have them.

About 16,000 women have abortions each year because their pregnancies were the result of rape or incest, 1 percent had abortions because they had been told that the fetus had a health defect, and 12 percent had an abortion because they feared that the child may have had such a defect. Seventy percent of women who have abortions intend to have children in the future (Alan Guttmacher Institute, 1993).

TABLE 5-36 Contraceptive Methods Used by Women, by Type: 1988

Method	Number of Users (1,000)	Percentage of Contraception Users
Sterilization	13,686	39.2
Tubal ligation	9,617	27.5
Vasectomy	4,069	11.7
Pill	10,734	30.7
Condom	5,093	14.6
Diaphragm	2,000	5.7
Periodic abstinence	806	2.3
Withdrawal	778	2.2
IUD	703	2.0
Spermicides	637	1.8
Sponge	399	1.1
Other methods	76	0.4
Total	34,912	100.0

Note: IUD = intrauterine device.

Source: Reprinted from Alan Guttmacher Institute. (1993). *Facts in brief: Contraceptive use, abortion in the United States, teenage sexual and reproductive behavior* (p. 1). New York: Author.

Organ Transplants

Table 5-37 shows the number of organ transplants and grafts performed between 1981 and 1991. The most common procedures were bone and cornea grafts, followed by kidney transplants. The table shows the number of people awaiting transplants; despite awareness of the need for organs, relatively few are donated each year.

TABLE 5-37 **Organ Transplantations and Grafts, by Centers, People Waiting, and One-Year Survival Rates: Selected Years, 1981 to 1991**

Procedure	Number of Procedures							Number of Centers		Number of People Waiting, 1991	1-Year Survival Rates, 1990 (%)
	1981	1985	1987	1988	1989	1990	1991	1981	1991		
Transplant											
Heart	62	719	1,512	1,647	1,673	1,998	2,125	8	156	2,267	82[a]
Liver	26	602	1,199	1,680	2,160	2,534	2,954	1	93	1,679	74[a]
Kidney	4,883	7,695	8,967	9,123	8,890	9,433	9,949	157	237	19,416	93[a]
Heart–lung	5	30	41	74	67	52	51	—	84	155	53[a]
Lung	0	2	11	31	89	187	401	—	79	678	54[a]
Pancreas/ Islet cell	—	130	180	243	413	529	532	—	89	602	89[a]
Cornea grafts	15,500	26,300	35,930	36,900	38,464	40,631	41,393	—	108[b]	5,083	95[c]
Bone grafts	—	—	250,000	300,000	—	350,000	375,000	—	34	—	—
Skin grafts	—	—	5,000	5,200	—	5,500	5,200	—	25	—	—

Notes: Numbers are based on reports of procurement programs and transplant centers in the United States. — = not available.

Source: Reprinted from the U.S. Bureau of the Census. (1993). *Statistical abstract of the United States: 1993* (113th ed., p. 127). Austin, TX: Reference Press.

[a]One-year patient survival rates for transplants performed between October 1, 1987, and December 31, 1989.

[b]Eye banks.

[c]Success rate.

Health Maintenance

Health experts have identified six behaviors that appear to reduce illness and increase the health of those who follow all or most of them. The six practices are to eat breakfast, avoid snacking, exercise regularly, drink alcohol only moderately, avoid smoking, and maintain one's weight at a satisfactory level. Table 5-38 identifies the six characteristics and the percentage of the U.S. population that follow these guidelines. By and large, only a small percentage follow all six; eating breakfast is the only practice adopted by more than half the population.

TABLE 5-38 **Personal Health Practices, by Selected Characteristics: 1990**

		Percentage Who					
Characteristic	Total Persons (1,000)	Ate Breakfast[a]	Rarely Snacked	Exercised Regularly[b]	Had Two or More Drinks on Any Day[c]	Were Current Smoker	Were 20 Percent or More Above Weight[d]
All persons[e]	181,447	56.4	25.5	40.7	5.5	25.5	27.5
Gender							
Male	86,278	54.6	25.6	44.0	9.7	28.4	29.6
Female	95,169	58.0	25.4	37.7	1.7	22.8	25.6
Race							
White	155,301	57.8	25.8	41.5	5.8	25.6	26.7
Black	20,248	46.9	22.7	34.3	4.3	26.2	38.0
Hispanic origin							
Hispanic	14,314	52.5	29.3	34.9	4.6	23.0	27.6
Non-Hispanic	166,599	56.7	25.2	41.2	5.6	25.7	27.5
Marital status							
Currently married	117,413	57.8	25.3	39.4	5.3	24.6	29.2
Formerly married	30,439	61.5	31.2	34.3	5.3	30.3	29.1
Never married	33,413	46.9	20.9	51.3	6.6	24.3	19.8
Education level							
Less than 12 years	38,367	58.6	26.9	25.9	5.1	31.8	32.7
12 years	69,405	52.6	24.0	37.0	5.9	29.6	28.6
More than 12 years	73,244	58.8	26.4	52.1	5.4	18.3	23.8
Income							
Less than $10,000	18,469	54.1	27.6	32.9	4.8	31.6	29.3
$10,000 to $19,999	30,452	56.6	25.9	32.3	4.9	29.8	28.5
$20,000 to $34,999	40,216	55.2	25.1	40.5	5.8	26.9	28.2
$35,000 to $49,999	29,795	53.7	23.8	46.1	5.6	23.4	27.8
$50,000 or more	36,199	57.2	25.8	51.7	6.7	19.3	24.9

Source: Adapted from U.S. Bureau of the Census. (1993). *Statistical abstract of the United States: 1993* (113th ed., p. 139). Austin, TX: Reference Press.

[a]Almost every day.

[b]Or played sports regularly.

[c]On average per day in the past two weeks.

[d]Above desirable weight. Height and weight data are self-reported.

[e]Includes people whose characteristics are unknown.

Outpatient Services and Physician Office Visits

The use of ambulatory services is a critical factor in the American health care system. In 1991, there were 669.7 million visits to physicians, an average of 2.7 visits per U.S. resident. Table 5-39 shows the age, gender, race and ethnicity, and region of those who made the visits. Not surprisingly, the highest rates were for elderly people. Women had a higher rate of visits than men. African Americans of all ages had fewer visits per person than did white patients.

TABLE 5-39 **Physician Office Visits, by Patient's Age, Gender, Race and Ethnicity, and Geographic Region: 1991**

Patient Characteristic	Number of Visits (1,000)	Percentage Distribution	Number of Visits per Person per Year
All visits	669,689	100.0	2.7
Age			
Under 15 years	125,025	18.7	2.2
15–24 years	61,534	9.2	1.8
25–44 years	185,267	27.7	2.3
45–64 years	141,994	21.2	3.0
65–74 years	83,689	12.5	4.6
75 years and over	72,181	10.8	6.0
Gender and age			
Female	400,485	59.8	3.1
Under 15 years	60,157	9.0	2.2
15–24 years	40,447	6.0	2.3
25–44 years	122,449	18.3	3.0
45–64 years	83,210	12.4	3.4
65–74 years	49,475	7.4	4.9
75 years and over	44,747	6.7	5.9
Male	269,205	40.2	2.2
Under 15 years	64,868	9.7	2.3
15–24 years	21,088	3.1	1.2
25–44 years	62,818	9.4	1.6
45–64 years	58,783	8.8	2.6
65–74 years	34,214	5.1	4.2
75 years and over	27,434	4.1	6.1
Race and age			
White	587,800	87.8	2.8
Under 15 years	103,174	15.4	2.3
15–24 years	54,099	8.1	2.0
25–44 years	161,071	24.1	2.4
45–64 years	125,363	18.7	3.1
65–74 years	76,306	11.4	4.7
75 years and over	67,787	10.1	6.2
Black	58,494	8.7	1.9
Under 15 years	16,377	2.4	1.9
15–24 years	5,213	0.8	1.0
25–44 years	17,198	2.6	1.8
45–64 years	11,660	1.7	2.4
65–74 years	4,682	0.7	2.9
75 years and over	3,364	0.5	3.5
All other races			
Asian or Pacific Islander	20,127	3.0	—
American Indian, Eskimo, or Aleut	3,269	0.5	—
Geographic region			
Northeast	154,869	23.1	3.1
Midwest	166,680	24.9	2.8
South	193,071	28.8	2.3
West	155,070	23.2	2.8

Note: — = not available.

Source: Reprinted from Schappert, S. M. (1993). *National ambulatory medical care survey: 1991 summary* (p. 3). Hyattsville, MD: U.S. Public Health Service, National Center for Health Statistics.

Table 5-40 shows the kinds of specialists visited by patients in 1991. The largest percentage of visits were to general and family practice physicians, followed by internal medicine physicians and pediatricians. These three specializations treat the broadest range of health problems.

TABLE 5-40 **Physician Office Visits by Physician Specialty and Professional Identity: 1991**

Physician Specialty	Number of Visits (1,000)	Percentage Distribution	Number of Visits per 100 Persons per Year
All visits	669,689	100.0	269.3
General and family practice	164,857	24.6	66.3
Internal medicine	102,923	15.4	41.4
Pediatrics	74,646	11.1	30.0
Obstetrics and gynecology	56,834	8.5	22.9
Ophthalmology	41,207	6.2	16.6
Orthopedic surgery	35,932	5.4	14.4
Dermatology	29,659	4.4	11.9
General surgery	21,285	3.2	8.6
Otolaryngology	19,101	2.9	7.7
Psychiatry	15,720	2.3	6.3
Urological surgery	12,758	1.9	5.1
Cardiovascular diseases	11,629	1.7	4.7
Neurology	6,798	1.0	2.7
All other specialties	76,341	11.4	30.7
Professional identity			
Doctor of osteopathy	46,727	7.0	18.8
Doctor of medicine	622,962	93.0	250.5

Source: Reprinted from Schappert, S. M. (1993). *National ambulatory medical care survey: 1991 summary* (p. 4). Hyattsville, MD: U.S. Public Health Service, National Center for Health Statistics.

Women's health and the well-being of newborn children are related to the frequency of women's visits to obstetricians and gynecologists. According to Schappert (1993b), almost all women between ages 25 and 44 made such visits in 1989–90, a pattern that has been true since the mid-1970s. Figure 5-12 shows the office visits to obstetricians and gynecologists per 100 women per year by age. Table 5-41 indicates that the visit rates of African American women are significantly lower than the rates for white women.

The 20 principal reasons that people gave for seeing a physician are shown in Table 5-42. Unfortunately, two-thirds of the visits were for reasons that were not specified in the study. Table 5-43 shows the diagnoses of the patients who visited physicians in 1991. Patients had

FIGURE 5-12 **Annual Visit Rates to Obstetricians and Gynecologists, by Patient Age: Selected Years, 1975 to 1990**

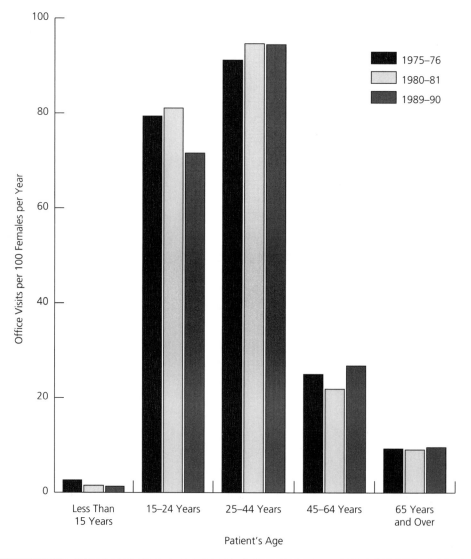

Note: Figures are based on two-year averages.

Source: Reprinted from Schappert, S. M. (1993). *Office visits to obstetricians and gynecologists: United States, 1989–90* (p. 4). Hyattsville, MD: U.S. Public Health Service, National Center for Health Statistics.

TABLE 5-41 Office Visits by Females to Obstetricians and Gynecologists, by Patient's Age and Race and Ethnicity: 1989–90

Patient Characteristic	Number of Visits (1,000)	Percentage Distribution	Visit Rate per 100 Females[a]
All visits	59,475	100.0	47.2
Age			
Less than 15 years	349	0.6	1.3
15–24 years	12,749	21.4	71.6
25–44 years	38,247	64.3	94.5
45–64 years	6,476	10.9	26.8
65 years and over	1,655	2.8	9.6
Race and age			
White	50,403	84.7	47.7
Less than 15 years	264	0.4	1.2
15–24 years	10,485	17.6	72.8
25–44 years	32,349	54.4	95.9
45–64 years	5,783	9.7	27.8
65 years and over	1,523	2.6	9.8
Black	5,113	8.6	31.8
Less than 15 years	64[b]	0.1[b]	1.5[b]
15–24 years	1,496	2.5	55.6
25–44 years	3,173	5.3	62.0
45–64 years	324	0.5	12.3
65 years and over	54[b]	0.1[b]	3.7[b]
Asian or Pacific Islander	1,763	3.0	c
American Indian or Alaskan Native	152	0.3	c
Unspecified	2,046	3.4	c

Source: Reprinted from Schappert, S. M. (1993). *Office visits to obstetricians and gynecologists: United States, 1989–90* (p. 7). Hyattsville, MD: U.S. Public Health Service, National Center for Health Statistics.

[a]Visit rates are based on U.S. Bureau of the Census estimates of the civilian, noninstitutionalized U.S. female population for July 1 of 1989 and 1990, averaged over the two-year period.

[b]Estimate does not meet standards of reliability.

[c]Numbers too small to compute a rate.

TABLE 5-42 The 20 Principal Reasons for Physician Office Visits: 1991

Reason for Visit	Number of Visits (1,000)	Percentage Distribution of Visits		
		All Visits	Female	Male
All visits	669,689	100.0	100.0	100.0
General medical examination	29,720	4.4	4.8	3.9
Cough	24,263	3.6	3.6	3.7
Routine prenatal examination	19,675	2.9	4.9	NA
Symptoms referable to throat	17,882	2.7	2.7	2.6
Postoperative visit	16,308	2.4	2.3	2.7
Earache or ear infection	13,404	2.0	1.9	2.1
Well-baby examination	13,276	2.0	1.7	2.4
Back symptoms	12,977	1.9	1.9	2.0
Skin rash	12,119	1.8	1.7	2.0
Stomach pain, cramps, and spasms	11,106	1.7	1.8	1.4
Fever	10,318	1.5	1.5	2.1
Headache, pain in head	10,128	1.5	1.2	1.5
Vision dysfunctions	10,011	1.5	1.5	1.5
Knee symptoms	9,522	1.4	1.2	1.7
Nasal congestion	8,444	1.3	1.1	1.5
Blood pressure test	7,645	1.1	1.2	1.1
Head cold, upper respiratory infection	7,616	1.1	1.1	1.2
Neck symptoms	7,193	1.1	1.0	1.1
Depression	7,060	1.1	1.2	0.9
Low back symptoms	7,051	1.1	0.8	1.4
All other reasons	413,971	61.8	60.9	63.2

Note: NA = not applicable.

Source: Adapted from Schappert, S. M. (1993). *National ambulatory medical care survey: 1991 summary* (p. 7). Hyattsville, MD: U.S. Public Health Service, National Center for Health Statistics.

a broad range of diagnoses, but the most common diagnosis was diseases of the respiratory system, followed by diseases of the nervous system and sense organs.

An important health-related behavior, smoking, was studied in connection with outpatient visits. As Table 5-44 shows, 10.1 percent of patients who made office visits smoked cigarettes; one-third of them were adults ages

45 to 64 years, and 58 percent were women.

Patients had a variety of means of paying for their visits. Table 5-45 shows the expected sources of payment. Over one-third expected to pay for their care with private or commercial health insurance, and the next largest number expected to pay for their care themselves. Medicare was the third largest expected payer, followed by health maintenance orga-

TABLE 5-43 Physician Office Visits, by Principal Diagnosis: 1991

Principal Diagnosis	Number of Visits (1,000)	Percentage Distribution
All visits	669,689	100.0
Infectious and parasitic diseases	24,570	3.7
Neoplasms	23,308	3.5
Endocrine, nutritional, and metabolic diseases and immunity disorders	27,312	4.1
Mental disorders	26,167	3.9
Diseases of the nervous system and sense organs	77,724	11.6
Diseases of the circulatory system	50,226	7.5
Diseases of the respiratory system	92,100	13.8
Diseases of the digestive system	22,724	3.4
Diseases of the genitourinary system	39,308	5.9
Diseases of the skin and subcutaneous tissue	39,578	5.9
Diseases of the musculoskeletal system and connective tissue	45,829	6.8
Symptoms, signs, and ill-defined conditions	25,694	3.8
Injury and poisoning	53,400	8.0
Supplementary classification	101,433	15.1
All other diagnoses	9,292	1.4
Unknown	11,025	1.6

Source: Adapted from Schappert, S. M. (1993). *National ambulatory medical care survey: 1991 summary* (p. 8). Hyattsville, MD: U.S. Public Health Service, National Center for Health Statistics.

TABLE 5-44 Physician Office Visits, by Patient's Cigarette-Smoking Status: 1991

Characteristic	Number of Visits (1,000)	Percentage Distribution
All visits	669,689	100.0
Does patient smoke cigarettes?		
Yes	67,674	10.1
No	416,771	62.2
Unknown	185,245	27.7
All visits by patients who smoke cigarettes	67,674	100.0
Age		
Under 15 years	237[a]	0.4[a]
15–24 years	6,131	9.1
25–44 years	27,939	41.3
45–64 years	22,652	33.5
65–74 years	7,575	11.2
75 years and over	3,139	4.6
Gender		
Female	39,308	58.1
Male	28,366	41.9

Source: Reprinted from Schappert, S. M. (1993). *National ambulatory medical care survey: 1991 summary* (p. 5). Hyattsville, MD: U.S. Public Health Service, National Center for Health Statistics.

[a]Estimate does not meet standards of reliability.

nizations or other prepaid programs. Medicaid accounted for 9.5 percent of the expected payments.

Most office visits resulted in prescriptions for medicines to treat patients. Tables 5-46 and 5-47 show the drugs mentioned most frequently in patients' records by a sample of physicians in 1991. Antibiotics (especially penicillin) were most often used. Various forms of analgesics or pain killers were second. According to Nelson (1993), 71 percent of the drugs physicians prescribed were by brand or trade names. Eighty-four percent of all drugs mentioned were prescription drugs. Table 5-48 lists the 50 drugs most commonly prescribed in U.S. office practice.

TABLE 5-45 **Physician Office Visits, by Patient's Expected Source of Payment: 1991**

Expected Source of Payment[a]	Number of Visits (1,000)	Percentage Distribution
All visits	669,689	100.0
Private or commercial insurance	239,425	35.8
Patient paid	157,834	23.6
Medicare	141,679	21.2
HMO or other prepaid	100,983	15.1
Medicaid	63,411	9.5
Other government	14,409	2.2
No charge	10,437	1.6
Other	27,390	4.1
Unknown	13,828	2.1

Source: Reprinted from Schappert, S. M. (1993). *National ambulatory medical care survey: 1991 summary* (p. 4). Hyattsville, MD: U.S. Public Health Service, National Center for Health Statistics.

[a]Number may exceed total number of visits because more than one source of payment may be coded for each visit.

TABLE 5-46 **The 20 Most Frequently Used Generic Substances: 1991**

Generic Substance	Number of Mentions (1,000)	Percentage Distribution	Therapeutic Classification
All drug mentions	804,615	100.0	
Amoxicillin	33,304	4.1	Penicillins
Acetaminophen	28,387	3.5	General analgesics
Erythromycin	16,060	2.0	Erythromycins and lincosamides
Hydrochlorothiazide	15,727	2.0	Diuretics
Aspirin	13,426	1.7	General analgesics
Ibuprofen	13,321	1.7	Antiarthritics
Phenylephrine	12,900	1.6	Nasal decongestants
Codeine	12,655	1.6	General analgesics
Phenylpropanolamine	11,734	1.5	Nasal decongestants
Albuterol	11,387	1.4	Bronchodilators, antiasthmatics
Digoxin	10,411	1.3	Cardiac glycosides
Naproxen	10,341	1.3	Antiarthritics
Guaifenesin	10,281	1.3	Antitussives, expectorants, mucolytics
Furosemide	10,257	1.3	Diuretics
Vitamin A	10,169	1.3	Vitamins, minerals
Riboflavin	9,402	1.2	Vitamins, minerals
Trimethoprim	9,343	1.2	Sulfanomides and trimethoprim
Sulfamethoxazole	9,223	1.1	Sulfanomides and trimethoprim
Ergocalciferol	9,165	1.1	Vitamins, minerals
Cefaclor	8,791	1.1	Cephalosporins

Note: "Drug mention" means appearance of the drug in a patient's record.

Source: Reprinted from Schappert, S. M. (1993). *National ambulatory medical care survey: 1991 summary* (p. 14). Hyattsville, MD: U.S. Public Health Service, National Center for Health Statistics.

Hospitals

Table 5-49 shows the hospital facilities available in each state in terms of the number of hospitals, beds, patients admitted, daily censuses, occupancy rates, outpatient visits, and personnel. Table 5-50 shows the number of community hospital beds per 100,000 population, occupancy rates, cost per day, and physicians per 100,000 population. A *community*

hospital is a nonfederal short-term general or special facility with six or more inpatient beds and an average stay of less than 60 days. North Dakota has the best ratio of beds per 100,000 population, and South Dakota is second. Massachusetts has the best ratio of physicians to population; Maryland is second, and New York is third. New York also has the highest occupancy rate for hospitals; Hawaii is second.

TABLE 5-47 **The 20 Drugs Most Frequently Prescribed at Office Visits, by Entry Name of Drug: 1991**

Entry Name of Drug[a]	Number of Mentions (1,000)	Percentage Distribution	Therapeutic Classification
All drug mentions	804,615	100.0	
Amoxicillin	18,017	2.2	Penicillins
Amoxil	9,653	1.2	Penicillins
Lasix	9,271	1.2	Diuretics
Ceclor	8,791	1.1	Cephalosporins
Allergy relief or shots	7,737	1.0	Diagnostics, nonradioactive and radiopaque
Prednisone	7,688	1.0	Adrenal corticosteroids
Synthroid	7,601	0.9	Agents used to treat thyroid disease
Lanoxin	7,566	0.9	Cardiac glycosides
Zantac	7,127	0.9	Agents used in disorders of upper GI tract
Motrin	7,033	0.9	Antiarthritics
Naprosyn	7,021	0.9	Antiarthritics
Diphtheria tetanus toxoids pertussis	6,996	0.9	Vaccines and antiserums
Premarin	6,879	0.9	Estrogens and progestins
Vasotec	6,632	0.8	Antihypertensive agents
Cardizem	6,516	0.8	Antianginal agents
Tylenol	6,330	0.8	General analgesics
Seldane	5,897	0.7	Antihistamines
Poliomyelitis vaccine	5,586	0.7	Vaccines and antiserums
Proventil	5,478	0.7	Bronchodilators, antiasthmatics
Keflex	5,422	0.7	Cephalosporins

Note: GI = gastrointestinal.

Source: Reprinted from Schappert, S. M. (1993). *National ambulatory medical care survey: 1991 summary* (p. 14). Hyattsville, MD: U.S. Public Health Service, National Center for Health Statistics.

[a]The entry made by the physician on the prescription or other medical records. This may be a trade name, generic name, or desired therapeutic effect.

TABLE 5-48 The 50 Drugs Most Frequently Used in Office Practice, by Entry Name, Number and Percentage of Mentions, Rank, and Therapeutic Use: 1990

Entry Name of Drug and Principal Generic Substance[a]	Number of Mentions (1,000)	Percentage Distribution	Therapeutic Use
All drugs	759,406	100.00	All therapeutic uses
Amoxicillin	17,891	2.36	Antibiotic
Amoxil (amoxicillin)	13,448	1.77	Antibiotic
Ceclor (cefaclor)	8,910	1.17	Antibiotic
Lasix (furosemide)	8,868	1.17	Diuretic, antihypertensive
Prednisone	7,830	1.03	Steroid replacement therapy, anti-inflammatory agent
Naprosyn (naproxen)	7,585	1.00	Nonsteroidal anti-inflammatory agent
Seldane (terfenadine)	7,251	0.95	Antihistaminic
Motrin (ibuprofen)	6,988	0.92	Nonsteroidal anti-inflammatory agent
Zantac (ranitidine)	6,501	0.86	Duodenal or gastric ulcer
Premarin (estrogens)	6,327	0.83	Estrogen replacement therapy
Lanoxin (digoxin)	6,275	0.83	Cardiotonic/digitalis
Vasotec (enalapril)	5,991	0.79	Antihypertensive
Aspirin or ASA	5,896	0.78	Analgesic, anti-inflammatory, antipyretic
Proventil (albuterol)	5,614	0.74	Bronchodilator
Dyazide (triamterene, hydro-chlorothiazide)	5,584	0.74	Diuretic, antihypertensive
Diphtheria tetanus toxoids pertussis	5,176	0.68	Immunization
Voltaren (diclofenac sodium)	5,160	0.68	Nonsteroidal anti-inflammatory agent
Tylenol (acetaminophen)	5,144	0.68	Analgesic
Synthroid (levothyroxine)	5,137	0.68	Thyroid hormone therapy
Xanax (alprazolam)	5,089	0.67	Anxiety disorders
Cardizem (ditiazem)	4,979	0.66	Cardiotonic/calcium channel blocking agent
Capoten (captopril)	4,785	0.63	Antihypertensive
Prozac (fluoxetine)	4,785	0.63	Antidepressant
Calan (verapamil)	4,755	0.63	Cardiotonic/calcium channel blocking agent
Ventolin (albuterol)	4,666	0.61	Bronchodilator
Theo-dur (theophylline)	4,600	0.61	Bronchodilator
Poliomyelitis vaccine	4,551	0.60	Immunization
Tavist (clemastine)	4,405	0.58	Antihistaminic
Keflex (cephalexin)	4,265	0.56	Antibiotic
Tenormin (atenolol)	4,231	0.56	Antihypertensive, angina pectoris
Vancenase (beclomethasone dipropinate)	4,106	0.54	Intranasal steroid
Inderal (propranolol)	3,970	0.52	Hypertension, angina pectoris, arrhythmia, migraine
Timaptic (timolol)	3,877	0.51	Glaucoma
Cipro (ciprofloxacin)	3,823	0.50	Antibiotic
Augmentin (amoxicillin, potassium clavulanate)	3,783	0.50	Antibiotic
Entex (phenylpropanolamine, phenylephrine, guaifenesin)	3,757	0.49	Cough preparation
Tylenol No. 3 (acetaminophen, codeine)	3,729	0.49	Analgesic
Procardia (nifedipine)	3,698	0.49	Cardiotonic/calcium channel blocking agent
Darvocet-N (propoxyphene, acetaminophen)	3,653	0.48	Analgesic
Duricef (cefadroxil)	3,573	0.47	Antibiotic
Micronase (glyburide)	3,434	0.45	Hypoglycemic
Tetracycline	3,383	0.45	Antibiotic
Ampicillin	3,310	0.44	Antibiotic
Erythromycin	3,260	0.43	Antibiotic
Coumadin (warfarin)	3,183	0.42	Anticoagulant
EES (erythromycin)	3,172	0.42	Antibiotic
Valium (diazepam)	3,168	0.42	Anxiety disorders
Benadryl (diphenhydramine)	3,150	0.41	Antihistaminic
Ortho-novum (norethindrone, estradiol, or mestranol)	3,041	0.40	Oral contraceptive
Tagamet (cimetidine)	3,014	0.40	Duodenal or gastric ulcer

Source: Adapted from Nelson, C. R. (1993). *Drug utilization in office practice: National ambulatory medical care survey, 1990* (p. 4). Hyattsville, MD: U.S. Public Health Service, National Center for Health Statistics.

[a]The trade or generic name used by the physician on the prescription or other medical records. The use of trade names is for identification only. Because of its nonspecific nature, the entry "Allergy relief or shots," with 4,184,000 mentions, is omitted.

TABLE 5-49 **Hospital Facilities, by State: 1991**

Region and State	Number of Hospitals		Beds (1,000)		Patients Admitted (million)		Average Daily Census (1,000)		Occupancy Rate[a]		Outpatient Visits (million)		Personnel[b] (1,000)
	Total	Community	Total	Community	Total	Community	Total	Community	Total	Community	Total	Community	
United States	6,634	5,342	1,196.8	923.9	33.6	31.1	827.1	611.0	69.1	66.1	387.7	322.0	4,164.9
Northeast	1,057	791	269.6	200.1	7.3	6.9	216.9	156.7	80.4	78.3	92.0	82.6	992.0
Connecticut	63	35	14.1	9.5	0.4	0.4	11.3	7.2	80.1	75.8	5.1	4.5	56.7
Maine	45	38	6.0	4.6	0.2	0.1	4.4	3.2	72.9	70.0	2.3	2.1	21.8
Massachusetts	154	101	31.9	21.7	0.9	0.8	24.4	15.8	76.3	73.0	12.0	10.6	123.9
New Hampshire	39	27	4.8	3.4	0.1	0.1	3.2	2.2	66.0	65.0	1.7	1.6	16.2
New Jersey	120	96	37.8	29.4	1.2	1.1	30.5	23.4	80.7	79.6	10.4	9.5	131.7
New York	298	231	102.0	75.2	2.5	2.3	88.2	63.8	86.5	84.8	34.2	30.3	370.7
Pennsylvania	301	236	66.3	51.4	1.9	1.8	49.7	37.4	75.0	72.7	23.9	22.0	244.4
Rhode Island	19	12	4.3	3.1	0.1	0.1	3.5	2.4	80.7	78.9	1.6	1.3	18.6
Vermont	18	15	2.3	1.8	0.1	0.1	1.7	1.2	72.5	68.3	0.8	0.7	8.0
Midwest	1,795	1,545	303.6	246.9	8.1	7.7	201.2	156.1	66.3	63.2	99.1	88.7	1,047.1
Illinois	249	209	57.1	45.1	1.6	1.5	39.5	29.9	69.2	66.3	19.2	17.0	204.2
Indiana	134	113	26.0	21.6	0.7	0.7	16.5	13.0	63.6	60.1	9.3	8.8	92.7
Iowa	133	123	17.0	14.1	0.4	0.4	10.9	8.5	64.2	60.2	4.9	4.7	51.1
Kansas	154	133	15.4	11.4	0.3	0.3	9.6	6.4	62.6	55.9	4.1	3.0	45.5
Michigan	205	175	39.5	32.9	1.1	1.1	26.7	21.6	67.7	65.4	17.6	16.4	155.9
Minnesota	162	148	23.9	19.1	0.6	0.5	16.7	12.9	69.6	67.7	5.2	4.7	66.5
Missouri	157	133	29.0	24.1	0.8	0.7	18.6	14.7	64.1	60.9	8.1	6.8	105.9
Nebraska	101	90	10.3	8.4	0.2	0.2	6.3	4.8	60.9	57.3	2.3	1.7	29.8
North Dakota	55	47	5.2	4.4	0.1	0.1	3.3	2.8	64.9	64.1	1.0	0.6	13.8
Ohio	228	193	51.3	42.8	1.5	1.5	33.8	27.0	65.9	63.0	18.9	17.6	193.4
South Dakota	64	52	5.5	4.3	0.1	0.1	3.4	2.6	62.4	61.9	1.3	0.8	14.6
Wisconsin	153	129	23.5	18.5	0.6	0.6	15.9	11.9	67.7	64.3	7.3	6.5	73.7
South	2,526	2,020	431.4	331.2	12.1	11.0	283.3	207.5	65.7	62.6	115.8	88.0	1,429.7
Alabama	137	119	23.4	18.7	0.6	0.6	15.6	11.6	66.7	62.1	6.0	4.8	72.3
Arkansas	101	88	13.3	11.1	0.4	0.3	8.3	6.7	62.3	60.6	2.8	2.3	40.9
Delaware	13	8	2.8	2.1	0.1	0.1	2.2	1.6	78.1	74.8	1.2	1.0	12.2
District of Columbia	17	11	7.5	4.3	0.2	0.2	6.1	3.3	81.0	76.6	2.1	1.1	29.1
Florida	296	227	62.9	50.5	1.7	1.6	39.7	31.1	63.2	61.6	15.8	12.3	212.4
Georgia	203	162	35.4	26.6	1.0	0.9	24.2	17.3	68.3	65.2	9.1	7.0	114.3
Kentucky	124	107	19.1	15.9	0.6	0.5	12.3	10.0	64.7	62.6	6.0	4.7	62.0
Louisiana	170	136	23.8	19.0	0.7	0.6	14.4	11.1	60.7	58.4	6.9	5.8	76.3
Maryland	81	51	19.9	13.3	0.6	0.6	15.2	10.1	76.3	75.6	6.1	4.4	76.5
Mississippi	113	102	17.2	13.0	0.6	0.4	10.9	7.5	63.3	57.5	3.1	2.2	43.9
North Carolina	155	117	30.0	22.0	0.9	0.8	22.2	15.9	73.9	72.3	8.7	6.6	109.3
Oklahoma	140	113	15.0	12.3	0.4	0.4	8.8	6.9	58.7	55.7	4.1	2.4	51.4

South Carolina	89	68	14.6	11.4	0.5	0.4	10.3	7.8	70.6	68.9	4.9	3.6	50.3
Tennessee	156	133	29.2	23.5	0.8	0.8	19.1	14.6	65.3	62.1	6.9	5.9	96.0
Texas	528	421	77.9	58.9	2.2	2.0	46.5	33.4	59.7	56.6	20.0	14.5	255.9
Virginia	136	98	29.1	20.2	0.8	0.7	20.7	13.3	71.1	65.8	8.7	6.6	94.7
West Virginia	67	59	10.4	8.3	0.3	0.3	6.9	5.3	66.2	63.7	3.3	3.0	32.2
West	1,256	986	192.2	145.7	6.0	5.4	125.7	90.7	65.4	62.2	80.8	62.8	696.1
Alaska	27	16	1.9	1.2	0.1	0.0	1.0	0.6	53.1	49.3	1.2	0.4	7.4
Arizona	93	61	13.6	9.7	0.5	0.4	8.6	6.0	63.6	61.8	5.1	3.1	48.0
California	552	440	105.1	79.8	3.3	3.1	69.9	50.4	66.5	63.1	42.9	35.6	380.6
Colorado	88	71	13.7	10.4	0.4	0.4	9.0	6.6	66.1	63.3	6.1	4.1	50.1
Hawaii	26	19	4.1	3.0	0.1	0.1	3.4	2.5	83.6	82.8	2.6	1.5	17.2
Idaho	49	41	4.0	3.3	0.1	0.1	2.5	1.9	60.8	57.4	1.4	1.2	12.1
Montana	61	53	4.7	4.4	0.1	0.1	3.0	2.8	63.4	63.1	1.1	0.9	13.0
Nevada	30	21	4.1	3.4	0.1	0.1	2.6	2.1	61.8	61.4	1.6	1.2	13.6
New Mexico	62	37	6.5	4.0	0.2	0.2	4.1	2.3	62.7	57.3	3.4	2.0	24.2
Oregon	73	66	10.1	7.8	0.3	0.3	6.2	4.3	61.7	55.1	3.8	3.4	37.8
Utah	53	42	5.6	4.4	0.2	0.2	3.4	2.6	60.1	58.3	3.1	2.8	21.8
Washington	110	92	15.7	12.0	0.5	0.5	10.3	7.5	65.7	62.9	8.0	5.9	63.2
Wyoming	32	27	3.0	2.2	0.1	0.0	1.7	1.1	56.1	51.3	0.7	0.6	7.1

Note: A community hospital is a nonfederal short-term general or special facility with six or more inpatient beds and an average stay of less than 60 days.

Source: Reprinted from U.S. Bureau of the Census. (1993). *Statistical abstract of the United States: 1993* (113th ed., p. 123). Austin, TX: Reference Press.

[a]Ratio of average daily census to every 100 beds.

[b]Includes full-time equivalents of part-time personnel.

Region and State	Community Hospitals,[a] 1991						Physicians, Rate per 100,000 Population,[a,d] 1990	
	Beds per 100,000 Population		Occupancy Rate[b]		Average Cost per Patient per Day[c]			
	Rate	Rank	Rate	Rank	Dollars	Rank	Rate	Rank
United States	366	NA	66.1	NA	752	NA	216	NA
Northeast	393	NA	78.3	NA	—	NA	280	NA
Connecticut	289	40	75.8	5	910	5	305	4
Maine	369	27	70.0	11	617	36	178	30
Massachusetts	361	28	73.0	8	880	9	337	1
New Hampshire	310	36	65.0	19	713	25	200	18
New Jersey	380	25	79.6	3	680	31	246	7
New York	417	18	84.8	1	694	27	315	3
Pennsylvania	430	16	72.7	9	732	22	235	10
Rhode Island	308	38	78.9	4	730	23	254	5
Vermont	316	35	68.3	13	621	35	253	6
Midwest	410	NA	63.2	NA	—	NA	190	NA
Illinois	391	20	66.3	15	770	17	212	14
Indiana	384	23	60.1	38	745	19	157	42
Iowa	506	5	60.2	37	538	45	151	43
Kansas	459	12	55.9	46	585	40	175	31
Michigan	351	29	65.4	17	792	15	185	27
Minnesota	431	15	67.7	14	582	41	220	11
Missouri	468	9	60.9	35	737	21	196	21
Nebraska	529	4	57.3	43	546	44	172	34
North Dakota	699	1	64.1	21	454	48	170	35
Ohio	391	20	63.0	26	782	16	196	21
South Dakota	605	2	61.9	31	436	50	140	47
Wisconsin	374	26	64.3	20	611	39	189	25
South	381	NA	62.6	NA	—	NA	192	NA
Alabama	458	13	62.1	29	637	34	158	40
Arkansas	468	9	60.6	36	571	42	150	44
Delaware	306	39	74.8	7	845	11	199	19
District of Columbia	722	NA	76.6	NA	1,038	NA	615	NA
Florida	381	24	61.6	33	836	13	208	16
Georgia	401	19	65.2	18	652	32	175	31
Kentucky	428	17	62.6	28	616	37	168	36
Louisiana	446	14	58.4	39	764	18	188	26
Maryland	275	41	75.6	6	740	20	334	2
Mississippi	503	6	57.5	41	479	47	133	49
North Carolina	327	31	72.3	10	651	33	190	24
Oklahoma	388	22	55.7	47	684	30	147	45
South Carolina	320	33	68.9	12	684	30	161	38
Tennessee	474	8	62.1	29	716	24	196	21
Texas	340	30	56.6	45	846	10	175	31
Virginia	322	32	65.8	16	701	26	213	12
West Virginia	460	11	63.7	22	612	38	166	37
West	269	NA	62.2	NA	—	NA	222	NA
Alaska	209	50	49.3	50	1,130	1	146	46
Arizona	259	46	61.8	32	955	3	197	20
California	263	44	63.1	24	1,037	2	244	8
Colorado	309	37	63.3	23	801	14	211	15
Hawaii	262	45	82.8	2	686	28	236	9
Idaho	319	34	57.4	42	565	43	125	50
Montana	541	3	63.1	24	437	49	158	40
Nevada	269	42	61.4	34	907	6	159	39
New Mexico	259	46	57.3	43	840	12	183	29
Oregon	268	43	55.1	48	896	8	205	17
Utah	249	48	58.3	40	915	4	185	27
Washington	239	49	62.9	27	904	7	213	12
Wyoming	475	7	51.3	49	489	46	139	48

Notes: A community hospital is a nonfederal short-term general or special facility with six or more inpatient beds and an average stay of less than 60 days. When states share the same rank, the next lower rank is omitted. Because of rounded data, states may have identical values shown, but different ranks. — = not available; NA = not applicable.

Source: Reprinted from U.S. Bureau of the Census. (1993). *Statistical abstract of the United States: 1993* (113th ed., p. xiv). Austin, TX: Reference Press.

[a]Source of this data is the American Hospital Association, Chicago (copyright).

[b]Ratio of the number of inpatients receiving treatment each day to every 100 beds; excludes newborns.

[c]Average cost to community hospitals, on the basis of total hospital expenses (payroll, employee benefits, professional fees, supplies, and so forth).

[d]Covers active nonfederal physicians and includes physicians not classified according to activity status.

Table 5-51 shows the average cost per patient to community hospitals from 1985 to 1991. As is clear from the table, costs for the whole nation and for each state increased significantly from 1985 through 1991.

TABLE 5-51 **Average Cost to Community Hospitals per Patient, by State: 1985, 1990, and 1991**

State	Average Cost per Day			Average Cost per Stay		
	1985	1990	1991	1985	1990	1991
United States	460	687	752	3,245	4,947	5,360
Alabama	389	588	637	2,653	4,175	4,455
Alaska	693	1,070	1,130	3,742	6,249	6,448
Arizona	591	867	955	3,547	4,877	5,212
Arkansas	381	534	571	2,292	3,730	3,927
California	654	939	1,037	4,050	5,709	6,169
Colorado	486	725	801	3,221	5,209	5,449
Connecticut	502	825	910	3,610	6,238	6,696
Delaware	474	771	845	3,357	5,112	5,748
District of Columbia	612	995	1,038	4,962	7,876	7,743
Florida	494	769	836	3,381	5,312	5,831
Georgia	386	630	652	2,501	4,303	4,677
Hawaii	420	638	686	3,522	6,048	6,553
Idaho	373	547	565	2,402	3,701	4,026
Illinois	498	717	770	3,607	5,253	5,570
Indiana	446	667	745	2,942	4,390	4,879
Iowa	359	495	538	2,735	4,135	4,527
Kansas	401	532	585	2,954	4,161	4,548
Kentucky	367	563	616	2,323	3,762	4,216
Louisiana	475	701	764	2,842	4,575	5,044
Maine	394	574	617	2,870	4,604	4,867
Maryland	443	678	740	3,237	4,640	4,835
Massachusetts	500	788	880	4,194	5,709	6,086
Michigan	507	716	792	3,666	5,358	5,750
Minnesota	369	536	582	3,302	4,782	5,035
Mississippi	319	439	479	2,037	3,116	3,454
Missouri	457	679	737	3,383	5,022	5,429
Montana	312	405	437	2,658	3,973	4,395
Nebraska	347	490	546	2,892	4,675	5,214
Nevada	677	854	907	3,953	5,511	5,883
New Hampshire	422	671	713	2,644	4,544	4,995
New Jersey	400	613	680	2,914	4,573	5,136
New Mexico	501	734	840	2,837	4,172	4,583
New York	419	641	694	3,930	6,397	6,823
North Carolina	356	595	651	2,416	4,408	4,759
North Dakota	322	427	454	2,918	4,468	4,898
Ohio	493	720	782	3,428	4,801	5,133
Oklahoma	455	632	684	2,814	4,302	4,547
Oregon	549	800	896	2,879	4,432	4,787
Pennsylvania	468	662	732	3,412	5,120	5,490
Rhode Island	447	663	730	3,432	4,839	5,063
South Carolina	358	590	684	2,508	4,168	4,868
South Dakota	282	391	436	2,442	3,905	4,436
Tennessee	397	633	716	2,709	4,340	4,859
Texas	461	752	846	2,799	4,663	5,179
Utah	556	832	915	2,799	4,409	4,688
Vermont	343	598	621	2,705	4,343	4,673
Virginia	399	635	701	2,862	4,408	4,875
Washington	546	817	904	3,062	4,519	5,035
West Virginia	399	565	612	2,520	3,918	4,319
Wisconsin	392	554	611	2,974	4,083	4,450
Wyoming	367	462	489	2,357	3,990	4,081

Source: Reprinted from U.S. Bureau of the Census. (1993). *Statistical abstract of the United States: 1993* (113th ed., p. 124). Austin, TX: Reference Press.

Table 5-52 provides information on the percentage of people without health insurance from 1988 to 1991 for all people in the United States and for certain categories of people based on poverty status, age, race and ethnicity, and marital status for 1988 to 1991. In 1991, 35.4 million Americans, or 14.1 percent of the population, did not have health insurance.

Conclusion

This lengthy chapter covers one of the most significant of all social welfare and social work issues—the health status and health care of the people of the United States. The major debate of the 1990s in social policy has been over health care and its provision.

TABLE 5-52 **People without Health Insurance, by Selected Characteristics: 1987 to 1991 (Numbers in millions)**

Characteristic and Year	Percent	Number
All people		
1987	12.9	31.0
1988	13.4	32.6
1989	13.6	33.3
1990	13.9	34.6
1991	14.1	35.4
Poor people		
1988	30.6	9.7
1989	30.3	9.5
1990	28.6	9.6
1991	28.6	10.2
Poor people under 18 years old		
1988	25.4	3.2
1989	24.9	3.1
1990	21.8	2.9
1991	20.5	2.9
White people		
1988	12.3	25.2
1989	12.5	25.8
1990	12.9	26.9
1991	12.9	27.1
Black people		
1988	19.6	5.9
1989	19.2	5.8
1990	19.7	6.1
1991	20.6	6.5
Hispanic people		
1988	31.8	6.4
1989	33.3	6.9
1990	32.4	6.9
1991	31.5	7.0
People in married-couple families		
1988	10.9	18.2
1989	10.8	18.3
1990	11.1	18.7
1991	11.2	19.0
People in poor married-couple families		
1988	38.7	4.3
1989	35.5	4.0
1990	35.7	4.2
1991	35.8	4.3
People in female-headed families		
1988	19.0	6.1
1989	20.0	6.5
1990	19.8	6.7
1991	19.7	6.9
People in poor female-headed families		
1988	20.6	2.5
1989	22.5	2.6
1990	18.4	2.3
1991	18.5	2.6

Source: Adapted with permission from Brimhall-Vargas, M. (1993). *Poverty tables 1991* (p. 83). Washington, DC: Center for Budget and Policy Priorities.

CHAPTER

6

MENTAL ILLNESS AND DEVELOPMENTAL DISABILITIES

Until the 1960s, public mental health services involved the housing and care of people defined as mentally ill in public mental hospitals funded primarily by state or local governments. Since the 1960s the mental health field has moved away from long-term hospitalization in public hospitals. The emphasis has been on "deinstitutionalization," or the movement of mentally ill people from institutions into other kinds of facilities or into the general community. Care and services provided through community mental health centers, nursing homes, and community general hospitals have steadily replaced much of the effort that was associated with public mental health services. Social workers play a role in the care provided in these and other programs.

There has also been a long tradition of care of mentally ill people by private hospitals and practitioners. Those who can afford private care, have sufficient funds to pay for it, and live in areas where such care is available use outpatient counseling and short-term hospital care to address their mental health needs.

This chapter provides information on the status of mental health services and providers and of people with mental illness and mental retardation. Much of the information is taken from the U.S. Department of Health and Human Services publication *Mental Health, United States, 1992* (Manderscheid & Sonnenschein, 1992). Some of the data are not as current as that provided in other chapters in this book. In some ways, information about mental health and developmental disabilities is also less detailed and comprehensive. Millions of decisions in a wide variety of settings are made each year about people with mental disabilities. Services are provided within and through public schools; through corrections programs and facilities; in courts

and law enforcement agencies; and within families, who arrange a multitude of mental health and developmental disability services for their family members with disabilities. Because services are so diverse and the data so difficult to collect, some of the most important information in the field is based on studies of relatively small samples that have not been replicated in recent years. Therefore, some of the data from the mid-1980s are the most currently available and the most reliable.

Deinstitutionalization

Perhaps the most important development in modern mental health services has been the deinstitutionalization of mentally ill people, which began in the 1960s for a variety of reasons and continues to be a major influence on mental health in the 1990s. As Table 6-1 shows, there has been a major decrease in inpatient beds, many of which were public mental hospital beds; a major increase in outpatient services; and an increase in "partial care services," which include hospital care for only part of a day, intermittent inpatient care for those who need it, and other new approaches to care.

Although it has been advocated and supported by social workers and other human services professionals, deinstitutionalization has had severe critics. In his book *Nowhere to Go*, E. F. Torrey (1988), a psychiatrist, blamed deinstitutionalization for the increasing incidence of homelessness in the United States. He suggested that the alternative community programs that were supposed to care for deinstitutionalized mentally ill people have not done so and that large numbers of such people are no longer followed by human services agencies.

Torrey also suggested that the deinstitutionalization movement shifted responsibility for mentally ill people from the states to the federal government. In 1963, before deinstitutionalization was widespread, the federal government paid only 2 percent of the cost of caring for mentally ill people. By 1985, however, the federal government was paying 38 percent of the costs. The states' responsibility, meanwhile, declined from 96 percent to 53 percent. Part of the reason for those

changes has been the development of Supplemental Security Income (see chapter 8), which provides monthly assistance to mentally ill people living in the community but not typically to patients in public mental hospitals. That program, along with direct grants for community mental health and Medicaid, accounts for much of the shift in responsibility.

TABLE 6-1 **Inpatient and Residential Treatment Beds, by Type of Mental Health Organization: Selected Years, 1970 to 1988**

Type of Organization	1970	1976	1980	1984	1986	1988
Number of inpatient beds						
All organizations	524,878	338,963	274,713	262,673	267,613	271,923
State and county mental hospitals	413,066	222,202	156,482	130,411	119,033	107,109
Private psychiatric hospitals	14,295	16,091	17,157	21,474	30,201	42,255
Nonfederal general hospitals with separate psychiatric services	22,394	28,706	29,384	46,045	45,808	48,421
VA medical centers	50,688	35,913	33,796	23,546	26,874	25,742
Federally funded community mental health centers	8,108	17,029	16,264	a	a	a
Residential treatment centers for emotionally disturbed children	15,129	18,029	20,197	16,745	24,547	25,173
All other organizations	1,198	993	1,433	24,452	21,150	23,223
Percent distribution of inpatient beds						
All organizations	100.0	100.0	100.0	100.0	100.0	100.0
State and county mental hospitals	78.7	65.6	57.0	49.6	44.5	39.4
Private psychiatric hospitals	2.7	4.7	6.6	8.2	11.3	15.5
Nonfederal general hospitals with separate psychiatric services	4.3	8.5	10.7	17.5	17.1	17.8
VA medical centers	9.7	10.6	12.3	9.0	10.0	9.5
Federally funded community mental health centers	1.5	5.0	5.5	a	a	a
Residential treatment centers for emotionally disturbed children	2.9	5.3	7.4	6.4	9.2	9.3
All other organizations	0.2	0.3	0.5	9.3	7.9	8.5
Inpatient beds per 100,000 civilian population						
All organizations	263.6	160.3	124.3	112.9	111.7	111.4
State and county mental hospitals	207.4	105.1	70.2	56.1	49.7	43.9
Private psychiatric hospitals	7.2	7.6	7.7	9.2	12.6	17.3
Nonfederal general hospitals with separate psychiatric services	11.2	13.6	13.7	19.8	19.1	19.8
VA medical centers	25.5	17.0	15.7	10.1	11.2	10.5
Federally funded community mental health centers	4.1	8.0	7.3	a	a	a
Residential treatment centers for emotionally disturbed children	7.6	8.5	9.1	7.2	10.3	10.3
All other organizations	0.6	0.5	0.6	10.5	8.8	9.5

Notes: The population used in the calculation of these rates is the January 1 civilian population of the United States for the respective years. VA = Veterans Administration.

Source: Reprinted from Manderscheid, R. W., & Sonnenschein, M. A. (Eds.). (1992). *Mental health, United States, 1992* (DHHS Publication No. SMA 92-1942, p. 24). Washington, DC: U.S. Government Printing Office.

[a]The inventory of federally funded community mental health centers was discontinued in 1981, and these organizations were subsumed under other categories.

Inpatient Services

The care of those who are defined as mentally ill has been treated as a public responsibility. However, the auspices of care for people with mental illness has been shifting from public to private sources, as shown in Table 6-1 and Figure 6-1. There were 413,066 state and county mental health facility beds in the United States in 1970; by 1988, that figure had dropped to 107,109. During that same period, however, private psychiatric hospital beds increased from 14,295 to 42,255. Likewise, the rate of public beds per 100,000 population dropped dramatically, whereas that of private beds more than doubled. Figure 6-1 compares the number of public state and county hospital beds to those provided by all organizations.

FIGURE 6-1 **Beds per 100,000 Civilian Population, All Mental Health Organizations and State and County Mental Hospitals: Selected Years, 1970 to 1988**

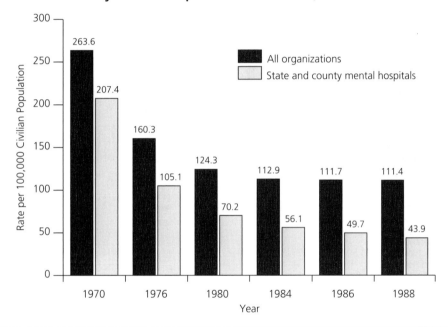

Source: Reprinted from Manderscheid, R. W., & Sonnenschein, M. A. (Eds). (1992). *Mental health, United States, 1992* (DHHS Publication No. SMA 92-1942, p. 2). Washington, DC: U.S. Government Printing Office.

Inpatient Population

Table 6-2 provides more information on the impact of deinstitutionalization on mental health facilities. In 1969 there were 468,831 inpatients in all facilities. By 1988, that figure had been cut to less than half, despite a growing population. The impact on state and county mental hospitals was even greater; their populations dropped from 367,629 to less than 100,000. On the other hand, private and general hospitals experienced an increase in admissions, as did residential treatment centers for children. Community mental health centers have provided only limited residential services—not enough even to report after 1979.

Figure 6-2 depicts the trends in inpatient admissions (both voluntary and involuntary) to mental health facilities. The overall admis-

TABLE 6-2 **Inpatient and Residential Treatment Census and Percentage Occupancy, by Type of Mental Health Organization: Selected Years, 1969 to 1988**

Type of Organization	1969	1975	1979	1983	1986	1988
Average daily inpatient census						
All organizations	468,831	287,588	233,384	224,169	228,530	227,836
State and county mental hospitals	367,629	193,380	138,600	116,236	107,056	99,869
Private psychiatric hospitals	11,608	12,058	13,901	16,467	23,475	29,698
Nonfederal general hospitals with psychiatric services	17,808	22,874	23,110	34,328	34,437	35,902
VA medical centers	47,140	32,123	28,693	20,342	21,242	19,602
Federally funded community mental health centers	5,270	10,186	9,886	a	a	a
Residential treatment centers for emotionally disturbed children	12,406	16,164	18,054	15,826	22,650	23,092
All other organizations	970	803	1,140	20,970	19,670	19,673
Percent occupancy						
All organizations	88.2	84.4	85.0	85.3	85.4	83.8
State and county mental hospitals	89.4	87.0	88.6	89.1	89.9	93.2
Private psychiatric hospitals	81.2	74.9	81.0	76.7	77.7	70.3
Nonfederal general hospitals with psychiatric services	79.5	79.7	78.6	74.6	75.2	74.1
VA medical centers	93.0	89.4	84.9	86.4	79.0	76.1
Federally funded community mental health centers	65.0	59.8	60.8	a	a	a
Residential treatment centers for emotionally disturbed children	82.0	89.7	89.4	94.5	92.3	91.7
All other organizations	81.0	80.9	79.6	85.8	93.0	84.7

Note: VA = Veterans Administration.

Source: Reprinted from Manderscheid, R. W., & Sonnenschein, M. A. (Eds.). (1992). *Mental health, United States, 1992* (DHHS Publication No. SMA 92-1942, p. 26). Washington, DC: U.S. Government Printing Office.

aThe inventory of federally funded community mental health centers was discontinued in 1981, and these organizations were subsumed under other categories.

sion rates are increasing—from 644.2 in 1969 to 819.1 per 100,000 population in 1988. However, admissions to state and county mental hospitals have steadily declined.

Table 6-3 shows the average daily number of inpatients and residential treatment center patients, by state, in 1983, 1986, and 1988. It covers people who were in three kinds of facilities during those years—state and county men-

tal hospitals, private psychiatric hospitals, and non–federal government general hospitals.

Table 6-4 provides information on the number of inpatients in Veterans Administration hospitals, children's residential treatment centers, and multiservice mental health agencies (such as community mental health centers) in 1983, 1986, and 1988. The table does not include children who were placed in spe-

FIGURE 6-2 **Inpatient Addition Rates, All Mental Health Organizations and State and County Mental Hospitals: Selected Years, 1969 to 1988**

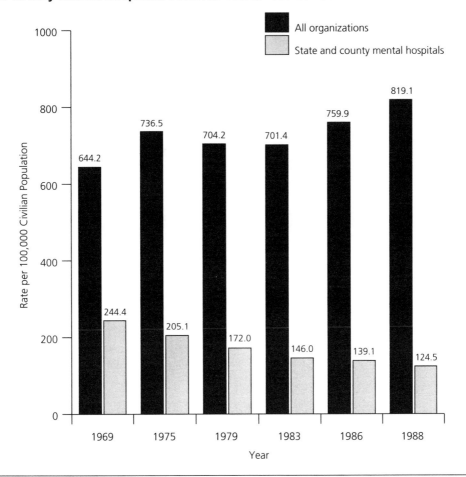

Source: Reprinted from Manderscheid, R. W., & Sonnenschein, M. A. (Eds.). (1992). *Mental health, United States, 1992* (DHHS Publication No. SMA 92-1942, p. 2). Washington, DC: U.S. Government Printing Office.

TABLE 6-3 Inpatient and Residential Mental Health Treatment Census in Mental, Psychiatric, and General Hospitals, by State: 1983, 1986, and 1988

State	All Organizations			State and County Mental Hospitals			Private Psychiatric Hospitals			Nonfederal General Hospital Psychiatric Services		
	1983	1986	1988	1983	1986	1988	1983	1986	1988	1983	1986	1988
United States	224,169	229,998	229,396	117,060	107,832	100,343	16,840	23,848	30,023	34,328	34,490	35,959
Alabama	3,833	3,846	4,183	2,077	1,864	1,933	177	214	300	402	529	677
Alaska	210	250	407	170	162	120	a	44	50	26	12	31
Arizona	1,795	2,404	3,027	336	492	526	42	206	678	259	241	175
Arkansas	876	1,259	1,262	285	260	218	a	85	255	168	173	155
California	16,709	20,014	17,953	5,895	5,147	4,492	1,673	3,087	3,134	2,773	2,352	2,618
Colorado	2,534	2,627	2,665	847	892	822	259	264	274	228	350	379
Connecticut	4,894	4,505	4,117	2,341	2,245	1,889	1,011	754	810	495	553	499
Delaware	700	697	745	517	511	485	37	45	76	69	75	75
District of Columbia	2,051	2,008	1,838	1,545	1,545	1,433	132	143	157	193	185	186
Florida	8,482	9,704	11,097	3,748	3,686	3,691	929	1,402	1,961	1,725	1,778	1,750
Georgia	8,066	5,554	5,942	4,257	2,806	2,351	1,015	1,205	1,451	546	583	671
Hawaii	434	467	451	239	227	223	77	41	76	70	148	84
Idaho	383	458	456	171	218	161	55	82	119	32	40	55
Illinois	8,306	8,590	9,278	4,014	3,766	4,091	545	607	695	1,884	2,037	2,240
Indiana	4,529	5,125	5,333	2,342	2,472	2,178	360	454	694	850	999	1,128
Iowa	2,200	2,586	2,736	853	834	760	a	a	56	685	699	659
Kansas	2,700	2,748	2,752	1,286	1,248	1,165	348	391	401	449	425	344
Kentucky	2,224	2,565	2,735	803	977	894	286	484	725	422	396	425
Louisiana	2,754	3,916	3,099	1,757	1,788	1,504	398	1,023	1,021	409	260	366
Maine	1,305	1,649	1,209	590	590	630	a	111	90	129	387	137
Maryland	4,678	4,878	4,338	2,770	2,545	2,234	554	637	634	614	623	635
Massachusetts	7,177	8,155	8,979	2,481	2,625	2,886	764	885	948	913	1,000	1,095
Michigan	8,466	9,047	9,984	4,105	4,400	3,431	537	758	638	1,426	1,629	2,072
Minnesota	3,930	3,703	4,005	1,527	1,809	2,146	58	58	80	1,068	875	741
Mississippi	2,739	2,150	2,276	1,739	1,418	1,384	26	91	138	292	184	198
Missouri	4,462	4,732	4,946	2,189	2,054	1,927	90	250	265	1,144	1,305	1,429
Montana	478	534	585	344	341	288	a	44	92	56	58	53
Nebraska	1,189	1,286	1,122	602	578	544	a	103	103	261	292	221
Nevada	302	345	478	82	118	175	68	107	183	54	49	37
New Hampshire	903	958	808	517	390	193	101	277	236	90	92	193
New Jersey	7,119	6,998	6,957	4,616	4,354	3,540	496	535	1,106	1,177	983	855
New Mexico	767	713	1,064	218	251	437	115	96	245	122	145	131
New York	32,721	33,301	31,386	23,692	22,131	21,036	737	1,000	1,216	3,710	4,032	4,214
North Carolina	8,767	5,892	5,484	2,992	2,832	2,806	291	605	a	734	778	860
North Dakota	676	649	591	526	509	427	a	a	a	110	88	110

Ohio	8,803	8,986	8,693	4,304	4,012	3,830	483	685	411	2,003	1,891	1,805
Oklahoma	1,996	1,767	2,143	1,221	906	788	239	245	358	373	380	706
Oregon	1,564	1,901	1,892	837	918	1,121	26	62	64	214	230	213
Pennsylvania	15,112	14,111	14,088	8,804	6,777	6,925	1,276	1,479	1,631	1,906	2,185	2,102
Rhode Island	745	696	623	421	278	213	149	156	151	42	52	54
South Carolina	3,460	2,795	2,570	2,928	2,166	1,746	75	209	244	316	261	369
South Dakota	642	816	920	377	391	415	a	a	a	40	77	61
Tennessee	3,417	3,718	3,092	1,822	1,637	1,641	187	498	835	627	675	758
Texas	12,707	12,525	12,043	5,411	4,270	3,639	1,590	2,498	4,141	2,173	1,872	1,683
Utah	923	1,095	1,428	294	302	309	a	54	353	203	283	281
Vermont	804	511	416	193	189	187	a	101	126	43	50	54
Virginia	6,029	6,162	6,439	3,652	3,353	3,051	959	1,081	1,088	640	696	748
Washington	2,529	2,717	2,736	1,257	1,427	1,344	96	90	130	435	459	417
West Virginia	1,485	1,318	1,158	1,022	640	521	67	55	109	257	271	304
Wisconsin	3,885	4,242	3,917	944	1,438	909	139	146	335	1,437	650	821
Wyoming	709	857	580	278	267	210	a	28	66	34	50	28
Puerto Rico	—	1,439	1,519	824	776	474	373	373	325	—	53	35

Note: — = not available.

Source: Reprinted from Manderscheid, R. W., & Sonnenschein, M. A. (Eds.). (1992). *Mental health, United States, 1992* (DHHS Publication No. SMA 92-1942, pp. 84–85). Washington, DC: U.S. Government Printing Office.

[a]Estimate does not meet standards of reliability.

TABLE 6-4 **Inpatient and Residential Mental Health Treatment Census in VA Medical Centers, Centers for Children, and Multiservice Organizations, by State: 1983, 1986, and 1988**

State	VA Medical Centers			RTCs for Emotionally Disturbed Children			Multiservice Mental Health Organizations		
	1983	1986	1988	1983	1986	1988	1983	1986	1988
United States	20,619	21,479	19,842	16,000	22,650	23,092	20,990	19,699	20,137
Alabama	589	730	737	125	122	167	463	387	369
Alaska	a	a	a	a	a	62	14	32	144
Arizona	111	145	142	681	832	1,062	366	488	444
Arkansas	269	380	355	10	69	98	144	292	181
California	1,349	1,698	1,482	2,594	2,485	3,279	2,425	5,245	2,948
Colorado	425	269	233	524	726	743	251	126	214
Connecticut	152	148	162	791	706	659	104	99	98
Delaware	a	a	a	77	45	57	a	21	52
District of Columbia	166	120	40	15	15	22	a	a	a
Florida	481	432	500	476	1,175	1,288	1,123	1,231	1,907
Georgia	788	403	430	66	127	77	1,394	430	962
Hawaii	a	a	a	36	39	37	12	12	31
Idaho	27	22	24	98	96	97	a	a	a
Illinois	941	739	903	410	950	919	512	491	430
Indiana	450	577	559	400	488	425	127	135	349
Iowa	373	350	571	162	352	238	127	351	452
Kansas	493	461	588	a	44	157	124	179	97
Kentucky	298	209	182	95	156	177	320	343	332
Louisiana	102	175	128	68	95	80	20	575	a
Maine	193	283	128	294	131	146	99	147	78
Maryland	388	615	324	352	398	470	a	60	41
Massachusetts	1,072	1,179	1,411	892	1,595	1,576	1,055	871	1,063
Michigan	459	450	793	750	960	1,250	1,189	850	1,800
Minnesota	738	262	315	362	578	616	177	121	107
Mississippi	476	277	353	a	a	6	206	180	197
Missouri	297	280	321	501	573	837	243	270	167
Montana	a	a	a	78	91	84	a	a	68
Nebraska	172	100	74	38	120	109	116	93	71
Nevada	18	18	30	52	53	53	28	a	a
New Hampshire	21	21	16	70	129	79	104	49	91
New Jersey	631	732	618	163	394	350	36	a	488
New Mexico	29	66	65	49	59	83	234	96	103
New York	1,816	1,940	1,612	1,506	3,078	2,655	1,260	1,120	653
North Carolina	199	609	510	69	53	42	4,482	1,015	517
North Dakota	a	a	a	a	52	a	40	a	54
Ohio	898	1,139	682	544	732	717	571	527	1,248
Oklahoma	76	90	85	a	29	56	87	117	150
Oregon	182	160	167	213	264	308	92	267	19
Pennsylvania	1,558	1,693	1,548	1,053	1,490	1,024	515	487	858
Rhode Island	37	37	20	50	136	180	46	37	5
South Carolina	57	86	63	58	47	57	26	26	91
South Dakota	122	174	291	83	120	83	20	54	70
Tennessee	667	683	408	a	60	78	114	165	182
Texas	1,569	1,832	1,199	570	674	562	1,394	1,379	819
Utah	96	96	76	188	221	143	142	139	266
Vermont	25	29	27	16	53	22	527	89	a
Virginia	433	406	414	172	389	340	173	237	798
Washington	352	229	269	342	309	218	47	203	358
West Virginia	55	52	38	30	129	62	54	171	124
Wisconsin	400	582	564	598	1,106	1,131	367	320	157
Wyoming	292	264	145	105	105	111	a	143	20
Puerto Rico	277	237	240	174	a	a	a	a	445

Notes: VA = Veterans Administration; RTC = residential treatment center.

Source: Reprinted from Manderscheid, R. W., & Sonnenschein, M. A. (Eds.). (1992). *Mental health, United States, 1992* (DHHS Publication No. SMA 92-1942, pp. 86–87). Washington, DC: U.S. Government Printing Office.

aEstimate does not meet standards of reliability.

cial residential facilities that would have been defined as schools rather than treatment centers or in similar facilities for adults.

Table 6-5 shows the race or ethnicity and gender of people who were inpatients in various kinds of psychiatric facilities in 1986. Men outnumbered women. Nearly 72 percent of all inpatients were white, but other races were disproportionately represented.

TABLE 6-5 **People under Psychiatric Inpatient Care, by Race, Gender, and Type of Service: 1986**

Race and Gender	Total, All Inpatient Services	Inpatient Psychiatric Service				
		State and County Mental Hospitals	Private Psychiatric Hospitals	VA Medical Centers	Nonfederal General Hospitals	Multiservice Mental Health Organizations
Number						
Total, all races	170,486	100,785	17,196	13,194	34,505	4,806
Male	100,756	60,654	8,397	12,855	16,144	2,706
Female	69,730	40,131	8,799	339	18,361	2,100
Total white	122,445	66,549	15,232	10,072	26,738	3,854
Male	67,975	36,890	7,511	9,733	11,858	1,983
Female	54,470	29,659	7,721	339	14,880	1,871
Total all other races	48,041	34,236	1,964	3,122	7,767	952
Male	32,781	23,764	886	3,122	4,286	723
Female	15,260	10,472	1,078	a	3,481	229
Percent distribution						
Total, all races	100.0	100.0	100.0	100.0	100.0	100.0
Male	59.1	60.2	48.8	97.4	46.8	56.3
Female	40.9	39.8	51.2	2.6	53.2	43.7
Total white	100.0	100.0	100.0	100.0	100.0	100.0
Male	55.5	55.4	49.3	96.6	44.3	51.5
Female	44.5	44.6	50.7	3.4	55.7	48.5
Total all other races	100.0	100.0	100.0	100.0	100.0	100.0
Male	68.2	69.4	45.1	100.0	55.2	75.9
Female	31.8	30.6	54.9	a	44.8	24.1
Rate per 100,000 civilian population						
Total, all races	71.2	42.1	7.2	5.5	14.4	2.0
Male	87.0	52.4	7.3	11.1	13.9	2.3
Female	56.4	32.5	7.1	0.3	14.9	1.7
Total white	60.3	32.8	7.5	5.0	13.2	1.9
Male	69.0	37.4	7.6	9.9	12.0	2.0
Female	52.2	28.4	7.4	0.3	14.3	1.8
Total all other races	132.0	94.0	5.4	8.6	21.3	2.6
Male	190.3	138.0	5.1	18.1	24.9	4.2
Female	79.6	54.6	5.6	a	18.1	1.2

Note: VA = Veterans Administration.

Source: Reprinted from Manderscheid, R. W., & Sonnenschein, M. A. (Eds.). (1992). *Mental health, United States, 1992* (DHHS Publication No. SMA 92-1942, p. 283). Washington, DC: U.S. Government Printing Office.

aEstimate does not meet standards of reliability.

Table 6-6 shows the diagnoses associated with a sample of inpatients in several kinds of facility. More than 40 percent were diagnosed with schizophrenia; the next largest percentage had affective disorders. Those with a diagnosis of schizophrenia are typically served in public rather than private facilities.

TABLE 6-6 **People under Psychiatric Inpatient Care, by Selected Principal Diagnoses and Type of Service: 1986**

Selected Principal Diagnoses	Total, All Inpatient Services	Inpatient Psychiatric Service				
		State and County Mental Hospitals	Private Psychiatric Hospitals	VA Medical Centers	Nonfederal General Hospitals	Multiservice Mental Health Organizations
Number						
Alcohol-related disorders	10,553	3,172	500	2,484	4,136	261
Drug-related disorders	5,046	1,624	590	527	2,035	a
Affective disorders	37,029	12,104	8,706	2,130	13,198	891
Schizophrenia	74,374	58,246	2,223	5,356	6,400	2,149
Personality disorders	4,148	2,646	601	255	558	a
Adjustment disorders	6,454	2,479	669	113	2,947	246
Organic disorders	9,368	6,882	470	793	1,042	181
Percent of total people under care						
Alcohol-related disorders	6.2	3.1	2.9	18.8	12.0	5.4
Drug-related disorders	3.0	1.6	3.4	4.0	5.9	a
Affective disorders	21.7	12.0	50.6	16.1	38.2	18.5
Schizophrenia	43.6	57.8	12.9	40.6	18.5	44.7
Personality disorders	2.4	2.6	3.5	1.9	1.6	a
Adjustment disorders	3.8	2.5	3.9	0.9	8.5	5.1
Organic disorders	5.5	6.8	2.7	6.0	3.0	3.8

Note: VA = Veterans Administration.

Source: Reprinted from Manderscheid, R. W., & Sonnenschein, M. A. (Eds.). (1992). *Mental health, United States, 1992* (DHHS Publication No. SMA 92-1942, p. 287). Washington, DC: U.S. Government Printing Office.

   [a]Estimate does not meet standards of reliability.

Table 6-7 lists age data on a sample of in-patients under care in April 1986. A large percentage of inpatients are young and middle-aged adults. There are differences among types of facilities. Inpatients in Veterans Administration hospitals tend to be older than inpatients in other facilities; those in private psychiatric hospitals are generally younger.

TABLE 6-7 **People under Psychiatric Inpatient Care, by Age and Type of Service: April 1, 1986**

Age	Total, All Inpatient Services	Inpatient Psychiatric Service				
		State and County Mental Hospitals	Private Psychiatric Hospitals	VA Medical Centers	Nonfederal General Hospitals	Multiservice Mental Health Organizations
Number						
Total, all ages	170,486	100,785	17,196	13,194	34,505	4,806
Under 18	16,679	6,872	7,020	a	2,013	774
18–24	20,053	11,939	2,150	230	5,103	631
25–44	81,374	49,715	4,778	7,160	17,250	2,471
45–64	32,964	20,002	1,766	4,248	6,315	633
65 and over	19,416	12,257	1,482	1,556	3,824	297
Percent distribution						
Total, all ages	100.0	100.0	100.0	100.0	100.0	100.0
Under 18	9.8	6.8	40.8	a	5.8	16.1
18–24	11.8	11.8	12.5	1.7	14.8	13.1
25–44	47.7	49.3	27.8	54.3	50.0	51.4
45–64	19.3	19.8	10.3	32.2	18.3	13.2
65 and over	11.4	12.2	8.6	11.8	11.1	6.2
Rate per 100,000 civilian population						
Total, all ages	71.2	42.1	7.2	5.5	14.4	2.0
Under 18	26.4	10.9	11.1	a	3.2	1.2
18–24	74.4	44.3	8.0	0.9	18.9	2.3
25–44	108.6	66.3	6.4	9.6	23.0	3.3
45–64	73.2	44.4	3.9	9.4	14.0	1.4
65 and over	66.6	42.0	5.1	5.3	13.1	1.0
Median age (years)	34	34	22	42	35	31

Note: VA = Veterans Administration.

Source: Reprinted from Manderscheid, R. W., & Sonnenschein, M. A. (Eds.). (1992). *Mental health, United States, 1992* (DHHS Publication No. SMA 92-1942, p. 285). Washington, DC: U.S. Government Printing Office.

aEstimate does not meet standards of reliability.

Length of Stay

Table 6-8 shows the median length of stay for people who left inpatient psychiatric services in 1986 by gender, race, diagnosis, and age. There were no apparent major differences in length of stay between men and women or white and nonwhite people. There were differences according to age, however. Younger people had longer stays than older people, al-though for those over age 65 and those under age 18 in state and county hospitals, the median number of days in hospitalization is exactly the same. Children stayed much longer in private psychiatric centers than did other age groups. Older people stayed longer in public hospitals and Veterans Administration facilities than they did in other kinds of facilities.

TABLE 6-8 **Median Days of Stay for People Terminated (Excluding Death) from Inpatient Psychiatric Service, by Race, Gender, Age, Selected Principal Diagnoses, and Type of Inpatient Psychiatric Service: 1986**

| Patient Characteristic | Total, All Inpatient Services | Inpatient Psychiatric Service | | | | |
		State and County Mental Hospitals	Private Psychiatric Hospitals	VA Medical Centers	Nonfederal General Hospitals	Multiservice Mental Health Organizations
Race and gender						
Total, all races	15	28	24	23	11	11
Male	15	27	24	23	9	11
Female	14	30	23	26	12	11
Total white	15	27	25	24	11	11
Male	15	25	26	23	10	11
Female	15	29	24	28	12	12
Total all other races	14	30	17	22	9	9
Male	16	30	17	22	8	11
Female	13	30	20	a	9	a
Age						
Under 18	26	43	43	a	12	a
18–24	12	27	24	22	8	10
25–44	14	28	19	22	10	11
45–64	16	24	21	24	12	10
65 and over	16	43	17	28	15	16
Selected principal diagnoses						
Alcohol-related disorders	8	15	24	22	5	6
Drug-related disorders	16	27	27	21	8	6
Affective disorders	16	33	24	24	13	13
Schizophrenia	19	37	18	23	13	17
Personality disorders	9	9	18	31	7	10
Adjustment disorders	8	9	18	12	7	5
Organic disorders	16	a	17	27	13	10

Note: VA = Veterans Administration.

Source: Reprinted from Manderscheid, R. W., & Sonnenschein, M. A. (Eds.). (1992). *Mental health, United States, 1992* (DHHS Publication No. SMA 92-1942, p. 288). Washington, DC: U.S. Government Printing Office.

aEstimate does not meet standards of reliability.

Table 6-9 provides information about specialized units for those with alcohol and drug abuse problems, including the kinds of clients served and services provided by such organizations.

TABLE 6-9 **Clients in Alcohol and Drug Abuse Treatment Units, by Type of Care and Unit Location: 1991**

Type of Care and Unit	Service Locations Reporting[a]	All Clients	Drug Abuse Clients Only	Alcoholism Clients Only	Clients with Both Problems
Total	8,928	811,819	237,008	365,147	209,664
Type of care					
Detoxification[b]					
Hospital inpatient	768	5,215	1,051	2,211	1,953
Free-standing residential	525	6,257	1,425	2,947	1,885
Rehabilitation/residential[c]					
Hospital inpatient	625	9,212	1,543	3,313	4,356
Short-term—30 days or less	895	17,929	3,150	7,449	7,330
Long-term—over 30 days	2,027	60,537	21,531	13,910	25,096
Ambulatory					
Outpatient	5,787	662,624	190,542	318,018	154,064
Intensive outpatient[d]	1,688	42,128	11,058	16,889	14,181
Detoxification[e]	253	7,917	6,708	410	799
Type of unit					
Community mental health care	1,287	133,670	32,854	68,293	32,523
Free-standing nonresidential	3,634	426,562	134,259	210,318	81,985
Hospital[f]	1,292	78,229	20,441	33,090	24,698
Correctional facility	219	39,270	12,784	4,826	21,660
Halfway house	775	15,830	2,374	6,574	6,882
Other residential facility	1,162	51,575	17,452	15,868	18,255
Other site	169	11,857	2,726	6,490	2,641
Multiple sites	390	54,826	14,118	19,688	21,020

Note: Data are based on the National Drug and Alcoholism Treatment Unit Survey (NDATUS), a census of all known drug abuse and alcoholism treatment facilities in the United States.

Source: Reprinted from U.S. Bureau of the Census. (1993). *Statistical abstract of the United States: 1993* (113th ed., p. 136). Austin, TX: Reference Press.

[a]Some units provide more than one type of treatment and are counted more than once in the total.

[b]24-hour care for the withdrawal and transition to ongoing treatment.

[c]Other than detoxification. Provides treatment services for dependency.

[d]"Intensive" outpatient involves at least two hours of treatment a day for at least three days a week.

[e]Less than 24-hour care.

[f]Includes general hospitals, alcoholism hospitals, mental and psychiatric hospitals, and other specialized hospitals.

Mental Health Expenditures

Figure 6-3 shows the trend in per capita expenditures in current and constant (adjusted to cancel inflation) dollars for state and county mental hospitals for selected years. It shows that expenditures per U.S. citizen for all mental health services have remained quite stable.

Total expenditures for all mental health organizations are shown in Figure 6-4. In con-stant dollars, expenditures have increased. However, expenditures by state and county mental hospitals have declined as expenditures by other mental health organizations have increased.

Figure 6-5 shows the changes in expenditures per capita for private psychiatric hospitals. In constant dollars, per capita expenditures increased 274% between 1979 and

FIGURE 6-3 **Expenditures per Capita in Current and Constant Dollars, All Mental Health Organizations: Selected Years, 1969 to 1988**

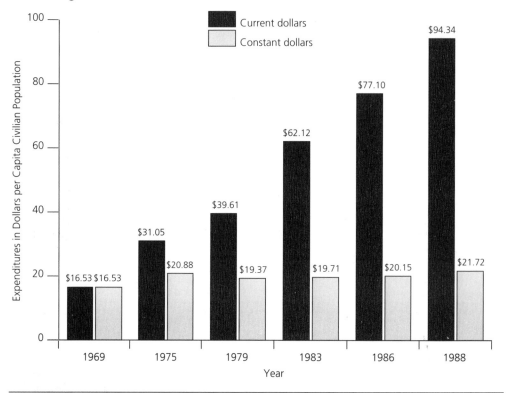

Source: Reprinted from Manderscheid, R. W., & Sonnenschein, M. A. (Eds.). (1992). *Mental health, United States, 1992* (DHHS Publication No. SMA 92-1942, p. 5). Washington, DC: U.S. Government Printing Office.

1988, a growth rate significantly greater than that of public hospitals. Similarly, expenditures for psychiatric services by general hospitals, where many of those in need of mental health care are now receiving those services, grew 180 percent, as Figure 6-6 shows.

Figure 6-7 shows the percentage of state government budgets used for mental health in 1990 in each state, ranked from lowest to highest expenditures. Figure 6-8 shows the state expenditures per capita for state mental health agencies in the same fiscal year.

FIGURE 6-4 **Annual Expenditures in Constant Dollars by All Mental Health Organizations, State and County Mental Hospitals, and All Other Organizations: Selected Years, 1969 to 1988**

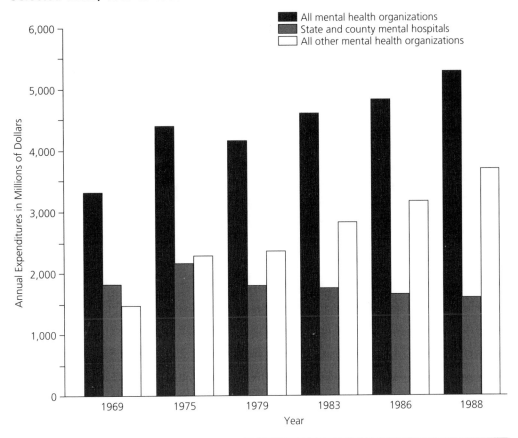

Source: Reprinted from Manderscheid, R. W., & Sonnenschein, M. A. (Eds.). (1992). *Mental health, United States, 1992* (DHHS Publication No. SMA 92-1942, p. 6). Washington, DC: U.S. Government Printing Office.

FIGURE 6-5 **Expenditures per Capita in Current and Constant Dollars by Private Psychiatric Hospitals: Selected Years, 1969 to 1988**

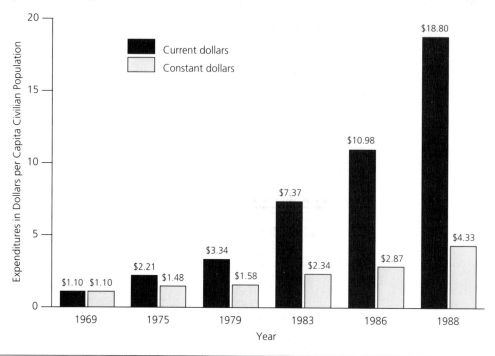

Source: Reprinted from Manderscheid, R. W., & Sonnenschein, M. A. (Eds.). (1992). *Mental health, United States, 1992* (DHHS Publication No. SMA 92-1942, p. 17). Washington, DC: U.S. Government Printing Office.

FIGURE 6-6 **Expenditures per Capita in Current and Constant Dollars by Separate Psychiatric Services of Nonfederal General Hospitals: Selected Years, 1969 to 1988**

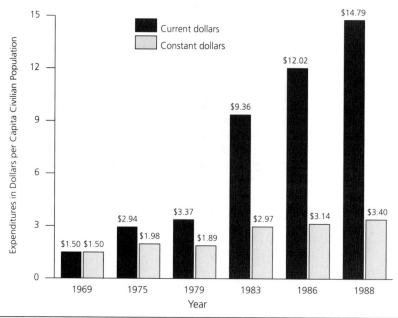

Source: Reprinted from Manderscheid, R. W., & Sonnenschein, M. A. (Eds.). (1992). *Mental health, United States, 1992* (DHHS Publication No. SMA 92-1942, p. 16). Washington, DC: U.S. Government Printing Office.

FIGURE 6-7 State Mental Health Expenditures as a Percentage of Total State Government Expenditures: 1990

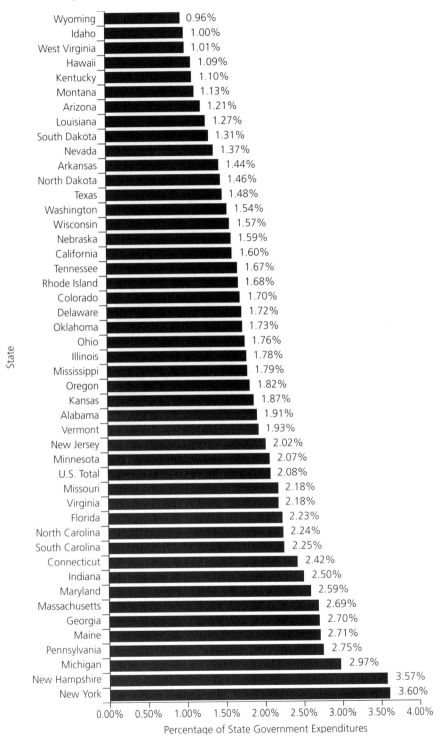

State	Percentage
Wyoming	0.96%
Idaho	1.00%
West Virginia	1.01%
Hawaii	1.09%
Kentucky	1.10%
Montana	1.13%
Arizona	1.21%
Louisiana	1.27%
South Dakota	1.31%
Nevada	1.37%
Arkansas	1.44%
North Dakota	1.46%
Texas	1.48%
Washington	1.54%
Wisconsin	1.57%
Nebraska	1.59%
California	1.60%
Tennessee	1.67%
Rhode Island	1.68%
Colorado	1.70%
Delaware	1.72%
Oklahoma	1.73%
Ohio	1.76%
Illinois	1.78%
Mississippi	1.79%
Oregon	1.82%
Kansas	1.87%
Alabama	1.91%
Vermont	1.93%
New Jersey	2.02%
Minnesota	2.07%
U.S. Total	2.08%
Missouri	2.18%
Virginia	2.18%
Florida	2.23%
North Carolina	2.24%
South Carolina	2.25%
Connecticut	2.42%
Indiana	2.50%
Maryland	2.59%
Massachusetts	2.69%
Georgia	2.70%
Maine	2.71%
Pennsylvania	2.75%
Michigan	2.97%
New Hampshire	3.57%
New York	3.60%

Percentage of State Government Expenditures

Source: Reprinted from Manderscheid, R. W., & Sonnenschein, M. A. (Eds.). (1992). *Mental health, United States, 1992* (DHHS Publication No. SMA 92-1942, p. 165). Washington, DC: U.S. Government Printing Office.

FIGURE 6-8 **State Mental Health Agency Expenditures per Capita: 1990**

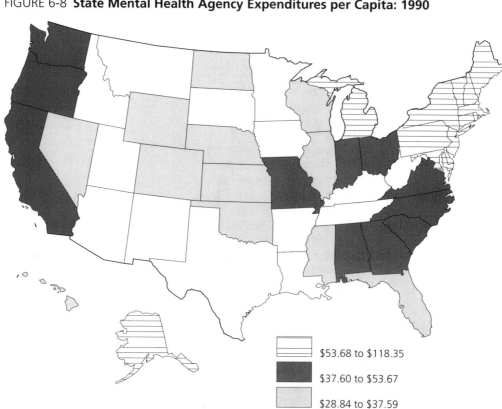

$53.68 to $118.35

$37.60 to $53.67

$28.84 to $37.59

Source: Reprinted from Manderscheid, R. W., & Sonnenschein, M. A. (Eds.). (1992). *Mental health, United States, 1992* (DHHS Publication No. SMA 92-1942, p. 168). Washington, DC: U.S. Government Printing Office.

Outpatient Services

As Table 6-10 indicates, the number of admissions to outpatient services and the number of outpatients under care far exceeded the number of admissions to inpatient facilities and the number of inpatients under care in 1986 (compare with Table 6-5). Some 1.4 million people were receiving outpatient services in April 1986. Roughly equal numbers of men and women were treated, and the rates by race do not appear to be substantially different. (This table and all others in this section are based on a patient sample.)

TABLE 6-10 **People under Outpatient Psychiatric Care, by Race, Gender, and Type of Service: 1986**

Race and Gender	Total, All Outpatient Services[a]	Outpatient Psychiatric Service					
		State and County Mental Hospitals	Private Psychiatric Hospitals	VA Medical Centers	Nonfederal General Hospitals	Multiservice Mental Health Organizations	Freestanding Outpatient Clinics
Number							
Total, all races	1,405,076	55,489	46,861	73,146	190,342	786,567	242,761
Male	683,789	26,908	19,074	69,174	71,739	378,668	114,149
Female	721,287	28,581	27,787	3,972	118,603	407,899	128,612
Total white	1,188,751	37,256	43,169	62,634	159,585	662,260	215,236
Male	562,355	18,172	16,492	58,761	60,429	304,572	100,646
Female	626,396	19,084	26,677	3,873	99,156	357,688	114,590
Total all other races	216,325	18,233	3,692	10,512	30,757	124,307	27,525
Male	121,434	8,736	2,582	10,413	11,310	74,096	13,503
Female	94,891	9,497	1,110	[b]	19,447	50,211	14,022
Percent distribution							
Total, all races	100.0	100.0	100.0	100.0	100.0	100.0	100.0
Male	48.7	48.5	40.7	94.6	37.7	48.1	47.0
Female	51.3	51.5	59.3	5.4	62.3	51.9	53.0
Total white	100.0	100.0	100.0	100.0	100.0	100.0	100.0
Male	47.3	48.8	38.2	93.8	37.9	46.0	46.8
Female	52.7	51.2	61.8	6.2	62.1	54.0	53.2
Total all other races	100.0	100.0	100.0	100.0	100.0	100.0	100.0
Male	56.1	47.9	69.9	99.1	36.8	59.6	49.1
Female	43.9	52.1	30.1	[b]	63.2	40.4	50.9
Rate per 100,000 civilian population							
Total, all races	578.0	23.2	19.6	30.6	79.5	328.6	101.4
Male	590.5	23.2	16.5	59.7	61.9	327.0	98.6
Female	583.7	23.1	22.5	3.2	96.0	330.1	104.1
Total white	585.7	18.4	21.3	30.9	78.6	326.3	106.0
Male	570.4	18.4	16.7	59.6	61.3	309.0	102.1
Female	600.1	18.3	25.6	3.7	95.0	342.6	109.8
Total all other races	594.2	50.1	10.1	28.9	84.5	341.5	75.6
Male	705.0	50.7	15.0	60.5	65.7	430.2	78.4
Female	494.7	49.5	5.8	[b]	101.4	261.8	73.1

Note: VA = Veterans Administration.

Source: Reprinted from Manderscheid, R. W., & Sonnenschein, M. A. (Eds.). (1992). *Mental health, United States, 1992* (DHHS Publication No. SMA 92-1942, p. 289). Washington, DC: U.S. Government Printing Office.

[a]Includes residential treatment centers for emotionally disturbed children.

[b]Estimate does not meet standards of reliability.

The diagnoses of outpatients studied in 1986 are presented in Table 6-11. Affective disorders are the most common diagnosis for outpatients, followed by schizophrenia. The ages of outpatients are shown in Table 6-12. Outpatient admissions, like inpatient admissions, are primarily of young and middle-aged adults. Young and elderly people with mental illness may be more likely to receive different

kinds of services. For example, young people may enter residential youth facilities or be served through their schools. In many cases, they may simply be cared for by their parents and avoid mental health services. Older people are less likely than young or middle-aged adults to have a spouse or other family member to care for them. Therefore, they may be committed to mental hospitals instead of be-

TABLE 6-11 **People under Outpatient Psychiatric Care, by Selected Principal Diagnoses and Type of Service: 1986**

		Outpatient Psychiatric Service					
Selected Principal Diagnoses	Total, All Outpatient Services[a]	State and County Mental Hospitals	Private Psychiatric Hospitals	VA Medical Centers	Nonfederal General Hospitals	Multiservice Mental Health Organizations	Freestanding Outpatient Clinics
Number							
Alcohol-related disorders	69,476	1,082	2,753	4,584	6,056	48,394	6,330
Drug-related disorders	26,551	b	b	4,170	4,542	9,880	4,824
Affective disorders	311,222	10,912	12,434	17,962	48,158	172,907	46,364
Schizophrenia	299,498	20,236	5,136	19,929	33,943	178,423	41,011
Personality disorders	84,519	b	2,196	1,342	10,761	51,303	14,884
Adjustment disorders	234,098	4,072	7,212	2,987	42,692	124,463	50,811
Social conditions	79,824	1,241	3,024	1,693	5,518	52,519	15,708
Percent of total people under care							
Alcohol-related disorders	4.9	1.9	5.9	6.3	3.2	6.2	2.6
Drug-related disorders	1.9	b	b	5.7	2.4	1.3	2.0
Affective disorders	22.1	19.7	26.5	24.6	25.3	22.0	19.1
Schizophrenia	21.3	36.5	11.0	27.2	17.8	22.7	16.9
Personality disorders	6.0	b	4.7	1.8	5.7	6.5	6.1
Adjustment disorders	16.7	7.3	15.4	4.1	22.4	15.8	20.9
Social conditions	5.7	2.2	6.5	2.3	2.9	6.7	6.5

Note: VA = Veterans Administration.

Source: Reprinted from Manderscheid, R. W., & Sonnenschein, M. A. (Eds.). (1992). *Mental health, United States, 1992* (DHHS Publication No. SMA 92-1942, p. 293). Washington, DC: U.S. Government Printing Office.

[a]Includes residential treatment centers for emotionally disturbed children.

[b]Estimate does not meet standards of reliability.

ing served through outpatient programs. To use an outpatient service, the person must have a residence in the community; transportation to the program; and, in many cases, someone to care for him or her in the community. These resources are more commonly available to young and middle-aged adults.

TABLE 6-12 **People under Outpatient Psychiatric Care, by Age and Type of Service: 1986**

| Age | Total, All Outpatient Services[a] | Outpatient Psychiatric Service | | | | | |
		State and County Mental Hospitals	Private Psychiatric Hospitals	VA Medical Centers	Nonfederal General Hospitals	Multiservice Mental Health Organizations	Freestanding Outpatient Clinics
Number							
Total, all ages	1,405,076	55,489	46,861	73,146	190,342	786,567	242,761
Under 18	229,149	6,494	11,949	[b]	35,180	115,034	56,678
18–24	130,574	5,679	5,569	633	11,723	83,697	22,499
25–44	644,917	23,901	22,076	33,852	74,419	381,622	105,180
45–64	309,963	12,649	4,170	27,187	50,556	165,328	49,435
65 and over	90,473	6,766	3,097	11,474	18,464	40,886	8,969
Percent distribution							
Total, all ages	100.0	100.0	100.0	100.0	100.0	100.0	100.0
Under 18	16.3	11.7	25.5	[c]	18.5	14.6	23.3
18–24	9.3	10.2	11.9	0.9	6.2	10.6	9.3
25–44	45.9	43.1	47.1	46.3	39.1	48.5	43.3
45–64	22.1	22.8	8.9	37.2	26.6	21.0	20.4
65 and over	6.4	12.2	6.6	15.7	9.7	5.2	3.7
Rate per 100,000 civilian population							
Total, all ages	587.0	23.2	19.6	30.6	79.5	328.6	101.4
Under 18	362.0	10.3	18.9	[c]	55.6	181.7	89.5
18–24	484.2	21.1	20.6	2.3	43.5	310.3	83.4
25–44	860.6	31.9	29.5	45.2	99.3	509.3	140.4
45–64	688.7	28.1	9.3	60.4	112.3	367.4	109.8
65 and over	310.2	23.2	10.6	39.3	63.3	140.2	30.8
Median age (years)	35	37	32	47	36	34	33

Source: Reprinted from Manderscheid, R. W., & Sonnenschein, M. A. (Eds.). (1992). *Mental health, United States, 1992* (DHHS Publication No. SMA 92-1942, p. 291). Washington, DC: U.S. Government Printing Office.

[a]Includes residential treatment centers for emotionally disturbed children.

[b]Estimate does not meet standards of reliability.

[c]Numbers too small to compute a rate.

Lengths of care for outpatients are listed in Table 6-13. The period of care is much longer for outpatients than for inpatients, which is an indicator of the transition from more expensive and more intensive care in hospitals to community- and family-based outpatient care.

TABLE 6-13 **Median Days of Stay for People Terminated (Excluding Deaths) from Outpatient Psychiatric Service, by Race, Gender, Selected Principal Diagnoses, and Type of Outpatient Psychiatric Service: 1986**

| Patient Characteristic | Total, All Outpatient Services[a] | Outpatient Psychiatric Service | | | | | |
		State and County Mental Hospitals	Private Psychiatric Hospitals	VA Medical Centers	Nonfederal General Hospitals	Multiservice Mental Health Organizations	Freestanding Outpatient Clinics
Race and gender							
Total, all races	157	b	171	98	132	165	170
Male	139	164	212	98	b	139	111
Female	171	357	171	91	108	205	200
Total white	155	249	171	96	131	156	174
Male	132	164	170	96	146	137	99
Female	177	499	171	91	108	194	213
Total all other races	157	44	317	142	157	192	112
Male	168	97	b	142	329	168	b
Female	157	44	118	b	157	221	107
Age (years)							
Under 18	136	103	183	b	91	142	176
18–24	135	b	135	b	108	156	103
25–44	158	274	171	70	164	151	174
45–64	180	398	b	105	71	208	211
65 and over	182	b	241	83	146	199	124
Selected principal diagnoses							
Alcohol-related disorders	113	436	b	b	270	98	164
Drug-related disorders	144	b	b	70	205	91	218
Affective disorders	183	277	183	143	244	180	297
Schizophrenia	250	249	135	115	294	297	178
Personality disorders	160	86	b	1	152	b	b
Adjustment disorders	157	144	b	72	120	167	174
Social conditions	122	288	231	180	b	142	81

Note: VA = Veterans Administration.

Source: Reprinted from Manderscheid, R. W., & Sonnenschein, M. A. (Eds.). (1992). *Mental health, United States, 1992* (DHHS Publication No. SMA 92-1942, p. 294). Washington, DC: U.S. Government Printing Office.

[a]Includes residential treatment centers for emotionally disturbed children.

[b]Numbers too small to compute a reliable median.

Private Psychiatrist Visits

An estimated 37.6 million office visits were scheduled with psychiatrists during the two-year period 1989–90. These visits did not include those with government-employed psychiatrists, such as those in community mental health centers, or with other physicians such as general practitioners and specialists in other fields who treat patients for psychiatric prob-lems. Psychiatrists received 2.7 percent of the office visits made to physicians during the period 1989–90. Ninety percent of patients were returning for treatment of a condition for which they had already seen the psychiatrist (Schappert, 1993c).

Table 6-14 provides basic demographic information about psychiatric patients in 1989–90 averaged across the two years. A dispropor-

TABLE 6-14 **Office Visits to Psychiatrists, by Selected Patient Characteristics and Geographic Region: 1989 to 1990**

Patient Characteristic	Number of Visits (1,000)	Percent Distribution	Visit Rate per 100 People
Age			
All ages	18,790	100.0	7.7
Under 15	940	5.0	1.7
15–24	1,484	7.9	4.2
25–44	9,065	48.2	11.4
45–64	5,950	31.7	12.8
65 and over	1,351	7.2	4.6
Gender and age			
Female, all ages	11,100	59.1	8.8
Under 15	229	1.2	0.9
15–24	918	4.9	5.2
25–44	5,497	29.3	13.6
45–64	3,466	18.4	14.4
65 and over	990	5.3	5.7
Male, all ages	7,690	40.9	6.5
Under 15	712	3.8	2.6
15–24	565	3.0	3.2
25–44	3,568	19.0	9.2
45–64	2,484	13.2	11.2
65 and over	361	1.9	2.9
Race			
White	17,355	92.4	8.4
Black	1,050	5.6	3.5
Asian and Pacific Islander	201	1.1	a
American Indian, Eskimo, and Aleut	58	0.3	a
Unspecified	126	0.7	a
Geographic region			
Northeast	6,325	33.7	12.8
Midwest	4,132	22.0	6.9
South	5,359	28.5	6.4
West	2,974	15.8	5.7

Note: Number of visits and visit rates are averaged over the two-year period.

Source: Reprinted from Schappert, S. M. (1993). *Office visits to psychiatrists: United States, 1989–90* (p. 3). Hyattsville, MD: U.S. Public Health Service, National Center for Health Statistics.

[a]Number too small to compute a reliable rate.

tionately large number of patients were white and in the 25- to 44-year age group, and the Northeast had by far the largest visit rate—12.8 per 100 population—in the country.

Two-thirds of the patients sought psychiatric treatment of specific problems, which are listed in Table 6-15. Depression is by far the leading problem, and anxiety or nervousness is second.

TABLE 6-15 **Office Visits to Psychiatrists, by the 20 Most Frequently Mentioned Principal Reasons for Visit: 1989 to 1990**

Principal Reason for Visit	Number of Visits (1,000)	Percent Distribution
All visits	18,790	100.0
Depression	5,303	28.2
Anxiety or nervousness	2,983	15.9
Psychotherapy	1,300	6.9
Other signs or symptoms relating to psychological and mental disorders	1,030	5.5
Marital problems	690	3.7
Behavioral disturbances	610	3.2
Medication, other and unspecified kinds	441	2.3
Parent–child problems	372	2.0
Anger	357	1.9
Disturbances of sleep	321	1.7
Social adjustment problems	319	1.7
Occupational problems	294	1.6
Psychosexual disorders	233	1.2
Problems with identity and self-esteem	227	1.2
Fears and phobias	223	1.2
Other problems of family relationship	219	1.2
Delusions or hallucinations	212	1.1
Functional psychoses	209	1.1
Counseling, not otherwise specified	194	1.0
Tiredness, exhaustion	184	1.0
All other reasons	3,070	16.3

Note: Number of visits is averaged for the two-year period.

Source: Reprinted from Schappert, S. M. (1993). *Office visits to psychiatrists: United States, 1989–90* (p. 6). Hyattsville, MD: U.S. Public Health Service, National Center for Health Statistics.

Grouped diagnoses given to the patients by gender are shown in Table 6-16. Mood disorders are the leading diagnoses, and among them depression is the most common. Anxiety disorders are second. Psychotic disorders, the most typical diagnoses of public mental health services patients and mental hospital residents, constitute less than 10 percent of the diagnoses, with no distinctions between men and women. Psychiatric diagnoses also typically include secondary diagnoses along with the principal designations; these are presented in Figure 6-9.

TABLE 6-16 **Office Visits to Psychiatrists, by Grouped Principal Diagnoses and Gender: 1989 to 1990**

Grouped Principal Diagnoses	Total		Female		Male	
	No.	%	No.	%	No.	%
All visits	18,790	100.0	11,100	100.0	7,690	100.0
Mental retardation, developmental disorders, and other childhood disorders	522	2.8	93	0.8	429	5.6
Hyperkinetic syndrome of childhood	352	1.9	56	0.5	296	3.9
Other	170	0.9	37[a]	0.3[a]	133	1.7
Delirium, dementia, and other mental disorders due to a general medical condition	81	0.4	64	0.6	17[a]	0.2[a]
Substance-related disorders	284	1.5	80	0.7	204	2.7
Schizophrenia and other (nonmood) psychotic disorders	1,651	8.8	974	8.8	676	8.8
Mood disorders	8,100	43.1	5,420	48.8	2,680	34.9
Bipolar disorders	1,160	6.2	797	7.2	363	4.7
Depressive disorders	6,920	36.8	4,603	41.5	2,317	30.1
Major depressive disorder	2,820	15.0	1,826	16.5	994	12.9
Dysthymia	3,054	16.3	2,011	18.1	1,043	13.6
Other depressive disorders	1,046	5.6	766	6.9	280	3.6
Other mood disorders	20[a]	0.1[a]	20[a]	0.2[a]	—	—
Anxiety disorders	2,511	13.4	1,503	13.5	1,008	13.1
Panic disorders	417	2.2	289	2.6	128	1.7
Obsessive–compulsive disorder	410	2.2	245	2.2	165	2.1
Other anxiety disorders	1,684	9.0	969	8.7	715	9.3
Adjustment disorders	1,457	7.8	756	6.8	700	9.1
Personality disorders	1,913	10.2	867	7.8	1,046	13.6
Other mental disorders	1,115	5.9	606	5.5	509	6.6
Other conditions that may be a focus of treatment	470	2.5	295	2.7	174	2.3
Ill-defined signs and symptoms and other nonpsychiatric medical conditions	558	3.0	375	3.4	183	2.4
Unknown	128	0.7	66	0.6	62	0.8

Notes: Number of visits is averaged for the two-year period. — = not available.

Source: Adapted from Schappert, S. M. (1993). *Office visits to psychiatrists: United States, 1989–90* (p. 7). Hyattsville, MD: U.S. Public Health Service, National Center for Health Statistics.

[a]Estimate does not meet standards of reliability.

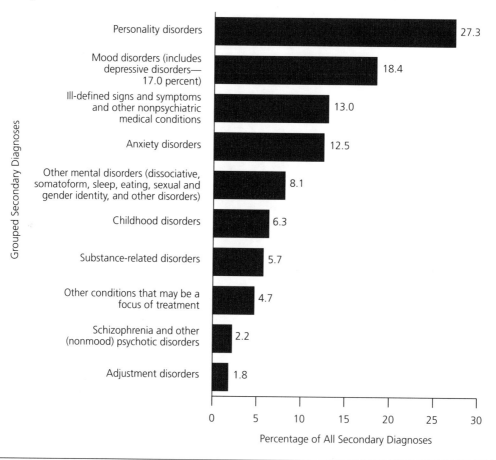

FIGURE 6-9 **Secondary Diagnoses at Psychiatrist Office Visits, by Diagnostic Group: 1989 to 1990**

Notes: Number of visits with secondary diagnoses = 6.827 million. Statistics are based on a two-year average.

Source: Reprinted from Schappert, S. M. (1993). *Office visits to psychiatrists: United States, 1989–90* (p. 9). Hyattsville, MD: U.S. Public Health Service, National Center for Health Statistics.

When the diagnostic data are grouped by age, children are most likely to be diagnosed with mental retardation, developmental disorders, and hyperkinetic syndrome (more commonly referred to as "attention deficit hyperactivity disorder"). The breakdown by age group is shown in Table 6-17.

TABLE 6-17 **Office Visits to Psychiatrists, by Grouped Principal Diagnoses and Age: 1989 to 1990**

Grouped Principal Diagnoses	Number of Visits (1,000)	Percent Distribution
Under 15 years		
All visits	940	100.0
Mental retardation, developmental disorders, and other childhood disorders	359	38.2
Hyperkinetic syndrome of childhood	289	30.8
Other	70	7.4
Adjustment disorders	171	18.1
Mood disorders	158	16.8
Depressive disorders	158	16.8
All other	252	26.8
15–24 years		
All visits	1,484	100.0
Mood disorders	535	36.1
Bipolar disorders	63	4.2
Depressive disorders	473	31.9
Adjustment disorders	228	15.3
Anxiety disorders	205	13.8
Mental retardation, developmental disorders, and other childhood disorders	104	7.0
All other	412	27.8
25–44 years		
All visits	9,065	100.0
Mood disorders	3,764	41.5
Bipolar disorders	605	6.7
Depressive disorders	3,152	34.8
Other mood disorders	8[a]	0.1[a]
Anxiety disorders	1,419	15.7
Panic disorders	199	2.2
Obsessive–compulsive disorder	194	2.1
Other anxiety disorders	1,026	11.3
Personality disorders	1,041	11.5
Schizophrenia and other (nonmood) psychotic disorders	786	8.7
Adjustment disorders	699	7.7
All other	1,356	15.0
45–64 years		
All visits	5,950	100.0
Mood disorders	2,795	47.0
Bipolar disorders	397	6.7
Depressive disorders	2,398	40.3
Anxiety disorders	699	11.8
Personality disorders	735	12.3
Adjustment disorders	322	5.4
All other	1,399	23.5
65 years and over		
All visits	1,351	100.0
Mood disorders	847	62.7
Bipolar disorders	95	7.1
Depressive disorders	740	54.8
Other mood disorders	12	0.9
All other	504	37.3

Note: Number of visits is averaged for the two-year period.

Source: Reprinted from Schappert, S. M. (1993). *Office visits to psychiatrists: United States, 1989–90* (p. 81). Hyattsville, MD: U.S. Public Health Service, National Center for Health Statistics.

[a]Estimate does not meet standards of reliability.

The kind of treatment provided for each diagnosis group is shown in Table 6-18. In almost all cases, patients receive psychotherapy either with or without medication. Table 6-19 shows the numbers of "drug mentions," or entry of a drug in a patient's record, by psychiatrists by generic name. The most frequently mentioned drug, fluoxetine hydrochloride, is the generic name for Prozac, a widely used antidepressant. Some of the medicines prescribed contain several drugs, each of which is included in the table separately. Antipsychotic and antianxiety drugs were among the most prescribed, after antidepressants.

Table 6-20 lists principal reasons for visits to psychiatrists and primary care and other physicians for psychiatric care.

TABLE 6-18 Office Visits to Psychiatrists, by Type of Therapy Ordered or Provided and Grouped Principal Diagnoses: 1989 to 1990

| | | Type of Therapy Ordered or Provided (% distribution) | | | |
Grouped Principal Diagnoses	Number of Visits (1,000)	Psycho-therapy with Medication	Psycho-therapy without Medication	Medication without Psycho-therapy[a]	Neither Psycho-therapy nor Medication[b]
All visits	18,790	45.6	43.9	4.6	5.9
Mental retardation, developmental disorders, and other childhood disorders	522	57.9	25.7	11.0	5.4[c]
Hyperkinetic syndrome of childhood	352	68.7	14.5	12.6	4.1[c]
Other	170	35.5	48.8	7.6[c]	8.1[c]
Delirium, dementia, and other mental disorders due to a general medical condition	81	55.1	37.0	7.9[c]	NA
Substance-related disorders	284	27.5	64.1	1.9[c]	6.4[c]
Schizophrenia and other (nonmood) psychotic disorders	1,651	64.2	16.7	16.8	2.4[c]
Mood disorders	8,100	58.5	35.6	3.8	2.1[a]
Bipolar disorders	1,160	72.9	21.5	5.6	NA
Depressive disorders	6,920	56.0	38.1	3.5	2.4
Major depressive disorder	2,820	78.6	12.8	6.4	2.1
Dysthymia	3,054	39.1	58.2	1.0[c]	1.7
Other depressive disorders	1,046	44.2	47.3	3.3[c]	5.2
Other mood disorders	20[c]	100.0	—	—	—
Anxiety disorders	2,511	47.1	47.1	2.3	3.4
Panic disorders	417	71.7	21.2	7.1[c]	—
Obsessive–compulsive disorder	410	53.2	35.9	2.9[c]	7.9[c]
Other anxiety disorders	1,684	40.1	56.1	1.0[c]	2.8
Adjustment disorders	1,457	18.2	74.6	3.1[c]	4.1
Personality disorders	1,913	13.0	72.6	0.9[c]	13.5
Other mental disorders	1,115	22.9	58.2	0.5[c]	18.4
Other conditions that may be a focus of treatment	470	30.6	47.6	3.4[c]	18.4
Ill-defined signs and symptoms and other nonpsychiatric medical conditions	558	37.2	33.3	5.8	23.6
Unknown	128	30.4	22.7[c]	29.3	17.6[c]

Notes: Number of visits is averaged for the two-year period. — = not available; NA = not applicable.

Source: Reprinted from Schappert, S. M. (1993). *Office visits to psychiatrists: United States, 1989–90* (p. 11). Hyattsville, MD: U.S. Public Health Service, National Center for Health Statistics.

[a]An average of 870,000 visits included medication without mention of psychotherapy. Of these, 47.7 percent reported other counseling advice ordered or provided at the visit, and 20.1 percent reported other nonmedication therapy at the visit.

[b]An average of 1.1 million visits did not include psychotherapy or medication therapy. However, 67.3 percent of these cited other nonmedication therapy, and 24.8 percent reported that other counseling or advice was ordered or provided.

[c]Estimate does not meet standards of reliability.

TABLE 6-19 **The 20 Generic Substances Most Frequently Used by Psychiatrists: 1989 to 1990**

Generic Substance	Number of Drug Mentions (1,000)	Percent Distribution	Therapeutic Classification
All mentions	15,933	100.0	
Fluoxetine hydrochloride	2,016	12.7	Antidepressants
Lithium	1,269	8.0	Antipsychotic drugs
Alprazolam	951	6.0	Antianxiety agents
Amitriptyline	851	5.3	Antidepressants
Imipramine	606	3.8	Antidepressants
Trazadone	558	3.5	Antidepressants
Thioridazine	553	3.5	Antipsychotic drugs
Nortriptyline	551	3.5	Antidepressants
Diazepam	526	3.3	Antianxiety agents
Desipramine	521	3.3	Antidepressants
Lorazepam	436	2.7	Antianxiety agents
Doxepin	433	2.7	Antidepressants
Trifluoperazine	420	2.6	Antipsychotic drugs
Haloperidol	344	2.2	Antipsychotic drugs
Perphenazine	308	1.9	Antidepressants
Chlorpromazine	293	1.8	Antipsychotic drugs
Temazepam	262	1.6	Sedatives and hypnotics
Benztropine	262	1.6	Drugs used in extrapyramidal movement disorders
Maprotiline	248[a]	0.0[a]	Antidepressants
Clonazepam	245[a]	0.0[a]	Anticonvulsants

Note: Number of drug mentions is averaged for the two-year period.

Source: Reprinted from Schappert, S. M. (1993). *Office visits to psychiatrists: United States, 1989–90* (p. 13). Hyattsville, MD: U.S. Public Health Service, National Center for Health Statistics.

[a]Estimate does not meet standards of reliability.

Mental Health Staff

Figure 6-10 shows the staffing patterns of mental health organizations by discipline from 1972 to 1988. Even though staffing at state mental hospitals decreased dramatically, from 223,886 to 180,161, the number of mental health staff in all organizations increased from 375,984 in 1972 to 531,072 in 1988 (Manderscheid & Sonnenschein, 1992). Pro-fessional patient care staff increased from 27 percent of total employees to 47 percent. Nurses, psychologists, and social workers increased in number, whereas psychiatrists declined slightly. Administrative and nonprofessional patient care staff experienced the greatest reductions. The same changes in staffing patterns occurred in private psychiatric hospitals, as Figure 6-11 shows.

TABLE 6-20 **Office Visits for Selected Principal Reasons for Visit and Grouped Principal Diagnoses, by Physician Specialty: 1989 to 1990**

Visit Characteristic	Number of Visits (1,000)	Total	Physician Specialty (% distribution)		
			Psychiatry	Primary Care	All Other Specialties
All visits	698,653	100.0	2.7	54.5	42.8
Principal reason for visit					
All symptoms referable to psychological and mental disorders	18,945	100.0	61.8	30.4	7.8
Depression	6,956	100.0	76.2	20.7	3.1[a]
Anxiety and nervousness	5,336	100.0	55.9	37.5	6.6
Disturbances of sleep	1,522	100.0	21.1	64.6	14.3[a]
Other signs or symptoms relating to psychological and mental disorders	1,365	100.0	75.5	19.9	4.6[a]
Behavioral disturbances	999	100.0	61.0	32.3	6.7[a]
Psychosexual disorders	891	100.0	26.1	17.4[a]	56.5
Anger	357	100.0	100.0	—	—
Fears and phobias	246	100.0	90.6	9.4[a]	—
Problems with identity and self-esteem	234	100.0	96.9	3.1[a]	—
Delusions or hallucinations	225	100.0	94.3	2.8[a]	2.9[a]
Grouped principal diagnoses					
Mental retardation, developmental disorders, and other childhood disorders	1,490	100.0	35.0	60.8	4.2[a]
Delirium, dementia, and other mental disorders due to a general medical condition	412	100.0	19.7[a]	44.0	36.2[a]
Substance-related disorders	988	100.0	28.7	65.3	6.0[a]
Schizophrenia and other (nonmood) psychotic disorders	2,100	100.0	78.6	18.3	3.1[a]
Mood disorders	10,914	100.0	74.2	21.8	4.0
Bipolar disorders	1,175	100.0	98.7	1.3[a]	—
Depressive disorders	9,718	100.0	71.2	24.3	4.4
Major depressive disorder	3,014	100.0	93.6	5.9[a]	0.6[a]
Dysthymia	3,757	100.0	81.3	16.5	2.3[a]
Other depressive disorders	2,947	100.0	35.5	53.3	11.2[a]
Other mood disorders	21[a]	100.0	95.1[a]	—	4.9[a]
Anxiety disorders	4,876	100.0	51.5	41.6	6.9[a]
Adjustment disorders	1,792	100.0	81.3	17.1	1.6[a]
Personality disorders	1,935	100.0	98.9	1.1[a]	0.1[a]
Other mental disorders	3,713	100.0	30.0	45.4	24.5
Other conditions that may be a focus of treatment	2,016	100.0	23.3	40.1	36.6
Ill-defined signs and symptoms and other nonpsychiatric medical conditions	654,311	100.0	0.1	55.5	44.5
Unknown	14,106	100.0	0.9[a]	54.6	44.5

Notes: Number of visits is averaged for the two-year period. — = not available.

Source: Reprinted from Schappert, S. M. (1993). *Office visits to psychiatrists: United States, 1989–90* (p. 10). Hyattsville, MD: U.S. Public Health Service, National Center for Health Statistics.

[a]Estimate does not meet standards of reliability.

Nursing Home and Residential Services

Many mentally ill people reside in nursing homes (also called "long-term-care facilities"), rather than in public mental hospitals or general hospital psychiatry units. Nursing home care is expensive, although it is much less expensive than inpatient hospital care. According to Wiener, Illston, and Hanley (1994), a year in a nursing home cost $37,000 in 1993. Although that is significantly less, at about $100 per day, than each day in a community hospital (see chapter 5), hospital stays are usually very brief. Furthermore, health insurance covers hospital stays but not typically nursing home residence. Wiener et al. stated that disabled elderly people are often surprised to find that "neither Medicare not private insurance

FIGURE 6-10 **Full-Time Equivalent Staff Employed in All Mental Health Organizations, by Discipline: Selected Years, 1972 to 1988**

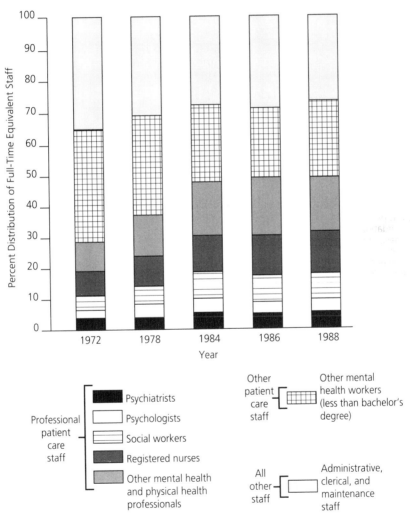

Source: Reprinted from Manderscheid, R. W., & Sonnenschein, M. A. (Eds.). (1992). *Mental health, United States, 1992* (DHHS Publication No. SMA 92-1942, p. 4). Washington, DC: U.S. Government Printing Office.

covers the costs of nursing home . . . care" (p. 2) and that only 4 percent to 5 percent of the elderly and a negligible portion of the nonelderly populations have private long-term-care insurance, a developing resource for paying for nursing home care. In 1993, a total of $54.7 billion was spent on nursing home care. Of that amount, $22.4 billion was paid by Medicaid, $4.3 billion by Medicare, and

$28.0 billion by patients themselves. They anticipated increases of over 100 percent in 1993 dollars by 2018 (Wiener et al., 1994).

Many mentally ill people also live in board and care homes, sometimes called "adult residential care facilities" or "adult foster homes." Board and care homes are usually less expensive, but they do not typically qualify for Medicaid or Medicare because their services

FIGURE 6-11 **Full-Time Equivalent Staff Employed in Private Psychiatric Hospitals, by Discipline: Selected Years, 1972 to 1988**

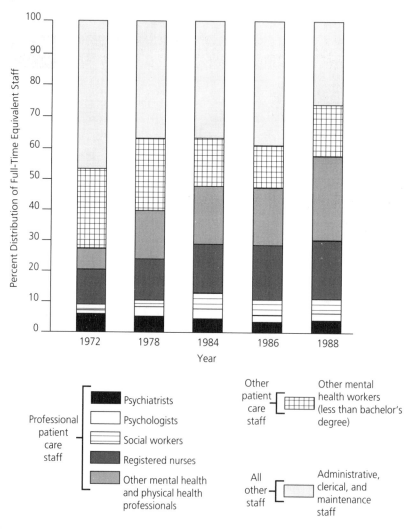

Source: Reprinted from Manderscheid, R. W., & Sonnenschein, M. A. (Eds.). (1992). *Mental health, United States, 1992* (DHHS Publication No. SMA 92-1942, p. 12). Washington, DC: U.S. Government Printing Office.

are not medical in nature—they are residential. Therefore, residents in such homes must pay out of their own resources, which typically include Supplemental Security Income or disability payments or both.

Figure 6-12 shows the percentage of mentally ill nursing home patients with each type of mental disorder in 1985. Table 6-21 shows selected characteristics of people with mental illness in nursing homes in 1985; the rates of each kind of cognitive disability per 1,000 nursing home residents, by age, are shown in Table 6-22.

In 1991 there were 46,942 nursing home and board and care facilities in the United States, with a total of 2 million beds and 1.9 million residents. One-third of the facilities were designated as nursing homes and two-

FIGURE 6-12 Mentally Ill Nursing Home Residents, by Type of Mental Disorder: 1985

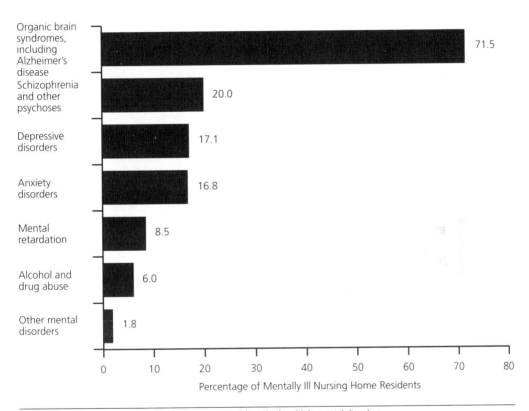

Note: Percentages total more than 100 because some residents had multiple mental disorders.

Source: Reprinted from Manderscheid, R. W., & Sonnenschein, M. A. (Eds.). (1990). *Mental health, United States, 1990* (DHHS Publication No. ADM 90-1708, Figure 6.2). Washington, DC: U.S. Government Printing Office.

thirds as board and care homes. However, nursing homes served more patients—1.5 million—than board and care homes (400,000). There were 609.3 beds in both kinds of facilities for every 1,000 people in the United States over age 85. Of the total nursing home residents in 1991, 38.7 percent were age 85 or over and 53.7 percent were between age 65 and 84. Only 0.2 percent were under 22 and 7.4 percent between age 22 and 64. For board and care homes, 15.6 percent were over age 85, 36.7 percent were between age 65 and 84, 43.4 percent were age 22 to 64, and 4.3 percent were under age 22 (Sirrocco, 1994).

TABLE 6-21 **Mentally Ill Nursing Home Residents: 1985**

Characteristic	No.	%
Total population	1,491,400	
Number with mental		
disorders	974,300	
Gender		
Female		72
Male		28
Age over age 65		87
Race		
White		92
Black and other		8
Diagnoses		
Organic brain syndromes		72
Schizophrenia and other		
psychoses		20
Anxiety disorders		17
Depressive disorders		17
Mental retardation		9
Alcohol and drug abuse		6
Other		2

Source: Adapted from Manderscheid, R. W., & Sonnenschein, M. A. (Eds.). (1990). *Mental health, United States, 1990* (DHHS Publication No. ADM 90-1708, p. 234). Washington, DC: U.S. Government Printing Office.

TABLE 6-22 **Cognitive Disabilities in Nursing Home Residents, by Age: 1985**

Cognitive Disability	Rate per 1,000 Residents			
	Under 65 Years	65–74 Years	75–84 Years	85 Years and Over
None	207	294	346	351
One or more	793	706	654	649
Organic brain syndromes	186	385	477	551
Alzheimer's disease and other degeneration of the brain	31[a]	82	66	40
Schizophrenia and other psychoses	316	212	103	74
Depressive disorders	178	186	159	108
Anxiety disorders	195	165	152	116
Alcohol and drug abuse	101	81	33	13
Mental retardation	263	98	27	1

Source: Reprinted from U.S. Department of Health and Human Services. (1992). *Health data on older Americans: United States, 1992* (p. 146). Hyattsville, MD: U.S. Public Health Service, National Center for Health Statistics.

[a]Estimate does not meet standards of reliability.

Adults with Serious Mental Illness

In 1989, 3.26 million adult Americans could be classified as having serious mental illness, defined as "any psychiatric disorder present during the past year that seriously interfered with one or more aspects of a person's daily life" (Manderscheid & Sonnenschein, 1992, p. 255). Socioeconomic and other information about this population is provided in Table 6-23. Nearly 80 percent of them had some current limitation on their activity, including work and discharging family responsibilities, because of their illness.

TABLE 6-23 Adults with Serious Mental Illness and Adults Currently Limited by Serious Mental Illness, by Selected Characteristics: 1989

| | Adult Household Population | | Adults with Serious Mental Illness (SMI) | | | | | |
| | | | Total | | | Currently Limited by SMI | | |
Characteristic	Number (1,000)	Percent Distribution	Number (1,000)	Percent Distribution	Rate per Thousand	Number (1,000)	Percent Distribution	Percent of Adults with SMI
Total[a]	179,529	100.0	3,264	100.0	18.2	2,571	100.0	78.8
Age (years)[a]								
18–24	25,401	14.2	361	11.1	14.2	291	11.3	80.6
25–34	42,814	23.9	707	21.7	16.5	501	19.5	70.8
35–44	35,982	20.0	744	22.8	20.7	600	23.3	80.6
45–64	46,114	25.7	919	28.2	19.9	749	29.1	81.5
65–69	9,903	5.5	142	4.4	14.3	99	3.9	70.0
70–74	7,925	4.4	102	3.1	12.9	82	3.2	79.8
75 and over	11,391	6.3	288	8.8	25.3	249	9.7	86.6
Gender[a]								
Male	85,257	47.5	1,320	40.4	15.5	1,105	43.0	83.7
Female	94,272	52.5	1,944	59.6	20.6	1,466	57.0	75.4
Race[a]								
White	153,763	85.6	2,812	86.1	18.3	2,194	85.3	78.0
Black	19,932	11.1	393	12.0	19.7	325	12.7	82.8
Other	5,834	3.2	59	1.8	10.1	52	2.0	87.1
Poverty status[b]								
Below poverty threshold	15,464	9.5	609	21.0	39.4	525	23.1	86.3
At or above poverty threshold	147,070	90.5	2,284	79.0	15.5	1,750	76.9	76.7
Education[b]								
Less than 12 years	39,809	22.4	1,083	33.8	27.2	937	37.3	86.5
12 years	68,563	38.6	1,120	34.9	16.3	866	34.5	77.4
More than 12 years	69,369	39.0	1,002	31.3	14.4	708	28.2	70.7
Respondent-assessed health status[b]								
Excellent	62,277	34.8	337	10.3	5.4	192	7.5	56.9
Very good	50,941	28.5	620	19.1	12.2	414	16.1	66.7
Good	43,769	24.5	812	24.9	18.6	617	24.1	75.9
Fair	15,565	8.7	755	23.2	48.5	648	25.3	85.9
Poor	6,207	3.5	734	22.5	118.3	695	27.1	94.7

Source: Reprinted from Manderscheid, R. W., & Sonnenschein, M. A. (Eds.). (1992). *Mental health, United States, 1992* (DHHS Publication No. SMA 92-1942, p. 252). Washington, DC: U.S. Government Printing Office.

[a]Includes people with unknown poverty status, education, or self-assessed health status.

[b]Percentage denominators exclude people with this characteristic unknown.

Table 6-24 shows selected characteristics of people with serious mental illness who had ever seen mental health professionals in 1989. Over three-fourths had seen a mental health professional, and almost all who had seen a professional received some form of government disability payment. More information about those who received disability payments is provided in Table 6-25. Many people with serious mental illness—22.7 percent—do not visit mental health professionals—ever. They may live in areas where there are no such professionals; they may not know how to gain access to such professionals; or they may not believe in them. They may rely on family physicians, clergy, family members, teachers, native healers, or many others for their help—or they may not receive help at all.

TABLE 6-24 **Adults with Serious Mental Illness Who Have Ever Seen a Mental Health Professional, by Selected Characteristics: 1989**

Characteristic	Number (1,000)	Percent Who Have Seen a Professional[a]
Total[b]	2,380	77.3
Age (years)		
18–24	276	80.3
25–34	503	75.8
35–44	630	87.6
45–64	719	82.5
65–69	89	68.5
70–74	70	69.5
75 and over	93	37.0
Gender		
Male	959	77.9
Female	1,421	76.8
Race		
White	2,042	76.8
Black	292	80.3
Other	46	79.7
Poverty status[c]		
Below poverty threshold	470	79.1
At or above poverty threshold	1,633	76.1
Education[c]		
Less than 12 years	766	74.9
12 years	804	76.4
More than 12 years	762	80.3
Respondent-assessed health status[c]		
Excellent	244	82.6
Very good	464	78.7
Good	606	78.2
Fair	533	74.4
Poor	530	75.8
Use of prescription medication for the mental disorder[d]		
Yes	1,648	88.2
No	657	76.7
Receipt of government disability payment[c]		
Yes	665	96.4
No	1,628	71.3

Source: Reprinted from Manderscheid, R. W., & Sonnenschein, M. A. (Eds.). (1992). *Mental health, United States, 1992* (DHHS Publication No. SMA 92-1942, p. 268). Washington, DC: U.S. Government Printing Office.

[a]All percentage denominators exclude people with unknown time since last seen by a mental health professional (184,000, or 5.6 percent of total adults with serious mental illness).

[b]Percentage denominator for total includes people with unknown poverty status, education, health status, prescription drug use, and disability pay.

[c]Percentage denominator excludes people with this characteristic unknown.

[d]Percentage denominator includes only people who have ever seen a doctor or other health professional and excludes people with this characteristic unknown.

TABLE 6-25 Adults with Serious Mental Illness Who Received Government Disability Payment for the Mental Disorder, by Selected Characteristics: 1989

Characteristic	Number (1,000)	Percent[a]
Total[b]	703	23.2
Age (years)		
18–24	38	11.0
25–34	123	19.1
35–44	198	28.3
45–64	298	35.1
65 and over	46	9.4
Gender		
Male	402	33.3
Female	301	16.6
Race		
White	537	20.5
Black	156	43.8
Other	10	22.7
Poverty status[c]		
Below poverty threshold	195	33.6
At or above poverty threshold	405	19.2
Education[c]		
Less than 12 years	317	30.9
12 years	212	20.8
More than 12 years	142	15.3
Respondent-assessed health status[c]		
Excellent	34	11.9
Very good	93	16.1
Good	140	18.3
Fair	193	27.3
Poor	241	35.1
Use of prescription medication in the past year for the mental illness[c]		
Yes	549	29.7
No	143	16.4
Last saw mental health professional for the mental disorder[c]		
Less than one month	385	38.7
One month to less than one year	188	23.2
One year or more	92	18.9
Never	25	3.6

Source: Reprinted from Manderscheid, R. W., & Sonnenschein, M. A. (Eds.). (1992). *Mental health, United States, 1992* (DHHS Publication No. SMA 92-1942, p. 265). Washington, DC: U.S. Government Printing Office.

[a]All percentage denominators exclude people with unknown receipt of disability payment (237,000, or 7.3 percent of adults with serious mental illness).

[b]Percentage denominator for total includes people with unknown poverty status, education, health status, time since last seen by a mental health professional, and use of prescription medication.

[c]Percentage denominator excludes people with this characteristic unknown.

Alcohol and Other Substance Abuse

Among the mental health issues of greatest concern in the United States is alcohol and other substance abuse. In employee assistance programs, 30 percent to 40 percent of people needing services require them for substance abuse, and about 60 percent to 65 percent of these use alcohol (Employee Assistance Programs Association [EAPA], 1992). Unfortunately, it is likely that most alcohol and substance abuse goes untreated.

According to the EAPA (1992), some 10.5 million Americans show signs of alcoholism or drug dependence, and 7.2 million have heavy drinking patterns that are associated with impaired health or social functioning. Almost 12 percent of the American work force reports heavy drinking, defined as five or more drinks per occasion on five or more days in the past 30 days.

Alcohol is involved in over half of all highway deaths, spouse abuse cases, and violent crime. Half of those convicted for murder or attempted murder had been drinking when they committed the crime. Alcohol is associated with more than a third of child abuse cases and with two-thirds of all drownings. Forty percent of traffic fatalities involve drivers with blood alcohol concentrations of .10 or higher (EAPA, 1992).

The use of illegal drugs, particularly marijuana, is also prevalent in the United States. As Table 6-26 indicates, about 4.8 percent of the population used marijuana in 1991. In addition, according to the EAPA (1992), 35.3 million people are dependent on prescription and nonprescription drugs.

TABLE 6-26 Percentages of People Who Have Used Selected Drugs, by Gender, Age, and Region: 1991

Substance and Age Group	Total[a]	Gender		Race and Ethnicity			Region			
		Male	Female	White[b]	Black[b]	Hispanic	Northeast	Midwest	South	West
Current users										
Cigarettes: Total	27.0	28.7	25.5	27.3	27.9	24.7	26.9	28.2	27.3	25.4
12 to 17 years old	10.8	11.8	9.8	12.7	4.4	8.7	11.6	12.4	10.2	9.5
18 to 25 years old	32.2	32.0	32.3	35.8	21.8	24.8	35.7	33.6	30.3	30.6
26 to 34 years old	32.9	34.8	31.1	33.3	36.9	28.6	32.6	34.4	35.9	26.9
35 years old and over	26.6	28.8	24.7	25.8	32.6	27.7	25.3	27.6	27.0	26.2
Alcohol: Total	50.9	58.1	44.3	52.7	43.7	47.5	56.3	52.3	44.0	56.3
12 to 17 years old	20.3	22.3	18.2	20.4	20.1	22.5	19.0	21.9	19.8	20.7
18 to 25 years old	63.6	69.7	57.8	67.2	56.0	52.8	71.1	65.2	57.7	65.7
26 to 34 years old	61.7	70.8	52.8	63.8	57.1	57.2	66.3	64.5	55.9	63.5
35 years old and over	49.5	57.4	42.5	50.9	40.3	47.8	55.3	50.5	41.1	57.2
Marijuana: Total	4.8	6.3	3.4	4.5	7.2	4.3	5.2	4.6	4.2	5.8
12 to 17 years old	4.3	5.0	3.7	4.4	4.5	4.6	3.7	4.6	3.9	5.5
18 to 25 years old	13.0	15.7	10.5	13.7	14.6	9.1	14.7	11.5	12.1	14.8
26 to 34 years old	7.0	9.5	4.5	6.6	11.9	4.2	6.2	7.6	5.6	9.2
35 years old and over	2.1	3.0	1.3	1.9	3.5	2.3	2.8	2.0	1.7	2.3
Cocaine: Total	0.9	1.3	0.6	0.7	1.8	1.6	0.9	0.9	0.8	1.3
12 to 17 years old	0.4	0.5	0.6	0.3	0.5	1.3	0.5	c	0.6	0.4
18 to 25 years old	2.0	2.8	1.3	1.7	3.1	2.7	1.5	2.1	1.8	3.0
26 to 34 years old	1.8	2.6	1.1	1.6	2.7	2.0	2.1	1.7	1.4	2.4
35 years old and over	0.5	0.6	0.3	0.2	1.3	1.0	0.4	0.6	0.4	0.6
Smokeless tobacco: Total	3.4	6.5	0.5	3.9	2.0	0.8	1.2	3.0	5.4	2.5
12 to 17 years old	3.0	5.4	0.5	3.9	0.8	1.1	0.9	3.8	3.8	2.5
18 to 25 years old	5.8	11.4	0.3	7.4	1.2	1.7	2.7	4.6	7.7	6.5
26 to 34 years old	3.6	7.1	0.2	4.3	1.5	0.8	0.9	2.9	6.0	3.0
35 years old and over	2.8	5.2	0.7	3.0	2.8	0.4	1.0	2.6	4.9	1.3
Ever used										
Crack: Total	1.9	2.6	1.3	1.5	4.3	2.1	1.8	2.0	1.5	2.6
12 to 17 years old	0.9	0.7	1.0	0.8	1.1	1.3	0.6	0.4	0.9	1.7
18 to 25 years old	3.8	4.7	2.8	3.7	4.7	3.3	4.6	3.1	3.1	5.0
26 to 34 years old	3.7	5.2	2.3	2.8	9.3	3.7	2.9	3.3	3.5	5.2
35 years old and over	1.0	1.6	0.6	0.8	3.0	1.1	1.0	1.6	0.6	1.3
Inhalants: Total	5.4	7.0	4.0	5.6	3.8	4.8	4.5	4.5	4.9	8.3
12 to 17 years old	7.0	7.0	7.0	7.6	5.1	6.6	5.1	6.8	7.6	7.9
18 to 25 years old	10.9	12.3	9.5	12.7	4.5	6.5	9.8	9.7	9.8	15.3

26 to 34 years old	9.2	12.1	6.3	10.3	4.6	6.3	7.7	6.6	9.1	13.5
35 years old and over	2.5	3.8	1.4	2.3	2.9	2.6	2.2	2.2	1.7	4.7
Hallucinogens: Total	8.1	10.1	6.2	8.9	4.1	6.4	7.5	7.9	6.0	12.6
12 to 17 years old	3.3	3.3	3.4	3.8	1.2	3.5	2.9	3.8	3.0	3.8
18 to 25 years old	13.1	15.4	11.0	15.8	5.4	7.5	11.7	12.1	10.5	20.8
26 to 34 years old	15.5	18.8	12.4	18.0	5.9	9.2	15.1	15.0	12.5	21.3
35 years old and over	5.2	7.0	3.5	5.4	3.7	5.5	4.8	5.2	3.3	8.8
Stimulants[c]: Total	7.0	8.2	5.9	7.9	3.3	4.8	4.4	6.2	6.5	11.5
12 to 17 years old	3.0	2.5	3.4	3.5	0.8	2.1	1.5	3.0	3.5	3.3
18 to 25 years old	9.4	9.8	8.9	11.3	3.2	5.1	5.0	10.5	9.1	13.2
26 to 34 years old	12.2	14.1	10.4	14.3	5.0	6.3	7.9	10.3	2.6	17.8
35 years old and over	5.4	6.8	4.2	5.8	3.3	4.7	3.6	4.5	4.5	10.1
Sedatives[c]: Total	4.3	4.8	3.8	4.6	3.0	3.0	3.3	3.6	3.9	6.7
12 to 17 years old	2.4	2.0	2.9	2.7	1.2	2.2	1.8	2.4	2.7	2.5
18 to 25 years old	4.3	4.5	4.1	5.1	2.4	2.3	2.1	5.5	4.4	5.0
26 to 34 years old	7.5	8.7	6.3	8.6	3.8	3.4	6.2	5.9	8.1	9.3
35 years old and over	3.5	4.0	3.1	3.5	3.4	3.3	2.8	2.7	2.7	6.8
Tranquilizers[c]: Total	5.6	5.9	5.2	6.1	3.1	3.9	4.2	4.7	5.6	7.9
12 to 17 years old	2.1	1.8	2.5	2.6	1.1	1.0	1.4	1.9	2.6	2.0
18 to 25 years old	7.4	7.5	7.4	8.8	3.9	3.7	6.2	7.8	7.9	7.6
26 to 34 years old	10.0	10.9	9.1	11.4	5.7	5.4	9.2	8.5	11.0	10.7
35 years old and over	4.2	4.6	3.9	4.4	2.4	4.2	2.5	3.2	3.8	7.9
Analgesics[c]: Total	6.1	6.8	5.4	6.5	4.7	3.9	4.0	6.8	5.3	8.7
12 to 17 years old	4.4	4.3	4.6	4.8	3.9	3.6	2.7	5.0	5.0	4.4
18 to 25 years old	10.2	10.6	9.8	11.4	6.8	6.3	6.0	11.6	9.7	13.8
26 to 34 years old	9.8	11.1	8.5	11.1	6.8	4.1	7.6	8.7	11.0	10.9
35 years old and over	4.1	4.8	3.5	4.2	3.3	3.0	2.6	5.3	2.4	7.4

Notes: Current users are those who used drugs at least once within the month prior to this study. Percentages are based on national samples of respondents residing in households and are subject to sampling variability.

Source: Reprinted from U.S. Bureau of the Census. (1993). *Statistical abstract of the United States: 1993* (113th ed., p. 137). Austin, TX: Reference Press.

[a]Includes other races, not shown separately.

[b]Non-Hispanic.

[c]Low precision; no estimate reported.

[d]Nonmedical use; does not include over-the-counter drugs.

Tables 6-26 and 6-27 describe the users of potentially harmful substances. According to U.S. Bureau of the Census data (1993) shown in Table 6-26, a slight majority of all Americans use alcohol in every region except the South, which has a smaller proportion of alcohol users. Cocaine and marijuana are used by very few people, although the largest percentages are among young adults ages 18 to 25. Only a tiny portion use cocaine, and less than 10 percent in every category (except young adult males) use smokeless tobacco. Inhalants, hallucinogens, stimulants, analgesics, and tranquilizers are used slightly more than other substances. As Table 6-27 shows, the percentage of people using almost all substances, both legal and illegal, has decreased since 1979.

TABLE 6-27 **Percentages of People Who Have Used Selected Drugs, by Age: Selected Years, 1974 to 1991**

Age and Type of Drug	Ever Used						Current User					
	1974	1979	1982	1985	1988	1991	1974	1979	1982	1985	1988	1991
12 to 17 years old												
Marijuana	23.0	30.9	26.7	23.6	17.4	13.0	12.0	16.7	11.5	12.0	6.4	4.3
Cocaine	3.6	5.4	6.5	4.9	3.4	2.4	1.0	1.4	1.6	1.5	1.1	0.4
Inhalants	8.5	9.8	—	9.2	8.8	7.0	0.7	2.0	—	3.4	2.0	1.8
Hallucinogens	6.0	7.1	5.2	3.3	3.5	3.3	1.3	2.2	1.4	1.2	0.8	0.8
Heroin	1.0	0.5	a	a	0.6	0.3	a	a	a	a	a	0.1
Stimulants[b]	5.0	3.4	6.7	5.6	4.2	3.0	1.0	1.2	2.6	1.6	1.2	0.5
Sedatives[b]	5.0	3.2	5.8	4.1	2.3	2.4	1.0	1.1	1.3	1.0	0.6	0.5
Tranquilizers[b]	3.0	4.1	4.9	4.8	2.0	2.1	1.0	0.6	0.9	0.6	0.2	0.4
Analgesics[b]	—	3.2	4.2	5.8	4.1	4.4	—	0.6	0.7	1.6	0.9	1.1
Alcohol	54.0	70.3	65.2	55.5	50.2	46.4	34.0	37.2	30.2	31.0	25.2	20.3
Cigarettes	52.0	54.1	49.5	45.2	42.3	37.9	25.0	12.1	14.7	15.3	11.8	10.8
18 to 25 years old												
Marijuana	52.7	68.2	64.1	60.3	56.4	50.5	25.2	35.4	27.4	21.8	15.5	13.0
Cocaine	12.7	27.5	28.3	25.2	19.7	17.9	3.1	9.3	6.8	7.6	4.5	2.0
Inhalants	9.2	16.5	—	12.4	12.5	10.9	a	1.2	—	0.8	1.7	1.5
Hallucinogens	16.6	25.1	21.1	11.3	13.8	13.1	2.5	4.4	1.7	1.9	1.9	1.2
Heroin	4.5	3.5	1.2	1.2	0.3	0.8	a	a	a	a	a	0.1
Stimulants[b]	17.0	18.2	18.0	17.1	11.3	9.4	3.7	3.5	4.7	3.7	2.4	0.8
Sedatives[b]	15.0	17.0	18.7	11.0	5.5	4.3	1.6	2.8	2.6	1.6	0.9	0.7
Tranquilizers[b]	10.0	15.8	15.1	12.0	7.8	7.4	1.2	2.1	1.6	1.6	1.0	0.6
Analgesics[b]	—	11.8	12.1	11.3	9.4	10.2	—	1.0	1.0	1.8	1.5	1.4
Alcohol	81.6	95.3	94.6	92.6	90.3	90.2	69.3	75.9	70.9	71.4	65.3	63.6
Cigarettes	68.8	82.8	76.9	75.6	75.0	71.2	48.8	42.6	39.5	36.8	35.2	32.2
26 years old and over												
Marijuana	9.9	19.6	23.0	27.2	30.7	32.7	2.0	6.0	6.6	6.1	3.9	3.3
Cocaine	0.9	4.3	8.5	9.5	9.9	11.6	a	0.9	1.2	2.0	0.9	0.8
Inhalants	1.2	3.9	—	5.0	3.9	4.2	a	0.5	—	0.5	0.2	0.3
Hallucinogens	1.3	4.5	6.4	6.2	6.6	7.8	a	a	a	a	a	0.1
Heroin	0.5	1.0	1.1	1.1	1.1	1.5	a	a	a	a	a	a
Stimulants[b]	3.0	5.8	6.2	7.9	6.6	7.1	a	0.5	0.6	0.7	0.5	0.2
Sedatives[b]	2.0	3.5	4.8	5.2	3.3	4.5	a	a	a	0.6	0.3	0.3
Tranquilizers[b]	2.0	3.1	3.6	7.2	4.5	5.7	a	a	a	1.0	0.6	0.5
Analgesics[b]	—	2.7	3.2	5.6	4.5	5.5	—	a	a	0.9	0.4	0.5
Alcohol	73.2	91.5	88.2	89.4	88.6	88.6	54.5	61.3	59.8	60.6	54.8	52.5
Cigarettes	65.4	83.0	78.7	80.5	79.6	77.6	39.1	36.9	34.6	32.8	29.8	28.2

Notes: Current users are those who used drugs at least once within the month prior to this study. Percentages are based on national samples of respondents residing in households and are subject to sampling variability. — = not available.

Source: Reprinted from U.S. Bureau of the Census. (1993). *Statistical abstract of the United States: 1993* (113th ed., p. 136). Austin, TX: Reference Press.

[a]Estimate does not meet standards of reliability.

[b]Nonmedical use; does not include over-the-counter drugs.

Mental Retardation

Services for people with mental retardation are also discussed in several other places in this book. Some material is included in chapter 2, Children, and in chapter 4, Education. Although mental retardation is not always included in discussions of mental health, many mentally retarded people are treated in mental health facilities or in nursing homes. In addition, many mentally ill people who are "dually diagnosed" also carry a diagnosis of mental retardation.

About 3 percent of the U.S. population is assumed to have mental retardation, but only 1 percent to 1.5 percent are actually diagnosed with this condition. The birth rate of children with IQs below 50 is 3.6 per 1,000 live births. In 80 percent of the cases, the cause of the mental retardation is unknown. The condition is not correlated with race, nationality, religion, or socioeconomic status. The incidence of familial retardation among children of couples in which both partners are mentally retarded is 40 percent; when one partner has mental retardation, the incidence is 20 percent among the offspring (Berkow et al., 1992).

Premature infants with gestations of less than 32 weeks and weights of less than 1.5 kilograms have a 10 percent to 50 percent chance of having mental retardation. Mental retardation is four times more prevalent among males than females.

In terms of the degree of mental retardation, those considered to have profound mental retardation have IQs of less than 20. Severe is defined as an IQ of 20 to 35; moderate, 36 to 51; and mild, 52 to 68. Seventy-five percent of all people with mental retardation have a mild form, 20 percent have a moderate form, and 5 percent have a severe or profound form (Berkow et al., 1992).

One of the more prevalent forms of mental retardation is Down syndrome, a chromosome disorder (National Down Syndrome Congress, 1988). Incidence is one in 700 live births (Berkow et al., 1992). The National Down Syndrome Congress estimated that 4,000 children are born with the condition each year.

Down syndrome is associated with the age of the mother. The incidence is one per 2,000 live births among women in the early childbearing years; after age 40, the incidence is one per 40 live births. However, just over 20 percent of children with Down syndrome are born to mothers older than 35, a group who give birth to only 7 percent to 8 percent of children (Berkow, 1992); 80 percent of children with Down syndrome are born to women under 35.

People with mental retardation have been deinstitutionalized at a rate that is comparable to that for the mentally ill population. Although mentally retarded people once tended to live in public institutions, they are now encouraged to live in the community with help from schools, clinics, workshops, and private facilities and support for their families. There has also been a growth of care in private facilities such as special residential schools and nursing homes. The trend in public institutions is away from large facilities toward smaller, more homelike facilities.

Table 6-28 shows the trends in residential care for people with mental retardation during selected years from 1970 and 1990. In the years shown, the rate of care in public institutions dropped almost out of existence, whereas care in private facilities increased dramatically. The private facilities housed approximately the same number in 1990 as the public facilities housed in 1970. The numbers of facilities in both state and private categories increased dramatically, much more than the numbers of residents, indicating that the facilities are much smaller and house fewer residents.

Of 31,431 board and care homes studied in 1991, 13,169 were for people with mental retardation. Unlike the age breakdown for the general population of such homes, in these homes nearly 80 percent of the residents were between ages 22 and 64; 10.1 percent were under age 22; 9.6 percent were ages 65 to 84; and only 1.2 percent were age 85 or over (Sirrocco, 1994).

Conclusion

Along with children and some older adults, those with mental disabilities are among the most vulnerable people in American society. An understanding of the conditions they live in is an important part of the knowledge base of social workers.

TABLE 6-28 **Residential Facilities for People with Mental Retardation: Selected Years, 1970 to 1990**

Item	State-Operated Facilities					Private Facilities[a]			
	1970	1980	1985	1989	1990	1977	1982	1989	1990
Number of facilities	190	394	881	1,305	1,321	10,219	14,605	38,657	41,547
Residents beginning of year	189,956	148,734	117,101	99,267	94,675	—	—	—	—
Admissions[b]	14,985	14,064	7,713	6,518	5,568	22,363	22,431	—	—
Deaths in institutions	3,496	2,142	1,537	1,205	1,143	891	920	—	—
Live releases[c]	14,702	16,225	10,310	7,479	7,679	12,384	12,999	—	—
Residents end of year	186,743	140,230	112,183	94,268	91,640	89,120	115,032	180,023	188,902
Rate per 100,000 population	92.5	62.2	47.5	38.5	34.7	40.9	50.0	73.4	76.0
Average daily residents	187,897	136,304	111,791	96,171	92,729	—	—	—	—
Maintenance expenditures per day per average daily resident (dollars)[d]	13	68	122	184	196	19[e]	37[e]	—	—

Notes: For years ending June 30. "People with mental retardation" refers to those who have been so designated by state governments in the process of placing them into residential facilities. — = not available.

Source: Reprinted from U.S. Bureau of the Census. (1993). *Statistical abstract of the United States: 1993* (113th ed., p. 129). Austin, TX: Reference Press.

[a]A privately operated living quarter which provides 24-hour, seven-days-a-week responsibility for room, board, and supervision of mentally retarded people. Excludes single-family homes providing services to a relative and nursing homes, boarding homes, and foster homes not formally licensed or contracted as mental retardation service providers.

[b]Includes readmissions and excludes transfers. Excludes people entering newly opened facilities.

[c]In 1970, represents excess of residents released alive from facility over those returning to facility. Beginning 1980, total live releases.

[d]Reporting facilities only; includes salaries and wages, purchased provisions, fuel, light, water, and so on.

[e]Represents average daily reimbursement rate per resident.

7

OLDER ADULTS

As chapters 1 and 2 show, the U.S. population is aging. In 1980, the over-65 population was 11.3 percent of the total, up from 9.8 percent in 1970. In 1992, according to the U.S. Bureau of the Census (1993), 12.6 percent of the population was 65 or older; by 2010, 13.3 percent will be.

The changes in the proportion of older people are important for a variety of reasons—among them that older people require more health and social services than do other age groups. It is axiomatic in human services planning that children and older people are the primary recipients of human services programs and entitlements due to social arrangements and physical realities that limit the ability of the young and the elderly to be self-sufficient. This chapter deals with some of the special issues facing older adults and the rest of the society in providing for older people.

Throughout this *Almanac,* attention is given to older adults because so many issues in social welfare are associated with aging. General information about the older adult population is provided in chapter 1. Health and mental health issues have powerful effects on older people, who are typically the heaviest users of health services. Chapters 5 and 6 detail use of those services. The need for economic assistance or income maintenance and the programs designed to provide them are discussed in chapter 8. Income assistance was initially developed in the United States to enhance the well-being of older people and is, therefore, a special concern for the elderly. Data on these issues are not duplicated in this chapter, which focuses on some special issues of aging.

The terminology for dealing with aging is diverse. Terms to describe older people include "the aged," "older adults," "senior citizens,"

and "the aging." In this chapter, the term "older adults" is used most frequently, although any of the others are acceptable in the social services literature. Definitions of aging also vary. The most common demarcation is age 65, suggesting that people who are older than 65 are included in that population. However, some age-based social security programs are available for people as young as 50. Some nondisabled people, such as widows, may receive social security at age 60. Some other programs treat people as young as 55 as older adults.

The American Association of Retired Persons (AARP), which has some 30 million members, admits people as young as 50. There is also increasing attention given to the rapidly growing older aging population, sometimes called the "old old"—those who are 85 and older.

There are some who believe that 65-year-olds cannot be called older adults in the context of the longer lifespan of the 1990s. Many people who are 70 and older lead fully employed, active lives. Therefore, definitions of the aging population are diverse.

Population Trends

Figure 7-1 shows the number of older adults in the United States, beginning in 1900 and with projections to the year 2030. Tables 7-1 and 7-2 provide further information about the number of older adults by age group and gender. The number of people age 65 and older will grow from nearly 32 million in 1990 to a projected 61.5 million in 2025. The population of older women will consistently exceed the population of older men at all ages. Of those age 85 and older, women will consistently outnumber men by almost two to one. Information on the elderly population by race and

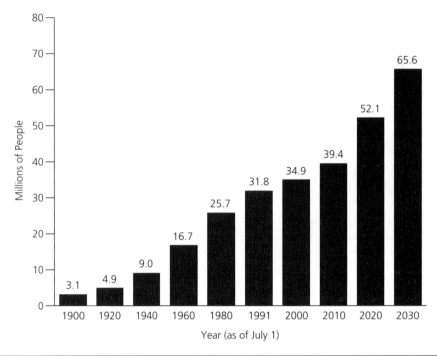

FIGURE 7-1 **Number of People Age 65 Years and Older: Selected Years, 1900 to 2030**

Source: Reprinted with permission from American Association of Retired Persons. (1992). *A profile of older Americans* (p. 2). Washington, DC: Author.

TABLE 7-1 **Elderly Population, by Percentage of Total Population, Age, and Gender: Selected Years, 1940 to 2025**

Category	1940	1950	1960	1970	1980	1990	2000[a]	2025[a]
Population 65 years and older (in thousands)	9,556	12,807	17,268	20,892	26,125	31,995	35,682	61,480
Percent of total population age 65 and older	6.8	8.0	9.1	9.7	11.1	12.3	12.6	18.8
Percent of total population age 75 and older	2.0	2.5	3.1	3.7	4.4	5.2	6.0	7.9
Percent of total population age 85 and older	0.3	0.4	0.5	0.7	1.0	1.3	1.6	2.1
Percent of the population age 65 and older who are								
Men 65 and older	48.4	46.8	44.5	41.6	40.3	40.8	41.6	44.3
Men 65 to 74	34.8	32.6	30.2	26.9	26.3	25.9	23.9	27.6
Men 75 to 84	11.9	12.2	12.2	12.4	11.3	12.1	14.0	13.2
Men 85 and older	1.7	2.0	2.2	2.4	2.8	2.9	3.6	3.5
Women 65 and older	51.6	53.2	55.5	58.4	59.7	59.2	58.4	55.7
Women 65 to 74	35.8	35.7	35.7	34.7	33.9	31.8	28.3	30.5
Women 75 to 84	13.4	14.7	16.3	19.2	19.3	19.8	21.1	17.7
Women 85 and older	2.3	2.8	3.5	4.6	6.5	7.5	9.0	7.4

Notes: Population data include total United States plus the outlying areas covered under the social security program and an adjustment for population undercount.

Source: Adapted from Committee on Ways and Means, U.S. House of Representatives. (1993). *Overview of entitlement programs: 1993 greenbook* (p. 1267). Washington, DC: U.S. Government Printing Office.

[a]Projection.

ethnicity, marital status, living arrangements, education, and labor force participation is provided in Table 7-3.

Table 7-4 shows the state-by-state elderly population in 1991 and the increases between 1980 and 1991. The table also shows the percentage of elderly people below the poverty level in 1989. Figure 7-2 shows the geographic concentrations of elderly people. Older adults are concentrated in the middle of the nation, from the Dakotas south to Arkansas, as well as in Florida, Pennsylvania, Rhode Island, and West Virginia.

TABLE 7-2 **Population Age 65 Years and Older, by Age Group and Gender: 1980, 1990, and 1991, and Projections for the Year 2000**

Age Group and Gender	Number (1,000)				Percent Distribution			
	1980	1990	1991	2000	1980	1990	1991	2000
People 65 years and over	25,549	31,079	31,754	34,886	100.0	100.0	100.0	100.0
65 to 69 years old	8,782	10,066	10,037	9,469	34.3	32.4	31.6	27.1
70 to 74 years old	6,798	7,980	8,242	8,789	26.6	25.7	26.0	25.2
75 to 79 years old	4,794	6,103	6,279	7,447	18.8	19.6	19.8	21.3
80 to 84 years old	2,935	3,909	4,035	4,892	11.5	12.6	12.7	14.0
85 years old and over	2,240	3,021	3,160	4,289	8.8	9.7	10.0	12.3
Males, 65 years and over	10,305	12,493	12,791	14,402	100.0	100.0	100.0	100.0
65 to 69 years old	3,903	4,508	4,491	4,369	37.8	36.1	35.1	30.3
70 to 74 years old	2,854	3,399	3,531	3,911	27.7	27.2	27.6	27.2
75 to 79 years old	1,848	2,389	2,482	3,100	18.0	19.1	19.4	21.5
80 to 84 years old	1,019	1,356	1,406	1,807	9.9	10.9	11.0	12.5
85 years old and over	682	841	881	1,215	6.6	6.7	6.9	8.4
Females, 65 years and over	15,245	18,586	18,962	20,484	100.0	100.0	100.0	100.0
65 to 69 years old	4,880	5,558	5,546	5,100	31.9	29.9	29.2	24.9
70 to 74 years old	3,945	4,580	4,712	4,878	25.9	24.6	24.8	23.8
75 to 79 years old	2,946	3,714	3,797	4,347	19.3	20.0	20.0	21.2
80 to 84 years old	1,916	2,553	2,629	3,086	12.6	13.7	13.9	15.1
85 years old and over	1,559	2,180	2,279	3,074	10.3	11.7	12.0	15.0

Note: Figures as of April, except 1991 and 2000 (as of July).

Source: Reprinted from U.S. Bureau of the Census. (1993). *Statistical abstract of the United States: 1993* (113th ed., p. 45). Austin, TX: Reference Press.

TABLE 7-3 **Characteristics of People Age 65 Years and Older, by Gender: Selected Years, 1980 to 1992**

Characteristic	Total				Male				Female			
	1980	1985	1990	1992	1980	1985	1990	1992	1980	1985	1990	1992
Total[a] (million)	24.2	26.8	29.6	30.6	9.9	11.0	12.3	12.8	14.2	15.8	17.2	17.8
White (million)	21.9	24.2	26.5	27.3	9.0	9.9	11.0	11.4	12.9	14.3	15.4	15.9
Black (million)	2.0	2.2	2.5	2.6	0.8	0.9	1.0	1.1	1.2	1.3	1.5	1.5
Percent below poverty level	15.2	12.4	11.4	12.4	11.1	8.7	7.8	7.9	17.9	15.0	13.9	15.5
Percent distribution Marital status												
Single	5.5	5.2	4.6	4.6	4.9	5.3	4.2	4.2	5.9	5.1	4.9	4.9
Married	55.4	55.2	56.1	55.8	78.0	77.2	76.5	75.9	39.5	39.9	41.4	41.2
Spouse present	53.6	53.4	54.1	54.1	76.1	75.0	74.2	73.8	37.9	38.3	39.7	39.8
Spouse absent	1.8	1.8	2.0	1.7	1.9	2.2	2.3	2.1	1.7	1.6	1.7	1.4
Widowed	35.7	35.6	34.2	34.4	13.5	13.8	14.2	15.0	51.2	50.7	48.6	48.3
Divorced	3.5	4.0	5.0	5.3	3.6	3.7	5.0	4.9	3.4	4.3	5.1	5.5
Family status												
In families	67.6	67.3	66.7	66.5	83.0	82.4	81.9	80.8	56.8	56.7	55.8	56.2
Nonfamily house-holders	31.2	31.1	31.9	32.0	15.7	15.4	16.6	17.1	42.0	42.1	42.8	42.7
Secondary individuals	1.2	1.6	1.4	1.5	1.3	2.2	1.5	2.1	1.1	1.1	1.4	1.1
Living arrangements												
Living in household	99.8	99.6	99.7	99.7	99.9	99.5	99.9	99.7	99.7	99.6	99.5	99.8
Living alone	30.3	30.2	31.0	31.1	14.9	14.7	15.7	16.3	41.0	41.1	42.0	41.8
Spouse present	53.6	53.4	54.1	54.1	76.1	75.0	74.3	73.8	37.9	38.3	39.7	39.8
Living with someone else	15.9	15.9	14.6	14.6	8.9	9.8	9.9	9.6	20.8	20.2	17.8	18.1
Not in household[b]	0.2	0.4	0.3	0.3	0.1	0.5	0.1	0.3	0.3	0.4	0.5	0.2
Years of school completed												
8 years or less	43.1	35.4	28.5	26.5	45.3	37.2	30.0	28.1	41.6	34.1	27.5	25.2
1 to 3 years of high school	16.2	16.5	16.1	15.7	15.5	15.7	15.7	14.9	16.7	17.0	16.4	16.3
4 years of high school	24.0	29.0	32.9	34.3	21.4	26.4	29.0	29.9	25.8	30.7	35.6	37.4
1 to 3 years of college	8.2	9.8	10.9	11.4	7.5	9.1	10.8	11.2	8.6	10.3	11.0	11.6
4 years or more of college	8.6	9.4	11.6	12.1	10.3	11.5	14.5	15.8	7.4	8.0	9.5	9.5
Labor force participation[c]												
Employed	12.2	10.4	11.5	11.2	18.4	15.3	15.9	15.6	7.8	7.0	8.4	8.0
Unemployed	0.4	0.3	0.4	0.4	0.6	0.5	0.5	0.5	0.3	0.2	0.3	0.4
Not in labor force	87.5	89.2	88.1	88.4	81.0	84.2	83.6	83.8	91.9	92.7	91.3	91.7

Source: Reprinted from U.S. Bureau of the Census. (1993). *Statistical abstract of the United States: 1993* (113th ed., p. 45). Austin, TX: Reference Press.

[a]Includes other races, not shown separately.

[b]In group quarters other than institutions.

[c]Annual averages of monthly figures.

TABLE 7-4 **Population over Age 65, by State: 1991**

State	Number (1,000)	Percentage of All Ages	Percentage Increase, 1980–91	Percentage Below Poverty Level, 1989
United States	31,754	12.6	24.3	12.8
Alabama	529	12.9	20.2	24.0
Alaska	24	4.2	105.1	7.6
Arizona	497	13.2	61.6	10.8
Arkansas	353	14.9	12.9	22.9
California	3,187	10.5	32.0	7.6
Colorado	340	10.1	37.5	11.0
Connecticut	451	13.7	23.7	7.2
Delaware	83	12.2	40.2	10.1
District of Columbia	77	12.8	3.5	17.2
Florida	2,432	18.3	44.1	10.8
Georgia	668	10.1	29.3	20.4
Hawaii	129	11.4	69.6	8.0
Idaho	124	12.0	32.8	11.5
Illinois	1,448	12.5	14.8	10.7
Indiana	708	12.6	21.0	10.8
Iowa	431	15.4	11.1	11.2
Kansas	346	13.9	13.1	12.0
Kentucky	472	12.7	15.1	20.6
Louisiana	474	11.2	17.3	24.1
Maine	166	13.4	17.7	14.0
Maryland	530	10.9	33.9	10.5
Massachusetts	824	13.7	13.5	9.4
Michigan	1,130	12.1	23.8	10.8
Minnesota	555	12.5	15.8	12.1
Mississippi	323	12.4	11.5	29.4
Missouri	726	14.1	12.0	14.8
Montana	108	13.4	28.1	12.5
Nebraska	225	14.1	9.4	12.2
Nevada	138	10.8	110.6	9.6
New Hampshire	128	11.6	24.2	10.2
New Jersey	1,041	13.4	21.1	8.5
New Mexico	168	10.9	45.1	16.5
New York	2,357	13.1	9.1	11.9
North Carolina	826	12.3	37.0	19.5
North Dakota	92	14.5	14.1	14.6
Ohio	1,432	13.1	22.5	10.7
Oklahoma	430	13.5	14.2	17.9
Oregon	401	13.7	32.3	10.1
Pennsylvania	1,858	15.5	21.4	10.6
Rhode Island	152	15.1	19.7	11.6
South Carolina	407	11.4	41.5	20.5
South Dakota	104	14.7	13.7	15.5
Tennessee	629	12.7	21.6	20.9
Texas	1,756	10.1	28.1	18.4
Utah	155	8.8	42.4	8.8
Vermont	67	11.9	15.5	12.4
Virginia	682	10.9	35.0	14.1
Washington	590	11.8	36.6	9.1
West Virginia	271	15.1	14.1	16.7
Wisconsin	661	13.3	17.1	9.1
Wyoming	49	10.6	30.7	10.7

Source: Reprinted with permission from American Association of Retired Persons. (1992). *A profile of older Americans* (p. 6). Washington, DC: Author.

FIGURE 7-2 **People Age 65 Years and Older as a Percentage of the Total Population, by State: 1991**

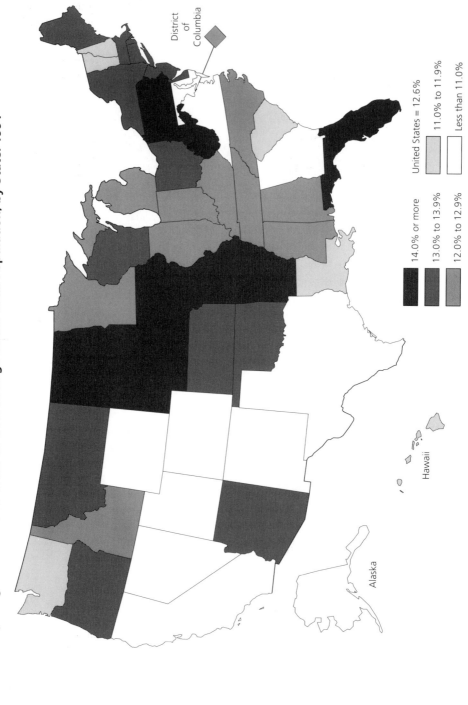

14.0% or more

13.0% to 13.9%

12.0% to 12.9%

United States = 12.6%

11.0% to 11.9%

Less than 11.0%

District of Columbia

Hawaii

Alaska

Source: Reprinted with permission from American Association of Retired Persons. (1992). *A profile of older Americans* (pp. 6–7). Washington, DC: Author.

Living Arrangements

The male–female differential among the elderly population leads to some marked differences in their living arrangements, as Figure 7-3 illustrates. According to the AARP pamphlet *A Profile of Older Americans: 1992,* 74 percent of men over age 65 lived with their spouses, whereas only 40 percent of their female counterparts lived with their spouses.

Seven percent of men lived with other relatives, but 16 percent of women did. More than twice as many women (44 percent) lived alone or with nonrelatives as men (18 percent). Although there are many explanations for these differences, the most significant is that women outlive their husbands. Figure 7-4 shows the marital status of people over age 65 in 1991. Only 41 percent of the women were married,

FIGURE 7-3 **Living Arrangements of People Age 65 Years and Older: 1991**

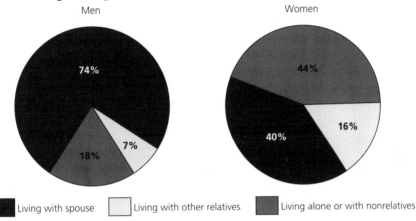

Source: Reprinted with permission from American Association of Retired Persons. (1992). *A profile of older Americans* (p. 4). Washington, DC: Author.

FIGURE 7-4 **Marital Status of People Age 65 Years and Older: 1991**

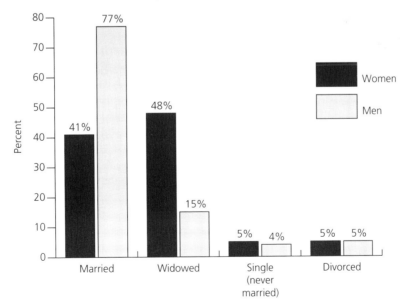

Source: Reprinted with permission from American Association of Retired Persons. (1992). *A profile of older Americans* (p. 3). Washington, DC: Author.

but 77 percent of the men were. Almost 50 percent of the women were widowed, but only 15 percent of the men were. The numbers of men and women who were never married or divorced were about equal. Table 7-5 shows the marital status of older adults in 1960, 1970, 1980, 1989, and 1991.

TABLE 7-5 **Marital Status of Older People, by Gender and Age Group: Selected Years, 1960 to 1991**

Gender and Marital Status	1960		1970		1980		1989		1991	
	65 to 74	75 and Over	65 to 74	75 and Over	65 to 74	75 and Over	65 to 74	75 and Over	65 to 74	75 and Over
Men (in thousands)	4,778	2,280	5,333	3,031	6,459	3,234	7,880	4,199	8,156	4,391
Marital status (percent distribution)										
Married, wife present	76.2	56.5	74.6	57.5	79.4	67.7	78.4	66.7	79.0	65.6
Married, wife absent	2.7	2.6	3.0	4.0	2.2	1.7	2.7	2.7	1.9	2.7
Widowed	12.7	31.6	11.0	30.4	8.5	24.0	8.9	23.4	9.2	24.8
Divorced	1.7	1.5	2.9	1.5	4.4	2.2	5.1	2.8	5.3	3.2
Never married	6.7	7.8	8.5	6.6	5.4	4.4	4.9	4.4	4.7	3.7
Women (in thousands)	5,529	3,054	6,741	4,608	8,549	5,411	9,867	7,077	10,081	7,464
Marital status (percent distribution)										
Married, husband present	43.5	20.6	43.8	18.9	48.1	22.1	51.4	24.3	51.4	24.0
Married, husband absent	2.1	1.2	1.6	1.9	2.0	1.2	1.8	1.4	1.9	1.3
Widowed	44.4	68.3	43.7	70.5	40.3	68.0	36.6	65.6	35.3	65.7
Divorced	1.7	1.2	3.0	1.3	4.0	2.3	5.7	2.9	6.6	3.5
Never married	8.4	8.6	7.9	7.4	5.6	6.4	4.5	5.8	4.8	5.5

Source: Reprinted from Committee on Ways and Means, U.S. House of Representatives. (1993). *Overview of entitlement programs: 1993 greenbook* (p. 1270). Washington, DC: U.S. Government Printing Office.

Poverty

Low economic status has historically been a problem for aging Americans. Table 7-6 shows the poverty rates among the older adult population by age, gender, and marital status. Elderly women are consistently less well off than men in each age group.

Public Expenditures for Older Adults

Table 7-7 shows estimates of federal spending on behalf of older people from 1965 through 1995. The table also shows the outlays per person, both as a percentage of total federal spending and as a percentage of the gross national product. In every case, these outlays have increased.

TABLE 7-6 **Poverty Rates among People Age 65 and Older by Age, Gender, and Marital Status: 1991**

Gender and Marital Status	65 and Over	65 to 74	75 to 84	85 and Over
Male total	7.9	7.6	8.0	10.8
Married	5.3	5.0	5.5	7.9
Widowed	15.0	15.3	15.1	13.8
Divorced, separated, or never married	17.3	18.5	13.3	a
Female total	15.5	13.1	17.8	22.7
Married	5.4	4.8	6.8	a
Widowed	21.2	19.9	22.0	22.8
Divorced, separated, or never married	27.4	28.1	24.0	a
Total	12.4	10.6	14.0	18.9

Source: Reprinted from Committee on Ways and Means, U.S. House of Representatives. (1993). *Overview of entitlement programs: 1993 greenbook* (p. 1275). Washington, DC: U.S. Government Printing Office.

[a] Estimate does not meet standards of reliability.

TABLE 7-7 **Estimated Federal Spending in Billions of Dollars for the Elderly Population under Selected Programs: Selected Years, 1965 to 1995**

Program	1965	1971	1975	1980	1985	1990	1995
Social security	—	27.1	51.8	81.2	137.9	192.5	260.0
Railroad retirement	—	1.7	2.8	3.6	4.8	3.5	3.4
Federal civilian retirement	—	2.3	5.5	7.8	13.7	21.1	26.1
Military retirement	—	0.7	1.1	1.8	3.9	7.4	9.7
Benefits for coal miners	—	0.1	0.2	1.3	1.4	1.3	1.1
Supplemental security income	—	1.4	1.8	2.3	3.6	3.5	5.7
Veterans pensions	—	0.9	1.5	3.3	5.7	7.4	9.1
Medicare	—	7.5	12.8	29.3	60.9	95.5	165.6
Medicaid	—	1.9	2.6	4.7	8.1	13.5	31.7
Food stamps	—	0.2	1.0	0.5	0.6	0.8	1.2
Housing assistance	—	0.2	0.4	2.3	4.5	6.1	7.9
Total	18.8	44.0	81.3	138.1	245.2	352.6	521.5
Total in 1990 dollars	71.3	134.1	192.9	221.6	295.9	352.6	443.1
Spending per aged person in 1990 dollars	3,860	6,540	8,500	8,620	10,370	11,290	13,190
Spending as a percentage of total federal outlays	15.9	20.9	24.5	23.4	25.9	28.2	33.1
Spending as a percentage of GDP	2.8	4.2	5.4	5.2	6.2	6.4	7.6

Notes: GDP = gross domestic product; — = not available.

Source: Adapted from Committee on Ways and Means, U.S. House of Representatives. (1993). *Overview of entitlement programs: 1993 greenbook* (p. 1564). Washington, DC: U.S. Government Printing Office.

Abuse and Neglect of Older Adults

In recent decades, it has become clear that many older people are victims of abuse and neglect. All states now have a public program charged with receiving reports on adult abuse and neglect and finding ways to prevent and treat such problems. For the past several years, the National Aging Resource Center on Elder Abuse (NARCEA) has collected data from public adult protective services programs and agencies to determine the nature and extent of such abuse and neglect against older people. The agencies surveyed include 54 jurisdictions—states, territories, the District of Columbia, and the Commonwealth of Puerto Rico.

NARCEA (Tatara, 1993a) found 227,000 reported cases of domestic elder abuse in 1991, an increase of 7.6 percent over 1990. That increase followed a consistent upward trend since 1986, when there were 117,000 reports. The five-year increase from 1986 to 1991 was 94 percent. The reporting jurisdictions included two elements of maltreatment: physical abuse and neglect. In addition, NARCEA estimated that there were 735,000 incidents of elder abuse in domestic settings, only a frac-

tion of which were reported to official agencies and the authorities.

Table 7-8 shows the sources of reports of elder abuse. Service providers were by far the largest group, followed by physicians or other health care professionals and other unspecified sources. The types of maltreatment reported are detailed in Table 7-9.

TABLE 7-8 **Elder Abuse, by Source of Report: 1990 and 1991**

	Percentage of Reports Made	
Reporter Category	1990	1991
Family member or relative	14.9	15.0
Friend or neighbor	8.8	8.2
Service provider	28.1	26.7
Physician or health care professional	17.0	18.0
Law enforcement	4.3	4.3
Clergy	0.1	0.1
Bank or business	0.2	0.2
Elder victim	5.6	4.6
All other types	18.7	21.0
Unknown or missing data	2.2	2.0

Note: Data are based on reports from 29 states in 1990 and 25 states in 1991. Due to rounding errors, the total is not exactly 100%.

Source: Reprinted with permission from Tatara, T. (1993). *Summaries of the statistical data on elder abuse in domestic settings for FY 90 and FY 91: A final report* (p. 15). Washington, DC: National Aging Resource Center on Elder Abuse.

TABLE 7-9 **Types of Maltreatment of the Elderly: 1990 and 1991**

	Percentage of Reports Made	
Type of Maltreatment	1990	1991
Physical abuse	20.3	19.1
Sexual abuse	0.6	0.6
Psychological or emotional abuse	11.6	13.8
Neglect	46.6	45.2
Financial or material exploitation	17.4	17.1
All other types	3.3	4.0
Unknown or missing data	0.2	0.2

Notes: Data are based on reports from 29 states in 1990 and 30 states in 1991. This analysis includes only the substantiated reports involving abuse victims and does not include self-neglect reports.

Source: Reprinted with permission from Tatara, T. (1993). *Summaries of the statistical data on elder abuse in domestic settings for FY 90 and FY 91: A final report* (p. 20). Washington, DC: National Aging Resource Center on Elder Abuse.

Various types of abusers are identified in Table 7-10. Adult children are the most frequent abusers, followed by spouses and other relatives. "All other categories" includes former spouses, current and former housemates, unrelated caregivers, and lovers.

Table 7-11 shows the age categories of victims in 1990 and 1991. The older the adult, the more likely it is that he or she will be a victim of abuse or neglect.

Self-abuse and neglect, which NARCEA defines as "abusive or neglectful conduct of an older person directed at himself/herself that threatens his/her health or safety" (Tatara, 1993a, p. 8), is one of the largest categories of maltreatment after physical abuse and neglect. One of the main reasons for intervention into adult domestic problem situations is the failure of the adult to care for himself or herself adequately. According to the reporting states, some 62 percent of self-neglecting elders in both 1990 and 1991 were women (Tatara, 1993a). Table 7-12 shows the ages of those who abused or neglected themselves in 1990 and 1991. Although the data are based on only 18 states in 1990 and 19 in 1991, they provide a useful estimate of the problem.

TABLE 7-10 **Perpetrators of Elder Abuse: 1990 and 1991**

	Percentage of Reports Made	
Abuser	1990	1991
Adult children	31.9	32.5
Grandchildren	4.0	4.2
Spouse	15.4	14.4
Sibling	2.6	2.5
Other relatives	13.0	12.5
Service provider	6.6	6.3
Friend or neighbor	7.3	7.5
All other categories	16.7	18.2
Unknown or missing data	2.5	2.0

Notes: Data are based on reports from 21 states. Due to rounding errors, the total is not exactly 100%.

Source: Reprinted with permission from Tatara, T. (1993). *Summaries of the statistical data on elder abuse in domestic settings for FY 90 and FY 91: A final report* (p. 22). Washington, DC: National Aging Resource Center on Elder Abuse.

TABLE 7-11 **Elder Abuse Victims, by Age Group: 1990 and 1991**

	Percentage of Reports Made	
Age (years)	1990	1991
60 to 64	7.8	7.6
65 to 69	11.2	10.5
70 to 74	15.0	15.5
75 to 79	17.4	17.1
80 to 84	19.2	19.4
85 and over	22.2	23.1
Missing data	7.2	6.8

Note: Data are based on reports from 22 states in 1990 and 25 states in 1991.

Source: Reprinted with permission from Tatara, T. (1993). *Summaries of the statistical data on elder abuse in domestic settings for FY 90 and FY 91: A final report* (p. 25). Washington, DC: National Aging Resource Center on Elder Abuse.

TABLE 7-12 **Percentage of Elderly Self-Abusers, by Age Group: 1990 and 1991**

	Percentage of Reports Made	
Age (years)	1990	1991
60 to 64	9.9	9.4
65 to 69	13.0	11.8
70 to 74	14.8	15.3
75 to 79	18.3	16.7
80 to 84	18.5	18.8
85 and over	18.0	20.3
Missing data	7.6	7.6

Notes: Data are based on reports from 18 states in 1990 and 19 states in 1991. Due to rounding errors, these totals are not exactly 100%.

Source: Reprinted with permission from Tatara, T. (1993). *Summaries of the statistical data on elder abuse in domestic settings for FY 90 and FY 91: A final report* (p. 28). Washington, DC: National Aging Resource Center on Elder Abuse.

Elderly Victims of Crime

Older people are also victims of crime, sometimes disproportionately to their percentage of the population. Table 7-13 shows the average rate of victimization of each 1,000 elderly people or households by gender, race and ethnicity, marital status, and type of crime. Household crime rates are significantly higher among African Americans than among white individuals and households.

TABLE 7-13 **Crime Victimization Rates of People Age 65 and Older, by Gender, Race, Marital Status, and Type of Crime: 1987–90**

	Number of Victimizations per 1,000 People or Households							
	Gender		Race		Marital Status			
Type of Crime	Male	Female	White	Black	Never Married	Widowed	Married	Divorced or Separated
Crimes of violence	4.9	3.4	3.6	7.6	3.0	4.2	7.6	11.3
Robbery	2.0	1.2	1.2	4.4	1.2	1.7	5.1	1.7
Aggravated assault	1.4	0.8	1.1	1.4	0.8	0.9	1.5	4.8
Simple assault	1.4	1.2	1.2	1.4	0.9	1.4	0.7	4.4
Crimes of theft	19.8	19.4	19.5	19.6	18.2	4.2	26.3	35.4
Personal larceny with contact	1.8	3.2	2.3	5.7	1.8	2.9	6.1	6.4
Personal larceny without contact	17.9	16.2	17.2	13.9	16.4	15.1	20.2	30.0
Household crimes[a]	82.2	74.3	70.9	154.1	77.6	75.1	71.1	110.4
Burglary	32.8	31.9	29.1	63.8	28.7	33.7	35.2	46.3
Household larceny	41.6	37.1	36.5	71.9	41.6	35.7	34.1	37.8
Motor vehicle theft	7.7	5.2	5.3	18.3	7.2	5.7	1.8	10.5

Note: Rates shown are the average annual rate for the three years.

Source: Reprinted from Bachman, R. (1992). *Elderly victims: Bureau of Justice Statistics special report* (p. 5). Washington, DC: U.S. Department of Justice, Bureau of Justice Statistics.

[a]Household crimes are categorized by gender, race, and marital status of the head of household.

Location of residence as a factor in the crime victimization of older people is described in Table 7-14. As with the rest of the population, those who live in cities experience greater crime rates than do suburban and rural residents. There are variations among older adults by age, as illustrated in Table 7-15. People age 75 and older were most likely to be victimized by violent crime at home, whereas those between ages 65 and 74 were most likely to be victimized on the street. Income is a factor in crime victimization, as shown in Table 7-16. The lower an elderly person's income, the more likely he or she was to be a victim of violent crime. However, lower-income elderly people were less likely to experience personal thefts or household crimes. Marital status was also a factor in some situations. Elderly people

TABLE 7-14 **Crime Victimization Rates of People Age 65 and Older, by Location of Residence, Home Ownership, and Type of Crime: 1987–90**

| | Number of Victimizations per 1,000 People or Households | | | | |
| | Location of Residence | | | Tenure | |
Type of Crime	City	Suburb	Rural	Own	Rent
Crimes of violence	7.1	2.9	2.2	3.1	7.7
Robbery	3.5	0.9	0.4	1.1	3.6
Aggravated assault	1.4	0.8	1.0	1.0	1.6
Simple assault	1.9	1.1	0.7	1.0	2.2
Crimes of theft	26.4	19.6	11.4	17.8	26.7
Personal larceny with contact	6.5	1.2	0.4	1.9	5.5
Personal larceny without contact	19.9	18.4	10.9	16.0	21.1
Household crimes	112.6	61.2	64.5	82.0	66.8
Burglary	42.4	25.6	30.7	33.6	28.3
Household larceny	57.3	31.2	31.3	42.1	30.9
Motor vehicle theft	12.8	4.3	2.5	6.2	7.5

Note: Rates shown are the average annual rate for the three years.

Source: Reprinted from Bachman, R. (1992). *Elderly victims: Bureau of Justice Statistics special report* (p. 5). Washington, DC: U.S. Department of Justice, Bureau of Justice Statistics.

TABLE 7-15 **Place Where Violent Crime Occurred, by Age of Victim and Type of Crime: 1987–90**

| | Percentage of Victims of Violent Crime | | | | | |
Type of Violent Crime	Total	At Home	Near Home	On the Street	In Commercial or Public Establishment	Elsewhere
All crimes of violence						
65–74	100	22	29	33	8	9
75 or older	100	33	28	25	14	11
Robbery						
65–74	100	14	27	40	7	12
75 or older	100	29	13	31	21	6
Assault						
65–74	100	24	30	29	15	8
75 or older	100	37	23	17	6	17

Note: Rates shown are the average annual rate for the three years.

Source: Reprinted from Bachman, R. (1992). *Elderly victims: Bureau of Justice Statistics special report* (p. 7). Washington, DC: U.S. Department of Justice, Bureau of Justice Statistics.

who were divorced or separated were more likely to be victims of all types of crimes than those who were married, widowed, or never married.

Conclusion

The older adult population is one of the major social welfare concerns in the United States. Health concerns, income, abuse, neglect, residential care, and many other issues all disproportionately affect older adults. As the average life span increases, more and more elderly people are caring for people who are even older than they are. Thus, it is not uncommon for people in their mid-60s to care for others in their 80s.

It is only in recent years that special attention has been given to the aging population. Part of the attention has resulted from their growing numbers, but a large part has resulted from the fact that older adults are more likely to be registered to vote than any other age group and are more likely to vote as well. Older people are also organized into groups such as AARP and the National Council on Aging, both of which are highly influential in Congress and in state legislatures.

This chapter provides some basic data on some of the special concerns and needs of older people in the United States today. When studied in tandem with information on the elderly population contained in other chapters, it can help provide a good understanding of the status, special needs, and programs for this large and growing group of Americans.

TABLE 7-16 **Crime Victimization Rates of People Age 65 and Older for Crimes of Violence, Crimes of Theft, and Household Crimes: 1987–90**

| | Number of Victimizations per 1,000 People or Households | | | | | |
| | Crimes of Violence | | Crimes of Theft | | Household Crimes | |
Characteristic	65–74	75+	65–74	75+	65–74	75+
Sex						
Male	5.2	4.4	22.4	14.8	86.9	73.1
Female	4.2	2.2	23.4	13.9	82.9	65.6
Race						
White	4.2	2.6	23.1	14.2	77.6	61.4
Black	13.9	6.5	36.7	16.1	156.8	149.6
Marital status						
Married	3.3	2.2	20.5	12.9	82.7	66.5
Widowed	5.6	3.1	24.6	13.0	83.3	68.5
Never married	8.1	7.0	30.8	20.2	73.3	67.7
Divorced or separated	13.1	6.2	34.9	36.5	116.6	92.2
Family income						
Less than $7,500	9.7	3.3	19.1	12.0	83.3	70.7
$7,500–$14,999	4.5	4.1	18.2	12.0	49.4	64.6
$15,000–$24,999	3.6	2.2	21.1	15.9	86.5	70.6
$25,000 or over	3.2	1.7	30.6	20.9	78.5	78.6

Note: Rates shown are the average annual rate for the three years.

Source: Reprinted from Bachman, R. (1992). *Elderly victims: Bureau of Justice Statistics special report* (p. 7). Washington, DC: U.S. Department of Justice, Bureau of Justice Statistics.

8

SOCIAL WELFARE, ECONOMIC ASSISTANCE, HOUSING, AND HOMELESSNESS

This chapter describes the needs of disadvantaged Americans and the programs designed to assist them.

Index of Social Health

One objective measure of the social problems and social needs of the nation is the annual *Index of Social Health* (Miringoff, 1993), published by the Fordham Institute for Innovation in Social Policy at the Fordham Graduate Center in Tarrytown, New York. The *Index* tracks 16 social problem areas, including infant mortality, drug abuse, high school dropout rates, average weekly earnings, unemployment, the impoverished elderly population, housing, and the gap between rich and poor. From the data, an index—a single figure—is developed and tracked over the years. The higher the figure, the better the nation's social health.

Figure 8-1 shows the index from 1970 through 1991. The index for 1991, 36.3, was the lowest ever. Eight of the 16 problems worsened, and three—child abuse, average weekly earnings, and out-of-pocket health costs for those over 65—were at their worst recorded level.

Family Strength Index

A comparable measure is the Family Strength Index (Ashcroft & Strauss, 1993), which was described in *Families First*, a report by a federal government study commission. Using such indicators as the percentages of married adults, intact first marriages, births to married parents, children living with their own married parents, and children living with two married parents, this index also showed a decline, dropping from 78 in 1970, to 71 in 1980, and to 66 in 1990, reflecting a decline in national family strength.

Entitlements

Few issues are of greater concern to social workers than social welfare and entitlement programs that assist people who have low incomes. Much of social work as we know it today can be traced to the national economic assistance services that began during the New Deal of the 1930s with the Social Security Act of 1935. Even social workers who serve in other fields, such as aging, health, mental health, child welfare, and corrections, invariably work closely with economic assistance programs. That is because the most serious problems faced by many clients of social agencies are fundamentally economic. Social workers seeking to resolve social problems must deal with economic programs and be familiar with income assistance services. People on probation and parole from corrections programs and their families, for example, often need assistance. Mental health clients often need financial assistance to meet their basic living costs. Many aged people face constant problems obtaining adequate nutrition and sufficient funds for such necessities as housing and transportation. Child welfare programs also help families who otherwise could not secure these basics. The programs are often called "entitlements," because they are available to people who meet specified criteria.

Unemployment and Unemployment Compensation

One of the fundamental causes of economic disadvantage is unemployment. Many of those who require assistance through programs such as Aid to Families with Dependent Children (AFDC) are in need because the family breadwinner is unemployed. Unemployment also can lead to poorer financial status later in life; those who do not hold jobs for one or more periods have smaller amounts available for their retirement or for their dependents if they die or become disabled. Unemployed people and their families who are unable to meet the strict asset limits and other requirements to qualify for AFDC constitute a special category of disadvantaged people. Table 8-1 shows the state-by-state rates of unemployment from 1983 through 1992. The figures are calculated as percentages of the work force who were unemployed in the years specified.

Unemployment insurance is provided for up to 26 weeks to workers who lose their jobs for reasons other than resigning or misbehavior; benefits may be extended under certain circumstances that vary with the times, the state, and the actions of the federal government. The benefits are paid from a fund that is collected from employers.

Table 8-2 provides some detailed information on the U.S. unemployment compensation program, which provides cash benefits and helps unemployed people find work. The table shows the national rates of civilian unemployment since 1982 and projections to 1994. Although the program is national, each

state determines its own program benefits and, to an extent, the amount of money each employer will contribute.

The numbers of people insured for unemployment are fewer than those who are unemployed. People who are self-employed, temporary workers, and workers in some kinds of jobs are not covered. Shapiro and Nichols (1992) pointed out that the shift from a manufacturing economy to a service economy reduces the numbers who can obtain unemployment compensation. Many service jobs are part-time, intermittent, and temporary and therefore do not qualify their holders for unemployment insurance. According to studies conducted by the Center on Budget and Policy Priorities (Shapiro & Nichols, 1992), benefits were less likely to be available in rural states. In the 15 most rural states, only 37 percent of unemployed people received benefits in 1991, compared to 51 percent in the 15 most urban states.

Table 8-2 contains figures dealing with the impact of unemployment compensation on the state trust fund, which reflects the money paid by the states to the federal government for un-

FIGURE 8-1 **Index of the Social Health of the United States, 1970 to 1991**

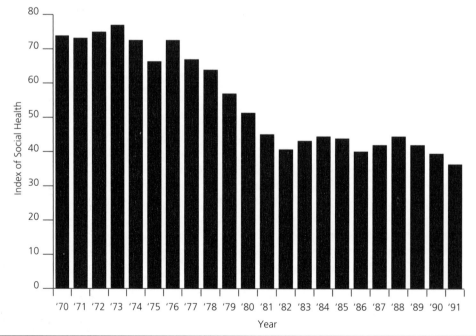

Source: Reprinted with permission from Miringoff, M. L. (1993). *The index of social health: Monitoring the social well-being of the nation* (p. 4). Tarrytown, NY: Fordham Institute for Innovation in Social Policy.

employment compensation. The negative figures for recent years suggest that the trust fund will lose part of its assets. However, unless unemployment is heavy and prolonged, the trust fund is large enough because of past contributions to pay out more than it takes in during poor economic times. The table also lists the cost of administering unemployment insurance and the U.S. Employment Service.

Table 8-3 shows the unemployment rates in each state in 1991 and the percentage of unemployed people who received benefits and the state rankings from lowest to highest. South Dakota had the lowest percentage of beneficiaries and Rhode Island the highest. Table 8-4 shows the amount and duration of weekly unemployment benefits for each of the states for 1992 and 1993. The range of weekly

TABLE 8-1 **Average Unemployment Rates, by State: 1983 to 1992**

State	1983	1984	1985	1986	1987	1988	1989	1990	1991	1992
Alabama	13.7	11.1	8.9	9.8	7.8	7.2	7.0	6.8	7.2	7.3
Alaska	10.3	10.0	9.7	10.8	10.8	9.3	6.7	6.9	8.5	9.1
Arizona	9.1	5.0	6.5	6.9	6.2	6.3	5.2	5.3	5.7	7.4
Arkansas	10.1	8.9	8.7	8.7	8.1	7.7	7.2	6.9	7.3	7.2
California	9.7	7.8	7.2	6.7	5.8	5.3	5.1	5.6	7.5	9.1
Colorado	6.6	5.6	5.9	7.4	7.7	6.4	5.8	4.9	5.0	5.9
Connecticut	6.0	4.6	4.9	3.8	3.3	3.0	3.7	5.1	6.7	7.5
Delaware	8.1	6.2	5.3	4.3	3.2	3.2	3.5	5.1	6.2	5.3
District of Columbia	11.7	9.0	8.4	7.7	6.3	5.0	5.0	6.6	7.7	8.4
Florida	8.6	6.3	6.0	5.7	5.3	5.0	5.6	5.9	7.3	8.2
Georgia	7.5	6.0	6.5	5.9	5.5	5.8	5.5	5.4	5.0	6.9
Hawaii	6.5	5.6	5.6	4.8	3.8	3.2	2.6	2.8	2.8	4.5
Idaho	9.8	7.2	7.9	8.7	8.0	5.8	5.1	5.8	6.1	6.5
Illinois	11.4	9.1	9.0	8.1	7.4	6.8	6.0	6.2	7.1	7.6
Indiana	11.1	8.6	7.9	6.7	6.4	5.3	4.7	5.3	5.9	6.6
Iowa	8.1	7.0	8.0	7.0	5.5	4.5	4.3	4.2	4.6	4.6
Kansas	6.1	5.2	5.0	5.4	4.9	4.8	4.0	4.4	4.4	4.2
Kentucky	11.7	9.3	9.5	9.3	8.8	7.9	6.2	5.8	7.4	6.9
Louisiana	11.8	10.0	11.5	13.1	12.0	10.9	7.9	6.2	7.1	8.1
Maine	9.0	6.1	5.4	5.3	4.4	3.8	4.1	5.1	7.5	7.1
Maryland	6.9	5.4	4.6	4.5	4.2	4.5	3.7	4.6	5.9	6.6
Massachusetts	6.9	4.8	3.9	3.8	3.2	3.3	4.0	6.0	9.0	8.5
Michigan	14.2	11.2	9.9	8.8	8.2	7.6	7.1	7.5	9.2	8.8
Minnesota	8.2	6.3	6.0	5.3	5.4	4.0	4.3	4.8	5.1	5.1
Mississippi	12.6	10.8	10.3	11.7	10.2	8.4	7.8	7.5	8.6	8.1
Missouri	9.9	7.2	6.4	6.1	6.3	5.7	5.5	5.7	6.6	5.7
Montana	8.8	7.4	7.7	8.1	7.4	6.8	5.9	5.8	6.9	6.7
Nebraska	5.7	4.4	5.5	5.0	4.9	3.6	3.1	2.2	2.7	3.0
Nevada	9.8	7.8	8.0	6.0	6.3	5.2	5.0	4.9	5.5	6.6
New Hampshire	5.4	4.3	3.9	2.8	2.5	2.4	3.5	5.6	7.2	7.5
New Jersey	7.8	6.2	5.7	5.0	4.0	3.8	4.1	5.0	6.6	8.4
New Mexico	10.1	7.5	8.8	9.2	8.9	7.8	6.7	6.3	6.9	6.8
New York	8.6	7.2	6.5	6.3	4.9	4.2	5.1	5.2	7.2	8.6
North Carolina	8.9	6.7	5.4	5.3	4.5	3.6	3.5	4.1	5.8	5.9
North Dakota	5.6	5.1	5.9	6.3	5.2	4.8	4.3	3.9	4.1	4.9
Ohio	12.2	9.4	8.9	8.1	7.0	6.0	5.5	5.7	6.4	7.2
Oklahoma	9.0	7.0	7.1	8.2	7.4	6.7	5.6	5.6	6.7	5.7
Oregon	10.8	9.4	8.8	8.5	6.2	5.8	5.7	5.5	6.0	7.5
Pennsylvania	11.8	9.1	8.0	6.8	5.7	5.1	4.5	5.4	6.9	7.5
Puerto Rico	23.4	20.7	21.8	18.9	16.8	15.0	14.6	14.2	16.0	16.7
Rhode Island	8.3	5.3	4.9	4.0	3.8	3.1	4.1	6.7	8.5	8.9
South Carolina	10.0	7.1	6.8	6.2	5.6	4.5	4.7	4.7	6.2	6.2
South Dakota	5.4	4.3	5.1	4.7	4.2	3.9	4.2	3.7	3.4	3.1
Tennessee	11.5	8.6	8.0	8.0	6.6	5.8	5.1	5.2	6.6	6.4
Texas	8.0	5.9	7.0	8.9	8.4	7.3	6.7	6.2	6.6	7.5
Utah	9.2	6.5	5.9	6.0	6.4	4.9	4.6	4.3	4.9	4.9
Vermont	6.9	5.2	4.8	4.7	3.6	2.8	3.7	5.0	6.4	6.6
Virginia	6.1	5.0	5.6	5.0	4.2	3.9	3.9	4.3	5.8	6.4
Washington	11.2	9.5	8.1	8.2	7.6	6.2	6.2	4.9	6.3	7.5
West Virginia	18.0	15.0	13.0	11.8	10.8	9.9	8.6	8.3	10.5	11.3
Wisconsin	10.4	7.3	7.2	7.0	6.1	4.3	4.4	4.4	5.4	5.1
Wyoming	8.4	6.3	7.1	9.0	8.6	6.3	6.3	5.4	5.1	5.5

Source: Reprinted from Committee on Ways and Means, U.S. House of Representatives. (1993). *Overview of entitlement programs: 1993 greenbook* (p. 531). Washington, DC: U.S. Government Printing Office.

TABLE 8-2 **Unemployment Compensation Program Statistics: 1982 to 1994**

	1982	1983	1984	1985	1987	1988	1989	1990	1991	1992	1993 (estimated)	1994 (projected)[a]
Total civilian unemployment rate (percent)	9.1	10.1	7.8	7.2	6.4	5.6	5.3	5.4	6.5	7.3	7.2	6.7
Insured unemployment rate (percent)[b]	4.4	4.3	2.9	2.9	2.5	2.2	2.1	2.3	3.1	3.2	2.8	2.8
Coverage (millions of individuals)	86.8	86.3	89.9	93.5	98.0	101.2	104.3	106.1	105.1	104.9	106.4	108.7
Average weekly benefit amount												
(current dollars)	114	120	119	123	134	140	145	154	163	167	171	177
In 1993 dollars	173	176	167	165	172	173	171	173	174	173	171	172
State unemployment compensation												
Beneficiaries (millions of individuals)	11.4	9.9	7.6	8.4	7.5	6.8	7.0	8.1	10.2	9.6	8.5	9.2
Regular benefit exhaustions (millions of individuals)	3.7	4.6	2.8	2.5	2.5	1.9	1.9	2.2	3.2	3.9	3.4	2.8
Regular benefits paid (billions of dollars)	19.3	20.8	13.3	14.3	15.0	13.2	13.5	16.8	24.4	25.6	23.0	24.1
Extended benefits (state share, billions of dollars)	0.93	1.21	0.03	0.03	0.04	0.04	c	0.03	0.01	0.02	0.00	0.01
State tax collections (billions of dollars)	12.8	14.4	19.0	20.0	19.1	18.3	17.3	16.0	15.3	17.6	19.9	21.8
State trust fund impact (income – outlays, billions of dollars)[d]	–7.50	–7.62	+5.70	+5.65	+4.11	+5.12	+3.80	–0.88	–9.13	–8.03	–3.12	–2.32
Federal unemployment compensation accounts												
Federal tax collections (billions of dollars)	3.18	3.58	5.02	4.44	5.08	5.50	4.45	5.36	5.33	5.41	5.40	5.56
Outlays: Federal extended benefits share plus federal supplemental benefits (billions of dollars)	0.97	6.80	3.01	1.27	0.04	0.04	c	0.03	0.01	11.15	12.33	2.08
State administrative costs (billions of dollars)												
Unemployment Insurance Service	1.42	1.70	1.58	1.58	1.56	1.61	1.71	1.74	1.95	2.49	2.59	2.44
Employment Service	0.68	0.72	0.76	0.92	0.90	0.95	1.00	1.01	1.05	1.02	1.10	1.09
Total administrative costs	2.10	2.42	2.31	2.50	2.46	2.56	2.71	2.75	3.00	3.51	3.69	3.53

Source: Reprinted from Committee on Ways and Means, U.S. House of Representatives. (1993). *Overview of entitlement programs: 1993 greenbook* (p. 475). Washington, DC: U.S. Government Printing Office.

[a]Projections are based on President Clinton's 1994 budget.

[b]The average number of workers claiming state unemployment compensation benefits as a percentage of all workers covered.

cLess than $5 million.

[d]Excludes interest earned.

benefit amounts is wide; the higher the earnings while employed, the larger the weekly benefit. Table 8-5 provides unemployment data based on varying definitions and measures of unemployment that take into account age, length of unemployment, underemployment, job-seeking behavior, and combinations of these factors from 1970 through 1992.

The 1991 unemployment rates in other industrialized nations were as follows (compare with 6.5 percent for the United States): Austria, 3.5; Denmark, 10.6; France, 9.3; Germany, 6.3; Greece, 7.3; Israel, 10.6; Japan, 2.1; Republic of Korea, 2.3; The Netherlands, 7.0; Norway, 4.7; Spain, 16.4; Sweden, 2.7; Switzerland, 1.3; and United Kingdom, 8.1 (International Labour Office, 1993).

TABLE 8-3 **Unemployment and Unemployment Insurance Protection, by State: 1991**

State	Percentage of Unemployed People Receiving Benefits	State Rank, from Lowest to Highest	Unemployment Rate in 1991
Alabama	32.4	13	7.2
Alaska	70.0	51	8.5
Arizona	37.0	19	5.7
Arkansas	40.1	25	7.3
California	50.4	38	7.5
Colorado	32.1	12	5.0
Connecticut	54.0	42	6.7
Delaware	34.8	18	6.2
District of Columbia	56.8	46	7.7
Florida	27.8	6	7.3
Georgia	44.1	34	5.0
Hawaii	55.3	44	2.8
Idaho	49.0	35	6.1
Illinois	37.9	21	7.1
Indiana	29.5	9	5.9
Iowa	37.0	20	4.6
Kansas	42.1	33	4.4
Kentucky	34.1	16	7.4
Louisiana	27.0	5	7.1
Maine	60.2	49	7.5
Maryland	41.6	31	5.9
Massachusetts	50.8	39	9.0
Michigan	41.0	30	9.2
Minnesota	41.9	32	5.1
Mississippi	29.5	10	8.6
Missouri	39.8	23	6.6
Montana	34.3	17	6.9
Nebraska	40.4	26	2.7
Nevada	58.3	47	5.5
New Hampshire	33.5	15	7.2
New Jersey	53.7	41	6.6
New Mexico	28.2	7	6.9
New York	49.3	37	7.2
North Carolina	40.8	28	5.8
North Dakota	40.0	24	4.1
Ohio	40.8	29	6.4
Oklahoma	21.6	2	6.7
Oregon	60.0	48	6.0
Pennsylvania	51.0	40	6.9
Rhode Island	64.1	50	8.5
South Carolina	39.6	22	6.2
South Dakota	20.8	1	3.4
Tennessee	40.4	27	6.6
Texas	26.0	4	6.6
Utah	29.0	8	4.9
Vermont	56.0	45	6.4
Virginia	24.0	3	5.8
Washington	55.2	43	6.3
West Virginia	31.1	11	10.5
Wisconsin	49.2	36	5.4
Wyoming	32.5	14	5.1

Source: Reprinted with permission from Shapiro, I., & Nichols, M. (1992). *Far from fixed: An analysis of the unemployment insurance system* (p. 16). Washington, DC: Center on Budget and Policy Priorities.

Aid to Families with Dependent Children

Perhaps the most significant of the income assistance programs is AFDC, which is designed to provide basic assistance to families with children who cannot support themselves otherwise. Each month, some 4.3 million families and 12.5 million individuals receive benefits through their state governments under this program. The program varies from state to state, although under the Family Support Act of 1988, some standardization has been developed. For example, all states must now provide assistance to families for whom the basis for needing assistance is unemployment. Until that legislation was implemented, about half of the states denied AFDC to families with adult breadwinners (usually fathers), even when they were unemployed.

TABLE 8-4 **Amount and Duration of Weekly Benefits for Total Unemployment under the Regular State Programs: 1992 and 1993**

State	1993 Weekly Benefit Amount ($)[a]		1992 Average Weekly Benefit ($)	1993 Potential Duration (weeks)		1992 Average Duration (weeks)
	Minimum	Maximum		Minimum	Maximum	
Alabama	22	165	121	15	26	11
Alaska	44–68	212–284	170	16	26	17
Arizona	40	185	147	12	26	16
Arkansas	43	240	151	9	26	13
California	40	230	152	14	26	18
Colorado	25	250	178	13	26	13
Connecticut	15–22	306–356	211	26	26	19
Delaware	20	245	181	24	26	15
District of Columbia	50	335	228	20	26	22
Florida	10	250	158	10	26	16
Georgia	37	185	148	9	26	11
Hawaii	5	322	240	26	26	15
Idaho	44	223	156	10	26	12
Illinois	51	227–300	183	26	26	19
Indiana	50	140–181	126	14	26	12
Iowa	30–36	200–245	170	11	26	14
Kansas	59	239	179	10	26	15
Kentucky	22	217	144	15	26	13
Louisiana	10	181	118	8	26	16
Maine	35–52	198–297	167	21	26	16
Maryland	25–33	223	180	26	26	18
Massachusetts	14–21	312–468	226	10	30	19
Michigan	42	293	211	15	26	13
Minnesota	38	279	198	10	26	16
Mississippi	30	165	123	13	26	14
Missouri	45	175	146	11	26	15
Montana	52	209	135	8	26	14
Nebraska	20	154	133	20	26	12
Nevada	16	217	168	12	26	16
New Hampshire	32	188	136	26	26	12
New Jersey	69	325	225	15	26	19
New Mexico	38	191	138	19	26	17
New York	40	300	197	26	26	21
North Carolina	22	267	158	13	26	11
North Dakota	43	212	146	12	26	14
Ohio	42	228–306	180	20	26	15
Oklahoma	16	229	159	20	26	14
Oregon	63	271	172	5	26	17
Pennsylvania	35–40	317–325	201	16	26	18
Puerto Rico	7	133	84	26	26	19
Rhode Island	41–51	294–367	206	15	26	16
South Carolina	20	193	143	15	26	13
South Dakota	28	154	128	18	26	11
Tennessee	30	170	124	12	26	13
Texas	40	245	176	9	26	16
Utah	14	240	174	10	26	13
Vermont	26	199	155	26	26	17
Virginia	65	208	164	12	26	13
Washington	68	273	176	16	30	18
West Virginia	24	270	163	26	26	15
Wisconsin	46	243	175	13	26	14
Wyoming	40	200	163	12	26	15

Source: Reprinted from Committee on Ways and Means, U.S. House of Representatives. (1993). *Overview of entitlement programs: 1993 greenbook* (pp. 501–502). Washington, DC: U.S. Government Printing Office.

[a] A range of amounts is shown for those states that provide dependents' allowances.

The amount of AFDC benefits varies dramatically from state to state. Table 8-6 shows average family grants ranging from $743 in Alaska to $122 in Mississippi. (Puerto Rico, with a monthly family grant of $104, is the absolute lowest.) The table also shows the per person payment, which can be somewhat misleading because of the administrative maximums on payments various states set. A state that pays family benefits only up to four people pays a lower monthly rate to individuals from larger families because they treat large families as if they were smaller.

Table 8-6 also shows the administrative costs of the program in each state. That figure reflects the costs of personnel and necessities such as office space, communications, and equipment. In many states, it also reflects the costs of some programs to help families find employment, to train personnel, and to provide counseling. In some states, administrative costs exceeded the average family benefit. Overall, the AFDC program cost nearly $27 billion in state and federal funds in 1992.

Table 8-7 shows the variations in benefits by family size. It should be noted that in most states, the increases are not proportional. Benefits go up significantly from two-person to three-person families, but as family size increases, the benefit changes do not increase as much, reflecting the belief that costs such as housing do not increase when an additional person is added to an existing family. In some states it may also reflect an effort to implement policies that discourage large families among AFDC recipients.

The table also demonstrates the wide variations among states. Alaska, which has a high cost of living, pays $1,025 per month for a family of four. Texas, where living costs are lower than Alaska's, but not dramatically, pays only $221 per month for the same size family. Each state determines a standard of need on the basis of the costs of essentials and then pays a percentage of that amount. Eleven states, New York City, and a New York county pay the full standard of need.

Table 8-8 adds a historical perspective to the AFDC program by showing the various payment levels for a family of three from 1970 through 1993. Table 8-9 shows that in constant dollars, benefits have declined rather

---

TABLE 8-5 **Unemployment Rates Based on Varying Definitions of Unemployment and the Labor Force: Selected Years, 1970 to 1992**

Measure	1970	1975	1980	1985	1986	1987	1988	1989	1990	1991	1992
People unemployed 15 weeks or longer as a percentage of the civilian labor force	0.8	2.7	1.7	2.0	1.9	1.7	1.3	1.1	1.2	1.9	2.6
Job losers as a percentage of the civilian labor force	2.2	4.7	3.7	3.6	3.4	3.0	2.5	2.4	2.7	3.7	4.2
Unemployed people 25 years and over as a percentage of the 25-and-over civilian labor force	3.3	6.0	5.1	5.6	5.4	4.8	4.3	4.0	4.4	5.4	6.1
Unemployed full-time job seekers as a percentage of the full-time civilian labor force	4.5	8.1	6.9	6.8	6.6	5.8	5.2	4.9	5.2	6.5	7.1
Total unemployed as a percentage of the labor force, including the resident Armed Forces[a]	4.8	8.3	7.0	7.1	6.9	6.1	5.4	5.2	5.4	6.6	7.3
Total unemployed as a percentage of the civilian labor force[a]	4.9	8.5	7.1	7.2	7.0	6.2	5.5	5.3	5.5	6.7	7.4
Total full-time job seekers plus 1/2 part-time job seekers plus 1/2 total on part-time for economic reasons as a percentage of the civilian labor force, less 1/2 of the part-time labor force	6.3	10.5	9.2	9.6	9.4	8.5	7.6	7.2	7.6	9.2	10.0
Total full-time job seekers plus 1/2 part-time job seekers plus 1/2 total on part-time for economic reasons plus discouraged workers as a percentage of the civilian labor force plus discouraged workers less 1/2 of the part-time labor force	7.1	11.6	10.1	10.6	10.3	9.3	8.4	7.9	8.2	10.0	10.8

Note: Numbers are annual averages of monthly figures.

Source: Reprinted from U.S. Bureau of the Census. (1993). *Statistical abstract of the United States: 1993* (113th ed., p. 415). Austin, TX: Reference Press.

[a]Current unemployment rate definition.

TABLE 8-6 Average Monthly Number of AFDC Families and Recipients, Total Benefit Payments and Administrative Costs, and Average Payment per Family and Recipient: 1992

State	Total Assistance Payments (millions of $)	Average Monthly Caseload (1,000)	Average Monthly Recipients (1,000)	Average Payment per Family	Average Payment per Recipient	Total Administrative Costs (millions of $)	Annual Administrative Cost per AFDC Family
United States	22,223.5	4,768.6	13,625.5	388	136	2,698.1	566
Alabama	85.1	50.6	141.9	140	50	20.6	407
Alaska	96.3	10.8	31.9	743	252	7.9	731
Arizona	242.6	63.6	180.5	318	112	33.8	531
Arkansas	61.1	26.8	75.1	190	68	10.9	407
California	5,828.3	806.1	2,306.5	603	211	484.3	601
Colorado	162.5	42.1	122.4	322	111	26.6	632
Connecticut	376.9	55.5	157.0	566	200	27.0	486
Delaware	37.3	10.7	26.5	290	117	6.9	645
District of Columbia	102.4	22.6	60.0	378	142	25.0	1,106
Florida	733.1	221.2	601.2	276	102	89.1	403
Georgia	420.3	136.0	388.0	258	90	52.9	389
Hawaii	125.3	16.5	50.4	633	207	10.2	618
Idaho	24.0	7.3	19.7	274	102	8.7	1,192
Illinois	882.6	228.6	687.6	322	107	74.4	325
Indiana	218.2	69.1	199.3	263	91	33.4	483
Iowa	164.3	37.2	102.7	368	133	15.6	419
Kansas	119.2	28.7	84.6	346	117	17.4	606
Kentucky	213.1	83.1	229.4	214	77	32.9	396
Louisiana	181.8	92.2	273.7	164	55	21.6	234
Maine	118.3	23.9	68.1	412	145	5.6	234
Maryland	333.3	79.8	220.8	348	126	45.6	571
Massachusetts	750.9	111.4	309.8	562	202	72.4	650
Michigan	1,162.0	225.6	674.2	429	144	162.1	719
Minnesota	387.0	63.7	191.8	506	168	59.6	936
Mississippi	88.8	60.8	177.3	122	42	20.1	331
Missouri	273.9	85.2	250.7	268	91	28.8	338
Montana	45.7	10.9	32.2	349	118	6.5	596
Nebraska	65.3	16.6	48.2	328	113	11.6	699
Nevada	41.0	11.9	32.2	287	106	9.4	790
New Hampshire	54.5	10.5	28.3	433	160	4.2	400
New Jersey	515.7	125.8	352.7	342	122	136.5	1,085
New Mexico	105.9	28.8	87.8	306	101	12.1	420
New York	2,927.2	397.2	1,117.0	614	218	459.1	1,156
North Carolina	335.3	121.4	313.5	230	89	51.9	428
North Dakota	27.5	6.4	18.3	358	125	3.4	531
Ohio	984.0	264.3	749.1	310	109	119.4	452
Oklahoma	169.2	46.8	134.9	301	105	43.1	921
Oregon	200.1	41.5	116.1	402	144	33.9	817
Pennsylvania	906.1	200.7	593.9	376	127	101.2	504
Puerto Rico	76.9	61.4	194.4	104	33	13.7	223
Rhode Island	128.4	21.3	59.4	502	180	5.6	263
South Carolina	119.2	49.7	139.6	200	71	17.1	344
South Dakota	25.2	7.2	20.4	292	103	3.5	486
Tennessee	205.8	95.2	266.1	180	64	28.5	299
Texas	516.5	265.8	757.9	162	57	36.3	238
Utah	75.5	17.9	51.8	351	121	14.0	782
Vermont	67.0	10.0	29.0	558	193	4.6	460
Virginia	224.8	70.7	188.4	265	99	36.9	522
Washington	605.9	96.4	273.5	524	185	60.8	631
West Virginia	120.1	40.5	118.6	247	84	6.1	151
Wisconsin	453.3	81.7	243.9	462	155	52.2	639
Wyoming	27.2	6.6	18.9	343	120	3.0	455

Note: AFDC = Aid to Families with Dependent Children.

Source: Reprinted from Committee on Ways and Means, U.S. House of Representatives. (1993). *Overview of entitlement programs: 1993 greenbook* (pp. 681–682). Washington, DC: U.S. Government Printing Office.

TABLE 8-7 Maximum Monthly AFDC Benefits, by Family Size: 1993

State	1-Person Family	2-Person Family	3-Person Family	4-Person Family	5-Person Family	6-Person Family
Alabama	$111	$137	$164	$194	$225	$252
Alaska[a]	515	821	923	1,025	1,127	1,229
Arizona	204	275	347	418	489	561
Arkansas	81	162	204	247	286	331
California	307	504	624	743	847	952
Colorado	214	280	356	432	512	590
Connecticut[a,b]	430	549	680	792	893	999
Delaware[a]	201	270	338	407	475	544
District of Columbia	258	321	409	499	575	676
Florida	180	241	303	364	426	487
Georgia	155	235	280	330	378	410
Hawaii	407	550	693	835	978	1,121
Idaho	208	254	315	357	399	433
Illinois[c]	212	268	367	414	485	545
Indiana	139	229	288	346	405	463
Iowa	183	361	426	495	548	610
Kansas[a]	267	352	429	497	558	619
Kentucky	162	196	228	285	333	376
Louisiana[d]	72	138	190	234	277	316
Maine	214	337	453	569	685	801
Maryland	159	280	359	432	501	551
Massachusetts[a]	352	446	539	628	720	814
Michigan[e]						
Washtenaw County	305	401	489	593	689	822
Wayne County	276	371	459	563	659	792
Minnesota[a]	250	437	532	621	697	773
Mississippi	60	96	120	144	168	192
Missouri	136	234	292	342	388	431
Montana	229	310	390	470	550	630
Nebraska[a]	222	293	364	435	506	577
Nevada	230	289	348	407	466	525
New Hampshire	388	451	516	575	631	707
New Jersey	162	322	424	488	552	616
New Mexico[a]	192	258	324	389	455	520
New York[a,f]						
Suffolk County	446	576	703	824	949	1,038
New York City	352	468	577	687	800	884
North Carolina	181	236	272	297	324	349
North Dakota[a]	217	326	401	491	558	616
Ohio	203	279	341	421	493	549
Oklahoma	200	251	324	402	470	538
Oregon[a]	310	395	460	565	660	755
Pennsylvania[g]	215	330	421	514	607	687
Puerto Rico	132	156	180	204	228	252
Rhode Island[a]	327	449	554	632	710	800
South Carolina	118	159	200	240	281	321
South Dakota	284	357	404	450	497	543
Tennessee	95	142	185	226	264	305
Texas	75	158	184	221	246	284
Utah	233	323	402	470	536	589
Vermont	452	554	659	740	829	887
Virginia[h]	220	294	354	410	488	518
Washington	349	440	546	642	740	841
West Virginia	145	201	249	312	360	413
Wisconsin[i]	248	440	517	617	708	766
Wyoming	195	320	360	390	450	510
Median State[j]	214	310	367	435	506	577

Notes: Maximum benefit paid for a family of given size with zero countable income in January 1993. Family members include one adult caretaker. AFDC = Aid to Families with Dependent Children.

Source: Reprinted from Committee on Ways and Means, U.S. House of Representatives. (1993). *Overview of entitlement programs: 1993 greenbook* (pp. 659–660). Washington, DC: U.S. Government Printing Office.

[a]States that pay 100 percent of the need standard. [b]Connecticut has three rent regions. Data shown are from rent region A, which has the highest rents. [c]Illinois divides itself into three distinct areas with regard to payment schedules. Data shown are from the Cook County area, which includes Chicago. [d]Louisiana has two payment schedules—one for urban areas, from which these data were taken, and one for rural areas. [e]Michigan has varied shelter maximums. Benefits shown are for Washtenaw County (Ann Arbor) and Wayne County (Detroit). [f]New York has payment schedules for each social service district. Amounts for Suffolk County and New York City are shown. The figures include energy payments. [g]Pennsylvania has four regions. The figures in the table are from region 1, which has the highest benefits. [h]Virginia has three payment schedules. The figures shown are from area 3, which has the highest benefits. [i]Wisconsin has two regions—one for urban areas, from which these data were taken, and one for rural areas. [j]Among 50 states and Washington, DC.

TABLE 8-8 **AFDC Maximum Benefit for a Three-Person Family, by State: Selected Years, 1970 to 1993**

State	1970[a]	1975	1980	1985	1987	1990	1991	1992	1993	Percent Change, 1970–93[b]
Alabama	65	108	118	118	118	118	124	149	164	−31
Alaska	328	350	457	719	749	846	891	924	923	−23
Arizona	138	163	202	233	293	293	293	334	347	−31
Arkansas	89	125	161	164	192	204	204	204	204	−37
California	186	293	473	555	617	694	694	663	624	−8
Colorado	193	217	290	346	346	356	356	356	356	−49
Connecticut	283	346	475	546	590	649	680	680	680	−34
Delaware	160	221	266	287	310	333	338	338	338	−42
District of Columbia	195	243	286	327	364	409	428	409	409	−43
Florida	114	144	195	240	264	294	294	303	303	−27
Georgia	107	123	164	208	256	273	280	280	280	−28
Hawaii	226	428	468	468	468	602	632	666	693	−16
Idaho	211	300	323	304	304	315	315	315	315	−59
Illinois	232	261	288	341	342	367	367	367	367	−57
Indiana	120	200	255	256	256	288	288	288	288	−34
Iowa	201	294	360	360	381	410	426	426	426	−42
Kansas	222	321	345	373	403	409	409	422	429	−47
Kentucky	147	185	188	197	197	228	228	228	228	−57
Louisiana	88	128	152	190	190	190	190	190	190	−41
Maine	135	176	280	370	405	453	453	453	453	−8
Maryland	162	200	270	313	345	396	406	377	359	−39
Massachusetts	268	259	379	396	491	539	539	539	539	−45
Michigan (Wayne County)	219	333	425	468	473	516	525	459	459	−43
Minnesota	256	330	417	524	532	532	532	532	532	−43
Mississippi	56	48	96	96	120	120	120	120	120	−41
Missouri	104	120	248	263	279	289	292	292	292	−23
Montana	202	201	259	332	354	359	370	390	390	−47
Nebraska	171	210	310	350	350	364	364	364	364	−42
Nevada	121	195	262	233	285	330	330	372	348	−21
New Hampshire	262	308	346	378	397	506	516	516	516	−46
New Jersey	302	310	360	385	404	424	424	424	424	−62
New Mexico	149	169	220	258	258	264	310	324	324	−40
New York City	279	332	394	474	497	577	577	577	577	−43
North Carolina	145	183	192	223	259	272	272	272	272	−49
North Dakota	213	283	334	371	371	386	401	401	401	−48
Ohio	161	204	263	290	302	334	334	334	341	−42
Oklahoma	152	217	282	282	310	325	341	341	324	−42
Oregon	184	337	282	386	397	432	444	460	460	−31
Pennsylvania	265	296	332	364	382	421	421	421	421	−56
Puerto Rico	43	43	44	90	90	90	90	180	180	+15
Rhode Island	229	278	340	479	503	543	554	554	554	−34
South Carolina	85	96	129	187	199	206	210	210	200	−36
South Dakota	264	289	321	329	366	377	385	404	404	−58
Tennessee	112	115	122	138	155	184	195	185	185	−55
Texas	148	116	116	167	184	184	184	184	184	−66
Utah	175	252	360	363	376	387	402	402	402	−37
Vermont	267	322	492	558	572	662	679	673	659	−32
Virginia	225	268	310	327	354	354	354	354	354	−57
Washington	258	315	458	476	492	501	531	531	546	−42
West Virginia	114	206	206	206	249	249	249	249	249	−40
Wisconsin	184	342	444	533	544	517	517	517	517	−23
Wyoming	213	235	315	360	360	360	360	360	360	−54
Median state income[c]	184	235	288	332	354	364	367	372	367	−45

Note: AFDC = Aid to Families with Dependent Children.

Source: Reprinted from Committee on Ways and Means, U.S. House of Representatives. (1993). *Overview of entitlement programs: 1993 greenbook* (pp. 666–667). Washington, DC: U.S. Government Printing Office.

[a]Data on three-person families were not published or reported before 1975. Thus, the 1970 data were derived by reducing the reported four-person maximum benefit amount by the proportional difference between three- and four-person AFDC maximum benefit as shown in the July 1975 Department of Health, Education and Welfare reports.

[b]Real percentage change.

[c]Among the 50 states and Washington, DC.

dramatically over the two decades. The median benefit in constant dollars for a family of four declined from $799 per month in 1970 to $435 per month in 1992.

Table 8-10 shows the federal share of the AFDC program from 1984 through 1994. The federal share is based on the state's per capita income. (There is a separate, limited contribution to the territories.) The minimum federal portion is 50 percent, no matter how wealthy the state might be. The federal share changes every two years. One can trace the economic fortunes of each state by examining its federal AFDC share. North Dakota, for example, had a relatively low 61.32 percent federal share in 1984–85 and a much higher rate of 71.13 in 1994, reflecting a decline in the state's economy, particularly in

TABLE 8-9 **Average AFDC Payment per Recipient and per Family and Maximum and Median Benefits for a Family of Four: Selected Years, 1970 to 1992**

Benefit	1970	1975	1980	1985	1990	1992
Average monthly benefit per family	178	210	274	339	389	388
In constant 1992 dollars	644	548	467	442	418	388
Average monthly benefit per person	46	63	94	116	135	136
In constant 1992 dollars	166	164	160	151	145	136
Median state benefit for a family unit of four with no income	221	264	350	399	432	435
In constant 1992 dollars	799	688	596	520	464	435

Notes: AFDC = Aid to Families with Dependent Children. Benefit amounts have not been reduced by child support enforcement collections.

Source: Adapted from Committee on Ways and Means, U.S. House of Representatives. (1993). *Overview of entitlement programs: 1993 greenbook* (p. 668). Washington, DC: U.S. Government Printing Office.

agriculture. Georgia and New Hampshire are examples of states that did better economically in those years and had substantial reductions in the federal share of AFDC.

Some of the characteristics of AFDC recipients as well as the character of their need for assistance are described in Tables 8-11 and 8-12. Table 8-11 provides detailed information on many of the most important charac-

teristics of AFDC recipients, such as the median length of time receiving assistance, the marital status of the heads of household, and the sizes of families. Table 8-12 shows the results of a 1983 study of the reasons people became recipients of AFDC and why they were terminated. Divorce or separation was the primary cause of need, and marriage was the most common reason for termination.

TABLE 8-10 **Federal Share of AFDC Benefit Payments: Selected Years, 1984 to 1994 (Percentage)**

State	1984–85	1988	1990	1991	1992	1993	1994
Alabama	72.14	73.29	73.21	72.73	72.93	71.45	71.22
Alaska	50.00	50.00	50.00	50.00	50.00	50.00	50.00
Arizona	61.21	62.12	60.99	61.72	62.61	65.89	65.90
Arkansas	73.65	74.21	74.58	75.12	75.66	74.41	74.46
California	50.00	50.00	50.00	50.00	50.00	50.00	50.00
Colorado	50.00	50.00	52.11	53.59	54.79	54.42	54.30
Connecticut	50.00	50.00	50.00	50.00	50.00	50.00	50.00
Delaware	50.00	51.90	50.00	50.00	50.12	50.00	50.00
District of Columbia	50.00	50.00	50.00	50.00	50.00	50.00	50.00
Florida	58.41	55.39	54.70	54.46	54.69	55.03	54.78
Georgia	67.43	63.84	62.09	61.34	61.78	62.08	62.47
Hawaii	50.00	53.71	54.50	54.14	52.57	50.00	50.00
Idaho	67.28	70.47	73.32	73.65	73.24	71.20	70.92
Illinois	50.00	50.00	50.00	50.00	50.00	50.00	50.00
Indiana	59.93	63.71	63.76	63.24	63.85	63.21	63.49
Iowa	55.24	62.75	62.52	63.41	65.04	62.74	63.33
Kansas	50.67	55.20	56.07	57.35	59.23	58.18	59.52
Kentucky	70.72	72.27	72.95	72.96	72.82	71.69	70.91
Louisiana	64.65	68.26	73.12	74.48	75.44	73.71	73.49
Maine	70.63	67.08	65.20	63.49	62.40	61.81	61.96
Maryland	50.00	50.00	50.00	50.00	50.00	50.00	50.00
Massachusetts	50.13	50.00	50.00	50.00	50.00	50.00	50.00
Michigan	50.70	56.48	54.54	54.17	55.41	55.84	56.37
Minnesota	52.67	53.98	52.74	53.43	54.43	54.93	54.65
Mississippi	77.63	79.65	80.18	79.93	79.99	79.01	78.85
Missouri	61.40	59.27	59.18	59.82	60.84	60.26	60.64
Montana	64.41	69.40	71.35	71.73	71.70	70.92	71.05
Nebraska	57.13	59.73	61.12	62.71	64.50	61.32	61.98
Nevada	50.00	50.25	50.00	50.00	50.00	52.28	50.31
New Hampshire	59.45	50.00	50.00	50.00	50.00	50.00	50.00
New Jersey	50.00	50.00	50.00	50.00	50.00	50.00	50.00
New Mexico	69.39	71.52	72.25	73.38	74.33	73.85	74.17
New York	50.88	50.00	50.00	50.00	50.00	50.00	50.00
North Carolina	69.54	68.68	67.46	66.60	66.52	65.92	65.14
North Dakota	61.32	64.87	67.52	70.00	72.75	72.21	71.13
Ohio	55.44	59.10	59.57	59.93	60.63	60.25	60.83
Oklahoma	58.47	63.33	68.29	69.65	70.74	69.67	70.39
Oregon	57.12	62.11	62.95	63.50	63.55	62.39	62.12
Pennsylvania	56.04	57.35	56.86	56.64	56.84	55.48	54.61
Puerto Rico	75.00	75.00	75.00	75.00	75.00	75.00	75.00
Rhode Island	58.17	54.85	55.15	53.74	53.29	53.64	53.87
South Carolina	73.51	73.49	73.07	72.58	72.66	71.28	71.08
South Dakota	68.31	70.43	70.90	71.69	72.59	70.27	69.50
Tennessee	70.66	70.64	69.64	68.57	68.41	67.57	67.15
Texas	54.37	56.91	61.23	63.53	64.18	64.44	64.18
Utah	70.84	73.73	74.70	74.89	75.11	75.29	74.35
Vermont	69.37	66.23	62.77	61.97	61.37	59.88	59.55
Virginia	56.53	51.34	50.00	50.00	50.00	50.00	50.00
Washington	50.00	53.21	53.88	54.21	54.98	55.02	54.24
West Virginia	70.57	74.84	76.61	77.00	77.68	76.29	75.72
Wisconsin	56.87	58.98	59.28	59.62	60.38	60.42	60.47
Wyoming	50.00	57.96	65.95	68.14	69.10	67.11	65.63

Note: AFDC = Aid to Families with Dependent Children.

Source: Reprinted from Committee on Ways and Means, U.S. House of Representatives. (1993). *Overview of entitlement programs: 1993 greenbook* (pp. 674–675). Washington, DC: U.S. Government Printing Office.

TABLE 8-11 Characteristics of AFDC Recipients: Selected Years, 1969 to 1991

Characteristic	1969	1973	1975	1979	1983[a]	1986[a]	1988[a]	1990[a]	1991[a]
Average family size (persons)	4.0	3.6	3.2	3.0	3.0	3.0	3.0	2.9	2.9
Number of child recipients (percentage of AFDC cases)									
One	26.6	—	37.9	42.3	43.4	42.7	42.5	42.2	42.2
Two	23.0	—	26.0	28.1	29.8	30.8	30.2	30.3	30.1
Three	17.7	—	16.1	15.6	15.2	15.9	15.8	15.8	16.2
Four or more	32.5	—	20.0	13.9	10.1	9.8	9.9	9.9	10.1
Unknown	—	—	—	—	1.5	0.8	1.7	1.4	1.5
Basis for eligibility (percentage of children)									
Parents present									
Incapacitated	11.7	10.2	7.7	5.3	3.4	3.2	3.7	3.6	3.8
Unemployed	4.6	4.1	3.7	4.1	8.7	7.4	6.5	6.4	7.1
Parents absent									
Death	5.5	5.0	3.7	2.2	1.8	1.9	1.8	1.6	1.8
Divorce or separation	43.3	46.5	48.3	44.7	38.5	36.3	34.6	32.9	32.5
No marriage tie	27.9	31.5	31.0	37.8	44.3	48.9	51.9	54.0	52.9
Other reason	3.5	3.6	4.0	5.9	1.4	2.4	1.6	1.9	1.9
Unknown	—	—	—	—	1.7	—	—	—	—
Education of mother (percentage of mothers)									
8th grade or less	29.4	—	16.7	9.5	—	4.8	5.5	5.8	5.6
1–3 years of HS	30.7	—	31.7	20.8	—	14.3	14.7	16.5	17.6
High school degree	16.0	—	23.7	18.8	—	17.3	17.5	19.3	20.4
Some college	2.0	—	3.9	2.7	—	3.4	3.9	5.7	6.1
College graduate	0.2	—	0.7	0.4	—	0.5	0.6	0.4	0.4
Unknown	21.6	—	23.3	47.8	—	59.7	58.3	52.3	49.9
Age of mother (percentage of mothers)									
Under 20	6.6	—	8.3	4.1[b]	3.6[b]	3.3[b]	3.4[b]	7.9	8.1
20 to 24	16.7	—	c	28.0[d]	28.6[d]	33.6[e]	32.2[e]	23.8[e]	23.4[e]
25 to 29	17.6	—	c	21.4	23.8	20.0[f]	19.4[f]	24.6[f]	23.8[f]
30 to 39	30.4	—	27.9	27.2	27.9	30.1	31.5	32.0	32.6
40 or over	25.0	—	17.6	15.4	15.7	13.0	13.4	11.7	12.1
Unknown	3.6	—	3.0	4.0	0.3	—	—	—	0.1
Ages of children (percentage of recipient children)									
Under 3	14.9	—	16.5	18.9	22.5	21.9	21.1	24.2	24.8
3 to 5	17.6	—	18.1	17.5	20.1	21.1	21.0	21.5	21.4
6 to 11	36.5	—	33.7	33.0	31.5	32.4	33.3	27.5	32.6
12 and over	31.0	—	30.9	29.8	25.5	24.3	22.4	21.3	21.4
Unknown	—	—	0.8	0.9	0.3	0.1	1.3	0.0	0.0
Mother's employment status (percentage)									
Full-time job	8.2	9.8	10.4	8.7	1.5	1.6	2.2	2.5	2.2
Part-time job	6.3	6.3	5.7	5.4	3.4	4.2	4.2	4.2	4.2
Presence of income (percentage of families)									
With earnings	—	16.3	14.6	12.8	5.7	7.5	8.4	8.2	7.9
No non-AFDC income	56.0	66.9	71.1	80.6	86.8	81.3	79.6	80.1	80.1
Median months on AFDC since most recent opening	23.0	27.0	31.0	29.0	26.0	27.0	26.3	23.0	21.9
Race (percentage of parents)[g]									
White	—	38.0	39.9	40.4	41.8	39.7	38.8	38.1	38.1
Black	45.2	45.8	44.3	43.1	43.8	40.7	39.8	39.7	38.8
Hispanic	—	13.4	12.2	13.6	12.0	14.4	15.7	16.6	17.4
Native American	1.3	1.1	1.1	1.4	1.0	1.3	1.4	1.3	1.3
Asian	—	—	0.5	1.0	1.5	2.3	2.4	2.8	2.8
Other and unknown	4.8	1.7	2.0	0.4	—	1.4	1.9	1.5	1.6
Incidence of households (percentage)									
Living in public housing	12.8	13.6	14.6	—	10.0	9.6	9.6	9.6	9.5
Participating in Food Stamp or donated food program	52.9	68.4	75.1	75.1	83.0	80.7	84.6	85.6	87.2
Including nonrecipient members	33.1	34.9	34.8	—	36.9	36.7	36.8	37.7	38.9
Father's relationship to youngest child (percentage)									
Not father	—	—	—	84.7	89.8	91.2	91.6	92.0	91.0
Natural father	—	—	c	9.6	—	—	—	—	—
Adoptive father	—	—	—	0.0	—	—	—	—	—
Stepfather	—	—	—	5.6	—	—	—	—	—

Notes: AFDC = Aid to Families with Dependent Children. — = not available.

Source: Reprinted from Committee on Ways and Means, U.S. House of Representatives. (1993). *Overview of entitlement programs: 1993 greenbook* (pp. 696–698). Washington, DC: U.S. Government Printing Office.

[a]Hawaii and the territories are not included in 1983; data after 1987 include the territories.

[b]Under age 19. Includes caretaker adult if mother is absent. Data for 1983–88 are for adult female recipients.

[c]The percentage for 20- to 29-year-olds was 43.1.

[d]The ages were 19–24 in 1979 and 1983. Includes other caretaker adult if mother is absent.

[e]In 1986 and 1988 this age group was 19–25.

[f]In 1986 and 1988 this age group was 26–29.

[g]For 1983, 12.6 percentage points where race was unknown were allocated proportionately across all categories.

TABLE 8-12 Events Associated with the Beginnings and Endings of AFDC Spells

Event	Percent
Beginnings	
Divorce or separation	45
Childless, unmarried woman becomes a female head with children	30
Earnings of female head fell	12
Earnings of others in family fell	3
Other income fell	1
Other (including unidentified)	9
All beginnings	100
Endings	
Marriage	35
Children leave parental home	11
Earnings of female head increased	21
Earnings of others in family increased	5
Transfer income increased	14
Other (including unidentified)	14
All endings	100

Note: AFDC = Aid to Families with Dependent Children.

Source: Reprinted from Committee on Ways and Means, U.S. House of Representatives. (1993). *Overview of entitlement programs: 1993 greenbook* (p. 725). Washington, DC: U.S. Government Printing Office.

Table 8-13 shows the economic consequences of employment for a single parent with two children who is receiving AFDC and food stamps. A minimum wage job would yield the family $2,720 more than welfare benefits; a $15,000 per year job would yield an additional income of $5,670. Table 8-14 shows the economic consequences of marriage for a single parent with two children who receives AFDC. The loss of benefits would yield a "marriage penalty" of 19 percent if the spouse earned minimum wage and 20 percent if the spouse earned $15,000 per year.

TABLE 8-13 Economic Incentive to Work for a Single Parent with Two Children: 1991

Source of Income	Minimum-Wage Job	$15,000 per Year Job
Unemployed		
Welfare income (AFDC and food stamps)	7,170	7,170
Total income when unemployed[a]	7,170	7,170
Employed		
Potential earnings	8,500	15,000
Work expenses	−1,250	−1,250
Welfare benefits lost	−5,120	−7,170
Change in taxes	590	−910
Total income when working	9,890	12,840
Net gain from work	2,720	5,670
Effective tax rate on work (percentage)	68	62

Notes: Amounts are given in 1991 dollars. AFDC = Aid to Families with Dependent Children.

Source: Reprinted from National Commission on Children. (1991). *Beyond rhetoric: A new American agenda for children and families* (p. 90). Washington, DC: U.S. Government Printing Office.

[a]Reflects combined incomes of welfare recipient and employed potential spouse.

TABLE 8-14 Economic Incentive to Marry for a Single Parent with Two Children: 1991

Source of Income	Spouse with a Minimum-Wage Job	Spouse with a $15,000 per Year Job
Unmarried		
Welfare (AFDC and food stamps)	7,170	7,170
Potential spouse's earnings	8,500	15,000
Work expenses	−1,000	−1,000
Taxes on potential spouse's income	−1,090	−2,570
Total income when unmarried	13,580	18,600
Married		
Welfare benefits lost	−4,220	−5,780
Loss of child support benefit	0	0
Change in taxes	1,680	2,090
Total income when married	11,040	14,910
Marriage penalty as a percentage of initial combined income	19	20

Note: AFDC = Aid to Families with Dependent Children.

Source: Reprinted from National Commission on Children. (1991). *Beyond rhetoric: A new American agenda for children and families* (p. 91). Washington, DC: U.S. Government Printing Office.

Child Support

A major reason for AFDC is the failure of absent parents to pay court-ordered support. As noted in the final report of the National Commission on Children (1991), *Beyond Rhetoric: A New American Agenda for Children and Families,* some observers believe that the failure of absent parents "to pay child support has become this nation's greatest source of financial insecurity" (p. 97). They also state that a better enforcement system could quadruple the amount now collected for child support.

As part of the AFDC program, the federal and state governments operate a child support enforcement program that helps caretaker parents obtain the child support that has been awarded them by the courts or, if such an order has not been made, to arrange for attorneys to help parents receive such orders. In some cases, the program helps parents establish the paternity of their children. In others, it helps locate parents, usually fathers, whose whereabouts are unknown by tracing their social security numbers when they obtain employment. Most of the administrative costs are paid by the federal government. A portion of the child support money collected for AFDC families is used to repay the state and federal governments for the family's benefits.

Table 8-15 lists child support enforcement program statistics from 1978 through 1992. The amounts collected have increased nearly eightfold. For every dollar spent administering the program, it has collected nearly $4. Over 11 percent of AFDC expenses were recovered in 1992, double the figure in 1980. The program has collected more money on behalf of non-AFDC families than AFDC recipients, and these efforts often prevent families from becoming AFDC recipients.

TABLE 8-15 **Child Support Collection Program Operations: Selected Years, 1978 to 1992**

	1978	1980	1982	1984	1986	1988	1990	1992
Total child support collections	$1,047	$1,478	$1,770	$2,378	$3,246	$4,605	$6,010	$7,951
In 1992 dollars	$2,282	$2,574	$2,585	$3,219	$4,137	$5,483	$6,505	$7,951
Total AFDC collections	$472	$603	$786	$1,000	$1,225	$1,486	$1,750	$2,253
Federal	$311	$246	$311	$402	$369	$449	$533	$737
State	$148	$274	$354	$448	$424	$525	$620	$786
Total non-AFDC collections	$575	$874	$984	$1,378	$2,019	$3,119	$4,260	$5,699
Total administrative expenditures	$312	$466	$612	$723	$941	$1,171	$1,606	$1,995
Federal	$236	$349	$459	$507	$633	$804	$1,061	$1,343
State	$76	$117	$153	$216	$308	$366	$545	$652
Federal incentive payments to states and localities	$54	$72	$107	$134	$158	$222	$264	$299
Average number of AFDC cases in which a collection was made	458	503	597	647	582	621	701	831
Average number of non-AFDC cases in which a collection was made	249	243	448	547	786	1,083	1,363	1,747
Number of parents located	454	643	779	875	1,046	1,388	2,062	3,704
Number of paternities established	111	144	173	219	245	307	393	515
Number of support obligations established	315	373	462	573	731	871	1,018	892
Percent of AFDC assistance payments recovered through child support collections	—	5.2	6.8	7.0	8.6	9.8	10.3	11.4
Total child support collections per dollar of total administrative expenses	$3.35	$3.17	$2.89	$3.29	$3.45	$3.93	$3.74	$3.99

Notes: All numbers are in thousands, and all dollar amounts are in millions. AFDC = Aid to Families with Dependent Children; — = not available.

Source: Reprinted from Committee on Ways and Means, U.S. House of Representatives. (1993). *Overview of entitlement programs: 1993 greenbook* (p. 742). Washington, DC: U.S. Government Printing Office.

Table 8-16 shows some of the demographic characteristics of women who received child support in 1989 (not necessarily with the assistance of the government child support enforcement program). The majority were married, separated, or divorced; less than one-fourth had never been married. About three-quarters of women awarded child support were collecting the payments to which they were entitled.

Emergency and General Assistance

A less prevalent but important aid program in which the federal government plays some role is emergency assistance, which is paid through the same agencies that provide AFDC. The program provides assistance on an emergency basis to people who meet specific federal requirements. Each state has different rules governing the program; as Table

TABLE 8-16 **Child Support Payments Awarded to and Received by Women with Children Present, by Selected Characteristics: 1989**

| | | | Supposed to Receive Child Support in 1989 | | | |
| | | | Actually Received Support in 1989 | | | |
Characteristic	Total (1,000)	Percent Awarded Child Support Payments	Total (1,000)	Percent	Mean Child Support ($)	Mean Income ($)
All women	9,955	57.7	4,953	75.2	2,995	16,171
Current marital status						
Married[a]	2,531	79.0	1,685	72.1	2,931	14,469
Divorced	3,056	76.8	2,123	77.0	3,322	19,456
Separated	1,352	47.9	527	79.7	3,060	14,891
Widowed[b]	65	c	34	c	c	c
Never married	2,950	23.9	583	73.2	1,888	9,495
Race or ethnicity						
White	6,905	67.5	4,048	76.5	3,132	16,632
Black	2,770	34.5	791	69.7	2,263	13,898
Hispanic origin[d]	1,112	40.6	364	69.8	2,965	14,758
Years of school completed						
Less than 12 years	2,372	36.9	741	66.7	1,754	8,201
High school completion	4,704	62.0	2,470	76.4	2,698	13,535
College						
1 to 3 years	1,988	65.0	1,139	76.6	3,338	18,462
4 years or more	891	74.5	603	77.9	4,850	30,872
Women below poverty level	3,206	43.3	1,190	68.3	1,889	5,047
Current marital status						
Married	176	72.2	106	67.0	2,275	4,351
Divorced	820	70.4	525	66.3	2,112	5,581
Separated	612	47.1	221	74.2	1,717	4,917
Widowed	8	c	4	c	c	c
Never married	1,590	24.5	334	68.6	1,553	4,543
Race or ethnicity						
White	1,763	54.6	827	67.8	1,972	5,010
Black	1,314	29.2	325	69.8	1,674	5,174
Hispanic origin[d]	536	33.0	148	63.5	1,824	4,958

Note: Data are for women with their own children under age 21 years from an absent father as of spring 1990.

Source: Adapted from Committee on Ways and Means, U.S. House of Representatives. (1993). *Overview of entitlement programs: 1993 greenbook* (p. 749). Washington, DC: U.S. Government Printing Office.

[a]Remarried women whose previous marriage ended in divorce.

[b]Widowed women whose previous marriage ended in divorce.

[c]Base less than 75,000.

[d]Persons of Hispanic origin may be of any race.

8-17 shows, some states had no programs at all between 1985 and 1992, whereas others had large programs. California had no cases in 1991 and 1992, for example, but the relatively small state of Oklahoma had 2,699 cases in 1992. The monthly dollar payments also vary dramatically.

General assistance programs, which are administered by some states and, in some cases, by county or local governments, provide certain kinds of aid that are based on need without special regard to the characteristics of families. In some places, the aid is "in kind," such as housing, food, or medical care, rather than in cash. In other places, it constitutes a monthly assistance check. The programs are so varied that they do not lend themselves to statistical analysis or tabular presentation.

TABLE 8-17 **Emergency Assistance: Total Caseload and Federal and State Payments: Selected Years, 1985 to 1992**

State	Average Monthly Caseload				Total Fiscal Year Payments ($1,000)				Monthly Dollar Payment per Family	
	1985[a]	1990	1991	1992[b]	1985	1990	1991	1992[b]	1985	1992
United States	32,500	55,514	58,962	52,906	156,565	377,942	305,999	266,989	401	421
Arizona	0	0	59	122	0	0	309	1,193	0	815
Arkansas	48	0	0	—	58	0	0	197	101	—
California	734	450	0	0	41,554	40,956	164[c]	247[c]	4,718	0
Colorado	0	0	0	852	0	0	0	2,602	0	255
Delaware	194	202	177	161	232	417	346	320	100	166
District of Columbia	968	1,682	1,821	1,780	2,381	9,591	10,544	2,995	205	140
Florida	0	2,095	1,913	848	0	8,828	8,253	3,633	0	357
Georgia	854	1,704	792	1,094	7,405	5,029	2,865	4,205	723	320
Hawaii	0	0	0	90	0	0	0	745	0	690
Illinois	1,161	1,998	3,037	1,724	2,295	3,218	6,034	4,799	165	232
Iowa	0	0	469	430	0	0	1,799	1,701	0	330
Kansas	159	197	228	206	394	515	534	514	206	208
Maine	304	259	386	461	1,007	1,184	1,114	1,158	276	209
Maryland	1,784	2,000	2,331	2,084	2,445	5,060	5,845	4,945	114	198
Massachusetts	4,584	5,336	5,171	3,721	17,678	58,970	46,745	37,850	321	848
Michigan	4,211	5,656	5,198	1,372	10,067	20,432	20,169	13,926	199	846
Minnesota	1,165	1,849	1,634	1,755	5,624	10,427	9,302	10,028	402	476
Missouri	0	0	0	—	0	0	0	758	0	—
Montana	72	60	70	75	386	162	232	270	446	300
Nebraska	181	253	201	186	646	1,641	1,205	1,110	297	497
Nevada	0	52	28	0	0	147	95	0	0	0
New Hampshire	0	46	46	244	0	386	154	882	0	301
New Jersey	601	3,820	5,125	6,577	2,171	50,902	47,188	52,271	301	662
New York	4,473	12,724	13,709	14,580	37,543	126,878	99,723	84,364	699	482
North Carolina	0	1,482	2,375	2,303	0	4,235	5,541	5,449	0	197
Ohio	5,037	4,330	4,408	4,011	11,778	6,339	9,162	7,767	195	161
Oklahoma	803	2,197	2,764	2,699	2,548	4,325	6,202	5,832	264	180
Oregon	1,312	1,758	1,711	1,532	3,415	4,869	4,927	4,246	217	231
Pennsylvania	32	1,512	1,771	525	92	4,705	6,013	2,636	239	418
Puerto Rico	1,069	538	388	354	247	126	489	250	33	59
Utah	0	106	120	120	0	257	402	620	0	430
Vermont	302	395	351	304	364	1,395	1,419	1,414	100	388
Virginia	18	15	24	43	63	57	70	89	290	172
Washington	727	511	622	537	3,327	2,437	3,122	2,731	381	424
West Virginia	1,202	1,201	1,014	1,225	1,521	1,529	1,571	1,764	105	120
Wisconsin	44	889	836	799	197	2,437	4,044	3,246	372	339
Wyoming	466	196	185	94	1,129	482	414	232	202	205

Notes: Not all states have emergency assistance programs. — = not available.

Source: Reprinted from Committee on Ways and Means, U.S. House of Representatives. (1993). *Overview of entitlement programs: 1993 greenbook* (p. 652–653). Washington, DC: U.S. Government Printing Office.

[a]Expenditure data for fiscal year 1985 do not include prior quarter adjustments.

[b]Data for fiscal year 1992 are preliminary.

[c]Represents prior year claims.

Social Security Benefits

Although it is not a program designed for poor people or specifically to maintain income, Old Age, Survivors, Disability, and Health Insurance (OASDHI), usually referred to by the generic term "social security," is probably the key factor in the nation's program to help people maintain themselves when they are unable to work. Covered workers, who include almost everyone in the United States, pay into the social security trust fund to a specified maximum amount based on their earnings each year. Workers pay 7.65 percent of their incomes up to $57,600, which is matched by their employers. Self-employed people pay 15.3 percent of their income. Workers' survivors, workers who become disabled, and retirees are compensated from those trust funds. In 1993 the maximum benefit, for someone who worked consistently at high-income levels, and retired at age 65, was $1,128 per month (Wright, 1993).

Table 8-18 shows the types of beneficiaries and their average monthly benefits in 1992. The largest group of beneficiaries, 62.1 percent, is retired workers, followed by widows and widowers of retired workers, disabled workers, and spouses of retired workers. As the table shows, the bulk of the funds go to retirees and their families. However, the program is also of great benefit to disabled workers and to the children of retired and disabled workers.

TABLE 8-18 **OASDI Beneficiaries and Benefit Payments: 1992**

Beneficiaries	Beneficiaries (1,000)	Percentage of All Beneficiaries	Average Monthly Benefit ($)
Retired workers	25,758	62.1	653
Wives and husbands of retired workers	3,112	7.5	337
Children of retired workers	432	1.0	285
Disabled workers	3,468	8.4	626
Wives and husbands of disabled workers	271	0.7	155
Children of disabled workers	1,151	2.8	170
Widowed mothers and fathers	294	0.7	438
Surviving children	1,808	4.4	432
Widows and widowers	5,074	12.2	608
Disabled widow(er)s	131	0.3	423
Parents	5	a	526
Special age—72	4	a	178
Total	41,507	100.0	589

Notes: Figures as of December. OASDI = Old-Age, Survivors and Disability Insurance.

Source: THE UNIVERSAL ALMANAC copyright 1993 by John W. Wright. Reprinted with permission of Andrews & McMeel, Kansas City, MO. All rights reserved.

aLess than 0.1 percent.

Table 8-19 lists the projected benefit levels for people who become disabled or retire at various ages. On the basis of the worker's marital status, age, earnings, and reasons for becoming a beneficiary, one can predict what the worker and his or her family or survivors might expect to receive. Of course, OASDHI formulas are quite complicated and involve a number of factors, such as total earnings, av-erage yearly earnings, and postretirement income. However, estimates such as those in Table 8-19 should assist in planning for retirement or for a family's well-being should a worker die or become disabled.

The trust funds that finance these social insurance programs are estimated to be viable until about 2020; that is, there are sufficient funds under the present program to pay the disability

TABLE 8-19 Approximate Monthly Retirement, Disability, and Survivor Benefits: 1993

Worker's Age, 1993	Worker's Family	Insured Worker's Earnings, 1992				
		$20,000	$30,000	$40,000	$50,000	$57,600+
Retirement benefits[a]						
45	Retired worker only	886	1,185	1,329	1,470	1,554
	Worker and spouse[b]	1,329	1,777	1,993	2,205	2,331
55	Retired worker only	803	1,078	1,183	1,270	1,315
	Worker and spouse[b]	1,204	1,617	1,774	1,905	1,972
65	Retired worker only	749	991	1,064	1,112	1,128
	Worker and spouse[b]	1,123	1,486	1,596	1,668	1,692
Disability benefits[c]						
25	Disabled worker only	751	1,009	1,130	1,252	1,319
	Disabled, with dependents[d]	1,127	1,513	1,696	1,878	1,979
35	Disabled worker only	746	1,003	1,126	1,246	1,293
	Disabled, with dependents[d]	1,120	1,505	1,689	1,869	1,940
45	Disabled worker only	745	1,002	1,117	1,201	1,228
	Disabled, with dependents[d]	1,118	1,503	1,676	1,801	1,848
55	Disabled worker only	745	993	1,079	1,135	1,154
	Disabled, with dependents[d]	1,118	1,490	1,618	1,703	1,731
64	Disabled worker only	737	972	1,045	1,090	1,105
	Disabled, with dependents[d]	1,105	1,458	1,567	1,635	1,657
Survivor benefits[e]						
35	Spouse and 1 child[f]	1,120	1,506	1,688	1,870	1,952
	Spouse and 2 children[g]	1,396	1,758	1,970	2,182	2,278
	1 child only	560	753	844	935	976
	Spouse at age 60[h]	534	718	805	891	931
45	Spouse and 1 child[f]	1,118	1,504	1,678	1,810	1,854
	Spouse and 2 children[g]	1,394	1,754	1,958	2,112	2,162
	1 child only	559	752	839	905	927
	Spouse at age 60	533	717	800	863	883
55	Spouse and 1 child[f]	1,118	1,490	1,618	1,702	1,730
	Spouse and 2 children[g]	1,394	1,737	1,887	1,986	2,019
	1 child only	559	745	809	851	865
	Spouse at age 60	533	710	771	811	825

Notes: Assumes steady earnings; actual benefits depend on the pattern of past and future earnings.

Source: THE UNIVERSAL ALMANAC copyright 1993 by John W. Wright. Reprinted with permission of Andrews & McMeel, Kansas City, MO. All rights reserved.

[a]If worker retires at normal retirement age with steady lifetime earnings.

[b]Spouse is assumed to be the same age as the worker. Spouse may qualify for a higher retirement benefit on the basis of his or her own work record.

[c]For workers with steady earnings and disabled in 1993.

[d]Includes spouse and child, the maximum family benefit.

[e]For workers with steady earnings who died in 1993.

[f]Benefits are the same for two children if no parent survives or if the surviving parent has substantial earnings.

[g]Equals maximum family benefit.

[h]Figures for 1993 only. Spouses turning 60 in the future would receive higher benefits.

and retirement benefits through 2020. In fact, large surpluses are available to cover the balance of this century and through about 2015. Beginning in about 2020, there may be a need for other resources such as taxes to cover the obligations. By 2040, the balance in the trust funds is projected to disappear. Table 8-20 shows the projections for the trust fund outlays, incomes, and balances through 1998.

Table 8-21 shows the total state-by-state social security payments in December 1992. It also shows the amounts spent in retirement, survivor, and disability benefits. Table 8-22 shows the number of social security beneficiaries by state in December 1992. A total of 41.5 million individuals received benefits that month.

Medicare is an important part of the social security system. It is primarily for older

TABLE 8-20 **Current Law Projections of the Old-Age and Survivors Insurance (OASI) and Disability Insurance (DI) Trust Fund Outlays, Incomes, and Balances on the Basis of the President's Fiscal Year 1994 Budget Assumptions 1992 to 1998 (In billions of dollars)**

Type of Insurance	1992	1993	1994	1995	1996	1997	1998
Old-age and survivors insurance							
Total outlays	256.2	270.1	283.6	296.1	308.6	321.4	334.4
Income[a]	307.1	319.3	346.5	366.2	387.6	409.4	431.3
Year-end balance	306.3	355.5	418.4	488.5	567.5	655.6	752.5
Start-of-year balance as percent of outlays	100	113	125	141	158	177	196
Disability insurance							
Total outlays	31.3	34.6	37.2	39.9	42.6	45.7	49.1
Income[a]	31.2	32.0	34.3	35.8	37.4	38.7	40.0
Year-end balance	12.9	10.3	7.4	3.3	b	b	b
Start-of-year balance as percent of outlays	42	37	28	19	8	b	b
Combined OASI and DI							
Total outlays	287.5	304.7	320.8	336.0	351.2	367.1	383.5
Income[a]	338.3	351.3	380.8	402.0	425.0	448.1	471.4
Year-end balance	319.2	365.8	425.8	491.8	565.6	646.7	734.5
Start-of-year balance as percent of outlays	93	105	114	127	140	154	169

Note: Estimates are based on economic assumptions in President Clinton's fiscal year 1994 budget.

Source: Reprinted from Committee on Ways and Means, U.S. House of Representatives. (1993). *Overview of entitlement programs: 1993 greenbook* (p. 85). Washington, DC: U.S. Government Printing Office.

[a]Income to the trust funds is budget authority and includes payroll tax receipts, interest on investments, and certain general fund transfers.

[b]The assets of the DI Trust Fund are estimated to be exhausted in 1996.

TABLE 8-21 Total Monthly OASDI Benefits, by Type of Benefit, Gender of Beneficiaries Ages 65 or Older, and State: December 1992 (In thousands of dollars)

State	Total	Retirement Benefits			Survivor Benefits		Disability Benefits			Beneficiaries Age 65 or Older	
		Retired Workers[a]	Wives and Husbands	Children	Widows and Widowers[b]	Children	Disabled Workers	Wives and Husbands	Children	Men	Women
United States[c]	24,441,927	16,811,061	1,047,524	123,175	3,269,653	781,617	2,171,044	41,920	195,933	9,016,992	10,059,464
Alabama	390,866	240,431	17,069	2,735	60,503	17,130	47,062	1,076	4,860	130,070	152,567
Alaska	21,130	13,727	693	161	2,196	1,744	2,330	37	242	7,753	6,754
Arizona	383,089	272,878	17,078	1,690	43,049	10,811	34,109	640	2,834	149,099	149,614
Arkansas	254,160	161,207	10,899	1,428	35,340	9,239	32,016	705	3,326	88,421	95,864
California	2,306,380	1,623,326	105,739	12,080	275,156	70,128	201,084	3,061	15,806	886,680	946,288
Colorado	262,006	174,476	13,216	1,036	34,174	8,768	27,433	493	2,410	96,842	102,004
Connecticut	363,070	275,611	11,677	1,590	40,955	8,552	22,725	271	1,689	141,469	161,760
Delaware	69,062	49,298	2,767	311	8,630	2,058	5,470	90	438	25,939	27,860
District of Columbia	39,820	27,725	1,194	187	5,100	1,726	3,675	19	194	12,989	19,033
Florida	1,687,235	1,247,292	70,435	6,660	195,369	37,626	117,778	2,223	9,852	680,836	695,164
Georgia	508,738	325,244	18,178	2,669	68,512	23,605	63,252	1,129	6,149	165,036	200,667
Hawaii	90,589	69,236	3,445	909	8,597	2,683	5,825	83	411	38,849	34,479
Idaho	95,147	66,272	4,821	467	11,646	3,204	7,825	170	742	38,072	36,447
Illinois	1,136,012	796,550	44,752	5,348	156,045	35,517	88,493	1,329	7,978	418,975	486,982
Indiana	584,606	400,479	23,848	2,866	80,104	18,987	52,204	955	5,163	209,453	241,879
Iowa	317,686	221,377	17,342	1,333	46,346	8,084	21,012	351	1,841	122,704	137,488
Kansas	256,354	181,365	12,681	1,075	35,447	7,350	16,685	251	1,500	99,258	111,444
Kentucky	355,269	210,016	16,661	1,965	56,614	13,625	49,716	1,467	5,205	117,244	134,180
Louisiana	354,769	200,514	19,710	2,483	62,760	18,335	44,141	1,500	5,326	120,577	130,090
Maine	122,750	84,572	5,244	564	16,128	3,416	11,635	231	960	45,124	50,299
Maryland	385,353	270,210	15,192	1,729	52,788	13,780	28,980	397	2,277	139,910	165,151
Massachusetts	612,918	442,621	21,241	2,475	75,908	14,338	51,763	727	3,845	223,840	275,702
Michigan	973,307	657,367	43,000	5,436	135,042	32,105	89,736	1,693	8,928	353,629	387,414
Minnesota	404,560	285,515	20,102	1,833	54,830	10,854	28,585	395	2,446	155,797	171,164
Mississippi	231,583	139,695	8,495	1,812	32,771	11,637	32,642	786	3,745	74,046	87,238
Missouri	547,902	373,939	23,008	2,564	75,196	17,190	50,324	914	4,767	196,884	228,824
Montana	82,048	54,624	4,232	385	10,928	2,690	8,205	197	787	31,586	31,314
Nebraska	161,415	113,450	8,464	615	22,804	4,379	10,535	159	1,009	62,631	70,053
Nevada	117,308	85,718	4,010	525	11,682	3,528	10,908	156	781	47,304	42,513
New Hampshire	104,188	76,875	3,537	397	11,640	2,782	8,121	126	710	39,165	43,816
New Jersey	840,797	621,434	25,712	3,403	101,831	22,378	60,406	887	4,746	318,673	370,554
New Mexico	125,220	81,362	6,696	828	16,310	5,315	13,010	370	1,329	46,186	45,332
New York	1,856,825	1,335,763	60,417	9,379	224,634	52,644	158,712	2,664	12,612	668,735	811,598
North Carolina	629,829	428,129	20,993	2,807	76,976	22,353	71,462	1,061	6,048	214,490	253,474
North Dakota	62,709	41,536	4,287	304	10,159	1,835	4,146	81	361	25,506	25,576

Continued on next page

TABLE 8-21 Continued

State	Total	Retirement Benefits			Survivor Benefits		Disability Benefits			Beneficiaries Age 65 or Older	
		Retired Workers[a]	Wives and Husbands	Children	Widows and Widowers[b]	Children	Disabled Workers	Wives and Husbands	Children	Men	Women
Ohio	1,121,895	739,185	56,980	5,649	176,382	33,961	98,740	2,003	8,995	412,922	462,104
Oklahoma	309,583	207,384	14,717	1,439	45,416	10,927	26,682	556	2,462	112,361	127,646
Oregon	314,444	227,569	14,040	1,338	37,203	8,259	23,729	416	1,890	124,282	128,022
Pennsylvania	1,420,633	1,001,526	61,728	5,796	210,113	35,390	96,785	1,929	7,366	536,160	617,118
Puerto Rico	207,206	103,584	11,045	2,899	26,426	12,075	43,597	1,610	5,970	65,918	56,535
Rhode Island	112,692	84,625	2,927	406	12,473	2,471	9,031	136	623	41,652	50,703
South Carolina	314,098	207,473	10,512	1,700	38,239	13,756	38,181	649	3,588	104,815	121,752
South Dakota	70,541	47,840	4,157	329	10,487	2,048	5,113	95	472	27,919	29,244
Tennessee	472,239	303,013	19,659	2,521	67,280	17,613	55,854	1,109	5,190	160,687	187,888
Texas	1,297,371	840,976	68,864	7,869	200,358	56,104	109,761	2,608	10,831	474,880	511,603
Utah	120,676	83,985	6,200	764	13,933	5,314	9,273	167	1,040	47,183	46,597
Vermont	53,634	37,466	2,194	246	6,923	1,553	4,756	90	406	19,835	22,134
Virginia	495,707	331,313	20,254	2,352	68,402	17,360	50,384	1,149	4,493	169,452	200,510
Washington	462,859	328,968	21,592	2,020	54,758	13,061	38,656	627	3,177	180,671	186,586
West Virginia	213,184	123,903	11,192	1,359	38,007	7,588	27,120	1,061	2,954	72,497	81,215
Wisconsin	527,465	373,911	22,584	2,529	68,638	14,079	41,132	673	3,919	200,676	218,244
Wyoming	38,821	26,781	1,735	154	4,911	1,482	3,369	63	326	14,931	14,721

Note: OASDI = Old-Age, Survivors, and Disability Insurance.

Source: Reprinted from U.S. Department of Health and Human Services, Social Security Administration, Office of Research and Statistics. (1993, November). *OASDI beneficiaries by state and county* (p. 2). Washington, DC: Author.

[a]Includes special age–72 beneficiaries.

[b]Includes disabled and nondisabled widows and widowers, widowed mothers and fathers, and parents.

[c]Totals include outlying areas not listed separately.

State	Total	Retirement Benefits			Survivor Benefits		Disability Benefits			Beneficiaries Ages 65 or Older	
		Retired Workers[a]	Wives and Husbands	Children	Widows and Widowers[b]	Children	Disabled Workers	Wives and Husbands	Children	Men	Women
United States[c]	41,507,201	25,761,409	3,111,515	431,936	5,504,647	1,807,998	3,467,783	270,674	1,151,239	12,180,671	18,250,664
Alabama	738,717	400,245	55,329	10,140	115,573	41,706	78,365	7,329	30,030	192,610	305,748
Alaska	37,275	21,195	2,230	669	3,963	3,858	3,684	262	1,414	10,847	12,324
Arizona	637,534	412,988	50,165	6,191	70,027	25,153	52,368	3,943	16,699	199,285	269,423
Arkansas	488,723	274,880	36,767	5,736	68,641	22,861	53,816	4,844	21,178	134,781	197,497
California	3,820,510	2,434,447	306,174	42,689	445,617	162,685	319,293	19,182	90,423	1,175,215	1,680,586
Colorado	454,528	274,391	39,579	3,563	57,071	19,178	43,805	3,083	14,015	133,361	192,439
Connecticut	546,534	385,100	30,284	4,567	61,505	18,303	35,750	1,775	9,250	170,530	262,506
Delaware	110,547	72,326	7,492	946	13,742	4,489	8,575	555	2,422	33,028	48,373
District of Columbia	77,590	50,074	3,964	741	10,142	4,861	6,581	127	1,100	21,270	37,980
Florida	2,804,407	1,915,349	206,396	23,180	317,713	87,719	185,658	13,457	54,935	913,071	1,262,324
Georgia	937,689	534,685	56,524	9,713	129,529	56,824	105,393	7,831	37,190	237,838	389,654
Hawaii	155,120	107,879	11,175	3,502	14,873	6,234	8,376	591	2,490	54,635	63,626
Idaho	165,692	104,548	14,492	1,637	19,442	7,375	12,525	1,097	4,576	52,866	69,505
Illinois	1,799,304	1,151,356	121,854	16,728	243,772	78,169	136,161	8,033	43,231	527,109	823,378
Indiana	945,927	587,640	66,377	8,648	127,223	40,438	80,850	5,876	28,875	268,524	417,710
Iowa	533,510	338,329	50,392	4,131	75,606	17,598	34,317	2,257	10,880	164,999	251,913
Kansas	421,097	271,404	35,355	3,395	56,912	16,201	27,581	1,584	8,665	129,605	198,569
Kentucky	671,557	349,416	55,374	7,473	106,522	32,296	79,497	9,546	31,433	175,714	270,521
Louisiana	678,196	329,383	62,125	9,567	115,906	45,661	69,971	9,974	35,609	175,078	264,497
Maine	223,597	140,817	16,265	1,939	28,287	7,930	20,394	1,645	6,320	65,697	98,229
Maryland	639,656	413,363	43,558	5,489	86,759	31,248	45,084	2,329	11,826	186,951	294,555
Massachusetts	1,009,098	675,647	59,409	7,966	120,934	32,188	84,697	4,948	23,309	295,903	482,691
Michigan	1,545,880	945,238	118,280	16,116	210,782	67,882	130,923	9,816	46,843	446,923	662,789
Minnesota	692,162	447,253	60,713	5,922	91,348	23,591	46,903	2,443	13,995	216,256	319,634
Mississippi	468,201	246,011	29,453	7,677	67,693	30,273	56,197	5,716	25,181	116,955	183,115
Missouri	945,251	585,386	68,977	8,687	127,590	39,701	81,369	5,851	27,690	270,980	422,328
Montana	143,864	86,411	12,780	1,327	18,297	6,216	12,939	1,227	4,667	44,410	59,318
Nebraska	274,881	176,385	24,771	2,007	37,462	9,703	17,383	1,093	6,077	85,429	129,462
Nevada	192,531	130,628	11,769	1,847	18,943	7,563	16,691	884	4,206	63,787	75,869
New Hampshire	170,805	116,992	9,844	1,213	18,704	5,820	13,103	876	4,253	51,579	77,274
New Jersey	1,274,199	868,832	68,638	10,108	155,706	48,945	92,199	5,344	24,427	385,189	601,365
New Mexico	234,336	132,540	21,701	3,375	29,807	13,681	21,391	2,649	9,192	67,540	90,148
New York	2,909,889	1,914,061	167,305	29,838	353,588	119,680	241,634	16,162	67,621	840,975	1,337,744
North Carolina	1,141,145	700,285	66,070	9,990	147,611	53,279	121,200	7,257	35,453	310,348	489,011
North Dakota	114,174	67,644	13,551	1,109	17,733	4,337	7,119	507	2,174	37,206	51,357
Ohio	1,857,615	1,106,754	162,089	17,579	282,374	74,389	151,966	11,988	50,476	540,647	829,755

Continued on next page

TABLE 8-22 **Continued**

State	Total	Retirement Benefits			Survivor Benefits		Disability Benefits			Beneficiaries Ages 65 or Older	
		Retired Workers[a]	Wives and Husbands	Children	Widows and Widowers[b]	Children	Disabled Workers	Wives and Husbands	Children	Men	Women
Oklahoma	552,439	333,880	45,780	5,239	80,630	25,297	43,293	3,613	14,707	161,281	243,884
Oregon	515,851	343,138	40,499	4,289	59,483	17,996	37,265	2,554	10,627	164,928	229,244
Pennsylvania	2,293,104	1,488,862	171,924	17,732	332,692	77,681	150,147	11,963	42,103	690,788	1,082,946
Puerto Rico	581,898	247,600	56,779	18,807	72,304	42,159	83,695	13,159	47,395	149,163	170,499
Rhode Island	185,412	130,088	8,280	1,315	20,137	5,568	15,129	980	3,915	54,869	88,968
South Carolina	574,197	339,317	32,568	5,998	73,954	33,489	63,571	4,426	20,874	150,834	235,892
South Dakota	131,218	80,010	13,441	1,247	18,713	5,121	8,908	648	3,130	41,884	58,792
Tennessee	869,875	496,820	61,749	9,191	125,913	42,234	94,455	7,653	31,860	233,664	367,474
Texas	2,320,492	1,330,662	210,405	31,453	350,435	132,621	178,181	17,914	68,821	662,833	978,366
Utah	205,797	127,651	17,910	2,619	22,442	12,196	15,029	1,128	6,822	62,588	85,325
Vermont	92,333	58,387	6,573	827	11,746	3,563	7,974	630	2,633	27,337	40,466
Virginia	884,080	535,208	62,701	8,244	123,262	39,504	81,846	7,349	25,966	242,634	381,676
Washington	749,219	486,200	60,620	6,342	86,333	27,897	60,520	3,752	17,555	234,818	329,295
West Virginia	378,877	192,268	34,586	4,787	66,729	17,152	40,438	6,252	16,665	101,167	154,778
Wisconsin	863,283	559,961	64,958	7,691	109,411	30,194	64,741	4,264	22,063	263,550	387,762
Wyoming	65,308	40,836	5,001	509	8,056	3,164	5,359	427	1,956	19,993	26,874

Note: OASDI = Old-Age, Survivors, and Disability Insurance.

Source: Reprinted from U.S. Department of Health and Human Services, Social Security Administration, Office of Research and Statistics. (1993, November). *OASDI beneficiaries by state and county* (p. 1). Washington, DC: Author.

[a] Includes special age-72 beneficiaries.

[b] Includes disabled and nondisabled widows and widowers, widowed mothers and fathers, and parents.

[c] Totals include outlying areas not listed separately.

people, but it also serves some disabled people. It pays for large parts of the costs of health care services, including hospitalization. Table 8-23 shows the number of Medicare recipients and the amount of benefits from 1975 through 1993.

Food Stamps

Perhaps the most flexible and available of all the income assistance programs is the Food Stamp program, which is administered by the U.S. Department of Agriculture. Under the program, low-income people obtain coupons that can be used for food in retail outlets throughout the United States. Eligibility is based strictly on available family funds and assets, so people in low-wage employment, adults who have no children, and others are eligible.

The Food Stamp program is the largest of the federal food assistance programs, which also include school breakfast and lunch assistance; the Special Supplemental Food Program for Women, Infants, and Children for pregnant women and families with young children; and nutrition assistance for elderly people. In 1992 some $21 billion in food stamps were issued to 25 million Americans (U.S. Bureau

of the Census, 1993). Recipients of AFDC, emergency assistance, and Supplemental Security Income (SSI) are among the recipients of food stamps, although it is not necessary for one to qualify for those programs to obtain food stamps.

Supplemental Security Income

For disadvantaged older adults and disabled people, the most important financial aid program is SSI, a federal program administered by the Social Security Administration. In the 1992–93 fiscal year, the SSI payment level was $434 for a single person and $652 for a married couple (Wright, 1993). The levels are adjusted each year on the basis of the cost of living. Table 8-24 shows the levels of payments from 1974 through 1993. Some states supplement these amounts, although they are not required to do so. Table 8-25 shows the subsidies provided to older couples with no income living independently by the states that provide them.

To receive benefits, a person must be blind, disabled, or elderly. Of the more than 5 million total recipients in 1992, some 4 million had disabilities (both physical and mental dis-

TABLE 8-23 **Medicare Recipients and Benefits: Selected Years, 1975 to 1993 (Numbers in thousands)**

Category	1975	1980	1985	1990	1991	1992	1993[a]
Enrollees with hospital insurance							
Total enrolled	23,842	27,539	30,067	33,071	33,836	34,425	35,078
Aged	21,795	24,571	27,123	29,801	30,456	30,365	31,329
Disabled	2,047	2,968	2,944	3,270	3,380	3,560	3,749
Total beneficiaries	5,362	6,664	6,840	6,750	6,810	7,465	7,635
Aged	4,906	5,943	6,168	6,070	6,110	6,730	6,860
Disabled	456	721	672	680	700	735	775
Average annual benefit ($)	327	863	1,587	1,987	2,024	2,341	2,567
Aged	326	853	1,563	1,971	2,007	2,320	2,552
Disabled	345	948	1,806	2,139	2,177	2,520	2,693
Enrollees with supplementary medical insurance							
Total enrolled	23,339	27,120	29,721	32,333	32,933	33,549	34,172
Aged	21,504	24,422	27,049	29,426	29,910	30,375	30,802
Disabled	1,835	2,698	2,672	2,907	3,023	3,174	3,370
Total beneficiaries	12,108	17,703	22,132	26,004	26,391	28,054	28,745
Aged	11,311	16,034	20,199	23,820	24,115	25,523	26,043
Disabled	797	1,669	1,933	2,184	2,276	2,531	2,702
Average annual benefit ($)	161	374	733	1,282	1,380	1,448	1,598
Aged	153	347	705	1,250	1,342	1,407	1,571
Disabled	259	615	1,021	1,602	1,758	1,841	1,847

Source: THE UNIVERSAL ALMANAC copyright 1993 by John W. Wright. Reprinted with permission of Andrews & McMeel, Kansas City, MO. All rights reserved.

[a]Projected.

abilities qualify), some 1.5 million were aged, and over 85,000 were blind (Wright, 1993). Recipients of SSI must also be economically disadvantaged. They may not have resources (such as savings) of more than $2,000 for an individual or $3,000 for a couple. They may own cars worth no more than $4,500. Their incomes, which may include AFDC, social security, other assistance or insurance pro- grams, and wages, must be less than the SSI payment level (Wright, 1993).

Different payments are made to people liv- ing independently and those who live with others. For example, nursing home residents and others who live in group facilities receive less than do those who are maintaining their own houses or apartments (the value of which, if owned, is not counted as a resource).

TABLE 8-24 **Federal Supplemental Security Income Benefit Levels: 1974 to 1993 (In dollars)**

		Eligibility Status					
		In Own Household			In Household of Another		
Year	In Medicaid Institution[a]	Single	Couple	Essential Person[b]	Single	Couple	Essential Person[b]
1974	25.00	146.00	219.00	73.00	97.34	146.00	48.67
1975	25.00	157.70	236.60	78.90	105.14	157.74	52.60
1976	25.00	167.80	251.80	84.00	111.87	167.87	56.00
1977	25.00	177.80	266.70	89.00	118.54	177.80	59.34
1978	25.00	189.40	284.10	94.80	126.27	189.40	63.20
1979	25.00	208.20	312.30	104.20	138.80	208.20	69.47
1980	25.00	238.00	357.00	119.20	158.67	238.00	79.47
1981	25.00	264.70	397.00	132.60	176.47	264.67	88.40
1982	25.00	284.30	426.40	142.50	189.54	284.27	95.00
1983	25.00	304.30	456.40	152.50	202.87	304.27	101.67
1984	25.00	314.00	472.00	157.00	209.34	314.67	104.67
1985	25.00	325.00	488.00	163.00	216.67	325.34	108.67
1986	25.00	336.00	504.00	168.00	224.00	336.00	112.00
1987	25.00	340.00	510.00	170.00	226.67	340.00	113.34
1988	25.00	354.00	532.00	177.00	236.00	354.67	118.00
1989	30.00	368.00	553.00	184.00	245.34	368.67	122.67
1990	30.00	386.00	579.00	193.00	257.34	386.00	128.67
1991	30.00	407.00	610.00	204.00	271.34	406.67	136.00
1992	30.00	422.00	633.00	211.00	281.34	422.00	140.67
1993	30.00	434.00	652.00	217.00	289.34	434.67	144.67

Source: Reprinted from Committee on Ways and Means, U.S. House of Representatives. (1993). *Overview of entitlement programs: 1993 greenbook* (p. 824). Washington, DC: U.S. Government Printing Office.

[a]Long-term-care facility that meets Medicaid's standards.

[b]Someone needed to care for ill or disabled person.

SSI recipients are generally also eligible for food stamps. Table 8-26 shows the combined benefits of individuals who receive SSI and food stamps, by state.

TABLE 8-25 **State Monthly SSI Supplements for Aged Couples with No Countable Income Living Independently: Selected Years, 1975 to 1993**

State	1975	1980	1985	1988	1989	1990	1991	1992	1993	Percent Change, 1975–93[a]
Alabama	9	0	0	0	0	0	0	0	0	−100
Alaska[b]	183	338	371	444	462	484	510	528	544	+13
California	251	389	448	534	563	588	557	557	488	−26
Colorado	133	229	278	292	299	309	293	323	328	−6
Connecticut[c]	—	—	—	602	551	525	522	461	—	—
District of Columbia	0	30	30	30	30	30	30	30	30	—
Hawaii	28	24	9	9	9	9	9	9	9	−88
Idaho	49	80	46	44	43	45	44	45	40	−69
Illinois[c]	—	—	—	—	—	—	—	—	—	—
Maine	15	15	15	15	15	15	15	15	15	−62
Massachusetts	173	214	202	202	202	202	202	202	202	−56
Michigan	18	36	40	45	45	45	46	21	21	−56
Minnesota[d]	38	44	66	66	66	88	132	129	126	+26
Nebraska	67	114	89	66	60	65	34	48	39	−78
Nevada	106	90	74	74	74	74	74	74	74	−73
New Hampshire	0	42	21	21	21	21	21	21	21	—
New Jersey	13	12	25	25	25	25	25	25	25	−27
New York	76	79	76	93	102	102	103	103	102	−49
Oklahoma	54	158	120	128	128	128	128	128	120	−15
Oregon	17	10	0	0	0	0	0	0	0	−100
Pennsylvania	30	49	49	49	49	49	49	49	49	−38
Rhode Island	59	79	102	111	115	120	121	127	120	−23
South Dakota	0	15	15	15	15	15	15	15	15	—
Utah	0	20	20	18	18	12	12	11	10	—
Vermont	61	76	96	106	109	115	118	118	110	−31
Washington[e]	40	44	37	22	22	22	22	22	22	−79
Wisconsin	105	161	161	166	166	166	166	146	146	−47
Wyoming	0	40	40	40	40	40	40	40	19	—
Median	57	63	66	66	60	65	49	49	30	−80

Notes: SSI = Supplemental Security Income; — = not available.

Source: Reprinted from Committee on Ways and Means, U.S. House of Representatives. (1993). *Overview of entitlement programs: 1993 greenbook* (p. 830). Washington, DC: U.S. Government Printing Office.

[a]The percentage change is in constant 1993 dollars.

[b]1975 and 1980—less if shelter costs less than $35 per month.

[c]State decides benefit on a case-by-case basis.

[d]State has various geographical payment levels. Level shown is for Hennepin County, the area with the largest number of SSI recipients.

[e]State has two geographical levels—highest levels are shown in table. Sum paid in King, Pierce, Kitsap, Snohomish, and Thurston Counties.

TABLE 8-26 Maximum Potential SSI and Food Stamp Benefits for Aged Individuals Living Independently: January 1993

State	Maximum SSI Benefit	Food Stamp Benefit	Combined Benefits Monthly	Combined Benefits Annual
Alabama	434	82	516	6,192
Alaska	808	73	881	10,572
Arizona	434	82	516	6,192
Arkansas	434	82	516	6,192
California	620	0[a]	620	7,440
Colorado	490	65	555	6,660
Connecticut[b]	747	0	747	8,964
Delaware	434	82	516	6,192
District of Columbia	449	78	527	6,324
Florida	434	82	516	6,192
Georgia	434	82	516	6,192
Hawaii	439	182	621	7,452
Idaho[c]	499	63	562	6,744
Illinois[d]	NA	NA	NA	NA
Indiana	434	82	516	6,192
Iowa	434	82	516	6,192
Kansas	434	82	516	6,192
Kentucky	434	82	516	6,192
Louisiana	434	82	516	6,192
Maine	444	79	523	6,276
Maryland	434	82	516	6,192
Massachusetts	563	43	606	7,272
Michigan	448	78	526	6,312
Minnesota	515	58	573	6,876
Mississippi[e]	434	82	516	6,192
Missouri	434	82	516	6,192
Montana	434	82	516	6,192
Nebraska	462	74	536	6,432
Nevada	470	71	541	6,492
New Hampshire	461	74	535	6,420
New Jersey	465	73	538	6,456
New Mexico	434	82	516	6,192
New York	520	56	576	6,192
North Carolina	434	82	516	6,192
North Dakota	NA	NA	NA	NA
Ohio	434	82	516	6,192
Oklahoma	494	64	558	6,696
Oregon	436	81	517	6,204
Pennsylvania	466	72	538	6,456
Rhode Island	498	63	561	6,732
South Carolina	434	82	516	6,192
South Dakota	449	78	527	6,324
Tennessee	434	82	516	6,192
Texas	434	82	516	6,192
Utah	439	81	520	6,240
Vermont[f]	491	65	556	6,672
Virginia	434	82	516	6,192
Washington[g]	462	74	536	6,432
West Virginia	434	82	516	6,192
Wisconsin	527	54	581	6,972
Wyoming	444	79	523	6,276

Notes: In most states these maximums apply also to blind or disabled recipients of Supplemental Security Income (SSI) who are living in their own households; however, some states provide different benefit schedules for each category. For one-person households, maximum food stamp benefits from October 1992 through September 1993 are $111 in the 48 contiguous states and the District of Columbia; $143 in Alaska (urban areas, benefit levels in rural Alaska are increased by about 50 percent to account for higher food prices in such areas); and $182 in Hawaii. For the 48 contiguous states and the District of Columbia, the calculation of benefits assumes a "standard" deduction of $127 per month; an excess shelter deduction of $200 per month (the maximum allowable for nonelderly, disabled households); and an excess medical expense deduction of $12 monthly (estimated from 1990 medical expense information). If smaller excess shelter costs were assumed, food stamp benefits would be smaller. For Alaska and Hawaii, higher deduction levels were used, as provided by law ($565 and $465, respectively, for combined standard and excess shelter allowance). NA = not applicable.

Source: Reprinted from Committee on Ways and Means, U.S. House of Representatives. (1993). *Overview of entitlement programs: 1993 greenbook* (pp. 831–832). Washington, DC: U.S. Government Printing Office.

[a]SSI recipients in California are ineligible for food stamps. California provides increased cash aid in lieu of stamps. [b]Individual budget process. [c]State disregards $20 of SSI payment in determining the state supplementary payment. [d]State decides benefits on a case-by-case basis. [e]Payment level for Hennepin County. State has two geographic payment levels—one for Hennepin County and the other for the remainder of the state. [f]State has two geographic payment levels—the highest are shown in the table. [g]Sum paid in King, Pierce, Kitsap, Snohomish, and Thurston counties.

Energy Assistance

One of the more important social welfare programs in recent years has been energy assistance for winter heating provided to low-income households. The cost of energy increased dramatically in the 1970s, at a rate much more rapid than inflation. Low-income people, especially those on fixed incomes, were often unable to pay their winter heating costs. As a consequence, the federal government established the Low-Income Home Energy Assistance Program, which provides funds to the states on the basis of the number of days the populations of each state require heating because of cold weather; the states in turn allocate the funds (or, in some cases, fuels) to clients. Some of the funds are used for home cooling during especially hot summers in warmer regions. Other funds are used for weatherization, such as home repairs and insulation to seal leaks of cold air, or installation of more modern heating equipment. Table 8-27 shows the record of appropriations by the federal government from 1981 to 1990. Table 8-28 shows the number of households that received the various benefits in 1988.

TABLE 8-27 **Federal Funding for the Low-Income Home Energy Assistance Program: 1981 to 1990**

Fiscal Year	Appropriations ($)
1981	1.850 billion
1982	1.875 billion
1983	1.975 billion
1984	2.075 billion
1985	2.100 billion
1986	2.010 billion
1987	1.825 billion
1988	1.532 billion
1989	1.383 billion
1990	1.393 billion

Source: Reprinted with permission from Center on Budget and Policy Priorities. (1991). *The low-income home energy assistance program: A review of participation rates and outreach activities* (p. 15). Washington, DC: American Association of Retired Persons.

TABLE 8-28 **Number of Households Receiving Benefits from the Low-Income Home Energy Assistance Program: 1988**

Type of Assistance	Households
Home heating	5,827,481
Home cooling	309,044
Heating crisis	981,775
Cooling crisis	57,750
Weatherization	156,770

Source: Reprinted with permission from Center on Budget and Policy Priorities. (1991). *The low-income home energy assistance program: A review of participation rates and outreach* (p. 18). Washington, DC: American Association of Retired Persons.

Housing

A critical social welfare issue for many Americans is housing. The number of new public housing units has dropped dramatically; these units primarily benefit low-income people. Figure 8-2 shows that there were 516,000 new public housing units constructed in 1977 and that by 1988 and 1989 only slightly more than 130,000 new units were built per year. Table 8-29 shows the number of occupied units and units under construction from 1970 through 1991. The increase in numbers of units has not been commensurate with population increases, particularly with the increase in the elderly population (Wright, 1993).

FIGURE 8-2 **New Housing Commitments of FmHA and HUD: 1977 to 1989**

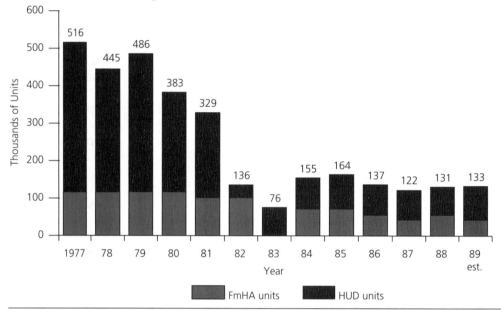

Notes: FmHA = Farmers Home Administration; HUD = Department of Housing and Urban Development.

Source: Reprinted with permission from Leonard, P. A., Dolbeare, C. N., & Lazere, E. B. (1989). *A place to call home: The crisis in housing for the poor* (p. 35). Washington, DC: Center on Budget and Policy Priorities and Low Income Housing Information Service.

TABLE 8-29 **Low-Income Public Housing Units, by Progress Stage: Selected Years, 1970 to 1991 (Numbers in thousands)**

Year	Total[a]	Occupied Units[b]	Under Construction
1970	1,155.3	893.5	126.8
Elderly	249.4	143.4	65.7
1980	1,321.1	1,195.6	20.9
Elderly	358.3	317.7	11.5
1985	1,378.0	1,344.6	9.6
Elderly	373.5	361.1	2.1
1989	1,205.0	1,137.5	7.8
Elderly	—	482.2	—
1990	1,305.3	1,028.1	7.6
Elderly	—	342.2	—
1991	1,304.9	1,200.9	7.5
Elderly	—	376.8	—

Notes: Housing for the elderly intended for persons age 62 years or older, disabled, or handicapped; includes Puerto Rico and the Virgin Islands. Covers units subsidized by the Department of Housing and Urban Development under annual contributions contracts. — = not available.

Source: Reprinted from U.S. Bureau of the Census. (1993). *Statistical abstract of the United States: 1993* (113th ed., p. 734). Austin, TX: Reference Press.

[a]Includes units to be constructed or to go directly "under management" because units with no rehabilitation needed are not shown separately.

[b]Under management or available for occupancy.

Much of the housing occupied by low-income renters and owners is either moderately or severely substandard as described by the U.S. Department of Housing and Urban Development. Severe and moderate substandard housing is defined in Figure 8-3. Figure 8-4 shows the percentage of units with physical problems. The problems of substandard housing are even more severe in rural areas.

Figure 8-5 illustrates the problem in nonmetropolitan areas.

Housing Assistance

Some analysts calculate that the major form of housing assistance in the United States is to homeowners through tax deductions for interest on home mortgages. Table 8-30 shows housing subsidies in 1988 in billions of dol-

---

FIGURE 8-3 **HUD's Definitions of Substandard Housing**

The Bureau of the Census and the U.S. Department of Housing and Urban Development classify housing units according to whether the units have physical or structural deficiencies. A unit is classified as having "severe" physical problems if it has one or more of the following five deficiencies:

- It lacks, within the unit, hot or cold water or a flush toilet, or both a bathtub and a shower.
- The heating equipment broke down at least three times in the previous winter for periods of six hours or more, and this resulted in the unit being uncomfortably cold for 24 hours or more.
- The unit has no electricity, or the unit has exposed wiring *and* has a room with no working wall outlet *and* also has had three blown fuses or tripped circuit breakers in the last 90 days.
- The unit has, in public areas (such as hallways and staircases), nonworking light fixtures *and* loose or missing steps *and* loose or missing railings and no elevator.
- The unit has at least five basic maintenance problems such as water leaks, holes in the floors or ceilings, peeling paint or broken plaster, or evidence of rats or mice in the last 90 days.

A unit is classified as having "moderate" physical problems if it does not have any of the severe problems, but has one or more of the following five deficiencies:

- On at least three occasions in the last three months, all flush toilets were broken down at the same time for at least six hours.
- The unit has unvented gas, oil, or kerosene heaters as its primary heating equipment.
- The unit lacks a sink, refrigerator, or either burners or an oven.
- The unit has three of the four hallway or staircase problems listed above.
- The unit has at least three of the basic maintenance problems listed above.

Note: HUD = Department of Housing and Urban Development.

Source: Reprinted with permission from Leonard, P. A., Dolbeare, C. N., & Lazere, E. B. (1989). *A place to call home: The crisis in housing for the poor* (p. 20). Washington, DC: Center on Budget and Policy Priorities and Low Income Housing Information Service.

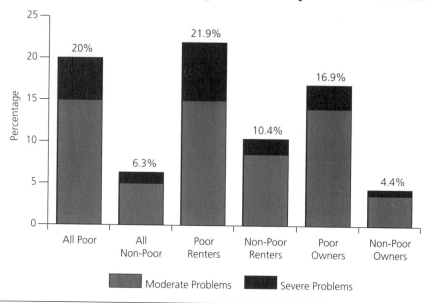

FIGURE 8-4 **Percentage of Public Housing Units with Physical Problems: 1985**

Source: Reprinted with permission from Leonard, P. A., Dolbeare, C. N., & Lazere, E. B. (1989). *A place to call home: The crisis in housing for the poor* (p. 21). Washington, DC: Center on Budget and Policy Priorities and Low Income Housing Information Service.

FIGURE 8-5 **Substandard Housing in Nonmetropolitan Areas: 1985**

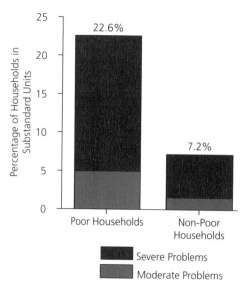

Source: Reprinted with permission from Lazere, E. B., Leonard, P. A., & Kravitz, L. L. (1989). *The other housing crisis: Sheltering the poor in rural America* (p. 25). Washington, DC: Center on Budget and Policy Priorities and Low Income Housing Information Service.

lars by annual income group. For those with incomes under $10,000, $10.1 billion was spent, most of it in direct expenditures for housing because low-income people do not often own houses or pay mortgages. However, those with incomes of $50,000 or more received no money in direct housing outlays but received over $33 billion in tax relief. The table shows that of all the money used to subsidize housing in the United States, only $13.8 billion goes into housing for the poor. Another $5 billion is provided in tax relief for people with incomes under $30,000 per year. Most housing assistance—some $45.6 billion—is spent in the form of tax deductions for those with incomes above $30,000 per year.

Table 8-31 shows the numbers of households that received housing assistance (exclud-

TABLE 8-30 Estimated Distribution of Housing Subsidies, by Household Income: 1988 (In billions of dollars)

| Annual Income | Tax Deductions | | Direct Outlays | Estimated Total | |
	Amount	Percentage		Amount	Percentage
Under $10,000	0.1	0.1	10.1	10.1	15.7
$10,000–$20,000	1.1	2.2	2.7	3.8	5.9
$20,000–$30,000	3.8	7.6	1.0	4.9	7.6
$30,000–$40,000	5.4	10.7	0.0	5.4	8.4
$40,000–$50,000	6.6	13.0	0.0	6.6	10.2
$50,000 and over	33.6	66.4	0.0	33.6	52.2

Source: Reprinted with permission from Leonard, P. A., Dolbeare, C. N., & Lazere, E. B. (1989). *A place to call home: The crisis in housing for the poor* (p. 33). Washington, DC: Center on Budget and Policy Priorities and Low Income Housing Information Service.

TABLE 8-31 Total Households Receiving Assistance, by Type of Subsidy: 1977 to 1993 (Numbers in thousands)

| Beginning of Fiscal Year | Assisted Renters | | | | Total Assisted Renters | Total Assisted Homeowners[a] | Total Assisted Homeowners and Renters[a] |
| | Existing Housing | | | New Construction | | | |
	Household Based	Project Based	Subtotal				
1977	162	105	268	1,825	2,092	1,071	3,164
1978	297	126	423	1,977	2,400	1,082	3,482
1979	427	175	602	2,052	2,654	1,095	3,749
1980	521	185	707	2,189	2,895	1,112	4,007
1981	599	221	820	2,379	3,012	1,127	4,139
1982	651	194	844	2,559	3,210	1,201	4,411
1983	691	265	955	2,702	3,443	1,226	4,668
1984	728	357	1,086	2,836	3,700	1,219	4,920
1985	749	431	1,180	2,931	3,887	1,193	5,080
1986	797	456	1,253	2,986	3,998	1,176	5,174
1987	893	473	1,366	3,047	4,175	1,126	5,301
1988	956	490	1,446	3,085	4,296	918	5,213
1989	1,025	509	1,534	3,117	4,402	892	5,295
1990	1,090	527	1,616	3,141	4,515	875	5,390
1991	1,137	540	1,678	3,180	4,613	853	5,465
1992	1,166	554	1,721	3,204	4,680	826	5,506
1993 (preliminary)	1,326	648	1,974	3,196	4,925	774	5,699

Note: Figures for total assisted renters have been adjusted since 1980 to avoid double-counting households receiving more than one subsidy.

Source: Reprinted from Committee on Ways and Means, U.S. House of Representatives. (1993). *Overview of entitlement programs: 1993 greenbook* (p. 1673). Washington, DC: U.S. Government Printing Office.

[a]Starting 1988, figures reflect a one-time decrease of 141,000 in the number of assisted homeowners because of asset sales by the Farmers Home Administration to private investors.

ing tax deductions for mortgage interest) from 1977 to 1993. Table 8-32 shows the monetary outlays by the U.S. Department of Housing and Urban Development from 1977 to 1992, with estimates for 1993. Again, the increases have been not nearly enough to keep up with population increases and inflation and maintain the program at its 1977 level.

Costs and Availability

Housing cost and availability are major social welfare issues, although they are not always defined as such. The cost of purchasing a house has doubled in 12 years, from an average of $76,000 in 1980 to $144,000 in 1992 (Wright, 1993). Table 8-33 shows the number of housing units available in 1991 by type and the year built; clearly, the number of hous-

TABLE 8-32 **Outlays for Housing Aid Administered by the U.S. Department of Housing and Urban Development, 1977 to 1993 (In millions of current and 1993 dollars)**

	Outlays	
Fiscal Year	Current Dollars	1993 Dollars
1977	2,928	6,751
1978	3,592	7,780
1979	4,189	8,332
1980	5,364	9,600
1981	6,733	10,950
1982	7,846	11,924
1983	9,419	13,706
1984	11,000	15,357
1985	25,064	33,748
1986	12,179	16,001
1987	12,509	15,975
1988	13,684	16,785
1989	14,466	16,940
1990	15,690	17,502
1991	16,897	17,942
1992	18,242	18,802
1993 (estimate)	19,977	19,977

Notes: The bulge in outlays in 1985 is caused by a change in the method of financing public housing, which generated close to $14 billion in one-time expenditures. This amount paid off—all at once—the capital cost of public housing construction and modernization activities undertaken between 1974 and 1985, which otherwise would have been paid off over a period of up to 40 years. Because of this one-time expenditure, however, future outlays for public housing will be lower than they would have been otherwise.

Source: Reprinted from Committee on Ways and Means, U.S. House of Representatives. (1993). *Overview of entitlement programs: 1993 greenbook* (p. 1675). Washington, DC: U.S. Government Printing Office.

TABLE 8-33 **Housing Units Available, by Type and Year Built: 1991**

Characteristic	Units (1,000)	Percentage of Units
Units in structure		
Single, detached	62,646	59.8
Single, attached	6,156	5.9
Mobile home or trailer	6,983	6.7
2 to 4	10,890	10.4
5 to 9	5,368	5.2
10 to 19	4,764	4.6
20 to 49	3,713	3.5
50 or more	4,073	3.9
Total units	104,592	100.0
Year built		
1919 or earlier	10,314	9.9
1920–29	5,677	5.4
1930–39	6,768	6.5
1940–49	8,607	8.2
1950–59	13,836	13.2
1960–69	16,161	15.4
1970–74	11,452	10.9
1975–79	12,146	11.6
1980–84	8,292	7.9
1985–89	8,951	8.6
1990–94	2,389	2.3
Median year built: 1964		

Note: Figures may not add to totals due to rounding.

Source: THE UNIVERSAL ALMANAC copyright 1993 by John W. Wright. Reprinted with permission of Andrews & McMeel, Kansas City, MO. All rights reserved.

ing units built in recent years is not enough to accommodate the growing population. From 1990 to 1994, the population was expected to increase 4 percent, but construction of housing units was anticipated to increase by only 2.3 percent (U.S. Bureau of the Census, 1993). Half of existing housing units in the United States were built in or before 1964.

The cost of housing is also an indicator of people's ability to afford housing. Table 8-34 shows the median sales price of one-family homes in selected metropolitan areas. Although prices have declined in some areas and have held steady in many, the overall cost of housing makes it difficult for people with modest incomes to purchase housing.

TABLE 8-34 **Median Sales Price of Existing One-Family Homes in Selected Metropolitan Areas: 1988, 1992, and 1993 (In thousands of dollars)**

Metropolitan Statistical Area	1988	1992	1993
Atlanta, GA	—	—	87.5
Baltimore, MD	88.7	113.4	113.2
Boston, MA	181.2	171.1	160.5
Chicago, IL	98.9	136.8	131.2
Cincinnati, OH	69.7	88.6	85.6
Cleveland, OH	69.2	90.7	89.2
Dallas, TX	90.8	91.3	89.5
Denver, CO	81.8	96.2	96.3
Detroit, MI	73.1	81.3	92.2
Houston, TX	61.8	80.2	78.0
Kansas City, MO–KS	70.5	79.5	79.1
Los Angeles area, CA	179.4	213.2	199.7
Miami–Hialeah, FL	82.9	97.1	98.0
Milwaukee, WI	74.5	97.0	98.4
Minneapolis– St. Paul, MN	85.2	94.2	96.4
New York– New Jersey– Long Island, NY–NJ–CT	183.8	172.7	168.0
Philadelphia, PA	102.4	117.0	108.9
Phoenix, AZ	80.0	86.8	86.3
Pittsburgh, PA	63.2	78.6	75.9
St. Louis, MO	78.1	83.2	80.9
San Diego, CA	147.8	145.7	175.5
San Francisco Bay Area, CA	212.6	254.8	249.3
Seattle–Tacoma, WA	88.7	183.8	145.0
Tampa– St. Petersburg– Clearwater, FL	65.6	72.6	69.9
Washington, DC–MD–VA	132.5	157.8	153.5

Note: — = not available.

Table 8-35 shows the characteristics of home buyers from 1976 through 1992. The average age of home buyers has increased, apparently because increases in the cost of homes have outpaced increases in incomes.

TABLE 8-35 **General Characteristics of Recent Home Buyers: Selected Years, 1976 to 1992**

Item	1976	1980	1985	1987	1988	1989	1990	1991	1992
Median purchase									
price ($)	43,340	68,714	90,400	99,260	121,910	129,800	131,200	134,300	141,000
First-time buyers	37,670	61,450	75,100	84,730	97,100	105,200	106,000	118,700	122,400
Repeat buyers	50,090	75,750	106,200	115,430	141,400	144,700	149,400	152,500	158,000
Average monthly									
mortgage									
payment ($)	329	599	896	939	1,008	1,054	1,127	1,144	1,064
Percentage of									
income	24.0	32.4	30.0	29.3	32.8	31.8	33.8	34.0	33.2
Percent buying									
New houses	15.1	22.4	23.8	23.8	26.2	21.8	21.2	19.7	20.5
Existing houses	84.9	77.6	76.2	76.2	73.8	78.2	78.8	80.3	79.5
Single-family									
houses	88.8	82.4	87.0	87.3	83.3	84.8	83.8	85.3	85.0
Condominiums[a]	11.2	17.6	10.6	12.5	12.4	13.5	13.1	11.5	13.1
For the first time	44.8	32.9	36.6	36.8	37.8	40.2	41.9	45.1	47.7
Average age (years)									
First-time buyers	28.1	28.3	28.4	29.6	30.3	29.6	30.5	30.7	31.0
Repeat buyers	35.9	36.4	38.4	39.1	38.9	39.4	39.1	39.8	40.8
Downpayment as a									
percentage of									
sales price	25.2	28.0	24.8	27.2	24.0	24.4	23.3	22.6	21.4
First-time buyers	18.0	20.5	11.4	20.4	14.6	15.8	15.7	14.7	14.3
Repeat buyers	30.8	32.7	32.7	31.3	29.7	30.3	28.9	29.1	28.0

Note: Figures are based on a sample survey and subject to sampling variability.

Source: Reprinted from U.S. Bureau of the Census. (1993). *Statistical abstract of the United States: 1993* (113th ed., p. 734). Austin, TX: Reference Press.

[a]Includes multiple-family houses.

Rental prices have increased as dramatically as housing sale prices, according to Table 8-36, which shows the fair market rents for existing housing in various metropolitan areas. The median purchase price for a house in the United States in 1980 was $68,714 and in 1990, $131,200, an increase of 91 percent (U.S. Bureau of the Census, 1993). Median rent in the United States in 1980 was $243 per month and in 1990, $447, an increase of 84 percent (U.S. Bureau of the Census, 1993). However, AFDC payments, incomes, and other factors that make rent payments possible have not kept up. Median household income in 1980 was $17,710. In 1990, it was $29,943, an increase of 69 percent.

TABLE 8-36 **Fair Market Monthly Rents for Existing Housing for Selected Metropolitan Areas: 1993 (In dollars)**

Metropolitan Area	1 Bedroom	2 Bedrooms	3 Bedrooms
Anaheim– Santa Ana, CA	751	883	1,104
Atlanta, GA	492	580	725
Baltimore, MD	504	593	742
Boston, MA	647	809	1,011
Chicago, IL	591	692	870
Cincinnati, OH	415	489	611
Cleveland, OH	429	505	632
Dallas, TX	485	571	713
Denver, CO	443	522	652
Detroit, MI	444	522	653
Fort Lauderdale– Hollywood– Pompano Beach, FL	573	674	843
Fresno, CA	479	565	705
Honolulu, HI	782	920	1,158
Houston, TX	414	488	612
Indianapolis, IN	432	508	635
Kansas City, MO–KS	416	489	611
Las Vegas, NV	583	687	862
Los Angeles– Long Beach, CA	704	829	1,036
Memphis, TN	383	451	562
Miami–Hialeah, FL	611	719	899
Milwaukee, WI	433	513	642
Minneapolis– St. Paul, MN	535	630	788
New Orleans, LA	383	451	564
New York, NY	579	681	854
Oklahoma City, OK	375	440	552
Philadelphia, PA–NJ	538	634	793
Phoenix, AZ	429	505	631
Pittsburgh, PA	386	454	568
Portland, OR	435	512	676
Sacramento, CA	497	595	864
St. Louis, MO	426	503	628
San Diego, CA	618	725	908
San Francisco, CA	845	1,002	1,247
San Jose, CA	780	920	1,149
Seattle, WA	536	630	813
Tampa– St. Petersburg– Clearwater, FL	453	534	665
Washington, DC–MD–VA	725	854	1,067
West Palm Beach– Boca Raton– Delray Beach, FL	477	556	680

Source: THE UNIVERSAL ALMANAC copyright 1993 by John W. Wright. Reprinted with permission of Andrews & McMeel, Kansas City, MO. All rights reserved.

Homelessness

Homelessness remains a major problem in the United States. Estimates of the numbers of homeless people range from 50,000 (the official figure of the U.S. Department of Housing and Urban Development) to 3 million. Studies have estimated that on a given night there are about 600,000 homeless people (Burt & Cohen, 1989) and that during the course of a year, between 1.3 and 2 million people are homeless for one or more nights (Wright, 1993). Table 8-37 lists characteristics of homeless adults in cities with populations over 100,000.

In a study conducted during the 1990 census, the U.S. Bureau of the Census visited 11,000 shelters and 24,000 street sites and found 228,621 homeless persons, 178,828 of

TABLE 8-37 **Characteristics of Homeless Adults in Cities with Populations over 100,000**

Characteristic	Homeless Adults (%)		
	Single	In Families	Total (%)
Total	77	8	85[a]
Sex			
Male	88	12	81
Female	12	88	19
Race or ethnicity			
Black	39	54	41
Hispanic	9	20	10
White	49	22	46
Other	3	4	3
Age			
18 to 30	NA	NA	30
31 to 50	NA	NA	51
51 to 65	NA	NA	16
66+	NA	NA	3
Marital status			
Married	9	23	10
Divorced or separated	30	25	29
Widowed	6	6	5
Never married	56	47	55
Medical history			
Mental hospitalization	20	11	19
Chemical dependency	35	12	33
Criminal history			
Jailed for 5 or more days	56	18	52
State or federal prison	26	2	24
Number of months homeless			
Mean	41.3	14.6	NA
Median	12.0	4.5	NA
Monthly cash income			
Mean	$146	$301	NA
Median	$64	$300	NA
Receiving benefits			
Food stamps	15	50	NA
Aid to Families with Dependent Children	1	33	NA
General assistance	10	33	NA
Eating habits (percentage)			
Eat less than once a day	8	1	7
Eat once a day	31	19	30
Eat twice a day	38	39	38
Eat three or more times a day	25	41	25
No food over a 2-day period, once a week	18	5	17

Notes: All data are from a study of 1,704 homeless persons who used services. NA = not applicable.

Source: Reprinted from Committee on Ways and Means, U.S. House of Representatives. (1993). *Overview of entitlement programs: 1993 greenbook.* Washington, DC: U.S. Government Printing Office.

[a]The remaining 15 percent of homeless individuals are children in homeless families.

whom were in emergency shelters. California had the highest number of homeless people (48,887); New York was second with 43,204, Florida had 10,299, and Pennsylvania had 9,549. New York City had an estimated 33,830 homeless people (Wright, 1993).

In a study of 28 major cities by the U.S. Conference of Mayors, it was concluded that the number of middle-aged men who are homeless is shrinking, whereas the number of homeless families with young children is growing rapidly. The study found that in the nation as a whole, 50 percent of the homeless population are single men, 35 percent are members of families, 12 percent are single women, and 3 percent are runaways or children who have been thrown out by their families. Children are about 24 percent of the population. Approximately 29 percent of the homeless population are mentally ill, and about 40 percent are substance abusers. Some 7 percent have AIDS or HIV-related illness. Eighteen percent of homeless people have full-time or part-time jobs, and 25 percent are veterans (Wright, 1993). According to the U.S. Department of Education, some 273,000 homeless people were school age, and 28 percent of them did not attend school regularly (Hill, 1990). Table 8-38 shows estimates of the size of the homeless populations in selected cities in 1990.

But the homeless population differs significantly from city to city. The largest number of homeless people in major cities such as Baltimore, Chicago, Detroit, New York, and St. Louis are people of color, whereas whites constitute the highest percentage in Milwaukee, Phoenix, Portland, and Ohio. Single men are 60 percent of the homeless population in Charleston, SC, Hartford, Minneapolis, Nashville, Phoenix, St. Paul, Salt Lake City, and San Diego; in Kansas City, MO, New York, Norfolk, and Trenton, NJ, single men are 30 percent or less of the homeless population (Institute of Medicine, Committee on Health Care for Homeless People, 1988). Families with children account for more than half the homeless population in Chicago, Kansas City, MO, New York, Norfolk, San Antonio, and Trenton. They are 20 percent or less in Boston, Hartford, Nashville, Portland, St. Paul, San Francisco, and San Juan.

American citizens consistently say that they are concerned about and sympathetic toward the homeless population. In a 1993 study that included a representative sample of 2,503 men and women ages 18 to 75, 56 percent reported that they believed that homeless people are not responsible for their situation, and 63 percent thought the main reason for homelessness is the breakdown of the American family (Clements, 1994). Three-fourths opined that homeless people are not assisted adequately by the government. Sixty-nine percent did not favor a legal procedure to forcibly remove homeless people from the streets, and two-thirds said they would donate money to assist homeless people if there were a category on their tax returns for doing so. Only 7 percent thought that homeless people are violent, but 60 percent said that the homeless contribute at least somewhat to the rising crime rate. Nearly a third believed that homeless people who are nonviolent but who are diagnosed as mentally ill should be institutionalized against their will.

Although the general responses were sympathetic, 16 percent said that they go out of their way to avoid homeless people; twice as

TABLE 8-38 **Estimates of the Homeless Population in Selected U.S. Cities: 1990**

Rank and City	Total	Number in Shelters	Number Visible on Street
1. New York	33,830	23,383	10,447
2. Los Angeles	7,706	4,597	3,109
3. Chicago	6,764	5,180	1,584
4. San Francisco	5,569	4,003	1,566
5. San Diego	4,947	2,846	2,101
6. Washington, DC	4,813	4,682	131
7. Philadelphia	4,485	3,416	1,069
8. Newark, NJ	2,816	1,974	842
9. Seattle	2,539	2,170	360
10. Atlanta	2,491	2,431	60
11. Boston	2,463	2,245	218
12. Houston	1,931	1,780	151
13. Phoenix, AZ	1,786	1,710	276
14. Portland, OR	1,702	1,553	149
15. Sacramento, CA	1,552	1,287	265
16. Baltimore	1,531	1,144	387
17. Dallas	1,493	1,200	293
18. Denver	1,269	1,169	100
19. Oklahoma City	1,250	1,016	234
20. Minneapolis	1,080	1,052	28

Source: THE UNIVERSAL ALMANAC copyright 1993 by John W. Wright. Reprinted with permission of Andrews & McMeel, Kansas City, MO. All rights reserved.

many of those who do so are white as are African American or Hispanic. When asked what they thought causes homelessness, 84 percent thought that drug and alcohol abuse are factors, and three-fourths thought that job loss is a factor. Over half mentioned that being released from mental hospitals resultes in homelessness, and nearly half said that homeless people do not want to work. A third blamed homelessness on cuts in government funding. When asked why they thought homeless people remain homeless, 41 percent of the respondents said that lack of job opportunities makes it difficult for homeless people to re-enter society. Twenty-eight percent thought that homeless people remain homeless because they lack affordable housing. Twenty-one percent thought that homeless people just didn't care, 21 percent thought that drug addiction was the reason, and 21 percent thought that unwillingness to work was the reason.

Fifty percent of study respondents with earnings of less than $20,000 a year believed they could become homeless if they lost their jobs; some 70 percent of them gave money to homeless people occasionally. People with incomes of over $75,000 did not view themselves as potentially homeless, and only 40 percent of them gave money to homeless people.

About two-thirds of the respondents said the government does not spend enough money on the homeless population, and approximately the same number said the government should build housing for homeless people. African Americans and Hispanics supported increased government housing to a greater extent (83 percent) than did white respondents (60 percent).

Race and Ethnicity of Social Welfare Beneficiaries

Table 8-39 shows the distribution of social welfare program recipients by race and ethnicity. White people constitute the majority of recipients of both social insurance and means-tested programs, with the exception of housing. Although minority groups in the United States experience a disproportionately large share of the social, economic, and health problems, half of those who are in need of help are white non-Hispanics. According to

Shapiro and Nichols (1992), the proportion of white poor people is growing more rapidly than the proportion of African American poor people. From 1989 to 1991, the white poor population grew by 14 percent, whereas the African American poor population grew by 10 percent. The Hispanic poor population increased by 17 percent, which may reflect the growth of the Hispanic population through immigration and a rise in the birth rates.

Poor white people are disproportionately rural. In rural areas, 69.7 percent of poor people are white, whereas only 43 percent of urban and metropolitan poor people are white. The majority of the poor people in 33 states are white, and white people are a plurality of the poor in seven states. In 28 states, 60 percent or more of the poor population is white. However, white people are twice as likely to be lifted out of poverty by government benefits than African Americans or Hispanics, according to Shapiro and Nichols (1992).

Federal Aid to State and Local Governments

The federal government provides assistance to states for a variety of programs. Table 8-40

TABLE 8-39 **Social Security Program Recipients, by Race and Ethnicity: 1991**

Program	Percentage Distribution		
	White	Black	Hispanic
Means-tested programs			
Cash assistance	48	32	15
Food stamps	46	33	17
Medicaid	47	31	17
Housing	38	43	14
Social insurance programs			
Social security	85	10	4
Medicare	84	20	4
Unemployment insurance	77	15	7

Note: "White" refers to "non-Hispanic white."

Source: Reprinted with permission from Shapiro, I. (1992). *White poverty in America* (p. 35). Washington, DC: Center on Budget and Policy Priorities.

| | Federal Aid[a] | | OE Compensatory Education[c] | EPA Waste Treatment Facilities Construction | HHS | | HUD | | ETA Employment Training | DOT Highway Trust Fund |
Region and State	Total	Per Capita[b] ($)			Administration for Children and Families[d]	Medicaid	Lower Income Housing Assistance[e]	Community Development		
Total[f]	174,448	684	5,813	2,367	25,548	67,740	10,775	2,957	6,570	14,843
Northeast										
Connecticut	2,593	790	64	32	340	1,030	226	37	99	351
Maine	1,047	847	32	22	142	448	77	15	38	79
Massachusetts	5,218	870	142	110	690	2,069	545	97	166	575
New Hampshire	935	842	15	19	76	561	49	9	22	58
New Jersey	5,217	670	199	71	686	2,100	439	89	213	402
New York	19,305	1,065	670	398	3,024	9,429	1,310	302	516	692
Pennsylvania	8,293	691	304	47	1,070	3,567	491	215	318	623
Rhode Island	986	981	23	10	123	403	103	17	37	117
Vermont	503	882	14	14	84	160	29	7	19	68
Midwest										
Illinois	6,937	596	290	153	994	2,077	592	171	349	540
Indiana	3,242	573	93	31	322	1,430	167	57	135	396
Iowa	1,660	590	46	25	228	595	70	38	63	238
Kansas	1,376	545	40	13	186	572	60	24	46	136
Michigan	6,004	636	240	162	1,169	2,243	286	114	317	394
Minnesota	2,894	646	67	43	453	1,087	195	56	98	267
Missouri	3,498	674	92	59	392	1,443	186	63	121	319
Nebraska	997	621	29	13	129	320	59	18	31	109
North Dakota	603	948	15	6	64	183	30	6	23	112
Ohio	7,064	641	224	103	1,177	2,950	485	146	287	486
South Dakota	601	845	19	11	57	176	41	9	21	100
Wisconsin	3,127	624	87	93	536	1,256	150	56	123	280
South										
Alabama	2,795	676	134	15	223	1,127	171	36	117	221
Arkansas	1,691	705	74	9	146	720	80	20	63	185
Delaware	425	617	17	10	53	123	36	4	18	60
District of Columbia	1,951	3,314	47	13	173	300	77	31	36	114
Florida	6,187	459	269	78	870	2,243	376	126	224	508
Georgia	4,028	597	179	35	549	1,581	247	62	127	332
Kentucky	2,951	786	111	21	360	1,355	170	42	100	176
Louisiana	4,417	1,030	148	26	380	2,498	164	55	100	304
Maryland	2,940	599	102	64	437	983	251	43	120	263
Mississippi	2,193	839	120	22	217	886	116	40	67	179

Continued on next page

TABLE 8-40 Continued

Region and State	Federal Aid[a] Total	Federal Aid[a] Per Capita[b] ($)	Office of Education Compensatory Education[c]	EPA Waste Treatment Facilities Construction	HHS Administration for Children and Families[d]	HHS Medicaid	HUD Lower Income Housing Assistance[e]	HUD Community Development	ETA Employment Training	DOT Highway Trust Fund
North Carolina	3,971	580	154	46	495	1,684	218	56	150	309
Oklahoma	2,066	643	59	21	286	786	138	20	67	186
South Carolina	2,393	664	96	17	222	1,129	119	30	83	192
Tennessee	3,658	728	132	33	316	1,642	186	55	116	308
Texas	9,645	546	380	75	983	4,041	491	185	319	885
Virginia	2,773	435	118	24	371	834	218	51	111	277
West Virginia	1,668	921	54	26	179	756	92	16	51	143
West										
Alaska	837	1,425	11	12	105	115	42	3	41	211
Arizona	2,235	583	62	23	377	786	135	31	91	189
California	19,738	639	541	193	5,036	6,142	1,191	340	830	1,688
Colorado	1,905	549	49	14	244	542	125	29	68	247
Hawaii	839	724	17	19	116	174	53	19	28	198
Idaho	694	650	18	10	76	210	30	8	36	110
Montana	765	929	15	16	85	210	33	7	28	157
Nevada	669	504	14	10	65	197	51	7	34	80
New Mexico	1,379	872	44	10	154	408	74	14	39	159
Oregon	2,050	688	48	24	314	567	103	24	96	210
Utah	1,042	575	21	2	132	352	35	16	46	108
Washington	3,374	657	65	58	593	1,170	151	37	143	401
Wyoming	593	1,271	8	4	44	85	13	3	19	103

Notes: Figures in millions of dollars, except per capita. Data are for fiscal year ending September 30. OE = Office of Education; EPA = Environmental Protection Agency; HHS = Department of Health and Human Services; HUD = Department of Housing and Urban Development; ETA = Employment and Training Administration, Job Training Partnership Act; DOT = Department of Transportation.

Source: Reprinted from U.S. Bureau of the Census. (1993). *Statistical abstract of the United States: 1993* (113th ed., p. 296). Austin, TX: Reference Press.

[a]Includes amounts not shown separately.

[b]Amounts are based on estimated resident population as of July 1.

[c]For the disadvantaged.

[d]Includes family support payments (Aid to Families with Dependent Children), social services block grants, children and family services, foster care and adoption assistance, low-income home energy assistance, community services block grants, refugee assistance, and assistance for legalized aliens.

[e]Includes public housing, housing payments (Section 8) to public agencies, and college housing.

[f]Includes undistributed amounts not shown separately.

shows allocations by federal government agencies to the states for social services, housing, health care, community development, employment training, and other functions. It also shows the per capita allocation by state. The District of Columbia, which is totally under federal jurisdiction, receives the largest per capita allocation; Virginia receives the smallest. Large portions of the funds allocated by the federal government are tied to state government appropriations of money that are subsequently matched by the federal government. The more the state is willing to contribute, the more the federal government provides in matching funds.

Conclusion

This chapter has covered some fundamental information for social workers—employment status, income, poverty, and programs that help reduce poverty through financial assistance. Poverty and its associated problems are basic, one may argue, to most social work services and most social problems. These are the areas from which social work emerged as a profession. Not only are many social workers engaged in work in these areas, the public also perceives these as the fundamental areas of concern that define the social work profession.

SOCIAL WORK: PROFESSIONAL ISSUES

The social work profession is about 100 years old, if one traces the history of the profession from the beginnings of professional education for practice (Hopps & Pinderhughes, 1987; Lloyd, 1987). The National Association of Social Workers (NASW), the major professional organization, was founded in 1955 in a merger of seven social work organizations: the American Association of Group Workers, the American Association of Medical Social Workers, the American Association of Psychiatric Social Workers, the American Association of Social Workers, the Association for the Study of Community Organization, the National Association of School Social Workers, and the Social Work Research Group.

According to the Bureau of Labor Statistics (BLS) of the U.S. Department of Labor (1993), the number of social workers will continue to grow through the period 1992 to 2005. As Table 9-1 indicates, there were more than 474,000 social workers in 1992, and BLS estimates that there will be between 634,593 and 680,798 social workers by 2005. The table includes only those who are employees and who work for salaries or wages. Another 10,000 social workers are self-employed now, according to the BLS, and small percentage increases are also predicted for that group during the coming decades.

The majority of social workers are employed by services organizations, especially social services (27 percent) and health services (26 percent), as Table 9-1 shows. Over 40 percent of social workers are employed directly by government, primarily local and state governments, but even many of those that are not classified as government employees are employed by agencies that are supported by government contracts.

Social Work Education

All states now have some legal regulation of the practice of social work, and many require that social workers be licensed. According to the Council on Social Work Education (CSWE) (Lennon, 1993), there are now 416 social work education programs in the United States employing 5,400 faculty members. Social work education programs are accredited by CSWE, which also collects, maintains, and disseminates information on these programs. Table 9-2 shows the aggregate figures on the accredited professional education programs. Table 9-3 shows the institutional auspices of social work education programs. Most are part of public colleges and universities. Table 9-4 shows the size of the institutions that have social work programs.

Social Work Faculty

Table 9-5 provides information on the gender and ages of social work faculty. The majority of the faculty are women; however, men constitute a higher percentage of the faculty than of the profession. Table 9-6 shows the race or ethnicity and gender of social work faculty by level of program. Table 9-7 correlates rank with race or ethnicity. Salary information by primary responsibility and level of program is provided in Table 9-8. The table shows that median salaries are significantly higher for faculty in graduate and joint programs than for those in exclusively baccalaureate programs. Although the salaries of undergraduate educators vary little in terms of medians, despite different responsibilities, the range is wide. Classroom instructors, for example, earned as little as $1,800 and as much as $70,280 in 1991–92. Similarly broad ranges may be seen for the salaries of graduate educators and administrators. The figures reflect the diversity of education and experience

TABLE 9-1 **Social Work Employment by Industry and Occupation: 1992, with Alternative Estimates Projected for the Year 2005**

	1992		2005 Estimates Number			Percent (moderate estimate)
Industry	Number	Percent	Low	Moderate	High	
Total, all industries	474,176	100.00	634,593	664,547	680,798	100.00
Agriculture, forestry, and fishing	a	a	a	a	a	a
Services	282,474	59.57	406,805	422,769	427,268	63.62
Health services	123,372	26.02	192,000	200,840	202,789	30.22
Offices of physicians, including osteopaths	7,025	1.48	11,342	11,828	11,993	1.78
Offices of other health practitioners	5,805	1.22	10,016	10,446	10,591	1.57
Nursing and personal care facilities	14,200	2.99	21,391	22,269	22,500	3.35
Hospitals, public and private	67,022	14.13	102,056	107,147	108,242	16.12
Medical and dental laboratories	51	0.01	74	77	78	0.01
Home health care services	4,257	0.90	8,568	8,923	8,980	1.34
Health and allied services	25,013	5.28	38,553	40,149	40,406	6.04
Education, public and private	22,572	4.76	34,206	35,965	37,313	5.41
Social services	126,546	26.69	167,522	172,569	173,627	25.97
Individual and miscellaneous social services	81,235	17.13	95,523	98,335	98,756	14.80
Job training and related services	8,721	1.84	13,311	13,853	13,964	2.08
Child day care services	4,601	0.97	8,049	8,259	8,288	1.24
Residential care	31,988	6.75	50,639	52,121	52,619	7.84
Membership organizations	9,983	2.11	13,077	13,395	13,539	2.02
Business and professional organizations	188	0.04	261	274	279	0.04
Labor organizations	86	0.02	83	84	85	0.01
Civic and social associations	5,993	1.26	8,085	8,246	8,340	1.24
Membership organizations	263	0.06	354	370	377	0.06
Religious organizations	3,453	0.73	4,294	4,420	4,457	0.67
Government	191,671	40.42	227,749	241,738	253,487	36.38
Federal government	4,999	1.05	4,631	4,892	5,078	0.74
State government, except education and hospitals	98,501	20.77	113,110	120,070	125,931	18.07
Local government, except education and hospitals	88,171	18.59	110,008	116,776	122,477	17.57

Source: Reprinted from U.S. Department of Labor, Bureau of Labor Statistics. (1993, November). *BLS releases new 1992–2005 employment projections* (p. 242). Washington, DC: Author.

[a]Fewer than 50 workers.

TABLE 9-2 Social Work Education Programs and Faculty, by Geographic Region and Level of Program: 1992

Region	Graduate Only Programs	Graduate Only Faculty	Joint Programs	Joint Faculty	Baccalaureate Programs	Baccalaureate Faculty	Total Programs	Total Faculty
1	6	249	5	88	19	109	30	446
2	6	321	6	381	33	179	45	881
3	3	108	11	359	41	175	55	642
4	5	127	9	246	54	259	68	632
5	5	178	17	593	64	334	86	1,105
6	4	123	8	245	34	167	46	535
7	1	59	5	155	32	140	38	354
8	2	69	3	51	10	55	15	175
9	4	142	10	285	9	45	23	472
10	1	45	3	78	6	35	10	158
Total	37	1,421	77	2,481	302	1,498	416	5,400

Notes: Region 1 = Connecticut, Maine, Massachusetts, New Hampshire, Rhode Island, Vermont; Region 2 = New Jersey, New York, Puerto Rico, Virgin Islands; Region 3 = Delaware, District of Columbia, Maryland, Pennsylvania, Virginia, West Virginia; Region 4 = Alabama, Florida, Georgia, Kentucky, Mississippi, North Carolina, South Carolina, Tennessee; Region 5 = Illinois, Indiana, Michigan, Minnesota, Ohio, Wisconsin; Region 6 = Arkansas, Louisiana, New Mexico, Oklahoma, Texas; Region 7 = Iowa, Kansas, Missouri, Nebraska; Region 8 = Colorado, Montana, North Dakota, South Dakota, Utah, Wyoming; Region 9 = Arizona, California, Hawaii, Nevada; Region 10 = Alaska, Idaho, Oregon, Washington.

Source: Reprinted with permission from Lennon, T. M. (1993). *Statistics on social work education in the United States: 1992* (p. 3). Alexandria, VA: Council on Social Work Education.

TABLE 9-3 Social Work Education Programs and Faculty, by Institutional Auspices and Level of Program: 1992

Institutional Auspices	Graduate Only Programs	Graduate Only Faculty	Joint Programs	Joint Faculty	Baccalaureate Programs	Baccalaureate Faculty	Total Programs	Total Faculty
Public								
State	17	526	61	1,889	149	893	227	3,308
Other	1	89	0	0	4	19	5	108
Private								
Church related	5	192	7	219	118	426	130	837
Other	14	614	9	373	31	160	54	1,147
Total	37	1,421	77	2,481	302	1,498	416	5,400

Source: Reprinted with permission from Lennon, T. M. (1993). *Statistics on social work education in the United States: 1992* (p. 4). Alexandria, VA: Council on Social Work Education.

TABLE 9-4 Social Work Education Programs, by Size of College or University Enrollment and Level of Program: 1992

Full-Time Enrollment	Graduate Only	Joint	Baccalaureate	Total
Under 2,000	5	0	95	100
2,000–4,999	4	9	72	85
5,000–9,999	6	8	59	73
10,000–19,999	7	19	56	82
20,000 and over	15	41	20	76
Total	37	77	302	416

Source: Reprinted with permission from Lennon, T. M. (1993). *Statistics on social work education in the United States: 1992* (p. 4). Alexandria, VA: Council on Social Work Education.

among educators and the financial resources among programs.

Undergraduate Social Work Education

Social work education at the undergraduate level has also grown in recent years. Since the 1970s bachelor of social work (BSW) programs have been eligible for accreditation by CSWE. Also, the fact that many master of social work (MSW) programs grant up to one year of advanced standing for BSW graduates has helped make undergraduate social work education attractive.

Statistics on undergraduate social work education are not as concrete as those for graduate education. Many students take a few social work courses as electives or minors or simply to explore their interest. However, the sta-

TABLE 9-5 **Social Work Program Faculty, by Gender, Age, and Level of Program: 1992**

Level of Program and Age	Male		Female		Total	
	No.	%	No.	%	No.	%
Graduate and joint						
Under 35	84	5.2	179	8.2	263	6.9
35–44	402	25.0	728	33.3	1,130	29.8
45–54	597	37.1	856	39.2	1,453	38.3
55 and older	526	32.7	422	19.3	948	25.0
Total	1,609	100.0	2,185	100.0	3,794	100.0
Baccalaureate						
Under 35	56	9.1	116	13.1	172	11.5
35–44	158	25.8	348	39.3	506	33.8
45–54	272	44.4	319	36.0	591	39.5
55 and older	127	20.7	102	11.5	229	15.3
Total	613	100.0	885	100.0	1,498	100.0

Source: Reprinted with permission from Lennon, T. M. (1993). *Statistics on social work education in the United States: 1992* (p. 9). Alexandria, VA: Council on Social Work Education.

TABLE 9-6 **Social Work Program Faculty, by Race or Ethnicity, Gender, and Level of Program: 1992**

Level of Program	Race or Ethnicity	Male		Female		Total	
		No.	%	No.	%	No.	%
Graduate	African American	210	13.1	320	14.7	530	14.0
and joint	Asian American	57	3.5	46	2.1	103	2.7
	Chicano/Mexican American	57	3.5	48	2.2	105	2.8
	Native American	14	0.9	17	0.8	31	0.8
	Puerto Rican	17	1.1	37	1.7	54	1.4
	Other minority	15	0.9	20	0.9	35	0.9
	Total minorities	370	23.0	488	22.4	858	22.6
	Foreign	2	0.1	3	0.1	5	0.1
	White	1,237	76.9	1,692	77.5	2,929	77.2
	Total	1,609	100.0	2,183	100.0	3,792	100.0
Baccalaureate	African American	80	13.1	202	22.9	282	18.9
	Asian American	11	1.8	6	0.7	17	1.1
	Chicano/Mexican American	15	2.4	12	1.4	27	1.8
	Native American	10	1.6	10	1.1	20	1.3
	Puerto Rican	9	1.5	35	4.0	44	2.9
	Other minority	9	1.5	10	1.1	19	1.3
	Total minorities	134	21.9	275	31.1	409	27.3
	Foreign	1	0.2	1	0.1	2	0.1
	White	478	78.0	607	68.7	1,085	72.5
	Total	613	100.0	883	100.0	1,496	100.0

Source: Reprinted with permission from Lennon, T. M. (1993). *Statistics on social work education in the United States: 1992* (p. 10). Alexandria, VA: Council on Social Work Education.

tistics on juniors and seniors enrolled in social work programs present a relatively good measure of the number of social work majors who will complete BSW degrees. Table 9-9 shows that 22,359 students in 1992 were enrolled in social work programs and that 9,510 students completed the programs and were awarded degrees; 23.1 percent of the graduates were members of minority groups.

Graduate Social Work Education

The oldest degree and still the most prevalent is the MSW, which is awarded by 114 public and private colleges and universities throughout the country. Doctoral education is a much smaller part of graduate social work education; as of 1990, 52 programs granted either a PhD in social work or a doctorate in social work (DSW) (Lennon, 1993).

TABLE 9-7 Social Work Program Faculty, by Rank, Race or Ethnicity, and Level of Program: 1992

| Level of Program | Rank | Percentage Distribution | | | | | | |
		African American	Asian American	Chicano/ Mexican American	Native American	Puerto Rican	Other and Foreign	White
Graduate	Professor	13.8	28.4	19.0	16.1	22.2	10.0	19.8
and joint	Associate professor	29.3	27.5	19.0	19.4	33.3	27.5	19.4
	Assistant professor	27.6	21.6	20.0	29.0	27.8	27.5	19.8
	Instructor	5.5	1.0	7.6	9.7	1.9	5.0	11.3
	Lecturer	8.3	9.8	19.0	19.4	5.6	10.0	12.7
	Other	15.5	11.8	15.2	6.5	9.3	20.0	17.0
	Total	100.0	100.0	100.0	100.0	100.0	100.0	100.0
	Number	529	102	105	31	54	40	2,926
Bacccalaureate	Professor	12.5	17.6	22.2	5.0	0.0	14.3	14.1
	Associate professor	24.6	29.4	25.9	20.0	36.4	14.3	26.3
	Assistant professor	35.7	47.1	18.5	35.0	22.7	42.9	32.7
	Instructor	10.7	5.9	11.1	20.0	9.1	9.5	10.9
	Lecturer	10.7	0.0	14.8	20.0	27.3	14.3	10.9
	Other	5.7	0.0	7.4	0.0	4.5	4.8	5.0
	Total	100.0	100.0	100.0	100.0	100.0	100.0	100.0
	Number	280	17	27	20	44	21	1,072

Source: Reprinted with permission from Lennon, T. M. (1993). *Statistics on social work education in the United States: 1992* (p. 16). Alexandria, VA: Council on Social Work Education.

TABLE 9-8 Salary Median and Range of Full-Time Social Work Program Faculty, by Primary Responsibility and Level of Program: 1992

| Level of Program | Primary Responsibility | Salary ($) | | | | |
| | | Adjusted for Months | | Unadjusted for Months | | |
		Median	Range	Median	Range	Number
Graduate	Classroom teaching	40,558	2,170–98,165	42,500	1,929–103,383	1,258
and joint	Classroom and field	32,265	10,000–61,347	34,000	5,050–75,835	58
	Field instruction/liaison	29,628	6,510–68,500	33,354	3,000–68,500	158
	Dean/director	56,250	29,045–110,455	73,882	27,000–143,500	91
	Associate dean/director	50,472	34,366–78,750	63,154	40,609–105,000	64
	Assistant dean/director	42,345	27,263–62,116	50,138	33,518–66,274	35
	Director of undergraduate program	39,274	27,756–78,344	42,197	29,048–87,049	45
	Director field instruction	34,424	14,488–62,820	43,480	19,317–69,800	75
	Assistant director, field instruction	31,459	4,500–47,600	35,744	4,500–51,306	26
	Director admissions/ minority recruitment	34,806	18,941–55,302	41,138	25,255–73,736	26
	Director continuing education/work study	33,028	12,750–67,502	36,688	17,000–90,002	12
	Other administration	46,086	8,516–88,292	50,836	11,355–98,102	121
Baccalaureate	Classroom teaching	32,000	1,800–70,280	32,880	1,800–73,000	408
	Classroom and field	31,500	8,212–44,800	32,000	3,650–44,800	41
	Field instruction/liaison	27,000	4,400–60,000	28,500	4,400–60,960	45
	Dean/director	36,500	18,000–97,300	39,336	22,800–97,300	228

Source: Reprinted with permission from Lennon, T. M. (1993). *Statistics on social work education in the United States: 1992* (p. 23). Alexandria, VA: Council on Social Work Education.

Table 9-10 shows that interest in graduate-level social work education increased between 1991 and 1992. However, although more candidates were accepted by graduate school programs in 1992, the number of students who actually registered increased only slightly.

TABLE 9-9 **Juniors and Seniors Enrolled Full-Time in Baccalaureate Programs and Students Awarded Baccalaureate Degrees, by Race or Ethnicity: 1992**

	Juniors and Seniors Enrolled		Students Awarded Degrees	
Race or Ethnicity	No.	%	No.	%
African American	3,695	16.5	1,320	13.9
Asian American	398	1.8	115	1.2
Chicano/Mexican American	915	4.1	279	2.9
Native American	273	1.2	109	1.1
Puerto Rican	620	2.8	278	2.9
Other minority	205	0.9	97	1.0
Total minorities	6,106	27.3	2,198	23.1
Foreign	115	0.5	46	0.5
White	16,138	72.2	7,266	76.4
Total	22,359	100.0	9,510	100.0

Source: Reprinted with permission from Lennon, T. M. (1993). *Statistics on social work education in the United States: 1992* (p. 28). Alexandria, VA: Council on Social Work Education.

TABLE 9-10 **Applications for Admissions to First-Year Status in Master's Degree Programs, by Action Taken: 1991 and 1992**

				Action Taken on Application					
		Total Received		Considered for Admission		Accepted		Registered	
Year	Program	No.	%	No.	%	No.	%	No.	%
1991	Full-time	23,839	100.0	21,463	90.0	13,915	58.4	8,472	35.5
	Part-time	9,622	100.0	8,361	86.9	5,814	60.4	4,454	46.3
	Total	33,461	100.0	29,824	89.1	19,729	59.0	12,926	38.6
1992	Full-time	28,493	100.0	25,021	87.8	14,465	50.8	8,472	29.7
	Part-time	11,273	100.0	9,992	88.6	6,374	56.5	4,944	43.9
	Total	39,766	100.0	35,013	88.0	20,839	52.4	13,416	33.7

Source: Reprinted with permission from Lennon, T. M. (1993). *Statistics on social work education in the United States: 1992* (p. 30). Alexandria, VA: Council on Social Work Education.

Table 9-11 shows the number of MSWs and doctoral degrees awarded from 1966–67 to 1991–92 by most of the accredited graduate social work education programs in the United States. As can be seen, there was a steady increase in the number of MSW degrees awarded until 1983–84, when the number was the lowest since 1973–74. The 1983–84 drop reflected the impact of the Reagan presidency on social services, as well as reductions in student aid programs and other practices and policies that discouraged the preparation of MSW-level social workers. The number of doctoral degrees awarded rose fairly steadily from 1965 to the 1980s but peaked in 1987–88.

In 1984–85, social work education began to grow again. Legislation passed by Congress, which remained a supporter of human services programs, increased the need for social workers. Although federal funds for many programs were reduced or not increased sufficiently to keep pace with increasing costs, many states began to replace federal funds with state funds so that social welfare programs could continue to operate and expand. An increasingly older population required more assistance in aging programs, hospitals, and long-term-care facilities. Longer sentences for crimes and an increasing tendency to incarcerate offenders required more social workers in the corrections field. Despite what appeared to be some political hostility toward federally funded human services, programs continued to expand. These factors increased the attractiveness of social work as a profession. In addition, the increased population of student-

TABLE 9-11 Graduate Students Awarded Master's and Doctoral Degrees: Academic Years 1966–67 through 1991–92

Academic Year	Master's Degree	Doctoral Degree
1966–67	4,279	54
1967–68	4,614	67
1968–69	5,060	89
1969–70	5,638	84
1970–71	6,284	129
1971–72	6,909	114
1972–73	7,387	112
1973–74	8,005	159
1974–75	8,824	155
1975–76	9,080	179
1976–77	9,254	179
1977–78	9,476	178
1978–79	10,080[a]	174[a]
1979–80	9,820	213[a]
1980–81	9,750	226
1981–82	9,556	284
1982–83	9,034[a]	227[a]
1983–84	8,053[a]	245[a]
1984–85	8,798[a]	181[a]
1985–86	8,134[a]	297[a]
1986–87	8,811[a]	195[a]
1987–88	9,891[a]	332
1988–89	9,509[a]	189[a]
1989–90	10,063[a]	247[a]
1990–91	10,969[a]	245
1991–92	11,582[a]	243[a]

Note: Response rate to survey = 104 of 106 master's programs and 49 of 52 doctoral programs.

Source: Reprinted with permission from Lennon, T. M. (1993). *Statistics on social work education in the United States: 1992* (p. 31). Alexandria, VA: Council on Social Work Education.

[a]Response rate was less than 100 percent.

age Americans added to the enrollment of students at all levels.

The gender and race or ethnicity of graduate social work students are detailed in Tables 9-12 and 9-13. Data are presented for those enrolled and for those who graduated. For MSW students, about 80 percent were women and about 80 percent were white. As the tables indicate, doctoral students were somewhat less likely to be female but more likely to be non-white or foreign. About one-third of doctoral students were men, and close to one-third were either foreign or members of minority groups.

TABLE 9-12 **Percentage Distribution of Master's and Doctoral Students, by Gender and Age: 1991**

Age (years)	Gender	Master's Students		Doctoral Students	
		Full-time	Part-Time	Full-Time	Part-Time
25 and under	Male	3.7	2.2	0.8	0.0
	Female	29.7	13.3	3.2	0.2
26–30	Male	4.3	4.5	3.8	1.2
	Female	18.1	18.4	9.7	4.5
31–40	Male	5.7	7.2	14.7	12.7
	Female	18.5	25.3	23.1	25.1
41 and over	Male	3.8	5.6	13.7	16.6
	Female	16.1	23.5	31.0	39.7
Total	Male	17.5	19.4	33.0	30.5
	Female	82.5	80.6	67.0	69.5
Total	Percent	100.0	100.0	100.0	100.0
	Number	20,551	10,711	897	995

Source: Reprinted with permission from Lennon, T. M. (1993). *Statistics on social work education in the United States: 1992* (p. 32). Alexandria, VA: Council on Social Work Education.

TABLE 9-13 **Percentage Distribution of Master's and Doctoral Students Enrolled and Students Awarded Degrees, by Race or Ethnicity: 1991**

Race or Ethnicity	Master's Students			Doctoral Students		
	Enrolled		Awarded Master's Degrees	Enrolled		Awarded Doctoral Degrees
	Full-Time	Part-Time		Full-Time	Part-Time	
African American	10.3	11.3	9.2	13.5	13.0	14.4
Asian American	2.1	1.9	1.8	2.2	1.5	1.2
Chicano/Mexican American	2.5	3.1	2.5	2.4	2.0	1.6
Native American	0.8	0.3	0.6	1.0	0.6	0.4
Puerto Rican	1.9	1.4	1.7	1.6	0.3	0.4
Other minority	1.2	1.6	1.4	1.4	1.4	1.2
Total minorities	18.8	19.6	17.1	22.1	18.8	19.3
Foreign	1.3	0.4	1.2	9.4	6.6	11.9
White	79.9	80.0	81.6	68.5	74.6	68.7
Total	100.0	100.0	100.0	100.0	100.0	100.0
Number	20,671	10,745	11,582	1,000	1,005	243

Source: Reprinted with permission from Lennon, T. M. (1993). *Statistics on social work education in the United States: 1992* (p. 33). Alexandria, VA: Council on Social Work Education.

The MSW curriculum has changed over the years in some programs from allowing students to concentrate only in methods of practice to allowing them to concentrate in "fields of practice" or "social problems." Table 9-14 shows the methods concentrations of MSW students in 1992, some of whom combined concentrations in methods with concentrations in fields of practice or social problems.

Over half the students were concentrating in direct practice, and another 8.9 percent were concentrating in "generic" or "generalist" practice; 16.3 percent had not yet determined what method they would choose. Only 3.1 percent were concentrating in administration and management, and only 2.1 percent were concentrating in community organization and planning, although another 7.5 percent were

TABLE 9-14 **Master's Degree Students, by Primary Methods Concentration: 1992**

| | Concentration Framework | | | | | | | |
| | Methods Only | | Methods Combined with Field of Practice or Social Problem | | Field of Practice or Social Problem Only (No Methods) | | Total | |
Method	No.	%	No.	%	No.	%	No.	%
Direct practice	4,660	54.6	12,333	56.2	NA	NA	16,993	54.0
Community organization and planning	195	2.3	475	2.2	NA	NA	670	2.1
Administration or management	315	3.7	669	3.0	NA	NA	984	3.1
Combination of direct practice with community organization and planning or administration or management	447	5.2	1,904	8.7	NA	NA	2,351	7.5
Combination of community organization and planning with administration or management	294	3.4	458	2.1	NA	NA	752	2.4
Generic	1,678	19.7	1,122	5.1	NA	NA	2,800	8.9
Other	358	4.2	440	2.0	NA	NA	798	2.5
Not yet determined	587	6.9	4,553	20.7	NA	NA	5,140	16.3
None (field of practice or social problem only)	NA	NA	NA	NA	978	100.0	978	3.1
Total	8,534	100.0	21,954	100.0	978	100.0	31,466	100.0

Note: NA = not applicable.

Source: Reprinted with permission from Lennon, T. M. (1993). *Statistics on social work education in the United States: 1992* (p. 34). Alexandria, VA: Council on Social Work Education.

in combined methods concentrations that included direct practice and either community organization and planning or administration and management.

In programs that had social-problem or field-of-practice concentrations, the largest number of students were in mental health, health, and family services—exceeded only by those who were not engaged in anything other than a methods concentration or who had not yet determined their field of practice, as Table 9-15 shows. Table 9-16 shows the field of practice of their field instruction placements.

TABLE 9-15 **Master's Degree Students, by Primary Field of Practice or Social Problem Concentration: 1992**

Concentration	No.	%
Aging/gerontological social work	792	2.5
Alcohol, drug, or substance abuse	488	1.6
Child welfare	2,148	6.8
Community planning	376	1.2
Corrections/criminal justice	216	0.7
Family services	2,482	7.9
Group services	136	0.4
Health	2,213	7.0
Occupational/industrial social work	207	0.7
Mental health or community mental health	4,041	12.8
Mental retardation	143	0.5
Public assistance/ public welfare	92	0.3
Rehabilitation	111	0.4
School social work	751	2.4
Other	1,264	4.0
Combinations	742	2.4
Not yet determined	6,730	21.4
None (methods concentration only)	8,534	27.1
Total	31,466	100.0

Source: Reprinted with permission from Lennon, T. M. (1993). *Statistics on social work education in the United States: 1992* (p. 35). Alexandria, VA: Council on Social Work Education.

TABLE 9-16 **Master's Degree Students, by Primary Field of Practice in Field Instruction: 1992**

Concentration	No.	%
Aging/gerontological social work	884	2.8
Alcohol, drug, or substance abuse	810	2.6
Child welfare	2,205	7.0
Community planning	561	1.8
Corrections/criminal justice	467	1.5
Family services	2,941	9.3
Group services	251	0.8
Health	2,956	9.4
Occupational/industrial social work	283	0.9
Mental health or community mental health	4,960	15.8
Mental retardation	280	0.9
Public assistance/ public welfare	293	0.9
Rehabilitation	235	0.7
School social work	1,349	4.3
Other	1,578	5.0
Not yet assigned field instruction	4,308	13.7
Not to be in field instruction this academic year	7,105	22.6
Total	31,466	100.0

Source: Reprinted with permission from Lennon, T. M. (1993). *Statistics on social work education in the United States: 1992* (p. 36). Alexandria, VA: Council on Social Work Education.

Profile of the NASW Membership

The BLS figures are for social worker positions, without regard to the educational preparation or professional identification of their incumbents. Federal government figures do not match the figures produced by NASW, which were developed by surveying some 135,000 NASW members. Figure 9-1 shows the differences between the BLS data and NASW's calculations for 1988 and 1991. The NASW figures reflect only those who qualify for NASW membership, which generally requires a social work degree. Not all those identified by the BLS qualify for NASW membership, and not all who qualify become members.

FIGURE 9-1 **NASW versus BLS Counts of Social Workers: 1988 and 1991**

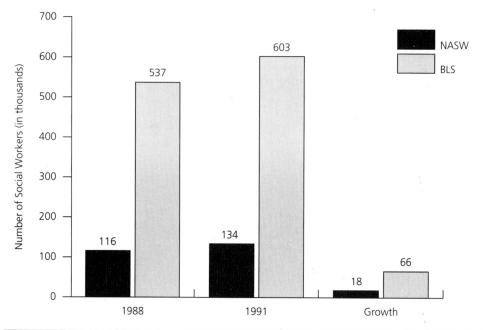

Notes: NASW = National Association of Social Workers; BLS = Bureau of Labor Statistics.

Source: Reprinted with permission from Gibelman, M., & Schervish, P. H. (1993). *Who we are: The social work labor force as reflected in the NASW membership* (p. 20). Washington, DC: NASW Press.

Both the BLS and the NASW studies agree that social workers are predominantly women. Figure 9-2 shows the 1988 and 1991 figures. The percentages of women they identify are roughly the same. The race or ethnicity of social workers who belonged to NASW in 1988 and 1994 is shown in Table 9-17. The membership is almost 90 percent white. The percentages of African Americans and Hispan-ics in the membership have increased slightly, but those of other groups have remained stable. More than 50 percent of the membership is over age 41, as shown in Figure 9-3. Most NASW members live on the east and west coasts. Table 9-18 shows the geographic distribution of members by region.

FIGURE 9-2 **NASW versus BLS Counts of Social Workers, by Gender: 1988 and 1991**

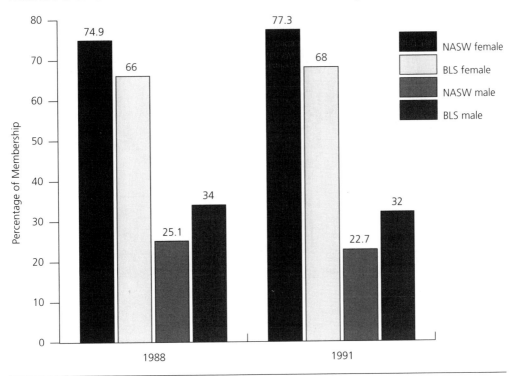

Notes: NASW = National Association of Social Workers; BLS = Bureau of Labor Statistics.

Source: Reprinted with permission from Gibelman, M., & Schervish, P. H. (1993). *Who we are: The social work labor force as reflected in the NASW membership* (p. 21). Washington, DC: NASW Press.

TABLE 9-17 **Race or Ethnicity of NASW Members: 1988 and 1994**

| Race or Ethnicity | 1988 | | 1994 | | % Change in Distribution |
	n	%	*n*	%	
White	81,632	88.4	120,568	87.5	−0.9
African American	5,254	5.7	8,496	6.2	0.5
Hispanic	2,206	2.4	3,961	2.9	0.5
Asian or Pacific Islander	1,427	1.5	2,236	1.6	0.1
Native American	463	0.5	785	0.6	0.1
Other	1,336	1.4	1,773	1.3	−0.1
Total respondents	92,318		137,819		

Notes: Percentages do not total 100 because of rounding. NASW = National Association of Social Workers.

Sources: 1988 data: Reprinted with permission from Gibelman, M., & Schervish, P. H. (1993). *Who we are: The social work labor force as reflected in the NASW membership* (p. 21). Washington, DC: NASW Press. 1994 data: National Association of Social Workers. (1994, October). Unpublished data from membership database.

FIGURE 9-3 Age of NASW Members: 1988 and 1991

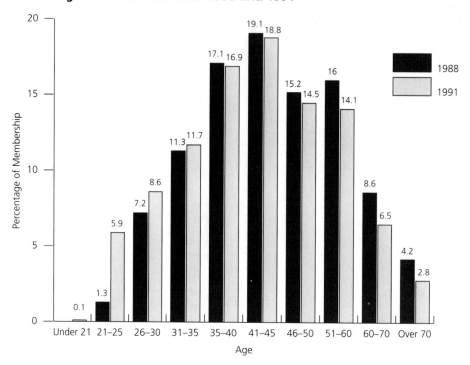

Note: NASW = National Association of Social Workers.

Source: Reprinted with permission from Gibelman, M., & Schervish, P. H. (1993). *Who we are: The social work labor force as reflected in the NASW membership* (p. 24). Washington, DC: NASW Press.

TABLE 9-18 Geographic Distribution of Working NASW Members: 1988 and 1994

Region	1988		1994	
	n	%	*n*	%
New England	9,112	10.6	15,081	10.7
Mid-Atlantic	20,738	24.2	24,511	17.4
East North Central	16,535	19.3	28,112	19.9
West North Central	5,502	6.4	9,128	6.5
South Atlantic	11,773	13.7	23,037	16.3
East South Central	2,461	2.9	5,388	3.8
West South Central	5,414	6.3	10,629	7.5
Mountain	3,632	4.2	7,642	5.4
Pacific	10,465	12.2	17,348	12.3
Territories	80	0.1	155	0.1
Total respondents	85,712		141,031	

Notes: Percentages do not total 100 because of rounding. New England = Connecticut, Maine, Massachusetts, New Hampshire, Rhode Island, Vermont; Mid-Atlantic = New Jersey, New York, Pennsylvania; East North Central = Illinois, Indiana, Michigan, Ohio, Wisconsin; West North Central = Iowa, Kansas, Minnesota, Missouri, Nebraska, North Dakota, South Dakota; South Atlantic = Delaware, District of Columbia, Florida, Georgia, Maryland, North Carolina, South Carolina, Virginia, West Virginia; East South Central = Alabama, Kentucky, Mississippi, Tennessee; West South Central = Arkansas, Louisiana, Oklahoma, Texas; Mountain = Arizona, Colorado, Idaho, Montana, Nevada, New Mexico, Utah, Wyoming; Pacific = Alaska, California, Hawaii, Oregon, Washington. NASW = National Association of Social Workers.

Sources: 1988 data: Reprinted with permission from Gibelman, M., & Schervish, P. H. (1993). *Who we are: The social work labor force as reflected in the NASW membership* (p. 48). Washington, DC: NASW Press. 1994 data: National Association of Social Workers. (1994, October). Unpublished data from membership database.

Table 9-19 shows the highest degrees held by NASW members in 1988 and 1994. The overwhelming majority of the membership hold master of social work degrees. Fewer than 10 percent of the members hold bachelor of social work degrees as their highest educational credential; some 5 percent hold doctorates. About half of NASW members hold the Academy of Certified Social Workers credential, which requires an MSW, supervised experience, and a passing grade on a standardized examination (Gibelman & Schervish, 1993b).

TABLE 9-19 **Highest Degrees Held by NASW Members: 1988 and 1994**

Highest Degree	1988		1994 (full members only)	
	n	%	*n*	%
BSW	8,417	7.8	2,933	3.1
MSW	93,979	87.5	89,229	93.2
DSW–PhD	5,058	4.7	3,540	3.7
Total respondents	107,454		95,702	

Notes: NASW = National Association of Social Workers; BSW = bachelor's degree in social work; MSW = master's degree in social work; DSW = doctor of social work; PhD = doctor of philosophy.

Sources: 1988 data: Reprinted with permission from Gibelman, M., & Schervish, P. H. (1993). *Who we are: The social work labor force as reflected in the NASW membership* (p. 22). Washington, DC: NASW Press. 1994 data: National Association of Social Workers. (1995, January). Unpublished data from membership database.

Employment

Over three-fourths of NASW members are employed full-time, according to Gibelman and Schervish (1993b). Most were employed in mental health, family, and children practice areas, as Table 9-20 demonstrates. With regard to the places they work, NASW members reported that they are primarily employed in agencies, hospitals, or clinics, with signifi-cant numbers having a secondary private practice. The settings are shown in Table 9-21. As Table 9-22 shows, the primary work of most NASW members is in direct practice, followed by management.

The historic categorization of social workers' specializations by method (such as casework, group work, community organization, and administration) is apparently evolving out

TABLE 9-20 Percentage of NASW Members, by Primary and Secondary Practice Areas: 1988 and 1994

| | 1988 | | 1994 | |
Area of Practice	Primary (n = 89,443)	Secondary (n = 35,666)	Primary (n = 101,899)	Secondary (n = 43,743)
Mental health	29.0	25.1	33.5	27.8
Children	17.0	12.0	16.5	12.8
Medical clinics	12.9	5.9	12.7	6.1
Family	12.2	20.6	10.6	17.9
Aged	5.3	6.3	4.6	5.3
Substance abuse	4.1	7.6	4.4	9.5
Schools	4.2	2.2	4.9	2.6
Mental retardation, developmental and physical disabilities	3.7	3.7	3.0	3.3
Corrections	1.5	1.5	1.2	1.5
Community organization–planning	1.6	2.8	1.1	2.2
Public assistance	1.0	0.8	0.8	0.6
Occupational	0.8	1.0	0.7	0.9
Groups	0.6	2.8	0.4	2.9
Other	0.9	1.0	5.6	6.7
Combined	5.2	6.7		

Note: NASW = National Association of Social Workers.

Sources: 1988 data: Reprinted with permission from Gibelman, M., & Schervish, P. H. (1993). *Who we are: The social work labor force as reflected in the NASW membership* (p. 28). Washington, DC: NASW Press. 1994 data: National Association of Social Workers. (1994, May). Unpublished data from the membership database.

TABLE 9-21 Percentage of NASW Members, by Primary and Secondary Practice Setting: 1988 and 1994

| | 1988 | | 1994 | |
Setting	Primary (n = 87,247)	Secondary (n = 27,555)	Primary (n = 99,572)	Secondary (n = 31,923)
Agency	26.0	10.6	22.6	10.5
Hospital	19.9	7.0	18.9	7.9
Medical clinic	16.2	12.6	16.7	12.5
Private solo practice	9.3	30.4	13.9	32.5
School	5.8	2.5	6.5	2.9
University	4.2	8.2	4.5	8.0
Private group practice	3.8	11.3	4.7	11.7
Group home	2.7	3.3	2.4	3.1
Institution	3.1	2.3	2.7	2.1
Nursing home	2.4	3.6	2.9	3.3
Non–social work setting	2.8	4.8	2.2	2.9
Court	1.5	0.5	1.3	1.8
Membership organizations	0.9	0.3	0.7	0.9

Notes: Percentages do not total 100 because of rounding. NASW = National Association of Social Workers.

Sources: 1988 data: Reprinted with permission from Gibelman, M., & Schervish, P. H. (1993). *Who we are: The social work labor force as reflected in the NASW membership* (p. 30). Washington, DC: NASW Press. 1994 data: National Association of Social Workers. (1994, May). Unpublished data from the membership database.

of existence. Figure 9-4 shows the specialties members identified themselves with in 1988 and 1991. Less than 25 percent identified themselves with a specific method. Some 75 percent said their specializations were generic or "other social work," which probably means that most social workers now view their work as involving a number of activities, depending on the needs of the clients they serve and the agencies that employ them. In addition, the fierce demarcations among individual, group, and community work may no longer exist.

In a study of the functions social workers perform in three job categories—direct service, supervisory, and administrative tasks—Teare and Sheafor (1992) provided additional insights into the ways in which social workers

TABLE 9-22 **Percentage of NASW Members, by Primary and Secondary Functions: 1988 and 1994**

| | 1988 | | 1994 | |
| | Primary | Secondary | Primary | Secondary |
Function	($n = 94,822$)	($n = 42,244$)	($n = 103,493$)	($n = 49,025$)
Direct service	64.1	32.6	68.7	33.5
Supervision	6.2	17.2	5.8	18.7
Management	16.8	10.2	15.1	9.8
Policy	0.5	2.5	0.5	2.2
Consultant	1.8	14.0	1.6	13.9
Research	0.5	2.2	0.5	2.2
Planning	0.5	2.6	0.4	2.0
Education	5.0	15.5	4.7	15.7
Non–social work	4.5	3.3	2.7	2.0

Notes: Percentages do not total 100 because of rounding. NASW = National Association of Social Workers.

Sources: 1988 data: Reprinted with permission from Gibelman, M., & Schervish, P. H. (1993). *Who we are: The social work labor force as reflected in the NASW membership* (p. 32). Washington, DC: NASW Press. 1994 data: National Association of Social Workers. (1994, May). Unpublished data from the membership database.

FIGURE 9-4 **Specialties of NASW Members: 1988 and 1991**

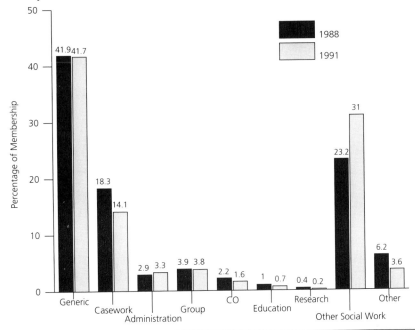

Notes: NASW = National Association of Social Workers; CO = community organization.

Source: Reprinted with permission from Gibelman, M., & Schervish, P. H. (1993). *Who we are: The social work labor force as reflected in the NASW membership* (p. 29). Washington, DC: NASW Press.

discharge their duties. Respondents from the three groups were asked to state how often they performed various functions and to rank them on a five-point scale (1 = not done; 2 = seldom; 3 = occasionally; 4 = frequently; 5 = almost always). The results are shown in Figures 9-5, 9-6, and 9-7. The numbers next to each graph bar represent the mean score for that function. For example, supervisors re-

sponded that they provided interpersonal help and staff supervision frequently (close to 4.0).

FIGURE 9-5 **MSW Direct Service Tasks**

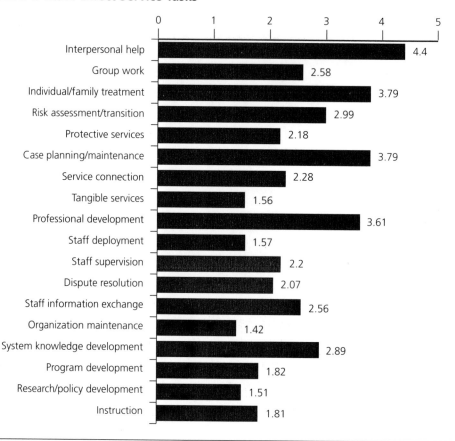

Notes: MSW = master's degree in social work. Scale ranges from 1 = not done to 5 = almost always done.

Source: Reprinted with permission from Teare, R. J., & Sheafor, B. W. (1992, March). *Social work practice: Reality versus fantasy*. Paper presented at the Annual Program Meeting of the Council on Social Work Education, Kansas City, MO.

FIGURE 9-6 **MSW Supervisory Tasks**

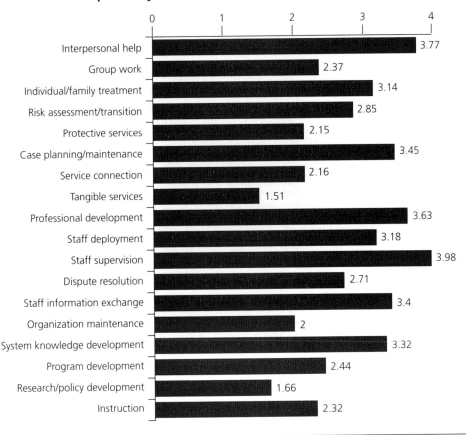

Notes: MSW = master's degree in social work. Scale ranges from 1 = not done to 5 = almost always done.

Source: Reprinted with permission from Teare, R. J., & Sheafor, B. W. (1992, March). *Social work practice: Reality versus fantasy.* Paper presented at the Annual Program Meeting of the Council on Social Work Education, Kansas City, MO.

FIGURE 9-7 **MSW Administrative Tasks**

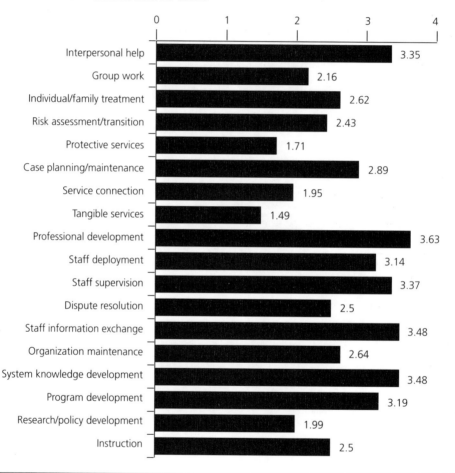

Task	Value
Interpersonal help	3.35
Group work	2.16
Individual/family treatment	2.62
Risk assessment/transition	2.43
Protective services	1.71
Case planning/maintenance	2.89
Service connection	1.95
Tangible services	1.49
Professional development	3.63
Staff deployment	3.14
Staff supervision	3.37
Dispute resolution	2.5
Staff information exchange	3.48
Organization maintenance	2.64
System knowledge development	3.48
Program development	3.19
Research/policy development	1.99
Instruction	2.5

Notes: MSW = master's degree in social work. Scale ranges from 1 = not done to 5 = almost always done.

Source: Reprinted with permission from Teare, R. J., & Sheafor, B. W. (1992, March). *Social work practice: Reality versus fantasy.* Paper presented at the Annual Program Meeting of the Council on Social Work Education, Kansas City, MO.

Salaries

NASW conducted a salary survey of its members in 1993 (Gibelman & Schervish, 1993a). Some 6 percent of the association's 145,448 members were included in the sample, and 42.8 percent of them (3,121 individuals) responded and were included in the data developed in May 1993. The researchers used a stratified sampling method in which about half of those surveyed had two years or less experience and the other half were from the rest of the membership, excluding certain groups such as student members, retired members, unemployed people, part-time workers, and those in other countries.

Gibelman and Schervish (1993a) found that most salary growth was in the first five years of employment. After that, salaries grew much more slowly and required about 10 years to match the growth rate of the first five. After 15 years, incomes appeared to level off, and there was little difference among people who had 15, 20, or more years of experience.

In 1993, 81.4 percent of NASW members who responded to the survey were women. Some 91 percent were white, 4.2 percent Af-rican American, 3.1 percent Hispanic, 1.3 percent Asian American, and 0.5 percent Native American. In terms of their highest degrees, 4.3 percent held BSWs, 86.9 percent had MSWs, 6.3 percent held doctorates in social work, and 2.5 percent held doctorates in other fields. In all, 95.1 percent of the sample held MSWs, including most of those with doctoral degrees.

Worker functions have an impact on earnings. Social work educators, managers, and researchers have higher earnings than those fulfilling other functions, as Table 9-23 shows. Tables 9-24 and 9-25 show the earnings of

TABLE 9-23 **Annual Income of Social Workers, by Function: 1993**

			Annual Primary Income			
Function	No.	%	25th Percentile	Median	Mean	75th Percentile
Direct service	2,227	71.6	$25,000	$29,000	$31,729	$34,000
Supervision	85	2.7	27,000	32,000	32,400	37,500
Management	509	16.4	30,000	36,000	39,079	45,000
Research	23	0.7	31,000	40,000	40,783	50,000
University teaching	132	4.2	36,000	43,000	48,265	54,750
Agency training	9	0.3	19,500	32,000	31,556	39,000
Policy	16	0.5	29,250	31,500	32,813	36,250
Community organization	26	0.8	24,500	27,500	29,154	33,750
Other	85	2.7	25,000	31,000	33,048	39,000

Source: Reprinted with permission from Gibelman, M., & Schervish, P. H. (1993). *What we earn: 1993 salary survey* (p. 28). Washington, DC: NASW Press.

the respondents by work setting and auspices. Those in private practice, university employees, and workers in business and industry had the highest earnings by work settings, and those who were self-employed, federal employees, and employees of military organizations had the highest earnings by auspices.

TABLE 9-24 **Percentage of Social Workers in Each Income Category, by Work Setting: 1993**

Work Setting	<25,000	26,000–30,000	31,000–35,000	36,000–40,000	41,000–50,000	51,000–60,000	>60,000
			Income ($)				
Business	10.6	21.1	7.9	10.5	26.3	13.2	10.5
Courts	23.7	26.3	26.3	10.5	7.9	a	5.3
Medical inpatient	11.2	32.6	31.3	12.7	9.1	2.1	1.1
Medical outpatient	17.6	29.6	21.8	16.2	11.2	1.4	2.1
Private group	19.2	18.3	14.4	13.5	14.4	7.7	12.5
Residential facility	29.5	30.0	14.8	9.9	4.5	a	a
Agency	38.1	25.1	16.5	9.7	6.7	2.3	a
University teaching	7.6	10.9	12.0	18.0	19.6	16.4	15.3
Mental health inpatient	17.6	32.9	26.7	11.9	7.6	1.4	2.0
Mental health outpatient	31.6	29.7	17.8	10.5	8.1	1.3	a
Managed care/HMO	7.3	24.4	22.0	17.1	26.8	2.4	a
Private solo	13.5	14.3	9.5	11.9	18.2	14.3	18.3
School	16.2	31.4	19.4	18.3	13.6	1.0	a

Note: HMO = health maintenance organization.
Source: Reprinted with permission from Gibelman, M., & Schervish, P. H. (1993). *What we earn: 1993 salary survey* (p. 26). Washington, DC: NASW Press.
aLess than 1 percent.

TABLE 9-25 **Annual Primary Income of Social Workers, by Auspices: 1993**

Auspice	No.	%	25th Percentile	Median	Mean	75th Percentile
			Annual Primary Income ($)			
Private not-for-profit	1,438	46.7	25,000	29,000	31,388	35,000
Public local	439	14.3	27,000	32,000	33,860	38,000
Public state	429	13.9	25,000	31,000	34,820	40,000
Public federal	50	1.6	31,000	35,000	36,300	41,000
Military	40	1.3	29,250	35,000	36,275	38,750
Private for-profit (self)	215	7.0	30,000	40,000	45,455	54,000
Private for-profit (organization)	466	15.1	27,000	31,000	33,261	36,000

Source: Reprinted with permission from Gibelman, M., & Schervish, P. H. (1993). *What we earn: 1993 salary survey* (p. 27). Washington, DC: NASW Press.

Table 9-26 shows the incomes of NASW members as reported in 1988, 1991, and 1993 surveys. Salaries show a generally upward trend; those earning less than $25,000 declined and those earning more rose, although 80 percent had 1993 incomes of less than $40,000. As might be expected, the higher the degree earned and the longer the work experience, the greater the earnings. Tables 9-27 and 9-28 illustrate the

TABLE 9-26 Primary Income Comparisons of NASW Members Who Work Full-Time: 1988, 1991, and 1993

Income Range	1988	1991	1993
Under $10,000	0.7	0.8	0.2
$10,000–$14,999	4.4	3.2	0.5
$15,000–$19,999	25.1	19.6	3.7
$20,000–$24,999	22.4	20.7	13.8
$25,000–$29,999	23.2	22.4	25.5
$30,000–$34,999	9.5	12.2	22.9
$35,000–$39,999	7.9	11.7	13.5
$40,000–$49,999	2.8	4.1	11.6
$50,000–$59,999	1.3	1.9	4.4
$60,000 and over	2.6	3.4	4.1

Note: NASW = National Association of Social Workers.

Source: Reprinted with permission from Gibelman, M., & Schervish, P. H. (1993). *What we earn: 1993 salary survey* (p. 19). Washington, DC: NASW Press.

TABLE 9-27 Income Distribution of NASW Members by Highest Degree: 1991 and 1993

	BSW		MSW		DSW/PhD	
Income	1991	1993	1991	1993	1991	1993
Under $10,000	3.7	0.8	0.6	0.3	0.5	0.5
$10,000–$19,999	66.2	43.9	20.8	2.4	5.1	0.0
$20,000–$29,999	22.7	48.0	45.0	42.6	26.1	2.5
$30,000–$39,999	5.8	5.3	24.6	39.3	35.3	21.2
$40,000 and over	1.6	3.0	8.8	12.8	32.9	70.7
Total	2,327	134	36,897	2,712	1,679	198

Notes: NASW = National Association of Social Workers; BSW = bachelor's degree in social work; MSW = master's degree in social work; DSW = doctor of social work; PhD = doctor of philosophy.

Source: Reprinted with permission from Gibelman, M., & Schervish, P. H. (1993). *What we earn: 1993 salary survey* (p. 21). Washington, DC: NASW Press.

TABLE 9-28 NASW Member Income, by Years of Experience: 1993

Years of Experience	Median ($)	Mode ($)	Midrange ($)
<1	27,000	28,000	23,000–30,000
2–3	28,000	30,000	25,000–33,000
4–5	33,000	30,000	28,000–38,000
6–10	35,000	30,000	30,000–42,000
11–15	45,000	40,000	36,500–54,750
16–20	50,000	38,000	41,250–62,500
21–25	51,000	40,000	42,000–68,000
>26	54,000	33,000	44,000–65,750

Notes: The midrange is achieved by excluding the highest 25 percent and the lowest 25 percent of reported salaries earned. NASW = National Association of Social Workers.

Source: Reprinted with permission from Gibelman, M., & Schervish, P. H. (1993). *What we earn: 1993 salary survey* (p. 21). Washington, DC: NASW Press.

incomes of respondents by their highest degrees in 1991 and 1993 and their median, modal, and midrange incomes by years of experience in 1993.

The study also reported on incomes by gender and race or ethnicity. As Table 9-29 shows, larger percentages of women (83.8 percent) earned salaries below $40,000 compared to men (62.8 percent).

Social workers of color—African Americans, Puerto Ricans, Asian Americans, and Chicanos—tended to earn slightly higher salaries than white and Native American social workers. Table 9-30 shows the breakdown by 25th and 75th percentiles and by median and mean earnings.

TABLE 9-29 **Income Distribution of NASW Members, by Gender: 1991 and 1993**

Income	Percentage Female		Percentage Male	
	1991	1993	1991	1993
<$10,000	0.9	0.2	0.6	0.2
$10,000–19,999	27.1	4.7	13.0	1.4
$20,000–29,999	44.6	42.1	38.3	26.8
$30,000–39,999	20.8	36.8	31.7	34.4
$40,000–49,999	3.1	10.2	6.9	17.5
$50,000–59,999	1.3	3.5	3.2	8.5
$60,000 and over	2.2	2.5	6.3	11.3
Total	28,190	2,519	10,467	576

Note: NASW = National Association of Social Workers.

Source: Reprinted with permission from Gibelman, M., & Schervish, P. H. (1993). *What we earn: 1993 salary survey* (p. 23). Washington, DC: NASW Press.

TABLE 9-30 **Annual Primary Income of NASW Members, by Race or Ethnicity: 1993**

Race or Ethnicity	No.	%	Annual Primary Income ($)			
			25th Percentile	Median	Mean	75th Percentile
White	2,818	90.9	25,250	30,000	33,580	37,000
African American	130	4.2	28,000	33,000	34,977	38,000
Asian	40	1.3	22,250	34,000	35,275	39,750
Puerto Rican	26	0.8	30,000	35,000	35,000	40,250
Chicano	27	0.9	28,000	35,000	35,115	39,750
Other Hispanic	42	1.4	27,000	32,500	35,333	42,250
Native American	17	0.5	24,500	30,000	31,941	42,500

Note: NASW = National Association of Social Workers.

Source: Reprinted with permission from Gibelman, M., & Schervish, P. H. (1993). *What we earn: 1993 salary survey* (p. 24). Washington, DC: NASW Press.

REFERENCES

Aguilar, S. M., & Hardy, A. M. (1993). *AIDS knowledge and attitudes for 1991: Data from the National Health Interview Study.* Hyattsville, MD: U.S. Public Health Service, National Center for Health Statistics.

Alan Guttmacher Institute. (1993). *Facts in brief: Contraceptive use, abortion in the United States, teenage sexual and reproductive behavior.* New York: Author.

American Association of Retired Persons. (1992). *A profile of older Americans.* Washington, DC: Author.

American Cancer Society. (1993). *Cancer facts and figures—1993.* Atlanta: Author.

American Heart Association. (1992). *1993 heart and stroke facts.* Dallas: Author.

American Humane Association, Children's Division. (1993). *Child abuse and neglect data: AHA fact sheet #1.* Englewood, CO: Author.

Ashcroft, J., & Strauss, A. (1993). *Families first: Report of the National Commission on America's Urban Families.* Washington, DC: U.S. Government Printing Office.

Associated Press. (1994). Juvenile cases on the increase. *Columbia State* [South Carolina], p. A3.

Association for Brain Tumor Research. (1991). *A primer of brain tumors: A patient's reference manual* (5th ed.). Chicago: Author.

Autism Society of America. (no date). *General information on autism.* Bethesda, MD: Author.

Bachman, R. (1992). *Elderly victims: Bureau of Justice Statistics special report.* Washington, DC: U.S. Department of Justice, Bureau of Justice Statistics.

Barancik, S., & Shapiro, S. (1992). *Where have all the dollars gone? A state-by-state analysis of income disparities over the 1980s.* Washington, DC: Center for Budget and Policy Priorities.

Bastian, L. D. (1992). *Criminal victimization 1991: Bureau of Justice Statistics bulletin.* Washington, DC: U.S. Department of Justice, Bureau of Justice Statistics.

Bayles, F. (1993, December 31). Youths fuel soaring homicide rate. *Columbia State* [South Carolina], pp. 1A, 8A.

Beck, A. J., Bonczar, T. P., & Gilliard, D. K. (1993). *Jail inmates 1992: Bureau of Justice Statistics Bulletin.* Washington, DC: U.S. Department of Justice, Bureau of Justice Statistics.

Beck, A., Gilliard, D., Greenfeld, L., Harlow, C., Hester, T., Jankowski, L., Snell, T., Stephan, J., & Morton, D. (1993). *Survey of state prison inmates, 1991.* Washington, DC: U.S. Department of Justice, Bureau of Justice Statistics.

Berkow, R. (Ed.-in-Chief). (1992). *The Merck manual of diagnosis and therapy* (16th ed.). Rahway, NJ: Merck Research Laboratories.

Blue Ribbon Task Force. (1993). *Gray plague of the twentieth century: Meeting the needs of individuals with Alzheimer's disease, their families and caregivers.* Columbia: School of Public Health, University of South Carolina.

Brimhall-Vargas, M. B. (1993). *Poverty tables 1991.* Washington, DC: Center for Budget and Policy Priorities.

Brinson, C. S. (1993, December 13). A mother in prison. *Columbia State* [South Carolina], pp. 1E, 6E–8E.

Burt, M. R. (1992). *Over the edge: The growth of homelessness in the 1980s.* New York and Washington, DC: Russell Sage Foundation and Urban Institute Press.

Burt, M. R., & Cohen, B. E. (1989). *America's homeless: Numbers, characteristics, and the programs that serve them.* Washington, DC: Urban Institute Press.

Center on Budget and Policy Priorities. (1991). *The low-income home energy assistance program: A review of participation rates and outreach activities.* Washington, DC: American Association of Retired Persons.

Centers for Disease Control and Prevention. (1993a, September). *Annual summary of births, marriages, divorces, and deaths: United States, 1992.* Hyattsville, MD: U.S. Public Health Service, National Center for Health Statistics.

Centers for Disease Control and Prevention. (1993b). *Births, marriages, divorces, and deaths for 1992.* Hyattsville, MD: U.S. Public Health Service, National Center for Health Statistics.

Centers for Disease Control and Prevention. (1993c, November 19). *Births, marriages, divorces, and deaths for June 1993.* Hyattsville, MD: U.S. Public Health Service, National Center for Health Statistics.

Centers for Disease Control and Prevention. (1993d). *HIV/AIDS Surveillance Report, 5*(3), 1–19.

Centers for Disease Control and Prevention. (1993e, February). *Prevalence of selected chronic conditions: United States, 1986–88.* Hyattsville, MD: U.S. Public Health Service, National Center for Health Statistics.

Centers for Disease Control and Prevention. (1994, July 21). *Monthly vital statistics report.* Hyattsville, MD: U.S. Public Health Service, National Center for Health Statistics.

Clayman, C. B. (Ed.). (1989). *The American Medical Association encyclopedia of medicine.* New York: Random House.

Clements, M. (1994, January 9). What Americans say about the homeless. *Parade,* pp. 4–6.

Cohen, R. L. (1992). *Drunk driving: Bureau of Justice Statistics special report, 1989 survey of inmates of local jails.* Washington, DC: U.S. Department of Justice, Bureau of Justice Statistics.

Committee on Ways and Means, U.S. House of Representatives. (1993). *Overview of entitlement programs: 1993 green book.* Washington, DC: U.S. Government Printing Office.

Conover, T. (1993, August 16). A reporter at large: Trucking through the AIDS belt. *New Yorker,* pp. 56–75.

Cystic Fibrosis Foundation. (1993). *Facts about CF.* Bethesda, MD: Author.

Edna McConnell Clark Foundation. (1993). *Americans behind bars.* New York: Author.

Employee Assistance Programs Association. (1992). *EAPA press file: Vital issues, alcoholism and other drug abuse in America and its workplaces.* Arlington, VA: Author.

Evangelauf, J. (Ed.). (1993, August 25). *The Chronicle of Higher Education almanac.* Washington, DC: Chronicle of Higher Education.

Federal Bureau of Investigation. (1993). *Crime in the United States, 1992.* Washington, DC: Author.

Fender, L., & Shaw, D. (1990). *The state of the states' children.* Washington, DC: National Governors' Association.

Fingerhut, L. A. (1993, March). *Firearm mortality among children, youth, and young adults 1–34 years of age, trends and current status: United States, 1985–90.* Hyattsville, MD: U.S. Public Health Service, National Center for Health Statistics.

Fingerhut, L. A., Jones, C., & Makuc, D. M. (1994). *Firearm and motor vehicle injury mortality—Variations by state, race, and ethnicity: United States, 1990–91.* Hyattsville, MD: U.S. Public Health Service, National Center for Health Statistics.

Gibelman, M., & Schervish, P. H. (1993a). *What we earn: 1993 salary survey.* Washington, DC: NASW Press.

Gibelman, M., & Schervish, P. H. (1993b). *Who we are: The social work labor force as reflected in the NASW membership.* Washington, DC: NASW Press.

Gilliard, D. K. (1993). *Prisoners in 1992.* Washington, DC: U.S. Department of Justice, Bureau of Justice Statistics.

Greenfeld, L. A. (1992). *Capital punishment 1991.* Washington, DC: U.S. Department of Justice, Bureau of Justice Statistics.

Greenfeld, L. A., & Minor-Harper, S. (1991). *Women in prison.* Washington, DC: U.S. Department of Justice, Bureau of Justice Statistics.

Hardman, P. K., & Morton, D. G. (1991). The link between developmental dyslexia, ADD and chemical dependency. *Environmental Medicine, 8*(3), 61–72.

Harris, G. E., & Bradford, J. B. (1987). Literacy. In A. Minahan (Ed.-in-Chief), *Encyclopedia of social work* (18th ed., Vol. 2, pp. 50–59). Silver Spring, MD: National Association of Social Workers.

Hill, G. (1990, May 22). School absent in many homeless lives. *Washington Post,* p. A21.

Hopps, J. G., & Pinderhughes, E. B. (1987). Profession of social work: Contemporary characteristics. In A. Minahan (Ed.-in-Chief), *Encyclopedia of social work* (18th ed., Vol. 2, pp. 351–366). Silver Spring, MD: National Association of Social Workers.

Institute of Medicine, Committee on Health Care for Homeless People. (1988). *Homelessness, health, and human needs.* Washington, DC: National Academy Press.

International Labour Office. (1993). *International Labour Office yearbook of labour statistics, 1992.* Geneva: Author.

Johnson, O. (Ed.). (1993). *The 1994 information please almanac.* New York: Houghton-Mifflin.

Kosmin, B. A., & Lachman, S. P. (1993). *One nation under God: Religion in contemporary American society.* New York: Harmony Books.

Kramer, M. (1993, December 20). Clinton's drug policy is a bust. *Time,* p. 35.

Lazere, E. B., Leonard, P. A., & Kravitz, L. L. (1989). *The other housing crisis: Sheltering the poor in rural America.* Washington, DC: Center on Budget and Policy Priorities and Low Income Housing Information Service.

Lennon, T. M. (1993). *Statistics on social work education in the United States: 1992.* Alexandria, VA: Council on Social Work Education.

Leonard, P. A., Dolbeare, C. N., & Lazere, E. B. (1989). *A place to call home: The crisis in housing for the poor.* Washington, DC: Center on Budget and Policy Priorities and Low Income Housing Information Service.

Levy, D. (1994, August 9). Some live long-term with HIV. *USA Today,* p. 1A.

Lloyd, G. A. (1987). Social work education. In A. Minahan (Ed.-in-Chief), *Encyclopedia of social work* (18th ed., Vol. 2, pp. 695–705). Silver Spring, MD: National Association of Social Workers.

Lloyd, G. A. (1990). AIDS and HIV: The syndrome and the virus. In L. Ginsberg (Ed.), *Encyclopedia of social work, 18th edition: 1990 supplement* (pp. 12–50). Silver Spring, MD: NASW Press.

Maguire, K., Pastore, A. L., & Flanagan, T. J. (1993). *Sourcebook of criminal justice statistics, 1992.* Washington, DC: U.S. Department of Justice, Bureau of Labor Statistics.

Manderscheid, R. W., & Sonnenschein, M. A. (Eds.). (1990). *Mental health, United States, 1990* (DHHS Publication No. ADM 90-1708). Washington, DC: U.S. Government Printing Office.

Manderscheid, R. W., & Sonnenschein, M. A. (Eds.). (1992). *Mental health, United States, 1992* (DHHS Publication No. SMA 92-1942). Washington, DC: U.S. Government Printing Office.

March of Dimes Birth Defects Foundation. (no date). *Thalassemia: Public health information sheet.* White Plains, NY: Author.

March of Dimes Birth Defects Foundation. (1986a). *Clubfoot.* White Plains, NY: Author.

March of Dimes Birth Defects Foundation. (1986b). *PKU: Public health education information sheet, genetic series.* White Plains, NY: Author.

March of Dimes Birth Defects Foundation. (1986c). *Rh disease: Public health education information sheet, genetic series.* White Plains, NY: Author.

March of Dimes Birth Defects Foundation. (1987). *Achondroplasia: Public health education information sheet.* White Plains, NY: Author.

March of Dimes Birth Defects Foundation. (1988a). *Cleft lip and palate: Public health education information sheet.* White Plains, NY: Author.

March of Dimes Birth Defects Foundation. (1988b). *Congenital heart defects: Public health education information sheet.* White Plains, NY: Author.

March of Dimes Birth Defects Foundation. (1992a). *The neurofibromatoses: Public health education information sheet.* White Plains, NY: Author.

March of Dimes Birth Defects Foundation. (1992b). *Sickle cell disease: Public health education information sheet.* White Plains, NY: Author.

March of Dimes Birth Defects Foundation. (1992c). *Spina bifida: Public health education information sheet.* White Plains, NY: Author.

March of Dimes Birth Defects Foundation. (1993). *Marfan syndrome: Public health education information sheet.* White Plains, NY: Author.

McCurdy, K., & Daro, D. (1993). *Current trends in child abuse reporting and fatalities: The results of the 1992 annual fifty state survey.* Chicago: National Committee for the Prevention of Child Abuse.

Miringoff, M. L. (1993). *The index of social health: Monitoring the social well-being of the nation.* Tarrytown, NY: Fordham Institute for Innovation in Social Policy.

Montgomery, L. (1994, January 8). Youths skeptical of crime summit. *Columbia State* [South Carolina], pp. 1A, 6A.

Mosher, W. D., & Pratt, W. F. (1992). *AIDS-related behavior among women 15–44 years of age: United States, 1988 and 1990.* Hyattsville, MD: U.S. Public Health Service, Centers for Disease Control and Prevention.

Moss, D. (1991, April 11). Practicing or not, many identify with religion. *USA Today,* p. 7A.

National Aphasia Association. (1993). *Fact sheet.* New York: Author.

National Center for Education Statistics. (1993). *Digest of education statistics 1993.* Washington, DC: Office of Educational Research and Improvement.

National Center for Health Statistics. (1993). *Health United States 1992 and healthy people 2000 review.* Hyattsville, MD: U.S. Public Health Service.

National Commission on Children. (1991). *Beyond rhetoric: A new American agenda for children and families.* Washington, DC: U.S. Government Printing Office.

National Diabetes Information Clearinghouse. (1993). *Statistics—Diabetes.* Bethesda, MD: Author.

National Down Syndrome Congress. (1988). *Facts about Down syndrome.* Park Ridge, IL: Author.

Nelson, C. R. (1993). *Drug utilization in office practice: National ambulatory medical care survey, 1990.* Hyattsville, MD: U.S. Public Health Service, National Center for Health Statistics.

Peterson, K. S. (1992, April 3). Child abuse deaths up 10% in '91. *USA Today,* p. 1D.

Pizzigatti, K. (1994). *Children's monitor.* Washington, DC: Child Welfare League of America.

Radin, C. A. (1994, August 9). AIDS work aims at longer life. *Columbia State* [South Carolina], pp. 1A, 11A.

Rand, M. R. (1993). *Crime and the nation's households, 1992: Bureau of Justice Statistics bulletin.* Washington, DC: U.S. Department of Justice, Bureau of Justice Statistics.

Ray, B. D. (1993). *Home education research fact sheet.* Salem, OR: National Home Education Research Institute.

Rensberger, B. (1993, December 30). Official suicide rates for blacks, women may not be accurate. *Columbia State* [South Carolina], p. 3D.

Schappert, S. M. (1993a). *National ambulatory medical care survey: 1991 summary.* Hyattsville, MD: U.S. Public Health Service, National Center for Health Statistics.

Schappert, S. M. (1993b). *Office visits to obstetricians and gynecologists: United States, 1989–90.* Hyattsville, MD: U.S. Public Health Service, National Center for Health Statistics.

Schappert, S. M. (1993c). *Office visits to psychiatrists: United States, 1989–90.* Hyattsville, MD: U.S. Public Health Service, National Center for Health Statistics.

Schoenborn, C. A., Marsh, S. L., & Hardy, A. M. (1994). *AIDS knowledge and attitudes for 1992: Data from the National Health Interview Survey.* Hyattsville, MD: U.S. Public Health Service, National Center for Health Statistics.

Shapiro, I. (1992). *White poverty in America.* Washington, DC: Center on Budget and Policy Priorities.

Shapiro, I., & Nichols, M. (1992). *Far from fixed: An analysis of the unemployment in-*

surance system. Washington, DC: Center on Budget and Policy Priorities.

Sirrocco, A. (1994). *Nursing homes and board and care homes: Data from the 1991 national health provider inventory.* Hyattsville, MD: U.S. Public Health Service, National Center for Health Statistics.

Sloan, M. (1993, August 9). Database. *U.S. News and World Report,* p. 14.

Snell, T. L. (1993). *Correctional populations in the United States, 1991.* Washington, DC: U.S. Department of Justice, Bureau of Justice Statistics.

Tatara, T. (1993a). *Summaries of the statistical data on elder abuse in domestic settings for FY 90 and FY 91: A final report.* Washington, DC: National Aging Resource Center on Elder Abuse.

Tatara, T. (1993b). *Voluntary cooperative information system research notes no. 9.* Washington, DC: American Public Welfare Association.

Teare, R. J., & Sheafor, B. W. (1992, March). *Social work practice: Reality versus fantasy.* Paper presented at the Annual Program Meeting of the Council on Social Work Education, Kansas City, MO.

Torrey, E. F. (1988). *Nowhere to go.* New York: Harper & Row.

U.S. Bureau of the Census. (1990). *Statistical abstract of the United States* (110th ed.). Washington, DC: U.S. Government Printing Office.

U.S. Bureau of the Census. (1993). *Statistical abstract of the United States: 1993* (113th ed.). Austin, TX: Reference Press.

U.S. Department of Education, National Center for Education Statistics. (1993). *Digest of education statistics.* Washington, DC: Author.

U.S. Department of Health and Human Services, National Center on Child Abuse and Neglect. (1993). *National child abuse and neglect data system working paper 2: 1991 summary data component.* Gaithersburg, MD: Author.

U.S. Department of Health and Human Ser-

vices. (1992). *Health data on older Americans: United States, 1992.* Hyattsville, MD: U.S. Public Health Service, National Center for Health Statistics.

U.S. Department of Health and Human Services, Social Security Administration, Office of Research and Statistics. (1993, November). *OASDI beneficiaries by state and county.* Washington, DC: Author.

U.S. Department of Justice. (1993). *Sourcebook of criminal justice statistics, 1992.* Washington, DC: U.S. Government Printing Office.

U.S. Department of Labor, Bureau of Labor Statistics. (1993, November 21). *BLS releases new 1992–2005 employment projections.* Washington, DC: Author.

Weiner, J. M., Illston, L. H., & Hanley, R. J. (1994). *Sharing the burden: Strategies for public and private long-term care.* Washington, DC: Brookings Institution.

Wilson, J. B. (1993). *Human immunodeficiency virus antibody testing in women 15–44 years of age: United States, 1990.* Hyattsville, MD: U.S. Public Health Service, Centers for Disease Control and Prevention.

Woodward, K. L. (1993, November 29). The rites of Americans. *Newsweek,* pp. 80–82.

Wright, J. W. (Ed.). (1993). *The universal almanac 1994.* Kansas City, MO: Andrews & McMeel.

Wright, L. (1994, July 25). Annals of politics: One drop of blood. *New Yorker,* pp. 46–55.

Zawitz, M. W., Klaus, P. A., Bachman, R., Bastian, L. D., DeBerry, M. M., Jr., Rand, M. R., & Taylor, B. M. (1993). *Highlights from 20 years of surveying crime victims: The National Crime Victimization Survey, 1973–92.* Washington, DC: U.S. Department of Justice, Bureau of Justice Statistics.

Zill, N., & Schoenborn, C. A. (1990). Developmental, learning, and emotional problems. In *Health of our nation's children, United States, 1988. Advance data* (No. 190). Washington, DC: U.S. Government Printing Office.

INDEX

North Carolina, 129. *See also* States
North Dakota, 93, 102, 321. *See also* States
Nursing homes, mental health care in, 285–288, *287–288*

O

Obstetrical/gynecological care, 244, *244, 245*
OCONUS, 67
Oklahoma, 327. *See also* States
Old Age, Survivors, Disability, and Health Insurance. *See* Social security program
Organ transplants, 240, *240*
Orphans, 86

P

Pennsylvania, 349. *See also* States
Population
    age distribution, 1, *5–9*
    age trends, 297
    ethnic ancestry, 12, *18*
    foreign-born, 12, *16–17*
    Hispanic, 9–12
    household demographics, 26–28, *29–36*
    international trends, 15–16, *27–28, 172–174*
    marital status, 28, 37, *37–42*, 39–43
    metropolitan/non-metropolitan distribution, 12–13, *19–24*
    mortality rates and causes, 170–176, *175–177*
    national trends, 1, *2*, 58
    political significance of census, 1–9
    projections, 1, *4*
    regional trends, 1
    religious affiliation, *47*, 47–53, *49–53*
    school-age, 133
    state profiles, 1, *3*
Poverty
    child population in, 80–81, *82*
    definition, 43
    elderly persons and, 299, *301*, 305, *305*
    family size and, 43, *43*
    of workers, 56, *57*
Prison population
    characteristics, *119*, 119–120, *121–123*
    family background, 120, *124*
    federal–state distribution, 114, 116
    incarceration rates, 114, *117–118*
    race/ethnicity of, *119*, 120, *121–124*, 124–126
    sentence characteristics, 120, *125*
    spending on, 120–124
    in state prisons, 116–120
    substance abuse background, 120, 124, *126*
    trends, 124

R

Race/ethnicity
    age–gender distribution, *7–9*
    AIDS distribution and, 202, *202–205*
    arrest statistics, 111, *115*
    cancer and, 186, *194*
    capital punishment and, 129–132, *130–132*
    census classification, 9
    child abuse and, 65, *71*
    crime victimization, 104
    criminal penalties and, 124–126
    educational outcomes and, *134, 142*
    elderly population, *300*
    family violence, 111
    firearm deaths and, 194–197
    higher education enrollments and, 154, *159–160, 163*
    homicide victimization and, 106, *107*
    household composition, 28, *33–34, 39*, 39–41, 58, *61, 62–64*
    income/poverty levels, *44*, 45, *48*
    infant mortality, 81, *82*
    labor force distribution, *55*, 55–56
    life expectancy, 170, *171*
    marital status, 41, *42*
    medical utilization, 242, *242*
    metropolitan populations, *25–26*
    national ancestry, 12, *18*
    preprimary school enrollment, *152*
    prison population, *119*, 120, *121–124*, 124–126
    proficiency test scores, *155*
    psychiatric service utilization, 263, *263*, 266, *266, 273, 276, 277*, 278
    school enrollment, *137–138*
    social work faculty, 354, *357*
    social work graduate students, 361, *361*
    social work profession, 365, *365*, 373, 376, *376*
    substance abuse and, *292–293*
    utilization of social welfare programs, 350, *350*
    youth population trends, 58, *60*
Rape, 90, *91–92, 93*, 106, *106*
    juvenile offenders, 127
    prison sentences, *125*
    state rates, *94–101*
    underreporting of, 102
Religious affiliation, *47*, 47–53, *49–53*
Respiratory disease, 225, 228, *229–230*
Rhode Island, 313. *See also* States
Robbery, 90, *91–92, 93*, 127. *See also* Crime
    state rates, *94–101*
    underreporting of, 102
Rural areas
    AIDS in, 202–203
    crime in, *94–101*, 102, 106

About the Author

Leon Ginsberg has been Carolina Research Professor in the College of Social Work, University of South Carolina, Columbia, since 1986. Before joining the University of South Carolina faculty, he served as associate professor of social work at the University of Oklahoma, Dean of the School of Social Work at West Virginia University, West Virginia Commissioner of Human Services in the administration of Governor Jay Rockefeller, and Chancellor of the West Virginia Board of Regents for Higher Education.

He has served as chair of the board of the National Center for Social Policy and Practice, as national secretary of the National Association of Social Workers, and as president of the American Public Welfare Association.

Ginsberg was a member of the board of editors of the 18th edition of the *Encyclopedia of Social Work* and chaired the editorial committee for the *1990 Supplement* to the encyclopedia. He is the coauthor with Anita Harbert of *Human Services for Older Adults,* editor of *Social Work in Rural Communities,* coeditor with Paul Keys of *New Management in Human Services,* and author of *The Practice of Social Work in Public Welfare* and *Understanding Social Problems, Policies, and Programs,* among other books and articles.

He holds a master's degree in social work from Tulane University and a PhD in political science from the University of Oklahoma.